Medical Internet of Things

Perspectives, Impact and Challenges

Editors

Amit Kumar Tyagi
National Forensic Sciences University
Gandhinagar, Gujarat, India

Shabnam Kumari
SRM Institute of Science and Technology
Kattankulathur, Chennai, Tamilnadu, India

CRC Press
Taylor & Francis Group
Boca Raton London New York

CRC Press is an imprint of the
Taylor & Francis Group, an **informa** business
A SCIENCE PUBLISHERS BOOK

First edition published 2026
by CRC Press
2385 NW Executive Center Drive, Suite 320, Boca Raton FL 33431

and by CRC Press
4 Park Square, Milton Park, Abingdon, Oxon, OX14 4RN

CRC Press is an imprint of Taylor & Francis Group, LLC

Library of Congress Cataloging-in-Publication Data (applied for)

ISBN: 978-1-041-08535-5 (hbk)
ISBN: 978-1-041-13683-5 (pbk)
ISBN: 978-1-003-67681-2 (ebk)

DOI: 10.1201/9781003676812

Typeset in Times New Roman
by Prime Publishing Services

Preface

The Medical Internet of Things (MIoT) stands at the forefront of a transformative era in healthcare, merging advanced connectivity, real-time data monitoring, and intelligent analytics to revolutionize how medical services are delivered and experienced. This book discusses huge potentials and critical importance of MIoT technologies in shaping the future of healthcare systems worldwide.

The COVID-19 pandemic underscored the urgent need for resilient, adaptive healthcare solutions that can operate effectively even under constrained conditions. MIoT emerged as an essential technology, enabling remote patient monitoring, telehealth services, and data-driven decision-making. By integrating mobile computing, smart sensors, and cloud infrastructures, MIoT devices facilitate continuous collection and analysis of vital health indicators, empowering physicians to diagnose, treat, and manage patient health with unprecedented accuracy and speed. These capabilities not only improve patient outcomes but also reduce healthcare costs, optimize clinical workflows, and extend care accessibility to underserved populations.

Beyond its immediate impacts, MIoT represents a critical foundation for future healthcare innovation. As medical devices become increasingly interconnected, the convergence of big data analytics, artificial intelligence, and edge computing within MIoT frameworks will drive personalized medicine, predictive diagnostics, and proactive disease management. Additionally, robotics and virtual simulations integrated with MIoT make the way for advanced surgical assistance and training, further enhancing healthcare quality and safety. We hope that this book will be more useful to our audience. For any issues/ error in our book, please contact us.

Till then Happy Learning!

Amit Kumar Tyagi
Shabnam Kumari

Contents

CHAPTER 1

Smart Hospital and Healthcare Facilities

Abikoye, Oluwakemi Christiana*(0000-0002-8912-6333), Usman-Hamza Fatimah Enehezei(0009-0004-1115-4555), Abdulraheem, Muyideen(0000-0003-4568-7566), Awotunde, Joseph Bamidele(0000-0002-1020-4432), Adebayo, Paul Olujide(0000-0002-4088-0634), Oladipo, Idowu Dauda(0000-0002-1472-2237) and Temitayo, Evelyn Damilola(0009-0006-5483-2891)

Department of Computer Science, University of Ilorin, Ilorin, Nigeria

1. Introduction

The healthcare industry is transforming with the advent of smart hospital and healthcare facility concepts. These facilities represent the convergence of advanced digital technologies, data analytics, and medical expertise, enhancing patient care, operational efficiency, and clinical outcomes. A smart hospital is not merely a facility equipped with modern medical devices; rather, it is a technologically integrated ecosystem that leverages tools such as the Internet of Things (IoT), Artificial Intelligence (AI), electronic health records (EHR), telemedicine, and automation to provide a more responsive, efficient, and patient-centric environment (Awotunde 2025). One of the fundamental features of a smart hospital is its ability to collect, process, and analyze large volumes of data in real time. Through IoT-enabled devices, vital signs and patient conditions can be continuously monitored, allowing healthcare professionals to receive timely alerts and make informed decisions (Kwon et al., 2022). Smart sensors and wearables provide seamless data transmission to centralized platforms, enabling early diagnosis and predictive analytics. For instance, AI algorithms can detect patterns in patient data to anticipate complications before they arise, ultimately reducing hospital readmissions and improving patient safety (Olalekan 2025).

Another significant aspect of a smart healthcare facility is the integration of automation and robotics. Automated medication dispensers, robotic surgery tools, and AI-driven diagnostic systems streamline clinical workflows, reduce human error,

*Corresponding author: abikoye.o@unilorin.edu.ng

DOI: 10.1201/9781003676812-1

and enhance precision in medical procedures. Additionally, hospital logistics can be improved with robotic systems that handle inventory, transport supplies, and perform routine tasks, allowing medical staff to concentrate on patient care. Telemedicine is another pillar of smart healthcare, expanding access to medical expertise beyond the confines of physical facilities. Virtual consultations, remote patient monitoring, and mobile health applications enable patients to receive care regardless of geographic location. This not only improves healthcare accessibility for rural and underserved populations but also reduces the burden on hospital infrastructure. The implementation of smart infrastructure also extends to facility management. Intelligent building systems regulate lighting, temperature, and ventilation to create a comfortable and energy-efficient environment. Furthermore, advanced security and access control systems enhance patient safety and data protection, critical in the increasingly digital healthcare landscape.

Smart hospitals integrated with AI, IoT, robotics, and advanced analytics offer transformative benefits that improve patient care, staff efficiency, and system-wide outcomes. By empowering real-time patient monitoring, connected wearables, smart beds, and sensor-equipped devices continuously track vital signs and environmental conditions. This enables early detection of complications, improved comfort, and proactive care interventions (Mustafa 2025). Leveraging AI and predictive analytics, smart systems analyze electronic health records and imaging feeds to identify patterns such as early sepsis risks or anomalies in diagnostics. This enhances clinical decision-making, reduces human error, and accelerates treatment (Balasubramanian et al., 2025).

Operational efficiency greatly increases through automation: digital registration, queue management, AI scheduling tools, and automated medication dispensing free up clinician time for direct patient interaction (Karrouk 2025). Real-time asset tracking via RFID and indoor navigation supports logistics, reducing wasted staff hours and equipment retrieval delays. For patient experience, smart hospitals foster seamless, more personalized care. Voice- or app-based room controls (lighting, temperature, blinds) promote comfort and autonomy. Telehealth platforms and virtual wards extend services remotely, enable post-operative monitoring, and reduce hospital admissions and readmissions (Das 2024). Crucially, cost savings and resource optimization follow. Predictive equipment maintenance minimizes downtime, telemedicine reduces in-person visits, and resource allocation becomes data-driven. This leads to more judicious use of beds, supplies, and staff while lowering operational costs (Al Jnainati et al., 2025). Overall, smart hospitals redefine healthcare by fostering early detection, precise diagnostics, efficient workflows, and improved patient empowerment. With global adoption accelerating and markets projected to reach $148 billion by 2029, these systems are poised to become the backbone of future healthcare infrastructure (Behl and Sampat 2025).

However, the transition to smart hospitals is not without challenges. High implementation costs, cybersecurity risks, and the need for skilled personnel to manage complex systems are significant considerations. Moreover, the integration of these technologies must be carried out with a strong focus on ethical standards, data privacy, and patient consent. Smart hospitals and healthcare facilities represent the future of modern medicine. They offer immense potential to revolutionize healthcare delivery by making it more efficient, personalized, and proactive. As technology evolves, the successful adoption of smart solutions will depend on thoughtful planning, investment, and collaboration among stakeholders, including healthcare providers, technologists, policymakers, and patients. Through this digital transformation, healthcare systems can not only improve patient outcomes but also achieve sustainability and resilience in the face of growing demands and global health challenges.

2. IOT in Hospital Asset Management

The Internet of Things (IoT) is at the forefront of an era characterized by intelligent automation and ubiquitous connectivity brought about by the rapid growth of digital technologies. To connect and exchange data with other devices and systems via the internet, a vast network of physical things equipped with sensors, software, and other technologies is known as the Internet of Things (Kumar and Patel 2017). This paradigm enables a wide range of commonplace objects, machines, and environments to have internet connectivity beyond conventional devices like computers and smartphones. This allows them to gather and share data in real-time without the need for human-to-human or human-to-computer interaction (Al-Fuqaha et al., 2015).

An IoT ecosystem is essentially made up of the following essential elements that work together:

1. Things (Sensors and Actuators): These are the actual devices that include sensors to collect information from their environment (such as temperature, location, and motion) and/or actuators to perform actions in response to received commands.
2. Connectivity: This layer includes a variety of communication technologies (such as Wi-Fi, Bluetooth, cellular, LoRaWAN, and RFID) that allow the "things" to connect to the internet and exchange data.
3. Data Processing: The gathered data is sent to a cloud platform or local servers, where it is processed, analyzed, and stored. Frequently, big data analytics and machine learning algorithms are used to extract insights.
4. User Interface/Applications: Lastly, end users can monitor, manage, and control the IoT devices and systems by using applications, dashboards, or alerts that display the processed data.

The proliferation of inexpensive sensors, the widespread availability of high-speed internet, the creation of reliable cloud computing infrastructures, and developments in data analytics and machine learning are some of the major technological enablers that have propelled the expansion of the Internet of Things. With the promise of increased productivity, better decision-making, and previously unheard-of degrees of automation, the Internet of Things is revolutionizing how we interact with our physical environment, from smart homes and linked cars to industrial automation and smart cities (Ray 2017). With IoT opening the door for a new era of digital health—often referred to as the Internet of Medical Things (IoMT) or Smart Healthcare—the healthcare industry stands to benefit greatly from this broad landscape. This entails applying IoT concepts to healthcare systems, medical devices,

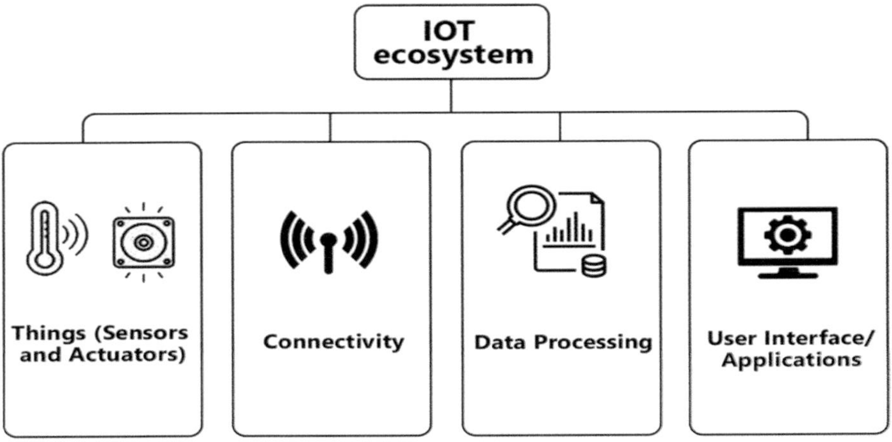

Figure 1: IoT ecosystem.

and hospital operations, particularly in the vital area of asset management. From life-saving medical equipment (such as ventilators, MRI machines, and defibrillators) and surgical instruments to wheelchairs, patient beds, and even consumables, hospital assets comprise a wide range of material and intangible resources essential to the provision of healthcare. Effective management of these resources is critical to patient care and the long-term viability of the hospital.

2.1. Challenges in Traditional Hospital Asset Management

Asset management is essential to delivering healthcare in an efficient and high-quality manner. Hospitals run intricate operations that largely depend on a wide range of medical tools, supplies, and equipment essential for diagnosing, treating, and caring for patients. However, traditional approaches to managing these assets are frequently laborious, manual, and rife with inefficiencies, resulting in serious operational difficulties, higher expenses, and, most importantly, possible compromises in patient safety and treatment quality.

The inability to track and locate equipment in real-time is one of the most widespread problems with traditional hospital asset management (Venu et al., 2022). Hospitals are dynamic because equipment is frequently moved between wards, operating rooms, labs, and maintenance departments. Employees often waste valuable time looking for lost or unavailable equipment when manual logs or sporadic physical inventory are used.. Particularly in emergency scenarios where prompt access to certain devices is essential, this "lost time" might result in delays in important medical procedures, which can have a detrimental effect on patient outcomes. Accurate inventory counts are also difficult due to the sheer amount and mobility of assets, which causes differences between reported and real stock levels.

Inefficient use of assets is another major problem. Hospitals frequently find it difficult to maximize the deployment of their equipment in the absence of real-time data on usage patterns. In one department, costly medical equipment may be underutilized, while in another, it may result in a scarcity or needless capital investment in new equipment or delays in patient care. On the other hand, excessive use of some equipment without adequate rotation or maintenance could result in early failure and increased wear and tear. Effective capacity planning and resource allocation are further hampered by the absence of insight into asset usage (Kumar, et al., 2023).

Lastly, the combination of these difficulties raises the risk of noncompliance and operational expenses. Reduced revenue from procedure delays, increased maintenance costs from lost work on reactive repairs, and inflated spending from needless equipment acquisitions are all consequences of ineffective asset management. Additionally, hospitals must comply with strict regulations about maintenance records, safety inspections, and equipment calibration. Manual systems raise the possibility of non-compliance, which could result in penalties, problems with certification, and above all, a compromise in patient safety (Kumar et al., 2023; Awotunde et al., 2025). A revolutionary approach to asset management is required to address these complex issues. This strategy should use cutting-edge technologies to give hospital operations real-time visibility, intelligent automation, and predictive capabilities.

2.2. Transformative Potential of IoT in Healthcare Asset Management

The emergence of the Internet of Things presents a groundbreaking answer to the numerous problems that traditional hospital asset management faces. Hospitals can move towards "Smart Hospitals" settings where networked devices and systems enable increased operational efficiency, better patient safety, and higher-quality care by incorporating IoT capabilities into healthcare infrastructure (Awotunde et al., 2025; Venu et al., 2022). IoT's revolutionary potential in hospital asset management is seen in several crucial areas:

First, IoT makes it possible to track the exact position of assets and see them in real time. Hospitals can continuously monitor the exact location of their assets by attaching or embedding small IoT devices, such as passive RFID tags or active Bluetooth Low Energy and Wi-Fi-enabled sensors, on medical equipment, instruments, and even consumables. Critical equipment, such as defibrillators, infusion pumps, or wheelchairs, will always be exactly where they are needed, when they are required, thanks to the elimination of the laborious manual equipment search process. This instant access to equipment improves patient care and results by drastically cutting down on procedure delays, particularly in urgent medical situations (Maged and Mohamed 2023; Rajwar et al., 2021).

Second, IoT makes inventory management and asset utilization more efficient. Equipment sensors can gather information on operating hours, idle periods, and consumption trends. Hospital administrators may learn a great deal about how often each piece of equipment is used thanks to this comprehensive data stream. They can discover underutilized assets that can be returned or repurposed, as well as overutilized ones that might need extra units or more frequent maintenance. These insights make it possible to allocate resources wisely, cut down on needless capital expenditures for new machinery, and guarantee that current assets are fully leveraged. To prevent stockouts and ensure that necessary supplies are always available, IoT-enabled smart shelves and bins for consumables may automatically monitor inventory levels and send out reorder warnings (Awotunde et al., 2025).

Finally, implementing IoT in hospital asset management improves regulatory compliance and results in significant cost savings. Hospitals can save a lot of money on capital expenditures, operating costs, and repair charges by optimizing utilization, reducing losses, and switching to predictive maintenance. Complying with strict healthcare rules and certification standards is made easier by automated data collection and digital record-keeping of asset movements, usage, and maintenance histories. A safer, more effective, and financially sustainable healthcare environment is promoted by hospitals meeting safety regulations and passing audits efficiently, thanks to openness and data integrity (Kumar et al., 2023; Darwish et al., 2025). To put it simply, IoT turns asset management from a labor-intensive, reactive process into a proactive, intelligent, and strategically optimized operation that immediately improves patient care results.

3. Smart Beds and IoT-Enabled Patient Rooms

Smart healthcare technologies use digital tools like AI, IoT, and data analysis to improve patient care and efficiency. These include wearable monitors, telemedicine platforms, and smart beds, enabling real-time monitoring and personalized treatment. The tools aim to enhance care, lower hospital readmissions, and improve patient outcomes by creating a connected and responsive healthcare system (Bhati, Deogade, and Kanyal 2023). Smart beds and IoT play important roles in modern patient care, making it safer and more comfortable. Smart beds have sensors that track patient vitals, movement, and positioning, which helps prevent falls and pressure ulcers (Recmanik et al., 2024). IoT in patient rooms connects devices like monitors and wearables, allowing healthcare teams to share data in real-time. This connectivity enables quicker responses, streamlines workflows, and improves the patient experience. The collected data also aids in predictive analytics, helping doctors make better decisions. Overall, smart beds and IoT lead to proactive and personalized healthcare (Abatal et al., 2024). The main goals of smart patient rooms are to boost patient safety, enhance care quality, and improve clinical workflows. These rooms use real-time data, automation, and connectivity to enable proactive actions, personalized care, and better resource management. This approach aims to improve patient outcomes and create a more responsive healthcare setting.

3.1. Smart Hospital Beds

Smart beds are advanced hospital beds that use technology to improve patient care and comfort. They possess several significant characteristics, including the ability to track vital signs like breathing and heart rate. The features can detect how a patient is positioned, and their movements help prevent falls or bedsores. The beds have the potential to automatically adjust positions remotely for comfort and medical needs.

Connection with Electronic Health Records (EHRs) and nurse call systems eases administration. With these beds, it is possible to alert staff if there are any issues with patient activity or vital signs (Areia et al., 2022). Lastly, continuous measurement of patient weight at intervals is observed and recorded.

3.1.1. Types of Smart Beds

There are various types of smart beds designed for specific patient needs and care settings.

- **ICU beds** are for critically ill patients, featuring constant monitoring and automated adjustments.
- **Med-surg beds** are used in general hospital wards, offering adjustable positions and fall detection.
- **Long-term** care beds focus on comfort and mobility for nursing home patients.
- **Bariatric smart beds** are for obese patients, providing wider surfaces and strong support.
- **Homecare smart beds** cater to patients at home and include remote monitoring and caregiver alerts, often controlled through mobile apps.

Table 1: Types of smart beds

Bed Type	Primary Use/Setting	Features
ICU Bed	Critically ill patients in the ICU	Constant monitoring, electric adjustability, CPR mode, integration with life support equipment, and rapid response features.
Med-Surg Bed	General hospital wards	Adjustable positions, fall detection, basic monitoring, suitable for a wide range of patients.
Long-Term Care Bed	Nursing homes, chronic care	Focus on comfort, mobility aids, low height for fall prevention, and ease of repositioning.
Bariatric Smart Bed	Obese patients in any setting	Wider surface, reinforced frame, high weight capacity, strong support, and electric controls.
Homecare Smart Bed	Patient homes	Remote monitoring, caregiver alerts, mobile app controls, adjustable positions, compact design.

Integrating smart beds with Electronic Health Records (EHRs) improves patient care by collecting real-time data like vital signs and movement (Bai, Gu, and Tang 2025). This data is sent to EHRs, reducing manual entry errors. Clinicians access current patient information quickly, enhancing decision-making and safety. EHR integration streamlines workflows, helping providers track trends and coordinate care for better patient outcomes.

3.2. IoT-Enabled Patient Rooms

The Internet of Things (IoT) in healthcare is a system of connected medical devices that gather and share health information in real time (Wu, Liu, Wang, and Bilal 2023). This includes devices like wearables, smart beds, and monitors with software and connectivity for continuous patient observation and interaction with healthcare professionals. IoT helps doctors make better decisions, improves health results for patients, and enables more effective and tailored care.

An IoT-enabled patient room uses smart technology to improve care and comfort. Key components include smart monitors for tracking vital signs and sending data to doctors; smart lighting that adjusts for patient needs; Heating, Ventilation, and Air Conditioning (HVAC) systems that control the room's environment; wearables that monitor health continuously; smart beds that adjust and send data; and voice-controlled systems for easy room management. Connected devices are key to enhancing patient experience and outcomes by monitoring vital signs, movement, and the environment. This real-time data allows for immediate medical response, enhancing patient comfort and safety. Patients can adjust room settings using voice commands, while clinicians benefit from better workflow and accurate patient information, reducing errors. Predictive analytics helps identify health risks early, leading to quicker recoveries and shorter hospital stays.

The main components include smart monitors for vital signs, smart lighting that adjusts automatically, HVAC systems for a comfortable environment, wearables that track activity and sleep, smart beds that respond to movement, and voice-controlled interfaces for patient assistance.

3.3. Key Functions and Benefits

Real-time monitoring in smart beds and IoT-enabled patient rooms tracks vital signs, movement, and posture through sensors (Iqubal et al., 2025). This monitoring helps detect health problems early, prevents falls, and allows for personalized care, improving patient safety, comfort, and the effectiveness of clinical responses in healthcare settings.

Smart beds and IoT-enabled patient rooms use sensors to monitor vital signs, movement, and posture. They alert healthcare staff when patients try to leave the bed or show instability. This helps staff respond quickly, lowering the risk of falls and injuries. These technologies can save hospitalization expenses while improving patient safety and treatment quality.

1. **Remote Adjustability and Patient Comfort:** Smart beds and IoT-enabled patient rooms let healthcare providers and patients control bed positions, lighting, and temperature from a distance. Haleem, Javaid, Singh, and Suman (2022) disclosed that customization helps patients feel more comfortable, recover better, and need less help from staff. Automated features can adjust posture to prevent pressure ulcers and improve circulation. By improving comfort and

giving patients more control, these technologies lead to better satisfaction and healthcare results.

2. **Data Collection for Predictive Analytics:** Data collection for predictive analytics in smart beds and IoT-enabled patient rooms involves continuously gathering health information like vital signs, movement patterns, and environmental conditions. This data is analyzed using AI and machine learning to spot early signs of complications, predict patient deterioration, and tailor treatment plans. Predictive analytics supports proactive interventions, which reduce emergencies and hospital readmissions. This approach optimizes the utilization of resources in healthcare settings, improves patient outcomes, and improves clinical judgments by transforming raw data into insightful knowledge.
3. **Improved Workflow Efficiency for Healthcare Staff:** Smart beds and IoT-enabled patient rooms help healthcare staff work more efficiently by automating routine tasks like monitoring and data collection. These systems provide real-time alerts and integrate smoothly with EHRs, cutting down on manual paperwork and letting staff focus on urgent care needs. Automation also improves communication, reduces mistakes, and allows for quicker responses, which helps healthcare professionals spend more time with patients. This leads to better productivity, less burnout, and higher-quality healthcare delivery.

3.4. Challenges and Limitations

Data privacy and cybersecurity are critical issues in smart healthcare. Protecting sensitive patient information from breaches is vital. To preserve confidence and stop illegal access or misuse, it is critical to guarantee secure data transport, storage, and adherence to laws like HIPAA.

1. **High Implementation and Maintenance Costs:** Many healthcare facilities face high costs when implementing and maintaining smart beds and IoT-enabled patient rooms. Expenses come from buying equipment, setting up infrastructure, regular software updates, and technical support. Smaller institutions with fewer resources may find it hard to afford these technologies, which limits their adoption, even though these tools have significant benefits.
2. **Integration with Legacy Systems:** Integrating smart beds and IoT technologies with old systems is challenging. Older hospitals and Electronic Health Records may not work well with new devices, requiring complicated updates or modifications.
3. **Staff Training and Acceptance:** Staff training and acceptance are major challenges when introducing smart beds and IoT-enabled patient rooms in healthcare. Healthcare professionals must be well educated to use new technologies and understand the data they generate. The adoption process may be slowed by resistance to change, fear of losing one's career, or a lack of digital skills. Continuous training and clear communication are vital to help staff feel confident, ensuring a smooth transition and making the most of these advancements.

4. Automation in Surgical Theaters

Automation in the surgical theater has revolutionized medical-surgical procedures by incorporating advanced technologies, including robotic systems and automated instruments. These tools enhance precision, increase efficiency, and improve patient safety by assisting surgeons and providing real-time data. This leads to fewer human errors, smoother workflows, and faster recoveries with fewer complications.

Recent progress in robotic surgical systems and automation technologies has considerably sharpened surgical accuracy and procedural outcomes (Nagy and Haidegger 2022). The benefits extend well beyond the operating table—patients experience less invasive interventions, surgeons enjoy enhanced capabilities, and policymakers can appreciate improvements in healthcare delivery at scale. This is not just evolution; it is a quiet revolution in the surgical suite.

Significantly, the focus has shifted from automating isolated tasks to developing collaborative systems that work alongside, rather than in place of, surgeons (Nagy and Haidegger 2022). These systems function more like trusted assistants than replacements—think of them as the high-tech equivalent of a well-trained surgical partner who never gets tired. As more hospitals adopt these technologies, it becomes increasingly important to examine not only the significant benefits they provide but also the challenges they pose in real-world clinical settings.

4.1. Benefits of Automation in Surgical Theaters

One of the most notable advancements in healthcare automation is the increased precision achieved during surgical interventions. Today, robotic systems enable surgeons to carry out procedures with a level of accuracy that surpasses traditional methods. (Dehghani and Kim 2021). This reduced precision error contributes to less tissue damage and minimizes the risk of complications. Summarily, surgical automation has post-surgical complications, such as infections and excessive bleeding.

Moreover, automation facilitates minimally invasive surgical techniques. These methods typically involve smaller incisions, resulting in reduced postoperative pain and a quicker recovery time. Minimally invasive surgery is a technique that enables surgeons to operate through small incisions, utilizing a camera and specialized instruments. In surgical automation, patients experience less discomfort and can return to their normal activities more quickly (Jinji 2023).

Beyond the surgical procedure, surgical automation of the surgical theater plays a vital role in enhancing preoperative planning and intraoperative guidance. New imaging technologies and real-time data analysis, which involve the immediate interpretation of data as it is collected, provide surgeons with important information and insights during the operation. (Ziyi et al., 2022). This support enables them to make more informed decisions during surgery, resulting in enhanced care and improved outcomes. Some of the benefits of automation in surgical theaters include:

1. Increased Precision and Accuracy: Surgical automation enhances surgical precision and reduces the risk of human error. Surgeons can navigate human

anatomy with robotic surgical systems and computer-assisted technology. (Nagy and Haidegger 2022; Yip and Das, 2018).

2. Enhanced Efficiency and Workflow: Automated systems streamline surgical planning, reduce human error, and accelerate processes, resulting in more efficient use of operating theaters and reduced waiting times (Diedhiou et al. 2020; Yip and Das, 2018).
3. Minimally Invasive Procedures: Robotic automation enables smaller incisions, improved visibility, and the ability to perform complex procedures with less trauma to patients, resulting in faster recovery and fewer complications (Ma et al., 2019).
4. Improved Safety: Automation can enhance safety by providing real-time biosignal monitoring, optimal control of instruments, and reducing the risk of human error during surgery (Yip and Das, 2018)
5. Reduced Surgeon Fatigue and Enhanced Comfort: Robotic systems can offload repetitive or physically demanding tasks, decreasing surgeon fatigue and enabling more comfortable and sustained performance during lengthy procedures (Battaglia et al., 2021).

4.2. Challenges in Integrating Automation in Surgical Theaters

Despite its numerous advantages, integrating automation into surgical practice presents its hurdles. One of the most immediate challenges is comprehensive training and adjustment among surgical teams. Learning to navigate new technologies requires time, effort, and resources—and let us face it, not everyone is eager to swap their trusted scalpel for a high-tech counterpart. Understandably, some clinicians may be hesitant, particularly when concerns linger about the reliability of automated systems.

Speaking of reliability, even the most sophisticated technologies are not immune to the occasional glitch. In the high-stakes environment of the operating room, a system malfunction can be more than just inconvenient—it can be dangerous. As such, surgical teams must be well-prepared to troubleshoot issues quickly and confidently when the unexpected arises.

Economic considerations also play a significant role in determining the widespread adoption of automation. While the long-term benefits, such as increased efficiency and improved outcomes, are compelling, the initial investment can be steep. Hospital administrators must carefully evaluate whether the potential returns justify the cost.

Another key factor is interoperability—the ability of new automated systems to communicate and function seamlessly with existing hospital infrastructure (Albouq et al., 2022). Think of it as getting all your smart devices to speak the same language; it is easier said than done, but crucial for smooth operations. Without this compatibility, even the most advanced technologies can disrupt workflows rather than improve them. Effective integration, though complex, is essential for reaping the full benefits of surgical automation.

The analysis in Table 2 examines the significant challenges encountered when integrating automation technologies into surgical theater environments.

Table 2: Integrating Automation in Surgical Theater Challenges

Technological Complexity	Cost and Resource Investment	Ethical and Legal Concerns	Cybersecurity Risks	Resistance to Change
Implementing sophisticated automation often requires seamless integration of multiple technologies, which can be highly challenging.	High implementation and maintenance costs create barriers for hospitals and clinics.	Automation raises questions about accountability and patient safety during surgeries.	Risks related to data breaches and hacking are amplified with connected systems.	Overcoming skepticism and adapting to new technologies by the surgical staff.
Interfacing robotic systems with existing medical devices	Procurement of advanced robotic systems with steep upfront costs	Liability in the event of machine errors or software malfunctions	Safeguarding patient data from cyber intrusions	Concerns among surgeons about loss of control
Ensuring real-time data processing and feedback	Training medical personnel on new automation technologies	Informed consent when using automated systems	Preventing unauthorized access to surgical automation tools	Adapting workflows to incorporate automation
Customization for diverse surgical procedures	Regular maintenance and software updates	Balancing human authority versus machine guidance	Ensuring uninterrupted system performance during surgeries	Reluctance to trust machine-driven precision over human skill

4.3. Future of Automation in Surgical Theaters

Artificial intelligence integration is projected to improve automated systems by enhancing procedural planning and offering real-time decision support during surgeries, setting the stage for future breakthroughs in surgical automation. As technology advances, the use of sophisticated analytics is expected to facilitate more complex surgical interventions, sparking growing interest in the revolutionary potential of artificial intelligence (AI) to improve surgical procedures.

Moreover, ongoing advancements in automation technology are poised to enhance the safety and quality of patient care. This development not only yields improved patient outcomes but also enhances the overall surgical experience. Therefore, the anticipated change in surgical techniques should present an optimistic outlook for the future of healthcare services. To illustrate the trend of its progression,

Table 3 provides an in-depth overview of the evolution of automation in surgical theaters over time, its current applications, and the promising trends we anticipate in the future.

Table 3: Historical and Future of Automation in Surgical Theaters

Historical Development	Current Applications	Future Projections
Explores the foundational technologies and innovations that set the stage for automation in surgical theaters	Highlights technologies used in surgical theaters today and their contributions to precision and efficiency	Examines anticipated advancements and their implications in transforming surgical theaters
Early adoption of mechanical tools in surgery	Robotic-assisted surgeries utilizing systems like Da Vinci (Johnson and Allaf, 2016)	Integration of fully autonomous robotic systems
Development of basic laparoscopic instruments	Real-time imaging and augmented reality for navigation using 4 and 5G	Use of 6G and beyond for faster data transmission and remote surgeries
Introduction of computer-assisted surgical devices	AI-driven predictive analytics for surgical decision-making	Enhanced AI models for personalized surgical strategies

Therefore, concerns about the future of surgical automation rely on society's needs. Now, research is moving toward more intelligent, adaptive, and collaborative robotic systems. Similarly, leveraging reinforcement learning and advanced sensing to improve autonomy and surgeon support is not left out of the plans.

The integration of automation in surgical theaters is ushering in a new era of surgical practice. This is evidenced by the benefits, such as improved precision, minimally invasive techniques, and enhanced planning capabilities. However, the researcher should also address challenges related to training, technical reliability, and costs. Furthermore, issues related to low latency, which are promised to be delivered with a 6G network (Das et al., 2022; Popovski et al., 2022), are significantly worth pursuing. Consequently, as the invention evolves within the healthcare system, adopting these innovations will be crucial for enhancing patient care and effectively addressing the complexities inherent in modern surgical environments. The future of automated surgery holds great promise, with the potential to significantly transform healthcare delivery for the better.

5. Hospital Administration and Workforce Management

Hospital administration and workforce are fundamental to healthcare systems worldwide. To grasp the relationship between these areas, it is essential to analyze how leadership, human resource strategies, and operational efficiency collaborate to create environments where top-notch patient care can flourish while ensuring financial stability.

Hospital administration is in charge of several facets of a medical facility, including financial management, quality improvement, procurement, and data analysis. Coordinating research projects, using evidence-based practices, and supporting hospital quality improvement initiatives all depend on it (Dubois and Singh, 2009; Kabene et al., 2006). This area of work focuses on overseeing the day-to-day activities and operations of hospitals and healthcare institutions, making sure that every department, from billing to the emergency room, runs efficiently in tandem. Effectively delivering high-quality healthcare services while protecting the organization's financial stability is the primary objective of hospital administration (Armstrong and Taylor, 2023; Kolié et al., 2023).

5.1. Scope of Hospital Administration

The realm of hospital administration is extensive and varied, covering a wide array of responsibilities, career opportunities, and organizational functions within the healthcare industry. Hospital administrators engage in the daily management of hospital operations and in a strategic capacity to shape healthcare provision, influence policy, and enhance patient outcomes.

1. **Hospital Management and Executive Leadership:** At the top tier, hospital administrators may hold positions such as Chief Executive Officers (CEOs), Chief Operating Officers (COOs), or Medical Directors, overseeing the strategic and operational direction of healthcare facilities. Their duties include long-term planning, ensuring adherence to healthcare regulations, supervising financial performance, managing risks, and fostering a culture of patient safety and high-quality care.

2. **Departmental Administration:** Administrators may also focus on specific departments, including:
    - **Human Resources (HR):** Tasked with the recruitment, training, and retention of healthcare staff.
    - **Finance**: Managing budgets, insurance claims, billing, and procurement processes.
    - **Patient Services**: Ensuring patient satisfaction, handling admissions, discharge protocols, and care coordination.
    - **Quality Control**: Overseeing healthcare outcomes and maintaining compliance with national standards and clinical regulations.

    Each of these domains necessitates specialized administrative knowledge to ensure effective internal operations and optimal utilization of resources.

3. **Health Policy, Planning, and Regulation:** Hospital administrators may collaborate with governmental bodies, NGOs, or international health organizations to assist in the development of health policies and healthcare strategies. These roles encompass:
    - Conducting a public health program needs assessments
    - Designing healthcare frameworks
    - Planning facility growth based on demographic needs

- Ensuring compliance with legal and accreditation standards

Administration plays a crucial role in macro-level decisions that affect entire communities and health systems.

4. **Healthcare Consultancy:** Hospital administrators can also serve as healthcare consultants, providing expert guidance to organizations to enhance service delivery, restructure processes, or implement new technologies. Consultants evaluate hospital operations, perform audits, and suggest actionable solutions in cost management, patient satisfaction, and operational efficiency.

5. **Research and Development (R&D):** Hospital administrators frequently contribute to clinical and health systems research by:
   - Supporting research teams with administrative management
   - Overseeing funding and grant proposals
   - Integrating evidence-based practices into everyday operations
   - Collaborating with academic institutions to innovate treatment protocols and hospital systems

   This role connects clinical innovation with practical hospital management.

5.2. Role of Hospital Administration

The administration of hospitals plays a crucial role in ensuring that healthcare institutions operate smoothly, effectively, and in alignment with legal and ethical guidelines. Although responsibilities can differ based on the facility's size, they generally encompass the following:

Strategic Planning: Hospital leaders establish long-term objectives, keep track of healthcare developments, and execute plans that improve hospital efficiency and patient satisfaction (Buchbinder and Shanks, 2019).

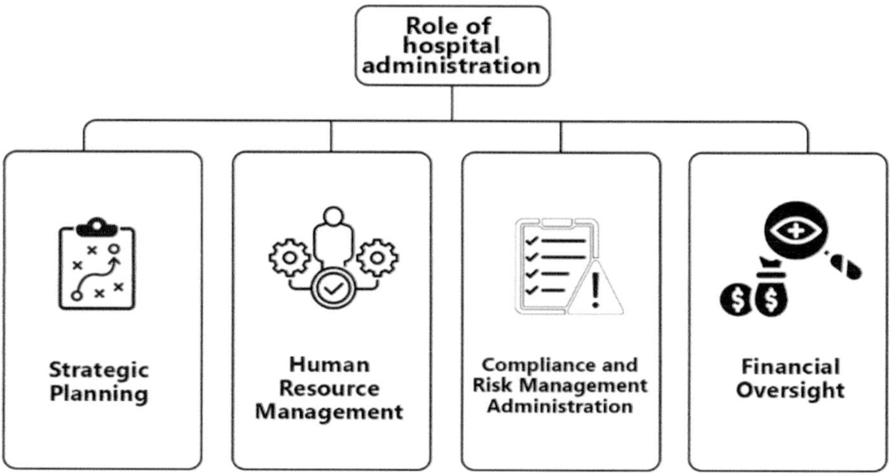

Figure 2: Role of hospital administration.

Human Resource Management: Human resource management is in charge of hiring, training, and retaining employees, ensuring that the hospital has the right people on board to meet patient needs (Kabene et al., 2006; Armstrong, 2006).

Compliance and Risk Management Administrators: Ensure that healthcare regulations and standards are followed while addressing risks associated with operations, patient safety, and legal issues (WHO, 2010).

Financial Oversight: They manage budgeting, purchasing, and resource distribution to sustain the hospital's financial stability (Nowicki, 2017). Patient Care Coordination Administrators collaborate with clinical teams to guarantee the smooth care delivery, thereby improving patient outcomes and satisfaction.

5.3. Workforce Management

WFM, or Workforce Management, is a system focused on staffing and scheduling to ensure an organization operates efficiently. In a large hospital setting, the volume of administrative tasks necessary for the smooth operation of each department is not only overwhelming but also critical for department functionality. Managing personnel and their schedules, along with various shifts, breaks, and backend operations, can all be effectively managed by a Workforce Management System. Essentially, the WFM system serves as an HR tool that aids in administrative tasks while also taking on important responsibilities such as filling open positions and managing payroll; it essentially monitors the workforce to promote the overall productivity of the organization (Code Brew Labs n.d.).

Key components of workforce management are:

Recruitment and Staffing: Hospitals must recruit qualified clinical and non-clinical personnel to meet care demands. Effective hiring ensures appropriate skills and credentials are matched to the workload (Zhu et al., 2024).

Figure 3: Key components of workforce management.

Workforce Planning and Scheduling: Hospitals engage in short- and long-term staffing plans based on patient volume and acuity. Tools help optimize schedules, considering skill mix, leave, and demand peaks.

Training and Development: Ongoing training ensures staff maintain competencies and adapt to care changes. Structured orientation and professional development close skill gaps and support growth.

Performance Management and Evaluation: Regular appraisals (confidential, semi-open, or open) align individual performance with hospital goals, promoting accountability and identifying areas for improvement.

Retention and Engagement: To reduce costly turnover, hospitals use strategies like flexible scheduling, competitive pay, and mentorship. A supportive environment improves staff satisfaction and retention. Importance of Workforce Management in Healthcare.

5.3.1. Technology and Automation of Workforce Management

Modern hospital personnel management is increasingly using advanced information systems that include scheduling, competency tracking, performance evaluation, and predictive analytics. These solutions provide real-time staffing level monitoring, automation of compliance tasks, and estimation of future manpower requirements.

By examining past data, patient flow, and employee preferences, artificial intelligence (AI) improves scheduling and produces effective and fulfilling schedules. Additionally, machine learning identifies patterns in employee turnover, enabling proactive retention tactics. However, issues including professional autonomy, privacy concerns, and the complexity of clinical decision-making make it difficult for technology to be adopted in the healthcare industry. Strong change management, extensive user training, and continuous improvement are necessary for an integration to be successful.

As noted by Zhu et al. (2024), innovations like electronic health records (EHRs), AI applications, and workforce management solutions can minimize human errors, enhance clinical results, and simplify care coordination. Predictive analytics can anticipate patient volumes, optimize shift assignments, and reveal opportunities for cross-training. Hospitals that implement AI-enhanced systems have reported decreased overtime and a better match between staff skills and patient requirements, particularly during emergencies like pandemics.

Common Challenges of the Healthcare Workforce

The management of the healthcare workforce encounters ongoing difficulties:

Staff Shortages: Numerous areas experience persistent shortages of nurses, doctors, and allied health professionals. These deficits put pressure on current staff and often necessitate the use of costly agency personnel. (Zhu et al., 2024) highlight "workforce shortages and high turnover" as key challenges faced in hospitals. The WHO anticipates a global deficit of approximately 11 million health workers by 2030, primarily in low-income nations. These shortages can result in unsafe nurse-to-patient ratios and postponed care.

Burnout and Workload: Intense workloads and stress contribute to clinician burnout, negatively affecting staff well-being and retention. Burnout among healthcare providers can have serious implications for patient safety and the quality of care. For instance, the NHS in England has reported instances of staff "crying with frustration and anger" due to constant pressures. Zhu et al. (2024) observe that disproportionate staff-to-patient ratios and excessive workloads may lower productivity and increase mistakes. Therefore, addressing burnout necessitates careful scheduling (to avoid excessive overtime), supportive programs, and sufficient staffing levels.

High Turnover: The high turnover of healthcare professionals incurs financial and operational burdens. Recruitment expenses (often amounting to tens of thousands per nurse) deplete budgets, and the loss of experienced personnel can compromise care continuity. Elevated turnover is frequently both a cause and a consequence of other issues: shortages worsen burnout, which in turn triggers departures. Thus, strategies for retention from recruitment to career advancement are crucial to disrupt the turnover cycle.

Regulatory Compliance: Hospitals must adhere to a multitude of regulations and accreditation standards related to staffing. These may include mandated staff-to-patient ratios, credentialing prerequisites, work-hour restrictions, and documentation guidelines. Noncompliance can threaten funding or accreditation. Zhu et al. (2024) stress that healthcare organizations must navigate complex legal and ethical requirements and comprehend relevant regulations concerning structural, procedural, and outcome standards. Workforce managers must ensure that schedules and staff credentials align with these regulatory obligations while maintaining adaptability.

5.3.2. Choosing a Workforce Management System

Integrating hospital administration with workforce management into an automated system can drastically reduce the workload in healthcare, improving efficiency and allowing staff to focus more on patient care. From experience, workforce management systems have become indispensable for various sectors, most notably in hospital settings. These systems go beyond simple schedule automation by considering staff availability, individual patient requirements, and the specific skills of each team member to ensure optimal task assignments. Both patients and healthcare professionals benefit greatly from having an automated system for workforce management and hospital administration.

5.3.3. Key Factors to Consider When Choosing a Workforce Management System for Healthcare Facilities

1. **Understand Your Facility's Unique Needs:** There is a need to understand your facility's unique needs to select the most suitable workforce management system for your healthcare facility. Thoroughly assess your facility's unique requirements by determining which workforce management areas require the most attention, and prioritize these to guide your selection. According to Miller (2024), selecting the right healthcare workforce management system entails

understanding the specific needs of your organization and ensuring the system supports seamless integration and user-friendly operations.

2. **Scalability and Integration Capabilities:** A healthcare management system, such as electronic health records (EHRs), human resource information systems (HRIS), or payroll software, can be integrated with existing systems to grow your healthcare organization. This healthcare system should scale with your organization. This compatibility supports operational continuity and future expansion without disruption.
3. **User-Friendly Interface:** A user-friendly platform that requires minimal training for your staff to operate efficiently is to be selected. A user-friendly interface reduces onboarding time and helps employees quickly adopt the system, which is highly important in rapidly changing healthcare environments.
4. **Data Security and Regulatory Compliance:** Since the nature of healthcare data is highly sensitive, it is crucial that the workforce management system adheres to data security standards and conforms with relevant healthcare regulations to safeguard patient and employee information.
5. **Staff Support and Training:** It is crucial to select vendors that provide ongoing technical support and detailed training resources to help your staff. It ensures that your team can fully leverage the software capabilities and efficiently adjust to updates or changes.

6. Application Challenges of Smart Hospitals and Healthcare Facilities

Implementing smart hospitals and healthcare facilities promises transformative benefits such as improved patient outcomes, streamlined operations, and enhanced staff efficiency; however, realizing this vision comes with a host of complex and interwoven challenges that span technology, infrastructure, finance, regulation, and people. At the heart of the difficulty lies the integration of disparate legacy systems with new technologies. Many hospitals, particularly in developing nations, operate on fragmented IT silos—where billing, diagnostics, monitoring, and records exist on isolated platforms. Efforts to modernize these systems often confront deeply entrenched, decades-old infrastructure that resists seamless integration. In countries like China, this fragmentation has led hospitals to build data "islands," undermining the very interoperability that smart hospitals require (Lakshumiah et al., 2025). Even in advanced healthcare economies, institutions like Denmark's hospitals have faced significant disruptions during transitions to systems like Epic, where poor localization and inadequate training led to clinical mishaps and operational chaos.

Closely tied to integration is the financial burden of deployment. The cost of high-technology systems spanning RFID asset trackers, AI-driven diagnostics, IoT sensors, and robust cybersecurity constitutes a significant hurdle. Deloitte projects that large hospitals may need to nearly double their IT budgets, pushing them from a modest 2–3% of operating costs to upwards of 4–5% annually (Salm et al., 2025).

This investment must go further than acquisition: ongoing maintenance, training, and upgrades deepen the financial strain. Lower-resourced facilities risk being left behind, as procurements can divert funds from other critical areas, perpetuating disparities in access to smart care.

Security and privacy challenges are central concerns, given the sensitive nature of health data. The proliferation of connected devices and cloud-based platforms heightens vulnerability to cyberattacks. Healthcare providers have witnessed a sharp rise in ransomware targeting hospitals, attacks that can halt care delivery and cost tens of millions in damages (Imoize et al., 2024). Regulatory compliance intensifies the challenge: frameworks like HIPAA in the U.S. and GDPR in the EU enforce stringent data protections, but industry practices often lag (Preston, 2022). The notorious breach of Change Healthcare in early 2024 exposed critical gaps in multifactor authentication and incident response preparedness (Aldosari, 2025). Thus, building a resilient cybersecurity posture demands technology investments and disciplined policy, oversight, and incident response capabilities.

Equally formidable are regulatory and ethical barriers that complicate deployment. Innovations like AI diagnosis tools, robotics, and telemedicine operate in regulatory gray zones where licensing, liability, and cross-border patient care raise thorny questions. The slow pace of regulation often cannot keep up with innovation, leaving hospitals to navigate uncertainty about reimbursement, malpractice, and legal accountability. Ethical considerations amplify the challenge: AI systems trained on biased data risk reinforcing health disparities, while invasions of privacy may reduce patient trust and compliance. On the infrastructure front, facility managers must retroactively embed smart building technologies such as IoT devices for ventilation, HVAC monitoring, and energy optimization into environments built long before such systems existed. These structures are complex, with 24/7 operations that cannot tolerate prolonged system downtime. Installing sensors, network backbones, and automation platforms often necessitates phased deployment that prolongs project timelines and complicates budgeting. Interdependencies, where a failure in one system can cascade into broader facility operations, heighten the stakes of these retrofits.

Technology proliferation itself presents challenges. Hospitals adopting IoT, edge computing, 5G, AI, and robotics must contend with heterogeneity in protocols and standards, Zigbee, Bluetooth, Wi-Fi, HL7, and FHIR, creating interoperability barriers and risking vendor lock-in (Bollineni et al., 2025). Orchestrating this complex architecture to guarantee quality of service, low latency for real-time alerts, and resiliency for critical devices is far from trivial. While cloud systems offer elasticity, they may not assure the immediate, high-assurance performance needed in clinical delivery, pushing some facilities to adopt fog computing layers and edge devices to maintain reliability (Ianculescu et al., 2025).

Human factors compound technical complexity. Successful adoption depends on clinicians and staff accepting new workflows, interfaces, and responsibilities. Yet resistance is widespread. Evidence suggests nurses spend up to 40% of their time on documentation, and the introduction of digital tools often intensifies this burden if not thoughtfully designed. Training must be continuous and deep, but resource-starved hospitals struggle to allocate time and funds. In extreme cases, part-time reliance on paper records persists, especially where reliable internet is not assured. Without frontline buy-in, smart solutions risk stagnation, even collapse. The demand for specialized skills exacerbates the problem. The deployment and upkeep of intricate smart ecosystems are hampered by a shortage of skilled IT and cybersecurity specialists with a thorough awareness of both healthcare operations and technology. Many hospitals resort to outsourcing to third-party vendors, which introduces its risks. External parties gain access to sensitive data and systems, and sponsored solutions may not fully align with unique organizational needs.

Despite these obstacles, progress continues. The Surat Municipal Corporation in India, under India's Smart Cities Mission, recently implemented a Hospital Management Information System that serves over 89,000 patients across multiple facilities and incorporates electronic health records, queue management, and mobile app access all within weeks of rollout. Apollo Hospitals is channeling greater portions of its digital budget into AI for documentation and diagnostics, aiming to free up critical clinician time. However, they still struggle with data standardization, EMR limitations, and proving ROI. Finally, transforming traditional hospitals into smart, digitally native health ecosystems is an intricate and gradual endeavor, like orchestrating a silent symphony amid the clinical chaos of care delivery. These institutions must simultaneously manage capital investments, regulatory compliance, cybersecurity defense, infrastructure modernization, and human change management. Fewer than 10% of hospitals currently meet the threshold of "smart." Yet with thoughtful strategy, cross-industry collaboration, and sustained institutional commitment, the vision of connected, resilient, patient-centric hospitals is steadily edging toward reality (Aman et al., 2024; Abdelsalam, 2025).

7. Conclusion

The transformation of traditional healthcare systems into smart hospitals and intelligent healthcare facilities represents a monumental leap toward the future of medicine. This evolution is not merely about adopting new technologies but about reimagining the entire healthcare ecosystem to be more responsive, efficient, and patient-centered. By integrating cutting-edge innovations such as the Internet of Things (IoT), Artificial Intelligence (AI), robotics, and automation, smart hospitals are redefining how care is delivered, managed, and experienced.

Smart hospitals enable real-time monitoring, predictive analytics, and personalized treatment plans that significantly enhance patient outcomes. Technologies like smart beds, IoT-enabled patient rooms, and automated surgical theaters are not only improving clinical precision and safety but also reducing human error, minimizing recovery times, and optimizing resource allocation. These advancements empower healthcare professionals with actionable insights, streamline workflows, and foster a more proactive approach to care delivery. Moreover, integrating digital tools in hospital administration and workforce management is revolutionizing operational efficiency. Automated scheduling, AI-driven performance tracking, and predictive staffing models are helping institutions manage human resources more effectively, reduce burnout, and ensure compliance with regulatory standards. These systems also support strategic planning and financial sustainability, which are critical in an era of rising healthcare demands and constrained budgets.

However, the journey toward fully realizing the potential of smart healthcare is fraught with challenges. High implementation and maintenance costs, cybersecurity vulnerabilities, interoperability issues, and resistance to change among healthcare staff are significant barriers. Additionally, ethical concerns surrounding data privacy, algorithmic bias, and patient consent must be addressed with robust governance frameworks and transparent policies. Despite these hurdles, the momentum toward digital transformation in healthcare is undeniable. Global trends indicate increasing investments in smart health infrastructure, with governments, private sectors, and academic institutions collaborating to drive innovation. Pilot programs and case studies from around the world demonstrate that with the right strategy, training, and stakeholder engagement, the transition to smart hospitals can be both feasible and impactful.

In conclusion, smart hospitals and healthcare facilities are not just a technological upgrade—they are a paradigm shift in how we perceive and practice medicine. They offer a vision of healthcare that is more connected, intelligent, and humane. As we move forward, this transformation must be guided by principles of equity, inclusivity, and sustainability to ensure that the benefits of smart healthcare are accessible to all. With continued innovation, investment, and collaboration, the dream of a truly smart, resilient, and patient-focused healthcare system is well within reach.

References

Abdelsalam, F. M. (2025). Blockchain Technology in the Healthcare Industry: An Empirical Study of Factors Influencing Organizational Adoption of Blockchain Technology. Doctoral dissertation, The University of North Carolina at Charlotte.

Abatal, A., Mzili, M., Mzili, T., Cherrat, K., Yassine, A., and Abualigah, L. (2024). Intelligent interconnected healthcare system: Integrating IoT and big data for personalized patient care. International Journal of Online & Biomedical Engineering, 20(11).

Aldosari, B. (2025). Cybersecurity in healthcare: New threat to patient safety. Cureus, 17(5).

Al-Fuqaha, A., Guizani, M., Mohammadi, M., Aledhari, M., and Ayyash, M. (2015). Internet of Things: A survey on enabling technologies, protocols, and applications. IEEE Communications Surveys & Tutorials, 17(4), 2347–2376.

Al Jnainati, M., Jnainati, J.A., Rath, S., Aujla, S., Nasir, E., Govindarajan, A., ... and Semy, M. (2025). Transforming paperwork with AI: Applications across healthcare and other industries. AI & Society, 1–14.

Albouq, S.S., Sen, A.A.A., Almashf, N., Yamin, M., Alshanqiti, A., and Bahbouh, N.M. (2022). A survey of interoperability challenges and solutions for dealing with them in IoT environment. IEEE Access, 10, 36416-36428. https://doi.org/10.1109/ACCESS.2022.3162219

Aman, A., Gupta, H., Kharub, M., and McDermott, O. (2024). Enablers for implementing big data analytics in the healthcare industry: Prioritization, classification, and implications for sustainable competitive advantages. IEEE Transactions on Engineering Management. Vol. n pp

Areia, C., King, E., Ede, J., Young, L., Tarassenko, L., Watkinson, P., and Vollam, S. (2022). Experiences of current vital signs monitoring practices and views of wearable monitoring: A qualitative study in patients and nurses. Journal of Advanced Nursing, 78(3), 810–822.

Armstrong, M. (2006). A Handbook of Human Resource Management Practice, 10th edition. Kogan Page, pp. 174.

Armstrong, M., and Taylor, S. (2023). Armstrong's handbook of human resource management practice: A guide to the theory and practice of people management. Kogan Page Publishers.

Awotunde, J.B. (2025). Introduction to smart hospital. *In:* Blockchain and Digital Twin for Smart Hospitals (pp. 1–35). Elsevier.

Bai, Y., Gu, B., and Tang, C. (2025). Enhancing real-time patient monitoring in intensive care units with deep learning and the Internet of Things. Big Data. https://doi.org/10.1089/big.2024.0113

Balasubramanian, S., Shukla, V., Islam, N., Upadhyay, A., and Duong, L. (2025). Applying artificial intelligence in healthcare: Lessons from the COVID-19 pandemic. International Journal of Production Research, 63(2), 594–627.

Battaglia, E., Boehm, J., Zheng, Y., Jamieson, A.R., Gahan, J., and Majewicz Fey, A. (2021). Rethinking autonomous surgery: Focusing on enhancement over autonomy. European Urology Focus, 7(4), 696–705. https://doi.org/10.1016/j.euf.2021.06.009

Behl, A., and Sampat, B. (Eds.). (2025). Digital Transformation: A Business Imperative. Taylor & Francis.

Bhati, D., Deogade, M.S., and Kanyal, D. (2023). Improving patient outcomes through effective hospital administration: A comprehensive review. Cureus, 15(10). e47731.

Bollineni, C., Sharma, M., Hazra, A., Kumari, P., Manipriya, S., and Tomar, A. (2025). IoT for next-generation smart healthcare: A comprehensive survey. IEEE Internet of Things Journal, 12(16), 32616-32639.

Buchbinder, S.B., Shanks, N.H., and Kite, B.J. (2019). Introduction to Health Care Management. Jones & Bartlett Learning.

Code Brew Labs. (n.d.). Workforce management systems in healthcare. Code Brew. https://www.code-brew.com/workforce-management-systems-in-healthcare/

Das, S. (2024). Applications of sensor technology in healthcare. *In:* Revolutionizing Healthcare Treatment with Sensor Technology (pp. 79-99). IGI Global.

Das, S.R., Sarma, S. Sen, Khuntia, M., Roy, I., Sinha, K., and Sinha, B.P. (2022). A novel routing strategy towards achieving ultra-low end-to-end latency in 6G networks. International Journal of Computer Networks and Communications, 14(1). https://doi.org/10.5121/ijcnc.2022.14101

Dehghani, H., and Kim, P.C.W. (2021). Robotic automation for surgery. Digital Surgery, 203–213. https://doi.org/10.1007/978-3-030-49100-0_15

Diedhiou, M., Tendeng, J., Barboza, D., Diallo, A.K., Diao, M., Camara, G., and Konate, I. (2020). Computer science in the management of operating theatres: A challenge for Sub-Saharan anaesthetists and resuscitation medical doctors. International Journal of Innovative Research in Medical Science, 5(06). https://doi.org/10.23958/ijirms/vol05-i06/882

Dubois, C.A., and Singh, D. (2009). From staff-mix to skill-mix and beyond: Towards a systemic approach to health workforce management. Human Resources for Health, 7(1), 87. https://doi.org/10.1186/1478-4491-7-87

Haleem, A., Javaid, M., Singh, R.P., and Suman, R. (2022). Medical 4.0 technologies for healthcare: Features, capabilities, and applications. Internet of Things and Cyber-Physical Systems, 2, 12–30.

Ianculescu, M., Constantin, V.Ș., Gușatu, A.M., Petrache, M.C., Mihăescu, A.G., Bica, O., and Alexandru, A. (2025). Enhancing connected health ecosystems through IoT-enabled monitoring technologies: A case study of the Monit4Healthy system. Sensors, 25(7), 2292.

Imoize, A.L., Meshram, C., Awotunde, J.B., Farhaoui, Y., and Do, D.T. (Eds.). (2024). Cybersecurity in Emerging Healthcare Systems. *In:* IET (pp. 1–746).

Iqubal, S., Khan, S., Pant, N., Sarkar, S., Rey, T., and Mohapatra, H. (2025). A study on IoT-enabled smart bed with brain-computer interface for elderly and paralyzed individuals. *In:* Future Innovations in the Convergence of AI and Internet of Things in Medicine (pp. 61–88). IGI Global Scientific Publishing.

Jinji, G. (2023). Self-recovery and automation. Artificial Self-Recovery and Autonomous Health of Machine, 45–61. https://doi.org/10.1007/978-981-19-4514-4_3

Johnson, M.H., and Allaf, M.E. (2016). The da Vinci surgical system. Atlas of Laparoscopic and Robotic Urologic Surgery, 39-42. https://doi.org/10.1016/B978-0-323-39326-3.00005-9

Kabene, S.M., Orchard, C., Howard, J.M., Soriano, M.A., and Leduc, R. (2006). The importance of human resources management in health care: A global context. Human Resources for Health, 4(1), 20. https://doi.org/10.1186/1478-4491-4-20

Karrouk, Y., Debasa, F., and Sanchez, L.M.F. (2025). The digital transformation of smart hospitals: Challenges and opportunities. Utilizing AI of Medical Things for Healthcare Security and Sustainability, 1–54.

Kolié, D., Van De Pas, R., Codjia, L., and Zurn, P. (2023). Increasing the availability of health workers in rural sub-Saharan Africa: A scoping review of rural pipeline programmes. Human Resources for Health, 21(1), 20. https://doi.org/10.1186/s12960-023-00801-z

Kumar, M., Kumar, A., Verma, S., Bhattacharya, P., Ghimire, D. et al. (2023). Healthcare Internet of Things (H-IoT): Current trends, future prospects, applications, challenges, and security issues. Electronics, 12(9), 2050.

Kumar and Patel. (2017). A survey on Internet of Things for healthcare. SAGE Open Medicine, 5, 205031211772652. (From https://journals.sagepub.com/doi/10.5772/61821.

Kwon, H., An, S., Lee, H.Y., Cha, W.C., Kim, S., Cho, M., and Kong, H.J. (2022). Review of smart hospital services in real healthcare environments. Healthcare Informatics Research, 28(1), 3–15.

Lakshumiah, A., Malaiarasan, A., Packianathan, R., Natarajan, S.K., and Arumugam, G. (2025). Application of Artificial Intelligence (AI) techniques for green transportation in smart city. *In:* Driving Green Transportation System Through Artificial Intelligence and Automation: Approaches, Technologies and Applications (pp. 335–358). Cham: Springer Nature Switzerland.

Ma, X., Song, C., Chiu, P.W., and Li, Z. (2019). Autonomous flexible endoscope for minimally invasive surgery with enhanced safety. IEEE Robotics and Automation Letters, 4(3), 2607–2613. https://doi.org/10.1109/LRA.2019.2895273

Maged and Mohamed. (2023). Role of Internet of Things (IoT) in enhancing patient safety in hospitals: A systematic review. Journal of Healthcare Engineering, 2023. https://pmc.ncbi.nlm.nih.gov/articles/PMC8890838/.

Mustafa, S.M.N. (2025). Leveraging artificial intelligence in healthcare: Safeguarding human rights through state policies. *In:* Intersection of Human Rights and AI in Healthcare (pp. 285–308). IGI Global Scientific Publishing.

Nagy, T.D., and Haidegger, T. (2022). Performance and capability assessment in surgical subtask automation. Sensors, 22(7). https://doi.org/10.3390/s22072501

Nowicki, M. (2017). Introduction to the Financial Management of Healthcare Organizations, Seventh Edition.

Olalekan Kehinde, A. (2025). Leveraging machine learning for predictive models in healthcare

to enhance patient outcome management. Int Res J Mod Eng Technol Sci, 7(1), 1465.
Popovski, P., Chiariotti, F., Huang, K., Kalor, A.E., Kountouris, M., Pappas, N., and Soret, B. (2022). A perspective on time toward wireless 6G. Proceedings of the IEEE, 110(8), 1116–1146. https://doi.org/10.1109/JPROC.2022.3190205
Preston, R. (2022). Stifling innovation: How global data protection regulation trends inhibit the growth of healthcare research and start-ups. Emory Int'l L. Rev., 37, 135.
Rajwar et al. (2021). Deploying Internet of Things in healthcare: A comprehensive survey. International Journal of Engineering Research & Technology (IJERT), 7(4). https://d1wqtxts1xzle7.cloudfront.net/70447818/20180925060202816-libre.pdf?1632852892=&response-content-disposition=inline%3B+filename%3DDeploying_Internet_of_Things_in_Healthca.pdf.
Ray. (2017). A survey on Internet of Things architectures, protocols, applications, recent advances, and future directions. Journal of Systems Architecture, 72, 1-24. https://www.sciencedirect.com/science/article/abs/pii/S2452414X16000066.
Recmanik, M., Martinek, R., Nedoma, J., Jaros, R., Pelc, M., Hajovsky, R. et al. (2024). A review of patient bed sensors for monitoring of vital signs. Sensors, 24(15), 4767.
Salm, M., Alwan, A., Lichtveld, M., García, P.J., Kilmarx, P.H., Sewankambo, N.K. et al. (2025). Reimagining global health: Accelerating change for a sustainable future. Annals of Global Health, 91(1), 6.
Ting, S.L., Kwok, S.K., Tsang, A.H., and Lee, W.B. (2011). Critical elements and lessons learnt from the implementation of an RFID-enabled healthcare management system in a medical organization. Journal of Medical Systems, 35(4), 657–669.
Venu et al. (2022). Investigation on Internet of Things (IoT): Technologies, challenges and applications in healthcare. International Journal of Research in Engineering and Science (IJRES), 10(8), 101–115.
Wu, X., Liu, C., Wang, L., and Bilal, M. (2023). Internet of things-enabled real-time health monitoring system using deep learning. Neural Computing and Applications, 1–12.
World Health Organization. (2010). World Health Statistics 2010. World Health Organization.
Yip, M., and Das, N. (2018). Robot Autonomy for Surgery. 281–313. https://doi.org/10.1142/9789813232266_0010
Zhu, Z., Zheng, W., Tang, N., and Zhong, W. (2024). Review of manpower management in healthcare system: Strategies, challenges, and innovations. Journal of Multidisciplinary Healthcare, 17, 5341–5351. https://doi.org/10.2147/JMDH.S497932
Ziyi, Z., Shuang, L., Shihao, Z., Zhikai, Z., and Yunrun, L. (2022). Opinion: Auxiliary role of medical imaging technology in clinical surgery. Frontiers in Surgery, 9. https://doi.org/10.3389/fsurg.2022.913427

CHAPTER
2

Benefits of Surgical Robots

R. Sivarethinamohan[1*(0000-0003-1918-8931)], P. Aranganathan[2(0000-0002-4132-5704)], B. Elamurugan[3(0000-0002-9747-1727)] and Aarti Mehta Sharma[1(0000-0002-8292-2839)]

[1] Symbiosis Centre for Management Studies, Bengaluru Campus, Symbiosis International (Deemed University), Pune, India
[2] Gnanam School of Business, Thanjavur, Tamil Nadu, India
[3] Department of Management Studies, Saveetha Institute of Medical and Technical Sciences, Chennai, India

1. Introduction

The surgical robotic arm's movements have a greater range of motion than a human hand. It decompresses hospital inpatient populations, improves patient care, and enhances existing surgical treatments. These sophisticated robotic systems provide surgeons unprecedented precision, flexibility, and control to perform minimally invasive procedures that reduce incision sizes, blood loss, and recovery times (Toader et al., 2023; da Silva et al., 2018). Surgical robots have well demonstrated their applicability across various medical disciplines, including general surgery, gynaecology, cardiothoracic surgery, and urology. They have revolutionized appendectomy, hysterectomy, mitral valve repair, gastric bypass, and hernia repairs with better visualization and precision, resulting in improved patient care (Chen et al., 2022).

Surgical robotic systems (SRS) overcome many of the limitations associated with traditional surgery, which often relies on the skill of individual surgeons and is impacted by factors such as hand tremors, fatigue, and limited imaging capabilities. It makes surgeries simpler and more accurate, resulting in shorter hospitalization. Reduced pain and discomfort, speedy recovery time, and return to normal activities (Suh et al., 2020). Additionally, robotic systems assist in standardising surgical performance and further accessibility to high-quality care through uniformity in procedures and better surgeon training. However, challenges persist, including poor adaptability to unpredictable complications, narrow visual fields, and small working spaces in minimally invasive surgery (Chen and Decary, 2020).

*Corresponding author: srmohan1213@gmail.com

DOI: 10.1201/9781003676812-2

Surgical robotics has already reached milestones, commencing with the PUMA 560 in 1985, which developed robotic precision in neurosurgical biopsies. The continuum of technological advancements of the da Vinci Surgical System and Mako platform allowed the development of refining robotic surgery's capabilities over time (Kwoh et al., 1988; Zhao et al., 2022). Today, surgical robots combine cutting-edge technologies like AI, AR, and IoT, which optimize surgical planning, improve on-site decision-making, and allow for timely data sharing, thus providing more value during an operation (Papaleo et al., 2023).

It lessens complications, including quick patient recovery, reduces infection risk, excessive blood loss and trauma, and postoperative pain, and quickens recovery. Hence, it can shorten hospital stays, reduce rare readmissions, and improve patient satisfaction. From an economic perspective, robotic systems enhance resource utilization and reduce healthcare costs by lowering the incidence of complications, streamlining procedures, and increasing surgical throughput (Toader et al., 2023). More than that, teleoperated systems have democratized access to healthcare by making remote surgeries in underserved regions possible to bridge gaps in the accessibility of healthcare (Chen et al., 2022).

The variety of available surgical robots is now oriented to specific clinical needs. The da Vinci system is still the leader in performing minimally invasive abdominal and pelvic surgeries, while Mako specializes in joint replacement, using 3D planning and haptic feedback. ROSA excels in orthopaedic and neurosurgical applications, offering advanced imaging for enhanced precision. The R-Universal orthopaedic system leverages AI for surgical planning and execution (Zhao et al., 2022). It nurtures surgical precision and integrates advanced tools to increase clinical, economic, and societal outcomes.

Advancements in medical technology are represented by surgical robots that help with procedures' precision, stability, and agility. Invasive techniques replace existing surgical practices to increase patient outcomes and surgical efficiency. Ongoing research and advancements are required to face current challenges and unlock further potential. Nowadays, surgical robotics ensures healthcare improvements for patients, surgeons, and the broader medical community. Therefore, proper investigation and examination are necessary to explore the continuous developments in this field. This chapter studies the benefits of various surgical robotic systems and their impact from clinical, economic, and societal perspectives. Further, this paper will add to the increasing number of articles in surgical robotics literature that help stakeholders understand the capabilities and limitations of such technologies. This chapter, discussing the latest advancements in robotic surgery, is supposed to help guide the design and implementation of more effective and accessible robotic solutions for health care.

2. Surgical Robots

Robotic surgery, also known as robotic-assisted surgery, is one of the most revolutionary innovations in modern medical technology. Today's most commonly used system combines a high-definition camera and precision surgical instruments attached to robotic arms. A specially trained surgeon carefully controls these arms through a console in the same room as the operating table. However, the system is capable of more than just physical proximity. It allows the console to be mounted remotely, thereby facilitating telesurgery and enabling surgeons in remote locations to perform surgical procedures comfortably while seated.

In contradistinction to popular belief, robots do not autonomously conduct robotic surgery. Instead, the surgeon has complete control over the robotic arms throughout the procedure. The robot is an enhanced instrument that complements the surgeon's abilities and accuracy. This partnership between the surgeon and the robotic technology is why the term "robotic-assisted surgery" is used—to reflect that the surgeon remains engaged with every step of the surgical process.

The history of robotic surgery is pretty deep, dating back several decades. A 2014 American Journal of Robotic Surgery report documented that the first robotic system to be used in surgery was in 1985. Then, Westinghouse Electric developed a robot called PUMA 200 to perform a brain biopsy (Shah et al., 2014). That was an early innovation toward surgical technology. Although a revolution, the PUMA 200 has become outdated, especially considering the systems available today. Of all the well-known and state-of-the-art models, perhaps the most prominent is the da Vinci Surgical System. Invented in 2000, this early version of the da Vinci system was the

Table 1: Historical Evolution of Surgical Robots

Year	Milestone
1985	The first robotic-assisted surgical system, PUMA 560, was used in a neurosurgical biopsy - an initial exploration of robotic capabilities in surgery.
1990s	Early research and development in robotic-assisted surgery. Focus on enhancing precision and control.
2000	Da Vinci Surgical System receives F.D.A. approval. Introduced for urological procedures, it marked the beginning of a new era in robotic surgery.
2003	Expansion of Da Vinci applications to gynaecology. Widening the range of procedures amenable to robotic assistance.
2008	Introduction of single-site surgery with Da Vinci. Enabled surgery through a single incision. Reduced scarring and improved cosmetic outcomes.
2010s	Growing adoption in various surgical specialties. Increased use in urology, gynaecology, and general surgery.
2014	FDA approval for the enhanced surgical system. Designed for minimally invasive surgery, and added to the options available to surgeons and hospitals.
2018	Continued advancements in robotic technology improved visualization, ergonomics, and agility. Surgeons gain greater control and precision.
2020	Increased adoption of robotic systems worldwide. Expanding applications in colorectal surgery, thoracic surgery, and enhanced training programs for surgeons using robotic platforms.
2023	Ongoing research and development for enhanced robotic-assisted technologies, and Integration of AI for smarter surgical assistance. Emphasis on improving accessibility in remote and underserved areas.

Source: Handa et al. (2024)

first robotic platform approved for general laparoscopic surgery, including minimal invasiveness with procedures within the abdomen or pelvis, and usually assisted with a camera.

With these technologies, surgeries have been much safer and more effective, allowing surgeons to execute much more complex procedures with higher precision and a less invasive approach. In addition, robotic technology has been modified and applied to almost all surgical specialties, such as neurosurgery (brain, spinal column, and peripheral nerve procedures), cardiothoracic surgeries, and ear, nose, and throat operations.

3. Benefits of Surgical Robots

The potential application of artificial intelligence (AI) and machine learning (ML) helps in surgical decision-making by enhancing the recognition of minute and complex anatomical structures. Robotic surgery is better than human surgery because of smaller incisions, reduced pain and discomfort, shorter hospital stays, faster recovery, fewer infections, and better outcomes. In complex procedures, such systems will offer greater control and accuracy. Besides, elongated high-definition cameras offer a clear view of the site of operation during robotic surgeries; therefore, with such clear and detailed imagery, fatigue for the surgeon is reduced, and it eliminates the issue of hand tremors that may take place during long operations, thus ensuring maximum accuracy during the operation.

For patients, minimally invasive techniques are prevalent in robotic surgery, translating into small incisions. Compared with a traditional surgical procedure, the traditional definition of patient advantages would include less pain, less scarring, quicker recovery periods, shorter hospital stays, and quicker returns to daily lives. Robotic surgery means less blood loss, fewer transfusions, and reduced risks of postoperative infections, thus safe and comfortable.

Advantages extend to certain cases, even in applicability. For instance, in the cases of prostatectomy, the ability of robotic surgery allows quicker recovery

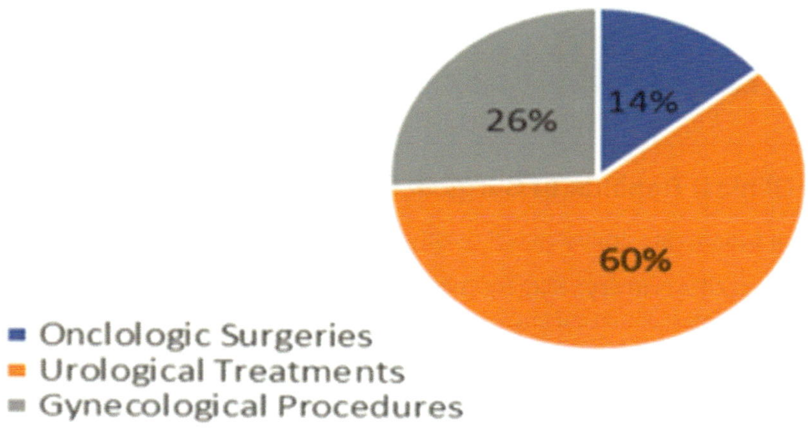

Figure 1: Major robotics surgeries.

of normal functions like urination and sexual health, helping patients regain their quality of life faster. It can foster patients' physical, emotional, and psychological recovery because of less downtime and a more straightforward healing process.

Robotic-assisted surgery integrates precision technology and minimally invasive approaches to provide a better surgical experience. Surgeons can get good visualization and better control, which reduces discomfort and results in quicker patient recovery.

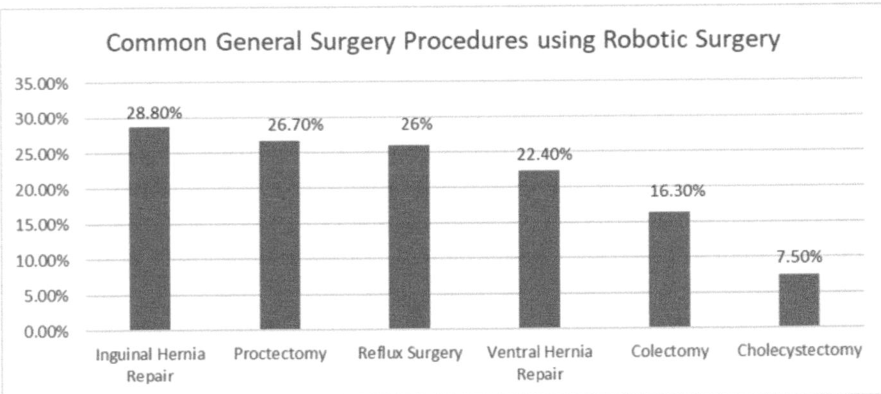

Figure 2: General surgery procedures followed in robotic surgery.

Figure 3 exhibits the clinical, economic, and societal benefits of robotic surgery, besides the ethical considerations.

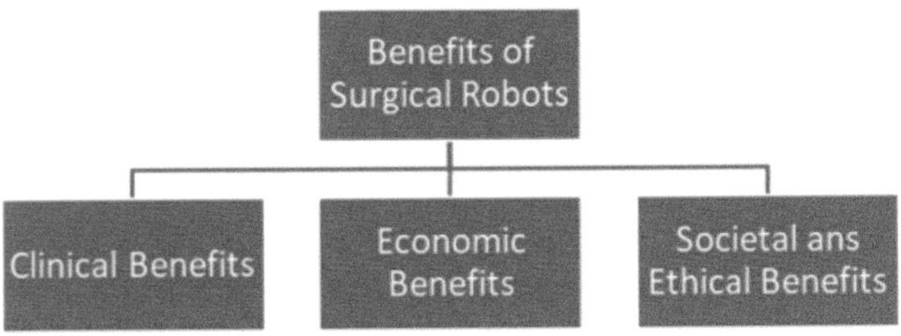

Figure 3: Benefits of surgical robots.

3.1. Clinical Benefits of Surgical Robots

Clinical benefits are discussed elaborately below.

(a) Enhanced Accuracy: Surgery robots have significantly upgraded the accuracy of medical interventions. Unlike human hands, robotic arms can make precise, controlled movements with sub-millimetre accuracy. In these procedures, slight inaccuracies could lead to tissue or organ damage; thus, having the capability to execute movements with unmatched precision is very important (Howe and Matsuoka, 1999; Thai et al., 2020).

The impact of human factors like hand tremors is easily eliminated with the use of robotic systems. Furthermore, robotic arms have a much longer range of motion than human hands. This means that surgeons can reach areas of the anatomy that are confined and difficult to access, such as deep within the brain or in complex spinal surgeries.

The benefits of robotic precision apply to various surgical areas, such as biopsies of brain lesions, hip joint replacements, and minimally invasive procedures. These systems enable surgeons to work through smaller incisions, leading to less tissue damage, smaller scars, and shorter recovery times. Hence, better surgical outcomes are achieved with robotic-assisted surgeries. They give the surgeons more confidence and control over the procedures as they are more critical for high-stakes operations (Howe and Matsuoka, 1999; Peters et al., 2018). Fewer surgical complications: Robotic surgery thus becomes indispensable as it reduces the complications of surgery through its ability to conduct minimally invasive, low-incision procedures. There is thus less risk of infection and less blood loss and scarring, all fears of traditional open surgery (Kim et al., 2021; Bankar and Keoliya, 2022). Moreover, accurate robotic systems mean even more invasive methods are not required, thus avoiding even more complications. In the field of vascular and endovascular surgery, for example, robotic assistance has decreased splenectomy during vascular exclusion and has improved the success of complex operations such as fenestrated stent grafting (Pietrabissa et al., 2011; Riga et al., 2009). In that way, surgery becomes safer, and patients stand a better chance of recovery with fewer long-term complications.

(b) Improved Surgeon Ergonomics: Robotic systems in surgery have brought significant advancements in surgeon ergonomics. These systems now remedy the physical challenges of the old method of surgery. They answer long, complicated procedures through which strain and discomfort cause fatigue and even long-term musculoskeletal injury among surgeons. Robotic assistance in surgery allows this treatment to be performed while seated at a console using an intuitive joystick or console-based controls, something that most ergonomically designed systems bring along. By this, it is possible to use relaxed postures and avoid awkward postures, which predispose surgeons to repetitive strain injury. Better ergonomic design provides superior control and precision, involving little physical restriction and better overall performance. Shortened Recovery Time: One of robotic surgery's most significant clinical advantages is that it reduces patients' recovery times. Because robotic-assisted surgeries are minimally invasive, their surgical trauma to the body, which forms relatively small incisions and blood loss, prevents infections from occurring in comparison with open surgeries. Consequently, healing is faster, hospital stays are shorter, and post-operative pain is lower. On top of that, robotic systems can perform highly accurate operations, adding up to less damage to tissue and even better healing pathways in the body. For the patient, this means returning to normal activities quickly, improving overall quality of life. These benefits are especially observed in complex areas such as orthopaedics, where robotic support ensures that prosthetics are aligned with higher precision, thus recovering patients faster and achieving better long-term results (Kim et al., 2021; Bankar and Keoliya, 2022). Therefore, robotic surgery benefits the patient and reduces the overall burden on healthcare systems due to a decrease in prolonged hospitalization and follow-up care.

(c) Customization and Adaptability: Adaptability is one of the central arguments of surgical robots, as they can be integrated into almost any operating room setting. In addition, not only does the modularity of their system allow tailoring to the speciality spectrum from cardiothoracic surgery to urology, but it also helps in allocating costs per function. Otherwise, surgical robots can even reach those remote or deprived localities where optimum expert care may have been extended. With telepresence, surgeons can perform complex operations while seated in a tiny office-linked room with full robotic assistance and try remotely to ensure that the patients in less-served areas receive the highest-quality surgical care (Teng et al., 2022). This is essential in filling the healthcare gap worldwide because it brings sophisticated surgical solutions to regions with no unique expertise or infrastructure.

The customization and adaptability of surgical robots empower surgeons to push medical innovation boundaries. Such systems are transforming the face of modern medicine by empowering precision, reducing risks, and extending access to expert care for patients all around the world. The incorporation of robotic systems into a variety of surgical applications is, therefore, improving surgical outcomes and transforming the field of modern medicine.

3.2. Economic Benefits of Surgical Robots

The economic benefits of surgical robots are described as follows:

(a) Long-Term Cost Savings: Studies have provided evidence that the upfront investments in robotic-assisted surgery are paid back through long-term savings. Increased implementation of robotic systems in healthcare would result in enormous cost savings through diminished expenses for surgical complication-related care, follow-up treatments, and longer hospital stays. For instance, studies in the United States estimated that adopting robot-assisted surgery could save about $1.5 to $6.5 billion yearly. The UK-based study on robotic prostate surgeries stated that even after the initial investment by the National Health Service over a 20-year duration, there would be a saving of more than £286 million. These savings come primarily from shorter hospital stays, fewer complications, and faster recovery times.

(b) Efficient Time Utilization: Robotic surgery reduces the time and resources used in any surgical procedure, thus economizing. According to research studies, robotic systems decrease operative time while the number of surgeries that can be performed within a specific duration increases (Dixon et al., 2021). In addition to improving operative efficiency, robotics has hastened recovery times for patients so that hospital stays are shorter. Such an approach improves healthcare provider costs while at the same time opening bed availability to admit more patients who need care. Moreover, the minimally invasive nature of the robotic procedures reduces the complications, mainly in terms of infections or repeat interventions, which also reduces the overall treatment cost.

For healthcare systems, such efficiencies translate into a cost-effective model that aligns both clinically and financially. This means reduced operating room costs and increased patient throughput in a hospital setting. For patients, these results mean quicker recoveries, reduced medical bills, and a faster return to normal activities. Robotic-assisted surgery addresses surgical and recovery processes, thus improving patient outcomes and simultaneously addressing the economic pressures healthcare providers face today. It is considered a transformative solution for sustainable surgical care.

A more excellent training opportunity has been presented with robotic surgery, where surgical professionals can receive improved training in skills. Surgical professionals need more rigorous training with these systems' new precision and intricacy. These are costly initial training and system maintenance investments, but provide continued learning and technical growth. Advanced simulation tools and real-time feedback during surgeries enable surgeons to hone their skills in a controlled, low-risk environment. This will improve surgical outcomes and increase patient safety (Marchegiani et al., 2023).

(c) Patient Satisfaction and Retention: Improved clinical outcomes and excellent patient experience, along with patient care, make procedures safer and more efficient, enhancing the overall experience for patients. Such a model shows examples; robotic prostatectomy results in a significant decrease by as much as 59% in the cases of infection after surgery while saving as much time in hospital care as conventional surgery (Patel et al., 2021). Thus, faster recovery of patients and minimally invasive processes increase the overall level of satisfaction. These results and a lower probability of complications increase the chances that a patient may trust a health provider enough to return for subsequent procedures. As access to this robotic surgery is expanded and opens its doors, the possibility is enhanced whereby these healthcare institutions have patients, in the long run, improving their financial status and credit score. By delivering superior patient experience through robotic-assisted procedures, healthcare providers can strengthen their relationships with patients and grow a loyal patient base for the future.

3.3. Societal and Ethical Benefits

(i) Societal Benefits of Robotic Surgery

The following are the societal benefits of the surgical robots:

(a) Improved Patient Outcomes: Robotic-assisted surgery has revolutionized patient care by greatly enhancing the precision and outcomes of surgical procedures. The technology employed in robotic systems allows surgeons to perform highly accurate and controlled surgeries, minimizing the likelihood of human error. This increased accuracy shortens the duration of the procedures and lessens the strain on patients and surgical teams. These developments improve the immediate success of surgeries and contribute to better long-term health outcomes for patients.

Studies by Lanfranco et al. (2004) and Saniotis and Henneberg (2021) also explain how robotic-assisted surgery leads to higher recovery rates and decreased post-operative complications. Smaller incisions lead to reduced blood loss and risks of infection, which contribute to faster healing and fewer follow-up procedure requirements. The lower trauma caused to the surrounding tissues enhances overall patient comfort and the sooner return to normal activities.

Such great value is achieved through its versatility across various specialties—from urology and gynecology to cardiothoracic and neurosurgery. Robotic-assisted surgery raises the standard for surgeries everywhere by providing consistent and high-quality outcomes. It is currently setting a new benchmark for patient care by personalizing surgeries, prostheses, and more.

The very dimension of adaptability in various specialities, from urology and gynaecology to cardiothoracic and neurosurgery, makes them very precious. Robotic surgery ensures consistency and quality outcomes in surgery all over and is raising the standards for individualizing patient treatment in terms of outcomes in patient care today.

Increased Access to Advanced Care: Such an approach will enhance public welfare since robotic-assisted surgery provides an access mode for advanced healthcare services. Robotic technology can also narrow the gap between rural and urban healthcare systems, through which advanced surgical procedures could reach residents of underserved population areas when more patients and providers have access to the technology. Such evidence is particularly relevant for rural and economically disadvantaged patients, who usually cannot access specialty surgery-related care services and specialized professionals.

The remote setting benefits from added robotic systems distributed in more hospitals, where onboard procedures such as minimally invasive surgeries, once limited to urban centres, could now be available. Healthcare democratization will be invoked, so the newest medical treatments are no longer geographically bound. The combination of technologies, such as telepresence, allows highly skilled surgeons to conduct robotic-assisted surgeries worldwide, ensuring advanced care for resource-deprived settings.

Moniz and Maia's (2014) research indicates the transformative potential of robotic surgery to level the healthcare playing field. Ensuring that unequal service provision for state-of-the-art treatments no longer becomes a privilege of the urban or affluent population, robotic technology facilitates high-quality surgical care for all patients from all geographical locations or financial statuses.

(b) Efficiency and Cost Savings: Surgical procedures using robotic tools have transformed healthcare efficiency and cost. In critical care settings, these technologies enhance surgical workflow by improving accuracy and reducing the need for follow-up treatment. These outcomes result in improved patient outcomes and, equally importantly, in major economies in the health system.

The efficiency with which robotic systems use resources is brought about by the nature of operative time, which is often shortened, and the relatively fewer days a hospital would have housed an unfortunate patient who has undergone surgery. It hastens recovery, minimizes complications, and alleviates the financial burden of post-surgical patient care. Robotic surgery leads to lower mortality and less economic burden due to extended hospital stays and post-operative complications (Teng et al., 2022). Thus, quality care can be provided by cheaper spending on hospital expenses.

Research has shown that robotic surgery is accurate and minimally invasive, and thus reduces the number of reoperations, allowing hospitals to utilize their resources better. This makes patient care optimal and increases patient stay in hospitals to cope with the growing demand for health care. Such a scenario in a particular region over a certain period may enable sustainable healthcare development through robotic applications, providing better quality patient care while reducing financial impacts on healthcare providers and systems.

(ii) Ethical Benefits of Robotic Surgery

The surgical robots come with the following ethical benefits:

(a) The ethical benefits of surgical robots include enhanced safety. With improved precision and control during surgery, robotic devices can significantly reduce the risk of surgical errors. These machines perform more precise and less invasive surgeries, lowering complications and reducing the chances of human error. According to studies conducted by Lanfranco et al. (2004) and Moniz and Maia (2014), the patient's safety during surgery is increased as the robotic system improves surgical results and decreases the risk of complications.

(b) Informed Consent and Autonomy: Such surgery needs to have clear communication on precise informed consent and the autonomy of patients. The increasing involvement of artificial intelligence and robots in surgical treatment surely means providing and making the patients aware of the different procedures, risks involved in the operation, and the intervention of robots during their surgery. Providing access to information has trained people, as noted by Chappell and Teven (2023), in requiring healthcare professionals to ensure that the patients understand the technology used and consent with a complete understanding of their options. This principle would likely empower patients to make informed decisions while honoring their autonomy.

(c) Bioethics Reflection: Robotics integration into surgery also brings about an important discussion of bioethics. Advanced technology being used more in medicine also raises the issue of relationships between technology, health practitioners, and patients. Therefore, ethical implications are placed on relying on machines to make crucial medical decisions and the risks involved with that dependency. As asserted by Siqueira-Batista et al. in 2016, these bioethical reflections are crucial in allowing surgical technology to be harnessed responsibly and ethically toward both patient welfare and evolving the healthcare professionals' role within such a high-tech setting.

(iii) Ethical Considerations in Robotic Surgery

Robotic-assisted surgery is becoming more common, making a strong regulatory and ethical framework essential. This framework addresses patient safety, data privacy, and accountability for surgical complications. Implementing these sophisticated technologies in the health sector requires clear-cut guidelines that safeguard patients and healthcare professionals' ethical practices and legal responsibilities. Mughal (2022) also accentuated the need to devise comprehensive legislation regulating surgical robotics with ethical standards maintenance within this evolving area.

Above all, it requires clear guidelines to integrate these advanced technologies into healthcare, focusing on ethical practices for patients and healthcare professionals and their legal responsibilities. Besides, according to Mughal (2022), there is indeed an even greater urgency for developing comprehensive legislation regarding the regulation of surgical robotics and maintaining ethical standards within this evolving field.

(a) Skill Dependency and Job Displacement: The ever-growing dependence on robotic systems in surgery raises some ethical questions about the future roles of human healthcare professionals. Robotic technology proves to be an asset in terms of surgical precision; however, this could cause the loss of traditional surgical skills among medical professionals. Increasing dependence on machines for complex procedures may result in the loss of expertise in manual surgery, bringing health professionals close to total dependence on that technology. This also leads to job losses in health services because automation removes many traditional human roles. According to Saniotis and Henneberg (2021) and Mughal (2022), issues of ethics revolve around and caution against what should not be a “throwaway mentality” for the worthiness and relevance of human skills or socio-economic impact vis-à-vis new technologies.

(b) Access Inequality: Another ethical concern is the potential for increased healthcare inequality from robotic surgery systems’ high cost and complexity. While these technologies are revolutionary, they are also expensive and require specialized training, which limits their availability in low-resource settings. The significant financial burden associated with acquiring and maintaining robotic systems may worsen disparities in healthcare access, particularly in underserved or economically disadvantaged areas. Moniz and Maia (2014) argue that careful planning and equitable distribution of these technologies are essential to ensure that advancements in healthcare do not exacerbate social inequities. This includes finding ways for health systems to make robotic surgery accessible to all patients, regardless of socioeconomic status.

4. Future Potential and Innovations

Surgical robots are changing the landscape of medicine by delivering remarkable improvements in precision, efficiency, and patient outcomes. Embracing this technology enhances surgical performance and elevates the standard of care for patients. Emerging technologies, expanded applications, and global integration are leading to further development of robotic surgery in addressing existing challenges and opening new frontiers in healthcare.

(i) Emerging Technologies: Robotic surgery is one of the most significant strides medical technology has achieved. The da Vinci Surgical System has changed this practice over the last twenty years by improving surgeons’ cognitive and physical skills (Peters et al., 2018; Hoeckelmann et al., 2015). Platforms that integrate with the regular surgery practice provide more minimally invasive procedures and better recovery times, making outcomes superior (Lanfranco et al., 2004).

The future of surgical robotics is centred around several key advancements:

(a) **Smaller and more accessible systems:** Compact, cost-effective, and user-friendly robots will make advanced procedures more accessible.

(b) **AI integration:** Artificial intelligence will make decisions better with real-time analytics to improve surgical precision and safety (Ashrafian et al., 2017; Panesar et al., 2019).

(c) **Real-time imaging and haptic feedback:** Visualization and intuitive feedback will provide surgeons seamless interaction with robotic systems (Liu and Liu, 2012; Chang et al., 2018).

(d) **Virtual and augmented reality:** Such instruments will enhance preoperative planning and intraoperative navigation by making surgeons more aware of the surgical site.

Applications Expanding Robotic surgery continues to be expanded across all speciality departments. It has become applicable even to complex areas such as cranial neurosurgery and oncologic surgeries, starting with general surgery and orthopaedics. With unmatched precision in the control of instruments, it eradicates human errors involved during minimally invasive cancer surgery, as Bal et al. (2021) and Lendvay et al. (2013 mentioned. There has also been a rethinking of surgery by introducing innovations such as NOTES (natural orifice transluminal endoscopic surgery) and magnetic endoscopes that reshape how surgeries are done. Many procedures, such as colonoscopy, have become non-invasive and less harmful for individuals with inflammatory bowel disease (IBD.

(ii) Global Reach and Accessibility: The impact of robotic surgery on a global scale is enormous and provides better outcomes, but it faces issues like high costs and a lack of accessibility. Economic barriers have been one of the traditional barriers, but improvements in affordability and accessibility are likely to lead to growth, especially in developing countries (Camarillo et al., 2004; Lanfranco et al., 2004). Telesurgery is an innovation addressing global disparities as surgeons perform procedures from remote locations. This approach has significant potential for underserved areas but needs regulatory frameworks to sort out the issues of safety, liability, and communication (Lendvay et al., 2013).

(iii) Potential Innovations: Looking ahead, several innovations are poised to transform robotic surgery further:

(a) **Advances in surgical planning:** AI-driven diagnostics and other advanced imaging techniques will optimize preoperative strategies.

(b) **Real-time intraoperative guidance:** Advanced navigation tools will give surgeons precise, dynamic guidance during procedures.

(c) **Improved adoption in developing countries:** Affordability and miniaturization will make robotic surgery more widely available in resource-limited countries.

(d) **Autonomous robots:** Semi-autonomous and autonomous systems will allow robots to perform complicated tasks with minimal human intervention.

(e) **Cost efficiency:** The prices of robotic systems will fall dramatically with better manufacturing processes and competition, and thus open up these technologies to more users.

Surgical robotics is probably the most potent innovator in the medical field today and may one day change healthcare worldwide. With artificial intelligence, extended reality, and advanced imaging, robot-assisted surgery has reduced average

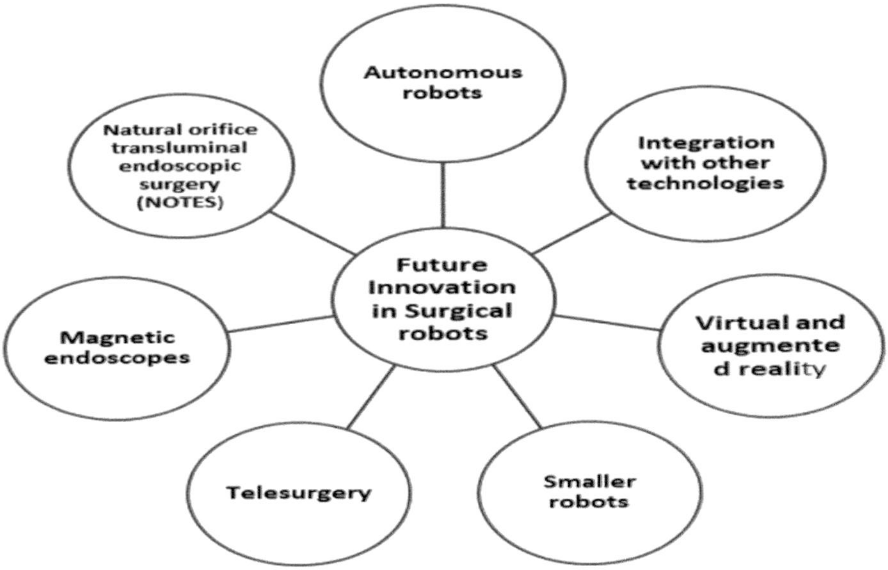

Figure 4: Future innovations in surgical robots.

error dramatically, leading to less pain during recovery, lower risk of infection, and reduced blood loss.

5. Challenges and Limitations

Surgical robots have some drawbacks and barriers that researchers hope to address in the future. These include the following limitations:

(i) Cost and Accessibility: Since robotic surgery revolutionized the medical field by providing exceptional precision, improved recovery times, and lower patient trauma, the most important barrier to broad acceptance, despite all these advantages, remains the price of the robotic systems. The Da Vinci Surgical System is a surgical robot that costs millions of dollars; training and maintenance costs even more. Hence, the heavy up-front investment restricts the use of robotic surgery even in smaller hospitals/resource-poor settings, as such centres depend on wealthier institutions or specialized centres (Tan et al., 2018; Coelho et al., 2024). Robotic surgery costs have been incurred by buying and maintaining the robotic system, and increased operating theatre time. Another point was that robots take longer to set up and prolong the time a surgeon spends on the patient during surgery, which can increase operating costs (Tan et al., 2018). All these inefficiencies in time and the cost of the apparatus put a heavy burden on the shoulders of robotic surgery. The dramatic example can be especially noted in a field such as reconstructive microsurgery, where robotic systems are rarely used.

Despite the many benefits of surgical robots, they are costly and, therefore, cannot be accessed by many medical centres, especially in developing countries or rural regions. In that regard, many patients cannot reach the latest technological advances in surgical care, which creates a disparity in healthcare availability. Tan et al. (2018) and Coelho et al. (2024) point out that unless the cost of the robotic system decreases and makes it an affordable item for hospitals, the growth of robotic surgery in some specialities will still be restricted. One probable answer is found in more cost-effective robotic systems and the introduction of artificial intelligence that can standardize surgical practices, reduce time spent in operations, and reduce costs.

(ii) Learning Curve and Adoption: The other barrier to adopting robotic surgery within clinical practice is the very steep learning curve for surgeons. Indeed, no matter how sophisticated the level of precision, the myriad benefits these systems possess come with the need to acquire specific skills and heavy training to work effectively on a given robotic system. Surgeons must undergo considerable training and practice, simulating experience, mentorship, and real-time surgery on robotic systems to become masters of such systems (Ashrafian et al., 2017). Such an immense investment in training can slow the rate at which such robotic surgeries are adopted into hospitals and surgical centres.

The time to master surgical robots can vary significantly based on the surgeon's experience and the system's complexity. Ashrafian et al. (2017) observe that even though most surgeons are proficient in open surgery, training in robotic-assisted surgery requires different skills, such as learning the interface of the technology, handling robotic instruments, and interpreting 3D imaging systems. This can be a huge obstacle, especially in less resource-intensive hospitals. Further, there is no proper standardized training program, and the need for certification makes adapting challenging.

The impact of this learning curve is not only on the surgeons but also on the healthcare system as a whole. Time and resources spent training surgeons to operate on robotic systems, along with necessary support for adopting new technologies, delay the benefits of robotic surgery in clinical practice. Moreover, a lack of knowledge in some areas can be another source of inequality in access to advanced surgical treatments. Since surgical robots are getting highly advanced, there is an urgent need to develop comprehensive training programs, provide practical experiences, and minimize the period of learning for surgeons so that the transition to robotic surgery becomes easy and accessible to a more significant extent for healthcare providers (Ashrafian et al., 2017).

(iii) Ethical and Regulatory Hurdles: Robotic surgery has a myriad of hurdles—financial, technical, ethical, and legal—that must be tackled for its safe and fair introduction into clinical practice. Perhaps the most significant ethical concern relates to the possible dehumanization of surgery. As robotic systems take over manual tasks, weakening the doctor-patient bond would harm personalized care. Enayati et al. (2016) pointed out that while robotic systems enhance fidelity and minimize human error, they do not replace the human element of compassion, judgment, or discretion.

An acute concern with robotic surgery lies in the safety of the patients, especially in terms of liability in case of malfunction. It is hard to ascertain whose fault it is, the machine, the surgeon, or the designer of the entire system, especially in the context of AI and machine learning embedded in robotic systems (Seetohul et al.,

2023; Seetohul and Shafiee 2022). Liaison and accountability concerning these technologies must be worked out to minimize risks.

Regulatory hurdles and time-consuming approval processes prevent the adoption of robotic surgery and delay hospital implementation (Enayati et al., 2016). Timely revisions can address ease and quick approvals without compromising safety.

Tan et al. (2018) and Coelho et al. (2024) witnessed that the high costs of robotic systems and well-resourced healthcare settings worsen existing healthcare inequality.

6. Conclusion

Surgical robots allow the machine to translate the surgeon's movements into real-time precision, greater visualization, and more dexterity. Such advanced systems allow the surgeon to perform even the most complex procedures with great accuracy, decreasing complications, shortening recovery time, and extending the realm of intricate surgeries such as neurosurgery, cardiac surgery, and minimally invasive operations. Robotic surgery advancement improved the quality and care and reduced hand tremors. However, smaller hospitals still prevent surgical robots due to the comprehensive approvals and costs related to purchasing and keeping robotic systems. Attach practice costs in training surgeons to operate these systems; the amounts keep piling up. Moreover, robotic integration within healthcare work processes would require substantial changes, thereby confining the utilization of such robotic systems only to high-end medical centres and preventing underserved populations from the service. Notwithstanding these limitations, the projected long-term returns—fewer complications, higher efficiency, and lower overall costs—would be worth the investment. Cost-effective designs and broadening accessibility promise to make robotic surgery less exclusive shortly.

Moreover, robotic surgery supports and improves the accuracy and agility of human surgeons during medical procedures and maximizes the efficiency of health services by increasing patient comfort and safety, cutting down the length of stay at the hospital, and freeing the beds for more needy cases. It is a breakthrough in surgical technology. Surgeons can provide a minimally invasive option for common conditions in gynecologic, urologic, general, and cardiothoracic surgery. As technology advances, its adoption grows more extensive across various medical fields. It comprises disparities in healthcare and improves outcomes for rural populations or disadvantaged groups in society. Equitable access and use will thus be guaranteed through ethical and regulatory oversight. With the incorporation of artificial intelligence, surgical robots promise, at best, to provide real-time data analysis, predictive insights, and personalized care; thus, they all herald a new dawn in modern medicine and a new era in global healthcare delivery.

References

Ashrafian, H., Clancy, O., Grover, V.K., and Darzi, A. (2017). The evolution of robotic surgery:

Surgical and anaesthetic aspects. British Journal of Anaesthesia, 119, i72–i84. https://doi.org/10.1093/bja/aex383

Ball, T., Gonzalez-Martinez, J., Zemmar, A., Sweid, A., Chandra, S., VanSickle, D. et al. (2021). Operative strategies in neurosurgical robotics. Operative Neurosurgery, 21(3), 371–380. https://doi.org/10.1093/ons/opaa426.

Bankar, G., and Keoliya, A. (2022). Robot-assisted surgery in gynecology. Cureus, 14. https://doi.org/10.7759/cureus.29190.

Camarillo, D., Krummel, T., and Salisbury, J. (2004). Robotic technology in surgery: Past, present, and future. American Journal of Surgery, 188(4A Suppl), 2S-15S. https://doi.org/10.1016/J.AMJSURG.2004.08.025.

Chang, K.D., Hathiramani, S.S., and Khandwala, Y.S. (2018). Novel robotic systems and future directions. Indian Journal of Urology, 34(2), 88–95. https://doi.org/10.4103/iju.IJU_332_17

Chappell, A., and Teven, C. (2023). How should surgeons consider emerging innovations in artificial intelligence and robotics? AMA Journal of Ethics, 25(8), E589–597. https://doi.org/10.1001/amajethics.2023.589.

Chen, K., Zhang, J., Beeraka, N.M., Sinelnikov, M.Y., Zhang, X., Cao, Y., and Lu, P. (2022). Robot-assisted minimally invasive breast surgery: Recent evidence with comparative clinical outcomes. Journal of Clinical Medicine, 11(7), 1827. https://doi.org/10.3390/jcm11071827.

Coelho, M., Peltz, T., Hunt, J., and Gianoutsos, M. (2024). Robotic surgery in plastic surgery: A review of its potential. Australasian Journal of Plastic Surgery. https://doi.org/10.34239/ajops.115362.

da Silva, R.M., de Souza, J.R.R., Simões, M.A.C., and de Campos, J.A.P. (2018). Framework for modeling autonomous multi-robots systems. *In:* 2018 Latin American Robotic Symposium, 2018 Brazilian Symposium on Robotics and 2018 Workshop on Robotics in Education (LARS/SBR/WRE) (pp. 13–18). João Pessoa, Brazil.

Dixon, L., Biggs, S., Turner, B., Embury-Young, Y., Wood, F., Leandro, L. et al. (2021). 1113 Surgical innovators or spin doctors: Reporting of expectations for robotic gastrointestinal surgery. British Journal of Surgery. https://doi.org/10.1093/bjs/znab259.808.

Enayati, N., De Momi, E., and Ferrigno, G. (2016). Haptics in robot-assisted surgery: Challenges and benefits. IEEE Reviews in Biomedical Engineering, 9, 49–65. https://doi.org/10.1109/RBME.2016.2538080.

Handa, A., Gaidhane, A., and Choudhari, S.G. (2024). Role of robotic-assisted surgery in public health: Its advantages and challenges. Cureus, Jun 23; 16(6), e62958. doi: 10.7759/cureus.62958. PMID: 39050344; PMCID: PMC11265954.

Hoeckelmann, M., Rudas, I.J., Fiorini, P., Kirchner, F., and Haidegger, T. (2015). Current capabilities and development potential in surgical robotics. International Journal of Advanced Robotic Systems, 12(5), 61. https://doi.org/10.5772/61633.

Howe, R., and Matsuoka, Y. (1999). Robotics for surgery. Annual Review of Biomedical Engineering, 1, 211–240 https://doi.org/10.1146/ANNUREV.BIOENG.1.1.211.

Kim, J., Yang, S., Kim, S., and Kim, H. (2021). Application of robots in general surgery. Journal of the Korean Medical Association. https://doi.org/10.5124/jkma.2021.64.10.678.

Kwoh, Y.S., Hou, J., Jonckheere, E.A., and Hayati, S. (1988). A robot with improved absolute positioning accuracy for CT-guided stereotactic brain surgery. IEEE Transactions on Biomedical Engineering, 35(2), 153–160. https://doi.org/10.1109/10.1354.

Lanfranco, A., Castellanos, A., Desai, J., and Meyers, W. (2004). Robotic surgery: A current perspective. Annals of Surgery, 239, 14–21. https://doi.org/10.1097/01.sla.0000103020.19595.7d.

Liu, Y., and Liu, J. (2012). Surgical robotics: A look-back of latest advancement and bio-inspired ways to tackle existing challenges. Frontiers of Mechanical Engineering, 7(4), 376–384. https://doi.org/10.1007/s11465-012-0352-1.

Madhani, A., Niemeyer, G., and Salisbury, J. (1998). The Black Falcon: A teleoperated surgical instrument for minimally invasive surgery. Proceedings. 1998 IEEE/RSJ International Conference on Intelligent Robots and Systems. Innovations in Theory, Practice and Applications (Cat. No.98CH36190), 2, 936–944. https://doi.org/10.1109/IROS.1998.727320.

Marchegiani, F., Siragusa, L., Zadoroznyj, A., Laterza, V., Mangana, O., Schena, C. et al. (2023). New robotic platforms in general surgery: What's the current clinical scenario? Medicina, 59. https://doi.org/10.3390/medicina59071264.

Moniz, A., Maia, M., Kirner, E., Krings, B., and Decker, M. (2014). Robots in surgery: From the laboratory towards health care. *In:* Proceedings of the International Conference 'Going Beyond the Laboratory – Ethical and Societal Challenges for Robotics (GBTL 2014)' (pp. 1–8). Oldenburg, Germany. Karlsruhe Institute of Technology (KIT). https://doi.org/10.5445/IR/100004920.

Mughal, H. (2022). Ethical challenges facing autonomous surgical robots. British Journal of Surgery. https://doi.org/10.1093/bjs/znac039.205.

Panesar, S., Cagle, Y., Chander, D., Morey, J., Fernandez-Miranda, J., and Kliot, M. (2019). Artificial intelligence and the future of surgical robotics. Annals of Surgery, 270(2), 223–226. https://doi.org/10.1097/SLA.0000000000003262.

Papaleo, E.D., D'Alonzo, M., Fiori, F., Piombino, V., Falato, E., Pilato, F. et al. (2023). Integration of proprioception in upper limb prostheses through non-invasive strategies: A review. Journal of NeuroEngineering and Rehabilitation, 20(1), 118.

Patel, S., Rovers, M., Sedelaar, M., Zusterzeel, P., Verhagen, A., Rosman, C., and Grutters, J. (2021). How can robot-assisted surgery provide value for money? BMJ Surgery, Interventions, & Health Technologies, 3. https://doi.org/10.1136/bmjsit-2020-000042.

Peters, B., Armijo, P., Krause, C., Choudhury, S., and Oleynikov, D. (2018). Review of emerging surgical robotic technology. Surgical Endoscopy, 32, 1636–1655. https://doi.org/10.1007/s00464-018-6079-2.

Pietrabissa, A., Morelli, L., Ferrari, M., Peri, A., Ferrari, V., Moglia, A. et al. (2010). Mixed reality for robotic treatment of a splenic artery aneurysm. Surgical Endoscopy, 24, 1204. https://doi.org/10.1007/s00464-009-0703-0.

Riga, C., Cheshire, N., Hamady, M., and Bicknell, C. (2009). The role of robotic endovascular catheters in fenestrated stent grafting. Journal of Vascular Surgery, 51(4), 810–819; discussion 819–820. https://doi.org/10.1016/j.jvs.2009.08.101.

Saniotis, A., and Henneberg, M. (2021). Neurosurgical robots and ethical challenges to medicine. Ethics in Science and Environmental Politics. https://doi.org/10.3354/ESEP00197.

Seetohul, J., and Shafiee, M. (2022). Snake robots for surgical applications: A review. Robotics, 11, 57. https://doi.org/10.3390/robotics11030057.

Seetohul, J., Shafiee, M., and Sirlantzis, K. (2023). Augmented Reality (AR) for surgical robotic and autonomous systems: State of the art, challenges, and solutions. Sensors (Basel, Switzerland), 23. https://doi.org/10.3390/s23136202.

Siqueira-Batista, R., Souza, C., Maia, P., and Siqueira, S. (2016). Robotic surgery: Bioethical aspects. Arquivos Brasileiros de Cirurgia Digestiva: ABCD, 29, 287– 290. https://doi.org/10.1590/0102-6720201600040018.

Suh, J.H., Kotecha, R., Chao, S.T., Ahluwalia, M.S., Sahgal, A., and Chang, E.L. (2020). Robotic surgery systems. Nature Reviews Clinical Oncology, 17(5), 279–295. https://doi.org/10.1038/s41571-020-0341-8.

Tan, Y., Liverneaux, P., and Wong, J. (2018). Current limitations of surgical robotics in reconstructive plastic microsurgery. Frontiers in Surgery, 5. https://doi.org/10.3389/fsurg.2018.00022.

Teng, R., Ding, Y., and See, K. (2022). Use of robots in critical care: Systematic review. Journal of Medical Internet Research, 24. https://doi.org/10.2196/33380.

Thai, M., Phan, P., Wong, S., Lovell, N., and Nho, T. (2020). Advanced intelligent systems for surgical robotics. Advanced Intelligent Systems, 2. https://doi.org/10.1002/aisy.201900138.

Toader, C., Eva, L., Tataru, C.I., Covache-Busuioc, R.A., Bratu, B.G., Dumitrascu, D.I. et al. (2023, October 1). Frontiers of cranial base surgery: Integrating technique, technology, and teamwork for the future of neurosurgery. Brain Sciences, 13(10), 1495. https://doi.org/10.3390/brainsci13101495.

Zhao, Y., Mei, Z., Luo, X., Mao, J., Zhao, Q., Liu, G., and Wu, D. (2022). Remote vascular interventional surgery robotics: A literature review. Quantitative Imaging in Medicine and Surgery, 12(4), 2552–2574. https://doi.org/10.21037/qims-21-792.

CHAPTER

3

Monitoring Medication Adherence: Methods, Tools, and Outcomes

Radha R.*(0000-0001-9822-0949), Sharanya S.(0000-0003-2442-3246) and A Rehash Rushmi Pavitra(0000-0002-1220-1497)

Department of Data Science and Business Systems, SRM Institute of Science and Technology, Kattankulathur, Chengalpattu District, Tamil Nadu – 603203

1. Introduction

The average lifespan increases human quality of life, as evidenced by developed nations that recently recorded a sharp increase in elderly people. The Worldwide population related to people of the age group greater than 60 years is steadily increasing, and a 25% increase is expected by 2050, in contrast with 2013. While society ages, healthcare overheads increase drastically, requiring long-term planning and management. Assistive health technology (AHT) use has steadily expanded, drawing attention to keeping the elderly or aging population healthy (Patel and Smith, 2024). Thus, these advancements and societal needs have paved the way for designing quality health care systems that are expected to provide better treatment plans and monitoring systems. Technological advancements will revolutionize how we monitor healthy and unhealthy individuals' daily activities and behaviors with new approaches by integrating various domains (Smith et al., 2023). A key subset of medication adherence is human well-being and health maintenance; much research is developing around this subset, which has greatly aided in structuring this chapter.

Several approaches are required for healthy aging, which is considered a foremost challenge. Providing the correct medication is the most important strategy for managing a person's behavior, which forms the main methodology for managing the ailments. To achieve the desired good health, one must accept and take the medication as prescribed by the professionals involved in the healthcare industry. Medication adherence is still a common issue in the health care sector, specifically related to the aging population. Many chronic ailments are major health concerns

*Corresponding author: radhadoss25@gmail.com

DOI: 10.1201/9781003676812-3

for 50% of the aging population. Healthy outcome improvements are purely based on repetitive overseeing and evaluation of the patient's adherence, which has pros and cons. The article's main objective is to provide deep insights into medication adherence observing methods, which paved the path for further improvements (Zhao et al., 2023).

The review presented here shadows a looped incremental stage, and hence found innovative readings about medication adherence observing methodologies and methods in the gauged studies. Recent years have seen several effective attempts to stop drug adherence oversight, as seen in (Zhao et al., 2023). However, in this chapter, we are not discussing these commercial processes.

The objective of the best strategy used by medication adherence supervising methods is to improve healthcare schemes. This chapter is sectioned into various sections based on the objective of overseeing or sensing healthcare systems. This chapter compares medication adherence overseeing methods and approaches concerning accuracy, vitality competence, and user ease. This chapter presents the need for investigators and scientists of healthcare overseeing engineering and medical societies, which spotlights the prominence of technology in medication adherence systems. The chapter is structured to provide an overview of medication adherence ideas and review relevant literature. The chapter presents the differences between various approaches, the challenges, and future trends associated with them. Various dimensions related to medication adherence, which can improve the healthcare system in evaluating the health aspect of patients with illnesses, are shown below.

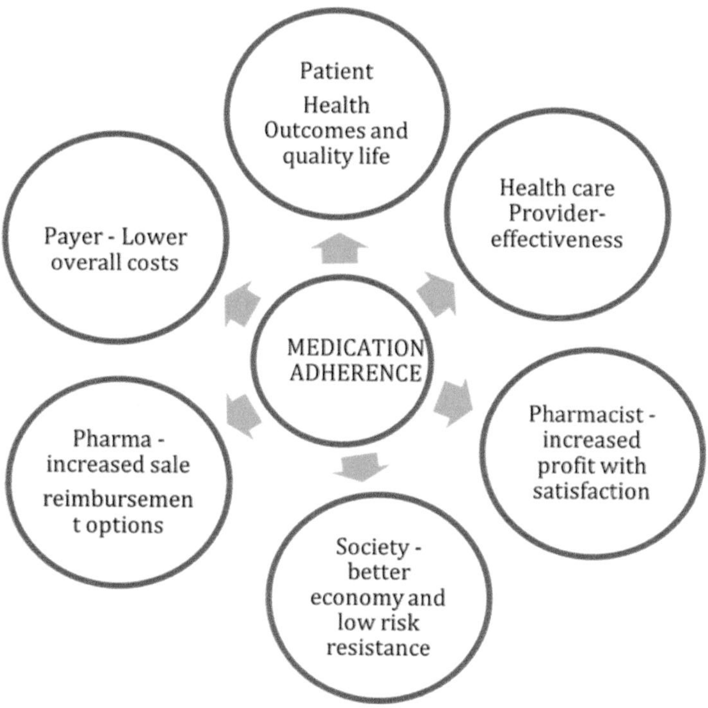

Figure 1: Various aspects of prescription adherence.

2. Background

2.1. Prescription Adherence

Self-medication etiquette of a person taking the prescription is defined as the process of medication adherence. The intake process of medicine by a patient is naturally referred to as medication adherence, quantified by the healthcare professional to include slot, measurement, and the rate of recurrence (Williams and Lee 2023). The other side of following up is non-adherence, referring to the non-intake of medication as measured, which includes unsteady, missed prescriptions, and inadequate medication use. The research showed that non-intake of medication leads to unwanted results in the rise of drug conflict, faster development of disease, various irretrievable health hitches, and increased death rates.

The various approaches show many advantages of following a prescription schedule. The patients suffering from infectious diseases with greater adherence to the prescribed medication have lower health issues, and many treatments have larger benefits with potentially energetic medical outcomes. The opposite side of following improper medication of a patient with chronic illness comes with degradation of the patient's health, which hypothetically leads to disability or death.

2.2. Prescription Adherence Overseeing

Following the prescription is the best way to take the medicine correctly, and sticking to the schedule as prescribed is necessary for proper administration, dosage frequency, and other important details. Several reports indicate that more than 50% of elderly people never get the medication as prescribed, or they do not use the medicines they bought as per the prescription. It is also noted that poor usage or follow-up of prescriptions is one of the major reasons for chronic illnesses among the elderly population (Lee et al., 2024). In some countries, it is noted that more than a lakh deaths are recorded annually, and billions of dollars are spent on healthcare systems every year. Various methods are available to monitor prescription adherence, as it has been shown to improve health outcomes. Improving adherence to medical treatment would enhance both health benefits and economic savings.

Two important factors are considered while dealing with medication adherence. The primary factor is overseeing, defined as calculation, quantification, capacity, or appraisal. Overseeing medication monitors a patient's behavior when taking medicine, making it a primary role. The secondary factor is involvement, which improves following adherence to correcting or checking the deviation of the intake of medicine as prescribed. The other is related to psychological and social factors that disturb the behavior of patients with ill health. This part of medication adherence is not discussed in this chapter.

Two methods are used to measure medication adherence: direct and indirect approaches. A direct opinion of a patient's lab detection of the medications, which includes patient bodily fluids and medication consumption, is part of the former approach that uses the qualification of adherence. The straight opinion of laboratory findings of the non-harmful biomarkers is available in medicine in dried body fluids, along with the presence of harmful biomarkers. Patients' reporting, counting the pills consumed by patients, and frequency of medicine replacements using digital medicine tracking systems are indirect mechanisms of prescription adherence (Chen et al., 2023). There is no one fitting standard for optimal prescription adherence overseeing. Both methods have their own merits and demerits; the former is precise, invasive, and comes with loaded costs, while the latter is less expensive and provides better estimates of prescription adherence. The methods depend on the steadiness of the user; these aspects are considered while selecting the adherence quantification mechanisms.

2.3. Reasons for Using Technology-Based Solutions

Prescription non-adherence can be eliminated and mandates the involvement of various aspects. To achieve significant growth in adherence, the primary focus is on the monitoring mechanism's dependability and utility. Physical tactics need focus and determination from the patient. Although simple biochemical techniques require subjects to supply bodily fluids in the lab, drawing blood samples is a more significant problem for clinic patients. Some of the key obstacles to prescription adherence identified through review of the past work are presented in the figure below.

Figure 2: List of identified barriers related to prescription adherence.

Faster development of Cyber-Physical Systems (CPS) for patient monitoring systems involves rare detecting and overseeing strategies embedded with mobile equipment such as smart medication bottles, fitness bands, and other wearables. The amalgamation of smart overseeing strategies with interventions that prompt the patients when a deviation is spotted to identify better prescription adherence. In contrast to physical mechanisms, digital mechanisms provide an approach with minimal cost and determination of interest from users. In conclusion, the correctness of methods is essential for a person providing health care systems (WHO 2023). The era of the Internet of Things (IoT), which favored device connectivity over the internet, is considered a prominent domain. This connectivity makes it possible to provide the collected information of the person with or without illness over the consumption of medicine, including activities like alerting and reminders for refilling.

Digital systems for healthcare management are movable units that save time, along with prolonged overseeing with the advantage of non-restriction of user time. Even though these digital models are highly feasible and cost-effective, they come with loads of limitations as well as failure in some cases, which is a burden for the person using them. So, there is a need for optimized digital models for examining medication adherence, along with extra efforts that require accurate and cost-reduced digital adherence mechanisms. The statistics related to refilling prescribed medicines for patients suffering from illnesses can be studied from the National Association of Chain Drug Stores.

3. Review of Earlier Work

Continuous checking and evaluation of prescription adherence is a major task. Based on the aberrations identified, enhancements are made to the existing models. A wide range of research has been conducted to study the prescription adherence issues faced by people suffering from illnesses. However, they are mostly related to laboratory analysis, although a few are related to digital models. Prescription adherence monitoring and enhancements receive less attention than with traditional approaches. The technological solutions presented and explained in the reviews are related to prescription adherence calculation and its merits/ demerits. There is a complete discussion on CPS together with the architecture of the system, expansion of hardware capabilities, and analysis of data collected through the systems related to healthcare management (Brown et al., 2024). One effective way to lower the costs of sustaining a healthcare system to treat chronic illnesses is to maintain medication adherence, as illustrated in Fig. 3.

Few studies are related to technological advancement concerning adherence overseeing and development. Digital methods of prescription measurements, alongside smart tablet applications for prescription adherence, are automated systems. The aged population uses digital technologies that notify them of their pharmaceutical procedures in addition to different adherence quantification systems. Numerous research studies related to clinical examinations of chronic illnesses that impact a significant number of people are presented using these adherence measurement tools. These studies also revealed information concerning the analysis of data collected through electronic medication models, along with their stability and expansion of their usability.

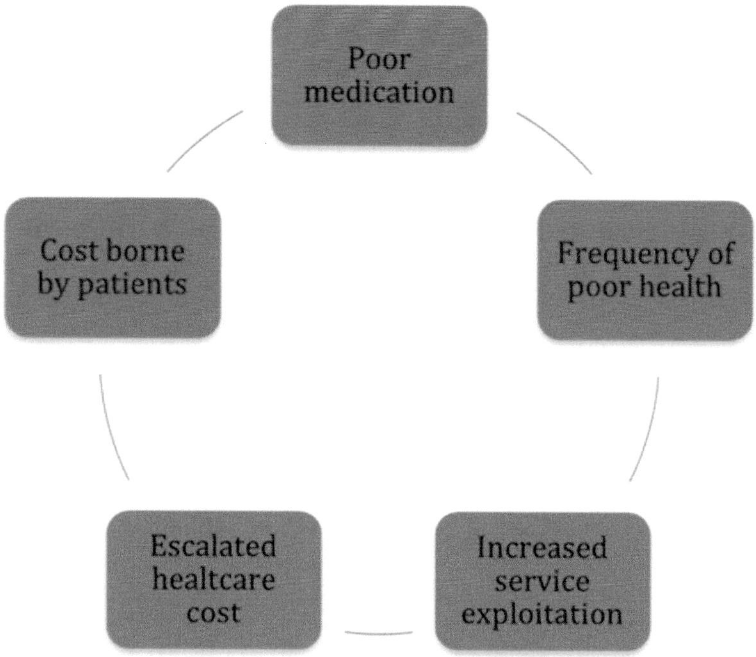

Figure 3: Process of medication adherence in the healthcare sector.

4. Prescription Method: A Review

Non-adherence to medication is a complex and extensive topic, which leads us to conclude that many factors interfere with improving prescription adherence. The use of technology should be suggested to improve adherence by offering caring tools. This offers timely supervision to generate important insights into the behavior of people with disorders. Many systems related to health-related proposals, as well as prescription adherence mechanisms, have been presented in the past that exploited monitoring and tracing methods. Various schemes for overseeing models for consuming medicine use emergent skills.

4.1. Systems Embedded with Sensors

Factors such as dimensions, fee, and power consumed by minor adhoc devices are the reasons for the decline in the magnitude of these devices. These days, adhoc or digital devices are bought at considerably lower cost. Daily activities are recorded, and the data are connected to software that can process this data with the help of embedded wearable sensor devices. These can offer privacy, safety, and day-to-day background activities are assessed, observed to manage the healthcare system requirements of the person suffering from illness. The aggregation of CPS and IoT's main components is a crucial factor in developing the latest IoT-enabled healthcare CPS systems.

The gap that covers the distance between the physical and digital worlds is filled by sensor grids and their subsets, which act as exceptional tools. Professionals in human health management employ sensor models to efficiently collect data over an extended period and daily. The analysis of a person taking medicine is an auspicious usage of the domain that monitors and evaluates these systems (Gracia et al., 2023; Ruppar 2020). Use of sensor embedded devices for calculating the efficiency of healthcare monitoring devices along with the drug consumption frequency monitor which are used by people with critical illnesses. Consistency in quantification, secluded observing ability, and background alertness are some of the factors used to evaluate these systems. The major categories in monitoring these models are fixed and wearable forms. The former are tied to pillboxes or bottles or in some other objects, while the wearables are feather-light and are tied to the body of the person suffering from illnesses. The latter is more aggressive in embedding with various uses of healthcare models, which follows prescription adherence evaluation.

4.2. Intelligent Drug Container

Containers used to hold drugs or bottles used for pills equipped with sensors are designed for observing the intake of medicine and the related actions. The oldest design, MedTracker, features a seven-day multi-grid box with needles inserted in each grid for convenient and comfortable access. These devices are equipped with sensors that detect when the compartments are not sealed properly, using the needles that act as a switch that triggers a microcontroller. The Bluetooth technology transmits the data collected by the controller to the software loaded in the system. The Bluetooth methods, which are straightforward and error-proof since they are made to treat an opened lid as an occurrence similar to drug intake, update this data continuously into the system every few hours.

Pillsense is another mechanism that uses a printable 3D drug storage bottle embedded with attracting sensors that act as a switch, an accelerometer with a load cell, with a PIP-Tag mote, which acts as a stand to collect the data from the sensors used and transfer the same without the need for a wired system to connect a computational system. They rely on notion-aggregate sensing, where the switch is used for evaluating the cap removal, while the accelerometer identifies the spontaneous consumption of the drug through hand-mouth activity, and the load cell checks for the weight of the pill bottle. Pillbox is designed as a 7-day grid box with a microcontroller, along with a ZigBee non-wired module, and a battery with an accelerometer. The data collected is transferred to a laptop of the person taking medicine; however, no proven results have been presented (Gray et al., 2019). These methods move toward removing involvement and adding sensors to the physical body, ensuring that the accelerometer sensor is used to retain accuracy and the patient's well-being. The device is not equipped to provide information about whether the drug is consumed by the person who is suffering from illness.

4.3. Wearable Devices Embedded with Sensors

The cost and smart spots of observation in inertial measurement units are the advancement of modern times; they are an aggregated product with accelerometers, sensors that calculate and measure geometrical coordinates, along with magnetometers. Motion detection is widely used in applications applicable in the healthcare industry, which track and record the activities of the affected person's wellbeing. Prescription adherence can be assessed using a variety of wearable technologies, which are commonly categorized as wristbands and neckbands. The former device is worn around the neck like a pendant with a piezoelectric sensor, a board for radio frequency, and a battery. These sensors actively track stress brought on by drug use, which produces voltage as a protective mechanism. The collected statistics are transmitted through Bluetooth to a device where the algorithm for classification is executed. Social recognition and a novel design for commercial intelligent medications that just need to be worn around the neck, with skin contact present the most challenging obstacles. Another mechanism is the usage of acoustic sensors in wearable devices; they are used for monitoring diet intake processes. Even though it needs more exploration, an acoustic-based approach aims at accumulating acoustic data by consuming or injecting activities related to the consumption of the diet. These are done by a microphone receiver placed near the throat that collects and analyzes the data, which then classifies the data based on the algorithm. Another approach where RFID in the form of a flex sensor with microphones is used to sense the moments on the throat area, which evaluates the usage of medication (Stirratt et al., 2018).

The latter device is tied to the wrist. These customized sensors come with a scaled-down version of the IMU and are utilized for tracking purposes in addition to being attractive items. Wearable and personalized sensors are used in various healthcare evaluation studies, which take into consideration drug consumption. IMUs have been massively used since these devices have larger capabilities for strength, path, and angle of movements, in addition to drug intake through a 3D management system. Whether or not treatment plans are involved, gathering this kind of data helps with the design and summarization of users' physical motions.

The model designed by Texas Instruments is utilized to gather and transmit signals from the onboard accelerometer. These inputs are used along with signal processing and classification of the data for the prescription of drug consumption. The 3-axis accelerometer and gyroscope, which Samsung Electronics used in a smartwatch, were also used in exposing pill bottles, subtraction of drug from the bottle, and pouring of drug along with water. Twisting the cap and turning the wrist of a wearable device face up while pouring medication from the container in the other hand are two of the main behaviors that have been identified. Accelerometers and gyroscopes in smart devices collect and transfer the readings related to drug intake. Using one or two smart watches on one or both hands, a decision tree algorithm analyzes wrist movement to determine drug ingestion.

The data from accelerometers embedded in smart devices is evaluated to identify whether the activity involves taking a drug with water or consuming water, or wiping of water droplets on lips while drinking water. Even though these smart devices can capture the data related to pill intake, there are still some challenging issues, like promptly identifying twist opening the pill bottle and consumption of drinking water. The smart device tied to the hand, along with IMUs, is capable of recording this, as well as a transmitter and receiver setup to transmit reminder messages for drug intake. The transmitter-receiver setup also enables the user to reschedule the time for drug intake or vocally respond to the reminders. The Android apps that are designed for the above activity come with multi-language support. The evaluation and data collection within the user's living environment is a significant benefit of this device's design and use, which also contributes to improved accuracy. The success of these devices design relies on user acceptance of these wearable gadgets, which effectively meets the need to position sensors close to the affected person's skin.

4.4. Consumable Biosensors

Consumables that can be swallowed by users enter the digestive system when they come into contact with fluids in the stomach. They release a chip, which could be an RFID or IC, to collect information about drug consumption. The way it reacts and is observed is recorded with the help of signals transmitted when these embedded objects interact with gastric juices. Such devices consumed orally, are biosensors; the research concerning these biosensors is still in its initial stage. The pros of biosensor usage are that they are capable of identifying parallel intake of medicine and their reactions with greater accuracy (Mohammed et al., 2018). They also offer no-cost involved methods for evaluating the prescription, where every prescription is different from one another. However, the one major requirement is that the device has to be secured to the affected person's body, which provides secured and non-public data to be transferred to the system with algorithms to analyze this data. These devices, however, are non-heavier evaluation tools that consume minimal energy for the same.

4.5. Vicinity Calculation Device

IoT devices are good at calculating the closeness based on some technology-supported algorithms. The devices are used regularly to observe the closeness of these devices to other things in the environment. The two types of non-wired communication mechanisms are RFID and NFC; both are undersized range contactless techniques. These devices are designed with an RFID tag for systems, an RFID reader, and LEDs. Glowing LEDs help the patient remember the time for medicine. Thus, they record the information about the drug taken from the pill box/bottle by calculating the distance range from the RFID reader. A caretaker or medical practitioner can follow the activities of the ill person in consuming the tablets. The same concepts are used to take stock of medicine and calculate the time for a refill or send in a refill request to a pharmacist.

These devices come with their pros and cons. The major advantage of the devices is that they gather the drug intake time, occurrence, and extent of prescribed medication (Mohammed et al., 2018). Older people consider these devices for closeness detection, which is non-invasive. Since RFID tags are embedded in drug containers for the intake of prescription medicine. The medication system's primary feature is its use of drug containers, which use RFID readers to determine the distance between them. RFID readers are used to collect information about the circumstances that result in patients with illnesses consuming medication.

4.6. Visualization system

Computer vision and processing technology of images are used in the development of various procedures for activities related to human representation and cataloguing. The applications of healthcare mechanisms in smart surroundings or homes where ambient assistive living techniques. One way of evaluating intake of medicine usage is to design modules to identify and keep track of inhabitants, signals, signs, and topics. The camera mounted in the medication area is to observe the intake of drugs from drug bottles to monitor the intake of medicine at the right time. Methods used for identifying skin/ non-skin color classification based on identification algorithms. These methods first categorize the skin tone of the person identified in the camera. These algorithms also classify hand over mouth, i.e., intake pills with water activity and twisting of the bottle.

Another system for observing medicine intake where various scenarios, like twisting of the drug bottle, picking up the drug, drug consumption, and reverse twisting of the drug bottle. The classification methods for identifying a person also classify people based on skin tone distinction. The purpose of the work was the development of a method of background clampdown of the videos taken with low-doggedness cameras and implementation of this method in the process of monitoring the medication intake (Aldeer et al., 2018). The method was, however, not tested using more than one subject, and we are not told of the accuracy levels. Moreover, the accuracy of the system can be impacted in case of different color clothes used by the contributors because the tryouts have been carried out with a contributor of obscure clothes in contrast to the background. An alternate vision-based system designed a multi-level method to identify and track the mobile objects in medication intake. The mouth, the face, the hands, a glass of water, and the medicine bottle were the objects that were tracked in this system.

To accomplish this, background subtraction detection and tracking, segmentation of skin regions, and utilization of color information in detecting bottles are employed. Activity recognition achieved an average success rate of 98 percent based on a population of tri subjects. The authors in later work explicitly utilize two cameras in their objective of handling occlusion. In a different method, the detection of skin tone and second-order Hu moments to track body parts when taking medication is applied. Also, the Petri network is a specification related to forming of the intake of medication. Out of 12 video clips of taking medications, the system could identify nine. Thus, the authors recommended that more features should be included in the system to improve it further. Activities between hands were differentiated as bottle opening, whereas occlusion between either hand and face was taken as pill swallowing. A monitoring system comprising a digital scale and a camera that was presented in the literature in this field of visual systems is also depicted. A digital scale has been employed, whereby it constantly weighs and indicates the weight of the medication bottle.

A digital scale is employed, whereby it is continuously weighed to show the medication decanter weight. The scale has been filmed, and the image with the readings on the screen has been sent to a nearby computer using the camera. After getting the images, a computer then uses an image processing algorithm to process the weight of the bottle. Based on the trend of weight reduction in a bottle, the system can produce an alarm, reminding the patient to take medicine. It is worth mentioning that even though the given work is focused on vision analysis, there is no human subject tracking (Kalantar-Zadeh et al., 2018). This kind of system cannot foster mobility because of the condition that the medication bottle must be positioned on the weight scale at all times, thereby giving a narrow perspective. Moreover, it makes the user own a digital scale, a camera, and a computer.

A second photographic clinical trial utilizes Microsoft Kinect (Redmond, WA, USA) as a time-of-flight sensor to measure medication adherence in patients with Parkinson's. Microsoft Kinect is utilized in the approximation of nodules on the human anatomy during walking, subsequently acquiring the 3D coordinates of several skeletal intersections. The velocity and acceleration of each intersection were therefore calculated in a manner such that patient gesticulation is achieved. Different data mining algorithms are then used to categorize the data to distinguish between adherent and non-adherent patients. The clinical study involved seven patients with Parkinson's disease initially, before they took prescribed medications, and then after taking medications. More than 97% and 78% accuracies were obtained with an independently optimized classification model and global model, respectively. Limitations in use and accuracy of these approaches will be the key drawbacks of vision-based systems, although they will have an important role in AAL environments.

Moreover, vision-based methods can have multiple requirements that are costly. The other disadvantage, particularly with surveillance-video methods, is that it is very computationally expensive to train the system. Moreover, the deeper we get, the more users favor completely mobile gadgets. But on the contrary, mobility is not supported in vision-based approaches. Last but not least, a user must be in range of the camera, and certain areas of the body must not be covered (hands and face) so that the system can capture and identify these areas to detect an activity of medication taking.

4.7. Fusion-based Systems

A developed medication following system which was composed of a cylindrically designed 7-section pillbox, a wristband device, and a computer, all of which can communicate with one another wirelessly. The pillbox consists of an Arduino microcontroller, motor, ZigBee transceiver, and RFID reader. Moreover, every compartment has a diode and a photodiode to sense the pill exclusion. The job of the MCU is to drive the motor in the direction that will rotate the section concerning the user at the time when medication needs to be taken, and also when the RFID-based wristband is within proximity of the pillbox. The wristband has an IMU, an RFID tag, and an LED. Therefore, it is adopted in the gathering of motion data related to pill consumption and taking. Besides, the RFID proximity detection within the pillbox and the reminder functions are carried out by the RFID tag and the LED, respectively (Iancu and Iancu 2018). The IMU is only allowed to trial the motion data about the likely detection of hand gestures that correlate to pill taking once the wristband is detected within the vicinity of the pillbox. Lastly, to confirm the pill ejection, the photo diode supplies a voltage which should be measured by the MCU, with a certain level depending on the light detected.

A combination of RFID sensors with a camera is adopted to define the act of medication taking in an in-home setting. In this effort, the medication bottles have been tagged with RFID and are kept in a medicine cabinet, which incorporates an RFID reader. The RFID is utilized as an identification technology for the medication bottles, which are stored in the cabinet. Nevertheless, as soon as the bottle has been taken out of the medication cabinet and it is no longer kept within the range of the antenna of the reader, the RFID technology-based identification procedure can no longer be accomplished. The vision system is therefore employed in a manner that triggers the system when the medication bottle is outside the view of the reader. The camera serves the purpose of tracking and confirming the event of taking medication, depending on the detection of moving objects and the color model of the bottle.

4.8. Visual-Sensor Systems

The patient's activity has been monitored to trace the medication intake using assistive living techniques. An instance is iMEC, which is designed to detect medicine timing and pill taking. Ubiquitous sensors have been attached to some devices (refrigerator, microwave oven, chair, and bed) to predict the behavior of the patient. A pill removal detection has been practiced using a medicine case fitted with a camera. The combination of the data from these devices was eventually used in the confirmation of medication adherence. Another attempt to monitor medication adherence in people with dementia. This system employed a container attached with sensors and LEDs, and a Kinect. The pillbox is operated in a way that it recognizes two events: opening of the compartment and medication intake, and closing of the compartment. In the meantime, Kinect is mounted close to the medication compartment to identify two events: bringing the hand → mouth and bringing the water cup → mouth.

Therefore, the pillbox is designed with magnetic read sensors to sense the opening and closing of the compartments, whereas the LEDs are utilized to inform the patient on the appropriate medication section. Skeletal tracking feature of Kinect is utilized in retrieving the coordinates of various joint spots of the patient, head and hands included. Lastly, the authors tested the system with 20 subjects, with which they were able to obtain a recognition accuracy of between 92–100 percent, depending on the angle at which the patient was facing the Kinect. The technology of personal mobile devices has experienced a significant advancement over the past few years. The services introduced by mobile devices, like the various communications methods and user applications, have introduced a plethora of possibilities. Therefore, the industry of mobile applications has been racing, even in the field of healthcare promotion of older patients.

Specifically, various medication adherence-based automated reminder systems have been developed as mobile and tablet applications. In that regard, the sensor-app solution is a combination of sensor network-based and mobile-app-based medication adherence monitoring and tracking approach. A pillbox with several compartments is also equipped with an ambient light sensor attached to each of the compartments and a WiFi connection (Zullig et al., 2017; Dua et al., 2017). In addition, there is the development of a mobile application that has a medicine schedule. The mobile app and the pillbox are linked to an online source of data.

Therefore, the mobile application raises alarms at the time of medication until the patient either takes the medicine out of the pillbox or decides to postpone the act. Recently, a system based on the pillbox and involving the Arduino UNO WiFi and a load cell. The medication weight was reported to a server through the Internet. More so, a mobile app was designed that follows up the shift in the weight scale and reminds the patient to have a medicine intake if a weight change is detected.

5. Challenges

5.1. System Correctness

To improve the state of healthcare, there needs to be proper systems that identify user activity. This is not an exception in the case of medication adherence monitoring systems. Overall, the accuracy depends on the device used to capture the medication-taking activity. Moreover, the environment in which medication is taken may influence and restrict the technological level of the advances used. E.g., the system may work at low sampling rates in exchange for low energy consumption. But this is obtained by sacrificing data excellence. Accuracy comprises data quality, data precision, or data fidelity. The sampling frequency, the operation style of the sensor (when the system allows multiple operations and power approaches), and the responsibility cycling can be used to characterize data fidelity. To get high-accuracy data, the system needs to be at high fidelity. Nevertheless, high-fidelity systems drain the backup power rather quickly (when it is battery-powered), because their core must be configured to execute frequently to record the event being monitored accurately. Therefore, the management of energy consumption should be taken into account while designing a medication intake tracking system.

5.2. Power Consumption

A medication adherence monitoring system may be battery-operated, e.g., in sensor network-based systems, and mobile systems, e.g., smart watches, mobile phones, and tablets. This is a problem because the battery contains a restricted energy budget. From the system perspective, it will be expected that enough electric current is being supplied into the system to make it functional. Simultaneously, as a user, one would expect that the system lifetime would be as long as possible because application developers would have to either replace batteries regularly or resort to rechargeable batteries. This would probably be unsatisfactory to be accepted by the user and expensive. It should be noted that energy consumption might not be a critical issue depending on the type of technologies, since some might be passive or not driven by a battery.

Among various technologies, systems embedded with sensors come with a bottleneck, i.e., they are complex to energy consumption because they are supposed to be operated using small-sized batteries which have limited capacities. That is because Moore's law cannot be applied to the production of batteries and, therefore, the battery components remain limited. In addition, the normal sensor nodes are tiny and therefore, there is a lack of space where big batteries could be incorporated, and this restricts the cost of energy. Although there were very few studies that measured the energy usage of medication adherence monitoring systems, this remains core in this discussion because it can gravely impair functionality, efficacy of the system. One can think of this in the case of wearable systems that use non-replaceable batteries. Overall, a battery is a complicated system, which may be unpredictable when influenced by various factors and circumstances, such as temperature and the load applied to it.

5.3. User Acceptability

The perception of the user of a monitoring system greatly influences its successful adoption. Firstly, limitations concerning scientific advancement as energy consumption of batteries, mobility support, and others, are principal obstacles to the broad acceptance of the technology-based systems of medication adherence monitoring. Second, there are ethical issues like privacy and confidentiality. Users have an issue with behaviors being tracked, as, besides the taking of medications, there is the possibility of the information gathered being accessed by unauthorized users. Moreover, they, and particularly the older generation, have social, physical, demographic, and cultural inhibitions to using technology, which consequently inhibits the user from accepting modern technology. In that respect, we can relate active and passive detection systems. With active detection, the sensing device can be tied to the patient and must be worn and active throughout the medication activity. Such a system may be, e.g., a smartwatch. Conversely, passive sensing is carried out through an off-the-patient body system. However, one of the main specifications that the medication adherence systems should support to win the perception of the user is portability, which will be achieved by ensuring comfort. However, as previously said, most portable systems, such as wearable sensors, require the user's attention by being worn constantly and requiring the battery to be charged or changed regularly. At the same time, passive sensing systems are not precise and portable, yet indifferent to the battery replacement problem. To balance such a trade-off implication, it is necessary to have a portable, yet energy-efficient and accurate system.

5.4. Meddling, Endorsement, and Active Non-Compliance

There are two major issues in this respect because users can attempt to actively cheat the system by making it believe they are compliant when in reality they are not. Tampering happens when the medication is received by an unauthorized user. The initial hurdle is therefore an issue of authentication. Is the individual taking the drug who he says he is? There is a possibility of tampering when it comes to drugs that can be addictive, like opiates, and in that case, an addict or a dealer will have the motivation to cheat the system. Authentication, along with authorization, acts in the same way in computer security-Is this who she or he claims to be, and is she or he allowed to take the medication? Even though there is a lack of projects that have addressed these security issues in particular, a variety of wearables are explored, whether a wearable is worn by the individual it is intended for. The second group of strategies tries to keep the unlicensed persons at bay using physical barriers, in this case, by locking the pillboxes. Another group of strategies is not aimed at the prevention of unauthorized access, but is more auditing-oriented. As an illustration, the audit trail can be generated by learning the wrist movements of various individuals so that, subsequently, any tampering can be detected and remediated.

The other difficulty is the active non-compliance, that is, the cases where the rightful handler of the system acts to mislead it. This behavior is possible in case the user does not agree with the treatment advised by a medical professional, yet he or she pretends to agree instead of questioning the expertise of the latter. Since the system user is an authorized user but just refuses to take the prescription, active user impersonation is more difficult to handle. Video monitoring and other measures can be used, but basic steps, like putting a medicine in the mouth, pretending to gulp, and subsequently expelling it out at a later time, will fool most of the modern technologies.

5.5. Future Developments

The solutions are limited in one way or another, which is apparent from this review. In that way, the created system can utilize the potential of a synergy of technologies to reach the final objective. Nevertheless, the mentioned challenges can be overcome in the following way. To achieve the accurate monitoring of patient adherence, fine-grain sensors, like load cells, motion sensors to sense and categorize the gestures related to the hand-to-mouth movement, and switch or capacitive sensors to verify the cap opening and closure, are promising candidate technologies. An example of collaborative sensing that can be exploited to extend the lifetime of a battery-powered system is the integration of low-energy-consuming sensors with low fidelity of activity and high-fidelity-of-activity, but also high-energy-consuming sensors on the same platform, and making the decisions of which sensor and when to be on.

However, this requires sensor fusion algorithms that build a common model from various sensed and reported inputs—e.g., Bayesian inference. Moreover, because the wireless part of the wireless-enabled systems creates a bottleneck because it drains a significant amount of the battery energy, it is necessary to seek low-power communication technologies. For example, the Transmit Only (TO) solution can be used instead of Bluetooth or WiFi. The TO technique is a one-hop communication that does not require handshaking or an acknowledgment, therefore making the amount of energy needed to transmit a packet merely a few tens of microjoules. Lastly, user acceptability and comfort could be carefully achieved through designing a low-energy, smart, and wireless pill container.

6. Conclusion

A huge challenge in the health care sector is medication non-adherence. Lack of good adherence to medication causes wastage of healthcare resources and poor treatment results. It has therefore emerged as a desirable field of study among numerous researchers in multidisciplinary fields to devise novel monitoring and interventions that can sense and rectify medication-taking schedules once they go awry. In the present paper, we have discussed the technology-aided medication adherence monitoring techniques and systems. We also upon the benefits, drawbacks, and limitations connected with these methods, yet how that will convert into amended operational and clinical outcomes needs additional input and observations of patients and clinical practitioners alike. Based on this review, we can say that more efforts have to be put into improving those technology-based systems that can surmount such challenges, particularly the accuracy, comfort of use, and power consumption by the user. Last but not least, it appears in the paper that numerous additional clinical trials should be carried out over extensive periods and involving extensive sample groups to assess the precision of medicine adherence systems as well as their usability.

References

Aldeer, M., Martin, R.P., and Howard, R.E. (2018). PillSense: Designing a medication adherence monitoring system using pill bottle-mounted wireless sensors. *In:* Proceedings of the IEEE International Conference on Communications Workshops (ICC Workshops), pp. 20–24. Kansas City, MO, USA.

Brown, M., Daneala, M.I., and Haasnsen, R. (2024). Value-based care models and medication adherence incentives. Health Affairs, 43(4), 567–575.

Chen, X., Zhao, Y., and Curtis, J. (2023). Ingestible sensors for medication adherence: Current status and future directions. Advanced Drug Delivery Reviews, 194, 114728.

Dua, A., Weeks, W.A., Berstein, A., Azevedo, R.G., Ward, A., and Li, R. (2017). An in-vivo communication system for monitoring medication adherence. *In:* Proceedings of the Wireless Communications and Networking Conference (WCNC), pp. 1–6. San Francisco, CA, USA, 19–22.

Garcia, M. (2023). Impact of social determinants on medication non-adherence in underserved populations. JAMA Network Open, 6(8), e2332345.

Gray, C., Cooke, C.E., and Brandt, N. (2019). Evolution of the medicare Part D: Medication Therapy Management program from inception in 2006 to the present. Am Health Drug Benefits, 12(5): 243–251.

Green, L. (2024). Pharmacist-led interventions to improve medication adherence in chronic diseases: A meta-analysis. Journal of the American Pharmacists Association (JAPhA), 64(2), 102–115.

Iancu, I., and Iancu, B. (2018). Elderly in the digital era: Theoretical perspectives on assistive technologies. Technologies 2017, 5, 60.

Kalantar-Zadeh, K., Berean, K.J., Ha, N., Chrimes, A.F., Xu, K., Grando, D., and Taylor, K.M. (2018). A human pilot trial of ingestible electronic capsules capable of sensing different gases in the gut. Nat. Electron., 1, 79–87.

Lee, H., Chen, X., and Williams, Y. (2024). Smart pill bottles and IoT for real-time adherence tracking. IEEE Journal of Biomedical and Health Informatics, 28(3), 1456–1464.

Mohammed, H.B., Ibrahim, D., and Cavus, N. (2018). Mobile device-based smart medication reminder for older people with disabilities. Qual. Quant., 1, 79–87.

Patel, S., and Smith, A. (2024). Artificial intelligence in medication adherence monitoring: A systematic review. Journal of Medical Internet Research (JMIR), 26(1), e51234.

Ruppar, T. (2020). Meta-analysis: How to quantify and explain heterogeneity? Eur J Cardiovasc Nurs., 19(7), 646–652.

Smith, A., Curtis, J.R., and Danila, A. (2023). Blockchain technology for secure and transparent medication adherence tracking. Nature Digital Medicine, 6(45).

Stirratt, M.J., Curtis, J.R., Danila, M.I., Hansen, R., Miller, M.J., and Gakumo, C.A. (2018). Advancing the science and practice of medication adherence. J Gen. Intern. Med., 33, 216–222.

WHO (2023). Global Guidelines on Medication Adherence for Chronic Conditions. World Health Organization Technical Report Series, 1035.
Williams, R., and Lee, H. (2023). Behavioral nudges and medication adherence: A randomized controlled trial. Health Psychology, 42(5), 321–330.
Zhao, Y., Martin, R.P., and Howard, R.E. (2023). Mobile health apps for medication adherence: Efficacy and user engagement. npj Digital Medicine, 6(1), 112.
Zullig, L.L., Mendys, P., and Bosworth, H.B. (2017). Medication adherence: A practical measurement selection guide using case studies. Patient Educ. Couns, 690, 1468414.

CHAPTER
4

Integrating Smart Solutions for Healthcare and Environmental Surveillance

Mannat Singh(0009-0006-1845-4897), **Shreya Singh**(0009-0008-7088-0644) **and Hina Bansal***(0000-0003-1683-1581)

Centre for Computational Biology and Bioinformatics, Amity Institute of Biotechnology, Amity University, Noida – 201303, Uttar Pradesh, India

1. Introduction

Major improvements in health care services, especially in remote health monitoring, have been brought about by the development of information technology (IT) (Li et al., 2019). Early detection of high-risk disease impairments and illness prevention are two main goals of using physical sensor networks (Mohammadzadeh et al., 2020). These days, fast monitoring and control of patients' conditions through timely access and ongoing evaluation of patient's vital health signals is made possible by smart technologies and sophisticated instruments such as wearable sensors and smart wireless devices (Schunk et al., 2022). Many types of healthcare or medical treatment (such as telemedicine) depend on these smart device's ability to store and transfer data (Cristiano et al., 2018). Along with several other health-related features, wearable sensors are mostly used to monitor and track patients' health issues and conditions. To put it another way, the patient's physiological state, organ function, and the course of their illness are all represented by their vital health signs. Nursing care, diagnosis, treatment, and illness prevention are all greatly affected by the evaluation of these markers (Fan et al., 2019). If properly and quickly evaluated, these health data could serve as a helpful guide for effective and superior medical treatment. To enhance the prompt and continuous assessment of patient's health statuses and associated healthcare subsystems, numerous smart gadgets, Internet of Things (IoT), and artificial intelligence (AI)-based technologies have been created. Over the past

*Corresponding author: hinabansal@gmail.com

DOI: 10.1201/9781003676812-4

10 years, smart devices—more especially, wearable sensors—have garnered a lot of interest, mostly in the healthcare industry. From physical (body) indications, including heart rate (HR), blood pressure (BP), body temperature, respiration rate, and body mobility, these devices aim to extract therapeutically significant health-related data (Majumder et al., 2017). In other words, appropriate wearable sensors and wearable sensor networks are used to extract and share fundamental health information. Numerous health-related sensors make up wearable sensor networks (WSNs). The sensors of these networks are placed on different body parts and can be implanted or worn by the patient. To detect and document symptoms (health-related data), each of these sensors has certain requirements. But given the prevalence of various illnesses and disabilities, patient monitoring continuity is essential for timely medical delivery and intervention. As a result, one of the main applications of smart wearable technology in the healthcare industry is patient monitoring via WSNs.

Furthermore, the successful partnership between AI and healthcare has resulted in better patient care in a variety of areas, from quality medical treatment (Jamal et al., 2009) to hospital productivity and patient safety (Lee et al., 2013). Since the Internet of Things (IoT) has made it possible for objects (in this example, sensors) to transmit and analyse data (Jones, 2014), basic health-related data gathering can be partially or completely automated, relieving physicians of the burden of continuously profiling health examination data. Additionally, data is processed and stored on a distributed platform via IoT (Li, Xu and Zhao, 2014). Utilising this platform enables the creation and application of machine learning (ML) algorithms (Lewis and Denning, 2018) to manage hospital/medical resources by forecasting future patient demands and predicting issues with patient health status. A useful overview of an IoT-ML-powered delivery of healthcare systems.

2. Fundamental Technologies

2.1. Features of the Smart Environment

Smart environments arise employing a variety of critical technologies. The Internet of Things (IoT), Internet of Medical Things (IoMT), artificial intelligence (AI), machine learning, and sensor networks are all technologies that are transforming the way we conduct our lives and function.

The Internet of Things (IoT) is the foundation of smart environments, enabling automatic interaction across linked objects. In medical services, IoTs are attributed to medical technology, allowing for remote monitoring and data collection.

As illustrated in Figure 1. It comprises a variety of technological equipment and sensors that gather, convey, as well as handle health information. Gadgets with IoMT might be embedded into one's skin (smartwatches), attached to it, or integrated into the surroundings. IoMT systems are made up of medical sensors (such as smartwatches and wearables) that gather biological information, telecommunication components that transmit data, and data processing. Smart settings offer several advantages in a variety of industries, as illustrated in the graphic below. Smart settings offer various advantages across a wide range of sectors, as seen below. Sensor-enabled devices can track vital signs, detect emergencies, and allow chronic patients to live freely.

Real-time data automation and analysis can help you save energy and lessen your environmental impact. Intelligent environments can detect dangers to safety, blazes, and other disasters and send real-time alerts. Automated modifications depending on individual tastes or external factors increase comfort and convenience.

In essence, smart environment's distinctive characteristics, such as Efficacy, accessibility, digitisation, and ecological responsibility, reflect a watershed moment in the design and implementation of sophisticated both private and workplace locations, embracing sensor-driven treatments.

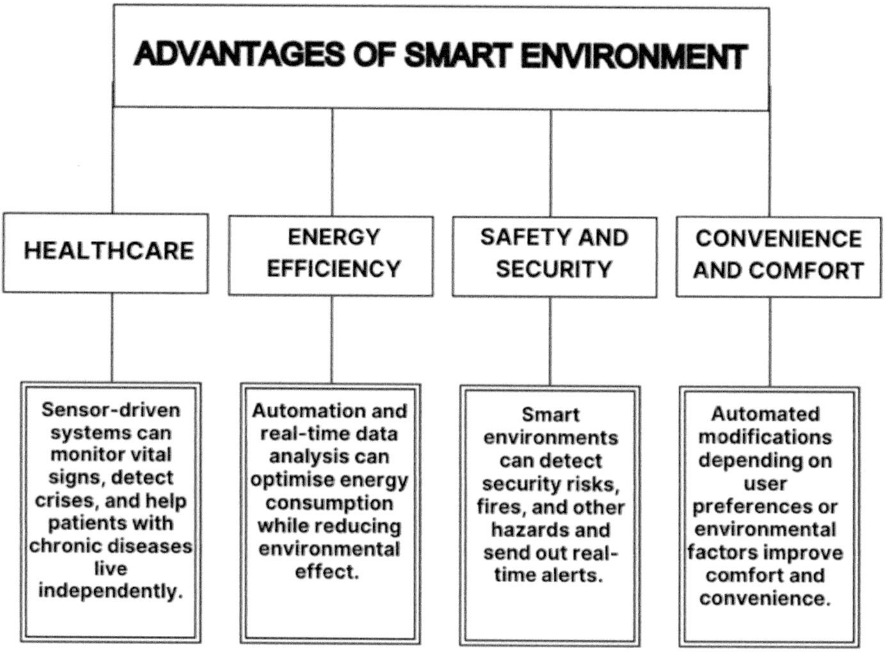

Figure 1: Depicts the advantages of a smart environment.

2.2. Elements of Modern Hospital and Healthcare Systems

Depending on the user's inclinations or circumstances in the environment, technology enablers improve convenience, ease, and thoughtful decision-making processes, with the primary goal of encouraging well-being and security while also providing personalised experiences. These benefits apply to a variety of businesses, encompassing wellness (e.g., continuous supervision), environmental sustainability, security and confidentiality, and overall user comfort. Smart hospital technology combined with smart buildings provides ground-breaking ideas to improve medical services. Healthcare practitioners can immediately share patient data within the smart building, which enhances cooperation. (Dharmar et al., 2013). Telemedicine services are being integrated into hospital infrastructure to allow for remote consultations and testing (Craig and Petterson, 2005). The use of automated systems for routine patient care tasks to improve healthcare workflows (Bort-Roig et al., 2014). RPM systems allow healthcare providers to remotely monitor their patient's health data, which improves chronic disease management. Remote prescription administration and pharmaceutical services are delivered through digital platforms. Real-time virtual consultations between healthcare practitioners and patients remove geographical barriers to healthcare access (McLean et al., 2013). Allows for asynchronous medical data transfer, making it easier for healthcare practitioners to collaborate. ("Telemedicine and the COVID-19 Pandemic, Lessons for the Future | Telemedicine and E-Health," 2021). Savvy Home Wellness Monitoring—These technologies span past wearables and create a whole wellness infrastructure in the comfort of your own home. Such unified systems employ a variety of detectors to track an expanded variety of biological factors, yielding a more comprehensive picture of a person's well-being. These data may include routines for sleeping, levels of activity at residence, as well as aspects of the environment that affect health. Smart home health monitoring systems assist both patients and carers by encouraging independent living and offering prompt interventions when necessary (Gold et al., 2018). Automated ways for controlling drug regimens and minimising mistakes. Telecare Systems are communication and alarm systems that allow for remote monitoring and rapid emergency response (Fothergill et al., 2023). Assistive robotics—designed to support users with everyday duties and allow them to live freely (Broadbent et al., 2009).

The incorporation of electronic health records into intelligent homes represents an unprecedented change in providing healthcare, since Interrelated Wellness Communities enable effortless incorporation of data on health from wearable devices and home surveillance equipment into larger healthcare infrastructure (Cabanillas-Carbonell et al., 2023). AI-Driven Gesundheit Insights are sophisticated insights that oversee vast data sets to deliver invaluable knowledge for personalised treatment (Table 1). represents essential elements of modern hospital and healthcare systems.

Table 1: Essential Elements of Modern Hospital and Healthcare Systems

Element	Description	Impact/Benefit
Smart Hospital Technology	Integration of intelligent building systems and smart healthcare infrastructure.	Enhances real-time data sharing and collaboration among healthcare professionals.
Telemedicine Services	Remote consultation, diagnosis, testing, and asynchronous data sharing.	Improves accessibility to healthcare, especially in remote or underserved areas.
Automated Patient Care Systems	Use of automation in routine healthcare workflows (e.g., vitals monitoring, admin tasks).	Streamlines processes, reduces human error, and improves efficiency.
Remote Patient Monitoring (RPM)	Systems to track patient health remotely, especially for chronic conditions.	Enables proactive and continuous care, reducing hospital visits.
Digital Prescription Platforms	Online systems for remote prescription management and delivery.	Ensures medication adherence and reduces prescription errors.

2.3. Technologies for Digital Twins

To address the concerns revealed by our contrasting evaluations of conventional and contemporary intelligent technologies, we propose an integrated methodology that maximizes dependability, safety, and user pleasure in smart environments. Our proposed strategy is based on the Intuitive Connectivity Framework (ICF), which combines essential technologies (e.g., IoT, AI), BMS, and HAS to address the limitations of both old and new smart systems (Clinic, 2023). Addressing Issues in Intelligent Environments. Our comparison study found weaknesses in both traditional and new smart workplaces. These limits include limited access, fewer operating system options, and data security issues. To address these concerns, we offer a comprehensive solution: the Innovative Networking Framework (ICF) and its most recent version (Al-Fuqaha et al., 2015). The Innovative Connectivity Framework (ICF) is a conceptual framework that overcomes healthcare industry restrictions. It combines important technologies (IoT, AI) with existing infrastructure (BMS, HAS, and cyber-physical systems (CPS)) to provide a secure and user-friendly environment (Devon, 2015). This platform promotes seamless integration, real-time data sharing, and enhanced interoperability across healthcare devices and systems. This eventually improves decision-making, resource allocation, and patient outcomes (Vodyaho et al., 2024). The ICF uses complex protocols to provide seamless communication between devices, allowing for real-time data transmission and reducing connectivity bottlenecks (Höyhtyä, 2023).

3. Healthcare and Internet of Things

3.1. The Internet of Things

The IoT is an extensive system of varied communication devices that may interact and exchange data with other devices. IoT devices have disrupted the field of medical applications, as evidenced by the numerous challenges and problems encountered in the past. These IoT devices can supply a substantial volume of biological data, which may play a crucial role in creating automated systems for medical data collection.

Integrating IoT devices with advanced Machine Learning (ML) algorithms transforms big data into a critical resource for enhancing health systems in diagnosis, treatment, and decision-making processes. The Internet of Everything (IoE), which includes patient monitoring and surveillance as well as symptomatic therapy, has gained attention due to its usage in biomedical applications [4]. Furthermore, the creation of small sensors in the medical field that continuously monitor patients' vital signs is enhancing system security and has great potential for early diagnosis and treatment (Kumar et al., 2023).

The Internet of Things is built on four fundamental components: sensors that gather data, devices that manage and exchange that data, and complex data processing algorithms that extract relevant data (Mervat Abu-Elkheir, Hayajneh, and Ali, 2013). This dynamic synergy between hardware and software enables IoT to bridge the physical and digital worlds, offering innovative solutions to everyday challenges and creating opportunities for enhanced automation, predictive maintenance, and personalized experiences (Atadoga et al., n.d.).

3.2. Internet of Things in the Health Sector

IoT technologies have numerous uses in the healthcare sector and are transforming patient care and management. Smartwatches, fitness trackers, and other wearable medical devices have become essential tools for those who want to keep an eye on their vital signs, sleep habits, and level of physical activity. By enabling patients to take an active role in their health management, these gadgets encourage an active approach to wellbeing (Estrela et al., 2018; Rayan et al., 2021).

To reduce the strain on hospital beds and medical personnel, non-critical patients may be monitored remotely from their homes rather than in hospitals. Those who live in remote regions may utilize it to improve their access to healthcare, or it could help older people stay in their homes longer. In essence, it can help people always have more control over their health and reduce the strain on healthcare facilities while expanding access to healthcare services. A practical approach to monitoring blood glucose levels in diabetics was proposed.

When using this method, patients must manually obtain blood glucose measurements at certain periods. Two types of blood-glucose anomalies are then investigated. Abnormal blood glucose levels are followed by a missing blood glucose measurement. Depending on how serious the irregularity is, the system decides who should be informed: the patient, family members and caregivers, or emergency medical personnel, such as physicians. This approach is possible and useful, even if automating blood-glucose readings might improve it even more (Raymond et al., 2024).

Using prefabricated parts and a specially built antenna, a heart attack detection gadget was developed. The A microcontroller processes cardiac activity picked up by an ECG sensor (Bhat and Bhat, 2017). Via Bluetooth, the user's device gets this data, performs additional analysis, and shows its findings in an application. According to the authors, developing tools to predict heart attacks might improve the approach. Assessing respiratory rate, which is known to help predict a heart attack, might lead to even greater benefits (Baker, Xiang, and Atkinson, 2017).

IoT devices offer a variety of new opportunities for individuals to monitor themselves and for medical professionals to monitor their patients. Therefore, there are benefits and drawbacks to the variety of wearable IoT devices for medical practitioners and their patients.

3.2.1. Connected Inhalers

Attacks that occur suddenly and without much notice are common in conditions like asthma or COPD. To assist medical practitioners in determining the reason for an attack, patients can benefit from IoT-connected inhalers that record the frequency of episodes and collect ambient data. Additionally, linked inhalers can alert patients when they abuse the device or leave it at home, increasing the likelihood that they will have an attack without it (Asmaul Hosna et al., 2022).

3.2.2. Ingestible Sensors

Gathering information from inside the body of an individual is typically a disorganized and upsetting procedure. For example, nobody enjoys having a probe or camera put into their intestinal tract. Ingestible sensors allow for far less intrusive data collection from the digestive and other systems. For example, they help identify the cause of internal bleeding or give information about the PH levels of the stomach. These devices need to be manageable in size. Additionally, they must dissolve or be readily absorbed by the human body. Many companies are putting a lot of effort into creating ingestible sensors that meet these specifications (Asmaul Hosna et al., 2022).

3.2.3. Connected Contact Lenses

A passive, non-intrusive method of gathering medical data is through smart contact lenses. They could also feature microcameras that let users snap images with their eyes, which is possibly why Google and other businesses have patented connected contact lenses. Whether they are used for other purposes or to improve health outcomes, smart lenses have the potential to make people's eyes a potent tool for digital interactions ("10 Internet of Things (IoT) Healthcare Examples," 2024).

3.3. Model for Healthcare in the Future Internet of Things

According to an analysis of current IoT-based healthcare systems, wearable sensors, particularly wireless and externally worn sensors, are used to track patient health. However, these technologies are limited to a particular physical site. To provide patients with a convenient and non-intrusive approach to monitor their health, all required sensors should be integrated as small, portable, and externally wearable nodes. For an IoT healthcare system, communications are also essential, including short-range technologies like Bluetooth and long-range technologies like LTE. Because machine learning algorithms are used to sift through massive volumes of data, spot trends in sickness, and provide diagnosis and treatment suggestions, cloud storage is crucial for big data healthcare systems.

Medicine has already been impacted by the IoT. You will be able to observe it directly in certain modern hospitals. Insulin pens, linked inhalers, and ingestible sensors are a few examples. Communication between devices allows for data transfer and action calls. This makes it possible for medical personnel to react more quickly. Additionally, doctors may now offer 24/7 remote medical care thanks to the IoT. Better patient care is the outcome. In this instance, the lives saved are attributable to ingenuity and technological progress.

However, by reducing expenses and boosting productivity, IoT might enhance healthcare in the future. It can aid in the development of equipment that is more patient-focused and tailored. Additionally, IoT will help patients receive more individualized care and better access to data, which will reduce hospital visits ("IoT Healthcare: The Future Landscape of Healthcare Industry," 2024). Here, the present technology's advantages and disadvantages are discussed, along with suggestions for future research areas.

3.3.1. Wearable Healthcare Systems

Nodes of sensor technology that measure vital parameters are known as wearable sensors. Since vital signs are the main indicators for evaluating critical health, it is advised to use sensors that can measure them, such as pulse, respiration rate, and body temperature. These extra sensors may be utilized as, in addition to the three vital signs, blood pressure and oxygen levels are often recorded. For systems aimed at a particular condition, special-purpose sensors like blood-glucose, fall detection, and joint angle sensors may be used. The central node receives data from the sensor node (Mohammadzadeh et al., 2020). After processing this data and maybe making certain decisions, it sends the data to an outside site. Since a dedicated central node with just features pertinent to a healthcare IoT system may extend battery life, it would be preferable to a smartphone. As shown in Table 2.

Table 2: Overview of the Proposed Model

Stage	Process/Components
1. Data Collection	Patient with a wireless body area network (WBAN)
2. Data Transmission	Central Node
3. Data Processing	LPWAN Base Station
4. Decision Making	Machine Learning Enabled Cloud
5. Action and Monitoring	General Practitioner, Specialist, Nurse, Carer

3.3.2. Body Temperature Sensors

The third crucial sign, the temperature of the person, can be used to diagnose a variety of illnesses, including hypothermia, heat stroke, and fever. Therefore, a wearable medical system must include body temperature as a useful diagnostic tool. Thermosensor-type devices are employed in all current body temperature measurement research. Positive-temperature-coefficient (PTC) detectors were considered alongside the typical negative-temperature-coefficient (NTC) type temperature sensors. Each experiment showed that thermometers can measure a fair range of degrees with acceptable error levels for monitoring the health of individuals. Therefore, it is highly recommended that future system designers continue to use these types of sensors. The accuracy of heat detection is limited by the sensor's proximity to the human body.

To construct sensors that could be put right onto human skin, several studies concentrated on creating thin, flexible polymers with an adhesive backing.

3.4. IOT Application for the Healthcare Industry

- Implanted glucose monitoring systems: Diabetes patients can use implanted devices with detectors to check their blood sugar levels in real time. To help anticipate possible problems and notify patients when their blood sugar levels are low, these devices keep track of past data. (Reddy et al., 2023).
- Activity Trackers During Cancer Treatment: During cancer treatment, wearable activity trackers keep tabs on patients' whereabouts, level of exhaustion, and appetite. Based on the replies of each patient, the data gathered helps medical practitioners customize and modify treatment strategies.
- Heart Monitors with Reporting: IoT-enabled heart monitors can report abnormalities to medical professionals and continuously monitor cardiac activity, which helps identify any cardiac problems early.

- Medical Alert Systems: Wearable medical alert gadgets can identify crises, including falls, and instantly warn emergency services or selected contacts.
- Ingestible Sensors: Patients can now consume sensory devices that look like tablets. The sensors provide information to a patient's smartphone app after consumption, which helps them follow prescription dosage instructions. Due to human mistakes or forgetfulness, most medicines are not taken as prescribed. This ingestible sensor is designed to guarantee that patients are taking the appropriate drugs at times that are suitable in the proper amounts. Furthermore, certain ingestible sensors are being used to better accurately identify diseases, including irritable bowel syndrome and colon cancer.
- Medicine Dispensers: Patients can now get devices implanted that give them steady doses of medicine all day long. Patients will be notified when they need to renew their medicines. Missing prescriptions can also be reported to doctors during regular visits.
- Wireless sensors: Wireless sensors deployed in labs and hospital freezers ensure that blood samples, cold medications, and other biomedical supplies are always kept at the proper temperatures.
- Monitored Inhalers: IoT inhalers are alerting patients about their behaviors or events that potentially trigger asthma episodes by sending information to their tablets or cellphones. Their doctors may also be given access to the information. Additionally, patients are urged to use the included inhalers to take their medicines. (Schwartz 2015).

3.5. Application of IoTs in Environment Monitoring

Figure 2 shows the various applications of IoT in environmental monitoring

a. **Evaluation of Water Quality:** IoT-based systems monitor the water's quality in a variety of locations, such as city drinking water sources, stormwater and groundwater systems, agricultural irrigation, and municipal water treatment facilities. These systems support efficient water resource management and pollution control.

Figure 2: Depicts the various applications of IoT in environmental monitoring.

b. Methane, carbon monoxide, contaminants, and other dangerous gases are detected by IoT devices to monitor the quality of the air. In urban planning, industrial operations, and environmental preservation initiatives, this monitoring is essential.

c. **Energy Monitoring:** IoT technology provides energy monitoring, which can help with conservation efforts. Through the provision of information and management tools, these technologies contribute to better energy use, lower consumption, and sustainability.

d. **Toxic Gas Detection:** IoT-based toxic gas detection systems examine the air quality in industrial settings to find combustible, hazardous, and toxic gases, enabling early environmental damage identification and prevention.

4. The Implementation State of Intelligent Healthcare

Smart medical care, which makes use of wearable technology, is a health service system that connects people, resources, and healthcare facilities by using mobile internet and IoT to dynamically access information. It then makes use of this data to adapt to the needs of the medical habitat and manage it intelligently. Collaboration is encouraged, access to essential services is guaranteed, decision-making is informed, and resources are managed effectively with smart healthcare, as shown in Table 3.

Table 3: Application and Implementation States of Intelligent Healthcare

Application	Implementation State	Examples/Remarks
AI-assisted Diagnosis	Widely implemented in pilot & clinical use	AI in radiology (X-ray, CT scan analysis), dermatology, and pathology
Telemedicine / Remote Consultation	Fully implemented in many regions	Used for rural healthcare, pandemic care (COVID-19), and follow-ups
Wearable Health Devices	Broad adoption in consumer & clinical use	Smartwatches, fitness trackers, ECG monitoring, glucose sensors
Robotics (Surgery/ Assistance)	Limited but growing	Robotic surgery (Da Vinci system), elderly care robots
Smart Hospital Systems	Early adoption in advanced hospitals	Automated beds, IoT-enabled monitoring, smart inventory management

Based on various needs, the use of smart healthcare can be categorized below.

4.1. Assisting Diagnosis and Treatment

Improvements in mixed reality, surgical robots, and artificial intelligence have enhanced the ability to identify and treat illnesses. The detection of hepatitis, lung cancer, and skin cancer is among the results of the creation of the clinical decision support system with artificial intelligence. The diagnosis results of artificial intelligence are more accurate than those of human doctors. Machine learning-based algorithms are often even more accurate than trained medical personnel, especially in pathology and imaging (Dhar and Ranganathan, 2015).

The application has been validated by experts, and smart diagnosis helps create a personalized treatment plan by giving a more accurate assessment of the patient's health and illness condition. During tumor treatment, the patient's radiation course can be dynamically monitored with smart radiomics (Dhar and Ranganathan, 2015).

4.2. Aiding in Diagnosis and Therapy

The traditional hospital- and doctor-centered approach to health care, however, appears to be unable to cope with the increasing number of patients and illnesses. The new medical management strategy under smart medical care places greater emphasis on patient self-management. Real-time patient self-monitoring, prompt medical behavior change, and prompt feedback on health data are all highly sought.

The creation of wearable and implantable smart gadgets, smart homes, and IoT-connected smart health information systems provides a solution to this issue.

Smart houses may provide home help for the elderly and disabled. Smart houses are special places to live with sensors and actuators integrated into the home's infrastructure to monitor health (Chan et al., 2009). Smart homes also perform functions that improve people's quality of life. Artificial intelligence and health monitoring are the two primary uses of smart homes in the medical field. While gathering health data, these technologies can offer a few fundamental services that can enhance the quality of life at home and help those in need of care become less dependent on physicians.

Patients may take control of their care by using applications and a health information platform. For instance, a wearable medical sensor is used by the Stress Detection and Alleviation system to continually monitor vital signs, including blood pressure (Liu et al., 2016).

4.3. Management of Healthcare

Health authorities must take the effort to collect patient data, compare it to the criteria of the authoritative body, and then publish the prediction findings for conventional sickness risk prediction to work. This method is a little slow and doesn't offer them any useful recommendations. Disease risk prediction in smart healthcare is dynamic and tailored to individual needs. Based on the results of their monitoring, patients and doctors may participate, actively monitor their risk of becoming ill and take certain preventative measures. The new sickness risk prediction model receives data through wearables and smart applications, uploads it to the cloud over a network, uses big data-based algorithms to evaluate it, and then uses a brief message service to provide consumers with real-time projections.

They support physicians and patients in making any required changes to their medical behaviors and lifestyles, as well as assisting decision-makers in developing regional health plans to achieve the goal of decreasing disease risk (Redfern, 2017).

4.4. Encouraging Drug Research

Using artificial intelligence and big data in scientific research will improve the accuracy and usefulness of drug development. The entire drug development process includes target screening, clinical trials, drug discovery, and other steps. To find effective action sites, several target molecules in the human body are manually crossed with currently available medications in classic pharmacological target screening. In addition to being sluggish, this approach is frequently disregarded. Artificial intelligence's automated medication and target impact screening has significantly sped up the screening procedure. Additionally, by rapidly accessing the most recent information from the outside world, the AI system can always improve or rectify the screening procedure (Liu et al., 2018). The main technique in drug discovery is high-throughput screening, in which several molecules are produced automatically and examined one at a time. However, the expense and risk rise in tandem with the number of compounds. A workable answer to this issue is the use of artificial intelligence in virtual drug testing. The number of drug compounds that are evaluated may be decreased by computer pre-screening. Clinical trials on medications employ a combination of big data, artificial intelligence, and the IoT (Tian et al., 2019).

5. Expansion of the Healthcare Industry in the Age of Big Data

In the healthcare industry, big data analytics has been utilized to improve quality of life, prevent avoidable deaths, cure epidemic diseases, and anticipate diseases (Wullianallur and Viju Raghupathi, 2014). Figure 3 illustrates the function of big data architecture in healthcare. Wearable IoT sensor data, temperature, climate, location, and medical data are all received by the system in a variety of formats, including semi-structured, unstructured, and structured data. After that, cloud computing is used to combine and visualise the data. Doctors, remote users, and ambulances receive the pre-processed data once it has been extracted, cleaned, and statistically analyzed in-database analytics. Big Data is the term for the vast amounts of organized and unstructured data that wearable sensor devices collect while continually monitoring users. " Sorting through vast amounts of data to find relevant information for decision-making is a challenging task. Higher latency is caused by cloud computing, which stores and manages data on a distant server housed online. Before the cloud collects, processes, and analyses data, a fog layer is added to lower latency and increase efficiency. Lastly, the data is saved on the cloud so that a quick choice may be made instantly. Network-connected IoT devices are used to gather and share big data, or "Big Data.". Big Data analytics and the IoT are essential components of the smart healthcare system in developing countries (Firouzi et al., 2017). Examined the use of wearable technology, sensors, and big data to inform these devices in the sophisticated healthcare system. Three distinct components that comprise the healthcare IoT system: (i) A body sensor area network that uses implanted or body-worn sensors to capture environmental data, including temperature, humidity, date, and time, as well as behavioural data about the patient.

(ii) A smart gateway that is connected to the Internet, like a fog layer or local access network, handles protocol conversion, data preprocessing, data mining and filtering, and patient local notifications. (iii) A cloud and big data support layer that stores, analyses, forecasts, and broadcasts a message to carers in case of an emergency.

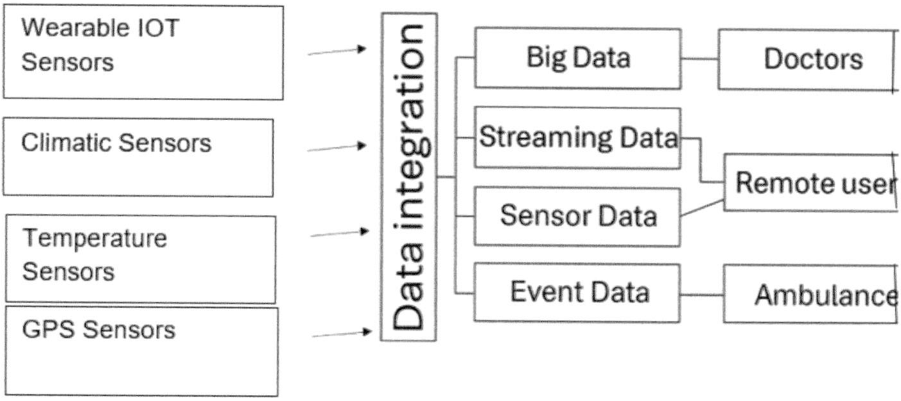

Figure 3: The function of big data architecture in healthcare.

6. Challenges to the Confidentiality of Patients in the Sophisticated Medical Environment

One may picture the risks to which patient data is exposed, given the many levels and different components of a typical healthcare solution (Ahmed and Rajput, 2020).

6.1. Social Engineering Attacks

6.1.1. Attacks Using Social Engineering

Hackers in this category rely on the psychological aspects of people. The objective may be the person's personal information or the information of the company they work for. To serve as the foundation for the password breach, a hacker may, for instance, watch a victim enter their password and request personal information, such as the spouse's name. Here is a list of the top five assaults that fall within this category.

1. **Phishing:** The victim of a phishing attack may click on a link or email that is delivered to them. The target is tricked into believing the email is from a trustworthy source, so they unintentionally click on it, even if some attacks are more complex than others. Ultimately, the user may provide the hackers with their bank login credentials or, worse, let them install dangerous software (such as viruses, worms, and trojans), exposing the victim and maybe their company.
2. **Pretexting:** This describes a hacker who is familiar with the victim's business history. They can begin by giving information that, in most cases, only a genuine person would be aware of (this can be done via email or phone). In

addition to lulling the victim into a false sense of security, the objective is to deceive them into disclosing important information that might expose them and their company.

3. **Baiting:** This technique is used by hackers to trick users into believing they are receiving something for nothing. The service could offer both digital and physical material (free movie access, USB, etc.). This kind of assault includes several document-sharing programs.

   The hackers use this to install software on their end after the user has used the service.
4. **Quid Pro Quo:** This tactic, which is comparable to baiting, provides free services or advantages in exchange. An email offering a credit card with a low interest rate may serve as an example.

   The victim and their company will be exposed when the user returns to a fictitious feeling of security.
5. **Tailgating:** This mostly describes the act of a hacker physically entering a venue by accompanying the victim in an attempt to win their confidence and provide them access. The FIPS 201 standard, which deals with Personal Identification Verification (PIV) cards, is published by NIST.

6.2. Insider Threats

A member of a certain organization who behaves maliciously is referred to as an insider threat. Such an individual either gives an outsider access to the organization's digital assets or obtains information to which they are not allowed. According to the 2018 Verizon Data Breaches report, insider leaks of company information were the cause of 28% of data breaches. The hacker can enter the network, comprehend the healthcare organization's solution architecture, and get patient data by installing undesired software, providing legitimate login credentials, or gaining physical entry to the building.

6.3. Denial of Service (DOS)

A denial-of-service attack is when a hacker floods the system with so many requests that the service stops working. Take a hacker, for instance, who floods a hospital's network with requests, rendering the system unworkable for staff members. An organization may be attacked from within or beyond. Such assaults would focus on the data's accessibility and may be expensive for a specific company that needs real-time data access. Given that healthcare institutions rely on real-time notifications for patients in critical condition, it is conceivable that this might lead to irreversible fatalities.

6.4. Viruses, Trojans, and Worms

Hackers construct harmful software, also referred to as malware, to make victims execute it. The malware is categorized into three main groups.

Virus: A virus is malicious software that infiltrates another program on the victim's computer after being downloaded. As a result, the victim's data is at risk as the malicious software will launch whenever the victim launches the program in question.

Worm: A worm is a malicious piece of software that the hacker somehow gets onto the victim's computer, much like a virus. A worm, on the other hand, does not have to affix itself to any other software to function. Furthermore, it may spread to other devices that are on the same network and replicate itself.

Trojan: A Trojan is a piece of software that, once installed on a victim's computer, grants access to third parties. An employee with access to a company network might unintentionally provide an outside hacker with unrestricted access to the company's assets.

7. Impact Evaluation and Prospects

Virtual well-being, location-based services, and smart settings have all been integrated to make revolutionary improvements that have a substantial impact on people, healthcare systems, and businesses, as illustrated by Figure 4. Case examples demonstrate the practical advantages of this combination.

Intelligent buildings: Autonomous energy management can reduce energy expenses by up to 30%. Real-time health monitoring allows for early detection of health concerns and quick intervention (Hanafi et al., 2024).

Effective Medical Institutions: Real-time data interchange cuts treatment and diagnostic times by approximately 20%. Automated patient-care systems can increase performance by 15%.

Retailers who implement indoor placement solutions for personalized marketing might enhance client engagement by 20%. Emergency services that use geographic

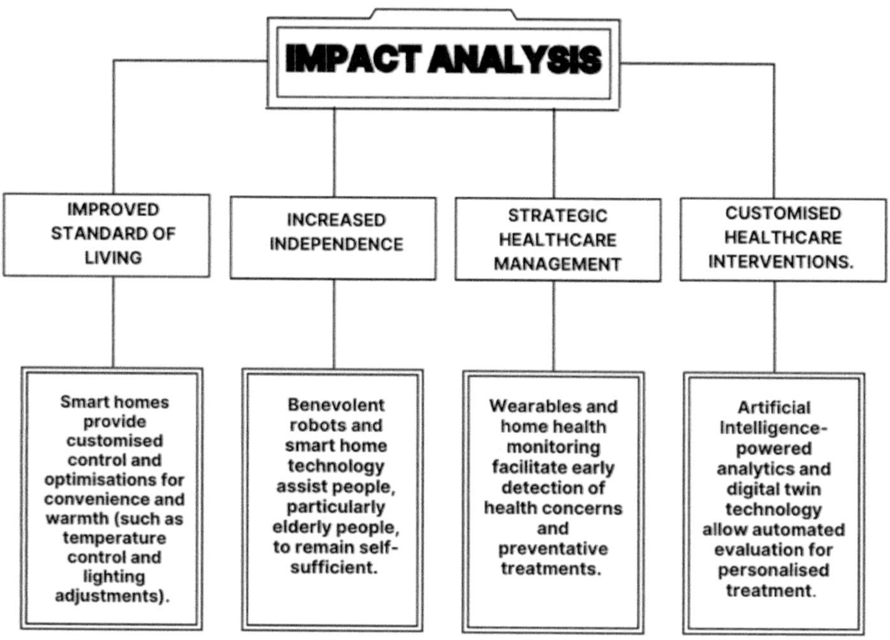

Figure 4: Shows the impact analysis.

data for rapid response can reduce response times by 25%. These case studies exhibit increased productivity and ease for individuals, indicating an improvement in health care and business procedures as a result of technological improvements.

The real-world impact goes beyond convenience, causing a significant shift in how we live, receive medical care, and run businesses (Miles, 2001). Transcend Facilitation denotes a considerable transformation. While convenience is undoubtedly essential, the overall impact is far greater. This technological innovation is changing the way we live, receive healthcare, and do business.

8. Challenges and Prospects for Future Research

Smart healthcare monitoring, which combines IoT, AI, and cloud computing, enables real-time patient tracking, early disease identification, and individualized treatments. However, its execution faces substantial challenges, as shown in Figure 5.

1. **Privacy & Data Security:** Due to its extreme sensitivity, patient data is a popular target for cyberattacks. It is difficult to ensure adherence to data protection regulations such as GDPR (EU) and HIPAA (USA).

   The confidentiality and confidence of patients may be compromised by unauthorized access or breaches of data.
2. **Problems with Interoperability:** Data exchange is challenging since different healthcare organizations utilize different EHR systems. Integration issues arise from a lack of standards among IoT medical devices.

   The ability of wearables, cloud platforms, and hospital systems to communicate seamlessly is still lacking.
3. **Overloading and Handling Data:** Constant health monitoring creates vast amounts of data. When health care providers are overburdened, it might be difficult to assess and reach useful findings.

   Strong artificial intelligence and large data technologies are necessary to successfully filter and handle patient data. ("Smart Healthcare: Challenges and Potential Solutions Using Internet of Things (IoT) and Big Data Analytics | Emerald Insight," 2019).
4. **Integration Difficulty:** Incorporating new technologies into existing intelligent networks can be difficult and require considerable infrastructure changes. Automating integration procedures is crucial for improving adoption. To facilitate integration without requiring significant infrastructure modifications, research should concentrate on developing modular and flexible solutions.
5. **User-Centric Design:** Usability is still a problem even with greater capabilities. The application of user-centered design methodologies is necessary to bridge the gap between technological capability and consumer demand. This includes doing user experience research to better understand consumer desires and preferences, as well as implementing basic design components and user feedback approaches into smart settings (Smart Things, 2025).
6. Versatility and affordability persist as issues, particularly when deploying intelligent settings in a variety of geopolitical contexts. Developing cost-

effective and adaptable implementation tactics is critical for broad acceptance and societal benefits (Google Books, 2019). Research should concentrate on low-cost technology and creative deployment tactics targeted to various socioeconomic circumstances.

7. **Ethical Consideration:** IoMT presents ethical issues around the usage of personally identifiable information. As medical devices collect more patient data, the risk of personal information being exploited or unlawfully obtained for non-healthcare purposes increases. This brings concerns about patient permission and control of wellness data.
8. **Policy and Uniformity Issues:** Policies and consistency improve healthcare quality by ensuring that services are provided consistently. By requiring all healthcare professionals to adhere to the same rules, they also improve patient safety while reducing expenses and mistakes. It guarantees that medical professionals will always offer premium treatment at a reasonable cost. Uniformity enhances patient safety, reduces medical errors, streamlines operations, and increases overall quality. It is estimated that around 51% of all medical devices made today are subject to Food and Drug Administration (FDA) rules (Rodziewicz et al., 2024), which disrupts medical delivery by restricting

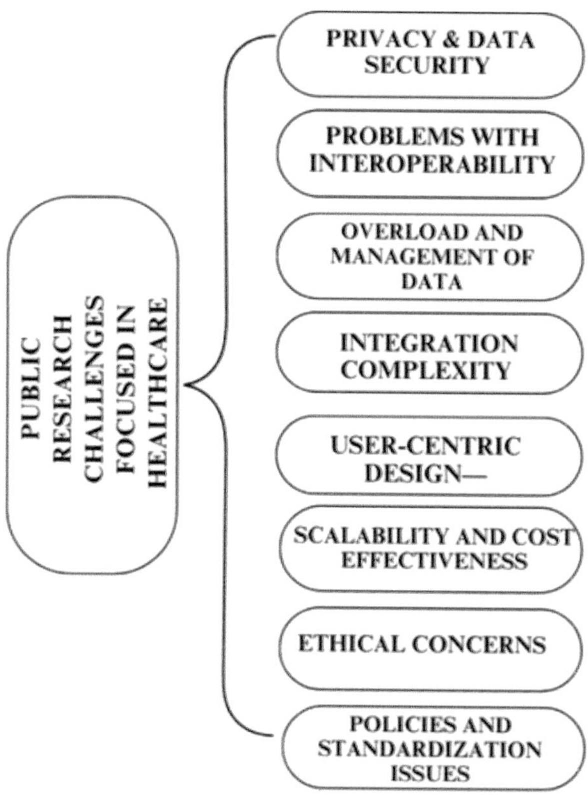

Figure 5: Depicts the challenges focused on healthcare.

IoMT capacity. Many other services, such as electronic medical records, need to be standardised. To do this, organisations like as the Information Technologies and Innovation Foundations (IETF), the Internet Protocol for Smart Objects (IPSO) Alliance, and the European Telecommunications Standards Institute (ETSI) interact through IoT technology working groups (Rayes and Salam 2022). These companies work with mobile and electronic healthcare providers, as well as Internet of Things experts, to offer standardised IoT-based healthcare services. Furthermore, the medical sector is decentralised, with various parties pursuing competing interests and agendas, making it impossible to establish a unified policy. Despite these limitations, healthcare regulations and standards provide numerous benefits. They strive to ensure that patients receive unified, good therapy regardless of where they are served, resulting in better patient outcomes.

Despite the challenges, smart healthcare systems have the potential to improve patient outcomes and healthcare delivery (Kraus, Schiavone, Pluzhnikova, & Invernizzi, 2021). By addressing security, interoperability, and ethical concerns, healthcare can become more innovative, efficient, and accessible to all. An excellent method for recording blood glucose levels in diabetics was proposed. Patients utilising this system must manually obtain blood glucose levels at predefined times. Two types of blood-glucose anomalies are then taken into consideration. A missing blood glucose reading is a sequel, and abnormal blood glucose levels are the first. After evaluating the abnormality's severity, the system decides who should be notified: the patient, family members and carers, or emergency medical personnel, such as doctors. Although automated blood glucose measurements have the potential to improve the procedure, they are also viable and practical (Khan, 2024).

A gadget for detecting heart attacks was built with readily available components and a custom antenna. An ECG sensor monitors heart activity and sends the data to a microcontroller for processing (Bauzha et al., 2019). The user's smartphone gets this data over Bluetooth, processes it, and shows the ECG results via an app. The researchers hope that developing strategies for anticipating heart attacks will help improve the strategy. Additional improvements could be achieved by assessing respiratory rate, which is known to aid in the prediction of a heart attack (Baker et al., 2017).

9. Future Prospects

The use of wearable biosensors, blockchain, IoT, 5G, and AI in smart healthcare monitoring is poised to revolutionize patient care. Through the analysis of real-time patient data, AI-driven predictive analytics will make it possible to detect diseases early and provide individualized treatment. By guaranteeing dependable, quick data transfer, 5G and edge computing will enhance telemedicine (Sharma et al., 2020). Wearable biosensors will improve remote monitoring by non-invasively monitoring vitals, including blood pressure and glucose (Kim et al., 2021).

Blockchain will improve interoperability and data security, guaranteeing secure sharing of medical records (Kuo et al., 2017). Healthcare processes will be streamlined by AI-driven automation and chatbots, which will lessen the workload for providers. But for broad use, issues including moral dilemmas, legal restrictions, and limitations in digital literacy need to be resolved (WHO, 2021).

Future healthcare will be more patient-centered, effective, and accessible as a result of the smooth integration of these technologies.

10. Conclusion

The integration of advanced technology into healthcare is altering the industry by enabling smart environments, digital twins, and extensive usage of the online world for improved performance, patient care, and operational efficiency. Machine learning, big data, and the Internet have changed today's healthcare systems. These improvements enable smart settings that allow for real-time monitoring, automation, and predictive analytics, making healthcare more proactive rather than reactive. The Internet of Things is vital in medical care because it links equipment, collects patient data, and allows for remote monitoring. IoT-powered wearable healthcare systems, such as smartwatches and fitness bands, help track vital signs, while body temperature sensors provide crucial health insights. These technologies are essential for a future healthcare paradigm that emphasizes real-time data analytics, automation, and seamless connectivity between equipment and medical experts. Furthermore, IoT extends beyond direct patient care by monitoring the surroundings to maintain optimal healthcare settings.

Smart healthcare applications have helped with diagnosis and treatment by utilizing AI-powered technologies to detect diseases early, offer personalized treatment strategies, and optimize hospital procedures. Smart platforms have also improved health management by allowing patients to easily track their symptoms and adhere to treatment programs. Predictive analytics also benefits illness prevention and risk monitoring by identifying patterns and mitigating health hazards before they become serious. The pharmaceutical business also benefits from technology, with digital solutions aiding in medication discovery, development, and testing. With the advancement of the healthcare business in the age of big data, healthcare institutions can now handle massive volumes of medical data, resulting in better decision-making, research, and treatment personalization. The application of massive data analytics for medical purposes improves predictive modelling, allowing healthcare professionals to forecast outbreaks, expedite hospital management, and optimize resource allocation. Despite these advances, significant obstacles remain. Given the volume of sensitive patient information transferred and kept digitally, data privacy and security are major considerations. Interoperability difficulties between healthcare systems and devices make it difficult to achieve seamless integration. Furthermore, the high cost of adopting smart technology, as well as the requirement for specialised skills, limit mainstream use. To ensure equitable and responsible use of technology in healthcare, ethical problems must be addressed, particularly those linked to AI-driven decision-making and patient autonomy. Heading into the future, AI, IoT, and big data analytics will most certainly continue to advance, boosting patient care and operating efficiency even more. Digital twins, which imitate real-world healthcare settings and patient situations, will improve treatment precision and medical simulations. Wearable technology will improve to give even more precise and real-time health monitoring, allowing patients to take more control of their health. Collaborations between healthcare institutions, tech businesses, and regulatory agencies will be critical as the industry evolves to create a secure, efficient, and patient-centered healthcare ecosystem. Finally, the digital transformation of healthcare is changing the industry by improving diagnosis, treatment, patient monitoring, and operational efficiency. IoT devices present several new ways for individuals to monitor themselves and for medical practitioners to monitor patients. As a result, the range of wearable IoT devices offers both advantages and disadvantages to healthcare professionals and their patients.

References

Ahmed, A., and Rajput, Q. (2020). Title of the article or book chapter. Title of the Journal or Book, volume number(issue number), page range. https://doi.org/xxxx

Al-Fuqaha, A., Guizani, M., Mohammadi, M., Aledhari, M., and Ayyash, M. (2015). Internet of Things: A survey on enabling technologies, protocols, and applications. IEEE Communications Surveys & Tutorials, 17(4), 2347–2376. https://doi.org/10.1109/comst.2015.2444095

Atadoga, A., Omaghomi, T., Elufioye, O., Odilibe, I., Daraojimba, A., and Owolabi, O. (n.d.). Internet of Things (IoT) in healthcare: A systematic review of use cases and benefits. International Journal of Science and Research Archive, 2024(01), 1511–1517. https://doi.org/10.30574/ijsra.2024.11.1.0243

Baker, S.B., Xiang, W., and Atkinson, I. (2017). Internet of Things for smart healthcare: Technologies, challenges, and opportunities. IEEE Access, 5, 26521–26544. https://doi.org/10.1109/access.2017.2775180

Bauzha, O., Sus, B., Sergiy Zagorodnyuk, S., and Stuchynska, N. (2019). *Electrocardiogram Measurement Complex Based on Microcontrollers and Wireless Networks*. 345–349. https://doi.org/10.1109/picst47496.2019.9061528

Bort-Roig, J., Gilson, N.D., Puig-Ribera, A., Contreras, R.S., and Trost, S.G. (2014). Measuring and influencing physical activity with smartphone technology: A systematic review. Sports Medicine, 44(5), 671–686. https://doi.org/10.1007/s40279-014-0142-5

Broadbent, E., Stafford, R., and MacDonald, B. (2009). Acceptance of healthcare robots for the older population: Review and future directions. International Journal of Social Robotics, 1(4), 319–330. https://doi.org/10.1007/s12369-009-0030-6

Cabanillas-Carbonell, M., Pérez-Martínez, J., and A. Yáñez, J. (2023). 5G technology in the digital transformation of healthcare, a systematic review. Sustainability, 15(4), 3178.

Chan, M., Campo, E., Estève, D., and Jean-Yves Fourniols. (2009). Smart homes—Current features and future perspectives. Maturitas, 64(2), 90–97. https://doi.org/10.1016/j.maturitas.2009.07.014

Clinic, C. (2023, March 9). Cleveland Clinic Opens New Cancer Center in Abu Dhabi. Retrieved February 18, 2025, from Cleveland Clinic website: https://newsroom.clevelandclinic.org/2023/03/09/cleveland-clinic-opens-new-cancer-center-in-abu-dhabi

Craig, J., and Petterson, V. (2005). Introduction to the practice of telemedicine. Journal of Telemedicine and Telecare, 11(1), 3–9. https://doi.org/10.1177/1357633x0501100102

Cristiano, Pasluosta, C.F., Björn Eskofier, Bandeira, D., and Rodrigo. (2018). Internet of

Health Things: Toward intelligent vital signs monitoring in hospital wards. Artificial Intelligence in Medicine, 89, 61–69. https://doi.org/10.1016/j.artmed.2018.05.005

Devon, D. (2015, July 14). Nest Smart Thermostat–Smart Heating control for your home & business. Retrieved February 1, 2025, from Intelligent Abodes website: https://www.intelligentabodes.co.uk/nest-smart-thermostat/

Dhar, J., and Ranganathan, A. (2015). Machine learning capabilities in medical diagnosis applications: Computational results for hepatitis disease. International Journal of Biomedical Engineering and Technology, 17(4), 330–330. https://doi.org/10.1504/ijbet.2015.069398

Dharmar, M., Kuppermann, N., Romano, P.S., Yang, N.H., Nesbitt, T.S., Phan, J., … Marcin, J.P. (2013). Telemedicine consultations and medication errors in rural emergency departments. Pediatrics, 132(6), 1090–1097. https://doi.org/10.1542/peds.2013-1374

Fan, Y., Xu, P., Jin, H., Ma, J., and Qin, L. (2019). Vital sign measurement in telemedicine rehabilitation based on intelligent wearable medical devices. IEEE Access, 7, 54819–54823. https://doi.org/10.1109/access.2019.2913189

Firouzi, F., Rahmani, A.M.K., Mankodiya, M. Badaroglu, Merrett, G.V., Wong, P., and Farahani, B. (2017). Internet-of-Things and big data for smarter healthcare: From device to architecture, applications and analytics. Future Generation Computer Systems, 78, 583–586. https://doi.org/10.1016/j.future.2017.09.016

Fothergill, L., Holland, C., Latham, Y., and Hayes, N. (2023). Understanding the value of a proactive telecare system in supporting older adults' independence at home: Qualitative interview study among key interest groups. Journal of Medical Internet Research, 25, e47997–e47997. https://doi.org/10.2196/47997

Gold, M., Amatniek, J., Carrillo, M.C., Cedarbaum, J.M., Hendrix, J.A., Miller, B.B., … Czaja, S.J. (2018). Digital technologies as biomarkers, clinical outcomes assessment, and recruitment tools in Alzheimer's disease clinical trials. Alzheimer S & Dementia Translational Research & Clinical Interventions, 4(1), 234–242. https://doi.org/10.1016/j.trci.2018.04.003

Google Books. (2019). Retrieved February 18, 2025, from Google.co.in website: https://www.google.co.in/books/edition/Renewable_Energy_Sources_and_Climate_Cha/qbYHzgEACAAJ?hl=en

Hanafi, A., Moawed, M., and Abdellatif, O. (2024). Advancing sustainable energy management: A comprehensive review of Artificial Intelligence techniques in building. Deleted Journal, 53(2), 26–46. https://doi.org/10.21608/erjsh.2023.226854.1196

Höyhtyä, M. (2023). Situational awareness for Industry 5.0 and mobile robotics: A review. OPAL (Open@LaTrobe), La Trobe University. https://doi.org/10.36227/techrxiv.22602028.v2

Internet of Things (IoT) Healthcare Examples. (2024, October 28). Retrieved February 3, 2025, from Ordr website: https://ordr.net/article/iot-healthcare-examples

Jamal, A., McKenzie, K., and Clark, M. (2009). The impact of health information technology on the quality of medical and health care: A systematic review. Health Information Management Journal, 38(3), 26–37. https://doi.org/10.1177/183335830903800305

Jones, N. (2014). Computer science: The learning machines. Nature, 505(7482), 146–148. https://doi.org/10.1038/505146a

Khan, F. (2024). Emerging trends and challenges of IoT in smart healthcare systems, smart cities and education. Sensors, 24(17), 5735. https://doi.org/10.3390/s24175735

Kim, J., Campbell, A.S., Esteban-Fernández, B., and Wang, J. (2019). Wearable biosensors for healthcare monitoring. Nature Biotechnology, 37(4), 389–406. https://doi.org/10.1038/s41587-019-0045-y

Kraus, S., Schiavone, F., Pluzhnikova, A., and Invernizzi, A.C. (2021). Digital transformation in healthcare: Analyzing the current state-of-research. Journal of Business Research, 123, 557–567. https://doi.org/10.1016/j.jbusres.2020.10.030

Kumar, M., Kumar, A., Verma, S., Bhattacharya, P., Deepak Ghimire, Kim, S., and Sanwar Hosen, A.S.M. (2023). Healthcare Internet of Things (H-IoT): Current trends, future prospects, applications, challenges, and security issues. Electronics, 12(9), 2050–2050. https://doi.org/10.3390/electronics12092050

Kuo, T.-T., Kim, H.-E., and Ohno-Machado, L. (2017). Blockchain distributed ledger technologies for biomedical and health care applications. Journal of the American Medical Informatics Association, 24(6), 1211–1220. https://doi.org/10.1093/jamia/ocx068

Lee, J., McCullough, J.S., and Town, R.J. (2013). The impact of health information technology on hospital productivity. The RAND Journal of Economics, 44(3), 545–568. https://doi.org/10.1111/1756-2171.12030

Lewis, T.G., and Denning, P.J. (2018). Learning machine learning. Communications of the ACM, 61(12), 24–27. https://doi.org/10.1145/3286868

Li, J., Ma, Q., Chan, A.H.S., and Man, S.S. (2019). Health monitoring through wearable technologies for older adults: Smart wearables acceptance model. Applied Ergonomics, 75, 162–169. https://doi.org/10.1016/j.apergo.2018.10.006

Li, S., Xu, L.D., and Zhao, S. (2014). The internet of things: A survey. Information Systems Frontiers, 17(2), 243–259. https://doi.org/10.1007/s10796-014-9492-7

Liu, J.T., and Liu, Y.H. (2018). Application of computer molecular simulation technology and artificial intelligence in drug development. Technol Innov Appl, 2, 46–47.

Liu, L., Stroulia, E., Nikolaidis, I., Miguel-Cruz, A., and Rincon, A.R. (2016). Smart homes and home health monitoring technologies for older adults: A systematic review. International Journal of Medical Informatics, 91, 44–59. https://doi.org/10.1016/j.ijmedinf.2016.04.007

Majumder, S., Mondal, T., and Deen, M. (2017). Wearable sensors for remote health monitoring. Sensors, 17(1), 130–130. https://doi.org/10.3390/s17010130

McLean, S., Sheikh, A., Cresswell, K., Nurmatov, U., Mukherjee, M., Hemmi, A., and Pagliari, C. (2013). The Impact of telehealthcare on the quality and safety of care: A systematic overview. PLoS ONE, 8(8), e71238. https://doi.org/10.1371/journal.pone.0071238

Miles, S. (2001). *Social Theory in the Real World.* SAGE. Retrieved from https://www.torrossa.com/en/resources/an/4913152

Mohammadzadeh, N., Gholamzadeh, M., Saeedi, S., and Rezayi, S. (2020). The application of wearable smart sensors for monitoring the vital signs of patients in epidemics: A systematic literature review. Journal of Ambient Intelligence and Humanized Computing, 14(5), 6027–6041. https://doi.org/10.1007/s12652-020-02656-x

Nguyen, H. (2024, May 8). IoT healthcare: The future landscape of healthcare industry. Savvycom Software. Retrieved from https://savvycomsoftware.com/blog/iot-healthcare-industry/

Rayan, R.A., Tsagkaris, C., and Iryna, R.B. (2021). The Internet of Things for healthcare: Applications, selected cases and challenges. IoT in Healthcare and Ambient Assisted Living, 1–15.

Rayes, A., and Salam, S. (2022). Industry organizations and standards landscape. Springer EBooks, 305–321. https://doi.org/10.1007/978-3-030-90158-5_11

Raymond, and Ganesan, B. (2024). *Digital Technology in Public Health and Rehabilitation Care.* Elsevier. Retrieved from https://www.who.int/publications/i/item/9789240020924

Redfern, J. (2017). Smart health and innovation: Facilitating health-related behaviour change. Proceedings of the Nutrition Society, 76(3), 328–332. https://doi.org/10.1017/s0029665117001094

Rodziewicz, T.L., Houseman, B., Sarosh Vaqar, and Hipskind, J.E. (2024, February 12). *Medical Error Reduction and Prevention.* Retrieved February 18, 2025, from Nih.gov website: https://www.ncbi.nlm.nih.gov/books/NBK499956/

Schunk, D., Malsy, M., and Zimmermann, M. (2022). Die Zusatzweiterbildung Klinische Akut- und Notfallmedizin. AINS - Anästhesiologie · Intensivmedizin · Notfallmedizin · Schmerztherapie, 57(07/08), 478–487. https://doi.org/10.1055/a-1545-2406

Schwartz, D. (2015). *IoT Applications in Healthcare*. Retrieved January 25, 2025, from Wirelesswatchdogs.com website: https://www.wirelesswatchdogs.com/blog/iot-applications-in-healthcare?utm_source=chatgpt.com

Smart Healthcare: Challenges and potential solutions using internet of things (IoT) and big data analytics | Emerald Insight. (2019). PSU Research Review, 4(2), 149–168. https://doi.org/10.1108//PRR

Smart Things. (2025). Retrieved February 18, 2025, from Google Books website: https://books.google.co.in/books?hl=en&lr=&id=-WLyUCBBUVAC&oi=fnd&pg=PP2&dq=.+This+includes+doing+user+experience+research+to+better+understand+consumer+needs+and+preferences,+as+well+as+implementing+basic+design+components+and+user+feedback+approaches+into+smart+settings.+&ots=HE12B5vslu&sig=gjXaMTvCbJM_pFVqiCLAsiXFKvU&redir_esc=y#v=onepage&q&f=false

Telemedicine and the COVID-19 Pandemic, Lessons for the Future | Telemedicine and e-Health. (2021). *Telemedicine and E-Health*. https://doi.org/10.1089/tmj.2020.29040

Tian, S., Yang, W., Le, M., Wang, P., Huang, W., and Ye, Z. (2019). Smart healthcare: Making medical care more intelligent. Global Health Journal, 3(3), 62–65. https://doi.org/10.1016/j.glohj.2019.07.001

Vodyaho, A., Zhukova, N., Delhibabu, R., and Subbotin, A. (2024). Continuous agile cyber–physical systems architectures based on digital twins. Future Generation Computer Systems, 153, 350–359. https://doi.org/10.1016/j.future.2023.11.024

Raghupathi, W., and Raghupathi, V. (2014). Big data analytics in healthcare: Promise and potential. Health Information Science and Systems, 2(1). https://doi.org/10.1186/2047-2501-2-3

CHAPTER

5

Data Privacy in Healthcare: A Focus on MIoT Devices

M. Muthulakshmi[1(0009-0009-2992-1704)], M. Bindhu[2(0009-0001-4801-1900)], V. Shyamala Susan[3*(0000-0002-3255-8725)] and I. Gusti Bagus Yosia Wiryakusuma[4(0000-0001-5845-8661)]

[1] Department of Commerce, A P C Mahalaxmi College for Women, Thoothukudi, India
[2] Department of History, A P C Mahalaxmi College for Women, Thoothukudi, India
[3] Department of Computer Science, A P C Mahalaxmi College for Women, Thoothukudi, India
[4] Department of International Business Management, Universitas Ciputra

1. Introduction to MIoT in Healthcare

Real-time monitoring, remote diagnostics, individualized treatment plans, and other capabilities have been made possible by integrating MIoT devices into healthcare, transforming the industry (Merih et al., 2023). Such advancement is best remembered for the merger of medical devices and applications with the Internet and the creation of infrastructure to allow the networking of health-related data (Gopinath et al., 2024). MIoT incorporates patient-worn equipment, telemonitoring units, and intelligent surgical tools, which increase patient participation and encourage proactive measures toward health (Sankaran and Kim, 2023).

Integrating MIoT into healthcare, which facilitates enhanced patient care and data collection, has expanded cost efficacy; however, a more concerning issue is the associated challenges of data privacy and security (Shahid et al., 2022). MIoT systems collect various types of data, covering personal health information and physiological, environmental, and behavioral data (Jiang et al., 2022). To identify potential privacy gaps caused by insufficient shielding mechanisms and barriers to anonymity, these aspects must be defined (Majeed and Lee, 2021).

A combination of technological approaches, regulations, and trust-building efforts is needed to address the issues posed by MIoT (AlAmr, 2024). Policies like HIPAA and GDPR play a vital role in safeguarding sensitive information that the MIoT systems gather and handle (Özçağdavul, 2024).

*Corresponding author: shyamalasusan@gmail.com

DOI: 10.1201/9781003676812-5

Moreover, trust is built when patients see transparency in how data is collected and used (AlAmr, 2024). The collection, storage, and sharing of health data should come with adequate consent and be explained to the patients so they can easily make competent choices to control their personal information (Sun et al., 2018).

Different groups like health practitioners, system designers, law enforcers, and the patients themselves capture the essence of securing MIoT systems used within the healthcare sector (Rajab et al., 2024). There are numerous possibilities with MIoT, yet they all come with growing issues needing to be solved, where prioritizing privacy and data protection will help greatly. This document explains the primary notions and usages of MIoT while focusing on its impact on the advancement of the health sector and the transformation of people's health.

2. Literature Survey

A literature survey on the privacy challenges in MIoT Systems, concerning several studies and frameworks, highlights the risks involved with the harvesting and sharing of sensitive information in MIoT contexts. This includes the study of existing anonymization techniques and their mitigation potential regarding privacy risks and ensuring compliance with HIPAA and GDPR (Majeed and Lee, 2021; Pawar et al., 2018). That analysis will concentrate on the possibilities of integrating these techniques into MIoT system design as a means of fostering data protection and user trust. The formulation of privacy frameworks rests on the evolving conditions of HIPAA and GDPR, which require extensive compliance and responsibility concerning data custodians and their operations. These strategies encourage the integration of technologies that meet regulatory standards as a means to promote trust among users and guarantee that privacy safeguards are persistent throughout data management lifecycles.

Anonymization or differential privacy, for instance, under MIoT falls under PETs, which deal with the protection of user data and serve as privacy enhancing technologies. A complete literature survey will be undertaken to assess the impact of such techniques to mitigate privacy risks and meet compliance with regulations (Pawar et al., 2018). This survey will emphasize gaps in the literature concerning the application of PETs in MIoT for privacy breaches and regulatory compliance with GDPR and HIPAA (Han and Lü, 2024). The survey will also discuss the consequences of data leaks and the need for strong privacy policies and frameworks to protect sensitive data. Moreover, it will study the relationship between anonymization approaches and legal compliance to identify barriers and possibilities for new investigations aimed at filling in the gaps.

The study will also cover a more speculative topic on how these technologies can help with privacy issues, calling for further development of MIoT-specific privacy-protecting strategies. By comparing the effectiveness of different anonymization techniques against compliance benchmarks, we intend to offer practical recommendations for decision-makers (Prokhorenkov, 2022). This will also include the assessment of microscopy advancements in PETs for MIoT applications concerning compliance with data protection by design and by default principles set by GDPR. In addition, we will analyze the impact of the implementation of these technologies on the privacy of the users and the functionality of MIoT systems.

3. Applications of MIoT Devices

The integration of MIoT in the healthcare sector comes with countless applications, including:

1. **Patient Monitoring:** The collection and analysis of a patient's vital signs and health metrics can now be performed continuously via MIoT devices. This proves even more valuable for patients with chronic conditions, as timely interventions become possible.
2. **Chronic Disease Management:** Modern MIoT technologies enable the effective management of chronic conditions like diabetes and heart disease by contemporaneously providing patients and healthcare practitioners with critical information on their health status, thus enabling necessary adjustments to the treatment plans.
3. **Telemedicine:** Remote consultations and diagnostics are made possible via MIoT devices, thereby improving telemedicine services. Patients can now be monitored from a distance, which lessens the need for actual attendance to healthcare facilities while increasing access to the healthcare they need.
4. **Wearable Devices:** Devices like smart watches and fitness trackers automatically monitor and provide data on physical activity, heart rate, and sleep, among other things. This data can be applied to self-health management and increased motivation to adopt healthier living.
5. **Smart Medical Instruments:** Smart medical devices that undertake certain activities on their own, improve efficiency in performing diagnostics, and subsequently, improve patient outcomes are a part of MIoT. Some of these include smart inhalers and connected insulin pens.
6. **Emergency Response:** MIoT can improve emergency response systems by communicating patients' conditions to first responders in real-time, thereby allowing for more informed and quicker decisions to be made during emergencies.
7. **Medication Management:** MIoT devices can assist in medication management by reminding patients to take their medications and tracking their adherence, considerably lowering the risks for complications.
8. **Health Data Analytics:** Information from MIoT devices can be analyzed to determine healthcare trends and to improve the strategies used in patient care and operations, making health analytics more efficient.
9. **Patient Engagement:** Patient engagement is improved with MIoT devices as they give access to their health data, empowering them to take more control of their health and thereby enhancing health outcomes.

In summary, MIoT devices improve service delivery in healthcare systems and provide better outcomes for patients while improving clinical efficiency. Figure 1 depicts some applications of MIoT devices.

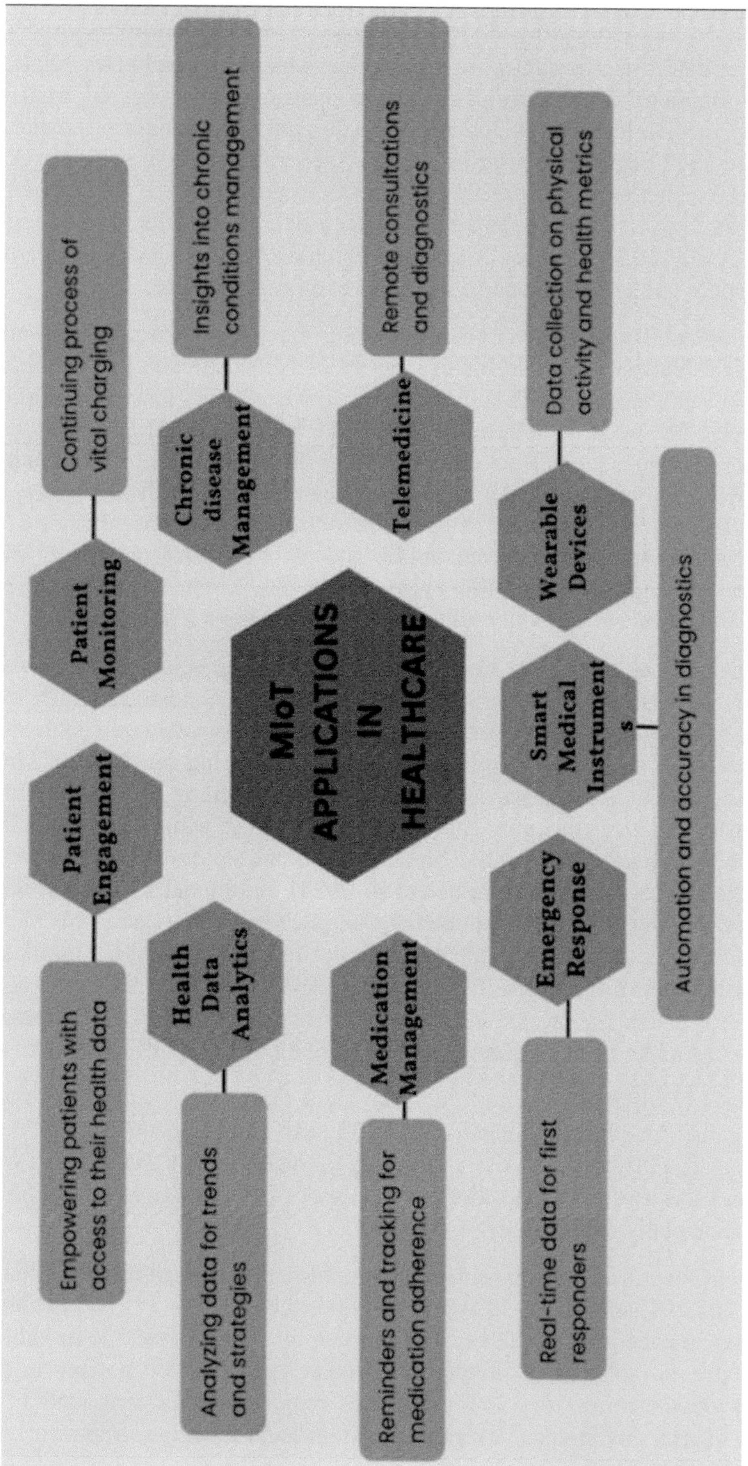

Figure 1: Applications of MIoT devices.

4. Types of Data Collected and Shared in MIoT

Considering the MIoT, the data types captured and shared are not limited to personal health information; rather, they also include real-time data received from other monitoring medical devices, which may include vital sign monitoring, medication compliance, and lifestyle activities. While the collation and scrutiny of this information can help improve patient outcomes considerably, there are also pertinent issues regarding privacy that demand advanced data protection from access and abuse (C et al., 2023). Devices otherwise known as MIoT or Medical Internet of Things devices gather a great scope of sensitive information, like:

1. Physiological Data: Apart from monitoring the patient's health, transmitting physiological data like heart rate, blood pressure, and glucose levels is also important. They can be analyzed by healthcare providers. However, such sensitive information requires adequate security measures for confidentiality and HIPAA and GDPR compliance (Said et al., n.d.; Bookert et al., 2022). To add, there should be controlled transmission of physiological information between devices and healthcare systems to prevent the acquisition of vital information without proper consent. Hence, there is a need to establish sufficient encryption and access control policies to protect information through its entire life cycle, while also emphasizing documenting processes from data collection through disposal (Jiang et al., 2022).

a. Signs such as heart rate, blood pressure, and oxygen saturation: These life signs being monitored can be tracked through MIoT devices, which in turn help in continuous monitoring of a patient's health status and enable critical action to be taken at the right time. Although clocking sensitive information can be beneficial, it poses serious privacy risks, thereby calling for stringent measures to maintain confidentiality and compliance with HIPAA and GDPR.
b. Data from wearing devices like fitness trackers and smartwatches (Shahid et al., 2022; Wani et al., 2024; Maqsood et al., 2024): Additionally, wearable devices that track physiological parameters have issues regarding data ownership and informed consent, where patients might not fully understand the implications of using their information. It is for this reason that more needs to be done to educate patients about the mechanisms of consent and data practices so that they can make informed decisions regarding their health information.

2. Personal Identifiable Information (PII): Once more, customers' MIoT systems scan and gather health data alongside other PII such as name, address, and contact information. The PII itself is at risk concerning the safety of one's identity, as well as privacy, and sensitive data protection policies specifically designed to counter such breaches are equally compelling.

a. Patient identification alongside demographics and medical history (Shahid et al., 2022; Khatib et al., 2024): In addition, the union of PII and health data forms an even greater risk because this combination is bound to be subjected to extreme violation of privacy if adequate measures are not put in place. This demonstrates why IoT companies require policies that tend to both sets of data governance, leveraging custom legal practices, frameworks, and industry standards.

3. Lifestyle Data: The advancement of MIoT devices captures lifestyle data, which inseparably integrates a person's day-to-day activities, eating and exercising habits, and health condition. While this information can be beneficial for tailored medicine, its unsolicited accumulation poses a risk of breaching user consent and being abused when shared without proper safeguards (Sivakumar et al., 2024). In this regard, organizations should be held accountable for crafting effective policies that govern the capture and application of lifestyle data geared towards informing users and enabling them to control their data. To this end, these users should be able to decide whether or not their data will be shared, which fosters responsible data stewardship and enhances confidence in data handling practices.

a. Diet, sleep, and activity levels are outlined as habits in (Shahid et al., 2023; Wani et al., 2024): Careful pathways involving user data participation and governance mechanisms require articulated privacy frameworks and consent processes. Showing users how data MIoT solutions collect, share, and utilize their lifestyle information increases trust and participation, where obtaining data privacy and security is prioritized.

4. Environmental Data: MIOT peripherals unobtrusively monitor and collect contextual environmental information, including air quality, temperature, ventilation, and other health-related parameters. Although this data is useful for understanding the influence of environmental factors on individual health, extreme caution poses privacy threats. Cleanliness should be exercised when it is linked to individual users. There is, therefore, a need for such devices to adopt sound data governance frameworks that protect the ethical use of exposure information without infringing on users' identity boundaries legally.

a. A smart home encompasses devices yielding more traditional health-related metrics such as temperature and air quality, which are important. Therefore, smart homes can contribute economically (Shahid et al., 2022; Khatib et al., 2024). As such, incorporating policies for information retention and sharing helps implement aggregation or anonymization techniques. Such organizations can mitigate the unintended consequences and risks around health-related environmental data capture.

This quote illustrates how the range of data gathered and privacy issues like MIoT systems must be addressed holistically. Relevant systems need to include strong user privacy policies, proactive SDRs, and open communications regarding collected information to effectively protect sensitive data and responsibly address the rise in use of the said systems. Figure 2 illustrates different types of data.

This information is shared between many parties, including mobile application vendors, networked sensors, and machine learning decryption service providers. These third parties participate to enhance user experience, streamline and advance healthcare services, and improve service delivery, management processes, and other organizational activities (Shahid et al., 2022; Wani et al., 2024; Maqsood et al., 2024).

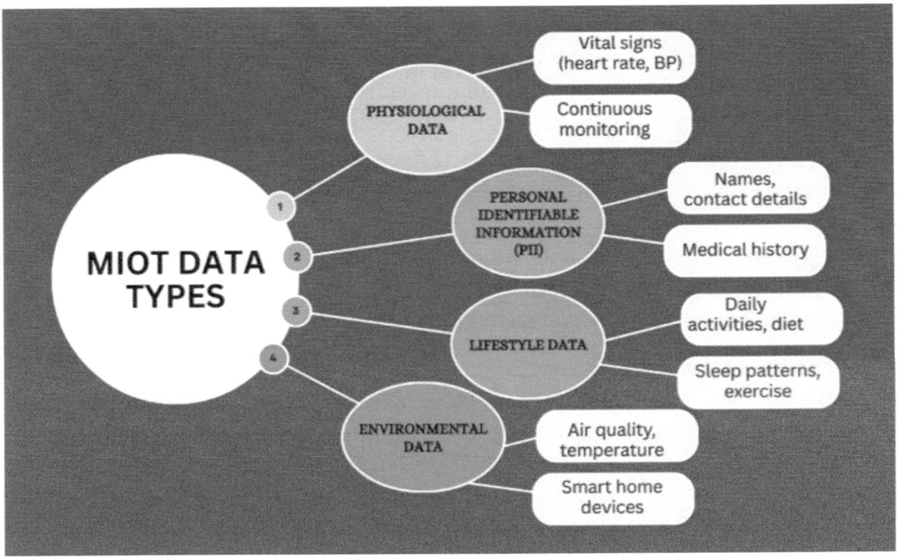

Figure 2: Different types of data.

5. Benefits of MIoT Technologies

Patients in health care systems receive better monitoring, chronic illness management, and operational MIoT efficiency. Proactive management strategies through real-time data enable timely intervention, improving health outcomes and reducing costs (Aslan, 2021; AIoMT Artificial Intelligence (AI) and Internet of Medical Things (IoMT), 2023). In addition to that, MIoT increases engagement through enablement. By giving power to individuals, they become active participants in a collaborative approach towards managing health, where they work with care providers, leading to better adherence with treatment. This increases health literacy and satisfaction with services. Moreover, MIoT technologies improve clinical workflows by automating mundane tasks and empowering data-driven decision processes (Maqsood et al., 2024; Khatib et al., 2024).

6. Risks and Challenges of MIoT

The most important and major issues of concern related to MIoT are the security and privacy of patient records. There is a high risk of unauthorized access and cyber-attack due to the connected nature of devices. To protect sensitive data and trust in MIoT technologies, strong strategies for encryption, secure authentication, and increased software updates are needed (Anil et al., 2023; Security and Privacy Issues in Internet of Things (IoT), 2023).

6.1. Privacy Risks in MIoT Systems

Despite the pros of MIoT, these privacy threats emerge as the most concerning issues. Before scrutinizing MIoT, exposure of sensitive information, unauthorized monitoring, and data abuse are the main privacy worries that escalate alongside the growth and development of MIoT systems (Emily Laidlaw, 2023). These have massive impacts on users and enterprises that hold confidential information as eroding user trust without robust measures, along with a user trust security framework safeguard.

1. Unauthorised Access: Healthcare service users of MIoT devices do not require any credentialed authentication, opening such patients to vulnerability owing to data exploitation (Wani et al., 2024). This results in control interfaces for MIoT devices that are unprotected, exposing patients to hacking with serious consequences, such as impersonation with forged medical documents, further worsening the already concerning situation. In controlled devices, organizations should implement reliable hardware identifiers to help restrict access.

2. Information Leaks: Concerning homes containing MIoT devices, vulnerabilities such as effortless access to repossession of the house, identity theft bypassing with fake documents as a 'doctor' impersonator, and illicit surveillance by outsiders are a few potential risks (Shahid et al., 2022; Li et al., 2024). Sensitive data, including health information, can be exposed in countless ways, from shredded healthcare workplace posters to neglected online forums, given the lack of confidentiality barriers. Thus, effective patient privacy safeguards and organizational breach concerns require a shift towards proactive cybersecurity planning, including perpetual risk assessment integrated with incident response management techniques.

3. Data Misuse: In addition, the sensitive information accommodating MIOT devices can lead not only to discrimination in healthcare services but also qualify as data misuse exploitation. This is why data governance policies, alongside ethical frameworks advocating for consent and transparency in data policies, legally become vital without infringing on the individual user's welfare.

4. Insider Threats: An employee or associate with working access to MIOT systems can deliberately or inadvertently manipulate patient information (Shahid et al., 2022; Li et al., 2024). Looking through the lens of insider threats, inadequate training coupled with shoddy intentions opens the doors for further complications. As a result, it becomes crucial for organizations to enforce strict access control policies in conjunction with activity monitoring. Changing the organizational culture to integrate with a heightened focus towards security can help ensure these data protection scaffolds are seamlessly and adequately integrated within the organization even further.

5. Device Vulnerabilities: The presence of legacy devices and older software within MIoT systems can further function as points of entry for cyberattacks (Wani et al., 2024; Maqsood et al., 2024). Businesses must place appropriate device management policies that pay attention to frequent updates and patches to counter those risks. Defending MIoT frameworks and protecting sensitive patient data greatly benefits from a comprehensive and active approach toward discovering and eliminating system weaknesses. Sadhu et al. (2022) observed how the combination of organizational and technological risk mitigation strategies creates a more secure MIoT environment with better privacy for all stakeholders. Technologies that enhance privacy alongside data governance frameworks and rising awareness of security among staff and system users promote stronger control over data and enhance security.

As a consequence of such issues, the adoption of strong security measures to protect sensitive patient information, along with other protective measures, robust privacy-enhancing technologies, and strong security controls, is imperative (Shahid et al., 2022; Wani et al., 2024; Li et al., 2024).

7. Technical Solutions for Data Privacy in MIoT

1. Blockchain Technology: The use of blockchain guarantees the security of MIoT data and also provides a long-term solution. Its decentralized system, along with an immutable and cryptographic technique, guarantees control over data integrity and transparency. An example of this would be medical data transactions where blockchain ensures compliance standards by designing self-sufficient audit trails (Gopinath et al., 2024; Awotunde et al., 2023). Also, Smart contracts, vital constituents of blockchain, can manage data access by automating control and consent approval, which helps in curtailing the chances of unauthorized information breach (Singla et al., 2024; "Acclimatization of mHealth Applications, Wireless Sensors, IoT in Healthcare: Focusing on Patient Privacy and Security in Legal Scenario," 2022).

2. Artificial Intelligence (AI): AI has two characteristics in MIoT. Primarily, it improves the quality of patient care and diagnostics. Secondly, it also deals with privacy and security issues. Solutions like federated learning enable data evaluation without notifying the patient due to AI taking control. Moreover, some protocols for AI-based trust management, like the Secure M-Trust Privacy (SMP) protocol, use cryptography as well as machine learning to ensure the safety of data while in transit (Sankaran and Kim, 2023). These are quite useful in MIoT systems having limited resources (Sankaran and Kim, 2023; Saxena and Mittal, 2022).

3. Data Fusion and Encryption: Fusing data, which improves efficiency, accuracy, and integrates information from various origins, is also a very promising approach in AI automation (Sadhukhan et al., 2024). Using fusion approaches minimizes the bulk of data to be sent and ensures that the accuracy of data processing in real time is improved (Sadhukhan et al., 2024). Ensuring safe data transmission and storage in MIoT ecosystems is still the primary method of data security. Advanced methods like homomorphic encryption and differential privacy, which help in analyzing and making new data without exposing sensitive or raw data, further strengthen the security of patients' data (Wani et al., 2024).

8. Regulatory Frameworks for Data Privacy

There are numerous governing concepts regulating the MIoT data, ensuring the patient's confidentiality in addition to securing the data integrity: HIPAA, or The Health Insurance Portability and Accountability Act sets up guidelines for safeguarding sensitive patient data within the United States because it requires that health care entities take protective measures to maintain the privacy and security of health information. Likewise, the GDPR or General Data Protection Regulation attempts to provide inclusive measures of protecting individual data in the EU, as it highlights consent and access to one's information, which is very important in MIoT systems (Shahid J., 2022).

Apart from HIPAA and GDPR, other regulations such as the California Consumer Privacy Act (CCPA) and Brazil's Lei Geral de Proteção de Dados (LGPD) also play critical roles in shaping the management of MIoT data and user data rights across different jurisdictions. Together, these regulations aim to strengthen workflows associated with sensitive data so that organizations achieve compliance and reduce risk exposure while building user trust in the MIoT framework.

1. The Health Insurance Portability and Accountability Act (HIPAA): HIPAA requires health care institutions to protect patient health information (PHI) by implementing sophisticated measures for data handling, preservation, and communication (Rockwern et al., 2021; Echenim and Joshi, 2023; Prasanna, 2025). Each healthcare provider and business associate is mandated to enforce administrative, physical, and technical controls to maintain the confidentiality, integrity, and availability of PHI. MIOT ecosystem compliance enhances health information privacy safeguards. Organisational compliance reduces risks related to legal liability, breaches, and patient trust after care MIOT technologies. These frameworks improve trust between patients and health care providers, aligned with MIOT technologies that systematically improve care outcomes. Healthcare entities like providers and insurers, as Covered Entities, are required to implement robust security controls like encryption and access controls for PHI (Echenim and Joshi, 2023; Rockwern et al., 2021).

2. General Data Protection Regulation (GDPR): GDPR governs the handling of personal information of individuals residing in the EU while enforcing strict regulations on data minimization, obtaining consent, and exercising the erasure clause (Chuang et al., 2023) (Echenim and Joshi, 2023; Özçağdavul, 2024). There is also a need to guarantee no opacity in the data acquisition and handling (Chuang et al., 2023; Özçağdavul, 2024).

8.1 Emerging and Regional Regulations

Countries such as Saudi Arabia have gone beyond GDPR and HIPAA to introduce Personal Data Protection Law (PDPL) and Essential Cybersecurity Controls (ECC) aimed at Health Data protection. These frameworks within this emerging region highlight the need to align national standards with internationally accepted best practices for data security (Alhoussari, 2025).

3. Other Regulations: Besides these, the European Union Medical Device Regulation (EU MDR) and guidelines from the U.S. Food and Drug Administration (FDA) also help safeguard the security and privacy of MIoT devices (Rajab et al., 2024; Shahid et al., 2022).

Following such regulations requires organizations to incorporate privacy-by-design, implement high-level security protocols, and schedule regular audits for complete adherence (Chuang et al., 2023) (Echenim and Joshi, 2023; Özçağdavul, 2024). Table 1 compares the different key regulations.

Table 1: Comparison of Key Regulations Governing MIoT Data

Regulation	Key Provisions	Citation
HIPAA	Protects PHI, mandates encryption, and access controls	(Rockwern et al., 2021; Echenim and Joshi, 2023; Prasanna, 2025)
GDPR	Emphasizes data minimization, consent, and the right to erasure	(Chuang et al., 2023; Echenim and Joshi, 2023; Özçağdavul, 2024)
EU MDR	Ensures the security and privacy of medical devices	(Rajab et al., 2024; Shahid et al., 2022)

9. Patient Trust in MIoT Ecosystems

9.1. Building Trust Through Transparency and Consent

The acceptance of MIoT technologies depends heavily on the trust that patients place. Trust is built when there is clear and transparent data collection and use disclosure. Patients must understand how their information is gathered, kept, and disseminated, as there must be appropriate consent policies (AlAmr, 2024). For instance, the active dialogue policies support patient participation in the consent processes, guaranteeing compliance with GDPR's consent management frameworks ("Acclimatization of mHealth Applications, Wireless Sensors, IoT in Healthcare: Focusing on Patient Privacy and Security in Legal Scenario," 2022).

9.2. Role of Security Awareness and Education

Alongside enabling trust to be built, fostering security awareness in patients and healthcare professionals remains a pivotal feature. Routine training sessions and effective communication plans filled with appropriate messaging can lessen the danger associated with sharing data (AlAmr, 2024). Moreover, protecting private information and other data security measures promoted by MIoT devices will help patients become more willing to use these devices (C et al., 2023).

9.3. Impact of Data Breaches on Trust

Data breaches involving MIoT systems can deeply damage the trust a patient has in a healthcare technological tool. It also brings tremendous ramifications, such as the loss of esteem from the healthcare system. To make sure a patient continues to trust the given healthcare provider, the provider must incorporate strong defenses like multi-factor authentication and encryption to protect the data stored (AlAmr, 2024; Sun et al., 2018).

10. Stakeholder Roles in Ensuring Data Privacy and Security

10.1. Healthcare Providers

The participation of healthcare professionals is critical when it comes to identifying the weaknesses of an MIoT system and guarding against them. They must consider best practices like compliance with regulatory frameworks through regular audits and training (Jiang et al., 2022). Moreover, they must also make sure that the relationship is built on the patient as a focus, meaning all processes involving data collection and sharing are based on ethical, socially accepted methodology and policies (AlAmr, 2024).

10.2. Technology Developers

MIoT devices and application developers have a responsibility to put security and privacy measures at the forefront of development, otherwise known as 'privacy by design'. That includes compliance with HL7 and FHIR standards concerning the security and sharing of information (Rajab et al., 2024). There needs to be a greater effort from the SMEs in utilizing these, such as GDPR and HIPAA compliance frameworks (Treacy et al., 2020).

10.3. Governments and Regulatory Bodies

There is a distinct lack of policies to protect MIoT data. Therefore, policymakers need to take action and develop comprehensive strategies for the privacy and protection of MIoT data. The collaboration of every stakeholder is vital in assisting to create consolidated policies and guidelines targeting the problems brought about by MIoT technology (Rajab et al., 2024; Alhoussari, 2025).

10.4. Patients

Patients are stakeholders in the MIoT domain and, therefore, must be in a position to make educated choices concerning their data. AlAmr (2024) notes that this includes an understanding of one's basic rights in the context of governance of data, including GDPR and HIPAA, as well as accountability and governance expectations.

11. Technical Solutions for Data Privacy

11.1. Privacy-enhancing Technologies and Anonymization

There are astonishingly relevant data pertaining to the myriad challenges linked to privacy and the MIoT. A selection of special agenda-setting documents has already been produced, among which it is worth stressing anonymity and deidentification methods, limitless encryption, and data guarding during transmission and storage. Additionally, several recently developed non-identifying data analysis methods like federated learning and secure multi-party computation serve to disguise the identity of users while ensuring their privacy, enhancing MIoT system security.

1. Encryption: It is crucial to protect sensitive data that is transferred between healthcare systems and MIoT devices. Organizations can use modern encryption techniques to encrypt sensitive data as it is being transmitted, preventing unauthorized individuals from accessing it. This is particularly significant in the scope of MIoT, where the magnitude of data exchanged is exchanged at a significant scale and the likelihood of breaches is high. Moreover, the application of end-to-end encryption in the system can aid in upholding data integrity and confidentiality by ensuring the protection of sensitive information from unauthorized individuals (Kim, 2017).

Emerging Privacy-Enhancing Technologies: Also, the creation of new methods aims to preserve privacy, such as differential privacy permits organizations to analyze huge datasets without the risk of revealing individual identities. Such methods fortify the protective measures and overcome regulatory challenges, which builds trust among users within MIoT. By employing these privacy-enhancing technologies (PETs) within management Internet of Things (MIoT) systems, organizations can create a powerful blueprint for protecting sensitive information while simultaneously optimizing healthcare results. This holistic approach not only addresses existing issues, but also sets anticipating user needs, sustains compliance with emerging unsolved problems regulations, and anticipates user needs.

To safeguard sensitive information from being disclosed without authorization, sensitive data is encrypted before dispatch or storage (Rockwern et al., 2021; Prasanna, 2025). Additionally, the integration of these technologies requires robust governance that applies and enforces legal requirements, which is critical for compliance. This approach will enhance the resolution of privacy issues while maximizing the benefits of advancements in MIoT.

Homomorphic encryption permits operations on encrypted information, maintaining privacy throughout the evaluation (Rockwern et al., 2021; Prasanna, 2025).

Therefore, the application of such sophisticated encryption models not only safeguards sensitive data but also allows organizations to analyze the data without jeopardizing user privacy. To effectively maneuver within the MIoT arena, the utilization of these technologies will be crucial to ensure the protection of data and the enhancement of user confidence as the landscape increasingly interlinks.

Along with these methods of encryption, organizations ought to consider adopting secure multi-party computation that enables computation without disclosure of the data among any of the parties. Such technologies could encourage the users' data privacy protections in MIoT systems.

2. Blockchain: Blockchain technology offers a new, less centralized approach to data organization, which improves security and confidentiality in MIoT systems. As a trustworthy audit trail in the event of potential unwanted access and data modification, the immutable ledger can help maintain data integrity and maintain a thorough record of sensitive information (Mampilly et al., 2024).

The advancement of blockchain technology gives a means that is secure, unchangeable, and transparent for tracking provenance while ensuring integrity (Digamber, 2024; Khan et al., 2025; Alsadhan et al., 2024). Its decentralized structure allows enhanced trust among users while carefully upholding privacy through cryptography. Blockchain technology addresses safety measures in the MIoT landscape by facilitating secure data exchange and creating immutable audit records for efficient compliance, bypassing issues (Lautert et al., 2020). Permitted blockchains can manage access restrictions, meet compliance, and contain ex-regulation obese attunele alignment restrictions (Alsadhan et al., 2024; Digamber, 2024).

3. Federated Learning (FL): Sensitive data from multiple MIoT devices is kept on their respective devices, enabling decentralization of model training. MIoT offers collaborative learning from the devices. No data is shared; only model updates, thus ensuring the information's secrecy and improvement of security within the MIoT framework.

FL facilitates decentralized collaboration in model development from various data locations without releasing sensitive information (Privacy-Enhancing Technologies in Federated Learning for the Internet of Healthcare Things: A Survey, 2023; Mosaiyebzadeh et al., 2023; R., 2023). This distributed system increases privacy and confidentiality while optimizing the efficiency of machine learning models, using diverse data sources without contradictory legal concerns. Through the adoption of federated learning, companies can promote the development of MIoT initiatives while keeping user information safe and confidential. This strategy aids in lowering the risk of data that can be exposed while retaining the accuracy of the model (Mosaiyebzadeh et al., 2023). Federated learning increases privacy as models can be constructed to fit specific user preferences without losing their anonymity, which is a significant advantage. Organizations can improve MIoT systems to help users without compromising the confidentiality and security of user data.

4. Differential Privacy: This is one of the most robust techniques that enables revealing useful information from a dataset while protecting individual private data. Adding noise guarantees that the offering or not offering a particular data does not change the effect of the outcome of the queries to be carried out on the data, which would expose him or her to danger (Mulder and Humbert, 2023; Cuff and Yu, 2016). The concept of differential privacy implies ensuring the confidentiality of sensitive information after identifying it by exposing it to a Specific Identifier (SI) (Kumar and Nilkant, 2024; Prasanna, 2025).

5. Data Anonymization: Their deployment improves confidentiality while providing meaningful data analysis, as individuals cannot be re-identified within datasets. Such measures also require the implementation of proper data governance frameworks to comply with privacy policies and build confidence among MIoT system users. Using PET frameworks allows organizations to impose stronger restrictions on MIoT frameworks—sensitive information can be withheld while still permitting data analysis to extract useful information. This approach underlines the importance of balancing privacy and utility as the MIoT ecosystem grows.

Techniques such as k-anonymity and l-diversity take away identifying markers to safeguard the patient's privacy (Prasanna, 2025). Privacy by design requires an accompanied layer that ensures constant monitoring and evaluation to adapt to evolving threats and regulatory shifts. Establishing a culture of privacy and proactive risk assessment enables organizations to bolster their defences against potential breaches while fostering trust within MIoT systems. Together, these measures mount a multi-layered approach to defend against privacy breaches while ensuring compliance with governing bodies.

Table 2 compares the different technical solutions (Rockwern et al., 2021; Digamber, 2024; Prasanna, 2025).

Table 2: Comparative Analysis of Technical Solutions

Solution	Description	Citation
Blockchain	Decentralized, immutable, and cryptographic security for data integrity.	(Gopinath et al., 2024; Awotunde et al., 2023; "Acclimatization of mHealth Applications, Wireless Sensors, IoT in Healthcare: Focusing on Patient Privacy and Security in Legal Scenario," 2022)
AI and Federated Learning	Enhances diagnostics and security through privacy-preserving data analysis.	(Sankaran and Kim, 2023; Saxena and Mittal, 2022)
Data Fusion	Reduces data volume and enhances real-time processing for optimized security.	(Sadhukhan et al., 2024)

12. Conclusion and Future Implications of MIoT in Healthcare

Our treatment systems can now deliver healthcare services with remote monitoring thanks to the integration of MIoT frameworks, which improves patient care and makes efficient use of resources. These devices collect data about the patient's condition in real time, which practically provides limitless opportunities for advancing healthcare services. The incorporation of MIoT frameworks into our treatment systems allows for the remote monitoring and delivery of healthcare services, which improves patient care and makes efficient use of resources. Trust must be built through open information about the technologies and concepts used, as well as providing access to the algorithms of action served by advanced technologies. Applying concise explanations, addressing patient data security concerns, and illustrating the application of privacy-preserving legal frameworks such as HIPAA and GDPR are equally crucial. Integration of medical IoT devices with AI and machine learning enables predictive treatment based on real-time data analysis and promises significant advancements in healthcare.

The formulation of interoperability protocols will be important to guarantee the integration of communications across various healthcare facilities and equipment to enable efficient data collection with the distributed systems, thereby improving the effectiveness of servicing patients. In relation to sensitive health data, there will be a strong focus on the patient information builder's technological gains and legal compliance strategies that foster trust and security in MIoT systems. Future innovations should focus on improving patients' participation in healthcare and decision-making processes. There will also be a greater need for countries to unify rules regarding MIoT data privacy and security to enable the use of MIoT technologies internationally while safeguarding patients' rights. Continuous education and awareness for the providers and the patients regarding MIoT technologies are required to address the misconceptions, a better understanding of the privacy of data, and responsible use of an individual's health information. Further research and sustained developmental efforts are needed to deal with emerging issues around MIoT, including risks to data security and ethical consequences of data use in healthcare. Finally, the device's sustainability and other ecological footprints must be addressed further.

References

AlAmr, M.I. (2024). Building patient trust through enhanced data security: A Saudi Arabian hospital case study. Galore International Journal of Applied Sciences and Humanities. https://doi.org/10.52403/gijash.20240405

Alhoussari, H. (2025). Securing health data in the digital age: Challenges, regulatory frameworks, and strategic solutions in Saudi Arabia. Journal of Ecohumanism, 4(1). https://doi.org/10.62754/joe.v4i1.6052

Alsadhan, A., Alsalamah, H.A., and Alhogail, A. (2024). A blockchain-based privacy-preserving model for IoMT medical systems. 2024 IEEE Blockchain Conference (BCCA). https://doi.org/10.1109/bcca62388.2024.10844473

Anil, A., Babu, A., Antony, J., Vilson, K.E., and Koshy, S. (2023). Security and privacy concern in IoT devices. International Journal of Engineering Technology and Management Sciences, 7(4). https://doi.org/10.46647/ijetms.2023.v07i04.065

Aslan, İ. (2021). Technologies and applications of Internet of Things (IoT) in healthcare. *In:* Emerging Advancements in Wireless Networks and IoT (pp. 312–329). IGI Global. https://doi.org/10.4018/978-1-7998-6673-2.ch018

Awotunde, J.B., Adeniyi, A.E., Falola, P.B., Imoize, A.L., Bandyopadhyay, A., Bhoi, A.K., and Rodríguez, D.Z. (2023). Artificial intelligence and blockchain for robust healthcare delivery: From the perspective of security and confidentiality. AI and Blockchain in Healthcare, 21. https://doi.org/10.1049/pbhe061e_ch21

Bookert, N., Bondurant, W., and Anwar, M. (2022). Data practices of Internet of Medical Things: A look from privacy policy perspectives. Smart Health, 26, 100342. https://doi.org/10.1016/j.smhl.2022.100342

Chuang, I., Huang, S., Hong, W.-H., and Kuo, Y.-H. (2023). An efficient GDPR-compliant data management for IoHT applications. 2023 IEEE International Conference on Communications Workshops (ICC Workshops). https://doi.org/10.1109/iccworkshops57953.2023.102835

Cuff, P., and Yu, L. (2016). Differential privacy as a mutual information constraint. Proceedings of the 2016 ACM SIGSAC Conference on Computer and Communications Security, 43–54. https://doi.org/10.1145/2976749.2978308

Digamber, K.M. (2024). Blockchain-based medical record sharing in healthcare IoT: Building trust and transparency through secure provenance tracking. Journal of Electrical Systems. https://doi.org/10.52783/jes.650

Echenim, K.U., and Joshi, K.P. (2023). IoT-Reg: A comprehensive knowledge graph for real-time IoT data privacy compliance. 2023 IEEE International Conference on Big Data. https://doi.org/10.1109/bigdata59044.2023.10386545

Gopinath, V., Rao, K.V., and Rao, S. (2024). Leveraging blockchain for securing and managing medical IoT data. *In:* Blockchain and AI in Healthcare, pp. 1–20. CRC Press. https://doi.org/10.58532/v3bgba1p1ch1

Han, Y.W., and Lü, X. (2024). Is data anonymization an effective way to protect privacy or not? International Journal of Computer Science and Information Technology, 4(3). https://doi.org/10.62051/ijcsit.v4n3.15

Jiang, R., Han, S., Shi, M., Gao, T., and Zhao, X. (2022). Healthcare big data privacy protection model based on risk-adaptive access control. Security and Communication Networks, 2022, Article 3086516. https://doi.org/10.1155/2022/3086516

Khan, A.A., Laghari, A.A., Alroobaea, R. et al. (2025). A lightweight scalable hybrid authentication framework for Internet of Medical Things (IoMT) using blockchain Hyperledger consortium network with edge computing. Scientific Reports, 15, 19856. https://doi.org/10.1038/s41598-025-05130-w

Khatib, I.A., Shamayleh, A., and Ndiaye, M. (2024). Healthcare and the Internet of Medical Things: Applications, trends, key challenges, and proposed resolutions. Informatics, 11(3), 47. https://doi.org/10.3390/informatics11030047

Kim, L. (2017). Cybersecurity awareness: Protecting data and patients. Nursing, 47(3), 68–69. https://doi.org/10.1097/01.NURSE.0000516242.05454.B

Kumar, H., and Nilkant, D. (2024). Privacy-preserving strategies for enhanced big data analytics in evolving healthcare environments. *In:* Big Data Analytics in Healthcare, pp. 245–260. CRC Press. https://doi.org/10.1201/9781032694375-17

Laidlaw, Emily. (2023). Technology mindfulness and the future of the tort of privacy. Osgoode Hall Law Journal, 60(3), 597–654. Doi: https://doi.org/10.60082/2817-5069.3925.

Lautert, F., Pigatto, D.F.G., and Gomes-Jr, L. (2020). Blockchain-based data provenance. 2020 Workshop on Blockchain and Distributed Ledger Technologies (WBLOCKCHAIN). https://doi.org/10.5753/wblockchain.2020.12975

Li, S., Baiocco, A., and Xu, S. (2024). Characterizing privacy risks in healthcare IoT systems. Proceedings of the 2024 International Conference on Privacy and Security in Healthcare IoT, 45–60.

Majeed, A., and Lee, S. (2021). Anonymization techniques for privacy preserving data publishing: A comprehensive survey. IEEE Access, 9, 8512–8545. https://doi.org/10.1109/ACCESS.2020.3045700

Mampilly, A.J., Manda, V.K., and Selvan, C.P. (2024). Blockchain in cybersecurity. In Advances in information security, privacy, and ethics (pp. 89–110). IGI Global. https://doi.org/10.4018/979-8-3693-9225-6.ch003

Maqsood, M.I., Dar, M.M., Shah, S.G.S., Javed, M.H., and Khan, H. (2024). A survey on the Internet of Medical Things (IoMT) privacy and security: Challenges, solutions, and future from a new perspective. Advances in Biotechnology and Bioscience, 4(4). https://doi.org/10.62019/abbdm.v4i4.279

Merih, Y.D., Aktan, M.E., and Akdoğan, E. (2023). Internet of Medical Things (IoMT): An overview and applications. In Emerging technologies in healthcare (pp. 245–260). Springer. https://doi.org/10.1007/978-981-99-6062-0_14

Mosaiyebzadeh, F., Pouriyeh, S., Parizi, R.M., Sheng, Q.Z., Han, M., Zhao, L., Sannino, G., and Batista, D.M. (2023). Privacy-enhancing technologies in federated learning for the Internet of Healthcare Things: A survey. Electronics, 12(5), 1103. https://doi.org/10.48550/arXiv.2303.14544

Mulder, V., and Humbert, M. (2023). Differential privacy. SpringerBriefs in Cybersecurity, 1–85. https://doi.org/10.1007/978-3-031-33386-6_27

Özçağdavul, M. (2024). General Data Protection Regulation compliance and privacy protection in wearable health devices: Challenges and solutions. Artuklu International Journal of Health Sciences, 1(1). https://doi.org/10.58252/artukluhealth.1566573

Pawar, A., Ahirrao, S., and Churi, P. (2018). Anonymization techniques for protecting privacy: A survey. 2018 IEEE PuneCon Conference. https://doi.org/10.1109/PUNECON.2018.8745425

Prasanna, G. L. (2025). Privacy preserving data sharing cloud-based healthcare systems. Indian Scientific Journal of Research in Engineering and Management, 4(4). https://doi.org/10.55041/ijsrem40474

Privacy-enhancing technologies in federated learning for the Internet of Healthcare Things: A survey. (2023). arXiv. https://doi.org/10.48550/arXiv.2303.14544

Prokhorenkov, D. (2022). Anonymization level and compliance for differential privacy: A systematic literature review. 2022 International Wireless Communications and Mobile Computing (IWCMC). https://doi.org/10.1109/iwcmc55113.2022.9824899

Rajab, R.M., Abuhmida, M., Wilson, I., and Ward, R. (2024). A review of IoMT security and privacy-related frameworks. Proceedings of the 23rd European Conference on Information Warfare and Security. https://doi.org/10.34190/eccws.23.1.2239

Rockwern, B., Johnson, D., and Sulmasy, L.S. (2021). Health information privacy, protection, and use in the expanding digital health ecosystem: A position paper of the American College of Physicians. Medical Informatics Committee and Ethics, Professionalism and Human Rights Committee of the American College of Physicians. Annals of Internal Medicine, 174(7), 1017–1024. https://doi.org/10.7326/M20-7639

Sadhu, P.K., Yanambaka, V.P., Abdelgawad, A., and Yelamarthi, K. (2022). Prospect of Internet of Medical Things: A review on security and privacy issues. Sensors, 22(15), 5517. https://doi.org/10.3390/s22155517

Sadhukhan, D., Ray, S., and Dasgupta, M. (2024). Data fusion in Internet of Medical Things: Towards trust management, security, and privacy. *In:* Data Fusion for Modern Applications, pp. 321–340. Elsevier. https://doi.org/10.1016/B978-0-44-313233-9.00018-7

Said, A.M., Yahyaoui, A., and Abdellatif, T. (2024). HIPAA and GDPR compliance in IoT healthcare systems. Proceedings of the 2024 International Conference on Privacy Regulations, 89–104. https://doi.org/10.1007/978-3-031-55729-3_16

Sankaran, K.S., and Kim, T.H. (2023). An improved AI-based secure M-trust privacy protocol for Medical Internet of Things in smart healthcare system. IEEE Internet of Things Journal. https://doi.org/10.1109/jiot.2023.3280592

Saxena, A., and Mittal, S. (2022). Internet of Medical Things (IoMT) security and privacy: A survey of recent advances and enabling technologies. Proceedings of the 14th International Conference on Contemporary Computing, 789–796. https://doi.org/10.1145/3549206.354930

Security and Privacy Issues in Internet of Things (IoT). (2023). TechRxiv. https://doi.org/10.36227/techrxiv.23512389

Shahid, J. (2022). Data protection and privacy of the internet of healthcare things. Applied Sciences, 12(4), 1927. https://doi.org/10.3390/app12041927

Shahid, R., uz Zaman, T., Thabit, F.M.A., and Can, O.E. (2022). Security and privacy challenges, issues, and enhancing techniques for Internet of Medical Things: A systematic review. Security and Privacy, 5(6), e409. https://doi.org/10.1002/spy2.409

Singla, D., Kumar, S., Dhingra, D., and Ghandhi, A. (2024). Blockchain-powered healthcare: Revolutionizing security and privacy in IoT-based systems. 2024 IEEE International Conference on Computing, Intelligence, and Communication Applications (ICCICA). https://doi.org/10.1109/ICCICA60014.2024.10585062

Sivakumar, C., Mone, V., and Abdumukhtor, R. (2024). Addressing privacy concerns with wearable health monitoring technology. Wiley Interdisciplinary Reviews: Data Mining and Knowledge Discovery, 14(2). https://doi.org/10.1002/widm.1535

Sun, W., Cai, Z., Li, Y., Liu, F., Fang, S., and Wang, G. (2018). Security and privacy in the medical Internet of Things: A review. Security and Communication Networks, 2018, 5978636. https://doi.org/10.1155/2018/5978636

Treacy, C., Loane, J., and McCaffery, F. (2020). A developer-driven framework for security and privacy in the Internet of Medical Things. Proceedings of the 15th International Conference on Evaluation of Novel Approaches to Software Engineering, 98283. https://www.scitepress.org/Papers/2020/98283/98283.pdf

Wani, N.A., Kumar, R., Mamta, Bedi, J. and Rida, I. (2024). Explainable AI-driven IoMT fusion: Unravelling techniques, opportunities, and challenges with explainable AI in healthcare. Information Fusion, 110, 102472. https://doi.org/10.1016/j.inffus.2024.102472

CHAPTER
6

Big Data-based Advancements in Prostate Cancer Imaging: Artificial Intelligence-based Segmentation of Ga-PSMA PET for Tumor Volume Assessment

Ritu Aggarwal[*(0000-0003-2809-0864)] **and Eshaan Aggarwal**[(0009-0005-9642-4477)]
Department of Computer Science and Engineering, Maharishi Markendeshwar Engineering College (MM (DU)) Mullana, India

1. Introduction

In a person, due to mutations, cancer is a genetic disease that originates in the prostate. The likelihood of mortality and patient recurrence depends on the quality of the treatment identified. Treatment of prostate cancer is very long and expensive. It is stressful and puts a toll on the patients themselves or their personal lives. The immune system rejects any weakened cells and prevents disease from entering the body. Through the lymph node, cancer cells rapidly grow and escape from the immune system, as wherever the cancer spreads, that area is deprived of an immune response. It is a challenge and a question of mortality. Many humans die from the treatment of this disease. In men, the diagnosis of the disease is due to a sudden increase in PSA level. Even with the assistance of professionals in the treatment planning of cerebral and corporal adversities of the disease, each individual has an imprecise prognosis (Hamm and Baumgärtner, 2023). It is classified into benign and malignant cells. Nearby tissues are not in danger if it is benign. Metastasis is an advanced stage of cancer in which the cancer spreads first to the lymph nodes and then to the human blood. A massive amount of data is being analysed and interpreted with the help of deep learning models. Various types of sample data, clinical data,

*Corresponding author: errituaggarwal@gmail.com

DOI: 10.1201/9781003676812-6

and genetic information that fall under the context of prostate cancer (Lim et al., 2023). Medical practitioners and the development of prediction models have various instances of prostate cancer with benign and malignant tumours, for which they have an effective method to detect and diagnose prostate cancer. Benign cancers are not hazardous, but malignant cells undergo metastasis and spread to other parts of the body. It gives no indications as it grows; the patients sense no irregularities in their bodies like continuous urination and fluid secretion in the prostate gland, semen in blood or urine (Boonseana et al., 2022). Prostate cancer risk increases in men after the age of 50. The risk increases if there is a family history of cancer, obesity, etc..

The chances of diagnosis are relatively higher than for other diseases. Disease prediction is based on the incidence rate, which jumps to nearly 60%. Patients are treated utilizing the data science paradigm, such as the Geasen group, Gleason score, and prostate-specific antigen levels, as part of their therapy process (Mehralivand et al., 2022). Patient-related data are considered and analysed based on the treatments recommended. With the aid of the therapy employed, the patient death rate can be studied. Deep learning and a predictive model can be used to examine the mortality rate of men who have prostate cancer. According to data, the number of disciplines in the computer science subject of healthcare has been reported. The ongoing evolution of the cancer case serves as the analysis's inspiration. There are numerous sections in this document.

2. Related Work

According to Hamm and Baumgärtner (2023), imaging samples and clinically important MRI scans are helpful for radiologic interpretation of prostate cancer. Data with limited clinical translation is lacking in AI. Bi-parametric MRI and biopsy are trained and tested on samples after the image classifications of different samples collected for prostate cancer images. Pi-RADS classifies benign and malignant tissue with the Gleason index value. Cross-validation techniques are used for detecting prostate cancer. The author achieved accuracy in terms of a greater performance rate.

In their study, Lim et al. (2023) presented a model that uses T2-weighted MRI sequence imaging data samples and ADC to identify and diagnose prostate cancer. To improve performance, the authors use a fusion model to incorporate clinical data to differentiate between benign and aggressive prostate cancer. Using the coefficient value, the model calculates the outcomes with 82 percent efficiency for identifying malignant lesions.Boonseana et al. (2022) have developed a model using machine learning techniques by applying various procedures, such as mpMRI/US, which is a guided biopsy with the transperineal approach, which has a 91.8% success rate for prostate cancer detection. The results of the biopsy tests are computed based on a systematic approach that improved the detection models. The authors proposed an accuracy of 87.2% with a prediction rate of 0.009. Prostate cancer detection rate could have more complicated as per diagnosis like other disease.

Mehralivand et al. (2022) have developed a model using an algorithm based on the training and testing of a model used for detecting the prostate at an early stage with the help of deep learning models and the labels, such as UNet, AHnet. The authors detect prostate cancer by finding lesions in biopsies' performance metrics.

525 patients were included for training and testing the validation algorithm. It obtained accuracy as for the LeNet model to achieve better performance.

A. Tejaswi et. al. (2022) and Hosseinzadeh et al. (2022) in this author proposed a model using a deep learning model that is based on a segmentation model. The results are based on the images of cells that receive prostate tissue at the time of biopsies. For cancer risk prediction multiple instances learning model is used on cell images. The results are based on the AUC characteristics.

Hosseinzadeh et. al. (2022 and Nematollahi et al. (2023) have developed a system model based on the MRI images. The author collected 2734 data samples for the detection of prostate cancer. The results are reported based on pirads factor. Performance relies only on the ROC values received.

Nematollahi et al. (2023) and Islam and Layek (2023) in their research have proposed using machine learning algorithms due to the diagnostic performance that works at a different rate. It achieved accuracy based on multiparametric MR imaging methods.

Talukder et al. (2020) (Ismail et al., 2020) have worked on brain tumours, that another kind of cancer that spreads rapidly in females. Manually identifying and detecting disease is not possible. It is possible with only an MRI. The author used an approach such as a deep learning model to detect the disease. Achieved an accuracy of 98.72, as in the case of the Xception algorithm used.

Ismail et.al. (2020) and Talukder et al. (2023) use various classification techniques to develop the system model. A modified logistic regression model and other clinical characteristics are considered based on PCA. The results show improvement in the prediction accuracy.

Talukder et al. and Bhattacharya et al. (2022) propose a combination of genetic diseases that can cause disability and death in humans. Cancer detection through machine learning and deep learning could speed up the identification of the disease by a hybrid feature selection model. It has high-performance filtering for the image cancer datasets. It achieved an accuracy of 98 % to the existing technologies used by the previous researchers.

Bhattacharya et al. (2022) and Eastham et al. (2022) proposed a model using automated methods for detecting prostate cancer by the MRI patient is as in early stages. If the Gleason pattern has have value of 3 or more, received patient is suffering from prostate cancer. Some pathological concepts are treatments are based on the observations of patient. In this work corsignia is used in MRI images to detect the disease at by their level assumption.

Hong et al. (2023) and Hosseinzadeh et al. (2022) proposed a data and work based on different samples received on the labelled data . it is in segmented form that using CNN. for validation and testing data Unet and dense net approach is implemented. It achieved 87 % accuracy from the current work

3. Proposed Flow Methodology

In this proposed work total of 4056 samples of prostate cancer were collected by an online repository of Machine learning, and a total of 58 attributes were selected for prediction and analysis report. The physicians used the medical images, which are called MRI scans report from the 4056 samples. These are divided into two main groups: one is prostate-related issues, and the other is called Brachytherapy. Strict privacy of images and other safety rules through HIPAA regulations are reviewed and approved.

The MRI scans have various views regarding the prostate cancer that are accessed by radiologists. In this research used a large collection of medical images in which patient data was used for developing the system model that helps to detect prostate cancer. It ensures privacy and data quality. It did the work accurately to identify the disease from MRI scans, as shown in Figure 1.

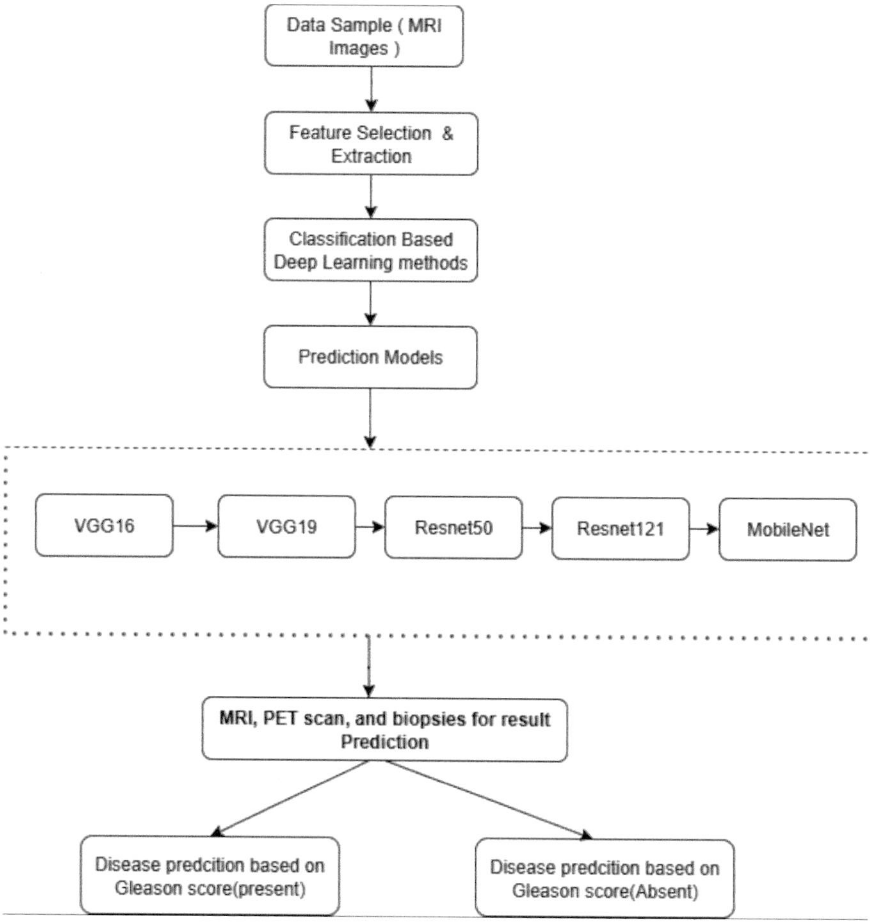

Figure 1: Proposed flow for disease detection.

3.1. Deep Learning Methods

In this proposed work, VGG16, VGG19, ResNet50, ResNet121, Mobilenet, and other machine learning classifiers etc. the results are implemented and analysed with decision tree, KNN, and SVM (Hosseinzadeh et al., 2022).

3.1.1. Feature Extraction

It is based on the detection of prostate cancer using deep learning and machine learning algorithms. It is a process of converting the unprocessed MRI images into significant predictions that capture the relevant patterns and erections to indicate prostate cancer with relevant features (Nematollahi et al., 2023). Input preparation has included the following procedure, such as first importing the MRI image that includes both benign and malignant prostate image samples. standardize all the pixel values with a range of stability of the model during the training. Spatial pooling methods could combine the information across the other dimensions used (Islam and Layek, 2023).

1. Eliminate the fully connected layers that are connected, namely the top layers, while keeping only with convolutional layers a pretrained models. Various extractors are used for selecting the feature from the dataset (Talukder et al., 2023).
2. It is necessary to standardize the feature vectors by improving the model convergence and generalization.
3. Various fusion techniques and feature vectors encapsulating crucial properties are enabled to diagnosis prostate cancer (Ismail et al., 2020).
4. Various correlation coefficient is used for feature extraction and selection.

4. Results and Discussion

In this prostate cancer disease detection first collect the samples of infected and healthy people data samples. T 1 exhibits MRI dataset samples according to statistics.

Table 1: MRI sample

Number of Attributes	Sample value
Healthy prostate number	800
Infected prostate	3000
MRI prostate	4000
Original images	7000
Human subject total no.	22

4.1. Estimation of Current System

It assesses the prostate-cancer disease after utilizing the deep leaning models used and machine learning classifiers. Early identification could save aperson's life and increase the morality rate in patients. The objective is improving the existing research by early detection of disease. This disease effects globally all the men. Petscan, MRI help to diagnose the disease and hormone therapy, robotic therapy could improve the life quality and life span in patients.

4.1.1. Data Collection

This study has been elaborated with MRI data samples that are accessible by the images of cancer samples. The dataset consists of many MRI sources with sequence numbers, such as subjective imaging, dispersion-weighted imaging, and disparity-improved imaging samples. In the data collection process, various feature samples are extracted and selected based on the images' characteristics, with clinical metadata accompanying the MRI data. The images are widely used to detect different aspects of cancer from multiple angles using MRI. As shown in Table 2, different feature extraction methods and reduced feature sets are used for analysis and implementation through deep learning.

Table 2: Machine-learning and deep learning classifiers with algorithm results

Algorithm_Type	Feature_before_extraction	Reduced _features
LR	3245	614
DT	2300	523
LDA	2634	520
Stacking classifier	3500	412

In the various algorithm are employed for detection of prostate cancer shown in Figure 2.

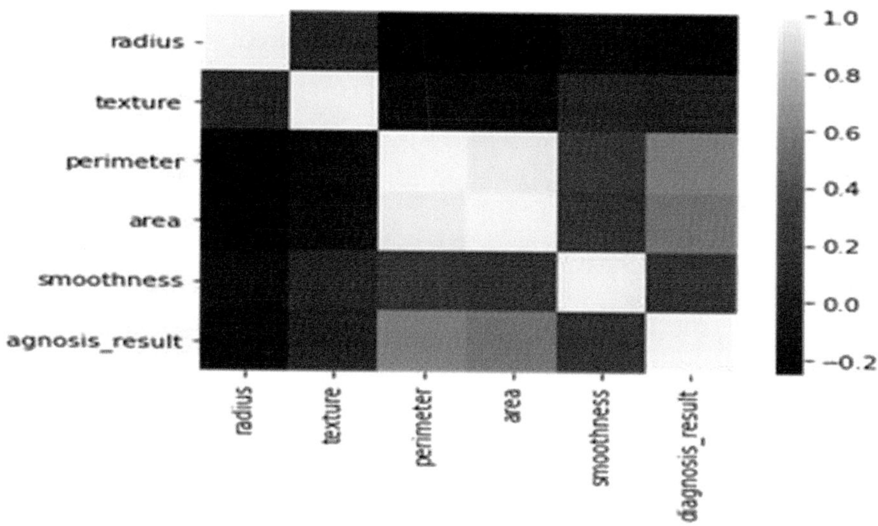

Figure 2: Correlation Graph for Prostate Cancer.

Figure 2 shows the results by correlating each attribute with their values after obtaining the different result data or value.

For prostate cancer disease, various predictions are shown in Figures 3 and 4, and two types of values are considered: true value and predicted value.

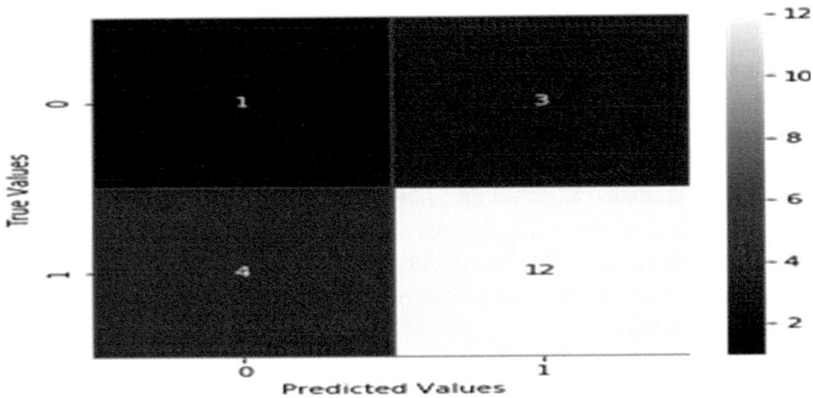

Figure 3: Prediction Results.

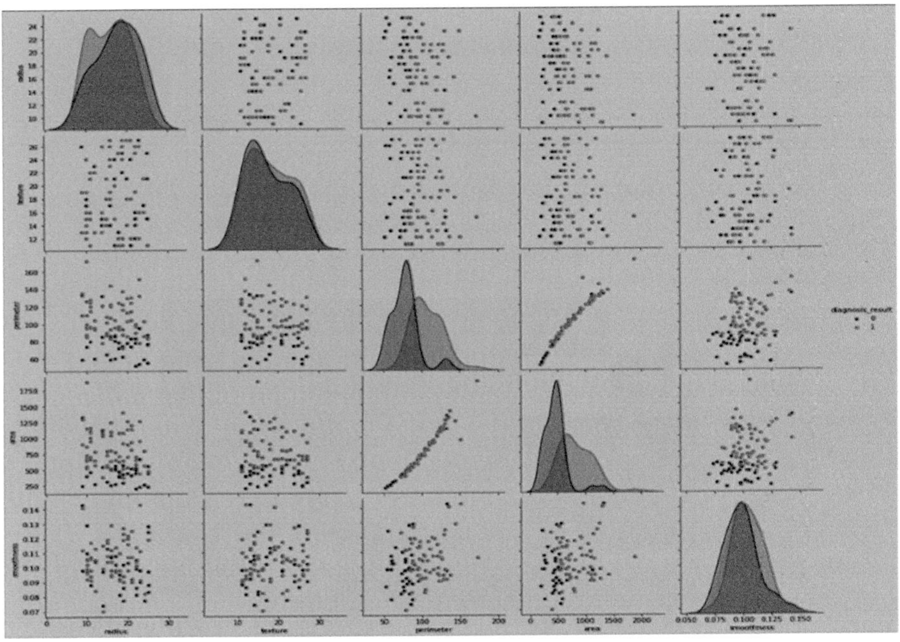

Figure 4: Implementation Resultant area graph for prostate cancer.

These are classifier used for implementation and their RPC curve generated according to value obtained.

Various classes are considered as following: for prostate cancer, various categories are used for detecting and diagnosing the disease in early stages with the help of MRI and PET-Scan. 0 means no tissue found or unknown, 1: benign tissue that have connected of epithelium and stroma combined. Radboud has 6 classes zero is for non-tissue, 1 is for benign stroma, 2 is healthy, 3 is cancerous, 4 have Gleason score 4 ,5 as a Gleason score 5. When merged all the class into a single one class have

0 have no symptoms and no detection which is as unknown, 1,2 considered as benign and 3,4,5 as cancerous stage.

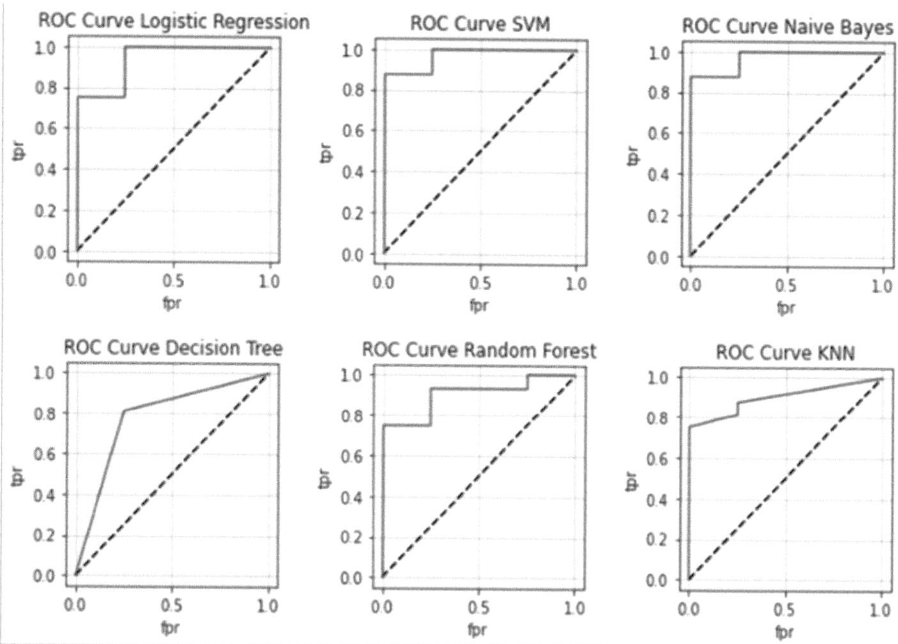

Figure 5: Result implementation classifier area graph for prostate cancer.

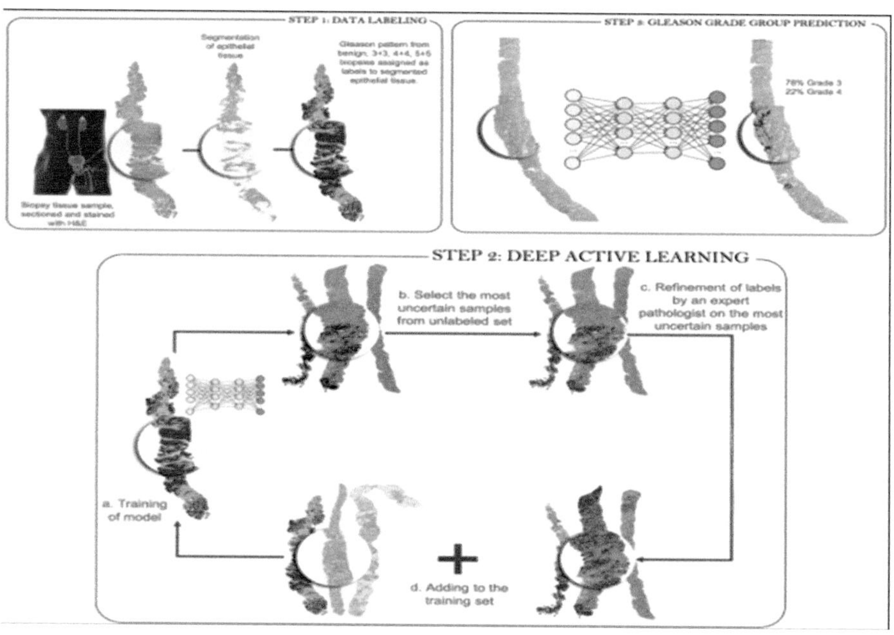

Figure 6: Implementation Result deep active learning for prostate cancer.

Figure 7 shows that various classes of prostate cancer are identified and computed by collecting the different samples according to the rated cancer classes.

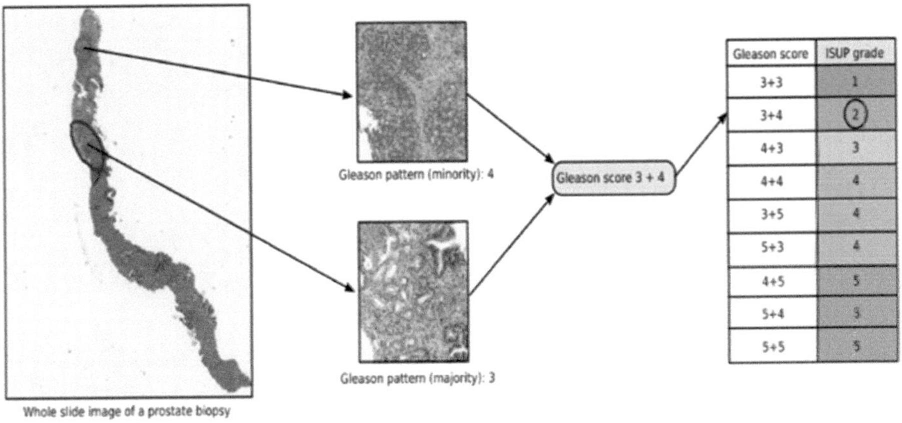

Figure 7: Cancer classes and stages.

4.1.2. Decision Tree Classifier

Various essential tools are used to check the prostate cancer by the decision tree classifier's effectiveness. It is utilized by classifier outcomes to train the model features retrieved by VGG16, VGG19, ResNet50, Rest50v2. It is used for implementation prostate cancer (Bhattacharya et al., 2022).

4.1.3. LDA

It is linear discriminant analysis to check the performance of LDA models. It is working to study the various features attained through LDA. It checks the cancerous and non-cancerous features by support of a confusion matrix in the MRI images (Eastham et al., 2022; Hong et al., 2023)..

4.1.4. Stacking Classifier

It is crucial to the development of the confusion matrix for cancer research diagnosis. It permits us to compute the presentation on the various feature reduction approaches. It is based on the ensemble learning algorithm. The classification performance was evaluated by different reduction techniques with deep learning models, using VGG16, VGG19, Resnet50, Resnet50V2, Mobilenet, and various classifiers of machine learning (Aggarwal et al., 2024; Hosseinzadeh et al., 2022).

4.1.5. Feature Importance

Different model classifiers are employed in this disease detection process to extract information and choose the most important features for prostate cancer disease detection. Finding the most important patterns in MRI data is the first step, since the majority of features point to the presence of prostate cancer. (Saha et al., 2023; Seibert et al., 2023). It relates the MRI to image properties, facilitating precise classification.

It selects the healthy and malignant prostate tissue (Aggarwal et al., 2023; Aggarwal et al., 2024) as shown in Figure 8.

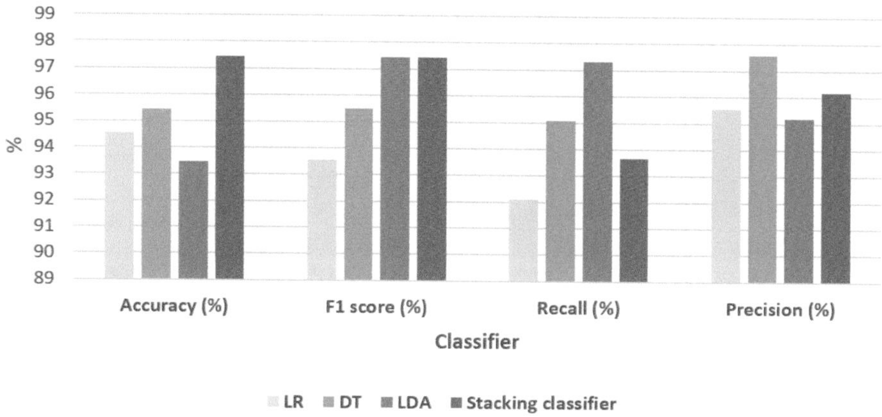

Figure 8: VGG16 results.

According to the results in Table 6.3 above, VGG16 uses deep learning algorithms like LR 94.53, LDA 93.45, Stacking classifier 97.45, and others.

The outcome of various machine learning classifiers, including LR 97.64, DT 96.49, LDA 94.47, Stacking classifier 96.46, etc., are displayed in Table 4 above, along with Figure 9.

Table 3: Results for VGG16 used in Prostate Cancer

Algorithm	Accuracy (%)	F1 score (%)	Recall (%)	Precision (%)
LR	94.53	93.56	92.11	95.56
DT	95.44	95.51	95.08	97.6
LDA	93.45	97.45	97.34	95.2
Stacking classifier	97.45	97.45	93.67	96.2

Table 4: Results for Deep learning VGG19 implementation

Algorithm	Accuracy (%)	F1 score (%)	Recall (%)	Precision (%)
LR	97.64	93.67	93.45	95.45
DT	96.49	95.58	92.08	97.68
LDA	94.47	95.46	97.34	95.28
Stacking classifier	96.46	96.46	97.89	96.89

Table 5 shows that the LR algorithm gives an accuracy of 95.78, the DT gives an accuracy of 95.34, LDA gives an accuracy of 96.15, and the stacking classifier gives 98.45, as shown in Figure 10.

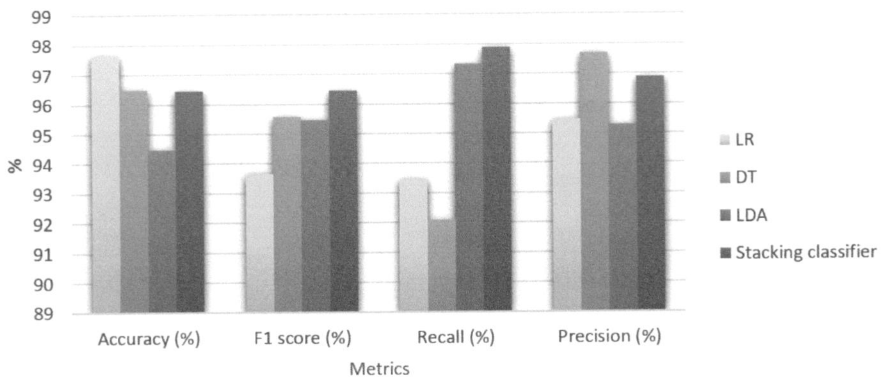

Figure 9: Implementation results VGG19.

Table 5: Implementation Results for Resnet50

Algorithm	Accuracy (%)	F1 score (%)	Recall (%)	Precision (%)
LR	95.78	93.56	94.78	95.56
DT	95.34	97.51	96.45	96.89
LDA	96.15	96.45	97.56	92.89
Stacking classifier	98.45	94.41	93.56	96.45

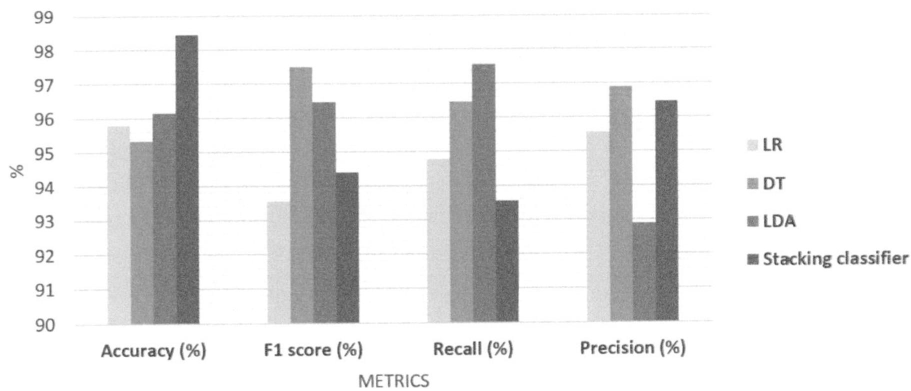

Figure 10: Implementation results VGG19.

As shown in Table 6, the results are as follows for the stacking classifier: 95.56, etc. For mobilenet, LR obtained an accuracy of 96.78, and the stacking classifier obtained 95.56, as shown in Figure 11.

The results are shown in Table 7, and the graphical implementation is shown in Figures 11 and 12 for Restnet50 V2 and mobilenet.

Table 6: Implementation Resnet50V2 results

Algorithm	Accuracy (%)	F1 score (%)	Recall (%)	Precision (%)
LR	96.78	93.67	90.12	96.23
DT	94.78	93.47	94.89	95.34
LDA	98.34	93.45	93.89	97.23
Stacking classifier	95.56	95.32	96.23	94.45

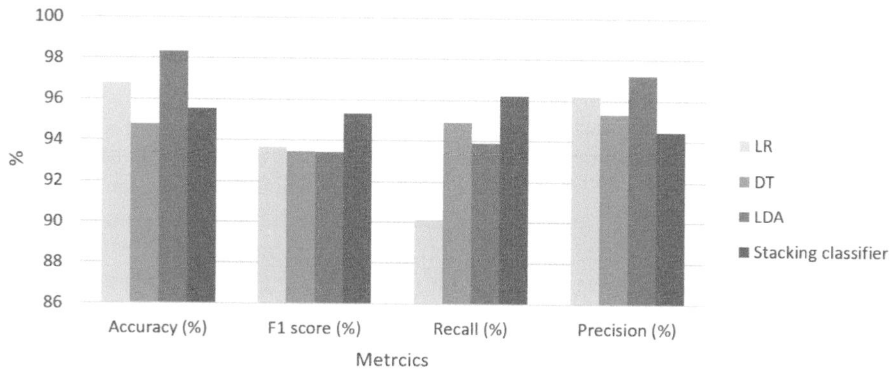

Figure 11: Implementation results Resnet50V2.

Table 7: Implementation Results Mobilenet

Algorithm	Accuracy (%)	F1 score (%)	Recall (%)	Precision (%)
LR	95.78	92.59	95.56	96.56
DT	95.89	95.61	96.67	97.86
LDA	97.43	96.67	97.48	96.89
Stacking classifier	98.99	97.67	94.67	96.82

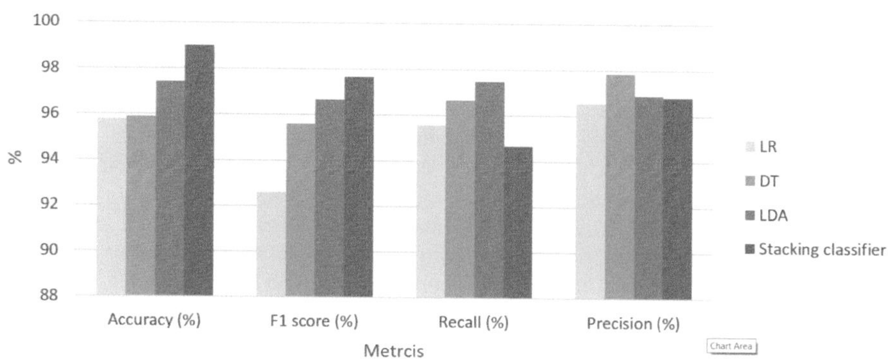

Figure 12: Results implementation of Mobilenet.

5. Conclusion and Findings

In the proposed work, feature extraction models or deep learning models are used to extract features by implementing sophisticated architectures such as MobileNet, ResNet50, ResNet121, and others to achieve greater performance and accuracy in results.

1. Various investigations are performing on by further optimization to further optimize the efficiency of disease detection model.
2. Pretrained models and other enhancing algorithms are used.
3. To allow information across many algorithms used for disease detection has achieved better results in terms of accuracy rate.

5.1. Future Work

In the future, prostate cancer detection will rely on deep learning algorithms and could improve by using fusion or multimodal approaches, which combine various data types such as biopsies, MRI, genetic information, and Petscan. These comprehensive methods can be used for analyzing and developing personalized risk assessments with other deep learning models. Using AI algorithms to analyse the various datasets and discover all the patterns.

References

Aggarwal, R., Aggarwal, E., Jain, A., Choudhury, T., and Kotecha, K. (2023). An automation perception for cotton crop disease detection using machine learning. 7th International Symposium on Innovative Approaches in Smart Technologies (ISAS), pp. 1–6. Istanbul, Türkiye. https://doi.org/10.1109/ISAS60782.2023.10391530

Aggarwal, R., Aggarwal, E., Jain, A., Aluvalu, R., Maheswari, U., and Choudhury, T. (2024). Deep learning image classification abiotic plant disease detection classification using MobileNet. 4th International Conference on Technological Advancements in Computational Sciences (ICTACS), pp. 526–530. Tashkent, Uzbekistan. https://doi.org/10.1109/ICTACS62700.2024.10841037

Bhattacharya, I., Seetharaman, A., Kunder, C., Shao, W., Chen, L.C., Soerensen, S.J.C. et al. 2022. Selective identification and localization of indolent and aggressive prostate cancers via corrsignia: An MRI-pathology correlation and deep learning framework. Medical Image Analysis, 75, Article ID 102288. https://doi.org/10.1016/j.media.2021.102288

Boonseana, S., Srinualnad, S., Leewansangtong, S., Sangtong, Tantranont, N., and Woranisarakul, V. (2022). Prostate cancer detection rate using MRI/ultrasound fusion-guided prostate biopsy in Siriraj Hospital. Insight Urology, 43(2), 128–133.

Choudhary, S.L., Aggarwal, R., Dixit, R.S., Duraisamy, B., Sundar, V.S.D. and Mane, S.B. (2025). HDLHDGAI: Hybridization of deep learning model for heart disease prediction using generative artificial intelligence. Journal of Machine and Computing, 102–110. https://doi.org/10.53759/7669/jmc202505008

Eastham, J.A., Auffenberg, G.B., Barocas, D.A., Chou, R., Crispino, T., Davis, J. W., . . . and Boorjian, S.A. (2022). Clinically localized prostate cancer: AUA/ASTRO guideline, part I: Introduction, risk assessment, staging, and risk-based management. The Journal of Urology, 208(1), 10–18. https://doi.org/10.1097/JU.0000000000002757

Hamm, C.A., and Baumgärtner, G.L. (2023). Interactive explainable deep learning model informs prostate cancer diagnosis at MRI. Radiology, 307(4), Article ID e222276. https://doi.org/10.1148/radiol.222276

Hong, S., Kim, S.H., Yoo, B., and Kim, J.Y. (2023). Deep learning algorithm for tumor segmentation and discrimination of clinically significant cancer in patients with prostate cancer. Current Oncology, 30(8), 7275–7285. https://doi.org/10.3390/curroncol30080528

Hosseinzadeh, M., Saha, A., Brand, P., Slootweg, I.R., de Rooij, M., and Huisman, H. (2022). Deep learning–assisted prostate cancer detection on bi-parametric MRI: Minimum training data size requirements and effect of prior knowledge. European Radiology, 32(4), 2224–2234. https://doi.org/10.1007/s00330-021-08320-y

Islam, R., and Layek, M.A. (2023). Stack ensemble mind: Enhancing well-being through accurate identification of human mental states using stack-based ensemble machine learning. Informatics in Medicine Unlocked, 43, Article ID 101405. https://doi.org/10.1016/j.imu.2023.101405

Ismail, M., Alam, M., Tahernezhadi, M., Vege, H.K., and Rajesh, P. (July 2020). A machine learning classification technique for predicting prostate cancer. *In:* Proceedings of the 2020 IEEE International Conference on Electro Information Technology (EIT), pp. 228–232. IEEE. https://doi.org/10.1109/EIT48999.2020.9208240

Lim, D.S., Kunder, C., Shao, W. et al. (2023). Mp55-12 improving automatic detection of prostate cancer on MRI with clinical history. Journal of Urology, 209(4).

Mehralivand, S., Yang, D., Harmon, S.A. et al. (2022). Deep learning based artificial intelligence for prostate cancer detection at biparametric MRI. Abdominal Radiology, 47(4), 1425–1434. https://doi.org/10.1007/s00261-022-03419-2

Tejaswi, A. (2022). Deep learning for prostate cancer risk prediction through image analysis of cells. https://www.divaportal.org/smash/get/diva2:1703702/FULLTEXT01.pdf.

Nematollahi, H., Moslehi, M., Aminolroayaei, F., Maleki, M., and Shahbazi-Gahrouei, D. (2023). Diagnostic performance evaluation of multiparametric magnetic resonance imaging in the detection of prostate cancer with supervised machine learning methods. Diagnostics, 13(4), 806. https://doi.org/10.3390/diagnostics13040806

Saha, A., Bosma, J., Twilt, J., van Ginneken, B., Yakar, D., Elschot, M., . . . and de Rooij, M. (2023, April). Artificial intelligence and radiologists at prostate cancer detection in MRI—The PI-CAI challenge. Medical Imaging with Deep Learning, Short Paper Track. https://openreview.net/forum?id=XfXcA9-0XxR.

Seibert, T.M., Garraway, I.P., Plym, A., Mahal, B.A., Giri, V., Jacobs, M.F., . . . and Morgan, T.M. (2023). Genetic risk prediction for prostate cancer: Implications for early detection and prevention. European Urology, 83(3), 241–248. https://doi.org/10.1016/j.eururo.2022.12.021

Talukder, M.A., Islam, M.M., Uddin, M.A., Akhter, A., Hasan, K.F., and Moni, M.A. (2022). Machine learning-based lung and mcolon cancer detection using deep feature extraction and ensemble learning. Expert Systems with Applications, 205, Article ID 117695. https://doi.org/10.1016/j.eswa.2022.117695

Talukder, M.A., Islam, M.M., Uddin, M.A. et al. (2023). An efficient deep learning model to categorize brain tumor using reconstruction and fine-tuning. Expert Systems with Applications, 230, Article ID 120534. https://doi.org/10.1016/j.eswa.2023.120534

CHAPTER

7

Healthcare Data and Analytics in Medical Internet of Things (MIoT)

R. Felista Sugirtha Lizy[1*(0000-0003-3648-0205)] **and I. Gusti Bagus Yosia Wiryakusuma**[2(0000-0001-5845-8661)]

[1] Department of Computer Science, A.P.C. Mahalaxmi College for Women, Thoothukudi, Tamil Nadu, India

[2] Department of International Business Management Universitas, Ciputra

1. Introduction

By way of a digital transformation, the healthcare industry is increasingly meeting the level of disruption associated with the emergence of "Internet of Things" (IoT) technologies that are largely applied to medical contexts – the Medical Internet of Things (MIoT). MIoT describes a network of connected medical devices, wearables, and sensors that continuously monitor the physiological characteristics of a patient, e.g., heart rate, blood glucose levels, oxygen saturation, etc.

The devices collect and produce enormous amounts of heterogeneous data in real time, providing an extraordinary opportunity to monitor health continuously, make early diagnoses, and tailor the treatment to the patient. Making meaningful inferences from these data troves will involve sophisticated data analytics.

This chapter explores the contours of health care data and analytics as a part of the MIoT ecosystem, the data sources, analytic methods, and the role of health care data analytics opportunities on health care delivery.

2. Literature Survey

Healthcare data analytics and the Medical Internet of Things (MIoT) have drawn much scholarly attention in the past ten years. This literature review focuses on documenting the most significant contributions, frameworks, and trends reported in

*Corresponding author: 21felistaa@gmail.com

DOI: 10.1201/9781003676812-7

scholarly and industry research, particularly concerning data generation, analytics methods, security issues, and real-world practice.

i. MIoT Data Generation and Characteristics

Literature discusses health care data produced by MIoT devices variably; there is consensus regarding the heterogeneity and quantity of data being generated. Aspects of MIoT data generation can be largely classified as continuous data, where Alotaibi et al. (2020) state it as continuous ECG, pressure, glucose data, etc. They highlight the necessity of effective data management strategies to absorb, store, or manage the volume of referred data flows in real time, as will be covered in detail.. In their research, Islam et al. (2015), reiterates the issue around developing dense and/or continuous data from multiple sources exaggerates the issue of variety as well as the quality of the data resulting from the sensors, as extraneous variables, noise, and missing observations must be managed or unnecessarily mislead pre-processing will have to take place to clean the data.

ii. MIoT Analytics Methods

Several researchers contribute to understanding how advanced analytics can be performed from MIoT data. Raghupathi and Raghupathi (2014) conducted a systematic review that identified the ways analytics were referred to, i.e., descriptive analytics, predictive analytics, and prescriptive analytics, and how machine learning (ML) and deep learning (DL) are key technologies in developing both diagnosis and prognosis.

For example, deep learning models, such as convolutional neural networks (CNNs), have been effectively utilized for medical imaging data from MIoT devices (Litjens et al., 2017). In addition, time series analysis using recurrent neural networks (RNN) and Long Short-Term Memory (LSTM) models for sensor-like data has shown potential for anomaly detection of the heart (Hannun et al., 2019).

iii. Real-time and Edge Analytics

To overcome the inherent latency in dealing with the transit of volumes of healthcare data, recent works support the recommendation for utilizing the edge-computing paradigm. Architectures that allow for partial pretreatment and analytics on the data source or close to the data generation location are highlighted by Shi et al. (2016). This allows more real-time decision-making in critical care monitoring. In turn, it reduces the bandwidth used over the network, as demonstrated in Satyanarayanan et al.'s study (Satyanarayanan et al., 2017).

iv. Security and Privacy Concerns

The privacy and security of MIoT's healthcare data appear to be a major research focus area. Zhang et al. (2018) examined MIoT potential vulnerabilities throughout MIoT networks, and supported encryption protocols and blockchain solutions for secure sharing of engagement activities. Factors like MIoT's adherence to regulatory framework (e.g., HIPAA and GDPR) further cloud the governing of MIoT data, as frontlined by Sun et al. (2020), and further described in Tang, Huang, and Tzeng (2022).

v. Applications and Use Cases

There have been several real-world examples of MIoT data analytics. The remote monitoring of patients with chronic diseases (e.g., diabetes, hypertension) is one of the most studied applications (Patel et al., 2012). Predictive maintenance of medical devices by developing analysis models can improve device availability and reliability (Chen et al., 2021). Public health surveillance with aggregated MIoT data has been shown to enhance epidemic prediction (Kumar et al., 2020).

vi. Gaps and Challenges in Current Research

Although there have been advancements, many open challenges still exist. The smooth transfer of data between MIoT platforms is hindered by the lack of standardized data formats and interoperability problems (Banaee et al., 2013).. How to manage large, multimodal healthcare datasets in real time while maintaining privacy is still being researched (Radanliev et al., 2020). Furthermore, there is a lack of research on explainable AI (XAI) techniques to address the explainability of AI/ML models employed in delicate healthcare decisions (Tjoa and Guan, 2020).

vii. Summary of Key Literature

Reference	Focus Area	Contribution	Limitations
Alotaibi et al. (2020)	MIoT data characteristics	Data volume and quality challenges	Limited real-time analytics focus
Raghupathi & Raghupathi (2014)	Analytics techniques	Categorization of healthcare analytics	Needs more MIoT-specific studies
Shi et al. (2016)	Edge computing in MIoT	Real-time analytics architectures	Early-stage implementations
Zhang et al. (2018)	Security and privacy	Blockchain for secure MIoT data	Scalability concerns
Hannun et al. (2019)	Deep learning for sensor data	Cardiac anomaly prediction	Model interpretability
Kumar et al. (2020)	Public health applications	Epidemic outbreak prediction	Data heterogeneity challenges

This survey characterizes the rapidly evolving and multidisciplinary nature of healthcare data analytics in MIoT. The integration of emerging technologies such as AI, edge computing, and blockchain is expected to develop new frameworks for overcoming old barriers. Future research is expected to focus thoroughly on scalable, interoperable, and transparent analytics frameworks that respect patient privacy and strive to improve healthcare outcomes.

3. Overview of MIoT in Healthcare

3.1. Definition and Scope

A specialized subset of the Internet of Things (IoT), the Medical Internet of Things (MIoT) addresses the electronic components and procedures of healthcare. MIoT uses the internet to connect to medical devices, sensors, and software applications to collect data from these devices and transmit and analyze function-related health data from patients. MIoT supports proactive communications between a patient, healthcare providers, and medical devices, supporting continuous monitoring of a patient, timely follow-up interventions, and data-based clinical decisions.

The MIoT can include such devices as implantable sensors that measure physiological parameters directly in the body, wearables that assess fitness and track physiological parameters externally, and smart equipment and devices in hospitals that can support optimizing and automating the facility's operations. MIoT's reach can include telemedicine and healthcare apps to allow remote diagnostics, consultations, and care management/patient education.

3.2. Key Components

MIoT systems have numerous essential components that work together to provide healthcare services:

- **Medical Devices or Sensors:** These devices collect data in the MIoT. These include every medical device capable of capturing physiological signals and health parameters, including ECG monitors, blood glucose sensors to monitor diabetes, pulse oximeters to measure oxygen saturation, smart inhalers to help with respiratory issues, and implantable devices such as a pacemaker, which continuously records the patients' physiological signals.
- **Communication Networks:** Communication is paramount in the MIoT. High reliability and low latency communications are important to ensure interoperability with wearables, sensors, and devices. For instance, 5G will enable a wireless connection with high speed and low latency appropriate for real-time streaming of massive volumes of data. Wi-Fi and Bluetooth Low Energy (BLE), which leverage Wi-Fi networks to provide short-range communication between several devices and the gateway to send data back to the MIoT, are further technologies.
- **Storage, Data, and Cloud Platforms:** Data collected from the MIoT will be transmitted to data repositories, which are often cloud-based. These cloud data platforms not only store large amounts of healthcare information, but they can also house scalable platforms for service and community data management, back-up, and access. By implementing cloud services, healthcare providers can have simultaneous access to patient data from the same platform, which enables collaborative patient care and continuity of care with health records being maintained over time.
- **Analytics Engines:** The ability to process and interpret healthcare data is the main benefit of MIoT. Analytics engines provide algorithms and software tools, such as machine learning and artificial intelligence models, that may examine gathered data for possible trends, abnormalities, and predictive powers. Analytics generates the information needed for decision support for diagnosis, treatment plans, and patient management.

3.3. Benefits of MIoT in Healthcare

The use of MIoT technology in healthcare offers many benefits (Figure 1) and is changing the traditional delivery of care:

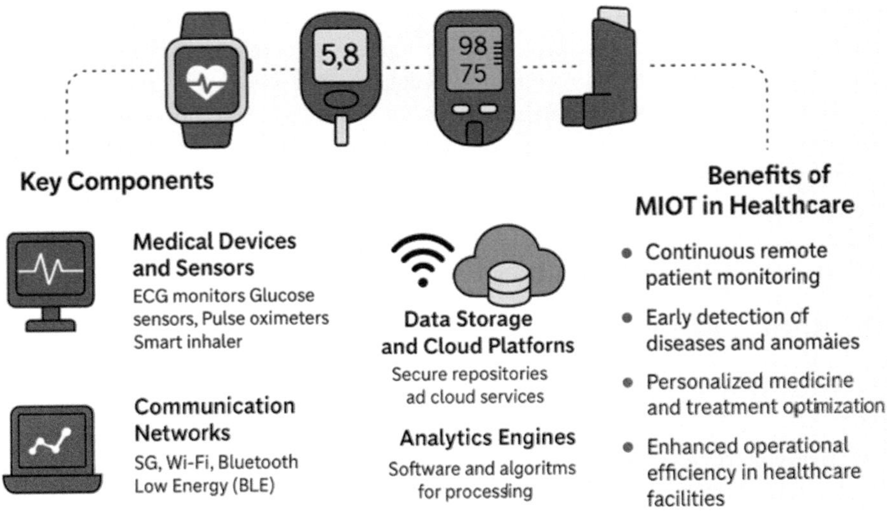

Figure 1: Overview of MIoT in healthcare.

- **Continuous Remote Patient Monitoring:** MIoT facilitates real-time monitoring of the patients' vital signs outside of the hospital environment, enabling clinicians to continue managing patients with chronic disease or post-operative recovery remotely. This means less time spent at the clinic or hospital and easier early intervention.
- **Detection of Diseases and Anomalies:** Detecting diseases and anomalies early on is crucial. MIoT systems are designed to keep a constant watch, analyzing complex data to spot any unusual patterns or early symptoms of health issues. We can significantly improve patient outcomes by rapidly detecting illnesses and offering preventive care.
- **Personalized Medicine and Optimized Treatments:** Better therapies may result from treatment plans that are carefully adapted to each patient's unique physiological condition and lifestyle circumstances. MIoT data is rich in patient insights and offers important facts about how each patient responds to their surroundings.
- **Better Efficiency in Care Delivery:** Smart hospital equipment and interrelated systems offer automated tasks (such as ordering medical supplies, keeping medical inventory, and managing daily resources) in place of administrators, showing a good deal of improvement in efficiency or quality of care through MIoT implementation.

4. Characteristics of Healthcare Data in MIoT

Healthcare data generated by Medical Internet of Things (MIoT) devices has several essential characteristics that distinguish it from traditional healthcare data. Two of the most pertinent characteristics are volume and velocity. Volume refers to the tendency for MIoT devices to continuously monitor a patient, resulting in the collection of a tremendous amount of data that translates into gigabytes (GB) or even terabytes (TB) per day in certain hospital environments with multiple smart devices. For example, the continuous monitoring of vital signs, movement, and a range of other physical and physiologic parameters may result in wearable monitors, implantable sensors, or smart beds that are constantly providing the volume of data back to a healthcare provider.

Furthermore, because MIoT data is created and sent in real-time, it frequently needs to be evaluated immediately or very soon to facilitate quick clinical choices. In particular, a device that detects an abnormal pulse or cardiac rhythm needs to interpret and deliver data in real-time so that a healthcare clinician can determine whether there is an emergency. MIoT data will always require the ability to process data at terribly high "data processing" speeds. The healthcare systems will often need the benefits of edge computing and low-latency networks for real-time processing and usage of MIoT data.

In terms of variety, MIoT healthcare data presents many different types of data elements. There are structured data, such as numbers (e.g., heart rate, temperature), semi-structured data, such as logs and metadata, and unstructured data, such as medical images and voice, and video recordings. Due to the variety of data types, new technologies like AI, ML, and NLP can be used to analyze and potentially combine different data types to create useful information.

The veracity of MIoT data deals with whether the data is accurate and can be trusted. If data is coming from sensors to the computer wirelessly, operational and data losses may occur, such as improper sensor functioning, interference, and loss of data altogether, resulting in unreliable data and bad diagnoses and treatment decisions. This makes data validation, calibration, and error checking processes important tasks to consider for MIoT systems (see Figure 2).

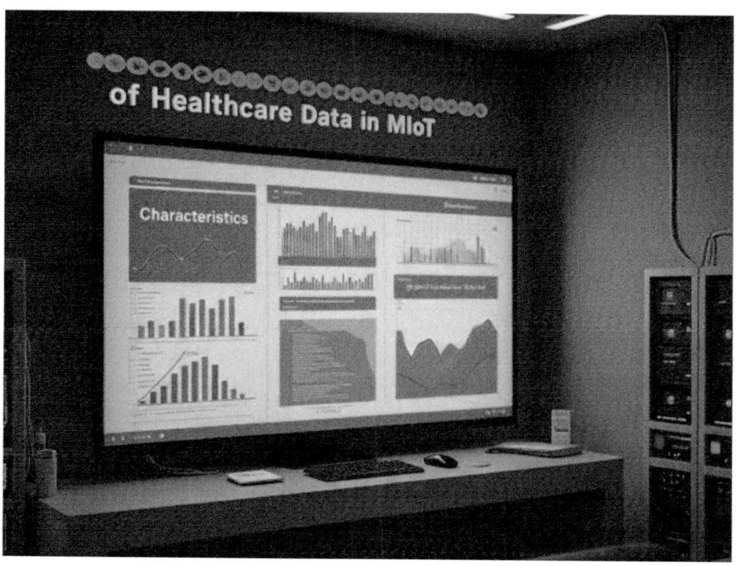

Figure 2: Characteristics of healthcare data in MIoT.

Lastly, privacy and security are serious concerns. The MIoT systems manage extremely sensitive patient information that needs to ensure compliance with established regulatory standards for data protection. In the United States, an example of a regulatory standard is HIPAA, while in the European Union, it is GDPR. Further, there is a risk in MIoT systems as a patient's data may be left exposed or become accessible through unauthorized access, which may occur due to hacking or a data breach during the transmission of data. Solutions for robust privacy and security may require specific features such as end-to-end encryption, secure access controls, and distributed ledger technology (Blockchain) for maintaining the integrity of the data. Audits to determine compliance and the weight of privacy laws will help to retain patients' trust in the MIoT system, while ensuring the confidentiality of their health data.

Table 1 contains a summary of the Attributes of Healthcare Data in MIoT. According to the provided description, it comprehensively summarizes each characteristic.

Table 1: The Characteristics of Healthcare Data in MIoT

Characteristic	Description	Example/Implication
High Volume	Continuous monitoring by MIoT devices leads to the generation of large-scale healthcare data, often in real time.	Smart ICU beds generate thousands of data points per minute.
High Velocity	Data is produced and transmitted in real time, requiring immediate processing for timely clinical actions.	Real-time arrhythmia detection triggers emergency alerts.
Variety	Data is heterogeneous, including structured, semi-structured, and unstructured formats such as numbers, logs, images, and audio.	Integration of heart rate readings, MRI scans, and patient voice notes using AI and machine learning techniques.
Veracity	Data quality can be inconsistent due to sensor errors, noise, environmental interference, or data loss during transmission.	Inaccurate data may lead to misdiagnosis; validation and cleaning are essential.
Privacy & Security	Data contains sensitive personal health information requiring strict protection and compliance with regulations like HIPAA and GDPR.	Use of encryption, access controls, and secure data protocols to prevent breaches and ensure confidentiality.

The nature of healthcare data in the MIoT environment presents specific difficulties, characteristics, and areas of concern, given the nature of healthcare data in MIoT—with the 5Vs, high volume, high velocity, variety, veracity, and privacy—special data management and strong compliance will help ensure safe and effective healthcare services.

5. Data Analytics Techniques in MIoT Healthcare

In the Medical Internet of Things (MIoT) ecosystem, there are numerous data analytics strategies available to provide context to the enormous quantity and complexity of healthcare information collected by smart devices in healthcare.

Data analytics is valuable for optimizing patient care, healthcare processes, and clinical decision-making (Figure 3). The main types are:

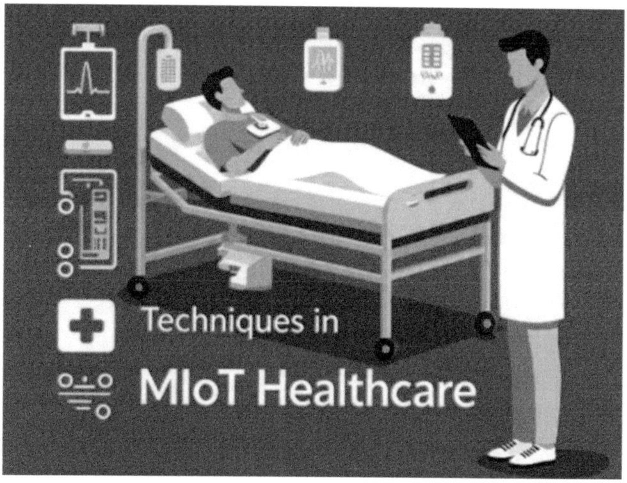

Figure 3: Data analytics techniques in MIoT healthcare.

5.1. Descriptive Analytics

Descriptive analytics assist in making sense of past events to identify past patterns and patient health patterns. While it provides an understanding of what has occurred, it can still be beneficial for reporting and monitoring.

Example: A clinician may want to evaluate whether a patient's blood pressure is stable or improving by determining his/her average blood pressure over the last week (Figure 4).

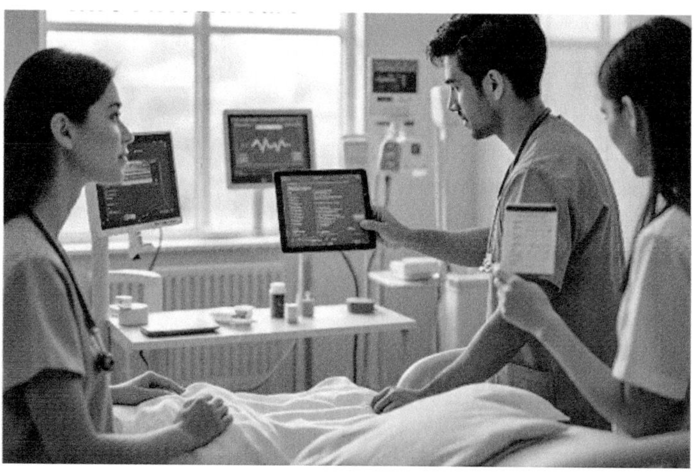

Figure 4: Descriptive analytics techniques in MIoT healthcare.

5.2. Diagnostic Analytics

The concept behind diagnostic analytics is figuring out the mnemonics and explanations for a health condition or an issue with device performance. Diagnostic analytics intends to explore the data even further to determine what may have created the health condition or device performance issue.

Example: Assessing data trends of heart rate data to determine the potential "cause" of erratic heartbeats, such as arrhythmia (Figure 5).

Figure 5: Diagnostic analytics techniques in MIoT healthcare.

5.3. Predictive Analytics

This technique uses machine learning and statistical models to predict future health situations and risks – allowing for less reactive care and more proactive care when anticipating the possibility of problems.

Example: Predicting the chances of stroke based on the current vital signs and history of the patient (Figure 6).

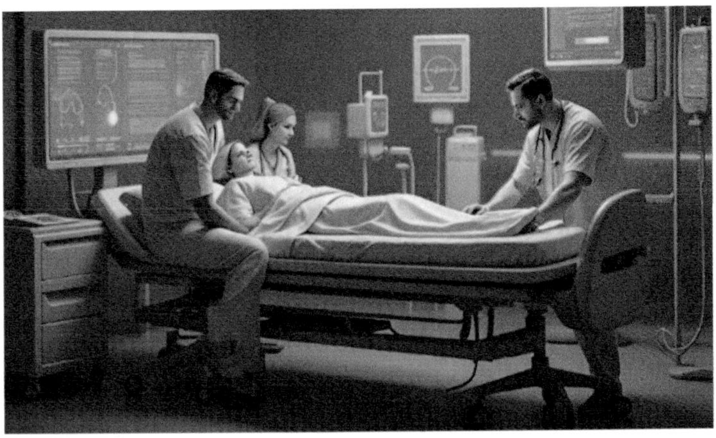

Figure 6: Predictive analytics techniques in MIoT healthcare.

5.4. Prescriptive Analytics

Prescriptive analytics goes even further, as this type of analysis focuses on recommending actions or treatment plans based on predictions (s) alone. If predictive analysis involves lots of data and searching for similar cases to guide a decision, prescriptive analysis must provide treatment recommendations. This analysis will provide support for personalized medicine and the decision-making process.

Example: Content recommending dose or dietary changes after analyzing trends in glucose levels (Figure 7).

Figure 7: Prescriptive analytics techniques in MIoT healthcare.

5.5. Real-time Analytics

Real-time analytics enables streaming data to be used as soon as it's available, allowing for notification and intervention during critical events. Real-time analytics is important when emergency response and near real-time notification are necessary for continuous patient monitoring.

Example: If a patient's oxygen saturation drops to a dangerous level, the system could instantly notify healthcare providers or emergency services (Figure 8).

These analytics techniques increase the efficiency, accuracy, and responsiveness of MIoT-powered healthcare systems to improve patient outcomes.

Table 2 provides examples and a clear relationship between the various data analytics approaches used in MIoT healthcare.

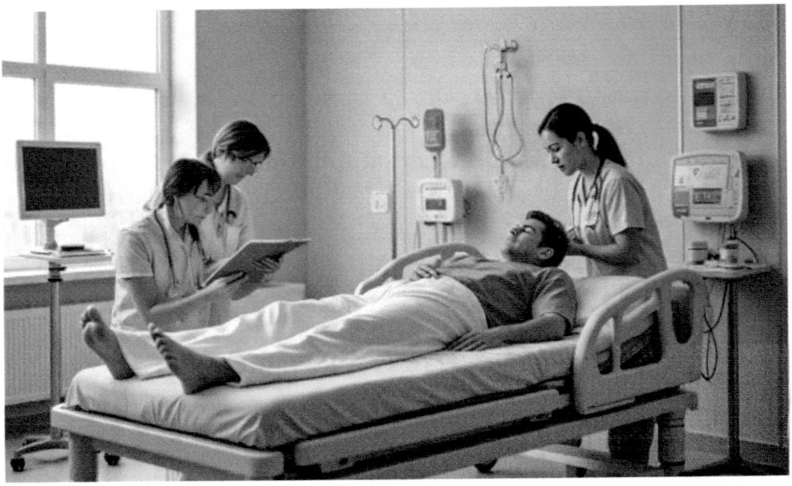

Figure 8: Real-time analytics techniques in MIoT healthcare.

Table 2: The Different Data Analytics Techniques in MIoT Healthcare

Technique	Purpose	Example in MIoT Healthcare
Descriptive Analytics	Summarizes historical data to identify trends or patterns	Calculating average blood pressure readings over a week to monitor patient stability
Diagnostic Analytics	Analyzes data to find causes of health issues or device faults	Investigating irregular heartbeats to determine if the patient has arrhythmia
Predictive Analytics	Forecasts future health events using ML/statistical models	Predicting the risk of a stroke using real-time vital signs and patient history
Prescriptive Analytics	Recommends treatment or actions based on predictive insights	Suggesting medication or insulin adjustments based on glucose monitoring trends
Real-time Analytics	Processes live data for immediate alerts and responses	Sending alerts to emergency services when oxygen saturation drops to a critical level

6. Key Analytics Methods and Tools in MIoT

In medical IoT, analytics is the key to success. It is imperative to employ the health data for wearables and sensors; what is required is methods to analyze and produce workable data.

6.1. Machine Learning

SVMs, Random Forests, and Neural Networks are the heavy-lifting team.. They are constantly spotting odd trends or identifying anomalies in your health data.

Let us take the Random Forests technique as an example. Imagine your Fitbit is constantly sending heart rate, blood pressure, O2 levels, etc. A good Random Forest model can examine all the data available and advise you to take medical precautions to prevent a medical episode such as a heart attack. Figure 9 is an example of how algorithms can decipher relevant information from 'noisy' data.

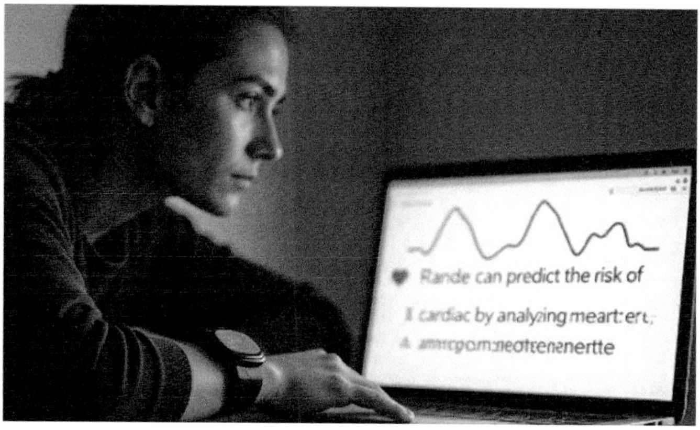

Figure 9: A random forest model – wearable devices.

6.2. Deep Learning

Deep learning techniques such as Convolutional Neural Networks (CNNs) and Recurrent Neural Networks (RNNs) can readily process complex datasets such as images and time series data.

For instance, a CNN can automatically identify tumors in a CT scan, and an RNN can monitor and predict abnormal breathing patterns by utilizing continuous data from a respiratory sensor (Figure 10).

Figure 10: CNN and RNN monitor.

6.3. Edge Analytics

Edge analytics involves processing data on MIoT devices or edge gateways, minimizing data transport latency and bandwidth overhead.

For example, direct access to blood sugar level data on a smart insulin pump that adjusts the delivery of insulin based on in-device blood sugar readings, not requiring cloud communication (refer to Figure 11).

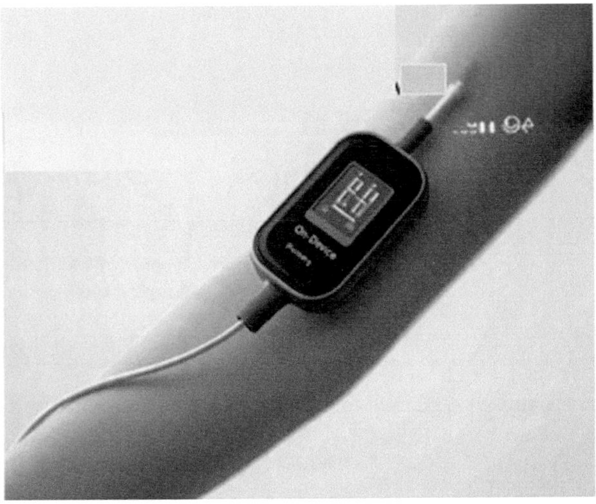

Figure 11: Smart insulin pump: seamless diabetes management.

6.4. Big Data Analytics Platforms

Platforms like Apache Hadoop and Apache Spark can handle and store MIoT data on a large scale. For example, hospitals utilize Apache Spark to process real-time emergency and ICU patient data from thousands of sensors to determine the long-term trends of ICU patient recoveries (see Figure 12).

Figure 12: Smarter healthcare, faster recovery: Apache Spark in action.

6.5. Data Visualization

Tools and dashboards with visuals transform complicated data into formats that health experts can easily understand.

Example: One hospital has a dashboard that shows, in real time, all the vitals of patients in a ward, using color-coded alerts for abnormal values, which allows doctors to easily see every patient who requires immediate attention (see Figure 13).

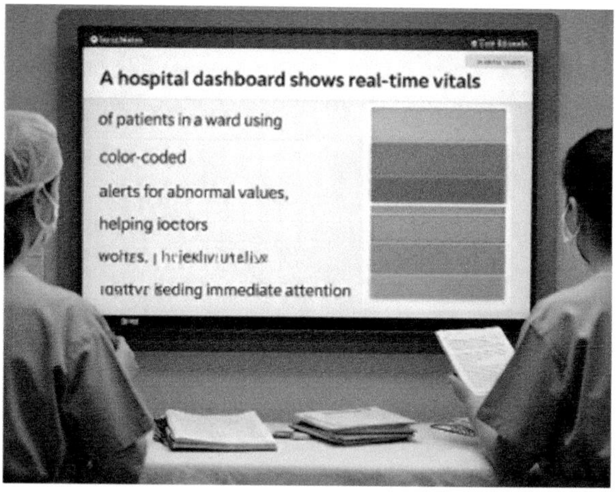

Figure 13: Real-time patient monitoring: swift response to critical needs.

In Table 3, we will summarize the Key Analytics Methods and Tools available in MIoT with descriptions and examples.

Table 3: The Key Analytics Methods and Tools in MIoT

Method/Tool	Description	Example
Machine Learning (ML)	Algorithms like SVM, Random Forest, and Neural Networks identify patterns and detect anomalies.	Random Forest predicting cardiac arrest risk from wearable sensor data.
Deep Learning	CNNs and RNNs analyze complex data such as medical images and time-series signals.	CNN detecting tumors in CT scans; RNN predicting abnormal breathing from respiratory sensor data.
Edge Analytics	Data is processed locally on devices or gateways to reduce latency and bandwidth usage.	Smart insulin pump adjusts dosage in real-time based on on-device glucose readings.
Big Data Analytics Platforms	Tools like Apache Hadoop and Spark enable scalable processing of large MIoT datasets.	Hospitals are analyzing ICU patient data trends using Apache Spark.
Data Visualization	Dashboards and visual analytics help healthcare professionals interpret complex data.	Real-time patient vital signs dashboard with color-coded alerts for immediate attention.

These tools and methods enable MIoT systems to provide health care services that are smarter, faster, and more accurate.

7. Challenges in Healthcare Data Analytics for MIoT

Data Privacy and Security is a major issue as MIoT devices handle sensitive personal patient data. They must ensure that data is encrypted, securely transmitted, compliant with standards such as HIPAA, and that they limit unauthorized access and data breaches.

Example: To ensure patient data confidentiality, a wearable health monitor encrypts data on the device before sending it to the cloud (Figure 14).

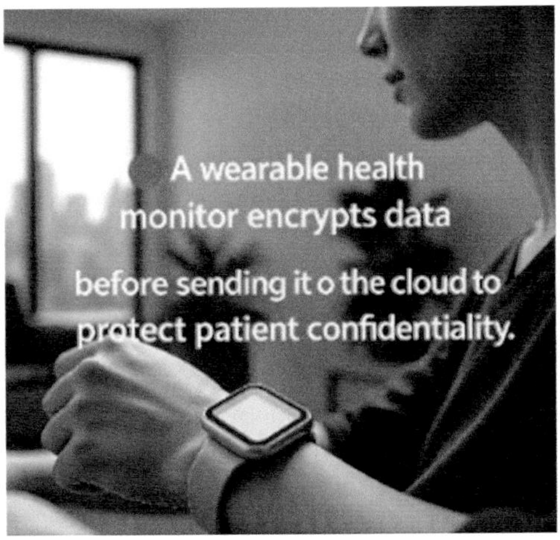

Figure 14: Secure health monitoring: encrypting data for patient privacy.

Interoperability consists of aggregating data from different MIoT devices and platforms, which utilize different communication protocols and data formats. The lack of standardization can impede fluid data sharing.

For example, the hospital struggles to aggregate data from different vendors' devices because the vendors' systems do not interact smoothly (Figure 15)

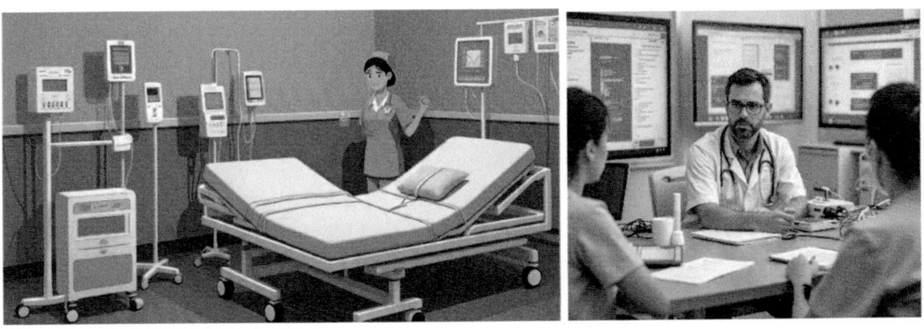

Figure 15: Interoperability challenges in healthcare data integration.

Data quality is commonly diminished through incomplete, noisy, or inconsistent data, caused by sensors subject to environmental conditions or errors in sensing devices. Poor quality data can lead to an invalid analysis.

Example: Motion artefacts from conflicting data markers of an ECG lead prevent accurate conclusions about heart conditions (Figure 16).

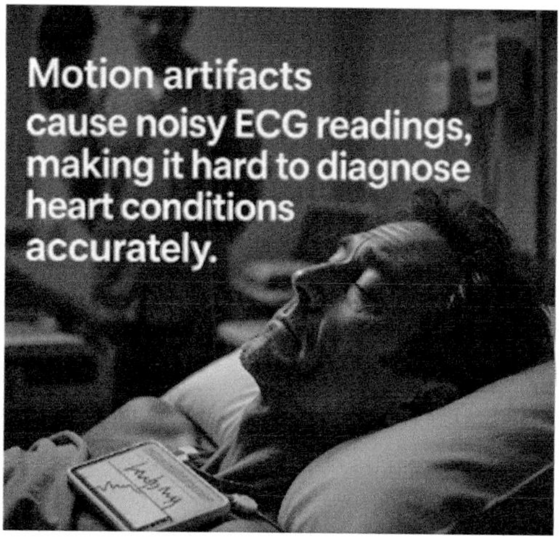

Figure 16: Noisy ECG signals: motion artifacts obscure diagnosis.

The massive data production from many devices in MIoT systems presents scalability problems. Such systems have an instantaneous need for robust infrastructure to save, process, and analyze the data quickly and effectively. Consider a case when a particular government health monitoring system must scale its cloud environment in real-time to receive data from millions of connected devices (see Figure 17).

Figure 17: Handling big health data: scalable cloud solutions.

Latency is the lag time between data generation and data analysis. Low latency is necessary for real-time healthcare decisions, but device and network computing limits will result in latency. The goal is to balance speed and resource constraints.

Example: A remote monitoring system performs local processing of critical patient alerts locally and is used to meet latency requirements rather than relying on cloud servers that are more distant and incur more latency (Figure 18).

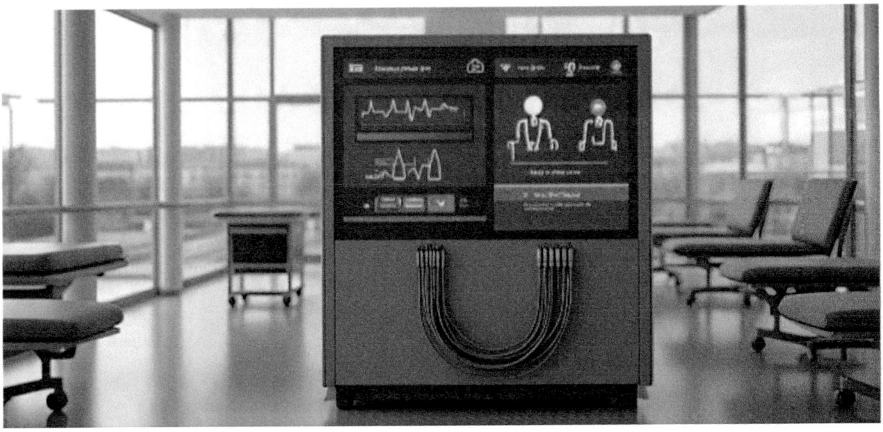

Figure 18: A remote monitoring system process.

Table 4 lists the Challenges in Healthcare Data Analytics in MIoT with definitions and examples.

Table 4: The Challenges in Healthcare Data Analytics for MIoT

Challenge	Description	Example
Data Privacy and Security	Protecting sensitive patient data through encryption, secure transmission, and regulatory compliance.	Wearable health monitors encrypt data before sending it to the cloud to ensure confidentiality.
Interoperability	Integrating diverse devices and platforms that use different protocols and data formats.	Hospitals struggle to combine data from multiple vendors due to incompatible systems.
Data Quality	Managing incomplete, noisy, or inconsistent data caused by sensor errors or environmental factors.	Noisy ECG readings caused by patient movement make accurate diagnosis difficult.
Scalability	Handling the large volume of data generated by numerous MIoT devices requires robust infrastructure.	National health systems are scaling cloud resources to process data from millions of devices.
Latency	Reducing delays in data processing to support real-time healthcare decisions despite resource limits.	Processing patient alerts locally on devices to minimize delay instead of relying on the cloud.

These challenges need to be overcome if we want to take full advantage of MIoT for healthcare.

8. Case Studies and Applications in MIoT Healthcare

The Medical Internet of Things (MIoT) has changed the way healthcare and public health approach healthcare delivery by allowing real-time collection, evaluation, and decision support from various interconnected medical devices. The domains of MIoT in practicum are extensive, ranging from patient care, equipment management, public health monitoring, program evaluation, and regulatory compliance. The role of MIoT in healthcare case studies demonstrates how these technologies are being used collectively to improve clinical outcomes, operational efficiencies, and provide timely responses (Table 5). Exploring examples such as remote patient monitoring, predictive maintenance of medical equipment, and forecasting of an epidemic outbreak can increase understanding of MIoT implications and effects on present-day healthcare systems.

Table 5: Case Studies and Applications in MIoT Healthcare

Application	Description	Example
Remote Patient Monitoring	Continuous collection of vitals for chronic disease management to reduce hospital visits.	Connected glucose monitors send real-time data to doctors for timely treatment adjustments.
Predictive Maintenance	Analytics predict equipment failures to avoid downtime and ensure continuous healthcare service.	MRI machines are monitored to schedule maintenance before breakdowns occur.
Epidemic Outbreak Prediction	Aggregated MIoT data supports early detection and containment of infectious disease outbreaks.	Wearable devices detect increased flu symptoms in a community, alerting health officials early.

8.1. Remote Patient Monitoring

Remote patient monitoring employs MIoT devices that continually collect vital signs, including blood pressure, glucose levels, and heart rate. Remote patient monitoring is especially helpful to patients managing chronic diseases like diabetes and hypertension, as it minimizes the need to frequently visit the hospital and allows healthcare providers to intervene and act sooner.

Example. A diabetic patient will use a connected glucose monitor so that the data from the monitor is sent directly to their doctor in real time, which allows doctors to adjust medications promptly (Figure 19).

8.2. Predictive Maintenance of Medical Equipment

By using analytics on MIoT device data, healthcare providers can determine when their equipment is likely to fail (for example, a ventilator or infusion pump) and perform proactive maintenance; thus, reducing downtime and ensuring the medical device remains available.

Figure 19: Diabetes management redefined: real-time data, timely adjustments.

For example, A hospital is using sensor data on its MRI machines to predict and schedule maintenance before the MRI machine breaks, and incurs significant service costs (Figure 20).

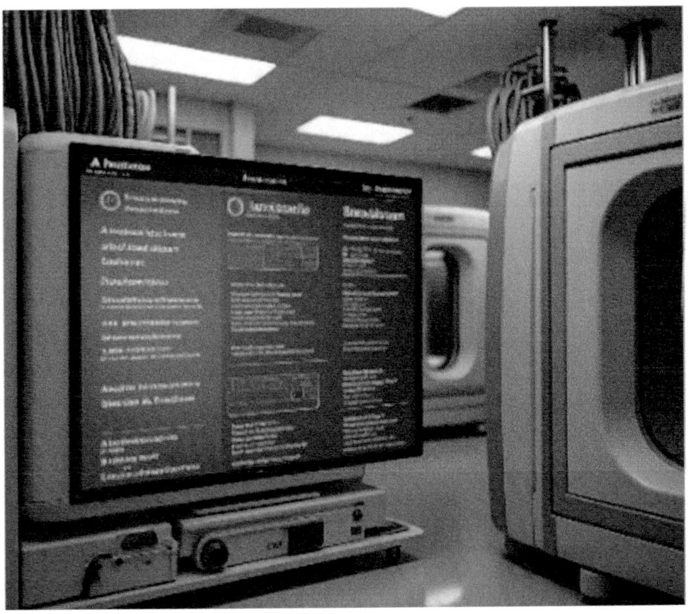

Figure 20: Sensor-driven insights: proactive MRI maintenance.

8.3. Epidemic Outbreak Prediction

As data from many MIoT devices is correlated and recorded, the early signs of infectious disease outbreaks can be determined by monitoring symptoms and vital signs in the context of populations. This allows for a quick and effective response to outbreaks by public health officials, allowing for containment of epidemic threats.

For example, the usage of wearable devices, by monitoring the temperature and respiratory rate of individuals across a wider community, an increase in flu-like symptoms and communicate as an early warning to health authorities (see Figure 21).

Figure 21: Tracking health trends: wearables support public health surveillance.

9. Future Trends and Research Directions

Integration with Artificial Intelligence (AI): The future of MIoT includes more sophisticated AI models that improve the accuracy of each prediction as well as provide more individualized healthcare. AIs will utilize the large amount of complex data being analyzed to customize a treatment plan based on an individual patient.

Example: Intricate algorithms delivered by AIs that improve the prediction of the patient's disease process based on the patient-specific MIoT data (Figure 22).

Figure 22: MIoT data meets AI: predicting disease progression.

Data Security Using Blockchain: Blockchain technology provides a decentralized way that is tamper-proof way to secure data collected in health care from MIoT devices. It allows for data traceability, privacy, and integrity without requiring a central authority.

Example: Using blockchain to securely record the health records of a patient using several MIoT devices, and to share that information among authorized providers (see Figure 23).

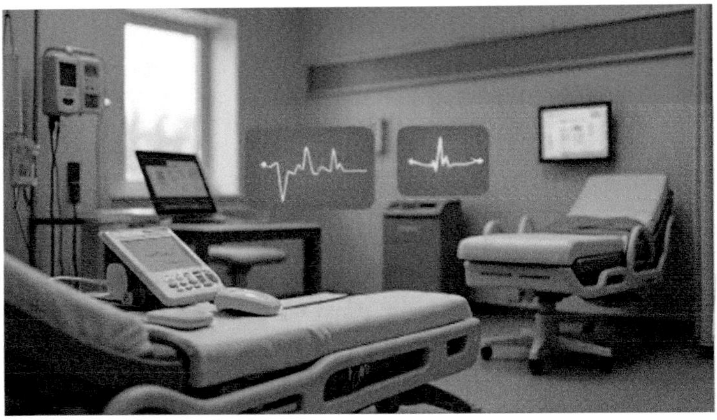

Figure 23: Secure health records: blockchain for MIoT data sharing.

The MIoT of 5G: The deployment of 5G networks will provide an ultra-low latency zone and bandwidth that is critical for real-time data transfer and analytics in healthcare. This will allow for faster responses and an improved ability to monitor remotely.

Example: Remote surgeries where MIoT devices allow for real-time surgery using video and sensor feedback, thanks to the 5G connection shown in Figure 24.

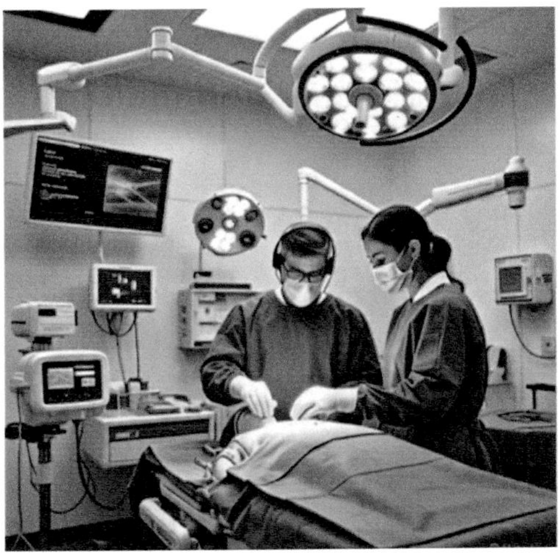

Figure 24: Remote surgery enabled by MIoT and 5G.

XAI (eXplainable AI): To develop trust in AI in healthcare, eXplainable AI methods are being developed to elucidate how AI models make their decisions (increased transparency) to facilitate a level of clinical acceptance of AI in healthcare.

Example: An AI system that predicts a diagnosis, but that also provides reasons behind its conclusions to physicians in an understandable way (see Figure 25).

Figure 25: AI system providing understandable diagnosis reasons.

Standardization Initiatives: Research continues to create unified protocols and standards to enable interoperability and secure data sharing across the many different MIoT devices and platforms. Consider the example of the adoption of common communication standards allowing different MIoT devices to work together within a hospital ecosystem (Figure 26).

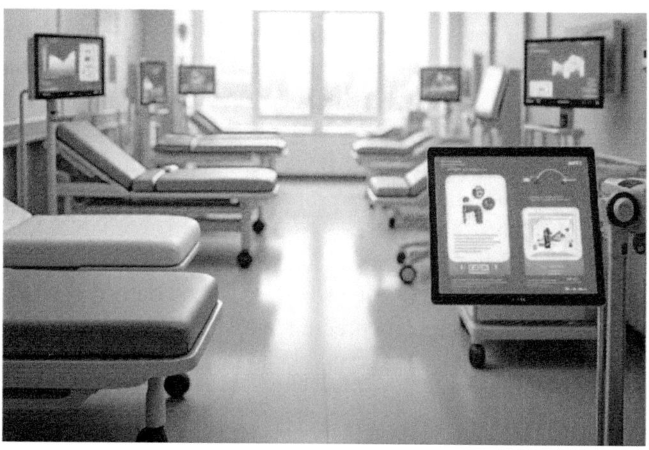

Figure 26: Harmonized MIoT ecosystem in hospitals.

Table 6 shows us the Future Trends and Research Directions in MIoT healthcare.

Table 6: The Future Trends and Research Directions

Trend/Direction	Description	Example
Integration with AI	Advanced AI models enhance predictive accuracy and personalized healthcare.	AI algorithms predicting disease progression using individual patient MIoT data.
Blockchain for Data Security	Distributed ledger technology secures data integrity and privacy without central control.	Using blockchain to securely share patient records from MIoT devices among healthcare providers.
5G-enabled MIoT	5G networks provide ultra-low latency and high bandwidth for real-time data transmission and analytics.	Remote surgeries with real-time sensor and video feedback enabled by 5G connectivity.
Explainable AI (XAI)	AI systems offer transparency by explaining their decision-making processes to build clinical trust.	AI diagnoses a condition while providing understandable reasons for its conclusions to doctors.
Standardization Efforts	Developing unified protocols for interoperability and secure data sharing across MIoT platforms.	Adoption of common standards enabling seamless communication between different MIoT devices in hospitals.

These emerging trends will be a force behind the next set of intelligent, secure, and efficient healthcare systems that will be driven by MIoT.

10. Conclusion

Healthcare data and analytics form the foundation of MIoT's transformative capacity to influence how we see and administer modern medicine. With MIoT, high volumes of real-time health data are analyzed to inform smarter, customized, and preventative healthcare. While privacy, interoperability, and data quality issues exist, prolific innovation opens new landscapes where healthcare is interconnected, proactive, and efficient.

Combine state-of-the-art technology from artificial intelligence, blockchain, and 5G connectivity into MIoT, and the possibilities grow exponentially, producing an ecosystem of new products and services based on secure, reliable, and responsive MIoT systems. The potential is limitless as healthcare providers eagerly embrace digital solutions that eventually result in better patient outcomes through prompt interventions, remote monitoring, and predictive maintenance of medical equipment.

Furthermore, current and ongoing work in the areas of standardization and explainable AI will ensure reasonable assurance to providers, patients, and all healthcare platforms that they can trust new solutions, focusing instead on collaboration, cooperation, and integration. Because MIoT encompasses data management and analytics as a system-wide approach, it can reduce costs by focusing attention on greater access for patients and households by giving them greater autonomy in controlling their health information.

Thus, MIoT will transform healthcare delivery by eliminating barriers between patients, providers, and technology, ultimately building a more resilient, fulfilling, and innovative healthcare environment for patients.

References

Alotaibi, E., Federico, P., and Wills, G. (2020). Internet of medical things: Review of recent advances and future challenges. Journal of Network and Computer Applications, 167, 102686. https://doi.org/10.1016/j.jnca.2020.102686

Banaee, H., Ahmed, M.U., and Loutfi, A. (2013). Data mining for wearable sensors in health monitoring systems: A review of recent trends and challenges. Sensors, 13(12), 17472–17500. https://doi.org/10.3390/s131217472

Chen, M., Hao, Y., Hwang, K., Wang, L., and Wang, L. (2021). Disease prediction by machine learning over big data from healthcare communities. IEEE Access, 7, 118517–118529. https://doi.org/10.1109/ACCESS.2019.2940023

Hannun, A.Y., Rajpurkar, P., Haghpanahi, M., Tison, G.H., Bourn, C., Turakhia, M.P., and Ng, A.Y. (2019). Cardiologist-level arrhythmia detection and classification in ambulatory electrocardiograms using a deep neural network. Nature Medicine, 25(1), 65–69. https://doi.org/10.1038/s41591-018-0268-3

Islam, S.M.R., Kwak, D., Kabir, M.H., Hossain, M., and Kwak, K.S. (2015). The Internet of things for health care: A comprehensive survey. IEEE Access, 3, 678–708. https://doi.org/10.1109/ACCESS.2015.2437951

Kumar, N., and Mallick, P.K. (2020). The Internet of things: Insights into the building blocks, component interactions, and architecture layers. Procedia Computer Science, 132, 109–117. https://doi.org/10.1016/j.procs.2018.05.199

Litjens, G., Kooi, T., Bejnordi, B.E., Setio, A.A., Ciompi, F., Ghafoorian, M., and Sánchez, C.I. (2017). A survey on deep learning in medical image analysis. Medical Image Analysis, 42, 60–88. https://doi.org/10.1016/j.media.2017.07.005

Patel, S., Park, H., Bonato, P., Chan, L., and Rodgers, M. (2012). A review of wearable sensors and systems with application in rehabilitation. Journal of NeuroEngineering and Rehabilitation, 9(1), 21. https://doi.org/10.1186/1743-0003-9-21

Radanliev, P., De Roure, D., Walton, R., Van Kleek, M., Montalvo, R.M., Cannady, S., and Nurse, J.R. (2020). Artificial intelligence and machine learning for COVID-19 – Real-time monitoring of social media and epidemic outbreak. Sensors, 20(16), 4334. https://doi.org/10.3390/s20164334

Raghupathi, W., and Raghupathi, V. (2014). Big data analytics in healthcare: Promise and potential. Health Information Science and Systems, 2(1), 3. https://doi.org/10.1186/2047-2501-2-3

Satyanarayanan, M., Bahl, P., Cáceres, R., and Davies, N. (2017). The case for edge computing. IEEE Pervasive Computing, 8(4), 37–43. https://doi.org/10.1109/MPRV.2009.82

Shi, W., Cao, J., Zhang, Q., Li, Y., and Xu, L. (2016). Edge computing: Vision and challenges. IEEE Internet of Things Journal, 3(5), 637–646. https://doi.org/10.1109/JIOT.2016.2579198

Sun, Y., Zhang, L., & Yao, S. (2020). Privacy-preserving in medical Internet of things: A survey. IEEE Internet of Things Journal, 7(7), 5826–5838. https://doi.org/10.1109/JIOT.2020.2967692

Tang, C., Huang, Y., and Tzeng, W. (2022). A privacy-aware access control scheme for healthcare IoT under GDPR and HIPAA compliance. *In:* Proceedings of the IEEE International Conference on Smart Healthcare Systems (ICSH 2022), pp. 145–152.

Tjoa, E., and Guan, C. (2020). A survey on Explainable Artificial Intelligence (XAI): Toward medical XAI. IEEE Transactions on Neural Networks and Learning Systems, 32(11), 4793–4813. https://doi.org/10.1109/TNNLS.2020.3027314

Zhang, R., Xue, R., and Liu, L. (2018). Security and privacy on Blockchain. ACM Computing Surveys, 52(3), 1–34. https://doi.org/10.1145/3195024

CHAPTER
8

Wearable and Implantable Medical Internet of Things Devices

Mohan Singh[1*(0000-0002-2973-3676)], **Seema Singh**[2(0009-0009-4776-2241)], **Kapil Dev Tyagi**[3(0000-0002-4596-2321)] **and Vaibhav Bhushan Tyagi**[4(0000-0001-8153-3607)]

[1] Department of ECE, G.L. Bajaj Institute of Technology and Management, Greater Noida – 201308, India
[2] Department of Education, Lloyd Institute of Management & Technology, Greater Noida – 201306, India
[3] Department of ECE, Jaypee Institute of Information Technology, Noida – 201309, India
[4] Department of ECE, ISBAT University, Kampala-8383, Uganda

1. Introduction

IoT (Internet of Things) has affected almost all aspects of modern life and changed the way we view technology and both our physical as well as environmental surroundings. At the same time, the Medical Internet of Things (MIoT) has developed as one of the most significant transformations in the healthcare industry, with the potential to fundamentally change the way medicine is practiced and improve health outcomes (Aledhari et al., 2022). IoT technology and Healthcare IoT data are already being used in various areas, such as telemedicine, remote patient monitoring, chronic disease management, and personalized care interventions. The advent of mobile devices and the wide accessibility of the Internet have brought to life a new technology era, where "things" talk to each other and connect to the Internet for many different purposes (Khan and Alam, 2021). Objects can now be accessed and controlled from a distance with the Internet of Things, improving accuracy, saving money, and optimizing performance, and have been adopted in smart homes, car navigation, health management, and smart cities, as shown in Figure 1.

IoT-based assets in the healthcare domain will help in real-time tracking, telemedicine, and online monitoring, improving patient assistance and reducing stress on healthcare infrastructure. This evolution further applies to wearable and

*Corresponding author: mohansingh571@gmail.com

DOI: 10.1201/9781003676812-8

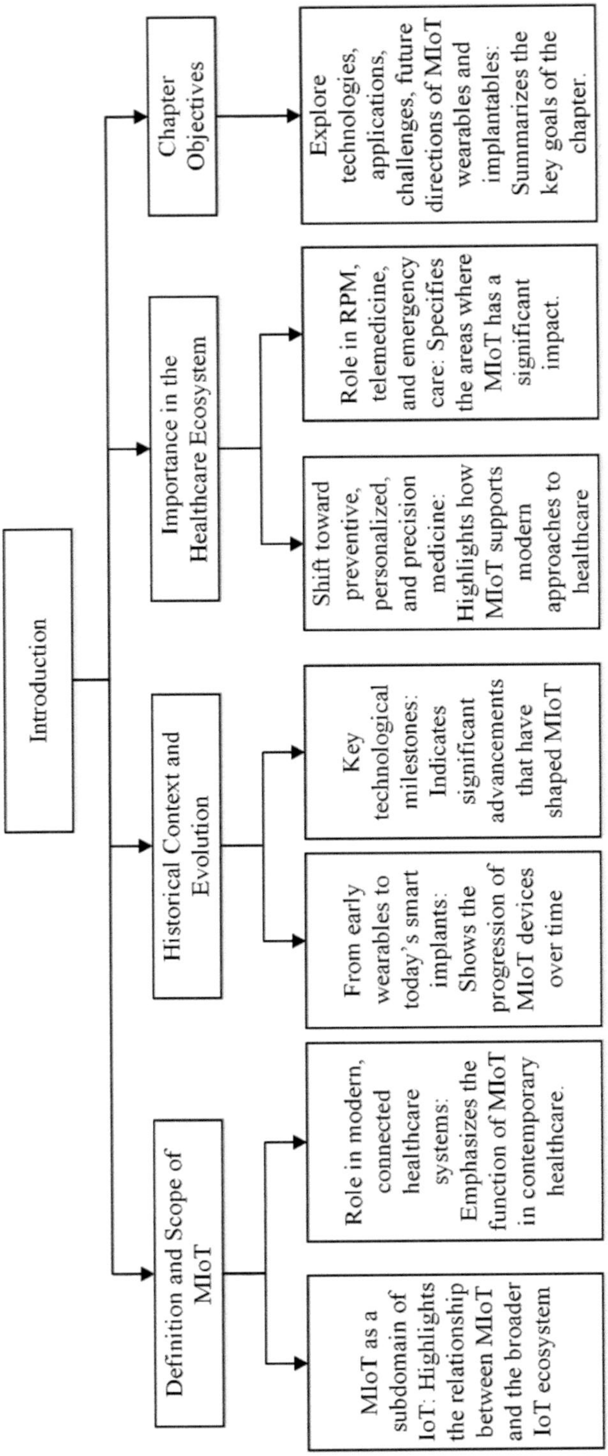

Figure 1: Introduction to MIoT.

implantable medical devices, signifying a major paradigm shift in the way health care is delivered (Haghi et al., 2017). Wearable and implantable medical devices enable continuous and remote monitoring of physiological parameters for early detection of abnormalities and personalized interventions.

1.1. Definition and Scope of MIoT

The Medical Internet of Things is a specific portion of the larger IoT environment that involves a network of connected medical devices and sensors that can communicate with other devices to collect, store, and transmit health data. MIoT systems have great potential to expand accessibility to patients, increase the quality of care, and lower healthcare expenditures.

- **Medical Internet of Things (MIoT) as an IoT Subdomain:** MIoT utilizes the IoT functionalities, with adaptations to the health domain requirements (wearable sensors, implantable devices, remote monitoring systems, etc.). MIoT systems comprise an architectural structure that includes several component modules, such as biosensors, communication modules, data processing units, and user interfaces, which work together to provide healthcare solutions. MIoT covers a variety of domains, including chronic disease management, remote patient monitoring (RPM), personalized drug delivery, and elderly care, with the opportunity to enhance patient outcomes and cut expenses in healthcare.
- **Role in Modern, Connected Healthcare Systems:** By guaranteeing ongoing patient monitoring for chronic conditions, the MIoT is transforming healthcare and enabling life-saving, rapid diagnosis in an emergency. With the advent of IoT solutions, the healthcare system has less work to do, enabling real-time patient care and monitoring. Integrating clinical, genetic, and environmental data might further improve healthcare issues in a variety of settings by enabling scalable and individualized patient care. Healthcare IoT is anticipated to reduce the cost of such services and enhance patient care and the overall user experience. This transformation allows for the monitoring of patients from the comfort of their own homes, and as patients recovering in their homes need to be monitored for physiological parameters continuously, it shows the need for tele-dermatology and restoration of IoT.

1.2. Historical Context and Evolution

This section details the evolution of medical (wearable and implantable) devices, which have been influenced by technology, changing health care paradigms, and evolving patient needs.

- **From Early Wearables (Striders) to Today's Smart Implants:** Early wearable devices, such as activity trackers for BMI, serve as the foundations to build more complex and integrated MIoT devices. The key to this integration of on-body and in-body devices has been advances in sensor technologies, wireless communication, and data analytics, leading to the development of smart implants that can deliver localized treatments and monitor physiological parameters in real-time.

- **Technological Milestones:** The evolution of MIoT was spurred on by several technological milestones, such as the miniaturization of sensors, low-power wireless communication protocols, and cloud computing platforms for storing and analyzing data.

1.3. Importance in the Healthcare Ecosystem

MIoT technology is becoming vital the health ecosystem, for patients, health service providers, and the healthcare system itself. MIoT enhances patient care with the continuous remote monitoring of vital signs, activity patterns, and medication adherence, allowing healthcare providers to monitor a patient's energy and identify early warning signs or potential health crises so they can intervene quickly (Li et al., 2024).

- **Shift Toward Preventive, Personalized, and Precision Medicine:** As MIoT enables the development of customized interventions and treatment modalities based on distinct patient characteristics and real-time physiological data, it aids in the shift to preventive, personalized, and precision medicine. The implementation of IoT for detailed, real-time health data allows the possibility of reformation in healthcare, in the form of early detection, personalized treatment, etc.
- **Role in Remote Patient Monitoring (RPM), Telemedicine, and Emergency Care:** MIoT plays an integral role in remote patient monitoring (RPM), telemedicine, and emergency care and significantly expands the reach of healthcare services, especially in remote or underserved areas. Wearable devices are crucial for the development of e-health, automating patient health data collection and allowing for analysis for health monitoring, disease diagnosis, and treatment analysis. The use of IoT can greatly enhance quality of life since the high information collected and real-time patient monitoring can prevent any reoccurring issues. Healthcare providers may get the critical data they require to make decisions and provide high-quality care due to MIoT's reliance on real-time monitoring and data-sharing platforms.

1.4. Chapter Objectives and Structure

This chapter aims to provide a comprehensive overview of wearable and implantable MIoT devices, including their fundamental components, parts, uses, difficulties, and potential future developments. To present a thorough understanding of this quickly developing field, this chapter will mostly concentrate on the underlying technology that powers MIoT, looking at sensor technologies, communication protocols, data analytics, and security considerations.

- **Explore Technologies, Applications, Challenges, and Future Directions of MIoT Wearables and Implantables:** This chapter will discuss the various technologies used in MIoT devices, their applications for healthcare, such as chronic disease management, remote patient monitoring, drug delivery, and elderly care, as well as challenges and future directions of MIoT wearables and implantables. To paint a comprehensive picture, this chapter will also highlight the complexities in MIoT implementation, such as data privacy and security concerns, strict compliance with regulations, and the demand for interconnectivity between devices, as well as between devices and systems.

2. Wearable Medical IoT Devices

A structured overview of wearable medical Internet of Things (IoT) devices in terms of different types, related technologies, applications, and examples is presented in Figure 2. The medical Internet of Things is shaped by the combination of wearable technology and telemedicine and telehealth.

2.1. Overview of Wearables in Healthcare

Integrating Wearable Medical Internet of Things (IoT) devices into healthcare systems can provide real-time monitoring of physiological parameters or activity patterns in ambulatory settings. They automatically gather patient health information,

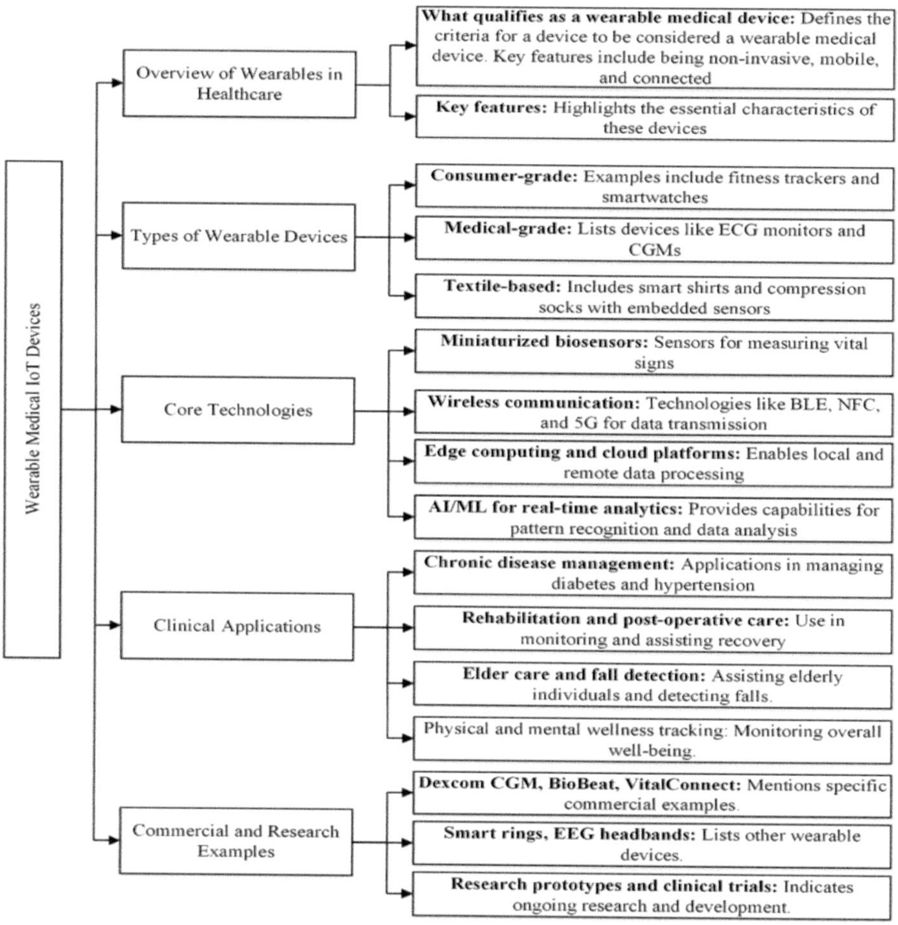

Figure 2: Wearable medical IoT devices.

removing the necessity for manual data gathering by healthcare practitioners and enabling medical personnel to interpret and process the data to track health, diagnose conditions, and deliver treatment. Wearable devices are shaking up how healthcare is managed, making it proactive, personalized, and accessible. IOS enhances the quality of life through real-time information collection and monitoring of the patients, which prevents further problems. Additionally, wearable technology is gaining attention from researchers worldwide. As the internet, smart devices, and big data continue to advance, smartwatches and bracelets are progressively playing a significant role in the healthcare industry (Liaqat et al., 2024).

- **What exactly are wearable medical devices?:** Wearable medical devices refer to any devices that are worn on the body for medical applications, such as diagnostic monitoring, therapeutic intervention, and rehabilitation. They are typically installed with a combination of sensors, processors, and communication interfaces, allowing them to capture, analyze, and pass through physiological information to medical professionals or individuals.
- **Key Features (Non-invasive, Mobile, Connected):** Wearables are appealing because they are non-invasive, can continuously collect data, and do not typically require major lifestyle changes or cause discomfort to the user, allowing them to be integrated into everyday life and improving adherence to monitoring regimens. Being able to move freely and perform daily activities (e.g., eating, sleeping, etc.), these wearable sensors provide a holistic and ecologically valid picture of health over an extended period by continuously measuring physiological parameters. Connectivity is an important aspect of smart wearables, allowing for data transfer to your phone, a cloud platform, or your healthcare provider network for remote monitoring and analytics.

2.2. Types of Wearable Devices and Their Applications

There has been an explosion in the number of available wearable medical devices with a wide variety of designs and use cases, to suit a broad range of monitoring or therapeutic needs. Wearable technology comes in different variants like wrist-worn, body-worn, head-worn, eye-worn, ear-worn, and clothing.

- **Consumer-grade:** Fitness trackers and smartwatches (e.g., Apple Watch, Fitbit) are common consumer-grade wearables that use sensors to track activity level, sleep, heart rate, and other physiological parameters. These devices enable individuals to monitor their activity levels, duration and quality of sleep, heart rate, and other physiological parameters so that they can make truly informed choices regarding their lifestyles and health behaviors. Lifestyle applications (Barua and Barua, 2021) are used to visually depict users' behaviors through dashboards that assist in tracking and maintaining adherence to dietary and medical data.
- **Medical-grade:** Medical-grade wearables are specialized wearables that provide clinical-grade data such as electrocardiograms (ECGs) and real-time blood glucose measurements. Examples include continuous glucose monitors that offer real-time glucose readings to facilitate diabetes management,

and wearable electrocardiogram monitors that detect and capture cardiac arrhythmias. Wearables are increasingly used to measure parameters, over 35 at the time of writing, and they are moving towards a technically sophisticated means to achieve this (Hasan et al., 2021). Medical-grade wearables measure vital signs, oxygen levels, electrocardiogram data, and other physiological parameters, and can send alerts and notifications to patients and healthcare providers if predefined thresholds are reached.

- **Textile-based Wearables (Smart Shirts, Compression Socks with Embedded Sensors):** The merging of sensors and electronics into textiles has opened the door to comfortable and unobtrusive wearable devices for long-term monitoring. They can monitor multiple physiological parameters such as heart rate, respiration rate, body temperature, and muscle activity, and can be embedded into clothing for continuous data collection. Sensors can also be embedded in fabrics to produce comfortable and stretchable wearable devices that facilitate continuous, wireless tracking of vital signs, such as respiratory rate, body temperature, and muscle activity over an extended duration (Angelucci et al., 2021).

2.3. Core Technologies Enabling Wearable MIoT Devices

Wearable MIoT devices feature a variety of integrated technologies to provide sensing, processing, and communication components that can potentially affect human activity recognition in people's daily lives.

- **Miniaturized Biosensors (for HR, BP, SpO2, etc.):** As a counterpart to the MCUs, miniaturized biosensors are one of the core components of wearable MIoT devices, which allow for the detection and quantitation of specific biomarkers in sweat, interstitial fluid, or other bodily fluids. Novel on-body bio-affinity bioassays and a range of time-slicing approaches are needed to diversify the range of biomarkers available for observation (Kim et al., 2019). The biological signals are converted to measurable electrical signals using different transduction mechanisms, including electrochemical, optical, and mechanical mechanisms. Electrochemical sensors detect changes in electrical signals due to the presence of analytes like glucose, lactate, and metabolite concentrations, while optical sensors quantify analytes by measuring changes in light absorption or fluorescence.
- **Wireless Communication (BLE, NFC, 5G):** Wireless technologies (Bluetooth, Wi-Fi, cellular, etc.) transmit data from wearables to smartphones, cloud, or healthcare provider networks. The data is then transferred to remote servers or healthcare providers via wireless communication protocols such as Bluetooth, Wi-Fi, ZigBee, and cellular technologies. Consider GSM for sampling point delocalization and DECT technology for local subnets. Employing this facility, this unit supports any such wearable device to monitor the patients and their data from anywhere in the world.
- **Edge Computing and Cloud Platforms:** When wearable devices have the edge computing capacity to process, analyze, or store data locally, it reduces the energy needed to send data continuously to the cloud while also improving latency. Edge computing minimizes latency on mission-critical applications and

enhances QoS. Wearable devices generate colossal amounts of data, and thus we spend a lot of time at cloud platforms that offer scalable storage and computing for data management and analytics in addition to allowing data sharing and collaboration among healthcare providers. The collected data is transmitted to a base station for further processing using existing wireless communication protocols (Ghamari et al., 2016).

- **AI/ML for Real-time Analytics and Pattern Recognition:** Artificial intelligence (AI) and machine learning (ML) algorithms help wearable MIoT devices to analyze and identify pattern recognition of data on a real-time basis, which further increases their diagnostic and predictive functionalities. Disease recognition from smartphone-uploaded images is obtained using machine learning. Anomaly detection, disease progression prediction, and personalized treatment plans via AI algorithms are achievable based on individual patient data. Deep learning–enabled signal processing has enabled gait analysis and posture perception to ensure harmony between humans and machines and help make contributions to smart healthcare applications. Machine learning has a unique potential for addressing complex healthcare problems, particularly in medical and assistive applications (Diab and Rodriguez-Villegas, 2022).

2.4. Clinical Applications of Wearable MIoT Devices

Wearable MIoT devices have numerous applications in clinical practice and are being utilized across multiple medical specialities to enhance patient care and improve healthcare delivery. Wearable technology can monitor coronavirus-infected patients and help surgeons and caregivers with real-time data. For practitioners to choose the best course of action, they may forecast patient data such as fitness trackers, medical records, health activities, body mass, temperature, and other health care-related information (Fouad et al., 2020).

- **Chronic Disease Management (Diabetes, Hypertension, Sleep Apnea):** Wearable devices are essential in managing chronic disease conditions (diabetes, CVD, respiratory). These devices can yield insights based on real-time monitoring of vital signs, activity levels, and medication adherence that can greatly contribute to understanding disease trajectories and treatment responses. For example, wearable ECG devices allow for continuous monitoring of heart rhythm and arrhythmias, leading to early interventions and avoiding adverse events. Similarly, cardiac patients can benefit from monitoring their physical activity via wearable sensors and receiving personalized feedback on how to establish healthier lifestyles and better glycemic control.
- **Rehabilitation and Post-operative Care:** Wearable sensors can monitor and remind patients of adherence to rehabilitation protocols, which helps therapists modify treatment plans according to patients' needs. Additionally, such devices can monitor healing progress, alerting to early signs of infection and notifying healthcare personnel for fast and effective treatment. Moreover, wearable sensors enable the evaluation of the efficacy of rehabilitation interventions and long-term outcome monitoring. Next-generation sensors can be used in applications to monitor muscle dynamics and neural activity during movement.

- **Elder Care and Fall Detection:** Wearables are particularly useful in monitoring elderly individuals and fall detection and monitoring, which is one of the leading causes of injuries and death in this demographic. When these devices sense a fall (by detecting changes in motion and orientation using accelerometers and gyroscopes), they can sound an alarm and alert caregivers or emergency services. Moreover, wearable sensors can track levels of activity, sleep, and social interactions to gain insights into the general health of older adults, which, in turn, can help detect potential health risks.
- **Physical and Mental Wellness Tracking:** Wearable devices track things like movement, how many steps you take, your heart rate, and how many calories you burn, encouraging more physical activity. Wearable devices allow individuals to monitor their sleep patterns, heart rate variability, and stress levels, giving them valuable feedback about their overall health. This information could enable the detection of health risks, including sleep apnea or chronic stress, and motivate people to change detrimental behavior. In addition, these wearable machines can offer individual feedback and suggestions for people to reach their fitness targets and enhance their health.

2.5. Commercial and Research Examples of MIoT Devices

A wide range of devices, commercial and research-grade, exists across the MIoT landscape, each fulfilling specific applications and user needs. Smartwatches and fitness trackers, the most common form factor of wearable MIoT technology, were formerly taken for granted but are now widely used by consumers and represent established and well-liked segments of the digital health business. These devices contain a variety of sensors such as accelerometers, gyroscopes, heart rate monitors, and GPS modules, enabling the monitoring of physical activity, sleep behaviors, and physiological parameters (Kao et al., 2019).

- **Dexcom CGM, BioBeat, VitalConnect:** The Dexcom continuous glucose monitoring system is a representative device for diabetes management. It offers real-time glucose monitoring using a subcutaneous sensor and transmits data wirelessly to a smartphone or a receiver. Healthcare and wearables, such as BioBeat provide a wrist-worn sensor that is capable of continually tracking vital signs, including heart rate, blood pressure, and respiratory rate, which allows for the early detection of anomalies and proactive handling of cardiovascular conditions. VitalConnect's HealthPatch MD is a single-use biosensor that is placed on the chest, and it permits continuous assessment of ECG, heart rate, respiratory rate, and activity levels, and thus can be used to give detailed physiological information for remote patient monitoring and clinical studies.
- **Smart Rings (e.g., Oura Ring), EEG Headbands:** Oura Ring is a wearable ring that tracks sleep, activity, and heart rate variability, offering insights into sleep quality, recovery, and overall health. Brainwave monitors, like those created by Muse, utilize electroencephalography (EEG) headbands that can track brain activity and provide feedback to the user in real time, helping them to boost focus, relaxation, and cognitive capacity.

- **Research Prototypes and Clinical Trials:** Various research groups and healthcare institutions are working on new MIoT devices across a variety of clinical applications. The most advanced prototypes employed in these fields include state-of-the-art sensing technologies, from biosensors and microfluidic devices to nanomaterials that can be used for continuous monitoring of different biomarkers and physiological parameters. There are ongoing clinical studies to evaluate the accuracy, reliability, and usefulness of MIoT devices in specific patient populations.

3. Bio-Sensing and Implantable Medical IoT Devices

Implantable Medical IoT devices are sensors inside the body for long-term measuring or treatment purposes; therefore, biocompatibility, power management, and optimization communication play important roles. Such devices comprise cardiac pacemakers and defibrillators, neurological deep brain stimulators (DBS) and brain-computer interfaces, drug delivery systems such as smart insulin pumps, and ingestible sensors for diagnostic purposes. Technology capabilities include MEMS, wireless power transmission systems, sealed telemetry systems, and biodegradable electronics. Applications include seizure anticipation, intelligent stents, pressure monitoring, and closed-loop drug administration. The clinical validation requires meeting FDA, CE Marking, and ISO regulations with robust cybersecurity and safety mechanisms as given in Table 1.

3.1. Introduction to Implantables

Implantable medical devices form a technologically advanced subset of MIoT innovations that are intended to reside in the human body to measure various physiological parameters, administer therapeutic interventions, or, most commonly, provide diagnostic information. In contrast to wearables, implantable sensors provide the benefit of continuous and long-term monitoring and can obtain physiological data that cannot be obtained from external sensors. The performance and effectiveness of implantable medical devices depend on the synergistic functioning of biocompatible materials, sophisticated sensing technologies, wireless communication mechanisms, and secure power management systems. These tools have brought improvements in the management of several chronic diseases, neurological disorders, and cardiac diseases.

- **Devices Placed Inside the Body for Long-term Monitoring or Therapeutic Purposes:** This includes implantable medical devices used for continuous monitoring or treatment of various conditions. Some common examples include pacemakers, implantable defibrillators, glucose monitors, and deep-brain stimulators. Electronic cardiac pacemakers and implantable cardioverter-defibrillators are life-saving devices that control heart rhythm and help prevent sudden cardiac death. Continuous glucose monitoring (CGM) provides up to real-time glucose readings for people with diabetes, allowing them to adjust insulin delivery and maintain glycemic control.

Table 1: Bio-Sensing and Implantable Medical IoT Devices

Category	Description
Introduction to Implantables	Implantable sensors that are placed inside the body for long-duration measurements or therapeutic action. Among the key design aspects are biocompatibility, power management, and efficient communication, among others.
Types of Implantable Devices	**Cardiac:** Pacemakers, defibrillators, heart monitors. **Neurological:** Deep brain stimulators, neuroprosthetics, brain-computer interfaces. **Drug delivery systems:** Palette on smart insulin pumps, micro-reservoirs. These are your ingestible sensors: pills for diagnostic assessments of gut health, temperature sensing, medication adherence, and more. Tissue or biomolecule detection has also utilized Optical sensors.
Enabling Technologies	Microelectromechanical systems; wireless power transfer (inductive/capacitive coupling, RF energy harvesting); telemetry systems for bi-directional communication; and biodegradable and stretchable electronics. New and improved biomedical applications are made via the utilization of soft, biocompatible, and resorbable materials.
Use Cases	Seizure prediction for epilepsy, smart stents, pressure sensors, and closed-loop drug delivery.
Clinical Validation and Regulatory Considerations	FDA Compliant, CE-marked, and ISO Compliant. It's also important to follow cybersecurity regulations and safety protocols.

- **Design Considerations – Biocompatibility, Power, and Communication:** The design of an implantable medical device involves considerations for biocompatibility, power delivery, and communication, ensuring that the device functions safely and effectively without causing damage to surrounding tissues. Implantable devices are deployed in the body to perform specific tasks autonomously, for long durations without requiring an external power supply provided They demand a sound power management integrated within them. Wireless communication capabilities enable data transmission from the implantable device to external monitoring systems or healthcare providers, facilitating remote patient management and timely interventions. The appropriate balance of these design considerations is a major determinant of the safety, efficacy, and lifecycle of implantable medical devices.

3.2. Types of Implantable Devices

Some implantable medical devices are designed without the requirement for certain solutions to clinical needs and therapeutic purposes. In real-time, implantable biosensors monitor biochemical parameters, including glucose, lactate, oxygen, and electrolytes. Such sensors use different sensing mechanisms based on electrochemical, optical, and enzymatic methods to identify and quantify the target analytes. Communication capabilities allow remote access to physiological data, enabling timely intervention and individualized treatment strategies. Such implantable drug delivery systems provide targeted and controlled release of medications at the specific site of action, leading to optimal therapeutic efficacy and the avoidance of systemic side effects. By utilizing the biocompatibility, programmability, and adaptability of such systems, drug delivery can be customized by a wide margin to be time-released, on-demand, or upon a physiological stimulus.

- **Cardiac – Pacemakers, Defibrillators, and Heart Monitors:** Pacemakers are small, battery-powered devices that are surgically implanted in the chest. These devices send electrical impulses to the heart, regulating its beats in patients with bradycardia or heart block. Defibrillators, which are also implanted in the chest, emit electrical pulses to bring an errant heart back to a rhythm in people at high risk of sudden cardiac arrest from ventricular fibrillation or ventricular tachycardia. Loop recorders, a type of implantable heart monitor, provide continuous monitoring of heart activity, allowing them to detect rarely occurring or asymptomatic arrhythmias and can help clinicians understand when and how to treat underlying cardiac conditions.
- **Neurological – Deep Brain Stimulators, Neuroprosthetics, Brain-Computer Interfaces (BCIs):** Deep brain stimulators are surgically implanted devices that deliver electrical impulses to targeted areas within the brain to alleviate certain symptoms of movement disorders such as Parkinson's disease, essential tremor, and dystonia. Neuroprosthetics are devices that are capable of replacing lost sensory or motor function in individuals with paralysis or amputation and can be implanted in the body. Brain-computer interfaces create a direct channel of communication between the brain and external devices that can allow people who are severely disabled to operate computers, wheelchairs, or prosthetic limbs with their minds. These implantable neurological devices could revolutionize the quality of life in patients fitted with different forms of debilitating neurological problems.
- **Drug Delivery Systems – Smart Insulin Pumps, Micro-reservoirs:** Smart insulin pumps are devices that are implanted and can automatically deliver insulin in response to continuous glucose monitoring, which can mimic the function of a healthy pancreas and result in better glycemic control in people with type 1 diabetes. Micro-reservoirs are miniaturized implantable devices that can store and release precise doses of medication over prolonged periods, allowing for controlled drug delivery for several therapeutic applications. Nevertheless, the use of these types of implantable drug delivery systems offers benefits over conventional drug administration methods, including better patient compliance, decreased side effects, and increased therapeutic efficacy (Pons-Faudoa et al., 2019).
- **Ingestible Sensors:** Ingestible sensors include diagnostic pills, temperature, and adherence. Ingestible sensors are pill-sized devices that can be swallowed. They are exposed to the gut environment while passing through the gastrointestinal tract and can provide localized diagnostic information in the gut. They can monitor the pH, the temperature, and the pressure for the presence of certain

biomarkers, helping to deliver the diagnosis of gastrointestinal disorders. Some ingestible sensors, for example, are intended to track medication adherence, reporting data back to healthcare providers to verify that patients are following the regimen. Smart implants are becoming rapidly impactful in healthcare systems; they create great opportunities for improving living standards, correcting defects, and even moving people with disabilities (Abyzova et al., 2023).

3.3. Enabling Technologies for Implantable MIoT Devices

The evolution of implantable MIoT devices hinges on a convergence of enabling technologies that collaboratively enhance their functionality, performance, and biocompatibility. Implantable devices involve a broad range of technologies, from materials science and microelectronics to wireless communication, power management, and data analytics. Through these various technologies, researchers can design powerful, inclusive devices that eventually should be safe, affordable, and easy to use. The use of biocompatible materials, including titanium, silicone, and polymers, is crucial for reducing undesired tissue reactions after insertion into the body and encouraging the long-term integration of implanted devices with surrounding tissues.

- **Microelectromechanical Systems (MEMS):** MEMS technology allows for scaling down sensors, actuators, and microfluidic elements, which helps design small, minimally invasive implantable devices. The MEMS-based sensors can measure various physiological parameters such as pressure, temperature, flow rate, and acceleration, which can be useful diagnostic information for personalized healthcare.
- **Wireless Power Transfer (Inductive/Capacitive Coupling, RF Energy Harvesting):** Wireless power transfer technologies, including inductive coupling and radiofrequency energy harvesting, allow for battery-free functioning of implantable devices, which minimizes the need for replacement batteries and improves reliability by mitigating potential dangers associated with battery leakage or failure. When it comes to pathological operations, they facilitate required data, making them helpful for real-time patient monitoring without the hassle of cable-based connections.
- **Telemetry Systems for Bidirectional Communication:** Telemetry systems allow for active two-way communication between immersed devices and external equipment, such as smartphones, computers, or medical equipment. These systems allow for remote monitoring of device performance, data being transmitted, and the programming, making personalized and adaptive healthcare management possible. The carrier signal can also provide power to the device, which is important for long-term use, e.g., cardiac pacemakers (Kassanos and Hourdakis, 2025).
- **Biodegradable and Stretchable Electronics:** Many devices that vanish are possible through the development of biodegradable materials, and flexible and stretchable electronics are helping to improve the integration of devices with biological tissues. Biodegradable electronics provide a different pathway toward transient medical devices that harmlessly dissolve within the body after doing

their job and do not need to be removed surgically. Conformable and durable implantable devices with minimal tissue irritation and optimal device operation can be achieved using stretchable electronics due to the dynamic motion of the body (Sayyad et al., 2024).

3.4. Use Cases and Applications

An overview of the applications of MIoT devices in proximity includes the similarity of applications in multiple specialties, such as diagnostic interventions, patient monitoring and management, or specific treatment delivery.

- **Prediction of Epilepsy Seizures:** By monitoring the brain activity, for example, devices can predict when a seizure occurs and give the patient time to either find a safe place where the seizure will not cause injury or to allow them to take medication. For example, implantable devices equipped with advanced signal processing algorithms can analyze patterns of brain activity to detect the onset of seizures in real-time with potential predictive capabilities to warn the patient before a seizure occurs (i.e. in time for the patient to take medication or get to a safe area if necessary). By utilizing the details of an individual's seizures in a real adaptive algorithm, they could change it to augment the individual's personal information, which will be beneficial for the individual and society.
- **Intelligent Stents and Pressure Sensors:** Implantable pressure sensors could be used to detect blood pressure inside the aneurysm, providing an early warning sign that a rupture is imminent. Smart stents with pressure sensors can measure blood flow in arteries and determine whether a blockage is present to alert healthcare providers early enough to prevent heart attacks and strokes. They can also administer localized therapy as drug treatment for that tissue area with high therapeutic activity and fewer side effects.
- **Closed-loop Drug Delivery:** These systems use implantable sensors and actuators to automatically control the release of drugs in response to real-time physiological feedback, intending to maintain optimal therapeutic concentrations while minimizing adverse effects. Such systems are especially valuable in chronic situations like diabetes, requiring tight control of insulin levels to maintain glycemia and avoid delayed complications.

3.5. Clinical Validation and Regulatory Considerations

In the clinical implementation of implantable MIoT devices, rigorous clinical validation and compliance with rigid regulatory standards will be an essential process to make sure that those devices are safe and effective for patients. Human subjects are crucial for the evaluation of performance, safety, and reliability of implantable devices and their effects on clinical outcomes and quality of life. The Food and Drug Administration in the United States, among other regulatory agencies, has developed comprehensive guidelines and protocols for the clearance and approval of medical devices, including implantable MIoT devices (Rushton, 2002).

- **FDA, CE Marking, ISO Standards:** Fundamental for implantable devices; safety and performance to be used for clinical use. This invasive characteristic of implantable drug-delivery systems exposes these devices to the highest scrutiny level. This process of obtaining regulatory approval can be challenging and lengthy, necessitating substantial documentation, testing, and clinical data. Furthermore, even after the clinical trials, it can be challenging to receive financial support, as reimbursement for goods and services is not assured (Bergsland et al., 2014).

- **Cybersecurity Standards and Safety Measures:** With MIoT devices being wireless, strong cybersecurity measures would be critical to protect patient information and prevent unauthorized access or manipulation of the device functionalities. Strict cyber-security regulatory compliance and safety guidelines have to intercede to protect against potential threats like as hacking, malware attacks, and data breaches. This requires the use of encryption, authentication, and access control methods that protect sensitive information from unauthorized access and control of device functions.

4. System Architecture and Data Ecosystem

Figure 3 depicts the important elements, along with their interconnections, of the MIoT system architecture and data landscape.

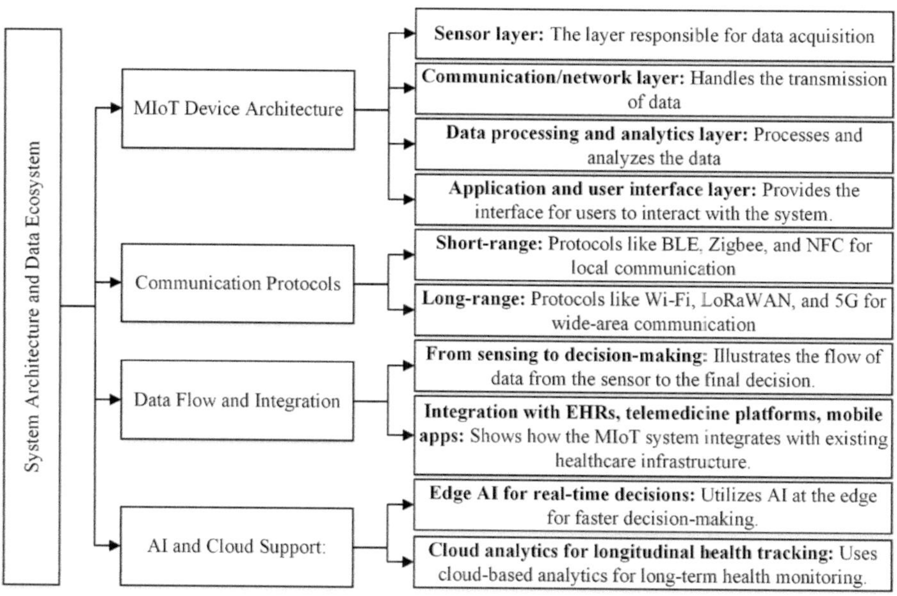

Figure 3: System architecture and data ecosystem.

4.1. MIoT Device Architecture

MIoT devices generally comprise several crucial components, which include sensors, processing units, communication modules, as well as power sources. Acquisition of physiological (vital signs, biochemical markers, activity level, etc.) data from the body via sensors. Microcontrollers or microprocessors receive data (or event) information and create decisions from that data using predetermined algorithms. Communication modules facilitate the wireless transfer of information to external devices or networks via Bluetooth, Wi-Fi, or cellular connectivity.

- **Sensor Layer (Transducers, Biosensors, MEMS):** The sensor layer sets the foundation of MIoT devices and allows for real-time acquisition of physiological data. Transducers transform physical or chemical signals into electrical ones that can be processed and analyzed, whereas biosensors can selectively identify and quantify specific biomolecules/analytes within the body. It leads to micro sensor and actuator systems of so-called Micro-Electro-Mechanical Systems technology, such systems can get compact and mobile features and become suitable for implantation.
- **Communication/Network Layer (Protocols, Interoperability, and Network Topologies):** The communication layer allows for wireless data transmission between MIoT devices within a network and the external world, enabling remote monitoring of devices, analysis of the data collected, and control over such devices. Standardised communication protocols, such as Bluetooth Low Energy, Zigbee, and Wi-Fi, are used to ensure that various platforms and devices can cooperate (Elijah et al., 2018). They provide a variety of network topologies, including mesh, star, tree, and others. These topologies determine how the MIoT devices connect with one another.
- **Data Processing and Analytics Layer (Cloud Computing, Edge Computing, Machine Learning):** The data processing and analytics layer is responsible for storing, processing, and analyzing the vast amounts of data generated by MIoT devices. These are embedded from Getty Images. However, solutions to these challenges are being developed — leading the way is the proliferation of cloud computing platforms and edge computing technology. Using machine learning algorithms, meaningful information can be extracted from the data in the form of event prediction, pattern identification, and treatment personalization.
- **Application and User Interface Layer:** Mobile apps, web dashboards, data visualization: The application and user interface layer enables access to MIoT data and interacts with device functions in a user-friendly manner. Patients, clinicians, and researchers can remotely monitor physiological data and treatment adherence or adjust device settings with mobile apps and web dashboards. Graphs, charts, heatmaps, and other visualization tools interpret complex data into meaningful processes of insight and allow managerial decision-making.

4.2. Communication Protocols and Standards

MIoT devices inherently rely on wireless communication, facilitating the communication of data and enabling remote monitoring. To meet the unique needs of MIoT applications, such as low power consumption, extended coverage, and enhanced reliability, sets of protocols and standards have been formulated. Choosing the right communication protocol will vary based on different parameters such as data rate, range, power, and security.

- **Short-range (BLE, Zigbee, NFC- WPAN):** These communication technologies are best suited for MIoT applications having low power consumption and proximity-based communication, such as Bluetooth Low Energy, Zigbee, and Near Field Communication. BLE allows devices to transmit data wirelessly over a 100-meter range while maintaining a low power consumption, making it suitable for use in wearable sensors and mobile health devices. Home health care and smart hospital applications require reliable and secure communication from dense environments in the home. Zigbee is a mesh network protocol that provides reliable delivery of information. NFC enables bidirectional communication between devices over short range without establishing a physical or wired connection.
- **Long-range (Wi-Fi, LoRaWAN, 5G-LPWAN):** Long-range communication technologies like Wi-Fi, LoRaWAN, and 5G have played an important role in transmitting the data over longer distances, enabling the MIoT application monitoring processes remotely (Kufakunesu et al., 2020). Wi-Fi is responsible for high bandwidth connectivity for data-intensive applications such as remote video monitoring and telemedicine within a short range. LoRaWAN (Long-Range Wide Area Network) is a low-power wide-area network protocol that allows long-range communication with low power consumption, making it ideal for applications like environmental monitoring and asset tracking. The latest generation of mobile networks revolutionizes the healthcare sector with advances in ultra-high data rate, very low latency, and large device density, including advanced MIoT applications: remote surgery and augmented-reality-assisted medical treatment.

4.3. Data Flow and Integration

As MIoT generates large amounts of data, proper management, storage, and analysis are necessary to extract significant insights and foster data-driven healthcare. Generally, MIoT systems follow a certain architecture for data flow, which comprises the following stages: data acquisition, data transmission, data storage, data processing, and, finally, data visualization. Data integration is important for combining data from different sources and formats, maintaining data consistency, and facilitating interoperability between different systems. The use of context-aware sensing, enabled by edge computing, strives to decrease energy usage based on the patient's state and context, so stability of energy usage and quality of data can be achieved (Amiri et al., 2020).

- **From Sensing to Decision-making:** MIoT devices use multiple sensors integrated into the human body, such as electrodes, accelerometers, and pressure sensors, to gather various physiological information. It then sends that data wirelessly to a central server or cloud platform where the data is stored and/or processed. For instance, data analytics techniques (i.e. machine learning and statistical analysis) are used to derive meaningful insights from the data (i.e. trend identification, anomaly detection, prediction, etc.). This actionable knowledge is subsequently delivered to doctors and patients via user-friendly platforms like mobile applications and web dashboards that enable evidence-based decision-making.

- **Integration with EHRs, Telemedicine Platforms, and Mobile Apps:** MIoT data can help facilitate sophisticated decision-making with more pertinent and contemporary patient data. MIoT data allows Telemedicine platforms to offer remote consultations, remote patient monitoring, and personalized care. Mobile applications can enable patients to manage their health, including the tracking of personal health data, medications, and communication with healthcare providers, thus promoting patient engagement and self-management.

4.4. AI and Cloud Support

The fusion of AI and cloud computing has transformed MIoT systems, facilitating sophisticated data analytics, personalized medicine, and remote health monitoring. The data generated by MIoT devices is vast in quantity, which makes it suitable to be processed and stored in a cloud computing environment for which expands its offering by providing economic infrastructure. Artificial intelligence algorithms can be trained on vast datasets to identify patterns, predict events, and provide personalized treatments, resulting in improved outcomes for patients and lowered healthcare costs.

- **Edge AI for Real-time Decisions:** In edge AI, data processing and decision-making occur at the edge of the source of the data, thus improving real-time performance and cutting latency. Edge AI algorithms can run on MIoT devices to detect anomalies, predict events, and recommend personalized actions, all of this without having to send data to the cloud. In this chapter, we assume that the reader is already well-versed in the most recent advancements in edge technology and understands how edge technology allows for local processing and storage of data instead of having to transfer all to cloud centers, thus reducing latency, energy consumption, and network congestion (Hayyolalam et al., 2021).
- **Cloud Analytics for Longitudinal Health Tracking:** Cloud analytics can also be used to analyze large amounts of data and identify trends over time, allowing for longitudinal health tracking and personalized healthcare. AI algorithms can glean data from thousands of sources, including those from MIoT devices, EHRs, and imaging data, and provide insight into risk factors, disease progression, and personalized treatment plans. The use of the cloud was adopted in healthcare and will continue to grow and gain strength in light of the growing utilization of smart devices attributed to IoT (Kang et al., 2018).

5. Challenges and Risks

The security risks and challenges of employing MIoT devices in healthcare need to be considered while developing a secure, safe, and effective solution. These challenges are technological, regulatory, ethical, and societal and require a multifaceted approach to address as discussed in Table 2.

Table 2: Challenges and Risks Description

Category	**Description**
Technical Challenges	Power persistence and battery life, sensor calibration and signal noise, and device interoperability.
Privacy and Cybersecurity Concerns	Security to avoid hacking and data breaches, encryption of data transmission and storage, and data protection laws like HIPAA and GDPR. The compromised devices can be used to hear activities or private conversations.
Ethical and Societal Issues	Continual surveillance and its psychological ramifications, questions of autonomy and consent (or the lack thereof, especially in groups that are at greater risk), and equal access to high-tech health care.
Regulatory and Standardization Barriers	Implementation of medical IoT regulations and no certification for AI decision-making in implants
Maintenance and Usability	The need to replace devices (due to battery life or old technology, etc.), and to train adequately both health care providers and patients.

5.1. Technical Challenges

MIoT devices also face technical challenges, such as interoperability, data security, power consumption, and communication reliability. Interoperability is the characteristic used to describe when MIoT devices or systems can communicate and exchange information without any problem. The sensitive nature of the data being collected and transmitted in MIoT systems makes data security paramount. Power is a quality of service (QoS) variable when it comes to MIoT devices, as wearable and implantable devices will typically need to last as long as possible between battery changes.

- **Power Limitations, Battery Life:** One of the biggest challenges to wearable and implantable MIoT devices is that they must be able to function autonomously for long periods without requiring new batteries to be fitted as needed. And then to maximize the lifetime of MIoT devices requires cutting-edge power management approaches like energy harvesting and low-power communication protocols. You can also help to reduce power consumption by using low-power microcontrollers and power-efficient algorithms.
- **MIoT Sensor Calibration and Signal Noise:** To ensure the accuracy and reliability of the data collected by MIoT devices, sensor calibration is essential. Signal noise corrupts the target data, and such measurements are unreliable. Signal processing, such as filtering and noise suppression algorithms, can be applied to reduce the influence of noise within the received signal.
- **Device Interoperability:** MIoT devices come from various manufacturers and use different communication protocols, which often hampers smooth data exchange. This is vital to help different MIoT devices and systems interoperate with each other, as standardized protocols and data formats need to be developed.

5.2. Privacy and Cybersecurity Concerns

Since MIoT systems can collect and transmit sensitive data, privacy and cybersecurity are among the main challenges facing these systems. The negative impact of data breaches on patients' data and unauthorized access to patients' data can have grave consequences such as identity theft, financial loss, and reputation damage. Security and privacy issues are major challenges that hinder the deployment of IoT, which can be addressed with adequate security and privacy mechanisms (Youm, 2017).

- **Risk of Hacking and Data Breaches:** MIoT devices can be hacked and breached because they are connected to the internet, and their security features may not be fully developed. This entails putting in place strong security protocols like encryption and authentication to safeguard MIoT devices against cyberattacks. IoT devices can be seized by attackers, and dangerous information can be captured by greedier attackers; communication layers can be attacked by denial-of-service attacks.
- **Transmission and Encryption Security:** Secure transmission and encryption are critical to helping prevent unauthorized access to patients' data during the transmission steps. You can use encryption algorithms like Advanced Encryption Standard and Rivest-Shamir-Adleman to encrypt data before transmitting it over the network. Proof of the identity of the new device on one side of the communication enables end-to-end encryption. Safe communication over the public network requires confidentiality, integrity, authenticity, and end-to-end security for the data generated from sensor-based devices (Hussain et al., 2021).
- **Ensuring Compliance with HIPAA, GDPR:** Compliance with regulations such as the Health Insurance Portability and Accountability Act (HIPAA) and the General Data Protection Regulation (GDPR) is essential to protect patient privacy and data security. These regulations establish strict standards for data protection and privacy, and healthcare organizations are required to adhere to these standards to avoid penalties and legal consequences. Thus, IoT solutions must ensure high-level privacy of personal data.

5.3. Ethical and Societal Issues

However, deploying MIoT devices brings several ethical and societal implications that need to be addressed. These problems start with data ownership, informed consent, and algorithmic bias.

- **Continuous Monitoring and Psychosocial Effect:** The continuous monitoring provided by MIoT devices may have psychological effects on patients, such as anxiety, stress, and loss of privacy. Providers of healthcare must be cognizant of these potential effects and offer counseling and support accordingly.
- **Autonomy and Consent, Especially in Vulnerable Populations:** Ensuring autonomy and obtaining informed consent from patients, particularly in vulnerable populations, will be important when approaching MIoT devices. Patients should be properly informed about what data is collected, how this data is used, and to whom it will be shared. They should equally be entitled to decline the use of MIoT devices or withdraw consent at any point.

- **Equity in Access to High-tech Healthcare:** As MIoT devices are deployed, we must pay attention to equity in access; the technology may not be as widely available in different segments of the population, especially underserved communities. It is indeed important to address that there are inequalities in access to MIoT devices and that not all patients have access to these technologies. IoT applications in healthcare should be designed while keeping in mind privacy and security to prevent legal and ethical issues.

5.4. Regulatory and Standardization Barriers

A clear regulatory framework and standardized protocols, however, are still lacking, and this can sap MIoT device development and penetration. However, the existing regulations and standards for MIoT devices create challenges toward widespread adoption for both manufacturers and healthcare professionals.

- **Lack of Global Harmonization in Medical Iot Regulation:** Manufacturers trying to market their medical IoT products internationally must navigate through a patchwork of fragmented global regulations. Different regulatory requirements in different countries can increase the cost and time it takes to develop a product and bring it to market.
- **Certified AI-driven Decisions in Implants:** Integrating Artificial Intelligence (AI) into implantable MIoT devices presents significant regulatory challenges, particularly for the certification and validation of AI-based decision-making algorithms. Thus, before these algorithms can safely and effectively be used in clinics and reliably promote unbiased practice, they must be required to capture and retain all relevant patient information. One of the major challenges in broad IoT adoption in healthcare is addressing issues around interoperability and standardization for IoT and healthcare systems.

5.5. Maintenance and Usability

There are certain challenges associated with MIoT devices, which can be difficult to maintain and utilize, especially in elderly or disabled patients. Usability and long-term maintenance of MIoT devices is a substantial challenge that cannot be overlooked, given the varying needs and capabilities of different patients, such as elders and disabled persons.

- **Need for Device Replacement (Battery, Outdated Tech):** MIoT device maintenance is complex due to the need for device replacement, upgrades, and disposal. Proper management of device lifecycles, including disposal, is important both for mitigating environmental impact and maintaining patient safety.
- **Training for Healthcare Providers and Patients:** Healthcare providers and patients should receive adequate training on the use of MIoT devices to ensure correct and safe usage. Training programs must be built on the requirements of specific user groups and address content from using the device to interpreting data to troubleshoot.

6. Future Trends and Opportunities

Wearing the Slim with eight actuators creates triggers and the sensation of demand. This covers integration of artificial intelligence and machine learning, nanomedicine and biosensors, complex energy harvesting, as well as the growth of remote patient monitoring. These advanced technologies are expected to pave the way for a new era that creates more proactive, personalized, and efficient healthcare solutions, as given in Table 3.

Table 3: MIoT Future Trends and Opportunities

Category	Description
Technological Advancements	Smart tattoos and epidermal electronics; Energy-harvesting wearables and implants; Microfluidics and non-invasive chemical sensing.
Convergence with Other Technologies	Predictive and precision medicine with AI + IoT + genomics; AR/VR + MIoT for surgical training and therapy; Blockchain for secure health data exchange.
Evolving Patient-Centric Models	Real-time feedback, self-managed care, remote diagnostics, decentralization of hospitals
Next-Generation Implantables	Nanosensors and neural dust; Bioelectronics for regeneration; Organ-on-a-chip and intelligent prosthetics
Global Health Impacts	Mobile health (mHealth) in low-resource settings; Wearables in pandemic management and disease surveillance.

Figure 4 represents the perspective of what could be the future of Medical IoT, but also the opportunities possible in the Medical IoT dream. IoT has the power to advance sustainable and green processes and enhance overall supply chain effectiveness.

6.1. Technological Advancements on the Horizon

AI and machine learning integration, nanomedicine, and advanced energy harvesting (the latter focusing on converting environmental energy into electrical energy) will propel next-generation MIoT devices, and advancements in these areas should make their way to market in the next few years. Incorporating the power of miniaturization methods combined with more advanced computational capabilities is changing the paradigm of MIoT devices, enabling the design of small yet capable devices capable of executing complex data algorithms on the service side.

- **Smart Tattoos and Epidermal Electronics:** Smart tattoos and epidermal electronics are an emerging field, promising continuous, non-invasive monitoring of various physiological parameters. These tools can be seamlessly integrated into the skin for real-time monitoring of vital signs, biomarkers, and drug levels.
- **Energy Harvesting Wearables and Implants:** Energy harvesting is a technology that will change hands in terms of MIOT devices; it will enable

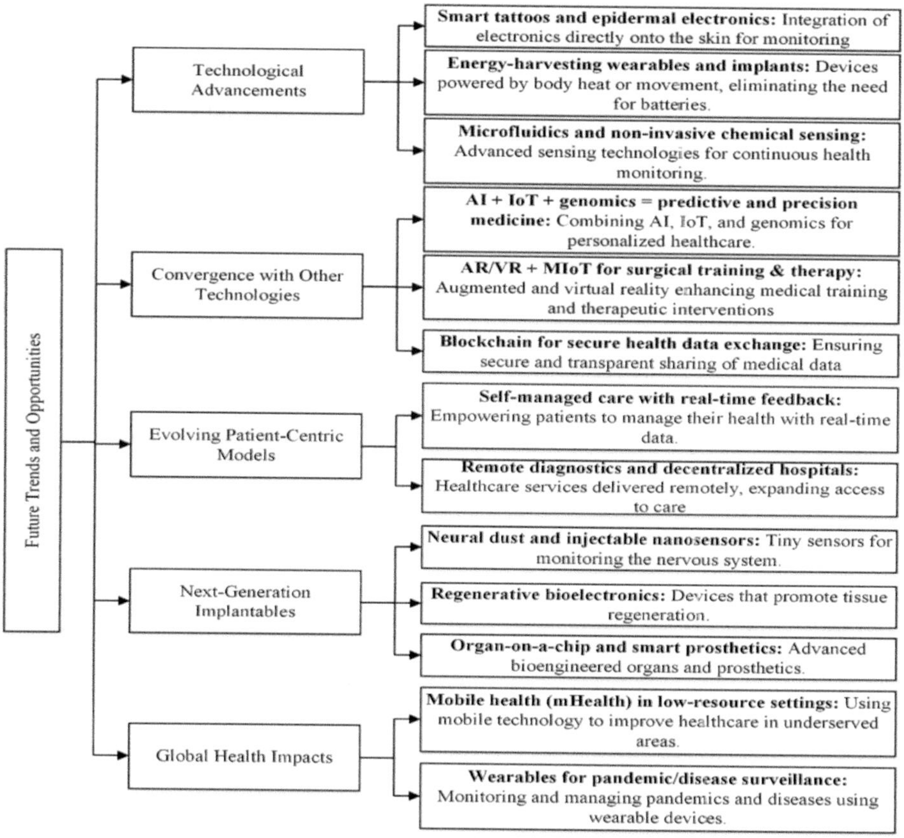

Figure 4: Future trends and opportunities of MIoT.

MIOT devices to live autonomously for months or even years without a battery replacement. Energy harvesting from body heat, motion, or ambient radio waves can be used to drive wearables and implants, eliminating the frequency of maintenance that these devices require and reducing the burden on the patient. In medical technology, new designs for flexible devices and packaging technologies, along with the trend toward ever-smaller silicon electronics, remain key factors (Kim et al., 2017).

- **Microfluidics and Non-invasive Chemical Sensing:** The combination of microfluidics and non-invasive chemical sensing technologies in multichannel MIoT devices enables real-time monitoring of a wide range of biomarkers in body fluids, including sweat, tears, and interstitial fluid. Such developments allow continuous, non-invasive monitoring of arterial blood gas and acid-base homeostasis (Vo and Trinh, 2024).

6.2. Convergence with Other Technologies

The integration of MIoT devices with other emerging technologies, like AI, blockchain, and 5G, is opening up new dimensions of possibilities and innovation in the health sector. The MIoT is also interacting with different technology domains, which helps in delivering innovative solutions for the healthcare system and patient handling. Parts of this innovative solution lie in this synergic relationship between technologies.

- **AI + IoT + Genomics = Predictive and Precision Medicine:** The combinations of AI + IoT + genomics are also paving the way for predictive and precision medicine, in which MIoT devices are integral in the acquisition and organization of physiological data to facilitate real-time data analysis using AI. When combined with genomic data, this information can offer a personalized perspective on a person's health risks and trigger tailored interventions. This alignment represents progress toward personalized medicine, which integrates an individual's genetic and physiological information to inform treatment and interventions.
- **AR/VR + MIoT for Surgical Training and Therapy:** These technologies are effectively used in surgical training and therapy in the MIoT process. The AR/VR nacelle can create a lifelike surgical environment for training, while the MIoT nacelle can enhance the realism and effectiveness of the training by supplying real-time physiological readings from the patient. The combination of MIoT devices with AR/VR is being leveraged in rehabilitation and pain management as well.
- **Blockchain for Secure Health Data Exchange:** By offering a decentralized, tamper-proof ledger for recording and sharing patient information, blockchain technology can improve the security and confidentiality of health data exchange in MIoT ecosystems. This guarantees the integrity and transparency of data while giving authorized users a secure and auditable way to share data. Smart contracts can also help to automate the policies for accessing and using data so that patients allow and use their data only as dictated by predefined rules and regulations (Abijaude et al., 2021).

6.3. Evolving Patient-Centric Models

MIoT devices are evolving to create patient-centric healthcare models that allow patients to manage their health and wellness. These models with a focus on patient-centricity, personalization, and access are driving them towards a more proactive and preventive way of care.

- **Real-time Feedback for Self-management of Care:** MIoT devices facilitate self-managed care through real-time health status delivery to the patient, enabling them to make informed decisions and adapt their lifestyles as appropriate. Monitoring of vitals, activity, and other relevant factors continuously enables patients to take an active role in managing chronic diseases, adhering to treatment cycles, and preventing complications. MIoT devices provide real-time feedback to the patients, assisting them with improved awareness and healthier behavior.
- **Remote Diagnostics and Decentralized Hospitals:** Micromobility Internet of Things (MIoT) devices have been used to enhance remote diagnostics and decentralized hospitals. MIoT devices allow remote patient monitoring and reduce hospital visits, which ultimately help improve the convenience and affordability of expensive healthcare services.

6.4. Next-Generation Implantables

To address new medical indications, implantable devices with enhanced sensing, energy harvesting, and therapeutic capabilities are being developed. Shape this product to fit the body, since using these devices to provide focused drug delivery, long-term monitoring, and individualized therapy will make the integration much easier.

- **Neural Dust and Injectable Nanosensors:** Neural dust and injectable nanosensors provide novel avenues for implantable technologies, allowing continuous monitoring of neural activity, as well as biochemical parameters, at an unrivalled resolution. The tiny sensors, some smaller than a grain of sand, can be embedded deep inside the body to collect real-time information on neural signals, glucose levels, and other biomarkers. Data is transmitted wirelessly to external devices where it can be analyzed and interpreted (Briganti and Le Moine, 2020).
- **Regenerative Bioelectronics:** Regenerative bioelectronics utilizes electrical signals in tandem with biological materials to promote tissue regeneration and enhance healing. They can emit electrical or chemical signals to encourage cell proliferation, tissue regeneration, and nerve regrowth.
- **Organ-on-a-Chip and Smart Prosthetics:** MIoT can help create artificial skin grafts or neocortex tissue to be used on prosthetic limbs that would mimic natural skin tissues and could be used for tactile or sensory experiences. MIoT sensors and actuators within smart prosthetics also enable real-time feedback and control, translating into enhanced ability and dexterity in artificial limbs.

6.5. Global Health Impacts

With the correct Internet of Things (IoT) devices, at the right time, in the right location, we can all help solve the world's biggest problems, improve remote monitoring, enable strategic disease prevention, and make healthcare more accessible, even in places with restrictions.MIoT telemedicine solutions play a crucial role in bridging the healthcare access gap for individuals located in remote and underserved regions where geographical factors and limited infrastructure prevent timely access to medical expertise and facilities (Lainjo, 2021).

- **Mobile Health (mHealth) in Low-Resource Settings:** In low-resource settings, the use of MIoT devices is crucial to mobile health as these devices provide economical and reachable healthcare solutions. Wearable sensors, smartphone-based diagnostics, and portable monitoring devices can all help diagnose diseases, monitor vital signs, and provide essential healthcare services in resource-poor communities. Smart farms employ IoT as a solution, while COVID-19 management systems also use IoT. (Biswas et al., 2021). This raises the increasing importance of telemedicine and the remote monitoring of patients using IoT.
- **Pandemic Management and Disease Surveillance:** Wearable sensors and MIoT devices could be employed for pandemic management and disease surveillance, providing real-time data on disease outbreaks, transmission

dynamics, and the effectiveness of public health interventions. Wearable real-time data can aid in updating public health policies, resource allocation, and effective interventions to restrain infectious disease spread.

7. Conclusion

Wearable and implantable Medical Internet of Things (MIoT) devices have the potential to transform healthcare to precision, preventive, and remote patient management. Wearable devices can be used for various purposes due to their non-invasive, mobile, and connected nature and in the case of implantable devices, it provides long-term monitoring and treatment with some implantable devices. Such devices deploy minuscule biosensors, wireless connectivity, edge computing, and AI/ML analytics to deliver real-time insights. MIoT reflects the ultimate integration where we can self-manage care, connected devices, medicines, telemedicine, and global healthcare systems. Yet, responsible innovation and interdisciplinary collaborative efforts are critical to overcoming technical hurdles, privacy and cybersecurity concerns, ethical and societal implications, and regulatory hurdles. Research disciplines in MIoT should inform future pathways of research, development, and deployment to effectively maximize the transformational impact of MIoT in pursuing technological advances, convergence with other technologies, and evolving patient-centric models.

References

Abijaude, J., Serra, H., Barretto, R., Bezerra, A., Sobreira, P., and Greve, F. (2021). Internet das coisas, blockchain e contratos inteligentes aplicados à saúde. Sociedade Brasileira de Computação. doi: 10.5753/sbc.7770.2.2.

Abyzova, E., Dogadina, E., Rodriguez, R.D., Petrov, I., Kolesnikova, Y., Zhou, M., and Sheremet, E. (2023). Beyond tissue replacement: The emerging role of smart implants in healthcare. Materials Today Bio, 22, 100784. doi: 10.1016/j.mtbio.2023.100784.

Aledhari, M., Razzak, R., Qolomany, B., Al-Fuqaha, A., and Saeed, F. (2022). Biomedical IoT: Enabling technologies, architectural elements, challenges, and future directions. IEEE Access, 10, 31306–31339. doi: 10.1109/access.2022.3159235.

Amiri, D., Anzanpour, A., Azimi, I., Levorato, M., Liljeberg, P., Dutt, N., and Rahmani, A.M. (2020). Context-aware sensing via dynamic programming for edge-assisted wearable systems. ACM Transactions on Computing for Healthcare, 1(2), 1–25. doi: 10.1145/3351286.

Angelucci, A., Cavicchioli, M., Cintorrino, I.A., Lauricella, G., Rossi, C., Strati, S., and Aliverti, A. (2021). Smart textiles and sensorized garments for physiological monitoring: A review of available solutions and techniques. Sensors, 21(3), 814. doi: 10.3390/s21030814.

Barua, S., and Barua, A. (2021). Understanding the determinants of wearable fitness technology adoption and use in a developing country: An empirical study. The Journal of Management Theory and Practice (JMTP), 78–87. doi: 10.37231/jmtp.2021.2.1.90.

Bergsland, J., Elle, O.J., and Fosse, E. (2014). Barriers to medical device innovation. Medical Devices: Evidence and Research, 205–209. doi: 10.2147/mder.s43369.

Biswas, M., Akhund, T.M.N.U., Ferdous, M.J., Kar, S., Anis, A., and Shanto, S.A. (2021, July). Biot: Blockchain based smart agriculture with internet of thing. *In:* 2021 Fifth World Conference on Smart Trends in Systems Security and Sustainability (WorldS4), pp. 75–80. IEEE. doi: 10.1109/worlds451998.2021.9513998.

Briganti, G., and Le Moine, O. (2020). Artificial intelligence in medicine: Today and tomorrow. Frontiers in Medicine, 7, 509744. doi: 10.3389/fmed.2020.00027.

Diab, M.S., and Rodriguez-Villegas, E. (2022). Embedded machine learning using microcontrollers in wearable and ambulatory systems for health and care applications: A review. IEEE Access, 10, 98450–98474. doi: 10.1109/access.2022.3206782.

Elijah, O., Rahman, T.A., Orikumhi, I., Leow, C.Y., and Hindia, M.N. (2018). An overview of Internet of Things (IoT) and data analytics in agriculture: Benefits and challenges. IEEE Internet of Things Journal, 5(5), 3758–3773. doi: 10.1109/jiot.2018.2844296.

Fouad, H., Hassanein, A.S., Soliman, A.M., and Al-Feel, H. (2020). Analyzing patient health information based on IoT sensor with AI for improving patient assistance in the future direction. Measurement, 159, 107757. doi: 10.1016/j.measurement.2020.107757.

Ghamari, M., Janko, B., Sherratt, R.S., Harwin, W., Piechockic, R., and Soltanpur, C. (2016). A survey on wireless body area networks for ehealthcare systems in residential environments. Sensors, 16(6), 831. doi: 10.3390/s16060831.

Haghi, M., Thurow, K., and Stoll, R. (2017). Wearable devices in medical internet of things: Scientific research and commercially available devices. Healthcare Informatics Research, 23(1), 4–15. doi: 10.4258/hir.2017.23.1.4.

Hasan, A., Klintworth, K., and Hajat, C. (2021). Wearable technology and health improvement. Occupational Medicine, 71(2), 53–55. doi: 10.1093/occmed/kqaa178.

Hayyolalam, V., Aloqaily, M., Özkasap, Ö., and Guizani, M. (2021). Edge intelligence for empowering IoT-based healthcare systems. IEEE Wireless Communications, 28(3), 6–14. doi: 10.1109/mwc.001.2000345.

Hussain, A., Ali, T., Althobiani, F., Draz, U., Irfan, M., Yasin, S., and Alqhtani, S. (2021). Security framework for IoT based real-time health applications. Electronics, 10(6), 719. doi: 10.3390/electronics10060719.

Kang, M., Park, E., Cho, B.H., and Lee, K.S. (2018). Recent patient health monitoring platforms incorporating Internet of things-enabled smart devices. International Neurology Journal, 22(Suppl 2), S76. doi: 10.5213/inj.1836144.072.

Kao, Y.S., Nawata, K., and Huang, C.Y. (2019). An exploration and confirmation of the factors influencing adoption of IoT-based wearable fitness trackers. International Journal of Environmental Research and Public Health, 16(18), 3227. doi: 10.3390/ijerph16183227.

Kassanos, P., and Hourdakis, E. (2025). Implantable passive sensors for biomedical applications. Sensors, 25(1), 133. doi: 10.3390/s25010133.

Khan, S., and Alam, M. (2021). Wearable Internet of Things for personalized healthcare: Study of trends and latent research. Health informatics: A computational perspective in healthcare, 43-60. doi: 10.1007/978-981-15-9735-0_3.

Kim, J., Campbell, A.S., de Ávila, B.E.F., and Wang, J. (2019). Wearable biosensors for healthcare monitoring. Nature Biotechnology, 37(4), 389–406. doi: 10.1038/s41587-019-0045-y.

Kim, J., Ghaffari, R., and Kim, D.H. (2017). The quest for miniaturized soft bioelectronic devices. Nature Biomedical Engineering, 1(3), 0049. doi: 10.1038/s41551-017-0049.

Kufakunesu, R., Hancke, G.P., and Abu-Mahfouz, A.M. (2020). A survey on adaptive data rate optimization in lorawan: Recent solutions and major challenges. Sensors, 20(18), 5044. doi: 10.3390/s20185044.

Lainjo, B. (2021). Thematic dynamics of Internet of Things (IoT): Impact on Digital Personalized Healthcare (PHC). International Journal of Women's Health Care, 6(3). doi: 10.33140/ijwhc.06.03.05.

Li, C., Wang, J., Wang, S., and Zhang, Y. (2024). A review of IoT applications in healthcare. Neurocomputing, 565, 127017. doi: 10.1016/j.neucom.2023.127017.

Liaqat, M., Mushtaq, M., Jamil, A., Mushtaq, M.M., Ali, H., Anwar, R., and Bokhari, S.F.H. (2024). Mobile health interventions: A frontier for mitigating the global burden of cardiovascular disease. Cureus, 16(6). doi: 10.7759/cureus.62157.

Pons-Faudoa, F.P., Ballerini, A., Sakamoto, J., and Grattoni, A. (2019). Advanced implantable drug delivery technologies: Transforming the clinical landscape of therapeutics for chronic diseases. Biomedical Microdevices, 21, 1–22. doi: 10.1007/s10544-019-0389-6.

Rushton, D.N. (2002). Electrical stimulation in the treatment of pain. Disability and Rehabilitation, 24(8), 407–415. doi: 10.2147/mder.s43369.

Sayyad, P.W., Park, S.J., and Ha, T.J. (2024). Recent advances in biosensors based on metal-oxide semiconductors system-integrated into bioelectronics. Biosensors and Bioelectronics, 116407. https://doi.org/10.1016/j.bios.2024.116407.

Vo, D.K., and Trinh, K.T.L. (2024). Advances in wearable biosensors for healthcare: Current trends, applications, and future perspectives. Biosensors, 14(11), 560. doi: 10.3390/bios14110560

Youm, H.Y. (2017). An overview of security and privacy issues for Internet of Things. IEICE TRANSACTIONS on Information and Systems, 100(8), 1649-1662. doi: 10.1587/transinf.2016ici0001.

CHAPTER

9

Ultrasound Medical Image Denoising Using Block-matching and 3D-filtering with the Alternating Direction Method of Multipliers

Karmanya Tyagi[1], Jishnu Saurav Mittapalli[1], Dhyani Desai[1], Aswathy Ravikumar[2(0000-0003-0897-6991)] and Harini Sriraman[1*(0000-0002-2192-8153)]

[1] School of Computer Science and Engineering, Vellore Institute of Technology, Chennai, India

[2] Senior AI Consultant, Sustainable Living Lab, Chennai, India

1. Introduction

High-frequency sound waves are employed in ultrasound imaging to visualize soft tissues, including internal organs, hence serving as a vital diagnostic tool for musculoskeletal, cardiac, and obstetrical disorders. The technique is highly preferred in the field of medical diagnostics due to its non-invasive nature, cost-effectiveness, and ability to provide real-time results, hence solidifying its status as a commonly employed diagnostic modality. As sound waves propagate through the body, they undergo reflection by various layers of tissue, resulting in the formation of pictures. Nevertheless, the quality of ultrasound images is hindered by various problems. These challenges include substantial loss of information during the process of signal reconstruction, the sensitivity of signal acquisition to direction, and the presence of inherent noise that obscures the intricate morphology of the specific anatomical region being targeted (John et al., 2021, Lakshminarayanan et al., 2023, Liu et al., 2021, Ravikumar and Sriraman, 2023a, 2023b).

A form of noise that is particularly damaging is speckle noise. This occurs as a result of the ultrasonic probe's signal dispersing throughout the organism. One major factor that reduces the clarity of ultrasound images is noise, which can

*Corresponding author: harini.s@vit.ac.in

DOI: 10.1201/9781003676812-9

mask important features and make the task of medical professionals more complex in the diagnostic process. Therefore, it is important to use advanced algorithms to successfully suppress speckle noise in US images since it is significant for the next post-processing steps and the actual visualization performed by healthcare providers.

Denoising medical images represents a critical operational step used to lower or remove noise since it preserves vital information, yet minimizes sensor-based electrical noise as well as digital quantization noise, together with environmental noise. Denoising seeks to clear important image structures so medical staff can make more accurate diagnoses, along with improved algorithm performance in image analysis (Mohd Sagheer and George, 2020). The implementation of denoising is crucial for multiple imaging technologies, including MRI, CT, X-ray systems and ultrasound.

Medical image denoising methods possess various strategies which require specific noise types and target goals for selection. Wavelet denoising achieves effective Gaussian noise reduction simultaneously with maintaining fine image structures according to Mohd Sagheer and George (2020). Total variation denoising stands out as a superior method for removing impulsive noise while protecting image edge definitions. Non-local means denoising generates successful results in managing multiple forms of noise by averaging matched image pixels.

The advanced image processing method BM3D performs a wide range of tasks throughout the image processing and computer vision fields by acting as Block-Matching and 3D-filtering. The technique undertakes a dual-stage operation involving matching image blocks before uniting them for the subsequent application of 3D-filtering methods to minimize noise interference. Image noise can be converted into a different domain, such as wavelets, through this method to enable filtering. An image returns to its original domain after processing, so the result becomes a denoised version. The BM3D model stands out as an effective solution for handling Gaussian, Poisson, and mixed Gaussian-Poisisson noises according to literature (Thakur et al., 2021).

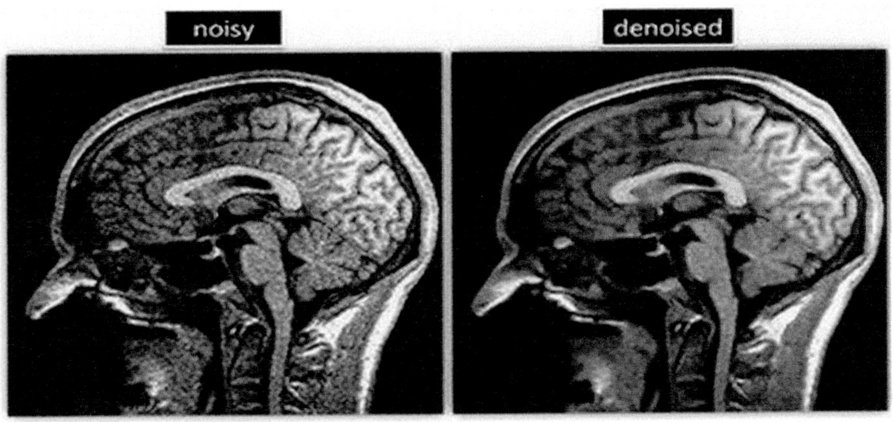

Figure 1: Sample image denoising (Polycystic ovary syndrome (PCOS), n.d.)

By implementing denoising techniques, the enhancement of picture quality not only facilitates precise diagnoses but also improves the efficacy of algorithms employed in image segmentation, registration, and feature extraction. Consequently, this leads to a reduction in the probability of diagnostic errors.

The process of medical image denoising plays a crucial role in improving the visual fidelity and precision of medical imaging. There are several techniques, such as wavelet denoising, total variation denoising, non-local means denoising, and BM3D, that can be employed to tackle diverse noise-related issues. The selection of a denoising methodology is contingent upon the particular noise characteristics and the desired outcome, hence making a substantial contribution to enhanced diagnostic methodologies and algorithmic efficacy (Hansen and Sørensen, 2013).

2. Background to Medical Imaging Techniques

Medical imaging techniques play a critical role in disease discovery and treatment approaches for numerous health conditions. MRI, CT scan and ultrasound imaging produce results that contain noise, which hides vital information, potentially leading to misinterpretations by medical practitioners (Elad and Aharon, 2006; Kaur and Dong, 2023; Tan et al., 2024). Accurate and efficient denoising methods stand as the foundation of critical importance because of their crucial role in medical imaging procedures. Developing powerful and resilient image denoising systems constitutes the essential problem for preserving critical medical information in clinical images. The development needs to resolve the complex medical image nature and multiple noise types while ensuring computational efficiency for real-time clinical application of denoising techniques. The main purpose behind this work is to create better diagnostic accuracy. Speckle noise in ultrasound pictures creates such a significant visual disruption that the necessary diagnostic information is hidden from view. Medical image denoising processes that achieve efficiency make it easier for clinicians to detect and understand essential clinical details more rapidly. The accuracy of precise measurement determines what treatment options will be available to patients because it enables proper identification of their medical issues. Enhanced image quality acts as a vital interest factor (Baby and Ravikumar, n.d.). Medical examinations need high-quality ultrasound picture acquisition because professionals can perform accurate evaluations. Enhanced image quality methods allow healthcare professionals to perform examinations of soft tissues and organs, leading to vital medical assessments, thus making these techniques essential for their work. The current generation of image denoising methods restores images with better clarity, thus accelerating medical identification operations. Medical time-sensitive detection systems prove essential to providing better treatment choices and improved patient results in heart diseases, together with various cancer types (Lakshminarayanan et al., 2023). The project delivers assistance to complex image processing workflows through segmentation methods, together with registration techniques and 3D reconstruction operations. Medical procedures today regarding examinations and treatment planning completely rely on noise-free, high-quality images to be successful. The quality of ultrasound images leads to better patient outcomes in a positive manner. Medical diagnoses based on dependable methods let healthcare providers deliver unique treatment plans per patient requirement, which minimizes the medical consequences arising from late or incorrect medical assessments (Ravikumar and Sriraman, 2023c).

3. Existing Methods

The literature contains a variety of research methodologies addressing medical image denoising. Two widely implemented methods are among those used for medical image denoising, that is Filter filter-based and model-based methods.

The filtering-based approach applies different types of filters to noisy images to eliminate noise contamination. Gaussian filters, together with median filters and wavelet filters, constitute examples of filters employed in image denoising applications. Simple image denoising techniques that offer quick application produce limited efficiency against all types of noise while enabling possible degradation of image details. The filtering-based technology stands as the simplest standard approach to achieve image denoising. Several filters are directly applied to noisy images through these methods to decrease noise while safeguarding the maximum amount of original detail (Fan et al., 2019).

The Gaussian filter performs image smoothing through pixel value averaging operations, which depend on Gaussian distribution weights within the kernel. Gaussian noise reduction performance is excellent, but the filters have a detrimental effect on image details, which leads to decreased resolution. The median filter operates by selecting the middle pixel value from a defined neighborhood for each pixel value replacement. The elimination of salt-and-pepper noise occurs efficiently through this filtering approach, and the outcome retains higher image clarity levels than Gaussian filters can achieve. A picture decomposed through wavelet filters allows for selective denoising of its frequency components since it separates the image into multiple frequency sub-bands. The method performs optimally in preserving edges plus intricate image details while reducing noise, thus making it appropriate for medical image applications with complex noise problems.

Model-based Methods

Mathematical models serve to represent the noise and image characteristics for denoising purposes (Arsalan et al., 2018). The developed models serve as tools to estimate noise-free original images from their corrupted versions. The category of model-based methods includes Bayesian methods, together with total variation methods and non-local means methods. Model-based denoising works through mathematical modeling, which includes representations for images and the noise affecting them. Advanced techniques in denoising use structural image properties together with noise assumptions to achieve superior results. Bayesian techniques establish statistical models which forecast noisy observation likelihoods while bringing in previous knowledge about noise distributions for clean image estimation. The effectiveness of Bayesian approaches is well-demonstrated, but these approaches usually require complex and time-consuming computations to function effectively. The objective of Total Variation (TV) methods is to simultaneously minimize detection signal variations and reduce noise in uniform sections while preserving the edges and keeping gradients steady in regions of high detail. The built-in property of TV techniques makes them very useful in medical imaging since edge preservation stands as a vital requirement. With non-local means algorithms, you get to find average pixel values by processing neighboring pixels that display similar patterns in the image. Studies show that this method proves highly successful at dealing with images featuring replicated textures and structure patterns in medical image applications.

Deep neural network training occurs through the utilization of large image databases with noise and uncontaminated versions for obtaining image de-noising capabilities. Different applications, such as image recognition, denoising and image synthesis, utilize deep learning techniques as an operational method. The denoising approaches consist of CNNs, DAEs and GANs. Picture denoising methods heavily rely on deep learning algorithms because today's world offers superior processing power together with large image collections. Neural networks become competent at cleansing noisy images through trained capabilities which enable image conversion between noisy and clean versions (Goodfellow et al., 2014; Ravikumar et al., 2023; Ravikumar and Sriraman, 2023b; Tian et al., 2020).

Diversified methods utilize two or more of the previously described approaches to result in enhanced denoising outcomes. A hybrid method incorporates low-frequency noise filtering techniques with high-frequency noise removal capabilities using models according to the literature (Tian et al., 2020). Diverse denoising algorithms receive their respective advantages through hybrid methods that merge multiple methodologies together for exploitation. The combination of filtering methods with model-based approaches permits low-frequency noise reduction using filters as the initial step, while model techniques support the outcome by eliminating high-frequency noise or enhancing edge features.

The process of pre-training deep learning models with images that undergo filtering helps them develop greater efficiency in learning, along with enhanced capabilities to withstand multiple types of noise. Denoising medical photographs adopts varied features within each strategy described throughout this discussion. Numerous factors related to the application's requirements determine the choice of noise reduction method, such as the noise type and whether processing requires real-time operation, combined with the required level of detail maintenance.

4. Proposed Method

The proposed system demonstrates how the BM3D algorithm connects to ADMM to reach superior algorithm performance. The ADMM provides an effective optimization technique able to solve diverse optimization problems, including image denoising (Andria et al., 2012; Chen et al., 2022; Dabov et al., 2007). The image denoising procedure of BM3D-ADMM is divided into two separate problems for block-matching operations and 3D-filtering operations. The ADMM algorithm serves to solve the optimization problems that appear in each subproblem. ADMM method's parallelization ability allows users to experience major speed improvements in their processes. Non-differentiable and nonlinear functions are manageable with the ADMM method because of its capability to suit the BM3D algorithm. Different research works have displayed how the BM3D-ADMM method successfully denoises Gaussian as well as Poisson and mixed Gaussian-Poisson noise types (Yang and Yu, 2021).

The image denoising in BM3D operates through collaborative filtering followed by aggregation, as depicted in Fig. 2. Similar image patches form 3D groups before the application of transform-domain denoising occurs to each group. Parallel data combination from denoised patches produces the final denoised image in the second step. ADMM serves in BM3D to conduct transform-domain denoising operations on the 3D patch groups through the collaborative filtering process. The collaborative filtering challenge presents itself as an optimized problem that includes necessary constraints. The ADMM algorithm divides the optimization task into two separate subproblems that run sequentially to each other.

The high-level overview of how ADMM is used in the BM3D algorithm for image denoising, as shown in the architecture Fig. 2:

- Divide the input noisy image into overlapping patches.
- Form 3D groups of similar patches.
- Apply a transform (e.g., discrete cosine transforms, wavelet transform) to each 3D patch group, yielding the transformed coefficients.
- Initialize the transformed coefficients and auxiliary variables for ADMM.
- Iterate the following steps until convergence:
    - Denoise the transformed coefficients by solving a denoising subproblem using ADMM.
    - Update the auxiliary variables based on the denoised coefficients.
    - Update the transformed coefficients based on the denoised coefficients and auxiliary variables.

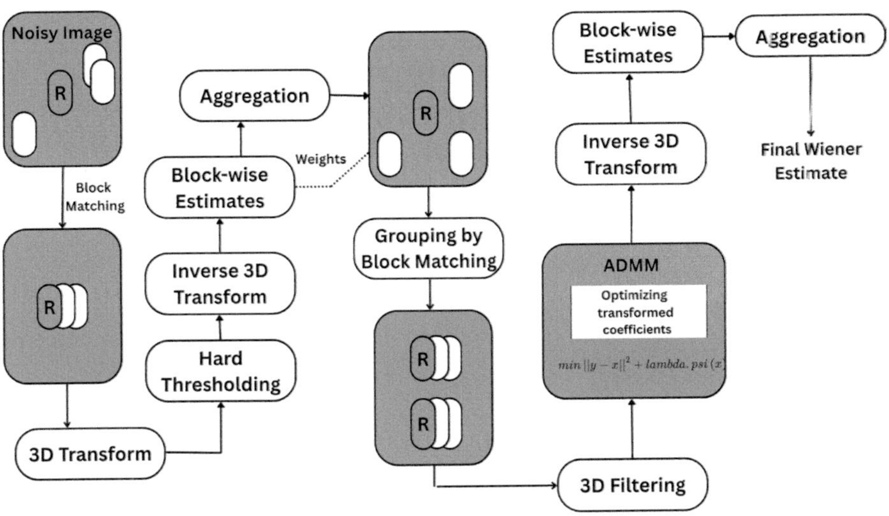

Figure 2: Proposed model.

- Inverse transform the denoised coefficients to obtain the denoised patches.
- Aggregate the denoised patches to reconstruct the final denoised image.

The denoising subproblem executes a cost function optimization that checks both the similar connection between noisy and denoised patches, known as the data fidelity term and a regularization term that supports smoothness or sparsity in transformed coefficients. The decomposition features of ADMM enable the handling of this problem through smaller, efficient subproblems. ADMM enables BM3D to leverage similar patch collaboration for achieving its effective denoising results. The optimization process between denoising operations and variable and coefficient updates leads to progressively better image denoising results.

i. BM3D

BM3D (Block-Matching 3D filtering) represents a well-established image denoising procedure which performs non-local block-matching operations followed by collaborative filtering steps. The algorithm implements two main blocks of operation, consisting of block-matching followed by collaborative filtering. Image blocks get partitioned during block-matching before the algorithm finds identical blocks in the image domain. The procedure creates a three-dimensional data array using blocks which have already been identified as matching each other. An estimate of the noise-free image appears after applying 3D filtering to the 3D data array through the collaborative filtering step. The image denoising technique known as Block-Matching 3D filtering, or the BM3D, serves as a commonly utilized method. The BM3D mathematical expression appears thus:

$$y = x + n \tag{1}$$

Where:
The observed image with noise appears under the variable "y" in the equation.
The image "x" refers to the original image without any noise.
The image noise appears as the variable "n" during the equation.

The BM3D algorithm carries out its process through two sequential stages, which form block-matching and collaborative filtering.

- Block matching: Blocks of image data receive overlapping regions before identical blocks are found through Euclidean distance analysis in this stage. The assembly process creates 3D groups using positions and scales of identically matching blocks.
- Collaborative filtering: The filtering process implements a 3D collaborative algorithm for every 3D group to compute a noise-free version of the image. This step requires a 3D collaborative filtering operation to complete its operation.
- The three-dimensional group undergoes frequency domain conversion through the implementation of the three-dimensional discrete cosine transform (DCT).
- A non-linear threshold is applied to transform coefficients to lower the signal noise level.
- When thresholding finishes the operation, the application uses inverse 3D DCT to switch back from the frequency domain into the spatial domain.

- All processed blocks unite into a single output image through the aggregation process.
- The mathematical expression of the BM3D algorithm appears as shown below:

$$\hat{x} = G(y) \tag{2}$$

Where:
The mathematical expression shows $\hat{x}$ as the estimated clean image.
The observed noisy image y is the notation for a variable in the equation.
The operator G implements the block-matching and collaborative filtering procedures as part of the BM3D denoising mechanism.

Extensive empirical evidence proves the effectiveness of the BM3D algorithm when removing Gaussian noise from images, while its functionality extends towards Poisson and impulse noise elimination as well.

ii. Optimization with ADMM

The extension of the BM3D algorithm named BD4M uses the ADMM (Alternating Direction Method of Multipliers) optimization framework to solve image denoising problems. The mathematical expression for BM3D with ADMM contains the following relationship:

$$\text{min\_}x \ ||y - x||^2\text{\_}2 + \lambda\Psi(x) \tag{3}$$

subject to $x = z$, $z = Tx + v$

Where the observed image suffering from noise contamination is symbolized by "y." The image denoising problem includes "x" as the variable that shows the original, uncorrupted image. During the process, the regularization parameter "λ" controls the relationship between the data fidelity term and the regularization term. The regularization term $\Psi(x)$ enables sparsity in wavelet space z, while the ADMM process requires the auxiliary variable z for implementation. In this context, the transform operator "T" facilitates the conversion of image "x" to wavelet domain space, while adding a noise term v to z produces the observed image y. The above equation uses the ADMM framework to compute three successive steps involving a soft-thresholding operator in the wavelet domain, and shrinkage operator in the wavelet domain and dual operator updates for the Lagrange multiplier. The iterative process stops at convergence to yield the noise-free image.

iii. Dataset

The preparation of data is essential when using learning-based denoising techniques. The training process requires adequate data samples, so this study collected many images from different medical modalities. A careful process was implemented for the data samples to include noise additions that made these samples suitable for future research purposes. The primary goal of this research was to increase the learning process generalizability in medical image classification through three separate class assignments. The research utilized image samples collected from many medical imaging modalities (Polycystic ovary syndrome (PCOS), n.d.) as depicted in Fig. 3.

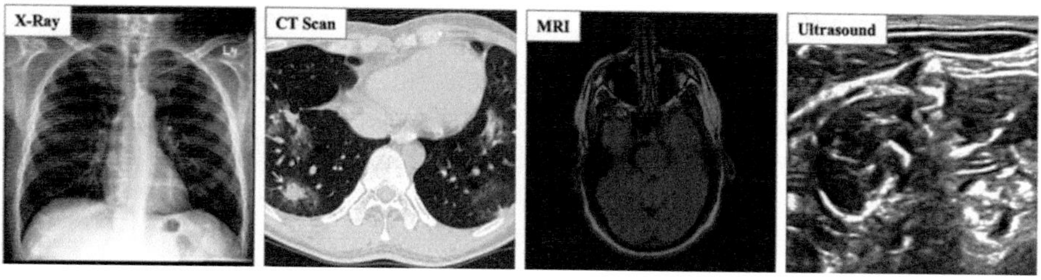

Figure 3: Different modality images.

The research data consists of Polycystic ovary syndrome (PCOS) information that presents as sporadic menstrual cycles with irregular periods and elevated androgen hormone levels. Numerous fluid-filled sacs named follicles appear in the ovaries, which frequently avoid regular egg release. Clinical and physical parameters required to diagnose PCOS and its associated fertility problems exist in the dataset collection.

5. Result Analysis

Executing an image denoising algorithm demands proper systematic implementation. The foundation for image denoising implementation begins with importing the required libraries consisting of cv2, numpy, matplotlib, pyplot and skimage metrics. The algorithm requires several parameter initializations for its operation, which include matching thresholds alongside block sizes and step sizes, in addition to window sizes and Kaiser window parameters. The program contains functions that initialize arrays used for image and weight matrices alongside the Kaiser window. The code defines three different functions, which enable block detection and search window setup and fast block matching operations. The algorithm executes its operations on each pixel block throughout the image, starting with fast block matching for block identification, then final refinement, followed by weighted average block calculations to produce the denoized output. The methodology described allowed us to create a successful algorithm for image denoising. The combination of ADMM with BM3D yielded superior results, which outperformed the original BM3D method through measures of peak signal-to-noise ratio and structural similarity index. The performance gains stem from the ADMM implementation that helps optimize both quality results and computational demands simultaneously. The implementation of ADMM enables the optimization problem to reach convergence at a faster rate than in the original BM3D approach. The optimization problem is solved more efficiently through the subproblems division, which the ADMM methodology achieves. Detectable image features maintain higher visibility in the BM3D with ADMM system when compared to the standard BM3D method. Image structures together with edges remain intact because non-local regularization functions form part of the ADMM method. Different noise levels do not impact the BM3D with the ADMM approach in the same way they affect the original BM3D algorithm. The ADMM method adjusts the regularization parameter according to the noise level.

The BM3D with ADMM approach functions as an effective algorithm for image denoising which provides superior denoising results along with accelerated speed and maintains spatial details accurately. The algorithm suffers from two main weaknesses which involve complex computational requirements and reduced performance when processing intricate types of noise. Figure 4 gives the comparison of the PSNR values existing between existing and proposed BM3D Approach.

Model	**σ**	**PSNR**
BM3D	10	30.290
BM3D-ADMM (Proposed)		***32.737***
BM3D	25	24.490
BM3D-ADMM (Proposed)		***28.585***
BM3D	50	21.880
BM3D-ADMM (Proposed)		***24.212***

Figure 4: Comparison with state of the art models.

After performing a qualitative assessment of image denoising at $\sigma = 10$, the proposed method was found to significantly enhance the perceptual quality of the resulting image when compared to the existing denoising techniques, as shown in Fig. 5.

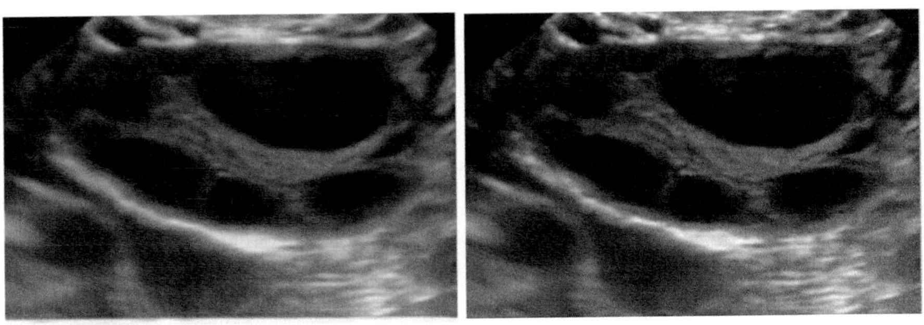

Figure 5: Noisy and denoised image using the $\sigma = 10$ BM3D method.

After a qualitative assessment of image denoising at $\sigma = 25$, the proposed method was found to offer a remarkable improvement in the perceptual quality of the resulting image when compared to the existing denoising method, as shown in Fig. 6.

The qualitative evaluation of image denoising at $\sigma = 50$ revealed that the proposed method significantly improved the perceptual quality of the resulting image when compared to the existing denoising technique, as shown in Fig. 7.

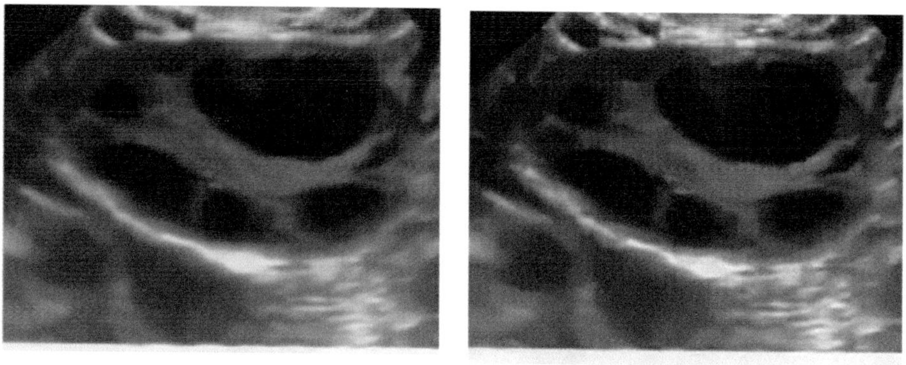

Figure 6: Noisy and denoised image using the σ = 25 BM3D method.

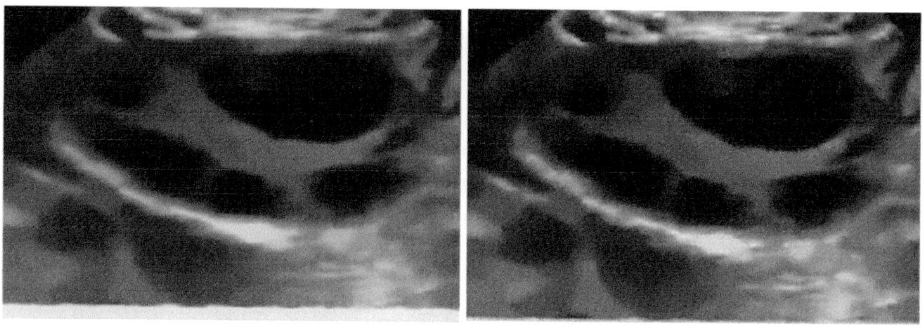

Figure 7: Noisy and denoised image using the σ = 50 BM3D method.

6. Discussion

The algorithm proves superior to wavelets along with total variation-based approaches for denoising because it generates better results based on visual inspection as well as quantitative PSNR and SSIM measurements. The main advantage of BM3D with ADMM arises from its ability to detect image structure similarities across different blocks, which permits the algorithm to effectively eliminate noise while maintaining edge fidelity. The algorithm implements a block-matching system together with collaborative filtering, which provides an efficient framework to process big image collections. The implementation success of BM3D when using the ADMM algorithm comes with essential operational limitations. To execute this algorithm, comprehensive computing power becomes necessary, which hinders real-time processing capabilities. Users who lack experience need several parameter controls to operate the algorithm successfully. The combination of BM3D with ADMM proves itself to be a leading image denoising technology suitable for many medical imaging needs. BM3D with ADMM shows increasing practical value for the future because modern technology provides improved computational power alongside algorithm enhancement. ADMM applied with BM3D establishes an efficient system for image denoising with multiple practical uses. The accuracy of medical diagnosis remains impeded by noises detected within MRI and CT scans and ultrasound images in clinical environments. Medical diagnostic accuracy of images is enhanced through the utilization of BM3D with ADMM as an effective medical noise reduction method.

7. Conclusion

BM3D with ADMM functions as an effective image denoising algorithm to remove noise effectively from images without disturbing their details and structures. The combination of block-matching 3D filtering with alternating direction method of multipliers results in a noise removal system which achieves the highest level of performance among its peers as of right now. The algorithm shows high performance in managing different types of noise events as well as maintaining stability in image content and noise characteristics. The algorithm shows simple implementation properties which enable application across different fields, including medical imaging, video processing and computer vision. Moderate opportunities exist to achieve essential discoveries across multiple image processing domains because of the promising future applications of BM3D with ADMM image denoising technology. The continuous expansion of computational power allows the possibility to optimize this algorithm for real-time operations, which would suit both medical imaging diagnostics and live video solutions. The combination of BM3D with ADMM can enhance virtual immersions through augmented and virtual realities by improving the visual presentation quality. The algorithm can be adapted to apply in space-based astronomical imaging to enhance both the clarity and detail quality of captured space images. An implementation of machine learning together with deep learning technology enables automatic parameter adjustment of BM3D with ADMM using image characteristics and noise patterns as variables. The system becomes more flexible through this method while also demonstrating higher performance potential. Future improvements to BM3D with ADMM will establish advanced standards for photographic denoising quality across different domains.

References

Andria, G., Attivissimo, F., Cavone, G., Giaquinto, N., and Lanzolla, A.M.L. (2012). Linear filtering of 2-D wavelet coefficients for denoising ultrasound medical images. Measurement, 45, 1792–1800. https://doi.org/10.1016/j.measurement.2012.04.005

Arsalan, M., Naqvi, R.A., Kim, D.S., Nguyen, P.H., Owais, M., and Park, K.R. (2018). IrisDenseNet: Robust iris segmentation using densely connected fully convolutional networks in the images by visible light and near-infrared light camera sensors. Sensors, 18. https://doi.org/10.3390/s18051501

Baby, K., and Ravikumar, A. (n.d.). Big data: An ultimate solution in health care. International Journal of Computer Applications, 106.

Chen, R.J., Chen, T.Y., Lipkova, J., Wang, J.J., Williamson, D.F.K., Lu, M.Y. et al. (2022). Algorithm Fairness in AI for Medicine and Healthcare. https://doi.org/10.48550/arXiv.2110.00603

Dabov, K., Foi, A., Katkovnik, V., and Egiazarian, K. (2007). Image denoising by sparse 3-D transform-domain collaborative filtering. IEEE Transactions on Image Processing, 16, 2080–2095. https://doi.org/10.1109/TIP.2007.901238

Elad, M., and Aharon, M. (2006). Image denoising via sparse and redundant representations over learned dictionaries. IEEE Transactions on Image Processing, 15, 3736–3745. https://doi.org/10.1109/TIP.2006.881969

Fan, L., Zhang, F., Fan, H., and Zhang, C. (2019). Brief review of image denoising techniques. Visual Computing for Industry, Biomedicine, and Art, 2, 7. https://doi.org/10.1186/s42492-019-0016-7

Goodfellow, I.J., Pouget-Abadie, J., Mirza, M., Xu, B., Warde-Farley, D., Ozair, S. et al. (2014). Generative Adversarial Networks [WWW Document]. arXiv.org. URL https://arxiv.org/abs/1406.2661v1 (accessed 6.20.25).

Hansen, M.S., and Sørensen, T.S. (2013). Gadgetron: An open source framework for medical image reconstruction. Magnetic Resonance in Medicine, 69, 1768–1776. https://doi.org/10.1002/mrm.24389

John, J., Ravikumar, A., and Abraham, B. (2021). Prostate cancer prediction from multiple pretrained computer vision model. Health and Technology, 11, 1003–1011. https://doi.org/10.1007/s12553-021-00586-y

Kaur, A., and Dong, G. (2023). A complete review on image denoising techniques for medical images. Neural Processing Letters, 55, 7807–7850. https://doi.org/10.1007/s11063-023-11286-1

Lakshminarayanan, V., Ravikumar, A., Sriraman, H., Alla, S., and Chattu, V.K. (2023). Health care equity through intelligent edge computing and augmented reality/virtual reality: A systematic review. Journal of Multidisciplinary Healthcare, 16, 2839–2859. https://doi.org/10.2147/JMDH.S419923

Liu, B., Xu, Z., Wang, Q., Niu, X., Chan, W.X., Hadi, W., and Yap, C.H. (2021. A denoising and enhancing method framework for 4D ultrasound images of human fetal heart. Quant Imaging Med Surg, 11, 1567–1585. https://doi.org/10.21037/qims-20-818

Mohd Sagheer, S.V., and George, S.N. (2020). A review on medical image denoising algorithms. Biomedical Signal Processing and Control, 61, 102036. https://doi.org/10.1016/j.bspc.2020.102036

Polycystic ovary syndrome (PCOS) [WWW Document] (n.d.). URL https://www.kaggle.com/datasets/prasoonkottarathil/polycystic-ovary-syndrome-pcos (accessed 6.20.25).

Ravikumar, A., and Sriraman, H. (2023a). Attenuate class imbalance problem for pneumonia diagnosis using ensemble parallel stacked pre-trained models. CMC, 75, 891–909. https://doi.org/10.32604/cmc.2023.035848

Ravikumar, A., and Sriraman, H. (2023b). Preserve privacy-HD. *In:* Privacy Preservation of Genomic and Medical Data. John Wiley & Sons, Ltd, pp. 189–212. https://doi.org/10.1002/9781394213726.ch9

Ravikumar, A., and Sriraman, H. (2023c). Computationally efficient neural rendering for generator adversarial networks using a multi-GPU cluster in a cloud environment. IEEE Access, 11, 45559–45571. https://doi.org/10.1109/ACCESS.2023.3274201

Ravikumar, A., Sriraman, H., Lokesh, S., and Maruthi Sai Saketh, P. (2023). Identifying pitfalls and solutions in parallelizing long short-term memory network on graphical processing unit by comparing with tensor processing unit parallelism. pp. 111–125. *In:* Smys, S., Kamel, K.A., Palanisamy, R. (Eds.), Inventive Computation and Information Technologies. Springer Nature, Singapore, https://doi.org/10.1007/978-981-19-7402-1_9

Tan, F., Delfino, J.G., and Zeng, R. (2024). Evaluating machine learning-based MRI reconstruction using digital image quality phantoms. Bioengineering, 11, 614. https://doi.org/10.3390/bioengineering11060614

Thakur, R.S., Chatterjee, S., Yadav, R.N., and Gupta, L. (2021). Image de-noising with machine learning: A review. IEEE Access, 9, 93338–93363. https://doi.org/10.1109/ACCESS.2021.3092425

Tian, C., Fei, L., Zheng, W., Xu, Y., Zuo, W., and Lin, C.-W. (2020). Deep learning on image denoising: An overview. Neural Networks, 131, 251–275. https://doi.org/10.1016/j.neunet.2020.07.025

Yang, R., and Yu, Y. (2021). Artificial convolutional neural network in object detection and semantic segmentation for medical imaging analysis. Front. Oncol. 11. https://doi.org/10.3389/fonc.2021.638182

CHAPTER

10

Role of 5G and Future Connectivity in MIoT

A. Vasuki[1(0000-0002-4397-6244)], Vijayakumar Ponnusamy[2*(0000-0002-3929-8495)] and Nemanja Zdravkovic[3(0000-0002-2631-6308)]

[1] Department of Electronics and Communication Engineering, SRM Institute of Science and Technology, Vadapalani, Chennai – 600026, India

[2] Department of Electronics and Communication Engineering, SRM Institute of Science and Technology, Kattankulathur, Chengalpattu – 603203, India

[3] Faculty of Information Technology, Metropolitan University, Serbia

1. Introduction

IoT applications will be distributed across a variety of devices, bolstering the infrastructure of a smart city (Akpakwu, 2017). These devices will cover every aspect of society from different municipal sectors, so it will be necessary to use widely accessible citywide networks to gather and disseminate the generated data. 5G has expanded its purpose to communicate more than simply with individuals in anticipation of this need. In contrast to technologies like LoRa and SigFox, the resultant 5G IoT enables organizations of all sizes to start up IoT services without having to install their network infrastructure, which adds to the success of the smart city ecosystem. Many 5G-enabled smart city services are expected to advance the integration of 5G and IoT. The on-building 5G mobile network will face hitherto unheard-of difficulties as a result of this development, which will also affect the 5G normative effort. This chapter covers the fundamental concepts of massive IoT, key technologies in IoT, the need for 5G in Massive IoT, the Connectivity model of 5G in massive IoT, and challenges in integrating 5G technologies and massive IoT.

Massive IoT: In 5G, the term "massive IoT," or "massive machine-type communications," or "mMTC," refers to the interconnection of numerous battery-powered devices that are typically left alone, have low complexity, are less sensitive to delays, and offer data across cellular networks at a low cost (BICS, 2025). These

*Corresponding author: vijayakp@srmist.edu.in

DOI: 10.1201/9781003676812-10

devices, many of which are sensors, are made to be low-cost and energy-efficient. They deal with small volumes of data, frequently not sent to the cloud regularly. Scalability and adaptability are the main characteristics of massive IoT, enabling communication between billions of machines, objects, and devices. Due to their long battery life and often low throughput speeds, these devices are ideal for deployment over wide geographic areas. The data acquired provides insights that have the potential to improve business practices and address difficult problems. The major applications of massive IoT and conventional IoT are illustrated in Figure 1.

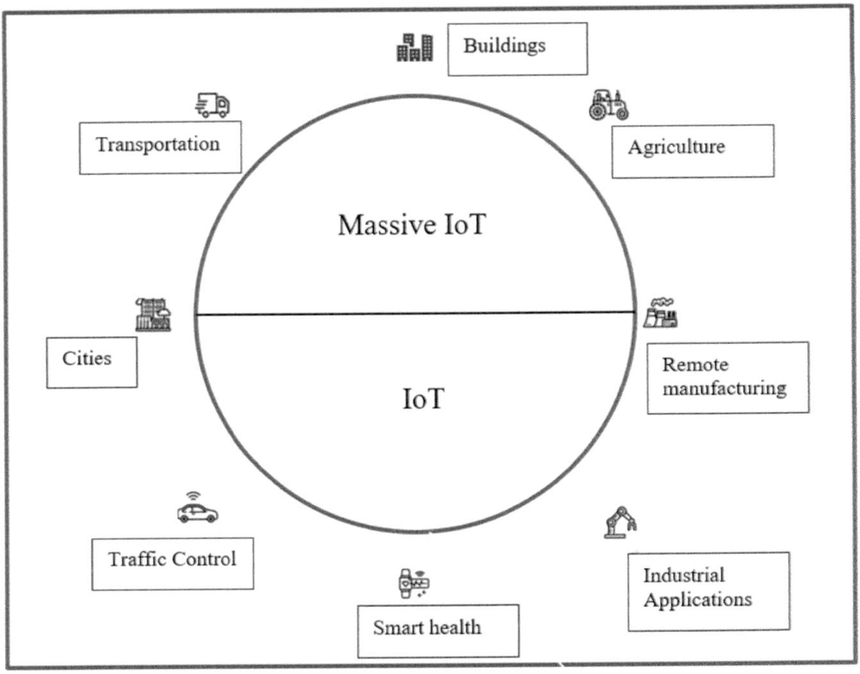

Figure 1: Applications of IoT and massive IoT.

Key Technologies of Massive IoT: Low Power Wide Area Networks enable large-scale IoT installations (LPWAN). LPWANs are wireless communication technologies designed to provide long-range connections with the least power. They allow electronics to function for years on a single battery.

Two primary LPWAN technologies are:

- **LTE-M:** These provide a blend of bandwidth, power efficiency, and mobility and are tailored for Internet of Things devices.
- **NB-IoT:** Narrowband IoT (NB-IoT) is a low-bandwidth technology designed for stationary devices that require extensive coverage and extended battery life.

eSIM and iSIM: Conventional physical SIM cards are evolving to meet the demands of a society that is becoming more linked. Embedded SIM(eSIM and iSIM (integrated SIM) technologies facilitate the deployment and management of large numbers of IoT devices.

Since embedded SIMs are built directly into the device, there is no need for a traditional SIM card and tray. Important space is conserved in this way, allowing for design innovations like smaller wearables or larger batteries. Because eSIMs have fewer holes in the device, they also reduce the possibility of water or dust damage.

e-SIM Push Model: Fleet managers or service providers centrally manage eSIMs for IoT installations, managing carrier changes using a specialised platform. Operational effectiveness and smooth connection are guaranteed by this strategy.

Global Connectivity with Flexibility: International deployments are made hassle-free by combining local SIM profiles with global connectivity, streamlining operations while preserving flexibility.

No Connectivity Lock-in: By removing reliance on a single connection provider, eSIM provides flexibility and acts as a "insurance model" to protect against unforeseen service interruptions.

Diverse Integration Options: For a more efficient onboarding process, companies may choose to use pre-integrated alternatives or use their own Subscription Management Secure Routing (SR) and Subscription Management Data Preparation (SM-DP) solutions.

Embedded SIM-in Factory: A single worldwide hardware configuration is made possible by the incorporated eSIMs during production. This facilitates quicker device manufacture for widespread deployments, lowers expenses, and streamlines logistics.

Simple Global Deployment: Devices with a global bootstrap profile may connect to the internet instantly and from any location. For fast-moving sectors like automotive, logistics, and smart city infrastructure, this guarantees smooth onboarding without manual SIM provisioning or region-specific variations.

Flexibility with no Lock-in: Without having to physically touch the device, eSIMs enable the remote provisioning of local operational profiles, allowing businesses to choose or switch network providers depending on factors like cost, performance, or regulations. This dynamic flexibility is crucial to ensure that IoT investments are future-proof.

i-SIM: The next step in SIM technology development is called Integrated SIM, or iSIM. iSIM is a miniature SIM integrated into the device's System on a Chip (SoC), in contrast to conventional or even embedded SIMs (eSIM). This saves space, lowers expenses, and improves security by integrating the SIM functionality into the device's operating system.

iSIM is perfect for ultra-compact IoT devices like wearables, asset trackers, and industrial sensors since it takes up no extra space. It also simplifies production and logistics by allowing devices to be deployed globally with a single hardware configuration and to instantly connect to a mobile network upon activation.

With even more integration than eSIM, iSIM enables remote provisioning, lifecycle management, and over-the-air upgrades, making it a potent facilitator of secure, scalable, and economical Massive IoT installations.

Simplified Manufacturing and Logistics: Since devices with eSIMs or iSIMs may connect to any suitable network, manufacturers no longer need to build several device types for various network operators.

Easier Remote Management: By remotely updating device network profiles over the air, service providers may do away with the need for expensive and time-consuming physical SIM card replacements at the conclusion of mobile network operator (MNO) contracts.

Streamlined Installation: SIM-embedded devices may choose the best MNO network at the deployment location automatically, making installation easier and requiring less human setup and testing.

Instant Connectivity: When combined with rapid activation services, eSIMs and iSIMs provide fast access to new services, improving the client experience.

Flexibility and Scalability: With eSIM/iSIM-enabled virtual SIM cards, installations may be scaled up or down without the logistical hassles of actual SIM cards, and connection management is made more flexible.

2. Key Techniques of MIoT

The standard architecture for these IoT-enabled applications consists of three fundamental layers (Guo et al., 2021): perceptual, network, and application, as shown in Figure 2. The perception layer refers to the physical systems where Internet of Things devices collect data and interact with their environment to carry out control actions. The network layer connects to the Internet of Things' communication networks, which include wireless access networks and the Internet, to locate and link IoT devices to edge/cloud servers for data or control information transfer. The application layer is the term used to describe the edge computing systems that manage data processing, storage, and decision-making for control determination.

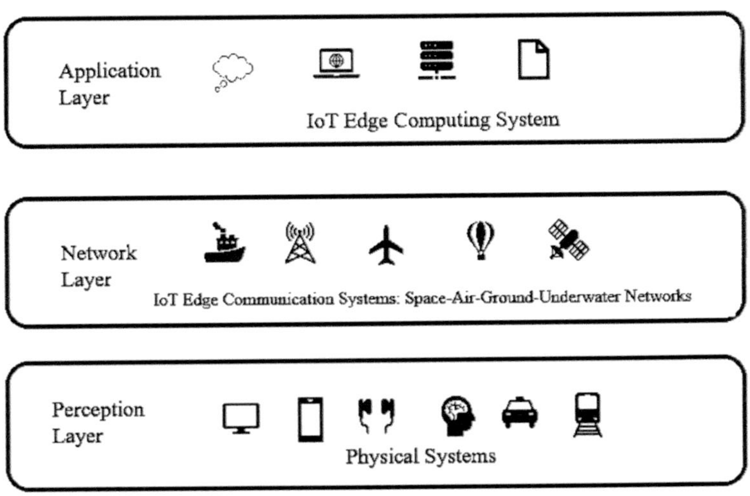

Figure 2: Architecture of IoT.

The standard IoT and the Massive IoT are different in several ways. The main difference between the IoT and Massive IoT is listed in Table 1. Massive IoT is a novel method of networking that links a large number of devices.

Although the phrase has been around since 2018, its relevance has increased with the rise of 5G and LPWANs.

Massive IoT is an ecosystem that makes enormous amounts of data more accessible and useful for enterprises by using cloud and edge computing, big data analytics, and AI. It is projected that 73.1 ZB of data (IDC) would be generated by IoT devices by 2030 (Cheikh et al., 2025). That is around four times the 18.3 ZB produced in 2019 (Shafique et al., 2020). Numerous connections, small data quantities, sporadic transmissions, inexpensive devices, and strict energy consumption regulations are characteristics of the massive IoT. Wearable technology, smart buildings, smart meters, fleet management, transportation logistics, industrial monitoring, and agriculture are a few examples.

Table 1: Difference between IoT and Massive IoT

Parameter	IoT	Massive IoT
Scalability	Cover a wider variety of applications at different sizes	Entails linking devices on a large scale, both in terms of the quantity of data gathered and the number of devices
Device characteristics	May have more power needs and a wider variety of capabilities	Makes use of inexpensive, simple devices that use little power and have extended battery lives. These devices are designed to transmit small amounts of data infrequently
Data handling	Uses machine learning methods	Frequently relies on cloud and edge computing, big data analytics, and AI to manage and extract value from the vast amounts of data generated by numerous devices
Transmission frequency	Might require more regular or continuous data exchange	Represented by unusual transmissions

3. Role of 5G in MIoT

Figure 3 shows the key factors that allow 5G to be integrated into large IoT wireless networks.

Increased Capacity and Density: 4G LTE capability is exceeded by 5G, which can handle an extraordinarily high density of connected devices—up to one million per square kilometre. This is an essential need for the extensive implementation of IoT.

Lower Latency: Compared to Critical IoT, Massive IoT often has less demanding latency requirements. Some applications that need more real-time responsiveness may still benefit from 5G's ultra-low latency capabilities.

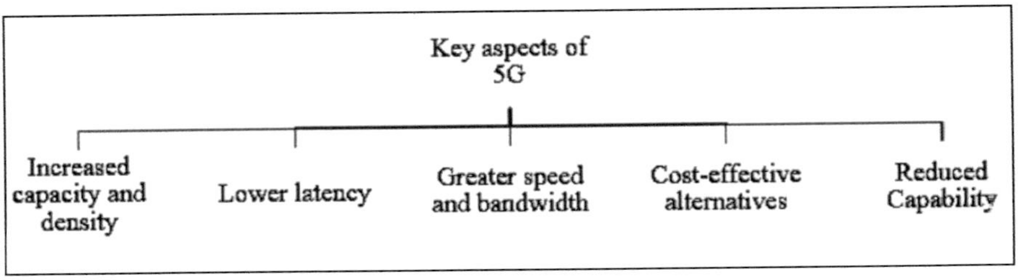

Figure 3: Key aspects of 5G.

Greater Speed and Bandwidth: Large IoT devices often transmit small amounts of data. However, the increased speed and capacity of 5G might expedite network access and possibly support future applications that require a bit more data.

Cost-effective Alternatives: For many Massive IoT use cases, the growing popularity of NB-IoT and LTE-M, which are backed by 5G core networks, offers more affordable options than conventional 4G/LTE.

Reduced Capability: Reduced Capability features in 5G are specifically made to optimize 5G for IoT devices by striking a compromise between performance and battery consumption.

Massive Access in IoT: The access of various applications in 5G enhances massive IoT, as illustrated in Figure 4. Due to the limited radio spectrum, different wireless devices need to employ different access methods in order to share the same bandwidth (Chen et al., 2020). In general, many variables, including device requirements and channel conditions, affect multiple access performance.

First, fading, interference, and noise may occur on the wireless channel, which may have a major impact on the dependability and efficiency of access. Second, the choice of appropriate access protocols and approaches is influenced by the devices' quality-of-service (QoS) needs, such as rate and latency, as various access schemes must coordinate many devices. In addition to the anticipated enormous quantity of IoT devices, the following crucial service attributes propel the transition from multiple access to massive access.

- **Sporadic traffic:** Bursty wireless traffic is caused by IoT devices that don't always have data to send. Idle devices don't connect to the network to save energy. Typically, each period sees a random number of devices connect to the network.
- **Small payload:** Small amounts of data of various sizes are seldom generated by most of the IoT applications. Short-packet transmission is the preferred method for increasing the efficiency of resource consumption.
- **Low power:** IoT devices should ideally have batteries that last longer than 20 years. IoT devices must employ an intelligent transmit power approach to reduce power consumption.
- **Ubiquitous distribution:** IoT devices are spread out over a large area, both in urban and rural regions, to serve a variety of applications. Wide wireless coverage is thus required.

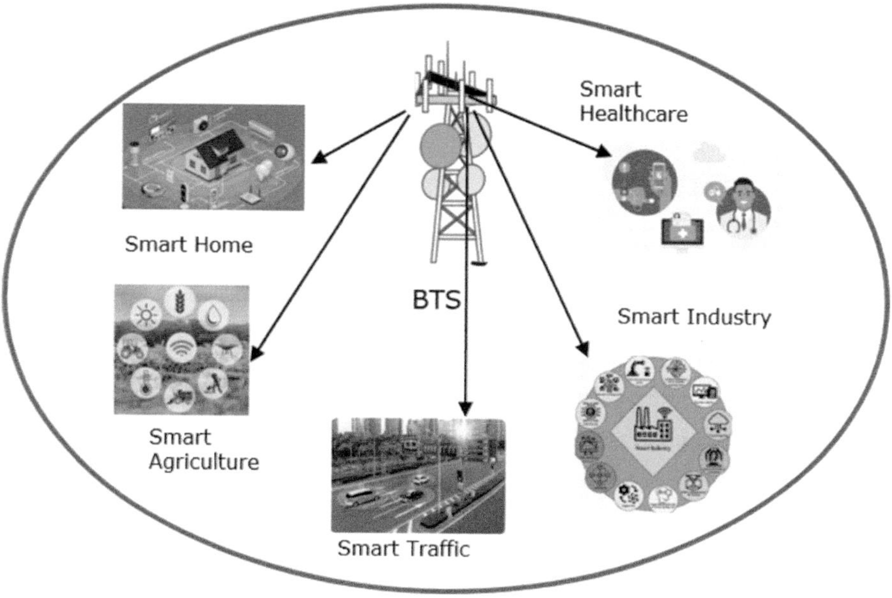

Figure 4: Massive IoT based 5G system.

- **Limited capability:** Most IoT devices are wireless nodes with simple architectures and little to no energy storage. Stated differently, advanced signal processing procedures are beyond the financial means of IoT devices.
- **Stringent latency constraint:** Certain IoT applications have strict latency requirements. Low-latency access methods are necessary to satisfy the latency requirements of such Internet of Things applications.
- **Heterogeneous QoS requirements:** IoT devices vary widely across many application domains. For instance, a car in a smart traffic system and a tiny temperature sensor have somewhat distinct QoS needs, which result in various wireless access requirements.

4. Connectivity Model of MIoT in 5G System

The work presented in (Condoluci et al., 2018) provides the connectivity model for massive IoT in 5G systems. Both 4G EPS and 5GS depend on connection-oriented connectivity models as illustrated in Figure 5, and it is evident from a high-level but not superficial comparison that both systems anticipate at least one tunnel per User Equipment (UE) between AN and UPF.

A thorough assessment of these models (Condoluci et al., 2018) must include different access distributions across time intervals ranging from tens of seconds to tens of hours, as traffic patterns are mostly device-triggered. A device density of 103 to 105 UE/km^2, or up to 106 devices per cell, is often envisioned in MIoT deployment scenarios. Since each device activation requires the transmission of data

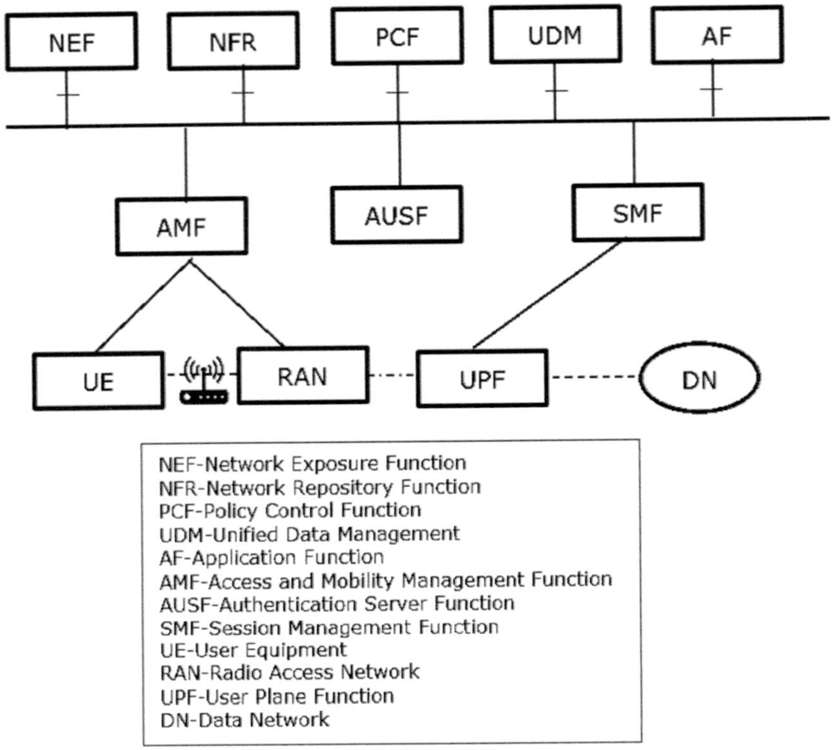

Figure 5: 5 G-enabled IoT system service reference architecture.

ranging from 102 to 104 bits, the uplink (UL) is where the bulk of the UP traffic is expected to occur.

Networks would need to support three to four orders of magnitude more connections than Mobile Broadband (MBB) use cases, even though each connected device would result in data traffic that is five to eight orders of magnitude lower than 4G smartphones.

Furthermore, it should be noted that the formation of bearers/Protocol Data Unit (PDU) sessions requires time, computation, and storage resources for both User Plane (UP) and Control Plane (CP) entities (3GPP et al., 2011; 3GPP et al., 2016). Only a target maximum number of bearers (106–107) can be handled concurrently by 4G UP network components SGW/PGW (and, most likely, early 5G UPFs), and their complexity and expense rise in tandem.

Establishing the device class, which outlines the device's communication requirements, is the first stage. Since devices in the same class have comparable communication requirements, the network must manage data transmission for them similarly. Second, the idea of a Virtual Device (VD) is presented. A VD is a logical entity at the CN side representing the collection of many UEs that are all camped on the same cell and are part of the same device class.

With the help of the VD idea, several UEs of the same class may be managed at CN as a "single device," with a single state machine controlling their behaviour.

For a given device class, the network may modify the maximum number of UEs connected to a VD. Devices collected by a VD are all members of the same device class. Finally, the Aggregate Core Network Bearer (ACNB) concept is introduced, which uses the CN UPFs to send UP data to the external DN from the RAN function.

Each VD includes an ACNB that sends data from the RAN/DN Gateway to the DN Gateway/RAN that was formed by or from each of the UEs that comprise the VD. An activity timer is connected to each ACNB for a certain device class, and it is restarted with each data transmission. When the activity period is over, the VD is de-allocated and the ACNB is freed.

Figure 4 shows how the ACNB is made when a first device has to be connected via a certain AN. It also shows how other MIoT devices of the same class connecting over the same AN may use the same ACNB to tunnel UP data.

5. Challenges in Implementing 5G – Massive IoT

In this section, the challenges in the implementation of 5G in massive IoT are discussed (Goswami et al., 2024).

Infrastructure Development: Large-scale 5G-enhanced IoT implementation is fraught with difficulties, chief among them being the development of infrastructure. To provide the high-speed, low-latency connection required for Internet of Things applications, 5G networks, in contrast to earlier generations, depend on a dense network of tiny cells, compact antennas, and transmitters positioned much closer together than conventional cell towers (Tiwari et al., 2023; Mondal et al., 2024).

Because telecom companies must develop and maintain these tiny cells in both heavily populated urban areas and sparsely inhabited rural areas, this need results in large capital costs. In urban areas, this may include installing equipment on already-existing structures and streetlights, which, while efficient, calls for meticulous preparation and collaboration with the local government (Scalise et al., 2024). The financial and logistical difficulties are even more noticeable in rural regions, where cell sites are further apart, which might postpone or restrict 5G penetration in these areas.

Security and Privacy Concerns: As millions of devices connect to the Internet of Things thanks to 5G, the network's susceptibility to cyberattacks is greatly increased. The total attack surface that cybercriminals may access increases significantly as every device, whether it be an autonomous car, smart sensor, or linked medical device, becomes a possible point of entry (Beyrouthy et al., 2024).

To preserve the integrity and operation of the larger IoT ecosystem, it is imperative to provide strong security for these devices and the data they process. Advanced encryption and authentication procedures must be implemented in order to safeguard data while it is in transit and at rest, since traditional security measures alone are inadequate for such complex situations. Robust authentication confirms the identification of devices and users, lowering the danger of spoofing and unwanted access, while encryption makes sure that data is unavailable to unauthorized users (Sahoo et al., 2024).

Spectrum Allocation and Management: 5G networks must function in a variety of frequency bands, each of which has a distinct function within the network, to provide the speed, connection, and low latency that have been promised (Singh & Kaunert, 2024). Low-frequency bands are perfect for connecting devices across large regions, whether in rural Internet of Things applications or large-scale urban coverage, since they provide broad coverage and can pass through buildings and other obstructions.

However, for dense, data-intensive applications like driverless cars, smart factories, or augmented reality systems, ultra-high speeds are provided by high-frequency bands, sometimes referred to as millimeter (mm) waves (Fadhel et al., 2024; Mondal and Goswami, 2024). However, to maintain coverage and performance in highly concentrated locations, these high frequencies need the dense deployment of tiny cells and antennas due to their limited range and difficulty with physical barriers.

6. Conclusion

By offering the speed, dependability, and connection required to enable a broad variety of applications across several sectors, 5G technologies are poised to completely transform the Internet of Things. 5G-enhanced IoT has the potential to revolutionize how we live and work, from smart cities and healthcare to industrial automation and beyond. However, achieving this potential requires tackling important issues, including spectrum management, security and privacy issues, and infrastructure development.

The combination of 5G with cutting-edge technologies like blockchain, edge computing, and AI will significantly expand the possibilities of IoT as the technology develops, opening the door for breakthroughs and uses.

5G-enhanced IoT has a bright future, but realizing its full potential will demand concerted efforts from all parties involved.

References

3GPP. (2011 Nov.). Cellular system support for ultra-low complexity and low throughput Internet of Things (CIoT) (Release 13). TR 45.820 V13.1.0.

3GPP. (2016 Sep.). Feasibility study on new services and markets technology enablers for massive Internet of Things, Stage 1 (Release 14). TR 22.861 V14.1.0.

Akpakwu, Godfrey Anuga, Bruno J. Silva, Gerhard P. Hancke, and Adnan M. Abu-Mahfouz. (2017). A survey on 5G networks for the Internet of Things: Communication technologies and challenges. IEEE Access, 6, 3619–3647.

Beyrouthy, T., Mostafa, N., Roshdy, A., Karar, A.S., and Alkork, S. (2024). Review of EEG-based biometrics in 5G-IoT: Current trends and future prospects. Applied Sciences, 14(2), 534. https://www.mdpi.com/2076 3417/14/2/534

BICS. (2025). https://www.bics.com/blog/understanding-massive-iot/

Cheikh, Imane, Sébastien Roy, Essaid Sabir, and Rachid Aouami. (2025). Energy, Scalability, Data and Security in Massive IoT: Current Landscape and Future Directions. arXiv preprint arXiv:2505.03036.

Chen, Xiaoming, Derrick Wing Kwan Ng, Wei Yu, Erik G. Larsson, Naofal Al-Dhahir, and Robert Schober. (2020). Massive access for 5G and beyond. IEEE Journal on Selected Areas in Communications, 39(3), 615–637.

Condoluci, Massimo, Riccardo Trivisonno, Toktam Mahmoodi, and Xueli An. (2018). MIoT connectivity solutions for enhanced 5G systems. In: 2018 IEEE International Conference on Communications (ICC), pp. 1–7. IEEE.

Exploring the Vital Role of AI in Cybersecurity | CCS Learning Academy. (n.d.). Retrieved February 7, 2024, from https://www.ccslearningacademy.com/role-of-ai-in-cyber-security/

Fadhel, M.A., Duhaim, A.M., Saihood, A., Sewify, A., Al-Hamadani, M.N.A., Albahri, A.S., … Gu, Y. (2024). Comprehensive systematic review of information fusion methods in smart cities and urban environments. Information Fusion, 107, 102317. DOI: 10.1016/j.inffus.2024.102317.

Goswami, Shankha Shubhra, and Surajit Mondal. (2024). The role of 5G in enhancing IOT connectivity: A systematic review on applications, challenges, and future prospects. Big Data and Computing Visions, 4(4), 314–325.

Guo, Fengxian, F. Richard Yu, Heli Zhang, Xi Li, Hong Ji, and Victor CM Leung. (2021). Enabling massive IoT toward 6G: A comprehensive survey. IEEE Internet of Things Journal, 8(15), 11891–11915.

Mondal, S., and Goswami, S.S. (2024). The evolution of blockchain technology: Applications, challenges, and future directions. Decision Making Advances, 2(1), 274–281. https://www.dma journal.org/index.php/dema/article/view/43/33.

Sahoo, S.K., Goswami, S.S., and Halder, R. (2024). Supplier selection in the age of industry 4.0: A review on MCDM applications and trends. Decision Making Advances, 2(1), 32–47.

Scalise, P., Boeding, M., Hempel, M., Sharif, H., Delloiacovo, J., and Reed, J. (2024). A systematic survey on 5G and 6G security considerations, challenges, trends, and research areas. Future Internet, 16(3), 67.

Shafique, Kinza, Bilal A. Khawaja, Farah Sabir, Sameer Qazi, and Muhammad Mustaqim. (2020). Internet of things (IoT) for next-generation smart systems: A review of current challenges, future trends and prospects for emerging 5G-IoT scenarios. IEEE Access, 8, 23022–23040.

Singh, B., and Kaunert, C. (2024). Integration of cutting-edge technologies such as Internet of Things (IoT) and 5G in health monitoring systems: A comprehensive legal analysis and futuristic outcomes. GLS Law Journal, 6(1), 13–20.

Tiwari, P., Gahlaut, V., Kaushik, M., Rani, P., Shastri, A., and Singh, B. (2023). Advancing 5G connectivity: A comprehensive review of MIMO antennas for 5G applications. International Journal of Antennas and Propagation, 1(1), 5906721.

CHAPTER
11

Pharmacovigilance-driven Personalized Treatment Using Genomic and Medical IoT Data

Prerna Mishra(0000-0003-2895-6146)
Department of CSE, IIIT Nagpur, Nagpur – 441108, Maharashtra, India

1. Introduction: Education at the Crossroads of Transformation

Healthcare isn't what it used to be, and that's a good thing. Across the globe, systems are moving away from the old, reactive models and towards proactive and personalized models based on real-time data. At the heart of this shift are Decision Support Systems (DSS). This smart computational system helps clinicians make better and faster decisions by extracting patient data, clinical guidelines, and predictive algorithms (Musen et al., 2014). While early versions of DSS were mostly rule-based and fairly rigid, today's systems are more intelligent, adaptive, and capable of learning from the massive volumes of diverse healthcare data we now generate.

The real breakthrough has come with the inclusion of Artificial Intelligence (AI) into these systems. Machine learning (ML), deep learning (DL), and natural language processing (NLP) are allowing us to go beyond by detecting subtle patterns, making personalized predictions, and handling the kind of complexity that's typical in real-world clinical care (Hirani et al., 2024). With these capabilities, AI-powered DSS are now being used to support everything from diagnosis and risk prediction to selecting therapies and catching potential adverse events before they happen. Rising in parallel with AI is the growing influence of the Medical Internet of Things (MIoT). MIoT is a web of interconnected smart devices, i.e., wearables, biosensors, and home monitors that don't just track health stats but continuously stream them to cloud platforms (Matayong et al., 2025). These tools are already changing how we

Email: pmishra@iiitn.ac.in

DOI: 10.1201/9781003676812-11

monitor patients. Whether a patient is within the hospital premises or at home, they make it possible to detect warning signs early and respond before things escalate (Tariq, 2024).

On bringing AI and MIoT together, we get intelligent, real-time, context-aware decision systems that don't just analyze data but also interpret its context. These hybrid systems can draw from continuous vitals, past medical records, even genomic or behavioral insights to issue timely alerts, guide clinical decisions, and personalize care pathways (Punugoti et al., 2023). These systems not only work towards improving their efficiency, but they are also more focused on the transformation of how we deliver care, especially when it comes to prevention and chronic disease management. However, there are some challenges too, such as these systems must deal with noisy, non-uniform data, maintain clinical accuracy, meet real-time demands, and still be explainable to doctors and regulators. Nowhere are these demands more visible than in areas like post-prescription pharmacovigilance, where systems are expected to catch adverse drug events (ADEs) as they happen and adapt to highly variable patient conditions. This chapter takes a closer look at how various technologies, AI, MIoT, and data science are converging to build smarter healthcare.

This chapter focuses especially on a flexible, real-time framework for pharmacovigilance and ADE detection, and explores how it fits into the larger vision of delivering safer, more personalized, and more responsive care.

2. Foundations of Medical IoT and AI-driven DSS

2.1. Medical IoT Architecture and Infrastructure

The MIoT represents an interconnected ecosystem of intelligent biomedical devices, edge processors, communication networks, and cloud-based analytics platforms that enable continuous, real-time monitoring of patients both inside and outside clinical settings (Atzori et al., 2010; Islam et al., 2015). A typical MIoT architecture is composed of three fundamental layers:

- **Perception (Sensing) Layer:** This layer includes biosensors and wearable/implantable devices that collect vital signs, environmental parameters, and behavioral data, such as ECG patches, glucose monitors, smart pill dispensers, and smart inhalers.
- **Network Layer:** This layer facilitates secure transmission of data using low-power wide-area networks (LPWAN), Wi-Fi, Bluetooth Low Energy (BLE), and healthcare-specific protocols like IEEE 11073. Middleware components ensure data compression, fault-tolerant streaming, and protocol interoperability.
- **Application Layer:** This layer hosts intelligent services such as AI-based diagnostics, real-time alert generation, data visualization dashboards, and cloud/edge analytics pipelines.

Modern MIoT systems are increasingly adopting fog and edge computing paradigms to process critical health data closer to the data source, minimizing latency and ensuring timely interventions (Rehman et al., 2025; Punugoti et al., 2023).

2.2. Multimodal Health Data Captured by MIoT

MIoT infrastructures enable the collection and fusion of a wide range of heterogeneous data sources, critical for context-aware and patient-centric decision-making, such as,

- **Physiological Data:** These are vital parameters such as heart rate, blood pressure, body temperature, respiratory rate, oxygen saturation, and glucose levels.
- **Behavioral and Environmental Data:** These are activity patterns, sleep cycles, medication adherence, air quality, and geo-location information.
- **Clinical and Administrative Records:** These are structured and unstructured components of Electronic Health Records (EHR), including diagnoses, medications, lab reports, imaging, and clinical narratives.
- **Genomic and Pharmacogenomic Profiles:** These are genetic variants (e.g., CYP450) that influence drug metabolism, treatment response, and adverse event susceptibility (Jyothi, 2023).

These diverse modalities, when processed in real time, provide a rich substrate for personalized and adaptive decision support.

2.3. Evolution of Decision Support Systems in Healthcare

Older clinical decision support systems (DSS) were built on well-defined rules drawn from expert guidelines and medical consensus. These rule-based systems were easy to understand and trusted by clinicians. But these systems were rigid, i.e., once made, they couldn't easily adapt to the unique nuances of different patients, especially those from underrepresented or complex subgroups (Musen et al., 2014).

The real turning point came with the rise of machine learning. Unlike rule-based models, ML could learn patterns from real patient data. The methods, like logistic regression, random forests, and gradient boosting, began to make accurate predictions about disease risks, treatment responses, or hospital readmission based on large historical datasets. Then came deep learning frameworks, which worked as a game changer, especially for data types that were too messy or complex for traditional ML. For some high-dimensional inputs like MRI scans, ECG signals, or free-text clinical notes, these learning models could automatically extract meaningful patterns from such data without the need for handcrafted features (Kabir et al., 2023).

Another major step forward was in natural language processing. For decades, a huge chunk of clinical data, such as doctors' notes, medical reports, discharge summaries, or radiology reports, was trapped in unstructured text. Through NLP, these data types were interpreted, making it searchable and useful through techniques like named entity recognition (NER), relationship extraction, and sentiment analysis (Amirahmadi et al., 2023). Now, DSS could understand what clinicians were writing and extract actionable insights from it. Together, these AI technologies transformed DSS from being static rule-followers into dynamic, learning-based systems. They're no longer just diagnostic aids, but these technologies in together become intelligent companions in care, capable of offering personalized recommendations that evolve as new data flows in.

2.4. Taxonomy of AI-Driven DSS in Clinical Contexts

AI-based DSS can be categorized based on their function in the clinical workflow. Each type benefits from real-time, longitudinal data capture afforded by MIoT, which extends their functionality beyond static snapshots to dynamic, continuously updated inferences. Categories of AI-based DSS are:

- **Diagnostic DSS:** This aids in disease detection using symptom profiles, lab results, imaging, or biomarker data (e.g., early-stage cancer detection from CT scans).
- **Therapeutic DSS:** This supports clinicians in selecting optimal drugs or procedures, guided by patient history, pharmacogenomics, and drug-drug interaction models.
- **Monitoring DSS:** This continuously assesses patient status to detect deterioration, adverse events, or deviations from expected recovery trajectories (e.g., sepsis prediction using multimodal ICU streams).

2.5. Convergence of MIoT and AI: Toward Intelligent, Real-time DSS

The convergence of MIoT and AI transforms traditional DSS into intelligent, real-time, and patient-aware platforms. Edge-enabled analytics reduce response times in emergency scenarios, while cloud-based deep learning models continuously improve through federated learning and population-scale retraining. This synergy enables:

Proactive Care: Early detection of abnormalities before symptom onset.

Personalized Interventions: Recommendations tailored to genomic risk factors, lifestyle habits, and comorbidities.

Real-time Alerting: Event-driven notifications to caregivers and clinicians via secure messaging or integrated hospital systems.

Such systems form the backbone of advanced clinical decision-making pipelines and pave the way for new applications such as remote diagnostics and home-based chronic care management.

3. Clinical Applications of AI-driven DSS in MIoT

AI-Driven DSS integrated with MIoT has found significant relevance across diverse clinical domains. These systems, by leveraging real-time sensor data, cloud analytics, and intelligent models, enable proactive interventions, patient-specific recommendations, and early detection of deteriorating health conditions (Chakraborty et al., 2024). This section presents key application areas where AI-empowered DSS in MIoT environments are being deployed effectively.

3.1. Chronic Disease Management

Chronic illnesses such as diabetes and hypertension demand continuous monitoring and adaptive care. MIoT-enabled devices like wearable glucometers and smart blood pressure monitors transmit time-series data to DSS platforms that apply predictive analytics for disease progression modeling (Schmidt et al., 2016). For instance, AI models can process blood glucose trends alongside lifestyle inputs (diet, exercise, sleep) to recommend insulin dosages or alert patients about hypo/hyperglycemic events (Rong et al., 2020). In hypertension management, DSS tools integrate systolic/diastolic readings with medication adherence data to adjust therapy plans dynamically, leveraging decision trees or Bayesian networks (Chiang et al., 2021).

3.2. Acute Care Monitoring

Acute care scenarios such as sepsis or myocardial infarction require high-frequency monitoring and fast response. MIoT systems equipped with edge-processing devices analyze patient vitals (e.g., temperature, heart rate, SpO2, lactate levels) in real time (Rathi et al., 2021). AI-based DSS platforms detect subtle deteriorations that precede sepsis onset using early warning scores and recurrent neural networks trained on ICU datasets. For cardiac events, multimodal inputs including ECG waveforms, chest pain logs, and historical comorbidities are integrated through CNN-LSTM hybrid models to flag possible heart attack symptoms (Shashikumar et al., 2017).

3.3. Personalized Drug Therapy

For precision medicine, AI techniques were integrated with MIoT systems and pharmacogenomic data, allowing DSS tools to tailor drug therapies at the individual level (Silva et al., 2024). For each individual, these systems evaluate metabolic genotypes, current drug regimens, and sensor-reported physiological responses to predict adverse reactions or efficacy mismatches. AI classifiers trained on historical ADE data aid in suggesting alternative drugs or dosage adjustments. The framework also supports decision-making in polypharmacy scenarios, especially in geriatric or comorbid populations (Ye et al., 2024).

3.4. Elderly and Home-based Monitoring

AI-driven DSS combined with MIoT is revolutionizing elderly care through remote monitoring and cognitive assessment. Smart homes are equipped with motion sensors, pressure mats, voice detection systems, and wearable accelerometers to monitor fall risks, sleep disorders, or wandering behavior in dementia patients (Matayong et al., 2025). Cognitive decline is assessed through speech pattern analysis, interaction frequency with home appliances, and deviations from routine behavior using anomaly detection algorithms. DSS platforms generate alerts for caregivers or recommend clinical evaluations when early signs of cognitive impairment are detected (Qian et al., 2021). These application domains highlight how current MIoT systems are redefining decision-making capabilities across the healthcare continuum. The next section presents a dedicated framework focused on real-time pharmacovigilance, which is an increasingly crucial component of modern DSS ecosystems.

4. Real-Time Pharmacovigilance and ADE Detection

Pharmacovigilance refers to the science and activities associated with the detection, assessment, understanding, and prevention of adverse drug effects or any other drug-related problems [World Health Organization 2002]. Although traditional pharmacovigilance systems rely primarily on voluntary reports from clinicians or patients, they suffer from serious limitations, including under-reporting, retrospective bias, and lack of real-time insights (Al Meslamani, 2023). Real-time pharmacovigilance leverages continuous monitoring of physiological and contextual data using MIoT, paired with intelligent models for risk prediction and clinical alerting (Uddin and Munni, 2021).

MIoT systems integrate wearable devices, smart medication dispensers, and ambient sensors that stream time-series data on patient vitals, drug intake, and environmental context. When this is aligned with EHR data and genomic profiles, it enables a holistic understanding of potential drug-related risks. Examples of sensor contributions include:

- **Wearables:** Capture vitals like ECG, SpO2, skin conductance, and body temperature to identify abnormal responses post-medication.
- **Smart Pillboxes:** Log dosage adherence and missed medication events.
- **Inhaler Sensors:** Record actuation frequency and inhalation patterns, useful in monitoring respiratory ADEs in asthma or COPD patients.

These sensor streams are fed into AI-based DSS engines that analyze multimodal data for spatiotemporal ADE pattern detection. AI-enabled DSS modules are designed to alert clinicians when the real-time ADE likelihood surpasses a predefined threshold, suggest drug alternatives or dosage modifications based on patient history and drug-gene interactions, and learn from ongoing patient responses to refine models (online learning or federated personalization).

4.1. System Architecture of MIoT-enabled Real-time Pharmacovigilance

The system architecture illustrated in Figure 1 represents a multilayered, modular pipeline that enables continuous monitoring, intelligent inference, and clinical decision-making in pharmacovigilance. At its foundation lies the *Data Collection Layer*, which includes a range of MIoT-enabled devices such as body-worn physiological sensors (e.g., heart rate monitors, blood pressure cuffs), smart pill dispensers, and digitally connected inhalers. These devices generate high-frequency, patient-specific data streams that capture both medication usage patterns and physiological responses in real-time. The *Data Transmission Layer* ensures that this information is securely relayed to edge or cloud-based systems using lightweight communication protocols such as Bluetooth Low Energy (BLE), WiFi, or long-range wide-area networks (LoRaWAN), depending on the application context. Privacy-preserving mechanisms and encryption standards are applied to maintain HIPAA-compliant data security during transmission.

The *Data Processing Layer* acts as the intelligence core of the architecture. Here, advanced AI models trained on historical EHRs, ADE-labeled datasets, and contextual MIoT sensor data are deployed on either edge nodes or scalable cloud platforms to perform real-time analytics. These models not only detect binary ADE occurrences

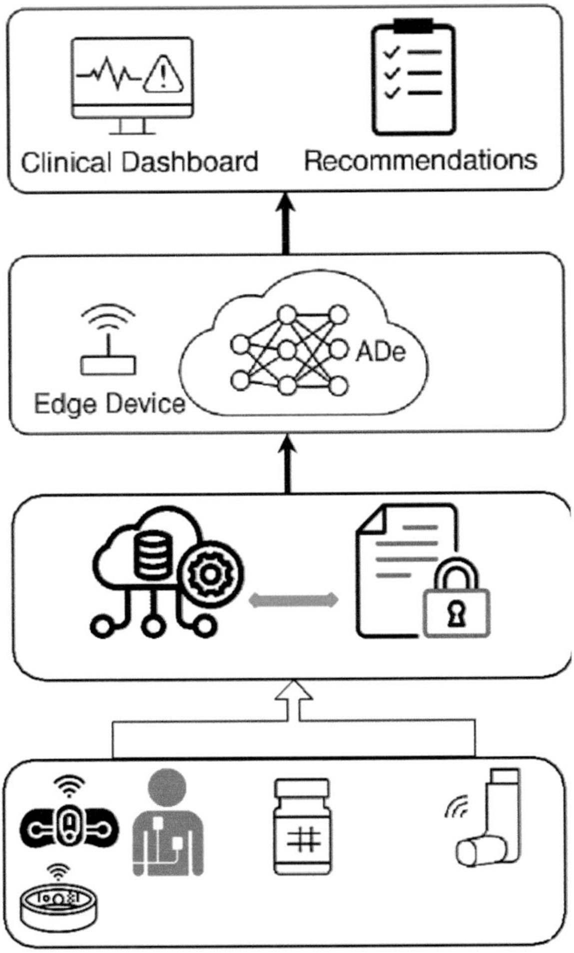

Figure 1: System architecture of MIoT-enabled real-time pharmacovigilance.

but also perform severity stratification and time-to-event estimation, leveraging both multimodal inputs and temporal learning frameworks. This layer is optimized for low-latency processing to support actionable insights with minimal delay. Finally, the *Decision Support Layer* synthesizes the model outputs into clinically meaningful recommendations. This includes risk-scored alerts for potential ADEs, escalation pathways for severe events, and visual summaries integrated into EHR dashboards for clinician review. Additionally, alerts can be configured to trigger automated workflows such as dosage adjustments or recommendations for alternative therapies, effectively closing the loop from detection to intervention.

Overall, this architecture supports scalable, personalized pharmacovigilance by bridging continuous MIoT sensing, AI-based inference, and real-time clinical action—making it particularly suited for dynamic care environments such as home-based chronic disease management or post-discharge monitoring.

4.2. ADE Severity Estimation and Time-to-Event Prediction

Modern decision support systems in pharmacovigilance are evolving beyond simply identifying whether an ADE has occurred. A more advanced and clinically valuable approach involves estimating the potential severity of the ADE and predicting when it is likely to manifest. These two capabilities are critical for enabling timely and appropriate medical intervention.

Within the data processing layer of the architecture, the severity estimation is performed using supervised machine learning models designed for ordinal classification. These models are trained to categorize ADEs into three levels, such as mild (for example, short-term nausea), moderate (such as extended dizziness), or severe (life-threatening reactions like anaphylaxis). They rely on annotated electronic health records combined with real-time physiological data obtained from MIoT devices. Models that use probabilistic graphical frameworks and regression techniques are particularly helpful here, as they provide interpretable results aligned with clinical judgment. In addition to classifying severity, DSS can also model the temporal aspect of pharmacovigilance by predicting when an ADE might occur. This is achieved using sequence-aware deep learning architectures such as BiLSTM networks and Temporal Convolutional Networks (TCNs). These models are capable of processing continuous streams of time-series data, sensor outputs, and medication administration timelines to estimate the likelihood and approximate onset time of an ADE (Table 1). This capability is commonly referred to as time-to-ADE prediction (Figure 2).

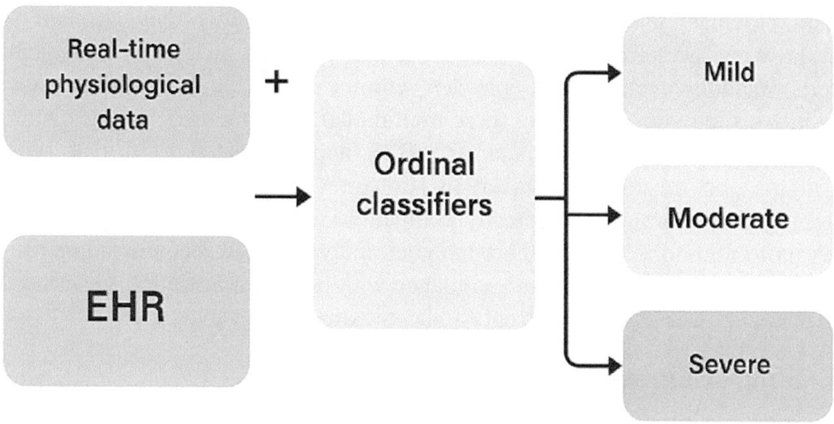

Figure 2: ADE severity classification pipeline.

By integrating the two dimensions of severity and timing in ADE, the systems can now support clinicians in making proactive decisions. For instance, if a patient is identified as being at high risk for a severe ADE within a short time frame, clinicians can respond in advance by changing the treatment plan, initiating diagnostics, or preparing contingency care. This predictive capability improves the safety and personalization of therapeutic interventions (Scaboro et al., 2023).

Table 1: Key Features of AI Models Used in ADE Detection

AI Model	Input Data	Task	Interpretability	Use Case Example
Bi-LSTM	Time-series from sensors	Time-to-ADE prediction	Moderate	Cardiovascular ADE detection
Ordinal Regression	EHR + vitals	Severity classification	High	Dose-adjustment recommendations
CNN-NLP Hybrid	Clinical notes	ADE entity extraction	Medium	ADE cause analysis in oncology

4.3. Integration with Personalized Treatment Plans

Personalization is a cornerstone of the proposed real-time pharmacovigilance architecture, particularly within the Decision Support Layer, where clinical outputs are tailored to each individual's biological and contextual profile. The system leverages genomic information, such as single nucleotide polymorphisms in drug-metabolizing enzymes (e.g., CYP450 variants), to model individual drug response variability. These variants are either preloaded into the patient profile or dynamically accessed through linked genomic repositories.

Simultaneously, real-time physiological data such as heart rate variability, respiratory rate, or skin temperature from wearable sensors provides a granular, moment-to-moment understanding of how a patient is responding to a given medication regimen. This continuous monitoring helps identify deviations from normal baselines that may signal subclinical ADEs before they escalate. The final layer of personalization stems from the patient's EHR-based medication history, including prior ADE episodes, chronic comorbidities, and concurrent drug interactions. By integrating these multimodal data streams, such as genomic, physiological, and historical data, the DSS applies personalized risk scoring algorithms and treatment optimization strategies. For example, it may suggest switching to a pharmacogenomically compatible alternative or modifying dosage intervals to minimize toxicity. Through such individualized recommendations, the system bridges real-time pharmacovigilance with precision medicine, ensuring that each therapeutic decision is both safe and contextually relevant.

4.4. Smart Remote Diagnosis and Treatment

Smart remote diagnosis and treatment expand healthcare delivery beyond the hospital by using Medical IoT technologies. This enables continuous, real-time patient monitoring and personalized therapeutic guidance. These models are particularly impactful for patients with chronic illnesses, mobility limitations, or those in remote areas who require consistent care.

The system is built on a multi-layered architecture. At the device level, wearable sensors such as ECG patches, blood pressure monitors, pulse oximeters, and smart inhalers collect vital data and medication usage trends. These readings are passed through local edge devices, like smartphones or home hubs, which handle initial filtering and quick processing. Cleaned and structured data is then transmitted securely to cloud-based platforms.

In the cloud, the AI models trained on large and diverse health datasets perform risk assessments and early diagnostics. These models identify subtle physiological changes that might indicate emerging adverse drug effects. For instance, a steady drop in blood pressure and reports of fatigue in a hypertensive patient may be flagged as an early warning. The system contextualizes such alerts using historical patterns from electronic health records and population data. AI techniques such as unsupervised learning detect personal deviations from baseline, while rule-based engines apply clinical logic. Natural language processing tools also interpret symptoms submitted through apps or voice assistants, adding to the system's decision-making capabilities.

One of the key advantages of this setup is its closed-loop treatment response. Clinicians can remotely adjust medications through integrated dashboards, which synchronize with smart dispensers or reminders at the patient's home. The system may also suggest lifestyle adjustments, such as hydration or rest, depending on the patient's condition. In case of emergencies, such as a drop in oxygen levels or abnormal heart rhythms, alerts are automatically sent to caregivers or nearby medical responders. This approach is already seeing success in fields like cardiology, pulmonology, and post-surgical care. Patients benefit from early detection, timely interventions, and reduced hospital readmissions, making healthcare more r esponsive and accessible.

4.4.1. Case Vignette: Early ADE Detection in a Hypertensive Patient

Mr. S, a 66-year-old retired teacher with a history of hypertension and atrial fibrillation, was recently prescribed metoprolol, a beta-blocker, following a routine cardiology consultation. At home, he used a MIoT-enabled health kit that included a smart blood pressure monitor, a wearable ECG patch, a sleep tracker, and a connected pillbox. Over several days, the system detected a steady decline in his blood pressure, from 130/85 to 105/65 mmHg, along with a slower heart rate, disrupted sleep, and self-reported fatigue. These data points were continuously processed by a cloud-based AI platform, which linked the physiological changes to his medication schedule and known drug response patterns. The system generated an alert, with a clear explanation of the concern, and sent it to Mr. S's physician. A teleconsultation was promptly scheduled. After reviewing the evidence, the doctor adjusted his treatment plan, switching to a more suitable medication. Crucially, this intervention took place before any serious symptoms appeared. The case highlights how MIoT and AI can enable early detection of adverse drug effects, helping patients avoid unnecessary hospital visits and improving clinical outcomes through timely, personalized care.

4.5. Integration of the MIoT Framework with Existing Healthcare Systems

For effective real-time pharmacovigilance, the MIoT framework must work smoothly with existing healthcare systems. It should bridge itself easily with EHRs, hospital information systems, telehealth platforms, and clinical workflows. This seamless integration ensures that clinicians can use the system without disrupting their routine, helping build trust and encouraging adoption.

A key requirement here is data interoperability. Using standards like HL7 FHIR, SNOMED-CT, and LOINC allows MIoT devices to share information with EHRs in a structured and consistent way. For example, if the system detects an ADE from any sensor data, it can instantly log the incident in the patient's digital record. Clinicians can then access that information during checkups or follow-ups, without needing to navigate additional interfaces. The system's edge and cloud components can be deployed as microservices within hospital networks or accessed through secure APIs. This flexible design allows both small clinics and large hospitals to adopt the technology at their own pace. A clinic might begin by simply pulling data from smart wearables, while a more advanced setup could include full AI-driven ADE detection and prediction modules.

Clinical decision support is another important layer. Suggestions generated by AI techniques, such as dosage adjustments or alerts about drug interactions, must be presented clearly and accessibly. Integrating these outputs into familiar dashboards, like those used in Epic, Cerner, or openEHR systems, helps ensure that healthcare professionals can easily understand and act on the recommendations. In remote care, these alerts can also be linked to teleconsultation platforms, improving the quality of virtual visits. Data privacy and security are critical across all touchpoints. The integration must comply with laws such as HIPAA, GDPR, and local data regulations, ensuring that patient information is used responsibly (Table 2). Techniques like federated learning and edge AI allow personal data to remain on the device while still supporting powerful analytics.

Table 2: Privacy and Compliance Mechanisms in MIoT-AI Systems

Compliance Area	Technique Used	Standard Referenced	Applicable Layer
Data anonymization	Differential privacy	HIPAA, GDPR	Edge + cloud
Consent management	Blockchain audit trail	Local health law	User interface
Secure transmission	End-to-end encryption	TLS 1.3	Sensor to cloud
Access control	Role-based permissions	ISO/IEC 27001	Hospital integration

On the operational side, embedding the system into care routines such as chronic disease management, discharge planning, or medication review can streamline clinical workflows. For instance, alerts can be routed directly to pharmacists or care managers, while patients at home receive timely notifications or chatbot follow-ups. Pilot studies in outpatient clinics, home-health programs, or specialty units like oncology or geriatrics can demonstrate the system's value without requiring major changes. These early deployments also provide valuable feedback, helping refine the framework based on real-world needs and outcomes.

5. Evaluation Metrics, Datasets, and Case Study

The effectiveness of AI-driven DSS hinges on rigorous evaluation across multiple dimensions. These include predictive accuracy, responsiveness, interpretability, and regulatory readiness. This section elaborates on standard metrics, publicly available datasets, and a case study of a patient.

5.1. Evaluation Metrics

To assess the accuracy of ADE detection and classification models, the following conventional classification metrics are employed.

- **Accuracy:** The overall proportion of correct predictions among total predictions.
- **Precision:** The proportion of true positives among all predicted positives, indicating the model's ability to minimize false positives.
- **Recall (Sensitivity):** The proportion of true positives detected among all actual positives, reflecting the model's ability to capture real ADEs.
- **F1 Score:** The harmonic mean of precision and recall, especially useful in imbalanced datasets.
- **AUC-ROC:** The area under the receiver operating characteristic curve, measuring the trade-off between sensitivity and specificity.
- **Latency:** Time taken for data acquisition to result generation, which is crucial in real-time monitoring scenarios.
- **Throughput:** Number of ADE detection events processed per unit time, particularly relevant in high-volume hospital settings.
- **Usability Scores:** Based on surveys or System Usability Scale (SUS) to measure the ease-of-use and trustworthiness of clinical dashboards.

5.2. Datasets

Despite the critical importance of pharmacovigilance, large-scale public datasets integrating MIoT data with ADE labels are limited. Table 3 summarizes the available datasets, their task categories, data types used, use cases, strengths, and availability.

5.3. Case Study

To illustrate the effectiveness of the proposed MIoT-integrated AI-driven DSS, this section presents a case study of a hypertensive patient under polypharmacy monitoring.

The patient is 64 years old, suffering from hypertension, mild arrhythmia. His prescribed medications are a beta-blocker, a calcium channel blocker, and a statin. The devices used for monitoring his health stats were a smart pill dispenser, a wearable health tracker (Fitbit), and a smart sleep monitor. Timeline of events noted are:

- **Day 1-3:** Baseline vitals were logged. Blood pressure and sleep duration were within normal range.
- **Day 4-7:** Gradual decrease in systolic BP is noted (from 124 mmHg to 95 mmHg). Increased daytime fatigue, lower heart rate, and shorter sleep cycles were detected by wearable sensors.

Table 3: Benchmark Datasets for ADE Detection

Dataset	Category	Data Type	Use Case	Availability	Strengths
MIMIC-IV (Johnson et al., 2023)	NLP, Time-Series, Structured	ICU records: EHRs, vitals, meds	ADE detection, longitudinal studies, clinical trend analysis	PhysioNet (Restricted)	Rich multimodal temporal data, widely benchmarked, linked with ICD codes
FDA FAERS (U.S. Food and Drug Administration, 2023)	Structured	Voluntary post-marketing ADE reports	Large-scale pharmacovigilance, signal detection	Public	Huge coverage of marketed drugs, standardized MedDRA terms
n2c2 ADE Corpus (Henry et al., 2020)	NLP	Annotated discharge summaries (ADEs, drugs)	ADE extraction, entity span recognition	Research license	High-quality manual annotations, task-specific for ADE NLP
eICU Collaborative DB (Pollard et al., 2018)]	Time-Series, Structured	ICU timestamped vitals and meds	Real-time ADE risk modeling, time-to-event learning	PhysioNet (Restricted)	Rich temporal granularity, diverse hospitals, high-resolution data
SIDER (Kuhn et al., 2016)	Knowledge Base	Drug-ADE associations from package inserts	ADE linkage, semantic graph modeling	Public	Curated side-effect database, useful for baseline ADE mapping
OFFSIDES/ TWOSIDES (Tatonetti et al., 2012)	Structured, Knowledge Base	Drug-drug interaction and ADE co-occurrence	Signal prioritization, polypharmacy ADE risk	Public	Mined from real-world clinical settings, DDIfocused
i2b2 Corpora (Uzuner et al., 2011)	NLP	Annotated clinical narratives	Relation extraction, negation scope detection	Licensed (Research)	Advanced NLP challenge sets, realistic clinical language

DrugCentral/ DrugBank (Avram et al., 2021, Wishart et al., 2018)	Knowledge Base	Drug indications, targets, ADEs, interactions	Knowledge graph completion, reasoning over ADEs	Public API access	Regularly updated, rich with drug properties and cross-references
EU-ADR (Van Mulligen et al., 2013)	NLP	Biomedical literature with ADE relations	Literature mining, ADE causality inference	Public (Research)	Manually verified ADE-drug-disease triples
THIN (IQVIA 2015)	Time-Series, Structured	Longitudinal UK general practice EHRs	Long-term ADE tracking, population-based studies	Commercial	Rich metadata, demographic diversity, primary care setting
MarketScan (Health, 2021)	Structured	Claims + EHR + billing records	Large-scale pharmacoeconomic ADE studies	Commercial	Population-scale coverage, billing + clinical linkage

- **Day 8:** The DSS aggregates longitudinal data from the smart pill dispenser (confirming medication adherence), wearable vitals, and EHR history.

Using temporal AI models, the system associates these changes with a likely ADE triggered by the beta-blocker. Then, the DSS sends an alert to the clinician dashboard suggesting dosage reassessment or substitution. The beta-blocker dose was adjusted, resulting in improved vitals by Day 10. This scenario exemplifies the potential of multimodal, real-time monitoring in proactively flagging clinically relevant ADEs, which would otherwise be missed in manual surveillance. Figure 3 visualizes how sensor data traverses through the MIoT-AI pipeline to generate real-time alerts.

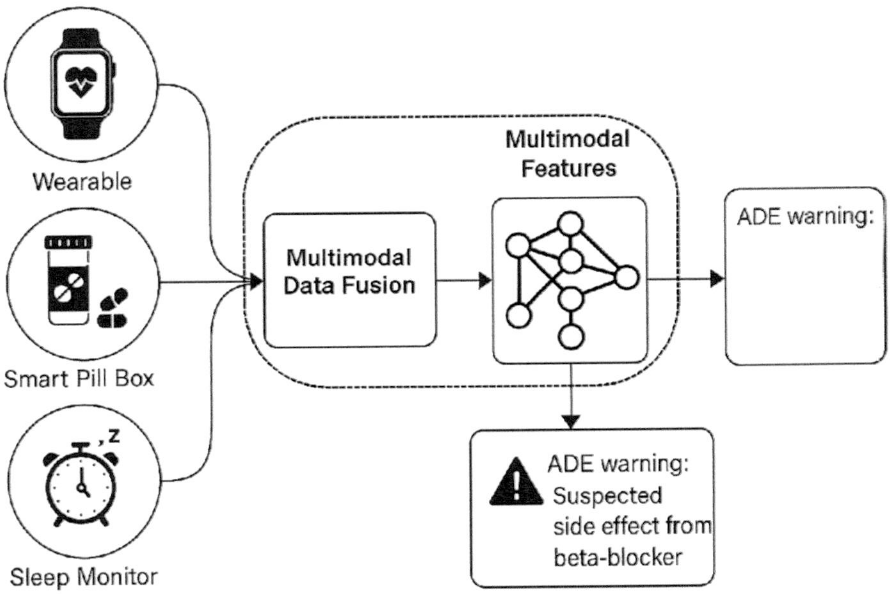

Figure 3: Sensor-to-ADE alert flow in MIoT-AI pharmacovigilance system.

6. Challenges and Limitations

Despite the promising capabilities of AI-driven DSS integrated with MIoT, several challenges persist across technological, clinical, regulatory, and societal dimensions; each of them is discussed below.

6.1. Data Heterogeneity and Interoperability

Clinical data is highly heterogeneous, spanning structured records (e.g., vitals, lab results), semistructured formats (e.g., prescriptions), and unstructured text (e.g., clinical notes). MIoT further adds streaming sensor data, making it difficult to harmonize information across sources (Amirahmadi et al., 2023). Lack of interoperability standards across devices and heterogeneous EHRs impedes seamless integration.

6.2. Data Privacy and Security

Real-time pharmacovigilance systems operate on sensitive health data. Ensuring compliance with data protection regulations such as HIPAA (Health Insurance Portability and Accountability Act) and GDPR (General Data Protection Regulation) is critical. The deployment of wearable and remote sensors raises concerns about unauthorized data access, device-level vulnerabilities, and cloud-level breaches (Rajkomar et al., 2018).

6.3. Clinical Validation and Acceptance

For AI-driven DSS to be adopted in real-world healthcare, they must undergo rigorous clinical validation. Clinicians often demand explainability and transparency before accepting model outputs into practice. The "black-box" nature of many deep learning models reduces their acceptability among medical professionals (Topol, 2019).

6.4. Regulatory and Legal Barriers

Despite recent interest by regulatory bodies in AI/ML-based Software as a Medical Device (SaMD) (Zinchenko et al., 2022), formal guidelines for AI-DSS in pharmacovigilance remain limited. Defining liability in cases where automated systems provide incorrect alerts or miss critical events is an ongoing legal dilemma.

6.5. Regulatory and Legal Barriers

While developed hospitals may adopt MIoT-based DSS, rural or under-resourced healthcare facilities often lack the infrastructure to deploy such systems. Power supply, connectivity, and skilled personnel are additional constraints. Solutions must be adaptable to diverse operational settings to ensure inclusivity.

7. Future Directions and Summary

7.1. Future Directions

To address current limitations and enhance the efficacy of AI-integrated MIoT systems in pharmacovigilance, several future research avenues can be brought into focus.

- **Federated Learning and Privacy-Preserving AI:** Distributed AI models, such as federated learning, allow hospitals to collaboratively train models on local data without sharing raw patient data, addressing privacy concerns while improving generalizability (Rahman et al., 2024).
- **Digital Twin Models:** Digital twins for patients, a real-time virtual replica of an individual's health, could enhance personalized drug response predictions and ADE risk assessment by simulating treatment outcomes based on multimodal data inputs.
- **Human-in-the-Loop Systems:** Involving clinicians directly in the decision-making loop can enhance trust and allow AI systems to learn from human feedback. This is particularly important for borderline ADE cases or novel drug reactions.

- **Emotion-Aware and Contextual AI:** Integrating affective computing into DSS can help monitor patient emotions and stress levels alongside physical health metrics. Such contextual understanding could improve ADE interpretation and patient compliance monitoring.
- **Cross-Institutional Benchmarking and Open Datasets:** The development of open-access benchmark datasets for ADE detection and real-time pharmacovigilance is essential to validate models and facilitate academic and industry collaboration.

7.2. Summary

This chapter explored the design, implementation, and evaluation of AI-driven Decision Support Systems in the context of Medical IoT for real-time pharmacovigilance. Starting with the fundamentals of MIoT and AI in healthcare, the chapter presented a detailed framework for ADE detection using multimodal data, including sensor signals, EHRs, and genomics. The integration of such systems enables proactive, personalized, and real-time patient safety management. While challenges in data quality, privacy, clinical integration, and scalability remain, emerging solutions like federated learning, digital twins, and human-in-the-loop AI offer promising paths forward. Continuous innovation and interdisciplinary collaboration are needed to realize the full potential of such intelligent systems to improve healthcare outcomes around the world.

References

Al Meslamani, A.Z. (2023). Underreporting of adverse drug events: A look into the extent, causes, and potential solutions. Expert Opinion on Drug Safety, 22(5), 351–354.

Amirahmadi, A., Ohlsson, M., and Etminani, K. (2023). Deep learning prediction models based on EHR trajectories: A systematic review. Journal of Biomedical Informatics, 144, 104430.

Atzori, L., Iera, A., and Morabito, G. (2010). The internet of things: A survey. Computer Networks, 54(15), 2787–2805.

Avram, S., Bologa, C.G., Holmes, J., Bocci, G., Wilson, T.B., Nguyen, D.-T. et al. (2021). Drugcentral 2021 supports drug discovery and repositioning. Nucleic Acids Research, 49(D1), D1160–D1169.

Chakraborty, C., Bhattacharya, M., Pal, S., and Lee, S.-S. (2024). From machine learning to deep learning: Advances of the recent data-driven paradigm shift in medicine and healthcare. Current Research in Biotechnology, 7, 100164.

Chiang, P.-H., Wong, M., and Dey, S. (2021). Using wearables and machine learning to enable personalized lifestyle recommendations to improve blood pressure. IEEE Journal of Translational Engineering in Health and Medicine, 9, 1–13.

Health, 2021 Merative (formerly IBM Watson Health). *MarketScan Research Databases*. 2022. Available at: https://www.ibm.com/us-en/marketplace/marketscan-research-databases. Accessed: 2025-06-11.

Henry, S., Wang, Y., Shen, F., and Uzuner, O. (2020). The 2019 national natural language processing (nlp) clinical challenges (n2c2)/open health. NLP (ohnlp) shared task on clinical concept normalization for clinical records, 27, 1529–1537.

Hirani, R., Noruzi, K., Khuram, H., Hussaini, A.S., Aifuwa, E.I., Ely, K.E. et al. (2024). Artificial intelligence and healthcare: A journey through history, present innovations, and future possibilities. Life, 14(5), 557.

IQVIA. (2015). The Health Improvement Network (thin). https://www.iqvia.com/solutions/real-world-evidence/our-data/the-health-improvement-network. Accessed: 2025-06-11.

Islam, S.R., Kwak, D., Kabir, M.H., Hossain, M., and Kwak, K.-S. (2015). The internet of things for health care: A comprehensive survey. IEEE Access, 3, 678–708.

Johnson, A.E., Bulgarelli, L., Shen, L., Gayles, A., Shammout, A., Horng, S. et al. (2023). Mimic-IV, a freely accessible electronic health record dataset. Scientific Data, 10(1), 1.

Jyothi, N. (2023). AI-enabled genomic biomarkers: The future of pharmaceutical industry and personalized medicine. Seybold Report Journal, 18(08), 54–72.

Kabir, R., Sivasubramanian, M., Hitch, G., Hakkim, S., Kainesie, J., Vinnakota, D. et al. (2023). "Deep Learning" for healthcare: Opportunities, threats, and challenges. *In:* Deep Learning in Personalized Healthcare and Decision Support (pp. 225–244). Academic Press.

Kuhn, M., Letunic, I., Jensen, L.J., and Bork, P. (2016). The sider database of drugs and side effects. Nucleic Acids Research, 44(D1), D1075–D1079.

Matayong, S., Jetwanna, K., Choksuchat, C., Choosawang, S., Trakulmaykee, N., Limsuwan, S., and Inthanuchit, K. (2025). IoT-based systems and applications for elderly healthcare: A systematic review. Universal Access in the Information Society, 24(1), 99–125.

Musen, M.A., Middleton, B., and Greenes, R. (2014). Clinical decision-support systems. *In:* Biomedical Informatics: Computer Applications in Health Care and Biomedicine. Fourth Edition (pp. 643–674). Springer London.

Pollard, T.J., Johnson, A.E., Raffa, J.D., Celi, L.A., Mark, R.G., and Badawi, O. (2018). The eICU collaborative research database, a freely available multi-center database for critical care research. Scientific Data, 5(1), 1–13.

Punugoti, R., Dutt, V., Anand, A., and Bhati, N. (2023). Exploring the impact of edge intelligence and IoT on healthcare: A comprehensive survey. *In:* 2023 International Conference on Sustainable Computing and Smart Systems (ICSCSS) (pp. 1108–1114). IEEE.

Qian, K., Zhang, Z., Yamamoto, Y., and Schuller, B.W. (2021). Artificial intelligence internet of things for the elderly: From assisted living to health-care monitoring. IEEE Signal Processing Magazine, 38(4), 78–88.

Rahman, A., Debnath, T., Kundu, D., Khan, M.S.I., Aishi, A.A., Sazzad, S. et al. (2024). Machine learning and deep learning-based approach in smart healthcare: Recent advances, applications, challenges and opportunities. AIMS Public Health, 11(1), 58.

Rajkomar, A., Oren, E., Chen, K., Dai, A.M., Hajaj, N., Hardt, M. et al. (2018). Scalable and accurate deep learning for electronic health records. npj Digital Medicine, 1(1), 1–10.

Rathi, V.K., Rajput, N.K., Mishra, S., Grover, B.A., Tiwari, P., Jaiswal, A.K., and Hossain, M.S. (2021). An edge AI-enabled IoT healthcare monitoring system for smart cities. Computers & Electrical Engineering, 96, 107524.

Rehman, A.U., Lu, S., Bin Heyat, M.B., Iqbal, M.S., Parveen, S., Bin Hayat, M.A. et al. (2025). Internet of things in healthcare research: Trends, innovations, security considerations, challenges and future strategy. International Journal of Intelligent Systems, 2025(1), 8546245.

Rong, G., Mendez, A., Assi, E.B., Zhao, B., and Sawan, M. (2020). Artificial intelligence in healthcare: Review and prediction case studies. Engineering, 6(3), 291–301.

Scaboro, S., Portelli, B., Chersoni, E., Santus, E., and Serra, G. (2023). Extensive evaluation of transformer-based architectures for adverse drug events extraction. KnowledgeBased Systems, 275, 110675.

Schmidt, H., Mah, C.L., Cook, B., Hoang, S., Taylor, E., Blacksher, E. et al. (2016). Chronic disease prevention and health promotion. *In:* Public Health Ethics: Cases Spanning the Globe, pp. 137–176.

Shashikumar, S.P., Stanley, M.D., Sadiq, I., Holder, A., Clifford, G.D., and Nemati, S. (2017). Early sepsis detection in critical care patients using multiscale blood pressure and heart rate dynamics. Journal of Electrocardiology, 50(6), 739–743.

Silva, L., Pacheco, T., Aráujo, E., Duarte, R.J., Ribeiro-Vaz, I., and Ferreirada Silva, R. (2024). Unveiling the future: Precision pharmacovigilance in the era of personalized medicine. International Journal of Clinical Pharmacy, 46(3), 755–760.

Tariq, M.U. (2024). Advanced wearable medical devices and their role in transformative remote health monitoring. *In:* Transformative Approaches to Patient Literacy and Healthcare Innovation (pp. 308–326). IGI Global Scientific Publishing.

Tatonetti, N.P., Ye, P.P., Daneshjou, R., and Altman, R.B. (2012). Datadriven prediction of drug effects and interactions. Science Translational Medicine, 4(125), 125ra31–125ra31.

Topol, E.J. (2019). High-performance medicine: The convergence of human and artificial intelligence. Nature Medicine, 25(1), 44–56.

Uddin, M.J. and Munni, M.N. (2021). Personalized patient safety management: Sensors and real-time data analysis. *In:* Vision, Sensing and Analytics: Integrative Approaches, pp. 267–305. Springer.

U.S. Food and Drug Administration. (2023). FDA adverse event reporting system (faers). Available: https://www.fda.gov/drugs/ questions-and-answers-fdas-adverse-event-reporting-system-faers.

Uzuner, O., Luo, Y., and Szolovits, P. (2011). Evaluating the state-of-the-art in automatic de-identification. Journal of the American Medical Informatics Association, 14, 550–563. Oxford University Press.

Van Mulligen, E.M., Fourrier-Reglat, A., Gurwitz, D., Molokhia, M., Nieto, A., Trifiro, G. et al. (2013). The EU-ADR corpus: Annotated drugs, diseases, targets, and their relationships. Journal of Biomedical Informatics, 46(5), 913–920.

Wishart, D.S., Feunang, Y.D., Guo, A.C., Lo, E.J., Marcu, A., Grant, J.R. et al. (2018). Drugbank: A comprehensive resource for in silico drug discovery and exploration. Nucleic Acids Research, 46(D1), D1074–D1082.

World Health Organization. (2002). The Importance of Pharmacovigilance: Safety Monitoring of Medicinal Products. World Health Organization, Geneva.

Ye, J., Woods, D., Jordan, N., and Starren, J. (2024). The role of artificial intelligence for the application of integrating electronic health records and patient-generated data in clinical decision support. AMIA Summits on Translational Science Proceedings, 2024, 459.

Zinchenko, V., Chetverikov, S., Akhmad, E., Arzamasov, K., Vladzymyrskyy, A., Andreychenko, A., and Morozov, S. (2022). Changes in software as a medical device based on artificial intelligence technologies. International Journal of Computer Assisted Radiology and Surgery, 17(10), 1969–1977.

CHAPTER
12

An Adaptive and Intelligent IoT Framework for Next Generation Rehabilitation

Sharanya S.[1*(0000-0003-2442-3246)], **Radha R.**[1(0000-0001-9822-0949)],
A Rehash Rushmi Pavitra[1(0000-0002-1220-1497)] **and Karthikeyan S.**[2(0000-0002-6873-9085)]

[1] Department of Data Science and Business Systems, SRM Institute of Science and Technology, Kattankulathur, Chennai – 603203

[2] Department of Aerospace Engineering, B S Crescent Institute of Science and Technology, Vandalur, Chennai – 600048

1. Introduction

The new demand for modern healthcare systems is to do more than just prevent people from dying by equipping their lives to fulfill their potential while optimizing their contribution to the family, community, and society. Developing and deploying innovative and disruptive technologies to help people regain their independence and fulfilling lives is the urgent need of the hour. Modern medical advancements have made remarkable increases in the survival rates from disorders, diseases, trauma, and injury (Laut et al., 2016). Nevertheless, survival is just the start, and the high survival rate has further envisaged the rehabilitation needs, which involve patients with diverse and complex medical conditions. The role of technology is paramount in the rehabilitation process, supporting a confined number of skilled healthcare practitioners, reducing hospital visits and stays, improving patient engagement with the rehabilitation procedures, and increasing independence, thereby improving the results. Accelerating recovery and aiding the patients to get back to work as well as normal life has a substantial social, economic, and personal impact (Kuroda et al., 2021).

The rehabilitation program is a network that connects healthcare providers, researchers, user groups, patients, industrial partners, and other supporting

*Corresponding author: nice_sharanya@yahoo.co.in

DOI: 10.1201/9781003676812-12

organizations, such as charities, policy makers, etc., to develop infrastructure and a community for advanced rehabilitation. By this connection, new inventive and innovative technologies with advanced materials can be developed without compromising mental and physical health (Herrera-Ligero et al., 2022). This supports the provision of innovative, affordable, and transformable solutions to address the issues of patients to lead fulfilling and independent lives. Any technological innovation in rehabilitation will focus on three key areas: the invention of advanced functional materials, the development of customized patient-specific devices and therapy, and implementing closed-loop monitoring and rehabilitation.

On the global front, the rehabilitation market size has surpassed USD 25.47 billion in 2023, and trend analysis in Figure 1 shows that in 2033, USD 52.90 billion must be expended for next-generation rehabilitation (Sakpal, 2024). This rehabilitation market is a critical component encompassing a wide spectrum of interventions, monitoring, and treatments focused on restoring mobility and function among individuals recovering from surgeries, injuries, or other physical impairments. The broad spectrum of rehabilitation includes a diverse range of stakeholders such as rehabilitation clinics, physical therapists, nursing homes, home healthcare providers, hospitals, etc. The grounded key service of rehabilitation is mainly focused on diagnosis, assessment, and devising personalized treatment plans involving manual therapy, exercise with modalities like electrical stimulation and ultrasound.

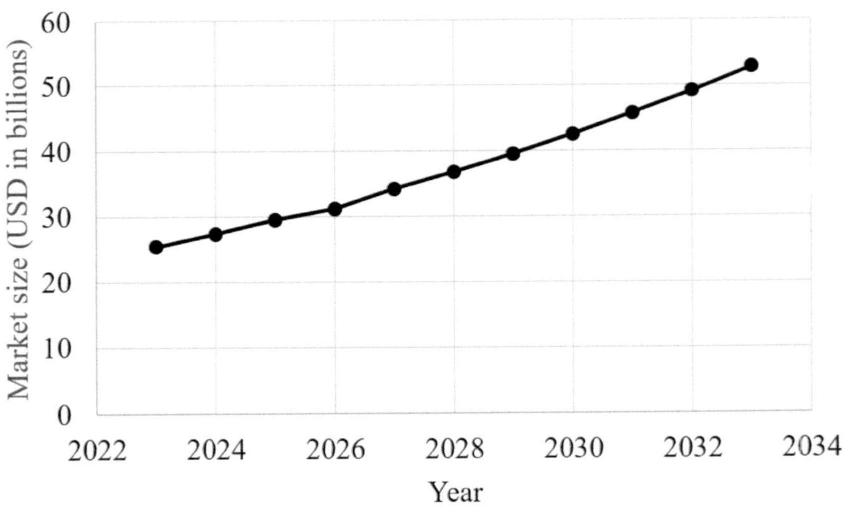

Figure 1: Trend analysis of the rehabilitation market.

Another notable point in the accelerating market growth is the increase in the aging population, which demands more rehabilitative care for conditions such as osteoarthritis, Alzheimer's, and stroke. In addition to this, technological advancements are reshaping the landscape of rehabilitation practices by integrating telehealth, virtual reality, robotics-assisted therapies, and wearable devices (Bowman et al., 2021). Nevertheless, challenges like shortages of skilled professionals, reimbursement issues, and medical costs are the chief obstacles to availing the rehabilitation services. Despite these numerous challenges, the rehabilitation market evolves dynamically and contributes to improving the patients' quality of life (Lorenz et al., 2024). The scope for rehabilitation is multifaceted. Some of the prominent genres that could foster rehabilitation are enumerated below:

- The acceleration of remote rehabilitation services has been driven by the expansion of telehealth, particularly in the post-pandemic era. The string continues as patients prefer more accessible and convenient ways to receive therapeutic services.
- Leveraging the technological advancements through the development of virtual reality (VR), wearable devices, augmented reality (AR), and mixed reality for monitoring, assessment, and rehabilitation has enhanced patient engagement, as these technologies provide the development and customization of personalized treatment (Zhao et al., 2024).
- The modern healthcare industry is planning a quick shift to value-based reimbursement models and outcome-focused care. So, the therapy providers emphasize more on patient outcomes by demonstrating their service efficacy in improving the functional abilities of the patient.
- Developments in genetic engineering and biomechanics have further facilitated the improvements in rehabilitation therapy by helping the therapist to devise more personalized and precise treatment procedures. To add to this, data-driven approaches help to tailor treatments based on individual needs.
- As there is an escalation in the aged population with chronic health conditions, there is a pressing demand for rehabilitation services to effectively manage health conditions like joint replacements, stroke, Alzheimer's, arthritis, etc. (Seijas et al., 2024). This trend is the primary driving force behind the innovations in geriatric rehabilitation techniques.

1.1. Scope of Technologies in Demand for Rehabilitation

The growing demand for customized rehabilitation services and innovative solutions provides researchers with different insights. Contemporary technologies like Internet of Things (IoT), artificial intelligence, computer vision, AR, VR, and gaming technologies have brought great shifts to the rehabilitation paradigm.

1.2. Solution Insights

Providing technology-based rehabilitation includes a wide range of equipment, interfaces, software, and services. The equipment encompasses mainly mobility aids, electrotherapy devices, heat therapy equipment, monitoring sensors, cameras, and exercise machines, supporting therapists in delivering quality treatment for the patients. Providing software solutions has become an integral part of the electronic health record systems. Some predominant software support includes telehealth platforms, online consultations, rehabilitation exercise programs, patient tracking, monitoring, and management etc. (Hergert et al., 2024). In addition, some of the services offered by therapists, such as physical therapy, occupational therapy, rehabilitation counselling, and speech therapy, are a crucial part of the rehabilitation solution.

1.3. Application Insights

There are many therapeutic applications supported by technological advancements to cater to patient-specific needs and conditions. For instance, orthopedic rehabilitation primarily focuses on improving musculoskeletal conditions to restore mobility and mitigate pain. On the other hand, neurological rehabilitation addresses conditions such as spinal cord injuries or stroke. The therapist engages the patients to enhance their motor functions along with cognitive abilities. There is a different turn for the cardiopulmonary rehabilitation asset that supports the patients with lung or heart impairments with breathing exercises. Pediatric rehabilitation helps children with delayed development to emphasize skill improvement and holistic development (Antoniadou et al., 2024).

1.4. End-user Insights

From the end user's perspective, hospitals provide inpatient rehabilitation services. On the other hand, the rehabilitation clinics and centers specialize in offering outpatient care. These centers customize the rehabilitation procedures to specific health conditions. After the pandemic era, home care settings are gaining momentum,

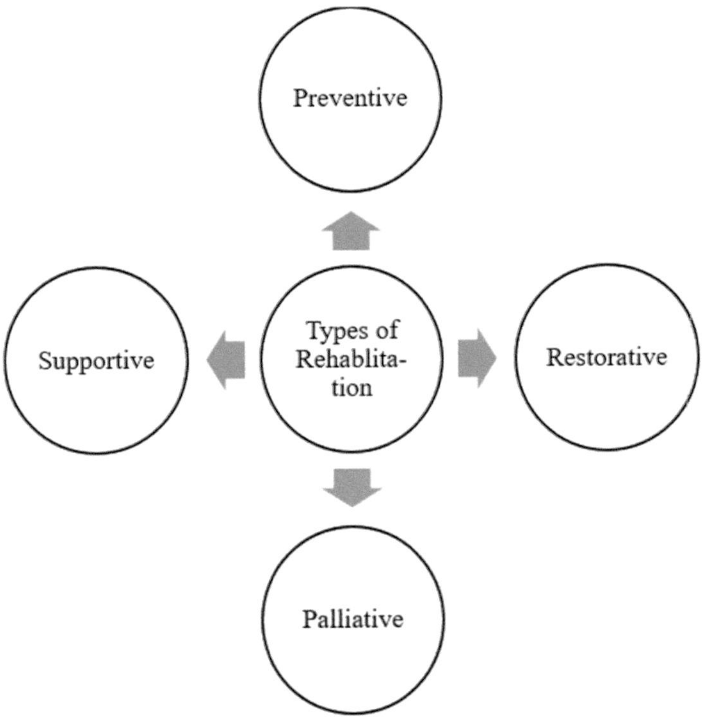

Figure 2: Types of rehabilitation.

and thereby, there is a steep increase in the demand for online consultations through telehealth platforms with remote guidance. Other genres such as nursing homes, schools, and sports medicine clinics also contribute to the rehabilitation market by rendering tailor-made rehabilitation services.

The domain of rehabilitation envisions different types of services based on the goals and approaches. The predominant types are shown in Figure 2. Preventive rehabilitation is primarily used for preventing disability and maintaining optimal function to avoid worsening health conditions. These types of rehabilitation are delivered for individuals at risk of functional decline, mostly in the elderly population. The outcomes include early intervention, lifestyle modification, and health promotion. The restorative rehabilitation is given to patients after an injury, surgery, or illness. This helps the patients regain their health. This type of therapy is more goal-oriented and intensive. Supportive rehabilitation helps individuals with progressive conditions to maintain their functionality. This is more common among people with incurable health conditions, and they focus on preventing more complications. Palliative rehabilitation enhances the quality of life and comfort in life-limiting conditions. These procedures primarily focus on emotional support, symptom management, and pain relief.

2. Medical Internet of Things in Rehabilitation

IoT is a technological system that connects people and things, thus fostering ample opportunities in making the world smarter. In the era of post-pandemic e-health, smart rehabilitation systems are setting a new standard. The IoT devices improve the rehabilitation therapy by rendering precise and customized care for the needy patients. The fusion of IoT technology and healthcare has accelerated automated treatments with remote monitoring facilities, which were once seen as a heavy burden to healthcare administration. Some of the predominant opportunities for integrating Medical IoT (MIoT) Devices in the healthcare sector are listed below:

- Including IoT devices as a part of therapeutic procedures and protocols greatly reduces the costs but improves efficacy.
- Personalized patient care is provisioned using precise and accurate IoT devices, which greatly reduce discomfort during the treatment. They also reduce the medical costs by decreasing travel and other related expenses for the patients and caretakers.
- Real-time patient monitoring is one of the most demanding services in patient healthcare. The MIoT devices can reliably deliver real-time data by continuously monitoring patients' physiological conditions. This vicious cycle is completed by the therapist providing health-related feedback and recommendations, who is well-informed about the patient's current health conditions through data collected by the MIoT devices.
- Integrating MIoT devices in inpatient patient-specific treatments helps store, collect, and analyze data, as well as track and monitor the patient's progress. This assists the therapist in fine-tuning their approach and guiding them to plan future treatment plans.

- Enhancing patient engagement is made possible by integrating MIoT devices into rehabilitation therapy. The real-time feedback mechanism, planning achievable goals, and promoting home-based exercises are some of the features that improve engagement levels.
- In addition to this, the gamification of exercises opens new opportunities for aged people to be more encouraged and enjoyable. Some of the notable applications of IoT in rehabilitation are shown in Figure 3.

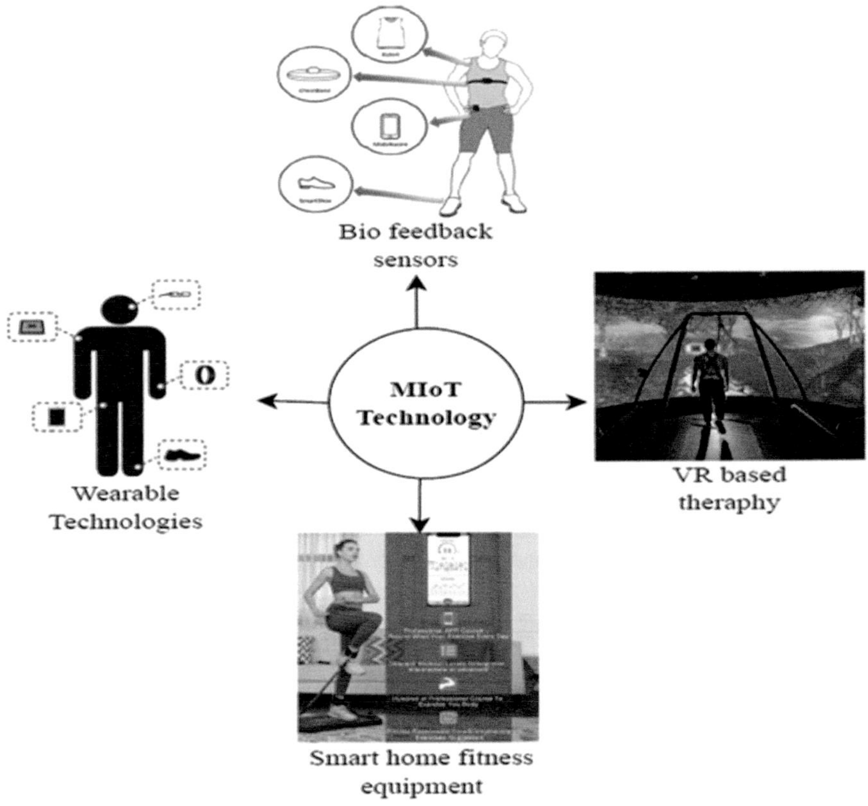

Figure 3: Applications of MIoT in rehabilitation.

Artificial Intelligence (AI) is emerging as a frontier in medicine through its capability to make a machine perform a task overseen by humans (Selvaraj et al., 2022). These algorithms are trained to think, learn, and can aid in various clinical practices, especially in rehabilitation. Also, including AI technologies greatly improves the quality of treatment by reducing medical errors. The inclusion of IoT and AI technologies is gaining momentum in the sector of rehabilitation to deliver patient-centric health care. Embracing these changes helps therapists succeed in their profession by including the AI-generated decisions (Kalani et al., 2024). AI is globally deployed to assist the assessment of neurological functions and supports the monitoring and recovery progress for patients with neurological disorders by providing customized feedback for the rehabilitation exercises, promoting accessibility through telerehabilitation and VR, and improving the efficacy of treatment for therapists. AI bridges the gap between the accessibility of services and the patients in need.

3. Literature Survey

AI and MIoT devices are increasingly used in rehabilitation therapy mainly to create patient-centered treatment plans, track progress, and enhance outcomes. The power of AI to analyze large amounts of medical data, including historical and real-time information, enables the development of personalized rehabilitation programs. Some of the notable works are discussed in this section.

Most of the existing rehabilitation techniques are based on exoskeletons, which impose stringent limitations on responsiveness, adaptability, and control. Sunil Jacob et al. (2021) proposed an AI-based exoskeleton system that collects data from various IoT devices to support paralyzed patients. The command for rehabilitation is generated through IoT with a simultaneous localization and mapping system to support the caretakers. Francesco Lanotte et al. (2023) present a comprehensive review of the prominent works in AI-based diagnosis, monitoring, and treatment in the context of rehabilitation. The work summarizes the limitations and challenges confronted by the smart rehabilitation system, which serves as a potential research problem.

Yang Han et al. developed an intelligent recommendation model for the rehabilitation of cancer patients by integrating a user-friendly recommendation system (Fan et al., 2014). A Convolutional Neural Network (CNN) was used to predict both the cause and the timing of cancer cell recurrence in patients. Response time is one of the critical factors in designing and developing a rehabilitation system, as the patient's needs must be catered to at a much quicker pace. An ontology-based automating design has been proposed by Yuan Jie Fan et al. (2014) to devise a customized rehabilitation strategy. The medical resources are reconfigured based on the patient's requirements and serve as a platform that interconnects multiple heterogeneous devices.

Sports rehabilitation is complex as it must consider musculoskeletal discomfort, disorders, and injuries. Real-time medical equipment is monitored using sensors, and the body area networks are deployed to collect physiological data of the sports person (Wu et al., 2025). The most challenging part of sports rehabilitation is the detection of playing position, cybersecurity, and game strategies. Integrating IoT with humanoid robots to promote motor skills is a pioneering achievement in the rehabilitation of disabled patients. The I-TROPHYTS is a sustainable medical robot that mimics the actions performed by physiotherapists to adaptively improve patients' motor skills (Moghbelan et al., 2024). The data from the physiotherapists is captured and modelled using ontology-based automatic reasoning.

The challenges faced by the rehabilitation sector are greatly mitigated by the inclusion of Machine Learning (ML) and Deep Learning (DL) techniques. A non-intrusive and intelligent sensing system that uses SensFloor, a smart carpet, with an inertial measurement unit to monitor the patient's back position (Monge et al.,

2023). The real-time data generated by the system is analyzed by the therapists using intelligent models specifically designed for gait balancing. The ML algorithms are used for suggesting tailor-made rehabilitation plans. Tele-rehabilitation has gained rapid momentum among clinicians and patients, as it holds great potential for cardiac rehabilitation. Shereena Shaji et al. (2024) designed a highly interactive and fail-safe system with real-time feedback for tele-cardiac rehabilitation. The MIoT devices are seamlessly integrated with AI-powered activity and anomaly detection models such as RESNET-18 and VGG 16. These models are deployed in clouds to avoid computational load on the end devices.

A narrowband smart medical system for rehabilitation of the lower limb exoskeleton is proposed by Linxiu Fan et al. (2021). The work comprises some significant research implications. The medical communication protocol and the required hardware and software are identified to integrate data from different platforms. Also, the system management software establishes seamless communication between various stakeholders of the rehabilitation system. Akash Gupta et al. (2021) have developed a smart post-operative hip fracture rehabilitation model that emphasizes hip physical movements and the associated events that go along with them. This IoT-based monitoring system comprises all the essential operating features. The detailed test results show its proficiency as a futuristic rehabilitation system.

Ioannis Vourganas et al. (2020) developed a customized patient-centric smart home-based rehabilitation system to assess the daily activities of patients with comorbidities. The interpretability and individualism of the model are provided by leveraging the gradient boosting method along with k-nearest neighbors. A significant feature of the model is its low computational footprint, which is the need of the hour. The ontological, behavioral, and value product design layers are investigated by Dan Yang et al. (2024) to build rehabilitation products. Cloud-based symbiotic data was generated, and an upper limb rehabilitation robot was developed by leveraging this big data.

Monitoring orthopedic rehabilitation exercises is critical, as it is necessary to monitor the patients during rehabilitation periods to avoid injuries. A new paradigm, which integrates IoT, DL, and edge computing to categorize the extension–flexion movement of the knee using ML models, is proposed by Evanthia Faliagka et al. (2023). The model exhibited excellent performance in modelling and labelling knee movements, even on low-energy platforms. Jie Yang et al. (2025) designed a wearable device by leveraging Micro Electromechanical Systems to collect real-time motion data along with signal processing and filtering techniques. Additionally, particle swarm optimization support vector machine is used as a classifier to label the motion patterns. Real-time analytics, system capacity, and performance make it more desirable for rehabilitation activities.

The integration of AI and IoT in building smart rehabilitation systems has created a significant advancement in modern healthcare systems. The existing literature portrays the inclining trend in deploying smart technologies to improve patient recovery with special emphasis on post-stroke therapy, post-cancer therapy, orthopedic rehabilitation, neurological disorders, and limb impairments. The IoT-based rehabilitation systems facilitate continuous monitoring with real-time feedback mechanisms to promote remote patient engagement, either through wearable devices or smart sensors. Often, these systems acquire physiological as well as biomechanical data to monitor and track patient activities, progress, and their adherence to the prescribed therapy protocols. AI techniques, including ML, DL, and computer vision models, are commonly used to investigate the collected data, predict outcomes, and develop patient-centric personalized rehabilitation plans. Many algorithms have been proposed and implemented for gesture recognition, anomaly detection, recovery trajectory prediction, and activity classification.

Several studies in the literature emphasize the deployment of intelligent feedback mechanisms, like virtual coaching, adaptive difficulty levels, and gamification, to further improve patient motivation and engagement. However, the rehabilitation system imparts multiple challenges like data privacy concerns, limited clinical validation, and interoperability issues. So, the proposed framework primarily focuses on developing standardized frameworks by integrating AI models to develop a generic, patient-centric IoT solution with better scalability, clinical efficacy, and usability.

4. An Adaptive Intelligent Rehabilitation Framework

This section briefs the operational workflow and design architecture of the proposed adaptive intelligent framework, which integrates the prowess of AI along with MIoT, AR, VR, and other assistive technologies to facilitate the formulation of customized patient-centric therapeutic procedures.

Figure 4 shows the overall architecture of the intelligent rehabilitation adaptive framework, which amalgamates contemporary and futuristic technologies to enable continuous monitoring of the patients, adaptive therapy planning by leveraging data-centric and AI-based algorithms to achieve better rehabilitation outcomes. The modules of the proposed framework are described below.

The input data for the proposed framework is collected from different stakeholders such as patients, therapists, and clinicians. However, patients are the pivotal focus of the proposed framework. The medical records of the patients are initially analyzed by expert clinicians and therapists to determine a device and recommend an initial therapy plan. Based on the assessment of the medical records, a more personalized patient-centric therapy plan is formulated by the physician. This plan is the initial intervention strategy, and this will be configured for real-time monitoring of the patient and their adaptive rehabilitation. The patient monitoring module incorporates advanced technologies that support intelligent and continuous monitoring of patients. Some of the potential technologies which could assist in supportive healthcare include:

- VR, AR, and mixed reality for rendering an effective immersive rehabilitation experience to the patients (Biswas et al., 2021).
- Use of assistive technologies, which includes an array of devices that help in patient recovery. These are complex and sophisticated tools which are designed with the focus store aid individuals suffering from various forms of sensory, cognitive, and physical impairments in discharging their daily tasks. These

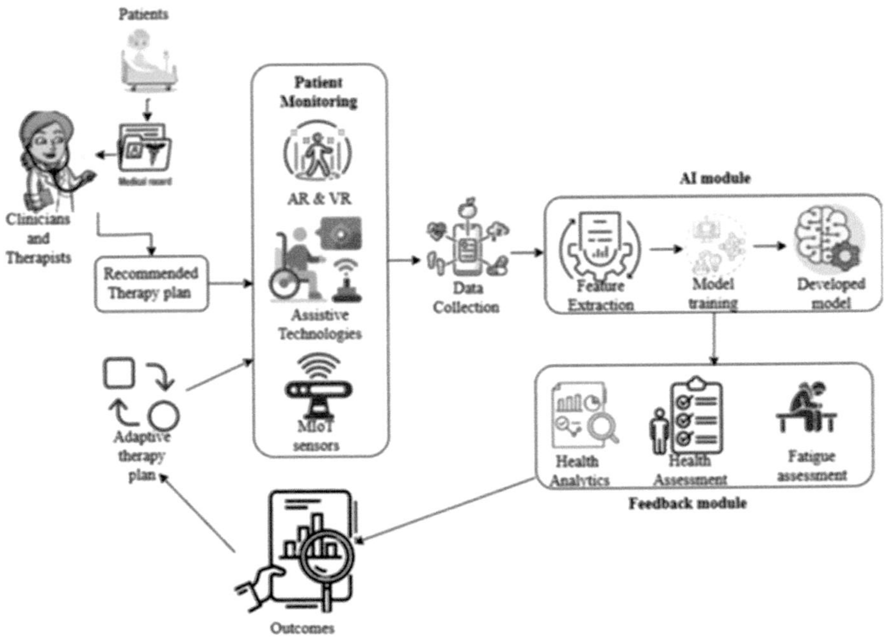

Figure 4: Proposed adaptive rehabilitation framework.

tools are very helpful in improving the engagement of the patients in therapy sessions. They support the therapy by improving patient interaction, facilitating continuous monitoring to support speedy recovery. The proposed rehabilitation framework provisions the integration of the following assistive technology tools and devices:

- **Mobility and Physical Rehabilitation Devices:** AI-powered wheelchairs and smart wheelchairs hold a special mention in physical rehabilitation, as these tools are equipped with sensors and other navigation aids to assess the mobility of the patient. They also play a predominant role in collecting data for planning future treatments. Exoskeletons and robotic suits are wearable robots that are commonly used by patients who have physical impairment or injury (Hassett et al., 2016). They assist the patients but movements such as balance, walking, and other limb movements. The next assistive device is robotic arm trainers, which play a key role in upper limb rehabilitation. They are used by patients affected by injury or stroke to promote their motion recovery.
- **Sensory and Cognitive Aids:** These are strategies and tools that are specifically designed and developed to support individuals who suffer from cognitive or sensory impairments. These tools can range from sample and compact devices like visual or hearing aids to more sophisticated and complex technologies like cognitive training programs or assistive listening devices. These aids are designed to improve the patient's potential to comprehend, perceive, process, and interact but the environment to improve their quality of life (Regan

et al., 2019). Some of the common devices doctors widely use in rehabilitation programs include speech-generating devices to help patients suffering from speech impairments respond and communicate with the environment. Brain-computer interfaces are sophisticated devices that translate the brain signals into control commands for the functional operation of assistive tools. AR and VR headsets are specifically designed to provide a comprehensive and immersive rehabilitation ecosystem for patients suffering from cognitive and physical disorders.

- **MIoT Integrated Wearables:** These are integrated wearables that connect to the Internet to transfer patients' health data to clinicians and therapists. They act as platforms for remote patient monitoring and data analysis. These are devices that are configured with smart sensors to track the body vitals, activity levels, and other health-related metrics, whose analysis will provide valuable insights to the patients as well as healthcare professionals. Some of the profound MIoT wearables include smart bins and fitness trackers, surface EMG sensors, gait and posture analyzers, etc. Smart bands and fitness trackers usually monitor the vital physiological properties such as sleep quality, step count, heart rate, etc. The surface EMG sensors are smart devices specifically designed to capture muscular activity for providing biofeedback in the motor rehabilitation process. The poster and gait analyzers are wearable sensors that track the body alignment and balance, along with walking patterns.
- **Daily Living Assistance Tools:** These tools are also a form of assistive technology specifically designed to support patients with permanent disabilities or limitations in performing their day-to-day tasks independently. The functions of these aids can vary from simple tools like reachers, dressing sticks to sophisticated devices like communication aids and smart wheelchairs. These tools are specifically developed to promote the functionalities such as dressing, mobility, toileting, and bathing of the patients. There is a wide array of daily living assistance tools available in the market. Some of them include an environmental control system that monitors, tracks, and controls the lighting of the room and doors, and helps the patients to handle appliances through touch or voice commands. Adaptive grips and utensils RA a form of assistive tools that help patients with limited dexterity to do tasks such as writing, eating, and grooming. Many times, the patient's forgetfulness adversely impacts the treatment procedures and their health developments. To address this issue, researchers have designed smart pill dispensers that automatically manage and remind patients to take their pills. This helps the patients to maintain the medication schedule.
- **Communication Aids:** Technically, they are also known as voice output communication aids or speech-generating communication systems. These tools help people and children to deal with language or speech difficulties in understanding or expressing dear thoughts to others. They include a wide range of techniques and devices from simple picture board representation to complex and automated speech-generating devices. Eye tracking devices are a form of communication aid that enables the control and communication of devices by tracking the eyeball movement. On the other hand, touch-screen-

based augmented and alternative communication devices are available to help patients with acute speech limitations.

The availability of various rehabilitation devices supports their integration into the proposed framework. These tools and technologies enable non-intrusive and remote monitoring of patient progress. They also assist clinicians in more accurately tracking and monitoring the complaints related to the suggested therapy and the performance metrics. Devices offer manifold advantages. They support real-time patient health data collection through continuous monitoring of the patients' activities and vitals. The embedded sensors in these devices facilitate the data collection process, which can be explored for future data analytics. The rehabilitation tools and devices promote patient engagement as they are highly responsive and interactive. These devices are more suitable for working in tandem with AI, ML, and DL models, and they can provide real-time feedback. Leveraging this feedback will help clinicians and therapists to design personalized and patient-centric treatment plans.

The health-related data generated from rehabilitation tools and devices are collected through smart platforms or devices for further data processing and analytics.

The proposed framework includes a generic AI module to enhance the decision-making process and therapy precision. The AI module comprises the key task of feature extraction. Feature extraction is a crucial process in ML models and data analysis, involving the identification and extraction of valuable and relevant information from unprocessed raw health data. The data acquired from different monitoring devices is transferred securely to the AI-based processing module. In this stage, the AI module performs the comprehensive feature extraction process to identify relevant attributes from the raw MIoT sensor data. The data generally comprises variations in heart rate, motion tracking movement patterns,etc. The features extracted from these data forms are the basis for configuring and training the AI models, which support clinical decision-making for clinicians and therapists. These key data features are identified and used to develop the AI model. The deployment of DL algorithms has eliminated the complex task of feature selection and extraction, as the DL models themselves automate the process of feature engineering. This has offered two advantages. Firstly, it saves a lot of time on feature extraction, and secondly, it helps avoid missing important trends and patterns in the underlying data. The next most important process is the training of AI models. ML or DL models are trained using real-time patient data. A massive amount of data is required for training the model, which is very difficult to acquire in real-time processing systems. Alternatively, pre-trained models are available, which can be directly deployed on the relevant data. Also, the advancements of generative AI technology have facilitated the massive production of synthetic data that could be leveraged for training the models. Once the model has been trained to achieve satisfactory accuracy, it can't be tested and deployed. The so-developed model has the potential for making intelligent predictions for therapy adaptation. Overall, the AI module performs multifaceted tasks. The extracted features from the health-related data are leveraged to design and train the AI models through a supervised learning approach. The AI models can assess the effectiveness of the recommended therapy, evaluate patients' mental and physical fatigue, and identify any deviations from the normal recovery pattern. Thus, the trained model forms the core part of the AI module, facilitating predictive as well as prescriptive analytics within the proposed intelligent rehabilitation framework.

The proposed model encompasses a feedback module. This module relies on a model's output to perform various important tasks. The feedback module processes patient health data to identify trends in progress, hence performing health-related analytics. The module asset also includes a health assessment, which entails assessing the patient's condition, progress, and recuperation. The module also encompasses fatigue assessment, which is the detection of mental or physical fatigue to prevent overexertion in patients.

The adaptive therapy loop is also included in the proposed intelligent rehabilitation framework, which gathers the insights from the feedback module to create an adaptive therapy plan. This induces dynamicity into the proposed architecture as the adaptive therapy plan is devised based on real-time data analytics, assessment, and fatigue analysis. This adaptive therapy plan is then fed into the monitoring module. Therapists and clinicians examine the feedback module's precise observations to create an adaptive therapy plan. This is the modification of the existing rehabilitation regime based on the patient's involvement, progress, and their evolving needs. This makes the rehabilitation therapy more dynamic and helps the patients to recover at a much faster pace. The dynamic adjustment of the therapeutic plan at a time, customized, more personalized, responsive, and adaptive care for the needy patients. In addition to this, the adaptation of the therapy plan minimizes the risk of mental and physical fatigue, which optimizes the speedy recovery of the patients.

Evaluation of the outcome of rehabilitation therapy is essential. The outcomes are generally analyzed to validate whether the therapy is effective for the patient. The result of the evaluation helps clinicians and therapists refine their future therapy plans and design customized, patient-centric treatment strategies. The monitoring system and the feedback module are subjected to assessment through multiple quantitative metrics. To validate the effectiveness of the outcome assessment, they are frequently reviewed by clinicians as well as therapists to further fine-tune the therapy strategies and to close the loop of the proposed intelligent rehabilitation framework. This continuous cycle of data gathering, analysis, and therapy adaptation promotes better patient engagement, therapy progression, and long-term speedy recovery.

Implementing the therapy in the proposed architecture begins with the analysis of patient records by the therapists and clinicians. Then, recommend personalized, patient-focused therapy plans based on the analysis findings. Clinicians use modern and cutting-edge assistive and supportive technology to create more interactive rehabilitation programs and exercises that gather comprehensive cognitive, behavioral, and physiological data. From the functional viewpoint, the collected data is transferred to a processing unit, the AI module in the proposed architecture. The relevant features from the health records are extracted from the data, and the developed AI models are trained on them to learn the patient performance patterns, trends, and other health indicators. Once the model is trained, it is used to evaluate the effectiveness of the recommended therapy plan.

Overall, the proposed architecture is a closed-loop system that uses customized care and AI-based data-driven decision-making to support adaptive rehabilitation. This improves both clinical efficiency and patient engagement.

5. Demystifying the Myths in AI-based Rehabilitation Practices

There are several myths and misconceptions about the widespread use of AI models in the rehabilitation process. There is a general opinion that AI will completely replace human therapists and clinicians, which will be harmful for treating patients with complete quality of care. However, this is false. The AI tools and techniques employed in any healthcare procedure will help clinicians and other healthcare providers by giving personalized feedback, tracking and monitoring the progress of the patients, and making healthcare recommendations and interventions more effective and personalized. Additionally, there is an assumption that implementing AI models and technologies is expensive and complicated. This becomes the more pressing issue in the context of rehabilitation, as there is a notion that emerging technologies would demand the complete replacement of the existing legacy systems. However, technological advancements worldwide are making AI more affordable, adaptable, accessible, and easier to integrate with legacy rehabilitation systems (Sharanya et al., 2022).

Also, an intense argument on reliability is being put forth regarding employing AI models in healthcare practices. The AI-based healthcare systems are carefully crafted, designed, and assessed with rigorous evaluation standards, protocols, and methods by different stakeholders. Also, ethical compliance and considerations are considered while designing any AI-based healthcare system. It is important to understand that the configuration and deployment of AI-based systems involve more rigorous assessment procedures, ongoing research, and ethical compliance, in addition to stakeholder involvement to create a more responsible AI. Nowadays, the AI models r evolving to become more explainable and transparent. They can now provide evidence and reasons for the actions, recommendations, and decisions.

6. Design Considerations of the Proposed System

The proposed intelligent AI-based adaptive rehabilitation framework is developed and designed to enhance patient engagement while enabling seamless remote monitoring to support adaptive therapy. The design guidelines for implementing the framework to meet clinical, technical, and patient-centered needs are discussed in this section. The selection of hardware and IoT devices plays a crucial role in the success of the system. Accelerometers, EMG sensors, and gyroscopes are more commonly used to collect real-time motion and physiological data from patients. The connectivity between these devices and the system is provided through low-power wireless communication protocols. Generally, ZigBee, Wi-Fi, and Bluetooth low energy protocols are leveraged to provide more secure and reliable data transmission in the health networks. Additionally, the microcontroller units embedded within the

MIoT devices must be energy efficient, apart from being capable of performing data compression and data filtering.

The integration of edge AI in the hospital premises will enhance the accessibility and availability of the rehabilitation models. Deploying lightweight ML and DL models with Federated learning facilitates more responsive real-time anomaly detection as well as activity recognition.

The proposed intelligent rehabilitation architecture can be extended to provide a therapist dashboard and a patient application. The therapist dashboard is a web interface that allows clinicians and therapists to monitor the overall process and progress of the patients. This helps them to adaptively reconfigure and adjust the therapy retention based on performance analytics. On the other hand, a mobile or web app can provide instructions to perform the exercises, track the progress, and give feedback to the patients by monitoring the audio-visual cues, apart from providing motivational notifications. Integration of this would make the system more robust and accessible. Also, designing the system with user-friendly navigation, multilingual support, and voice assistance will cater to the needs of a wide range of users.

The health-related data is very confidential, and hence special emphasis must be given to protecting the data. End-to-end encryption must be implemented for all transactions. Also, the patient data must be anonymized and stored by adhering to the health data standards. The implementation of role-based access control ensures that the confidential data can be accessed only by authorized users. Scalability is yet another concern of the proposed framework. Because the framework is completely modular, integrating additional sensors or AI technologies becomes seamless and easy. This introduces a great degree of dynamism into the rehabilitation process. Including cloud infrastructure as a part of the proposed rehabilitation framework facilitates horizontal scaling to serve the needs of more users without any significant performance degradation. Designing fault-tolerant parts using backup communication and implementing error recovery protocols will ensure the uninterrupted monitoring of the therapy. As the proposed rehabilitation framework includes many MIoT devices and wearable devices, special emphasis must be given to incorporating energy-efficient components and power optimization. The low-power modes and the sleep cycles of the devices must be extensively utilized to extend battery life. Also, configuring the components must be done based on their energy requirements without compromising performance.

7. Conclusions and Future Works

Rehabilitation technology is a part of healthcare that helps people regain and improve the functionality of their body parts after illness or injury. They can effectively augment the therapeutic care through various technologies like exoskeletons, remote monitoring, AI, AR, and VR. Integration of rehabilitation techniques with better accessibility helps in speedy recovery for long-term self-management. The chapter proposes an intelligent rehabilitation framework that amalgamates AI, MIoT, AR, and VR with other assistive technologies to provide a transformative approach. The proposed framework enables real-time data capturing and an adaptive feedback mechanism with remote monitoring of patients. This system could greatly enhance patient engagement, foster personalized therapeutic approaches, and empower therapists with more actionable insights. Scalable and modular architecture imbues great flexibility for covering a wide range of rehabilitation needs, thus making it more robust and generic. Overall, the proposed framework makes rehabilitation more affordable, accessible, user-centric, and more feasible in the post-pandemic era, which highlights the significance of virtual healthcare facilities. The proposed framework offers several futuristic opportunities. Integrating deep reinforcement learning algorithms along with multimodal data fusion will greatly healthy clinicians to improve the adaptiveness of the model. Clinical validation, which involves replicative clinical trials, should be conducted to validate the usability and efficacy of the proposed system in real world scenarios. Also, including haptic feedback along with AR/VR interfaces will greatly enhance patient engagement, interactivity, and motivation during the rehabilitation sessions. Gamification is one unexplored area, where game elements can be added to the therapeutic exercises to make the rehabilitation procedures more interesting and engaging to the patients.

References

Antoniadou, M., Granlund, M., and Andersson, A.K. (2024). Strategies used by professionals in pediatric rehabilitation to engage the child in the intervention process: A scoping review. Physical & Occupational Therapy in Pediatrics, 44(4), 461–488.

Biswas, P., Orero, P., Swaminathan, M., Krishnaswamy, K., and Robinson, P. (2021, May). Adaptive accessible AR/VR systems. *In:* Extended Abstracts of the 2021 CHI Conference on Human Factors in Computing Systems, pp. 1–7.

Bowman, T., Gervasoni, E., Arienti, C., Lazzarini, S.G., Negrini, S., Crea, S. et al. (2021). Wearable devices for biofeedback rehabilitation: A systematic review and meta-analysis to design application rules and estimate the effectiveness on balance and gait outcomes in neurological diseases. Sensors, 21(10), 3444. https://doi.org/10.3390/s21103444

Faliagka, E., Skarmintzos, V., Panagiotou, C., Syrimpeis, V., Antonopoulos, C.P., and Voros, N. (2023). Leveraging edge computing ML model implementation and IoT paradigm towards reliable postoperative rehabilitation monitoring. Electronics, 12(16), 3375.

Fan, L. (2021). Usage of narrowband internet of things in smart medicine and construction of robotic rehabilitation system. IEEE Access, 10, 6246–6259.

Fan, Y.J., Yin, Y.H., Da Xu, L., Zeng, Y., and Wu, F. (2014). IoT-based smart rehabilitation system. IEEE Transactions on Industrial Informatics, 10(2), 1568–1577.

Gupta, A., and Al-Anbuky, A. (2021). IoT-based patient movement monitoring: The post-operative hip fracture rehabilitation model. Future Internet, 13(8), 195.

Han, Y., Han, Z., Wu, J., Yu, Y., Gao, S., Hua, D., and Yang, A. (2020). Artificial intelligence recommendation system of cancer rehabilitation scheme based on IoT technology. IEEE Access, 8, 44924–44935.

Hassett, L., Van Den Berg, M., Lindley, R.I., Crotty, M., McCluskey, A., Van Der Ploeg, H.P. et al. (2016). Effect of affordable technology on physical activity levels and mobility outcomes in rehabilitation: A protocol for the Activity and MObility UsiNg Technology (AMOUNT) rehabilitation trial. BMJ Open, 6(6), e012074.

Hergert, B.C., Rana, A.N., Velasquez Jr, J.E., Johnson, A.E., Ali, S., Wong, K.A., and Teixeira, P.G. (2024). Post-traumatic amputations epidemiology and outcomes within the National Trauma Data Bank: Improved survival over time results in increased population in need of rehabilitation support. American Journal of Physical Medicine & Rehabilitation. https://doi.org/10.1097/PHM.0000000000002796 (if DOI available)

Herrera-Ligero, C., Chaler, J., and Bermejo-Bosch, I. (2022). Strengthening education in rehabilitation: Assessment technology and digitalization. Frontiers in Rehabilitation Sciences, 3, 883270. https://doi.org/10.3389/fresc.2022.883270

Jacob, S., Alagirisamy, M., Xi, C., Balasubramanian, V., Srinivasan, R., Jhanjhi, N.Z., and Islam, S.M. (2021). AI and IoT-enabled smart exoskeleton system for rehabilitation of paralyzed people in connected communities. IEEE Access, 9, 80340–80350.

Kalani, M., and Anjankar, A. (2024). Revolutionizing neurology: The role of artificial intelligence in advancing diagnosis and treatment. Cureus, 16(6). https://doi.org/10.7759/cureus.57488 (if DOI available)

Kuroda, Y., Young, M., Shoman, H., Punnoose, A., Norrish, A.R., and Khanduja, V. (2021). Advanced rehabilitation technology in orthopaedics—A narrative review. International Orthopaedics, 45, 1933-1940.

Lanotte, F., O'Brien, M.K., and Jayaraman, A. (2023). AI in rehabilitation medicine: Opportunities and challenges. Annals of Rehabilitation Medicine, 47(6), 444–458.

Laut, J., Porfiri, M., and Raghavan, P. (2016). The present and future of robotic technology in rehabilitation. Current Physical Medicine and Rehabilitation Reports, 4, 312-319.

Lorenz, E.A., Bråten Støen, A., Lie Fridheim, M., and Alsos, O.A. (2024). Design recommendations for XR-based motor rehabilitation exergames at home. Frontiers in Virtual Reality, 5, 1340072. https://doi.org/10.3389/frvir.2024.1340072

Moghbelan, Y., Esposito, A., Zyrianoff, I., Spaletta, G., Borgo, S., Masolo, C. et al. (2024). A smart motor rehabilitation system based on the Internet of Things and humanoid robotics. Applied Sciences, 14(24), 11489.

Monge, J., Ribeiro, G., Raimundo, A., Postolache, O., and Santos, J. (2023). AI-based smart sensing and AR for gait rehabilitation assessment. Information, 14(7), 355.

Regan, J., Frison, E., Collin, F., Dawes, P., Hann, M., Himmelsbach, I. et al. (2019). Individualised sensory intervention to improve quality of life in people with dementia and their companions (SENSE-Cog trial): Study protocol for a randomised controlled trial. Trials, 20, 1–15.

Sakpal, P. (2024, May 9). Physical Therapy Rehabilitation Market Size, Share, Report by 2033. LinkedIn. https://www.linkedin.com/pulse/physical-therapy-rehabilitation-market-prathamesh-sakpal-ktjif/

Seijas, V., Maritz, R., Mishra, S., Bernard, R.M., Fernandes, P., Lorenz, V. et al. (2024). Rehabilitation in primary care for an ageing population: A secondary analysis from a scoping review of rehabilitation delivery models. BMC Health Services Research, 24(1), 123. https://doi.org/10.1186/s12913-024-10398-3 (if DOI available)

Selvaraj, S., Prabhu Kavin, B., Kavitha, C., and Lai, W.C. (2022). A multiclass fault diagnosis framework using context-based multilayered Bayesian method for centrifugal pumps. Electronics, 11(23), 4014. https://doi.org/10.3390/electronics11234014

Shaji, S., Pathinarupothi, R.K., Guntha, R., Sankaran, R., Ishwar, P., Menon, K.U., and Ramesh, M.V. (2024). IoMT & AI enabled time critical system for tele-cardiac rehabilitation. IEEE Access, 12, 81122-81136.

Sharanya, S. (2022). A cyber physical system framework for industrial predictive maintenance using machine learning. *In:* Real-time Applications of Machine Learning in Cyber-Physical Systems, pp. 241–269. IGI Global Scientific Publishing. https://doi.org/10.4018/978-1-7998-8509-8.ch014 (if DOI available)

Vourganas, I., Stankovic, V., and Stankovic, L. (2020). Individualised responsible artificial intelligence for home-based rehabilitation. Sensors, 21(1), 2.

Wu, Z., Huang, Z., Tang, N., Wang, K., Bian, C., Li, D. et al. (2025). Research on sports injury rehabilitation detection based on IoT models for digital health care. Big Data, 13(2), 144–160.

Yang, D., and Fan, B. (2024, April). Design of intelligent rehabilitation products based on artificial intelligence. *In:* 2024 IEEE 4th International Conference on Electronic Communications, Internet of Things and Big Data (ICEIB), pp. 372–375. IEEE.

Yang, J., Hu, J., and Chen, W. (2025). IoT-enabled real-time health monitoring system for adolescent physical rehabilitation. Scientific Reports, 15(1), 1–15.

Zhao, S., Wei, W., and Gan, L. (2024, September). Research progress of exploring intelligent rehabilitation technology based on human-computer interaction. *In:* International Symposium on Artificial Intelligence and Robotics, pp. 100–109. Singapore: Springer Nature Singapore.

CHAPTER
13

Augmented and Virtual Reality in MIoT: Transforming Patient Care, Training, and Telemedicine

J. Vijila[1(0009-0002-8284-5009)], Godfrey Winster Sathianesan[1(0000-0001-9650-6628)], Gnanavel S.[1*(0000-0003-2344-0482)], M. Baskar[1(0000-0003-4655-7667)] and Mahmoud Elsisi[2,3(000-0002-0411-9637)]

[1] Department of Computing Technologies, School of Computing, Computer Science and Engineering, SRM Institute of Science and Technology, Kattankulathur, Chengalpattu District, Tamil Nadu, India
[2] Department of Electrical Engineering, National Kaohsiung University of Science and Technology, Kaohsiung City 807618, Taiwan
[3] Faculty of Engineering at Shoubra, Benha University, Cairo 11629, Egypt

1. Introduction

Integrating augmented reality (AR) and virtual reality (VR) in healthcare has revolutionized patient care, clinical practice, and diagnostics. These immersive technologies are improving the way medical professionals interact with data, improving accuracy and efficiency in procedures. The Medical Internet of Things (MIoT) further expands the capabilities of AR and VR by enabling real-time data collection, remote monitoring, and intelligent decision-making in clinical environments. As digital health continues to evolve, AR/VR combined with MIoT is expected to redefine modern healthcare by improving accessibility, reducing medical errors, and enhancing personalized treatment plans (Van Krevelen et al., 2010).

The influence of AR and VR on healthcare represents one of the most important contributions to medical trainee education. Traditional methods of learning are being augmented with increasingly interactive simulations, which allow medical students and students of medicine to practice difficult and advanced procedures in a low-stakes virtual experience. AR allows for real-time overlays of information while performing operations. VR simulations can provide experiences with hands-on work, such as

*Corresponding author: gnanaves1@srmist.edu.in

DOI: 10.1201/9781003676812-13

neurosurgery and related procedures delivered under an endoscope. The combination of AR and VR features with MIoT devices ensures that users get real-time feedback from real-world data, can continue upgrading their skills, and improve their decision-making capabilities.

Figure 1 illustrates the advantages and disadvantages of using augmented reality (AR) and virtual reality (VR) for medical training. Advantages identified include features like interactive simulations, a lower risk of injury while practicing, real-time feedback, training for advanced procedures, and better decision-making skills. The disadvantages encompass hurdles such as expenses, technical complications, accessibility concerns, the risk of technological reliance, and the necessity for continuous updates.

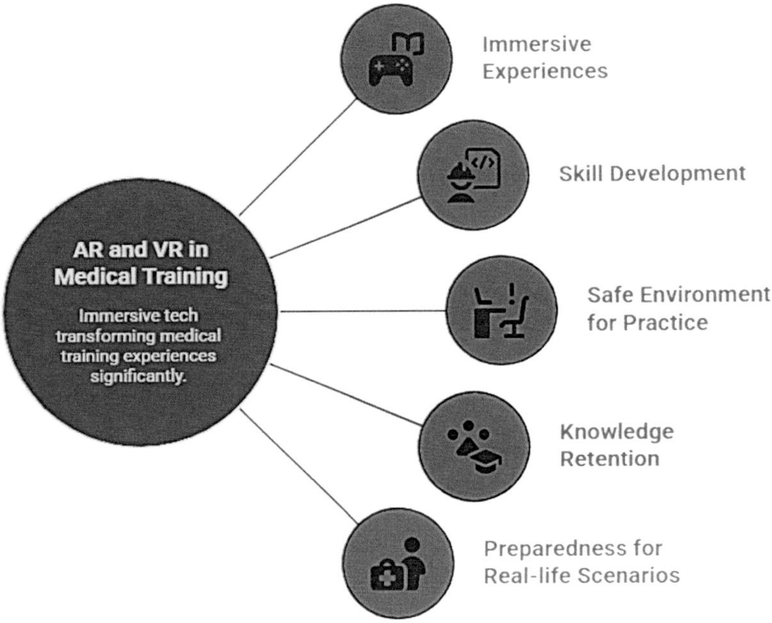

Figure 1: Illustrates AR and VR in medical training.

In addition to training and education, AR and VR have a significant impact on patient-focused areas like pain management, mental health therapy, and rehabilitation. VR exposure therapy is utilized to treat anxiety, phobias, and PTSD through controlled environments that are tailored for the patient. VR mitigations, during pain and anxiety management, dull the sensation of pain during clinical procedures, thus allowing the patient to feel more comfortable. There are AR-based programs for virtual physical therapy and rehabilitation, allowing patients to practice their recovery from injuries and surgeries to receive feedback and remedial guidance in real-time. When augmented to MIoT, it will allow for remote monitoring and recommendations for therapy, both in efficiency of time and in personalization for specific therapy.

1.1. The Role of AR and VR in Modern Healthcare

Augmented reality (AR) and virtual reality (VR) have been adapted into several medical applications such as surgical planning, rehabilitation, pain management, and medical training (Barsom et al., 2016). VR simulators allow medical students and professionals to practice complex procedures in a safe environment, providing them with improved performance when completing real surgeries. AR-enhanced surgeries help surgeons gain better accuracy through real-time overlays of the patient anatomy (Rauschnabel et al., 2022).

Figure 2 presents the use of AR and VR technologies in four major components of health care: diagnosis, treatment, recovery, and training. AR refers to the overlay of images in real time during diagnosis and surgery. VR is used for therapeutic recovery and training professionals. It centers on a patient-centered approach based on technology use. Overall, it improves clinical results, process precision, and the effectiveness of its application in healthcare. Table 1 summarizes key use cases of AR and VR in modern healthcare, highlighting the specific technologies and their associated benefits.

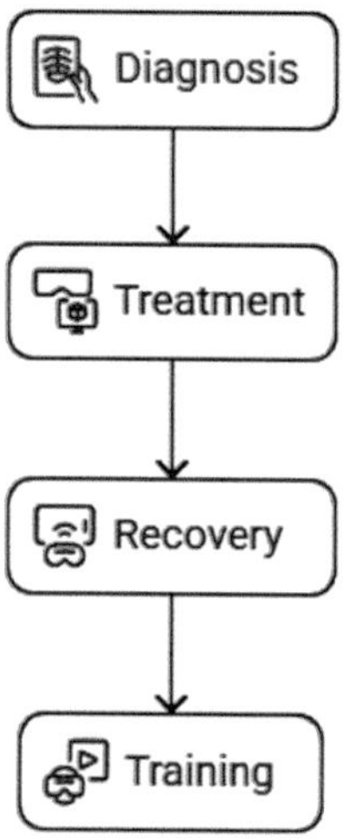

Figure 2: Role of AR/VR across the patient care spectrum.

Table 1: Applications of AR and VR in Modern Healthcare

Use Case	Technology	Benefit
Surgical Planning	AR	Real-time anatomical overlays for precision during operations
Medical Training	VR	Simulated environments for practicing surgeries without patient risk
Pain Management	VR	Reduces pain perception, an alternative to opioids
PTSD & Phobia Treatment	VR	Controlled exposure therapy sessions
Cognitive Rehabilitation	VR	Engaging exercises for stroke recovery improve motor and memory function

Furthermore, VR-based treatments have advanced patient involvement, like exposure therapy for post-traumatic stress disorder (PTSD), and cognitive rehabilitation for stroke patients. One research study demonstrated an up to 50% decrease in pain perception with VR treatment, contributing to an emerging alternative for opioid-based pain management solutions (Parsons and Rizzo, 2008).

1.2. How AR and VR Integrate with the Medical Internet of Things (MIoT)

The Medical Internet of Things (MIoT) consists of interconnected monitors that collect, analyze, and transmit health-related data to enhance clinical decision-making. AR and VR facetiously vie with the MIoT infrastructure, and mechanical devices interoperate with connectable devices:

- Wearable health-based monitors, such as smart watches and biosensors, that continually monitor patient vitals.
- Smart medical devices, i.e., artificial intelligence-based imaging devices that assist with diagnostics and treatment
- Cloud-based AI environments that can analyze greater amounts of patient-related data to produce predictive analytics (Ghasempour, 2019).

For example, Okay remote medicine-based AR applications allow physicians to visualize patient data remotely, and utilize imaging and the reconstruction of 3-dimensional imaging to assist a virtual consult (see Figure 3). VR-based remote surgeries have been successfully performed where the surgeon at one location performed surgery on a patient in a hospital at a separate location using robotic-assisted technology (Kamble, 2023).

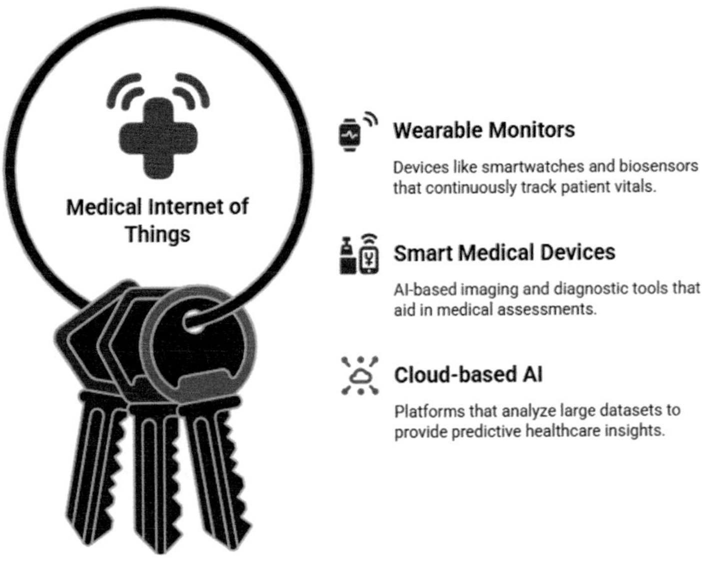

Figure 3: AR and VR integrate with the Medical Internet of Things (MIoT).

1.3. Transforming Diagnosis, Treatment, and Patient Care

The use of AR, VR, and MIoT is enhancing diagnosis, treatment planning, and individualized care:

Medical Imaging: AR technology places real-time patient data in and around diagnostic scans (MRI, CT), helping with visualization and decision-making.

Precision Surgery: AR aids minimally invasive surgery by displaying holographic projections of internal organs (Al-Jumeily et al., 2015).

Chronic Disease Management: VR-based cognitive therapy and distraction from pain methods appear helpful for chronic pain, anxiety, and neurologic disorders (Webster and Celik, 2014).

AR and VR are enhancing patient monitoring in real time with data-driven decision-making and ultimately enabling smarter, more connected healthcare systems, improving patient outcomes and streamlining medical workflows (Milgram and Kishino, 1994).

The diagram (Figure 4) presented in this chapter suggests ways that AR, VR, and MIoT technology are changing current healthcare practice. In the diagram, the light bulb represents new ideas, while each section of the image illustrates an important area of practice. Some of these areas of practice include medical training (for simulated scenarios and virtual worlds), disease diagnosis (more accurate and efficient), and MIoT integration (for patient-generated real-time data collection and remote patient monitoring). For patients, AR/VR helps create deep therapies and ways to get involved, while also making care fit each person and feel nicer. Together, these parts show how mixing tech you can step into with systems that talk to each other gives healthcare a new shape.

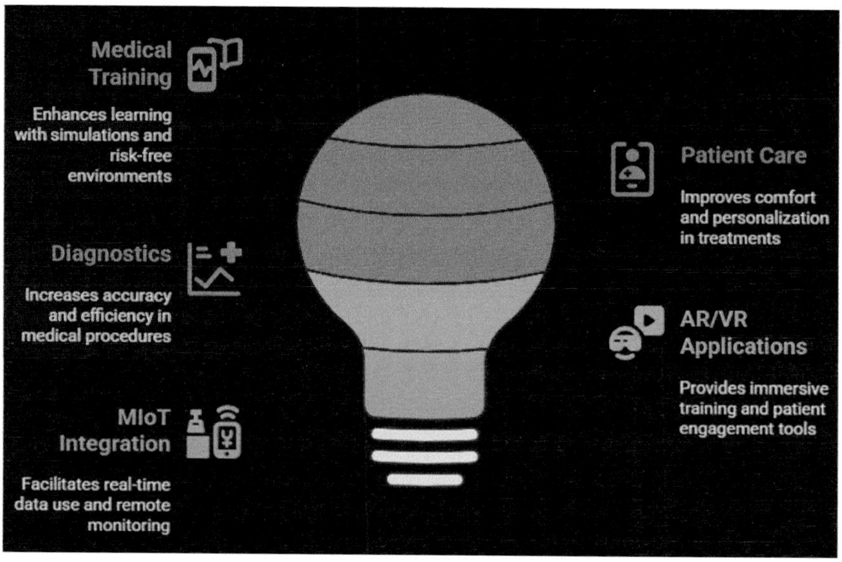

Figure 4: Transforming healthcare with AR, VR, and MIoT.

2. Understanding AR and VR in MIoT (Medical Internet of Things)

The intersection of Augmented Reality (AR), Virtual Reality (VR), and the Medical Internet of Things (MIoT) is transforming healthcare through the ability to make immersive, data-based medical experiences a reality. Combined, these technologies are reshaping clinical workflows, medical training, and patient care by allowing real-time interaction with medical information (Milgram and Kishino, 1994).

2.1. Key Technologies Behind AR and VR

Augmented Reality (AR) and Virtual Reality (VR) rely upon several underlying technologies that together create the immersive, interactive experiences that are possible. These technologies allow for the rendering of virtual environments in the digital domain and synchronous interaction with the real world—an absolute requirement for any medical application, where accuracy and immediate feedback are critically important (Webster and Celik, 2014). Figure 5 illustrates the foundational

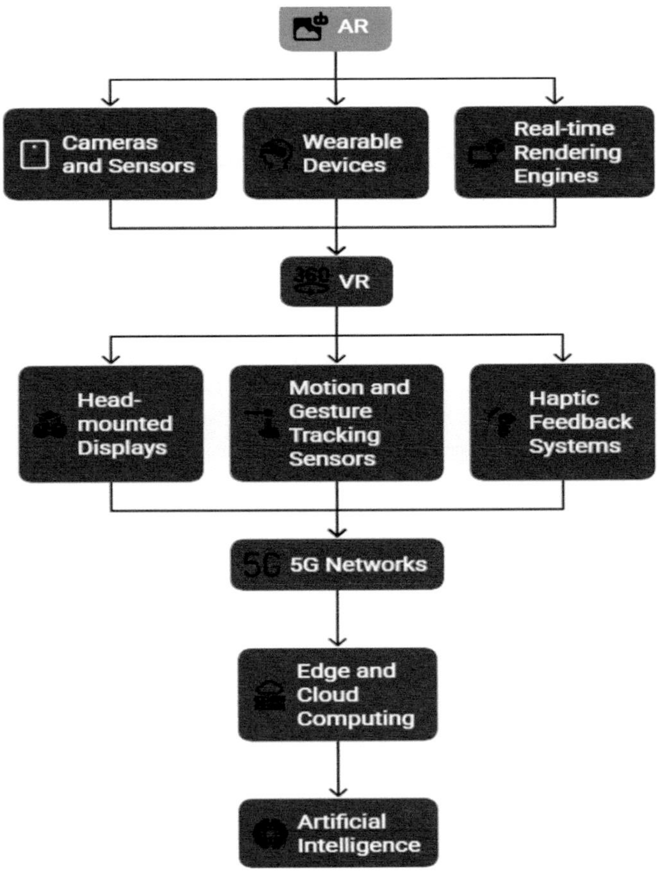

Figure 5: Foundational technologies behind AR and VR systems in medical applications.

technologies that enable AR and VR systems in medical applications, including cameras, wearable devices, rendering engines, tracking sensors, and haptic systems integrated with advanced 5G and AI-based networks.

Its effective operation depends on several fundamental technologies:

- Cameras and sensors to map and decipher the surroundings (Dehghan et al., 2020).
- Wearable devices provide hands-free access to superimposed data; examples of this are smart glasses (such as Microsoft HoloLens) (Aungst and Patel 2020).
- Recent studies such as IEEE BSN (2021) highlight how brain–computer interface (BCI) systems integrated with AR platforms can assess user attention and cognitive response during immersive medical training.
- Real-time rendering engines provide correct and seamless integration of digital content into the actual world (Haider et al., 2021).

Augmented Reality (AR) and Virtual Reality (VR) bring together hardware and software to create fully immersive and interactive experiences. Within the field of healthcare, these technologies can be implemented in a multitude of ways, ranging from preoperative planning to assisting patients with rehabilitation (Islam et al., 2021).

AR puts digital information—medical scans, vital signs, 3D models—right in front of us, making the real world around us better. It does this using software that creates images in real-time and cameras that map the surroundings, all packed into smart glasses like the Microsoft HoloLens (Al-Jumeily et al., 2015).

On the other side, VR drops users into a made-up world, often to practice or train for something. VR setups have headsets, devices that track movement, and systems that let you feel things all working together to create a lifelike world you can interact with (Webster and Celik, 2014).

Both AR and VR thrive on speedy networks like 5G, robust processors, and AI-powered software that quickly interpret and react to user inputs in real time (Karakostas et al., 2022).

2.2. How MIoT Enhances AR/VR Applications

The MIoT framework introduces an added dimension of interactivity and smarts in AR/VR technologies:

Data-Driven Spaces: MIoT integrates medical devices, wearables, and sensors, thereby establishing a system that constantly pipes patient data in real-time. AR/VR apps can source this data and render personalized context-aware content (Aungst and Patel, 2020).

Enhanced Remote Monitoring: VR environments can simulate real-world clinical scenarios, enabling remote patient monitoring and virtual consultations. AR can assist home caregivers by projecting real-time health metrics and procedural guides (Islam et al., 2021).

Surgical Planning and Training: MIoT-enabled imaging and diagnostic tools supply detailed patient-specific data. When combined with AR/VR, this supports more precise surgical simulations and anatomy visualization for education and preoperative planning (Milgram and Kishino, 1994).

Seamless Integration: MIoT ensures interoperability between devices and systems, allowing AR/VR tools to function in harmony with existing electronic health records (EHR), diagnostic tools, and therapeutic systems (Haider et al., 2021).

2.3. Real-Time Data Visualization and Decision-Making

The most revolutionary feature of AR/VR and MIoT convergence is visualization and response to real-time data:

Dynamic Dashboards: AR displays can project live vital signs, lab test results, and alerts on top of a clinician's view while they're performing procedures, enhancing situational awareness (Dehghan et al., 2020).

Decision Support Systems (DSS): Merging MIoT data with AR/VR enables clinicians to view decision-support tools that recommend treatment or highlight anomalies in real-time (Milgram and Kishino, 1994).

Critical Care Applications: In intensive and emergency care units, AR/VR systems can display complex information (ECG, oxygen saturation, etc.) understandably, enabling healthcare professionals to make faster, better-informed decisions (Islam et al., 2021).

Patient Engagement: AR/VR visualizations assist patients in gaining better comprehension of their medical conditions and treatment procedures, enhancing informed consent and compliance with care protocols (Milgram and Kishino, 1994).

3. Applications of AR and VR in Healthcare

With the evolution of technology, augmented and virtual reality are finding their place in healthcare, delivering medical services in a novel way and offering innovative solutions for diagnosis, treatment, education, and patient management. AR and VR are reshaping traditional healthcare methods into digitally upscaled experiential spaces through immersion, interactive platforms, and data-enriched environments. This chapter delves into the niche utility areas that AR and VR technologies have in healthcare, particularly when applied to areas of intersection with the Medical Internet of Things (MIoT), which can together set a precedent for a more intelligent and efficient medical system. As shown in Figure 6, AR and VR technologies are deeply integrated into multiple facets of healthcare, forming a connected ecosystem driven by MIoT. A consolidated comparison of AR and VR implementations across different healthcare applications is presented in Table 2 (Rajeshwaran and Bhushan, 2019; Sartaj et al., 2024).

3.1. Medical Training and Simulation

Immersion simulations and visualizations brought to life by AR and VR technologies have truly transformed medical education, enhancing the learning experience for both students and healthcare professionals. Traditional medical training often depends on static diagrams, cadaver dissections, or limited access to operating rooms. But by

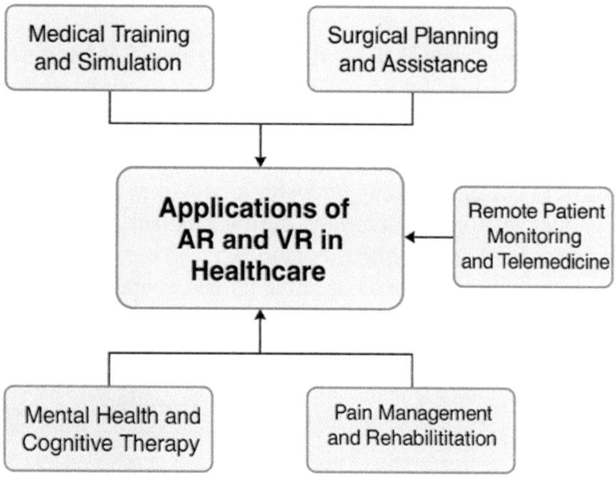

Figure 6: Applications of Augmented Reality (AR) and Virtual Reality (VR) in the Healthcare Ecosystem.

providing high-fidelity, interactive, and easily replicable virtual scenarios, AR and VR allow us to avoid these constraints (Barsom et al., 2016; Al-Jumeily et al., 2015; Dehghan et al., 2020).

Use Cases

- **Learning anatomy with virtual dissection:** Augmented reality tools like Complete Anatomy and Human Anatomy Atlas overlay interactive 3D representations of the human body that students can explore in real time (Rajeshwaran and Bhushan, 2019).
- **Surgical models:** High-fidelity, VR-based surgical simulators—like those on Osso VR and Touch Surgery—allow trainees to practice in a risk-free setting that performs procedures and provides haptic feedback and performance measures as if it were a real surgery (Barsom et al., 2016; Dehghan et al., 2020; Aungst and Patel, 2020).
- **Interactive clinical training:** VR environments can simulate scenarios like cardiac arrest, trauma retrieval to impart the skills of critical thinking and rapid decision-making required by medical professionals (Dehghan et al., 2020).

Advantages

- Improves retention with experiential learning.
- Supports real-time feedback and evaluation.
- Lessens reliance on actual patients and physical resources.

3.2. Surgical Planning and Assistance

AR and VR technologies now advance surgical procedures through their capabilities to improve doctor-planning stages and intra-operative guidance and real-time surgical decisions. Pre-operatively, surgeons gain precise three-dimensional visualization of personal patient anatomy so they can perform incisions with improved outcomes (IEEE Transactions on Medical Imaging, 2018).

Use Cases

The use of patient imaging data (MRI and CT scans) allows VR tools to generate 3D models of organs and tissues, which surgeons can use to study complex anatomies before surgical procedures (Aungst and Patel, 2020; IEEE Transactions on Medical Imaging, 2018).

- The Microsoft HoloLens, among other similar devices, enables surgeons to view real-time patient anatomical overlays during medical procedures. The precise positioning of screws and implants becomes a task easily achieved through AR technology in specific orthopedic treatments and spinal surgery (Van Krevelen et al., 2010).
- Real-time feedback and improved spatial awareness become possible during minimally invasive surgeries through the combined use of AR with fluoroscopy and live imaging (Van Krevelen et al., 2010; IEEE Transactions on Medical Imaging, 2018).

Benefits

- Improves surgical accuracy and confidence.
- Reduces the likelihood of complications.
- Medical staff need fewer invasive investigative procedures due to its use.

3.3. Remote Patient Monitoring and Telemedicine

Virtual healthcare services enhanced by AR/VR alongside MIoT technology allow healthcare professionals to monitor patients remotely and track patient health continuously, thus benefiting isolated populations. Healthcare providers use AR/VR interfaces to analyze real-time health data obtained from wearable IoT devices in remote patient monitoring (Islam et al., 2021; Hossain, 2020; Haider et al., 2021; Tuli et al., 2019; Barucha et al., 2022).

Use Cases

- Health organizations use VR systems to enable virtual consultations, which create shared immersive medical spaces for doctors and patients to meet. Health care sessions combine actual health metrics from diagnostic testing (Aungst and Patel, 2020).
- Field medics and paramedics implement AR goggles to display vital signs and injury facts and establish specialist connections during emergency procedures (Haider et al., 2021).
- Through VR headsets linked to IoT devices, patients under home care can access therapeutic care sessions with doctors or therapists (Islam et al., 2021; Barucha et al., 2022).

Impact:

- Enhances accessibility to healthcare services.
- Healthcare spending decreases because patients need fewer physical visits to medical facilities.
- The system provides preventive healthcare benefits through continuous patient monitoring activities.

3.4. Pain Management and Rehabilitation

Virtual Reality, together with Augmented Reality, demonstrates crucial importance when caring for patients with chronic pain and when delivering rehabilitation treatment. The technologies adjust what users sense or steer their body movements so people can regain focus from agony and enhance their healing time (IEEE Transactions on Medical Imaging, 2018).

Use Cases

- Secondly, VR Distraction Therapy provides burn patients as well as patients experiencing painful treatments with Snow World-type experiences, which function as cognitive distractors that reduce perceived pain (IEEE Transactions on Informative Technology in Biomedicine, 2010).
- Areas affected by stroke and orthopedic conditions utilize gamified VR spaces, which serve as platforms to conduct movement exercises to boost their patients' physical abilities and medical outcomes. MindMotion™ and XRHealth provide individualized rehabilitation service sessions, which track patient advancement (IEEE Transactions on Medical Imaging, 2018).
- AR-based Physiotherapy employs overlays, which use sensor data to supervise patients through exercises since it verifies correct body positioning while patients get sensor-based feedback (Van Krevelen et al., 2010).

Clinical Impact

- Decreases reliance on opioid medications.
- Increases therapy engagement and compliance.
- Enables remote and self-directed rehabilitation.

3.5. Mental Health and Cognitive Therapy

The mental health field is evolving because virtual reality allows the creation of therapeutic virtual world simulations, which offer secure therapeutic settings for psychological interventions and cognitive learning development (Parsons and Rizzo, 2008; Aungst and Patel, 2020; IEEE Transactions on Medical Imaging, 2018).

Use Cases

- PTSD patients, along with people battling phobias, receive exposure therapy treatment through VR technology by accessing virtual spaces simulating war zones and heights, and crowded environments to develop controlled desensitization (Parsons and Rizzo, 2008; IEEE Transactions on Medical Imaging, 2018).
- **Cognitive behavioral therapy (CBT):** VR applications guide users through CBT exercises, helping them recognize and modify negative thought patterns with immersive storytelling and virtual coaches (Aungst and Patel, 2020).
- Research published in IEEE Transactions on Neural Systems and Rehabilitation Engineering (2020) highlights that VR-based cognitive rehabilitation significantly enhances neural plasticity and functional recovery in patients with neurological disorders.

- **Mindfulness and meditation:** Guided meditation apps in VR, like TRIPP, offer calming visuals and sounds, aiding in stress reduction and emotional regulation (Aungst and Patel, 2020).

Advantages:

- Provides a safe, private, and controlled therapeutic environment.
- Offers high user engagement and realism.
- Extends mental health services to remote and underserved communities.

Table 2 provides a comparative overview of how Augmented Reality (AR) and Virtual Reality (VR) are applied across various healthcare domains, highlighting their specific use cases and associated benefits.

Table 2: Comparison of AR and VR Use Cases in Healthcare

Application Area	AR Use Case	VR Use Case	Benefits
Medical Training	Overlay anatomy in real-world view	Full-body virtual simulation of surgery	Interactive, repeatable learning
Surgical Assistance	Real-time overlay of organs during surgery	Pre-surgical planning in virtual 3D	Increased accuracy, reduced risks
Remote Monitoring	AR-assisted diagnostics by paramedics	Virtual teleconsultation rooms	Remote access, improved diagnostics
Pain Management	AR games during physical therapy	VR distraction for chronic/burn pain	Reduced reliance on medication
Rehabilitation	Guided exercises with AR overlays	Gamified therapy environments	Increased motivation, faster recovery
Mental Health	N/A	VR exposure therapy for phobias, PTSD	Safe, immersive treatment settings

4. Challenges in Implementing AR and VR in MIoT

The combination of Augmented Reality (AR) and Virtual Reality (VR) technology with Medical Internet of Things (MIoT) brings major advantages yet creates distinctive operational hurdles. Large-scale deployment, along with sustainable adoption, may face impediments from technical, ethical, financial, and regulatory challenges. AR/VR implementation for MIoT-based healthcare systems encounters various significant concerns together with implementation constraints (Al-Jumeily et al., 2015; Islam et al., 2021; Barucha et al., 2022). Table 3 summarizes the major challenges encountered in implementing AR and VR within MIoT environments, categorizing them by issue type, impact, and potential solutions.

4.1. Data Security and Privacy Risks

Due to live healthcare data exchanges between AR/VR technology and IoT systems, security standards must exist while maintaining patient privacy.

Table 3: Challenges in Implementing AR and VR in MIoT

Challenge	Issue	Impact	Potential Solution
Data Security and Privacy	Data breaches, unauthorized access	Loss of patient trust	End-to-end encryption, blockchain
Latency and System Response	High network delays, slow rendering	Poor user experience	Edge computing, 5G, compression techniques
Hardware and Cost	Expensive and uncomfortable devices	Low adoption, user fatigue	Cost-effective hardware, modular designs
Regulatory and Ethical Concerns	Lack of standards, unclear liability	Legal and ethical challenges	Regulatory engagement, digital ethics boards

Key Issues

- The exposure of personal data occurs frequently during AR/VR operations because of data breaches, and both identity theft and leaks can be risks when storage channels have vulnerabilities (Ghasempour, 2019; Dehghan et al., 2020).
- Weaker authentication standards enable unauthorized users to reach patient records and steal live video footage from AR/VR devices (Al-Jumeily et al., 2015).
- Users face a lack of clear understanding regarding the type and fate of collected data, thus leading to ethical issues regarding transparency and consent (Rajeshwaran and Bhushan, 2019).

Potential Solutions

- Medical data storage requires end-to-end encryption alongside secure APIs and blockchain technology for secure data logging (Ghasempour, 2019).
- Multi-factor authentication for device and user access (Dehghan et al., 2020).
- The adoption of privacy-ensuring machine learning methods like federated learning should be implemented (Rajeshwaran and Bhushan, 2019).

4.2. Latency and System Response Limitations

AR and VR applications still depend on real-time system response since it provides fluid interaction during important medical operations, including remote surgery and diagnostic imaging.

Key Issues

- Real-time feedback loses effectiveness in immersive environments since delays in data processing, combined with transmission problems, cause great latency issues (Al-Jumeily et al., 2015; Barucha et al., 2022).
- Network performance limitations rise sharply when users try to stream all 3D visuals together with sensor data and biometric information simultaneously, particularly in areas with limited network infrastructure (Al-Jumeily et al., 2015).
- Not all healthcare facilities can implement edge computing because they lack consistent access to strong local processing systems at their sites (Barucha et al., 2022).

Potential Solutions

- Deployment of 5G networks and edge AI chips for faster data processing (Al-Jumeily et al., 2015; Islam et al., 2021).
- Widespread bandwidth utilization optimization occurs through data compression methods and data prioritization algorithm implementations (Islam et al., 2021; Dehghan et al., 2020).
- Medical organizations should implement better cloud-edge hybrid systems that manage both speed and scalability effectively (Ghasempour, 2019).

4.3. Hardware and Cost Constraints

Healthcare institutions limit their adoption of AR/VR systems because the required hardware and infrastructure remain too expensive and complex to implement.

Key Issues

- High-quality AR glasses (HoloLens 2) and VR headsets (Oculus Quest Pro), as well as their high costs, restrict the devices' accessibility to many healthcare institutions (Al-Jumeily et al., 2015; Dehghan et al., 2020).
- Extended use of head-mounted devices through equipment and body-related ergonomics can trigger discomfort alongside fatigue symptoms and motion sickness, primarily among elderly and physically restricted patients (Ghasempour, 2019).
- There exists limited operational compatibility among medical IoT systems and AR/VR devices (Islam et al., 2021).

Potential Solutions

- The medical field requires cost-efficient lightweight devices that serve healthcare applications (Al-Jumeily et al., 2015).
- Patients can use combined Smartphone or tablet integration modular systems for AR/VR technology applications (Dehghan et al., 2020).
- Promotion of open standards for device interoperability and data exchange (Ghasempour, 2019; Islam et al., 2021).

4.4. Regulatory and Ethical Concerns

The combination of immersive AR/VR technologies along with real-time medical monitoring brings forward uncertainties regarding medical responsibility and consent procedures and regulatory control demands.

Key Issues

- There exists a major problem with the lack of standardized healthcare guidelines because existing regulations fail to keep up with the fast pace of modern technological developments, which results in incomplete standards (Islam et al., 2021).
- Extended use of virtual worlds leads to psychological distress, particularly among people with no protective mental resilience (Barucha et al., 2022).
- The specification of accountability becomes complicated during remote medical procedures when practitioners employ AR/VR technologies as they provide telemedicine services remotely (Al-Jumeily et al., 2015; Ghasempour, 2019).

Potential Solutions

- The organization seeks to connect with medical device regulatory bodies, including the FDA and EMA, to establish special guidelines for AR/VR systems (Islam et al., 2021; Al-Jumeily et al., 2015).
- Introduction of digital ethics committees for immersive healthcare solutions (Ghasempour, 2019; Dehghan et al., 2020).
- Emphasis on patient-centered design and ethical testing protocols (Al-Jumeily et al., 2015).

5. Recent Advancements and Innovations

The combination of AR/VR technologies with AI advancement and high-speed networks, together with cyber-physical systems, drives rapid innovation throughout the Medical Internet of Things (MIoT). These technological innovations improve medical solution interactivity while enhancing precision and personalization, and making healthcare more scalable, which leads to a major transformation in healthcare delivery and experience (Dehghan et al., 2020; Tuli et al., 2019). A visual summary of these technological advancements is presented in Figure 7.

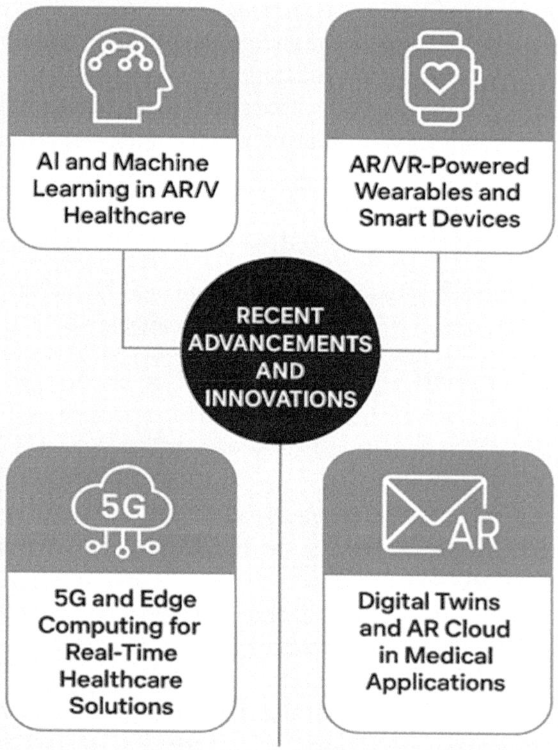

Figure 7: Visual overview of key advancements in AR/VR for MIoT.

A visual representation shows recent AR/VR innovations' interconnected role within MIoT. The visual representation presents four essential domains that comprise AI and ML alongside Wearables and Network Infrastructure with Digital Twins to enhance healthcare delivery. The structure makes it simple for readers to understand how new medical experience technologies function together as a synchronized network.

5.1. AI and Machine Learning in AR/VR Healthcare

The integration of artificial intelligence (AI) technology with machine learning algorithms within AR/VR platforms enables better diagnostic capabilities as well as outcome predictions and superior user experiences.

Key Innovations

- AI applies predictive analytics to wearable device patient data, which produces visualized expected outcomes (e.g., disease advancement) inside real-time AR/VR environments (Ghasempour, 2019; Al-Jumeily et al., 2015).
- Machine learning systems, through simulations, adapt difficulty levels according to the advancement rate of medical students and patient rehabilitation patients (Dehghan et al., 2020).
- AI helps AR systems detect organ tumors and anomalies directly during procedures through intelligent scene understanding to deliver improved accuracy in decision-making (Islam et al., 2021).
- AI software through Google Health uses an AR microscope to display detection insights for cancer directly in front of a pathologist's examination area (Al-Jumeily et al., 2015).

5.2. AR/VR-Powered Wearables and Smart Devices

Modern wearables and headsets equip biosensors and motion trackers, and contextual computing capabilities, which enhance immersive healthcare delivery.

Notable Devices and Features

- Through AR Glasses, medical staff receive real-time patient vital sign assessments that their wearable sensors transmit (Dehghan et al., 2020; Barucha et al., 2022).
- Patients undergo psychiatric treatments and cognitive therapy with VR headsets containing EEG or ECG sensors for measuring mental data in real time (Ghasempour, 2019).
- Doctors, together with physical therapy patients, utilize Haptic Feedback Devices to receive touch-based training that reinforces therapy development activities (Al-Jumeily et al., 2015).
- The smart devices serve to monitor patients continuously together with remote therapy and geographical boundary-defying realistic training functions (Islam et al., 2021; Tuli et al., 2019).

5.3. 5G and Edge Computing for Real-Time Healthcare Solutions

Low-latency networks and local computation are essential to support AR/VR's demands for high-speed, real-time data interaction.

Technological Benefits

- **5G connectivity:** Delivers high data throughput with ultra-low latency, crucial for remote surgeries and real-time diagnostics in AR/VR environments (Al-Jumeily et al., 2015; Islam et al., 2021).
- The IEEE Industrial Electronics Society (2021) emphasizes that integrating 5G edge computing with IoMT architectures is crucial to support real-time AR/VR applications in healthcare environments.
- **Edge computing:** Enables on-device or near-device data processing, reducing dependence on cloud and ensuring faster feedback loops in time-sensitive procedures (Dehghan et al., 2020).
- **Network slicing:** Prioritizes critical medical data streams in MIoT, ensuring uninterrupted AR/VR operations in emergencies (Liu et al., 2021).
- **Use case:** Remote robotic surgeries in 5G-enabled smart hospitals now leverage AR overlays with near-zero delay for precision execution (Al-Jumeily et al., 2015; Dehghan et al., 2020).

5.4. Digital Twins and AR Cloud in Medical Applications

Digital Twins and the AR Cloud represent transformative concepts that merge physical and virtual realities, enhancing modeling, simulation, and collaboration. Table 4 summarizes the recent advancements in AR/VR for MIoT-based healthcare systems, highlighting innovations, key features, and impact areas (Al-Jumeily et al., 2015; Islam et al., 2021).

Definitions and Applications

- **Digital twins:** Virtual replicas of human organs, systems, or even full patients, continuously updated using real-world IoT data. These twins can be explored using AR/VR for training, simulation, and pre-surgical planning (Nye, 2023).
- **AR cloud:** A shared 3D spatial map of environments (e.g., a hospital layout or surgical suite), enabling persistent, multi-user AR experiences and spatial memory in medical settings (Dehghan et al., 2020; Barucha et al., 2022).

Example: Siemens Healthineers and GE Healthcare are developing Digital Twin ecosystems for cardiac and pulmonary care simulations, allowing predictive interventions before physical symptoms arise (Tuli et al., 2019).

A summary of transformative innovations transforming future healthcare immersion appears in this table. The classification of these advancements includes their core technology along with essential features and real-world usage within Medical Internet of Things (MIoT) systems. AI technology, along with wearable devices working through next-generation networking systems and virtual modeling solutions, combine forces to enhance medical diagnosis accuracy and treatment effectiveness while creating real-time patient interaction possibilities (Ghasempour, 2019; Islam et al., 2021; Tuli et al., 2019).

Table 4: Recent Advancements in AR/VR for MIoT Healthcare

Innovation Area	Description	Key Features	Impact/Use Case
AI and Machine Learning	Integration of AI for smarter diagnostics and interaction in AR/VR	Predictive analytics, intelligent scene understanding	Cancer detection via AI-AR microscopes
Wearables and Smart Devices	Next-gen AR/ VR devices with sensors for real-time monitoring	Haptic feedback, EEG/ECG sensors, smart AR glasses	Remote cognitive therapy, surgical training
5G and Edge Computing	Enabling real-time AR/VR healthcare through high-speed, low-latency networks	5G, edge AI, network slicing	Remote surgeries, emergency diagnostics
Digital Twins and AR Cloud (IEEE Transactions on Consumer Electronics, 2025)	Creating virtual replicas and spatial maps for medical applications	3D simulations, spatial awareness, real-time updates	Pre-surgical planning, multi-user AR experiences

6. Future Trends and the Evolving Medical Landscape

AR/VR technologies in the Medical Internet of Things (MIoT) are advancing toward becoming necessary components that will form an integral part of standard healthcare infrastructure. The upcoming years will transform healthcare through several anticipated changes (Figure 8), which include connected hospital systems and customized treatment plans, and the wide adoption of AR/VR technology.

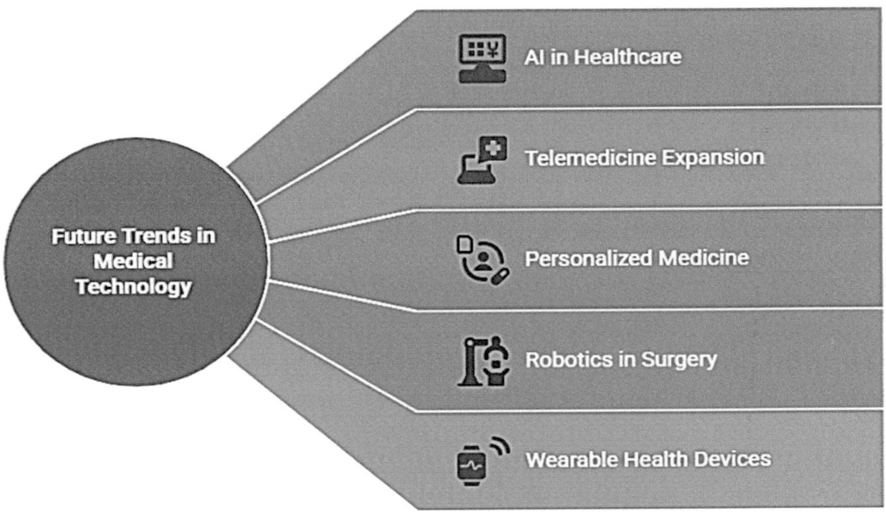

Figure 8: Future trends and the evolving medical landscape.

6.1. The Expansion of Digital Health and Connected Hospitals

The global shift toward digital health is reshaping hospitals into highly connected, intelligent environments where data flows seamlessly across devices, departments, and care teams.

Key Trends

- **Smart hospital infrastructure:** Integration of AR/VR with IoT for real-time monitoring, surgical guidance, and staff coordination (IEEE Digital Reality Initiative, 2021).
- **Telepresence and virtual wards:** Use of VR-based remote rounds and consultations for patients in isolation or rural areas.
- **Interoperable platforms:** Unified digital ecosystems that connect AR/VR tools with EHRs, diagnostics, and hospital management systems.
- **Future outlook:** Hospitals will increasingly operate like data-driven command centers, using AR/VR overlays to visualize patient flows, emergencies, and predictive analytics in real time.

6.2. Personalized Medicine Through AR/VR and MIoT

The future of medicine is deeply personal—and AR/VR technologies, empowered by real-time data from MIoT, are at the heart of this shift.

Emerging Capabilities

- **Digital avatars and twins:** Personalized 3D models of patients created from imaging and sensor data, used for individualized diagnosis, planning, and education.
- **Immersive patient engagement:** AR/VR environments tailored to specific therapeutic needs, cognitive conditions, or physical impairments (IEEE Computer Society, 1997).
- **Real-time feedback loops:** Continuous monitoring via wearable sensors provides instantaneous feedback to both clinicians and patients, creating dynamic treatment plans.
- **Impact:** This level of personalization supports more effective therapies, better adherence to treatment, and improved patient satisfaction.

6.3. The Road to Widespread Adoption of AR/VR in Healthcare

While the promise of AR/VR is clear, mainstream adoption will require overcoming both technical and cultural hurdles.

Enabling Factors

- **Affordability and accessibility:** Continued development of cost-effective, lightweight devices will be essential (Islam et al., 2021; Barucha et al., 2022).
- **Workforce training:** Upskilling clinicians and technicians to use immersive tools confidently and safely.
- **Regulatory frameworks:** Clear standards, safety protocols, and reimbursement models will facilitate trust and scalability.

- **Projection:** As AR/VR tools become easier to use and more deeply integrated with MIoT infrastructure, they will become as commonplace as stethoscopes—embedded into clinical workflows across disciplines (IEEE Transactions on Biomedical Engineering, 2020).

7. Conclusion

As AR and VR technologies continue to evolve alongside the expanding Medical Internet of Things (MIoT), their role in healthcare is becoming increasingly integral. This chapter has explored many innovations, such as AI integration, smart wearables, 5G-powered real-time systems, and digital twin models that are pushing the boundaries of immersive care. While these advancements offer exciting possibilities for training, diagnosis, treatment, and patient engagement, they also present notable challenges, including data privacy concerns, high hardware costs, latency limitations, and regulatory gaps. Despite these hurdles, the trajectory of AR/VR in healthcare remains promising. As the ecosystem becomes more connected and intelligent, AR/VR is poised to transform healthcare into a more personalized, predictive, and patient-centric experience, reshaping not only how care is delivered but also how it is understood and experienced in the future.

The Future of AR/VR in a Connected Healthcare Ecosystem

Looking ahead, AR and VR are set to become foundational components in the digital healthcare revolution. As MIoT environments grow smarter and more connected, these immersive technologies will shift from being optional innovations to essential clinical tools. Future developments will focus on:

- Hyper-personalized healthcare driven by digital twins and continuous biosensing.
- Intelligent, decentralized care models powered by edge AI and real-time AR visualizations.
- Equitable access through cost-effective, portable devices and scalable platforms.
- Ultimately, the convergence of AR/VR and MIoT signals a future where healthcare is not only more efficient but also more engaging, empowering, and human-centric.

References

Al-Jumeily, M., Hussain, A., and Alghamdi, A. (2015). Innovative trends of teaching and learning in smart education using augmented reality. *In:* Proceedings of the International Conference on Interactive Mobile Communication Technologies and Learning (IMCL), pp. 74–78.

Aleksandr Ometov, Viktoriia Shubina, Lucie Klus, Justyna Skibińska, Salwa Saafi, Pavel Pascacio (2023). A survey on wearable technology: History, state-of-the-art and current challenges. IEEE Access, 11: 12345–12368.

Aungst, P., and Patel, J.C. (2020). Integrating virtual reality into medical practice: A new era of healthcare. IEEE Pulse, 11(6), 18–23.

Barsom, E.Z., Graafland, M., and Schijven, M.P. (2016). Systematic review on the effectiveness of augmented reality applications in medical training. Surgical Endoscopy, 30: 4174–4183.

Bharucha, M.Z., Jaiswal, A., Kar, A.K., and Ilavarasan, P.V. (2022). Real-time digital twin framework for remote patient monitoring using wearable devices. IEEE Access, 10, 5040–5053. https://doi.org/10.1109/ACCESS.2021.3138777

Dehghan, J., Rezaei, M., and Tavakol, M. (2020). Applications of virtual reality in medical education and patient care: A brief review. IEEE Engineering in Medicine and Biology Magazine, 39(5), 36–42. https://doi.org/10.1109/MEMB.2020.3016712

Ghasempour. (2019). Internet of things in smart grid: Architecture, applications, services, key technologies, and challenges. Inventions, 4(1): 22.

Haider, M.R., Rahman, M.A., and Hassan, M.M. (2021). A secure IoT framework for smart healthcare monitoring. IEEE Internet of Things Journal, 8(21), 15940–15950.

Hossain, R.S., Amin, M.R., and Razzaque, M.A. (2020). 5G-based tactile internet for smart healthcare: A review. IEEE Access, 8, 213606–213627.

IEEE BSN. (2021). Best poster award: Assessing internal and external attention in AR using brain computer interfaces. IEEE BSN Conference 2021, MIT Media Lab.

IEEE Computer Society. (1997). A survey of augmented reality. Presence: Teleoperators and Virtual Environments, 6(4), 355–385, Computer Science.

IEEE Digital Reality Initiative. (2021). Digital twins: Ethical and societal implications. IEEE Future Directions. Home – IEEE Digital Reality+1Wikipedia+1.

IEEE Industrial Electronics Society. (2021). Special section on 5G edge computing enabled Internet of Medical Things. IEEE Transactions on Industrial Informatics, ITeN.

IEEE Transactions on Biomedical Engineering. (2020). Advancements in AR/VR for rehabilitation. 67(8), 2345–2356.

IEEE Transactions on Consumer Electronics. (2025). Special section on generative AI based wearable electronics devices for personalized healthcare, call for papers. Home – IEEE Consumer Technology Society.

IEEE Transactions on Information Technology in Biomedicine, Telemedicine and Remote Patient Monitoring. (2010). 14(3), 560–567.

IEEE Transactions on Medical Imaging, Deep Learning in Medical Image Analysis. (2018). 37(8), 1770–1780.

IEEE Transactions on Neural Systems and Rehabilitation Engineering, Virtual Reality-Based Cognitive Rehabilitation. (2020). 28(3), 1234–1242.

Islam, M.T., Pathan, S.N., and Andersson, K. (2021). A review on healthcare monitoring using Internet of Medical Things (IoMT), IEEE Access, 9, 3660–3682.

Kamble, S., Gunasekaran, R., and Belhadi, S. (2023). Digital twin technology for enhancing supply chain resilience and sustainability: A review and research agenda. Technological Forecasting and Social Change, 189, 122302.

Karakostas, K., Votis, K., Giakoumis, D., and Tzovaras, D. (2022). Digital twins in healthcare: Recent advances and challenges. IEEE Journal of Biomedical and Health Informatics, 26(1), 357–371. DOI: 10.1109/JBHI.2021.3107222

Liu, R., Wang, Y., Chen, J., and Zhang, J. (2021). An Overview of Human Activity Recognition Using Wearable Sensors: Healthcare and Artificial Intelligence. arXiv preprint arXiv:2103.15990. https://arxiv.org/abs/2103.15990

Milgram, P. and Kishino, F. (1994). A taxonomy of mixed reality visual displays. IEICE Transactions on Information and Systems, E77-D, 12, 1321–1329.

Nye, L. (2023). Digital Twins for Patient Care via Knowledge Graphs and Closed-form Continuous-time Liquid Neural Networks. arXiv preprint arXiv:2307.04772.

Parsons, T.D., and Rizzo, A.A. (2008). Affective outcomes of virtual reality exposure therapy for anxiety and specific phobias: A meta-analysis, Journal of Behavior Therapy and Experimental Psychiatry, 39(3), 250–261.

Rajeswaran, G., and Bhushan, R. (2019). Low latency and high throughput: Challenges and opportunities for 5G in remote medical applications. IEEE Communications Magazine, 57(5), 92–98.

Rauschnabel, P.A., Felix, S.C., and Hinsch, C. (2022). Augmented reality marketing: How mobile AR-apps can improve brands through inspiration. Journal of Retailing and Consumer Services, 58, 102312.

Sartaj, H., Ali, S., and Gjøby, J.M. (2024). Uncertainty-Aware Environment Simulation of Medical Devices Digital Twins. arXiv preprint arXiv:2410.03504.

Tuli, S., Basumatary, N., Gill, S.S., Kahani, M., Arya, R.C., Wander, G.S., and Buyya, R. (2019). HealthFog: An ensemble deep learning model for automated health monitoring in IoT. IEEE Transactions on Industrial Informatics, 15(1), 457–466. DOI: 10.1109/TII.2018.2869378

Van Krevelen, D.W.F., and Poelman, R. (2010). A survey of augmented reality technologies, applications and limitations. International Journal of Virtual Reality, 9(2), 1–20.

Webster, R.J., and Celik, H. (2014). Design of Medical Devices and Equipment. New York, NY, USA: Springer.

CHAPTER

14

Blockchain for Smart Healthcare: A Survey

Amit Kumar Tyagi[1], **Avinash Kumar Sharma**[2] **and Shrikant Tiwari**[3*]

[1] National Forensic Sciences University Gandhinagar, Gujarat, India

[2] Department of CSE, Sharda School of Engineering & Technology (SSET), Sharda University, Greater Noida, India

[3] School of Computing Science and Engineering (SCSE), Galgotias University, Greater Noida, Uttar Pradesh, India

1. Introduction to Blockchain and Smart Healthcare

Blockchain and smart healthcare offer a transformative approach to medical data management and patient care. By ensuring secure, transparent, and tamper-proof health records, blockchain enhances trust and data integrity. Smart healthcare systems leverage this technology to enable seamless data sharing, improved diagnostics, and personalized treatment. This integration fosters efficiency, privacy, and innovation across the healthcare ecosystem.

1.1. Blockchain's Fundamentals, Evolution, Benefits, and Limitations

Blockchain is a revolutionary digital technology that serves as a decentralized and distributed ledger system, enabling secure, transparent, and tamper-resistant recording of data and transactions. At its core, a blockchain consists of a chain of blocks, where each block contains a list of transactions, a timestamp, and a cryptographic hash of the previous block (Tripathi et al., 2020; Sharma et al., 2021; Tyagi et al., 2024a). This hash-based linking of blocks ensures the data immutability once it is added to the chain, as any attempt to alter one block would require changes to all subsequent blocks across all nodes in the network.

*Corresponding author: shrikanttiwari15@gmail.com

DOI: 10.1201/9781003676812-14

The decentralized nature of blockchain is one of its most defining features. Unlike traditional centralized systems that rely on a single authority or server, blockchain operates over a peer-to-peer (P2P) network. Each participant, or node, maintains a copy of the entire blockchain and follows a consensus mechanism to validate and agree upon the addition of new data. Popular consensus mechanisms include Proof of Work (PoW), Proof of Stake (PoS), and newer models like Delegated Proof of Stake (DPoS) and Practical Byzantine Fault Tolerance (PBFT), each varying in terms of efficiency, security, and scalability.

Blockchain ensures data integrity and security through cryptographic algorithms. Every transaction is encrypted and digitally signed using public-key cryptography, allowing only authorized users to initiate transactions. Once a transaction is validated and added to a block, it is practically immutable, meaning it cannot be altered or deleted without consensus from the network. This feature enhances trust among participants, especially in systems where parties may not know or fully trust one another.

Another fundamental component of blockchain is its transparency. In public blockchains, all transactions are visible to every participant, promoting accountability and auditability. Even in private or consortium blockchains, where access is restricted to selected participants, the shared ledger provides a single source of truth, reducing disputes and fraud. Smart contracts are self-executing contracts with predefined rules coded into the blockchain. They add another layer of functionality. These automate processes, reduce the need for intermediaries, and ensure that agreements are executed exactly as programmed.

Blockchain technology also incorporates fault tolerance and resilience. Since data is replicated across multiple nodes, the failure or compromise of a single node does not disrupt the network. This redundancy makes blockchain robust against data loss, cyber-attacks, and system failures. Additionally, because each block is time-stamped and linked to the one before, the blockchain provides a historical record of all transactions that can be traced and verified at any time.

The fundamental principles of blockchain—decentralization, immutability, transparency, security, and consensus—make it a powerful solution for a wide range of applications beyond cryptocurrencies. Its ability to provide a secure, shared, and trustworthy environment has positioned blockchain as a foundational technology in industries such as finance, healthcare, supply chain, voting systems, and digital identity management. As the technology matures, ongoing advancements aim to overcome existing challenges such as scalability, energy consumption, and regulatory uncertainty, paving the way for broader adoption and innovative use cases.

The evolution of blockchain technology has been marked by significant milestones, transforming it from a niche concept supporting digital currencies into a foundational technology with broad applications. The journey began in 2008 when an individual or group using the pseudonym Satoshi Nakamoto introduced Bitcoin, the first decentralized cryptocurrency, in a whitepaper titled "Bitcoin: A Peer-to-Peer Electronic Cash System." This marked the first generation of blockchain, where the primary focus was on enabling secure, decentralized digital currency transactions without the need for intermediaries like banks. Bitcoin's blockchain was designed as a public ledger to verify and record all transactions transparently.

The second generation of blockchain emerged with the launch of Ethereum in 2015 by Vitalik Buterin, which introduced the concept of smart contracts—self-executing contracts with the terms directly written into code. Ethereum's blockchain enabled developers to build decentralized applications (dApps), significantly expanding the potential use cases of the technology beyond just financial transactions. This shift opened up new avenues for industries such as supply chain, gaming, healthcare, insurance, and more.

As adoption grew, so did the need to address scalability, energy efficiency, and interoperability challenges. This led to the third generation of blockchain, characterized by innovations like Proof of Stake (PoS) consensus mechanisms (e.g., in Cardano and Ethereum 2.0), sharding, layer-2 solutions, and interoperable blockchain networks like Polkadot and Cosmos. These advancements aim to enhance transaction speed, reduce environmental impact, and allow different blockchain networks to communicate and work together seamlessly.

In recent years, blockchain has evolved further with the rise of Decentralized Finance (DeFi), Non-Fungible Tokens (NFTs), and Web3—the vision of a more user-controlled and decentralized internet. Institutions and governments have also begun exploring permissioned blockchains for use in digital identity, smart healthcare, e-voting, and central bank digital currencies (CBDCs). This ongoing evolution highlights blockchain's transition from a disruptive experiment to a mature, flexible technology poised to reshape industries and governance systems globally.

Blockchain technology offers a range of compelling benefits that make it attractive across various sectors. One of its most significant advantages is decentralization, which eliminates the need for a central authority by allowing peer-to-peer transactions. This enhances trust among participants, particularly in environments where parties may not fully know or trust each other. Another major benefit is immutability—once data is recorded on the blockchain, it cannot be altered or deleted, ensuring data integrity and preventing fraud. Transparency is also a core feature; in public blockchains, all transactions are visible to every node, enabling auditability and accountability. Furthermore, blockchain provides enhanced security through cryptographic techniques, making it highly resistant to hacking and data tampering. Smart contracts add automation to the system by executing agreements based on pre-defined conditions without intermediaries, thus improving efficiency and reducing operational costs. These benefits make blockchain particularly valuable in applications such as supply chain management, healthcare, finance, and digital identity.

Despite its strengths, blockchain also has several limitations. A key concern is scalability—many blockchains, especially those using Proof of Work (PoW), struggle to process a high volume of transactions quickly, leading to delays and increased fees. Energy consumption is another critical issue, particularly in PoW-based systems like Bitcoin, which require vast computational power and electricity. Additionally, blockchain faces integration challenges with existing legacy systems, which can be costly and complex. Data privacy can also be a concern, especially on public blockchains where transparency may conflict with the need to keep sensitive information confidential. Moreover, the lack of standardization and regulatory clarity hinders widespread adoption and creates legal uncertainties, especially in cross-border transactions. Lastly, the irreversibility of transactions can be problematic in cases of errors or fraud, as there is no central authority to reverse incorrect entries.

1.2. Smart Healthcare Definition, Evolution, Benefits and Challenges

Smart Healthcare refers to the integration of advanced technologies—such as the Internet of Things (IoT), Artificial Intelligence (AI), Big Data and Blockchain—into healthcare systems to enhance the delivery, efficiency and personalization of medical services (Amit et al., 2020; Amit et al., 2020b; Mishra et al., 2024; Supriya et al., 2024). It aims to improve patient outcomes, streamline clinical workflows, and enable real-time monitoring and data-driven decision-making through connected devices, electronic health records, remote diagnostics, and automated systems.

The evolution of smart healthcare has been driven by technological advancements and the growing demand for more efficient, personalized, and accessible medical services. It began with the digitization of health records through Electronic Health Records (EHRs), replacing paper-based systems and enabling better data management. The next phase involved telemedicine, allowing remote consultations and bridging the gap between patients and healthcare providers, especially in rural or underserved areas. The rise of mobile health (mHealth) and wearable devices enabled continuous health monitoring, empowering patients to take an active role in managing their health. More recently, the integration of Artificial Intelligence (AI), Machine Learning (ML), and Internet of Things (IoT) has enabled predictive analytics, early disease detection, and automated clinical decision support. Today, blockchain, cloud computing, and robotic surgery further push the boundaries, creating a connected and intelligent healthcare ecosystem. This ongoing evolution is transforming healthcare from reactive treatment to proactive, preventive, and precision-based care.

Smart healthcare offers numerous benefits that enhance the quality, accessibility, and efficiency of medical services. One of the primary advantages is improved patient care through real-time monitoring, personalized treatment plans, and early diagnosis enabled by AI and IoT devices. It also enhances operational efficiency by automating administrative tasks, reducing human error, and streamlining workflows. Remote healthcare solutions such as telemedicine increase accessibility, especially for patients in rural or underserved regions. Moreover, smart systems facilitate data-driven decision-making, leading to more accurate diagnoses and better health outcomes. However, smart healthcare also faces several challenges. Data privacy and security are major concerns, as sensitive health information is collected, stored, and transmitted across connected platforms. High implementation costs, lack of interoperability among devices and systems, and technological disparities between urban and rural healthcare infrastructure pose significant barriers. Additionally, regulatory hurdles, ethical concerns, and the need for digital literacy among both patients and healthcare providers continue to limit widespread adoption. Overcoming these challenges is essential for fully realizing the potential of smart healthcare.

Overall, smart healthcare is a revolution in the health sector with digital technology providing enhanced patient care, optimized operations, and better health outcomes. As enormous as the benefits are, the breakthrough of data security, interoperability, regulation, and ethical issues is needed to witness the full potential of smart healthcare.

1.3. Blockchain and IoT Integration in Smart Healthcare

The combination of blockchain technology and the Internet of Things (IoT) has enormous potential in revolutionizing the healthcare sector (Kumari et al., 2022; Tyagi et al., 2024c; Kumari et al., 2024; Tiwari et al., 2024b). Together, they can offer solutions for some of the issues created by data security, interoperability, trust, and transparency, and facilitate innovative healthcare solutions. An overview of blockchain and IoT integration into smart healthcare is as follows and shown in Figure 1.

- **Data Security and Integrity:** Blockchain's one-way hash function ensures IoT device data, such as medical wearables or sensors, remains secure and tamper-evident. Data written to the blockchain cannot be altered without the consensus of the network members, thus ensuring data integrity.
- **Data Ownership and Consent:** IoT-generated health data can be stored in a blockchain, thus ensuring patients control their data. Access permission to health data can be given and withdrawn, thus ensuring data privacy and Data Protection Act compliance.
- **Interoperability:** IoT devices and systems employ heterogeneous data formats. Blockchain can be used as a platform for storing and sharing healthcare

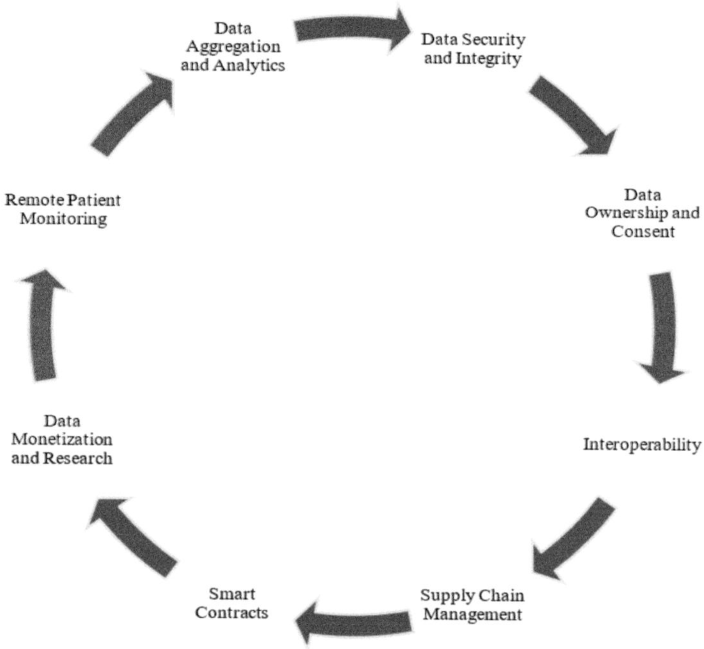

Figure 1: Blockchain and IoT integration into smart healthcare.

information and, thus, enables interoperability among heterogeneous IoT devices and healthcare organizations.

- **Supply Chain Management:** Blockchain can track drugs and medical devices from the manufacturer through a distributor, ensuring authenticity and preventing opportunities for counterfeit products to enter the supply chain.
- **Smart Contracts:** Smart contracts on the blockchain can automate healthcare tasks based on data from IoT devices. For example, a smart contract can automatically schedule a follow-up appointment after detecting critical signs from a patient's IoT sensors.
- **Data Monetization and Research:** Healthcare organizations can securely exchange, on a blockchain network, the data collected from IoT to researchers and other consumers. Incentives are offered to data owners in the form of rewards for providing data, thus offering incentives to contribute to medical research.
- **Remote Patient Monitoring:** IoT devices constantly monitor patients' health data, which can be securely routed to a blockchain-based EHR system. This allows physicians to view real-time data for timely interventions.
- **Data Aggregation and Analytics:** IoT sensors generate a large volume of data. Blockchain can aggregate this data and, with the assistance of AI and analytics, derive information useful for healthcare providers and researchers.

1.3.1. Challenges and Issues

Some of the challenges and issues are explained as follows:

- **Scalability:** Blockchain and IoT both can generate a large volume of data. The scalability of the combined system needs to be ensured.
- **Privacy and Consent:** Handling patient consent and data privacy while sharing data generated by IoT on a blockchain must be handled with care.
- **Security:** Security for IoT sensors needs to be ensured to prevent unauthorized access or modification of data before posting on the blockchain.
- **Cost:** It may be costly to deploy and maintain blockchain and IoT infrastructure.
- **Regulatory Compliance:** Healthcare regulations need to be considered and complied with while deploying blockchain and IoT solutions.

In brief, blockchain and IoT integration in smart healthcare can address most of the industry's problems while adding new functionality and improving patient care. Deployment must be successful with careful planning, security, and privacy considerations, and compliance with healthcare regulations.

2. Blockchain Applications: Healthcare Sector

Blockchain technology has been used in a variety of applications in healthcare, addressing some of the challenges related to data security, interoperability, transparency, and patient-centric care (M. Shamila et al., 2023; Madhav et al., 2022; Tiwari et al., 2024a; Tyagi et al., 2024g). Some of the primary blockchain applications in the healthcare sector are shown in Figure 2.

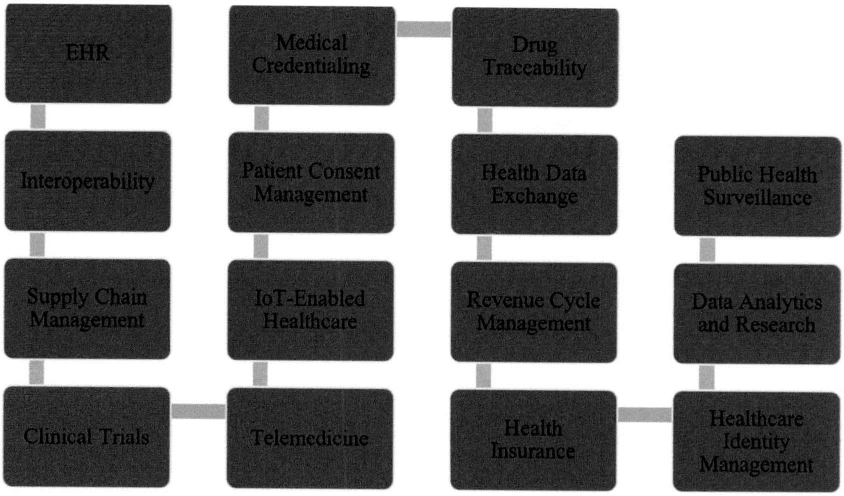

Figure 2: Blockchain applications in the healthcare sector.

- **EHR:** Blockchain can securely store and manage EHRs so that the integrity, accessibility, and portability of a patient's information are maintained among multiple providers. Patients have complete control over who gets access to their EHR and can provide access through smart contracts.
- **Interoperability:** Blockchain enables data interoperability by having a single platform for various healthcare systems and devices. Data can be easily exchanged among multiple healthcare consumers, enabling care coordination and minimizing errors.
- **Supply Chain Management:** Blockchain enables tracking and verification of the source and delivery of drugs, medical devices, and vaccines to prevent the introduction of spurious or substandard products in the supply chain.
- **Clinical Trials:** Blockchain provides transparency and trust in clinical trials through tamper-evident clinical trial data records. This makes the results tamper-proof and speeds up drug development.
- **Telemedicine:** Tamper-evident encryption and secure recording in the blockchain secure the patient data and provide remote delivery of healthcare services.
- **IoT-enabled Healthcare:** Such IoT devices as wearable health sensors can record patient data in real-time over a secure channel to blockchain-based electronic health records. The data is relayed to the healthcare providers so that the patients can be remotely monitored and interventions can be initiated in a timely fashion.
- **Patient Consent Management:** Blockchain-based smart contracts can grant, withdraw, or manage access to the patient's healthcare data and represent their consent choices.
- **Medical Credentialing:** Blockchain authenticates and transfers the healthcare provider's credentials more effectively, thus facilitating recruitment and streamlining administrative processes.

- **Drug Traceability:** Blockchain traces drugs in the supply chain for authenticity and safety, an important parameter in shielding the patient from the risk of drugs.
- **Health Data Exchange:** Patient health data can be exchanged securely with researchers to plan the patient's treatment and additional medical research.
- **Revenue Cycle Management:** Blockchain can automate and make billing and claims processing effective, thus saving the overhead of administrative processes and making the revenue cycle effective.
- **Health Insurance:** Smart contracts can automate the verification and processing of health insurance claims, avoid fraud, and make the claims process more effective.
- **Healthcare Identity Management:** Blockchain identity solutions can manage patients' and providers' secure identities, minimizing the risk of identity theft, thus improving access control.
- **Data Analytics and Research:** Blockchain can collect information on patients with health conditions from numerous information systems and give researchers a goldmine for epidemiological and medical research.
- **Public Health Surveillance:** Blockchain can manage the timely exchange of public health information and facilitate rapid response to outbreaks and emergencies due to health-related crises.

Though blockchain offers a broad range of benefits in healthcare, it is also a platform plagued with scalability issues, regulatory issues, and integration with legacy systems. As blockchain technology matures and becomes more acceptable, its uses in healthcare are bound to grow, transforming the industry into a safer, more efficient, and patient-centric environment. A few other uses of smart healthcare are Electronic Health Records (EHRs), Health Data Interoperability, Supply Chain Management in Healthcare, Drug Traceability and Prevention of Counterfeiting and Telemedicine, and Remote Patient Monitoring. Further, some other uses of Blockchain in Healthcare are: Patient Data Ownership and Control, Clinical Trials and Research Data, Healthcare Payment Systems, Medical Credentialing and Licensing, and Pharmaceuticals and Drug Safety.

3. Benefits, Limitations, Issues, and Challenges of Blockchain: Healthcare Sector

Blockchain technology has a lot in health, offering a lot in terms of its benefits, while it comes with limitations, issues, and challenges that should be put into consideration (Tyagi et al., 2020; Tyagi et al., 2024h; Tyagi et al., 2024i).

3.1. Benefits of Blockchain in Healthcare

Some of the benefits of Blockchain in healthcare are:

- **Data Security:** Blockchain provides data security through encryption and decentralized storage, which eradicates the fear of breach of patients' data and unauthorized access.
- **Data Integrity:** As the data is already written in the blockchain, it becomes immutable to avoid any type of modification in the medical records.

- **Interoperability:** Blockchain would offer a shared platform for storing health data to enable interoperability in systems and enable easy exchange among healthcare professionals.
- **Patient Control:** With this, a patient will be in control of the health data because access can be given or withdrawn, enhancing privacy and consent management.
- **File Transparency:** Blockchain's transparent and tamper-proof nature instills trust from patients, healthcare providers, and consumers, minimizing disputes and errors.
- **Administrative Efficiencies:** Claims processing, billing, and all administrative procedures can be streamlined using blockchain, minimizing administrative expenses and maximizing efficiency.
- **Clinical Trials:** Blockchain offers clear transparency and integrity of trials performed, which can speed up the development of a drug.
- Supply Chain Management: Tracking of pharmaceuticals and medical devices is possible through it, which significantly decreases the inclusion of counterfeit pharmaceuticals and other medical devices.
- **Telemedicine:** Secure recording of telemedicine consultations and prescriptions on blockchain provides an additional layer of security to patients during remote healthcare.
- **Smart Contracts:** Automating Healthcare Processes by using smart contracts helps simplify health system processes like handling insurance claims to consent for treating patients.

3.2. Limitations of Blockchain in Healthcare

Some of the Limitations of Blockchain in Healthcare are shown in Figure 3:

- **Scalability:** Public blockchain scalability issues, such as managing high volumes of healthcare data transactions.
- **Cost:** Setup and maintenance expenses of blockchain infrastructure, particularly for small healthcare providers, are costly.
- **Regulatory Compliance:** The healthcare sector is highly regulated, and the blockchain solution must be incorporated with existing law, which is difficult.
- **Interoperability:** Incorporating blockchain with the existing health sector systems and standards is difficult and time-consuming.

3.3. Problems and Challenges

Very few challenges and problems are shown in Figure 4.

- **Data Privacy:** Blockchain provides more data security, but data privacy is not automatic. Patient consent and anonymization issues are of the highest priority.
- **Identity Management:** Patient and provider identity management on the blockchain is necessary to avoid identity theft and fraud.
- **Adoption Barriers:** Awareness and knowledge about the advantages and applications of blockchain in the healthcare industry are needed for its mass adoption.

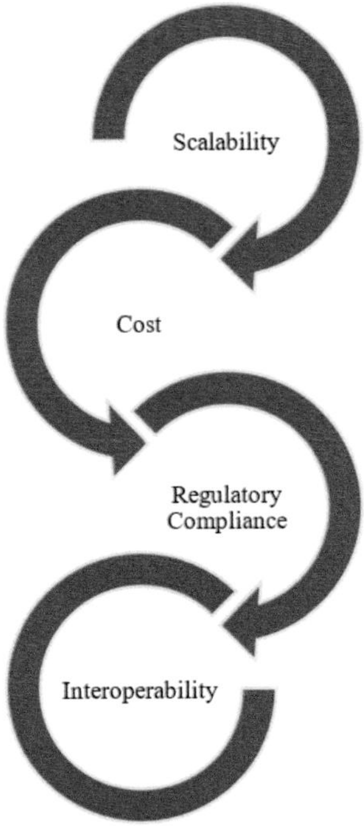

Figure 3: Blockchain limitations.

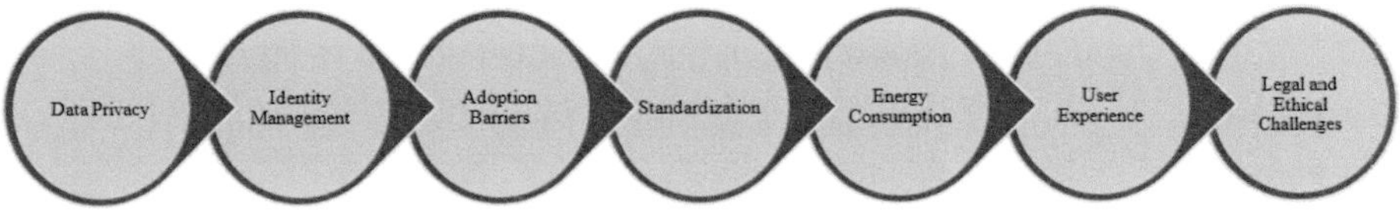

Figure 4: Blockchain challenges.

- **Standardization:** Industry standards for the adoption of blockchain and data formats are necessary for easy interoperability.
- **Energy Consumption:** Proof-of-work blockchains like Bitcoin and Ethereum are heavy consumers of energy, leading to environmental issues.
- **User Experience:** Blockchain solutions should be simple to use by healthcare providers and patients for easy adoption.
- **Legal and Ethical Challenges:** Application of the algorithm in decision-making, ownership, and responsibility in the event of a mistake are only a few of the ethical challenges that will arise.

Finally, blockchain can transform the health industry through security and confidentiality, interoperability, as well as efficiencies, but its adoption has to be made by overcoming existing constraints, in alignment with the regulatory progress, and enforcing data privacy so that it gets effectively implemented in day-to-day life.

4. Security, Privacy, Ethical, and Legal Issues Towards Using Blockchain in Smart Healthcare

In using blockchain technology in smart healthcare, several issues of highest priority in terms of security, privacy, ethics, and legality need to be taken care of to make the use of the technology responsible and effective (Tyagi et al., 2019; Gillala et al., 2019; Tyagi et al., 2024f; Tyagi et al., 2024e). Several of the most prominent issues in each of these domains are discussed below:

Security Issues

- **Network Security:** Secure the blockchain network itself, i.e., with strong cryptographic controls, node security, and 51% attack protection.
- **Smart Contract Security:** Strongly audit and test smart contracts to avoid vulnerabilities and potential exploits.
- **Access Control:** Use strong access controls to limit who can read, write, and execute transactions on the blockchain.
- **Data Encryption:** Use encryption methods to secure sensitive data in transit and at rest.
- **Incident Response:** Have a strong incident response plan in place to handle security breaches or unauthorized access.

Privacy Issues

- **Data Minimization:** Store and capture the absolute minimum of patient data on the blockchain to reduce exposure and potential breach.
- **Patient Consent:** Use strong consent management systems to maintain patients in control of who can access their health data and for what.
- **Data Anonymization:** Anonymize patient data or use techniques like differential privacy to hide individual identities.
- **Compliance:** Comply with healthcare data protection laws like HIPAA (in the United States) or GDPR (in Europe).

Ethical Issues

- **Informed Consent:** Properly inform patients on how their data will be used and provide a transparent opt-in or opt-out.
- **Transparency:** Provide transparency on data sharing practices and blockchain operations to create trust among patients and consumers.
- **Equity:** Consider the potential for blockchain technology to widen healthcare inequities and efforts to ensure equitable access and benefits.
- **Data Ownership:** Define data ownership regulations and provide patients' right of access, transfer, or deletion of their data from the blockchain.

Legal Issues and Regulatory Compliance

- **Regulatory Compliance:** Comply with local, national, and international healthcare law, including data protection, patient rights, and clinical trials law.
- **Data Portability:** Make blockchain systems data portable according to legislation like GDPR, which entitles patients to access and share their data.

- **Smart Contracts and Legal Frameworks:** Develop legal frameworks for smart contracts in a way that they are compliant with existing contractual legislation and regulation.
- **Liability and Dispute Resolution:** Provide clear liability frameworks in the event of errors or disputes in blockchain-based healthcare procedures.
- **Cross-Border Issues:** In the event of working abroad, consider international legal complexity, such as data sovereignty and jurisdictional variability.
- **Intellectual Property:** Provide solutions for intellectual property concerns about healthcare innovations and sharing data on the blockchain.
- **Regulatory Changes:** Adapt to changing regulations in the healthcare and blockchain space and modify systems accordingly.

Hence, deployment of blockchain in smart healthcare is a multidisciplinary process of technologists, legal professionals, ethicists, and healthcare workers. Interdisciplinary coordination and effective understanding of such issues are important to ensure that blockchain technology enhances healthcare without compromising the rights and privacy of patients.

5. Blockchain Consortia and Industry Initiatives towards Blockchain Integration in Smart Healthcare

Blockchain consortia and industry initiatives are chief drivers of the integration of blockchain technology in smart healthcare (Shruti et al., 2021; Sai et al., 2023; Tyagi et al., 2024c). These initiatives gather consumers across industries to design standards, disseminate best practices, and tackle common challenges. Some of the key blockchain consortia and initiatives focused on healthcare are discussed below, shown in Figure 5.

Hashed Health: Hashed Health is an organization that gathers healthcare organizations, tech companies, and blockchain specialists together to accelerate blockchain adoption in healthcare. They solve various use cases, such as supply chain management, identity management, and revenue cycle management.

Healthcare-Chain Coalition: It is an international coalition that focuses on encouraging the use of blockchain technology in healthcare. It strives to develop coordination among healthcare organizations, startups, and technology providers to encourage blockchain solutions for the sharing of health data and security.

Hyperledger Healthcare Working Group: It is part of the Hyperledger project of the Linux Foundation. The working group plans to develop open-source blockchain solutions for healthcare. It has membership from the health and tech communities and is working on interoperability, smart contracts, and data privacy.

MediLedger Project: It is specifically focused on enhancing the pharmaceutical supply chain with the assistance of blockchain technology. It brings together pharmaceutical companies, wholesalers, and healthcare providers to develop a secure and transparent supply chain network.

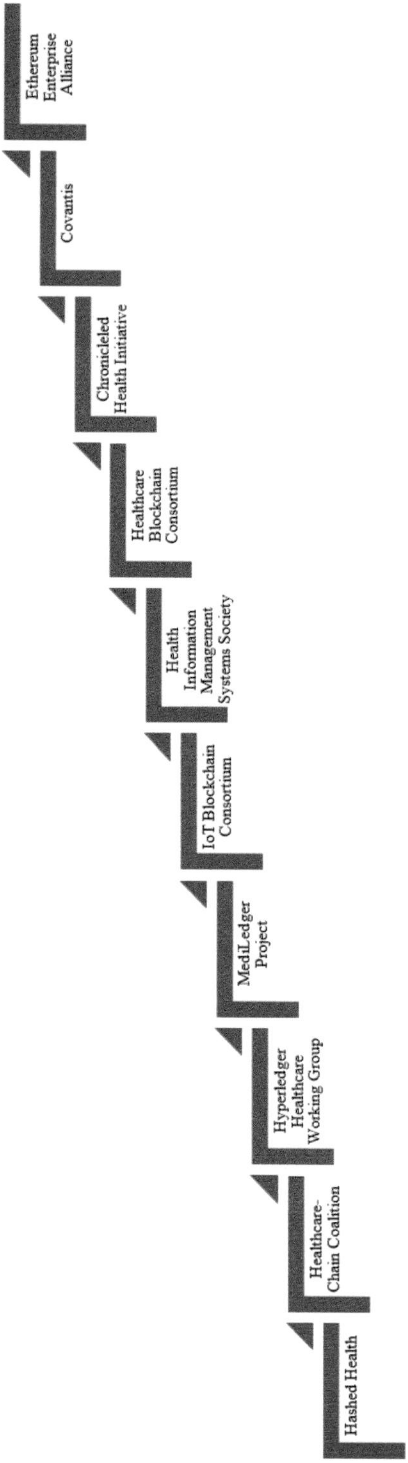

Figure 5: Blockchain consortia and initiatives.

IoT Blockchain Consortium: Not directly healthcare-oriented, this consortium is developing the intersection of blockchain and the Internet of Things (IoT), which has vast applications in healthcare. It is developing secure data exchange, device management, and data integrity.

Health Information Management Systems Society (HIMSS): HIMSS, an international nonprofit organization, promotes the use of information technology in healthcare. They have initiated discussions and education on the use of blockchain technology in managing health data and interoperability.

Healthcare Blockchain Consortium (HBC): HBC is an initiative by different healthcare organizations, including hospitals and academic institutions, to study and implement blockchain solutions for sharing healthcare data and security.

Chronicleled Health Initiative: This initiative, for the management of the pharmaceutical supply chain and anti-counterfeit drugs, uses blockchain and IoT technologies to enhance transparency and traceability in the healthcare supply chain.

Covantis: While primarily commodity trading and agriculture, Covantis is indirectly connected with pharmaceutical supply chain management. It invokes blockchain technology to bring transparency and efficiency to supply chain management.

Ethereum Enterprise Alliance (EEA): While not healthcare, EEA includes health industry stakeholders and forges Ethereum-based blockchain solutions. These solutions will find application in healthcare applications such as secure data exchange.

These consortia and initiatives thus bring together industry leaders, technology innovators, and regulators to work together and solve issues, and build blockchain standards and best practices for healthcare. Their efforts result in the responsible application of blockchain technology to smart healthcare, delivering data security, interoperability, and transparency, and addressing regulatory and ethical issues.

6. Future Trends and Emerging Technologies towards using Blockchain in Smart Healthcare

Blockchain application in smart healthcare continues to evolve, with several future trends and emerging technologies poised to shape its development (B. Gudeti et al., 2020; Amit Kumar et al., 2021; Kute et al., 2022a; Kute et al., 2022b; Nair et al., 2021; Chen et al., 2021). These trends will impact the industry by resolving existing issues and introducing innovative solutions. Some of the most important future trends and emerging technologies for blockchain in smart healthcare are shown in Figure 6.

Interoperability Standards: Standardization initiatives will increase to facilitate the free exchange of information between different healthcare systems and blockchains. Interoperable solutions will enhance care coordination, reduce errors, and enhance patient outcomes.

Blockchain and AI Synergy: Blockchain will be combined with AI and machine learning. AI algorithms will execute on healthcare data on the blockchain to

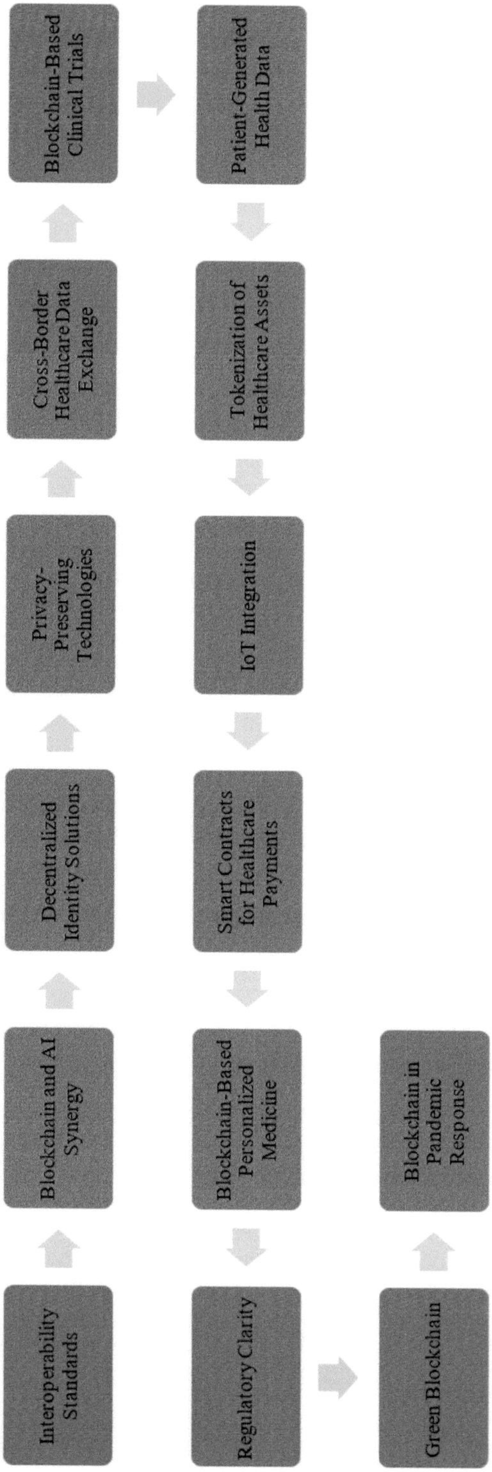

Figure 6: Blockchain future trends and emerging technologies.

deliver data for personalized care plans, predictive analytics, and population health management.

Decentralized Identity Solutions: Decentralized identity management solutions will gain popularity, enabling patients to own their identity and healthcare data. Patients can securely share access to specific healthcare providers or researchers.

Privacy-Preserving Technologies: Zero-knowledge proofs, homomorphic encryption, and other privacy-preserving technologies will be used to deploy blockchain systems to enhance patient privacy while enabling secure data analysis and sharing.

Cross-border Healthcare Data Exchange: Blockchain will enable cross-border healthcare data exchange, enabling patients to access medical records and receive treatment overseas and still comply with several regulatory requirements.

Blockchain-based Clinical Trials: Blockchain will be used in clinical trials to provide transparency, data integrity, and better patient recruitment. Decentralized trials based on real-world data will become common, accelerating drug development.

Patient-generated Health Data (PGHD): Blockchain will be used to store and manage PGHD securely from wearable devices, enabling continuous monitoring and providing real-time data for patient treatment.

Tokenization of Healthcare Assets: Healthcare assets such as insurance policies, medical records, and medicines will be tokenized on blockchain, enabling them to be more tradable, ownership verification easier, and data sharing easier.

IoT Integration: Blockchain integration with the IoT will enable secure and tamper-evident data transmission from sensors and medical devices. This will enable better-quality remote patient monitoring, preventive care, and early disease detection.

Smart Contracts for Healthcare Payments: Smart contracts will enable automation of healthcare payments, minimizing administrative burden, fraud, and billing errors.

Blockchain-based Personalized Medicine: Blockchain will be crucial in enabling research and development of personalized medicine through secure genomic and clinical data aggregation for targeted treatment.

Regulatory Clarity: As regulatory regimes become clearer, healthcare organizations will increasingly deploy blockchain solutions confidently. Regulators will provide standards of data compliance, privacy, and security.

Green Blockchain: Power-saving consensus algorithms and green blockchain platforms will be created to tackle the problem of the environmental cost of energy-intensive blockchain networks.

Blockchain in Pandemic Response: Blockchain will be used in contact tracing, vaccine tracking, and safe sharing of pandemic data, with people's privacy.

Thus, these future trends and technologies are the potential of blockchain in reshaping smart healthcare by enhancing data security, interoperability, patient-centered care, and research capabilities. However, scalability problems, regulatory hurdles, and adoption challenges need to be overcome to unlock the maximum potential of blockchain for healthcare. Thus, now the evolution of Blockchain in Healthcare can be observed in (Tyagi et al., 2024i; Tyagi et al., 2019).

6.1. Emerging Technologies Empowered the Smart Healthcare Sector for the Future Generation Society

Near-future emerging technologies will revolutionize smart healthcare and make it the backbone of next-generation care services by taking the quality of care to a new level. Some of the most influential emerging technologies empowering smart healthcare for the next-generation society are (Tyagi et al., 2024d; Tyagi et al., 2024b):

Artificial Intelligence and Machine Learning: AI and machine learning algorithms can examine the vast amount of medical data and, for instance, patient records, imaging, and genomics in an attempt to enhance diagnosis and suggestions for the treatment of patients. AI-based chatbots and virtual health assistants empower patient engagement and support.

IoT: IoT-based equipment, like wearable fitness devices and remote sensors, enables patients to be monitored in real time and data to be captured continuously. These also yield very useful data that can be used to provide personalized treatment and detect potential issues before they occur.

Telemedicine and Telehealth: Telemedicine refers to remote consultation, wherein medical guidance and treatment can be extended to patients without going to a healthcare facility. Telehealth involves remote monitoring and patient education services.

Blockchain Technology: Blockchain ensures the security, privacy, and integrity of health data. Blockchain is used for secure patient record management, consent management, drug tracking, and clinical trial management.

5G Connectivity: 5G networks enable low-latency, high-speed connectivity, which enables real-time data transfer for telemedicine, remote surgery, and IoT-based healthcare equipment. This technology offers better responsiveness to healthcare.

AI-aided Genomic Sequencing: Genomics can thus be used for formulating a personalized regimen for a patient, considering the accuracy that genomic sequencing possesses, and hence aided by AI. This gives maximum efficiency with minimum side effects of the treatment.

Virtual Reality (VR) and Augmented Reality (AR): VR and AR are used for medical training, planning for surgery, and pain management. Therapeutic use for the patient includes virtual rehabilitation and exposure therapy.

Surgical Robotics and Robotic Support: Robotic surgery and the robotic-assisted devices enable surgery to be precise and minimally invasive. A surgeon can perform intricate surgeries with better precision.

Healthcare 3D Printing: 3D printing enables customized prosthetics, implants, and medical models to be ready for pre-surgical planning. Patient-specific medical devices move at a faster pace.

Biotechnology Innovation: With biotechnology innovation, gene editing tools like CRISPR-Cas9 can cure genetic diseases and detect targeted therapies.

Medicine Nanotechnology: Nanoscale device and material development is enabling targeted medicine delivery, disease detection at an early stage, and high-resolution imaging to enhance treatment.

Healthcare Analytics and Big Data: Sophisticated analytics and big data solutions draw healthcare information for predictive data, patterns, and trends; facilitate population health management, resource planning, and disease surveillance.

Digital Health Records: PHRs and EHRs convert patient records into digital form, making it easy to transfer information from one healthcare provider to another, but giving more control to patients over their health information.

Voice and Natural Language Processing: Voice-controlled documentation, voice support for patient engagement, and access for disabled individuals are facilitated through voice recognition and natural language processing technologies.

Bioinformatics and Computational Biology: Bioinformatics software has the potential to assist in discovering medicines and determining which genetic factors cause a disease, due to its ability to process biological data of biology.

Regenerative Medicine: Regenerative treatments, such as stem cell therapy and tissue engineering, offer a cure for diseases that were once thought to be incurable.

Mental Health Technology: Digital technology for mental health, ranging from apps and chatbots to driving demand for mental health support and therapy.

Ethical and Privacy Enhancements: Standards and technologies for enhancing data privacy, informed consent, and ethical considerations of healthcare AI and data sharing.

Combining these next-generation technologies under smart healthcare thus promises to deliver more accessible, personalized, and effective services to the healthcare demands of future society. But it challenges data security, ethics, and regulatory compliance to carefully navigate to be maximally productive.

7. Conclusion

In this chapter, we have discussed many blockchain technology opportunities for the transformation of the healthcare industry towards an era of smart healthcare. Impressive qualities like decentralization, immutability, and cryptographic security of blockchain have been leveraged to overcome long-standing challenges that have plagued health care systems around the world. The contribution of blockchain towards smart healthcare is thus achieved in the creation of secure, interoperable, and tamper-proof EHRs. Blockchain technology has streamlined the pharma supply chain, improved the transparency of clinical trials, improved the scope of telemedicine, and transformed patient consent management. Such applications prove how blockchain is not some theory but an actual application with actual benefits for patients, healthcare providers, and consumers in the network. Our chapter has illuminated the existing state of blockchain adoption in healthcare, showing an increasingly visible number of projects as well as collaborations. However, there is still much to be done, especially in scalability and interoperability, not to mention usability; regulatory and ethical issues, like the protection of the privacy of data and regulation compliance, must be addressed with caution to ensure the responsible adoption of blockchain in health care systems. The chapter portrays a promising future of blockchain in smart healthcare. Emerging trends like the integration of blockchain with other emerging technologies like AI and IoT will further augment its capabilities.

References

Chen, Mengji, Taj Malook, Ateeq Ur Rehman, Yar Muhammad, Mohammad Dahman Alshehri, Aamir Akbar et al. (2021). Blockchain-enabled healthcare system for detection of diabetes. Journal of Information Security and Applications, 58, 102771.

Gillala, Rekha, Amit Kumar Tyagi and V. Krishna Reddy. (2019). A wide scale classification of class imbalance problem and its solutions: A systematic literature review. Journal of Computer Science, 15(7), pp. 886–929. ISSN Print: 1549-3636.

Gudeti, B., Mishra, S., Malik, S., Fernandez, T.F., Tyagi, A.K., and Kumari, S. (2020). A novel approach to predict chronic kidney disease using machine learning algorithms. 4th International Conference on Electronics, Communication and Aerospace Technology (ICECA), pp. 1630–1635, Coimbatore. doi: 10.1109/ICECA49313.2020.9297392.

Kumari, S. and Muthulakshmi, P. (2022). Transformative effects of big data on advanced data analytics: Open issues and critical challenges. Journal of Computer Science, 18(6), 463–479. https://doi.org/10.3844/jcssp.2022.463.479

Kumari, S., Tiwari, S., Naithani, K., & Subbiah, P. (2024). Internet of Things for smart agriculture: A survey. *In:* A. Naim (Ed.), AI Applications for Business, Medical and Agricultural Sustainability, pp. 100–121. IGI Global Scientific Publishing. https://doi.org/10.4018/979-8-3693-5266-3.ch005

Kute, S.S., Tyagi, A.K., and Aswathy, S.U. (2022a). Industry 4.0 Challenges in e-Healthcare applications and emerging technologies. *In:* Tyagi, A.K., Abraham, A., Kaklauskas, A. (eds.), Intelligent Interactive Multimedia Systems for e-Healthcare Applications. Springer, Singapore. https://doi.org/10.1007/978-981-16-6542-4_1

Kute, S.S., Tyagi, A.K., and Aswathy, S.U. (2022b). Security, privacy and trust issues in Internet of Things and machine learning based e-Healthcare. *In:* Tyagi, A.K., Abraham, A., Kaklauskas, A. (eds.), Intelligent Interactive Multimedia Systems for e-Healthcare Applications. Springer, Singapore. https://doi.org/10.1007/978-981-16-6542-4_15

Madhav, A.V.S., and Tyagi, A.K. (2022). The world with future technologies (post-COVID-19): Open issues, challenges and the road ahead. *In:* Tyagi, A.K., Abraham, A., Kaklauskas, A. (eds.), Intelligent Interactive Multimedia Systems for e-Healthcare Applications. Springer, Singapore. https://doi.org/10.1007/978-981-16-6542-4_22

Mishra, A.K., Tiwari, S., Tyagi, A.K., and Arowolo, M.O. (2024). Security, privacy, trust and provenance issues in Internet of Things–based edge environment. *In:* Pal, S., Savaglio,

C., Minerva, R., Delicato, F.C. (eds.), IoT Edge Intelligence. Internet of Things. Springer, Cham. https://doi.org/10.1007/978-3-031-58388-9_8

Nair, M.M., Kumari, S., Tyagi, A.K., and Sravanthi, K. (2021). Deep learning for medical image recognition: Open issues and a way to forward. *In:* Goyal, D., Gupta, A.K., Piuri, V., Ganzha, M., Paprzycki, M. (eds.), Proceedings of the Second International Conference on Information Management and Machine Intelligence. Lecture Notes in Networks and Systems, Vol. 166. Springer, Singapore. https://doi.org/10.1007/978-981-15-9689-6_38

Sai, G.H., Tripathi, K., and Tyagi, A.K. (2023). Internet of Things-based e-Health care: Key challenges and recommended solutions for future. *In:* Singh, P.K., Wierzchoń, S.T., Tanwar, S., Rodrigues, J.J.P.C., Ganzha, M. (eds.), Proceedings of Third International Conference on Computing, Communications and Cyber-Security. Lecture Notes in Networks and Systems, Vol. 421. Springer, Singapore. https://doi.org/10.1007/978-981-19-1142-2_37

Shamila, M., Vinuthna, K., and Amit Kumar Tyagi. (2023). Genomic privacy: Performance analysis, open issues and future research directions. *In:* Amit Kumar Tyagi, Ajith Abraham (eds.), Data Science for Genomics, pp. 249–263, Academic Press. https://doi.org/10.1016/B978-0-323-98352-5.00015-X.

Sharma, Ashutosh, Ravi Tomar, Naveen Chilamkurti, and Byung-Gyu Kim. (2020). Blockchain based smart contracts for Internet of Medical Things in e-Healthcare. Electronics, 9(10), 1609.

Shruti Kute, Amit Kumar Tyagi, Rohit Sahoo, and Shaveta Malik. (2021). Building a smart healthcare system using Internet of Things and machine learning. *In:* Big Data Management in Sensing: Applications in AI and IoT, pp. 159–178. River Publishers.

Supriya, M., Tyagi, A.K., Tiwari, S., and Richa. (2024). Sensor-based intelligent recommender systems for agricultural activities. *In:* A. Naim (ed.), AI Applications for Business, Medical and Agricultural Sustainability, pp. 197–235. IGI Global Scientific Publishing. https://doi.org/10.4018/979-8-3693-5266-3.ch008

Tiwari, S., Chidambaram, N., and Tyagi, A.K. (2024a). Need of 21st Century: A sustainable environment together with a smart environment. *In:* J. Thomas, G. Weber, R. Aguilar, E. Munapo, P. Vasant (eds.), Operational Research for Renewable Energy and Sustainable Environments, pp. 199–224. IGI Global Scientific Publishing. https://doi.org/10.4018/978-1-6684-9130-0.ch009

Tiwari, S., Reddy, R.R., and Tyagi, A.K. (2024b). Position of blockchain: Internet of Things-based Education 4.0 in Industry 5.0 – A discussion of issues and challenges. *In:* R. Pandey, N. Srivastava, & P. Chatterjee (eds.), Architecture and Technological Advancements of Education 4.0, pp. 292–311. IGI Global Scientific Publishing. https://doi.org/10.4018/978-1-6684-9285-7.ch013

Tripathi, Gautami, Mohd Abdul Ahad and Sara Paiva. (2020). S2HS-A blockchain based approach for smart healthcare system. Healthcare, 8(1), 100391.

Tyagi, A.K. and Go0yal, D. (2020). A survey of privacy leakage and security vulnerabilities in the Internet of Things. *In:* 5th International Conference on Communication and Electronics Systems (ICCES), pp. 386–394, doi: 10.1109/ICCES48766.2020.9137886

Tyagi, Amit Kumar and Rekha, G. (2019). Machine learning with big data. Proceedings of International Conference on Sustainable Computing in Science, Technology and Management (SUSCOM), Amity University Rajasthan, Jaipur, India, February 26–28, 2019. http://dx.doi.org/10.2139/ssrn.3356269

Tyagi, Amit Kumar, and Poonam Chahal. (2020). Artificial Intelligence and machine learning algorithms. *In:* Challenges and Applications for Implementing Machine Learning in Computer Vision. IGI Global. DOI: 10.4018/978-1-7998-0182-5.ch008

Tyagi, Amit Kumar, and Rekha, G. (2020b). Challenges of applying deep learning in real-world applications. *In:* Challenges and Applications for Implementing Machine Learning in Computer Vision, pp. 92–118. IGI Global DOI: 10.4018/978-1-7998-0182-5.ch004

Tyagi, Amit Kumar, Meenu Gupta, Aswathy, S.U., and Chetanya Ved. (2021). Healthcare solutions for smart era: An useful explanation from user's perspective. *In:* Recent Trends in Blockchain for Information Systems Security and Privacy. CRC Press.

Tyagi, A.K., and Tiwari, S. (2024a). The future of Artificial Intelligence in blockchain applications. *In:* P. Baby Maruthi, S. Prasad, A. Tyagi (eds.), Machine Learning Algorithms Using Scikit and TensorFlow Environments, pp. 346–373. IGI Global Scientific Publishing. https://doi.org/10.4018/978-1-6684-8531-6.ch018

Tyagi, A.K., Kumari, S., and Tiwari, S. (2024b). Internet of Things for smart healthcare: A survey. *In:* Arshi Naim (ed.), Future of AI in Medical Imaging, Chapter 02. IGI Global Publishing. DOI: 10.4018/979-8-3693-2359-5.ch002.

Tyagi, A.K., Simhan, V., and Tiwari, S. (2024c). Blockchain security in edge computing: Use cases, challenges and solutions. *In:* D. Lakshmi, A. Tyagi (eds.), Emerging Technologies and Security in Cloud Computing, pp. 105–134. IGI Global Scientific Publishing. https://doi.org/10.4018/979-8-3693-2081-5.ch005

Tyagi, A.K., Simhan, V., and Tiwari, S. (2024d). *In:* Abraham, A., Bajaj, A., Hanne, T., Siarry, P., Ma, K. (eds.), Intelligent Systems Design and Applications. ISDA 2023. Lecture Notes in Networks and Systems, Vol 1050, pp. 166–179. Springer, Cham. DOI: 10.1007/978-3-031-64847-2_15

Tyagi, A.K., Kumari, S., and Tiwari, S. (2024e). Blockchain for Internet of Things and machine learning-based automated sectors. *In:* A.K. Tyagi, S. Tiwari, S.K. Arumugam, A.K. Sharma (eds.), Artificial Intelligence-enabled Digital Twin for Smart Manufacturing. https://doi.org/10.1002/9781394303601.ch9

Tyagi, A.K., Kumari, S., Tiwari, S., and Subbiah, P. (2024f). Industry 5.0 at the core of society 5.0: A revolution in the modern era of the health care sector. *In:* Balaji Sundaramurthy, Padmalosani Dayalan (eds.), Sustainable Innovation for Industry 6.0. IGI Global Publishing. ISBN: 9798369331408, DOI: 10.4018/979-8-3693-3140-8.ch017.

Tyagi, A.K., Kumari, S., Rajasekaran, M., and Tiwari, S. (2024g). Blockchain for safety of internet of vehicles in smart transportation. *In:* A.K. Tyagi (Ed.), Digital Twin and Blockchain for Smart Cities. https://doi.org/10.1002/9781394303564.ch11

Tyagi, A.K., Naithani, K., and Tiwari, S. (2024h). Security and possible threats in today's online social networking platforms. *In:* S.K. Rathi, B. Keswani, R.K. Saxena, S.K. Kapoor, S. Gupta, R. Rawat (eds.), Online Social Networks in Business Frameworks. https://doi.org/10.1002/9781394231126.ch8

Tyagi, A.K., Tiwari, S., and Naithani, K. (2024i). Distributed systems and distributed ledger technology – An introduction. *In:* A.K. Tyagi, S. Tiwari, S.K. Arumugam, A.K. Sharma (eds.), Artificial Intelligence-Enabled Digital Twin for Smart Manufacturing. https://doi.org/10.1002/9781394303601.ch6

Tyagi, A.K., Tiwari, S., and Naithani, K. (2024j). Blockchain, AI and IoT for smart road traffic management system. *In:* A.K. Tyagi (ed.), Digital Twin and Blockchain for Smart Cities. https://doi.org/10.1002/9781394303564.ch10

CHAPTER
15

Integrating Blockchain and Digital Twin for Secure Drug Tracking and Personalized Medication in Smart Pharma

Avinash Sharma[1(0009-0003-1192-8381)], **Garima Mathur**[2*(0000-0002-8841-3920)], **Shumali Gupta**[3] **and Priyanka Jain**[2]

[1] Department of Computer Science & Engineering, Oriental College of Technology, Bhopal
[2] Department of Computer Science & Engineering with Cyber Security, Sagar Institute of Science & Technology, Bhopal
[3] Department of Computer Science & Engineering, Sagar Institute of Science & Technology, Bhopal

1. Introduction

Overview: In today's modern world, every individual deserves access to the best healthcare services and their basic fundamental right. As more and more new diseases are identified globally each day, a multitude of drugs with different names and labels are released onto the market. These drugs give the sufferer a brief reprieve from excruciating agony. These medications have many drawbacks rather than advantages, as the authenticity of the manufacturing organizations is ambiguous, unregistered, and deviates from established guidelines. According to WHO (Abbas et al., 2020; Harris et al., 2009), the use of these fake or substandard drugs is blamed for numerous deaths in underdeveloped nations, with children being the primary victims.

According to the data, US pharmaceutical businesses report a yearly loss of over $200 billion because of these counterfeit pharmaceuticals (Williams and McKnight, 2014). In addition to having numerous harmful side effects, these fraudulent pharmaceuticals might not support the patient's recovery from their illnesses. These

*Corresponding author: garimamathur@sistec.ac.in

DOI: 10.1201/9781003676812-15

medications are hazardous to public health. It is challenging to identify these counterfeit medications since they are distributed over several intricate networks. About 25% of the US government's $3.2 trillion budget, which is allotted to the healthcare industry, is used exclusively to manage safe supply chain procedures (Metcalf et al., 2019; Akunyili et al., 2004). Several professional opinions and recommendations have been made to address and prevent the problems caused by counterfeit drugs. Those suggestions include improved handling of supply chains and drug delivery, improved management and oversight of the drug market at the pharmacy and distributor, and making use of the most recent innovations to constantly observe drugs at every step of the supply chain (Dégardin et al., 2014; Blackstone et al., 2014).

Given the considerations, safe medication supply chain management is critical to avert this problem. The most effective solution to this issue is one that can trace and monitor the supply of pharmaceuticals at every stage, including the manufacturing of products, the distribution stage, the pharmacy, clinics, and consumers. This will help prevent the use of counterfeit drugs. Furthermore, Blockchain is the new cutting edge technological innovation that can manage the supply chain and track the products. Blockchain technology effectively tracks deliveries and secures supply chain operations (Khatoon et al., 2020; Soundarya et al., 2018).

Motivation and Objective: This paper introduces blockchain technology for secure medicine supply chain management utilizing the Hyperledger Fabric. To address counterfeiting, it can continuously track and monitor the drug distribution process. In addition to finding a solution for safe medication distribution, the objective is to give users the best medication possible. We created an AI-based system for drug recommendations based on a previously gathered dataset of feedback from consumers. Data was gathered from online sources, including user comments and opinions, and subsequently categorized based on the health conditions of the users.

Additionally, N-gram and LightGBM, training of two machine learning models, is done using that dataset to suggest the potential medications to system users. In a nutshell, our suggested system operates like this: We began by developing a new drug supply chain system using blockchain technology. Participants in the drug delivery smart pharmaceutical network, including suppliers, manufacturers, distributors, pharmacies, hospitals, and clinics, use the blockchain network to store and share information efficiently and securely. The system provides a user-friendly web interface for managing and tracking drugs. Furthermore, web apps connect to the blockchain network through the Hyperledger Composer REST API. By establishing the protocols in the access control policy and history, the suggested method accomplishes the verification and authentication of transaction requests.

Couch-DB is the finest solution to the data redundancy issue and offers distinct storage for every blockchain network node. It is utilized in this work to store a large number of transaction records. The finished solution gives users, including patients, the potential to authentically trace the origin of the medication. Our system's additional benefit is that, by using the algorithms based on machine learning, it can suggest the greatest and highest-rated medications to its users. Moreover, the blockchain network and the machine learning module are connected, allowing users of the proposed system to take advantage of both characteristics simultaneously.

Following that, the models can also be trained using the feedback and evaluations client web application provides, updating the recommendation outcomes.

Chapter's Organization: This chapter is structured to provide a clear and progressive understanding of the proposed solution.

Section 2 offers a foundational discussion on blockchain, detailing its underlying structure, operational framework, and the cryptographic principles that ensure its integrity. Section 3 delves into the use of blockchain within healthcare settings, emphasizing its role in maintaining the accuracy and reliability of pharmaceutical data and supporting patient-centered care. Section 4 outlines the architecture and development of the suggested drug supply chain and personalized recommendation platform, which integrates blockchain and machine learning technologies. Section 5 surveys prior research in this area, highlighting current contributions and pinpointing critical research gaps, particularly in the context of secure and intelligent healthcare systems. Section 6 explains how smart contracts are embedded within the system to automate processes, manage permissions, and maintain transparency. Section 7 discusses the application of blockchain in protecting digital twin data, with a specific focus on ensuring secure and accurate information in pharmaceutical operations. Section 8 concludes the work and suggests avenues for future enhancements, especially in areas such as performance optimization and advanced analytics for decision-making in healthcare.

2. Overview of Blockchain Technology

The term "blockchain" describes a data-linked list that is encrypted using a fixed key size of 256 and the standard cryptographic hash algorithm; each block's hash value is stored with its data in the subsequent block (Mathur et al., 2024; Mathur et al., 2024). A secure hash protects the previous block, which is referred to by each new block that is made and is placed at the end of the linked list that has been created (Sleiman et al., 2015; Khan et al., 2018). The blocks in the entire blockchain are spread out and stored peer-to-peer. Figure 1 illustrates the blockchain technique in its entirety. For encryption and decryption, each block contains a symmetric and an asymmetric key Mathur, Garima et al., 2020). Only the encryption method used to encrypt the message can be used to decrypt it. This will facilitate the development of immutability and dependable behavior (Zheng et al., 2017). The term "asymmetric cryptography" refers to this.

The key feature of blockchain technology that ensures data integrity is immutability. If someone could realize that they can't tamper with an organization's accounts and that many crimes could be avoided simply because of the blockchain's cryptographic hash, we can only imagine the positive impact it could have on payment systems. The definition of hashing is taking an arbitrary-length information string and returning a fixed-length result. A hashing algorithm for cryptocurrencies like Bitcoin generates a fixed-length response that accepts transactions as input. Internally, blockchain technology utilizes SHA 256 to generate hash values (Wang et al., 2019).

Across a network of computers, transactions can be securely, transparently, and impenetrably recorded thanks to blockchain technology, a decentralized and distributed ledger. The three main tenets of the blockchain are immutability (data cannot be changed once recorded), transparency (all parties can see the transactions), and security.

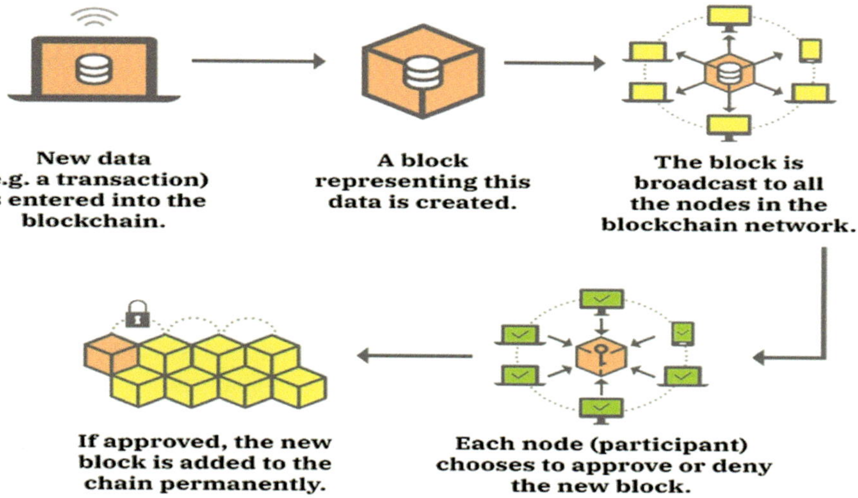

Figure 1: Process of blockchain.

We believe that implementing a framework supported by blockchain technology is the most efficient way to ensure the data integrity of the system that enables the transfer of healthcare data. This is due to the robust built-in security in blockchain technology that makes it impossible to tamper with data. This is all due to the technology's distributed nature and immutability that powers blockchain. The immutability and decentralized structure of the blockchain are likely to be the two most important factors in the development of this trend. The main approach of this research is to determine how to use blockchain technology to protect EHRs and ensure the security of cloud-based EHR data sharing and storage. This study's secondary goal is to determine how to improve healthcare using blockchain technology, which is related to the primary goal.

To generate hash values, the SHA256 algorithm and the POS consensus technique are both used. Furthermore, the Elliptic Curve Digital Signature Algorithm (ECDSA) is used to validate the records and ensure the accuracy of the data. When we are finished collecting data with a sensor, we store it in a database hosted in the cloud to protect it from prying eyes. We use a JavaScript class to provide a sophisticated method of protecting patient data that is available to both users and administrators. This method works for both categories. Before this can happen, the "nmp module" must be turned on. This module makes sure that only reliable data is sent from one node to another. The results of the evaluation show that the proposed structure for storing and exchanging electronic health records does not put data integrity at risk in any way.

Features of Blockchain: Some of the well-known features of blockchain are:

- **Data Integrity:** Data integrity is greatly improved by blockchain technology. Once a data-containing block is uploaded to the blockchain, it can only be amended with the agreement of all contributing nodes, making modifications that are not authorized quite impossible.
- **Decentralization and Transparency:** All transactions on the blockchain are transparent and verifiable by all users, and their decentralized structure guarantees that no single party has power over the entire network. This characteristic can promote mutual trust and cooperation among bioinformatics stakeholders.
- **Security Enhancement:** Data is shielded from fraud, manipulation, and unwanted access by the cryptographic encryption built into blockchain technology. This functionality has significance for databases of bioinformatics that handle sensitive medical data.
- **Better Interoperability:** In the field of bioinformatics, blockchain can greatly enhance interoperability across various databases and systems, promoting improved data exchange and cooperative research initiatives.
- **Audit Trails:** Because blockchain is immutable, every transaction has a verifiable audit trail. This is very helpful in biology for tracking changes to data and making sure regulations are followed.
- Blockchain-based smart contracts can reduce manual intervention and human error by automating several bioinformatics database operations, including data verification, access control, and protocol execution.
- **Impact on Stakeholders:** The use of blockchain technology will undoubtedly have an impact on stakeholders, as it will challenge established professional health record systems for managing data and call for modifications to workflows and operations.
- **Permissioned Blockchains:** Bioinformatics databases can be made safe and secure for data sharing and collaboration by implementing permissioned blockchains, in which only authorized parties can participate.

3. Blockchain Application

Researchers and industry professionals are interested in blockchain technology. A blockchain, to put it briefly, is an encrypted hash association and time-stamp-sealed publicly accessible ledger that is unchangeable (Zhang et al., 2018; Singh et al., 2016). Transaction activities can be facilitated without the requirement for a trusted third party because of its decentralized architecture, encryption algorithm, accountability, smart contracts, and resistance to manipulation (Holbl et al., 2018). To begin with, a blockchain uses a timestamp technique to allow tracing of data and verification, which provides a transparent and secure means of tracing an asset's possession before and throughout an activity (Chris et al., 2016).

Second, all participants can log and save data simultaneously thanks to the open-source sharing protocols integrated into the blockchain, guaranteeing that the recorded transactions are immutable in the past without the network's consent (Paul et al., 2014; Wang and Liu, 2015). Finally, a blockchain's decentralized architecture and governance make it very fault-tolerant and impervious to conspiratorial attacks. Additionally, a blockchain can safeguard users' privacy by utilizing asymmetric encryption, which allows data encryption using a private key, and cryptographic hash functions (Zyskind et al., 2015; Kosba et al., 2016; Meiklejohn et al., 2015).

Therefore, a blockchain offers a new means of addressing the challenges that occur in the building of large genomics data systems. It has the potential to enhance a big data platform for genomics in three different ways. A few use cases regarding healthcare in blockchain are described below (Figure 2).

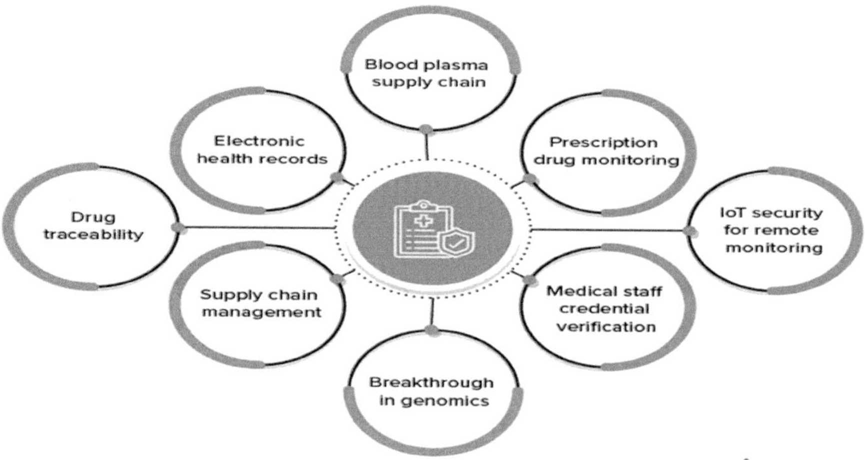

Figure 2: Application of blockchain in healthcare.

Data Ownership Enhanced by Traceability: The capacity to confirm a product's background, whereabouts, or intended application using official records of identification is known as traceability (Kim and Laskowski, 2018). Blockchain completely stores the whole process from initial generation of data to final storage by using timestamp technology to ensure data authenticity and validity (Lim et al., 2018). As a result, in blockchain, every bit of data may be identified as belonging to the specific data producer of generation, and the holding of the data can be independently verified using the record.

Smart Contracts and Anti-tampering Strengthen Data Sharing: The automated agreement consists of protocols that provide automatic communication between its parties. Any node can alter any record on the blockchain (Christidis et al., 2016). The antitampering function aids in implementing access and safeguarding the integrity of the data, hence guaranteeing the functioning of the agreement. The automated agreement code enables, validates, and regulates the bargaining and execution of an agreement or transaction (Li et al., 2017; Shabani et al., 2019; Xia et al., 2017). Therefore, the data-sharing mechanism may be reinforced by employing these two blockchain properties, encouraging users to give data for outside benefits.

Protection of Data and Privacy is enhanced by Decentralization and Encryption Algorithms: Trust is built, security concerns are decreased, and data is managed with the use of decentralized storage (Jin et al., 2019). One element of the security of digital data movement is a ciphered algorithm. Data security and privacy are robustly guaranteed by the blockchain encryption method (Kuo et al., 2017). For instance, Sun et al. (2018) suggested using blockchain technology to safeguard data confidentiality, privacy, and intellectual property in online education.

4. Application of Drug Management System in Smart Pharma

The pharmaceutical industry's medicine supply chain is now more secure and private thanks to blockchain technology's decentralized, dispersed nature. As depicted in Figure 3, the full management of the drug supply chain and recommendation (DSCMR) mechanism allows users to update and control all supply chain activities through participants and a blockchain network. Information regarding vendors, producers, traders, pharmacies, hospitals, doctors, and patients about system users is placed in the system based on blockchain. The DSCMR systems' components include raw materials, prescription drugs, orders, and record repositories. Every system user has access to a front-end built on a client application, allowing them to easily carry out transactions and interact with the blockchain network. Any relevant system participants can use the client application to monitor the medication dispatch updates during the entire DSCMR process.

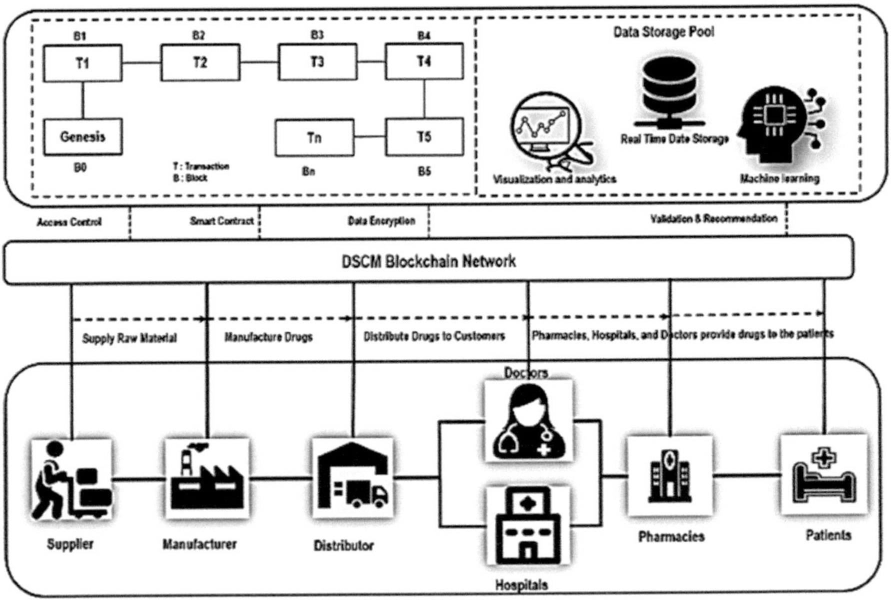

Figure 3: Drug SCM with blockchain.

Furthermore, a data storage pool contains a unique library of data called a stored-off blockchain. According to this research, the system's machine learning section should use the store-off storage pool. The algorithm that learns then advises the optimum prescription to our clients. Because of this, it's an ideal instrument for data analysis and visualization on this system and in projects involving medical institutions. Additionally, users of the system are granted authorization to view the full details of medications, raw materials, and other pertinent data, such as price, production date, expiration date, and so forth. Peer nodes in the system oversee running the agreement process to accomplish the goal of the distributed ledger's consistency. The drug firm in the system receives the basic material from the first supplier.

All the users in the system have a web portal that they may use to log in and finish a transaction. If a manufacturer places an order with a peer node in the network, the transaction can be verified. The supplier receives the order after the submitted transaction has been verified. The supplier then completes the order event confirmation when the raw material order is ready for delivery. But only if the customer thoroughly reviews a company's medical data can they perform those actions, which in the blockchain network are called permission rules.

In a different situation, a physician placing an order with a pharmaceutical company might follow the identical procedures outlined in the previously mentioned scenario and utilizing our suggested blockchain technology. First, the doctor's authentication; second, the transaction proposal is submitted; the manufacturers validate the transaction; finally, the doctor's transaction is confirmed; finally, a successful transaction updates the order status based on event message.

The distributed storing of information, where each block comprises several transactions, is the primary and most significant objective of the blockchain network. Security concerns lead to the hashing and encryption of these transactions during storage. The suggested system offers distributed ledger and smart contract functionality as a service to users using a service-oriented design. This management system and recommendation mechanism comprise the two main components of the proposed system, respectively.

The web application's front end allows end users (suppliers, distributors, pharmacies, doctors, manufacturers, and patients) to conduct transactions. They can order medications, obtain raw materials, update medication data, update, record, deliver medications, share data, track medications at every stage of supply, manage customers, and more. Preventing the sale of fake medications and giving end users access to a safe supply chain management system are the system's two main objectives. The approach we suggested is protected because it incorporates blockchain security and integrity management capabilities. Through the usage of this DSCMR system, each user can monitor the medication's distribution.

5. Related Work

Several previous studies have produced data demonstrating how blockchain technology can be used for various applications inside healthcare organizations, including the safe sharing of EHR. Several hospitals are actively collaborating on various blockchain-based research projects (Zghaibeh et al., 2020)—the advantages and use cases involved in blockchain technology in auditing, accounting, and corporate management (Secinaro et al., 2021). The researcher described the development of a piece of software known as a Healthcare Data Gateway (Kashyap et al., 2019). This platform, one of the most well-known private blockchains, aims to serve as a repository for each patient's unique medical records. This goal is specifically mentioned in the platform's white paper. Edge computing and blockchain technology are used for a distributed and cross-enterprise ecosystem to enable secure data and service exchanges between businesses. This ecosystem will be built using edge computing. Their efforts paved the way for the development of this ecosystem, which was made possible by edge computing. Researchers introduced the DASH application, which is developed with decentralized blockchain apps and is based on blockchain technology (Pandey and Litoriya, 2020). The application's major goal is to make the exchange of medical records secure and private (Nair and Bhagat, 2021; Griggs et al., 2018).

This Ethereum-based approach will use sensors to provide safe patient monitoring even for patients who live in remote areas. The notion of personal health records, or PHRs, which are based on open-source blockchain technology. Patients and doctors can swiftly exchange medical histories using this technology. A blockchain-powered, cloud-hosted app for managing and sharing individual patients' medical records (Mohanakurup et al., 2022). This application allows patients' medical records to be shared and stored. The same methodology was used to create this application. Within the framework of this system, patients have the authority to check their medical status, as well as the ability to interact with and exert control over those records. In the type of commercial transaction being discussed here, neither party is required to use the services of a middleman or any other type of intermediary. Researchers (Agrawal et al., 2022) describe how they built a blockchain-based artificial intelligence system. Medical professionals would be able to assess the overall effectiveness of patient care if they allowed them to choose their course of treatment. Patients would be able to choose their treatment options, the architecture that is now known as MedChain to ensure the confidentiality of patient records transmitted during consultations. Cryptography and blockchain technology, among other things, were incorporated into the architecture's design.

Any mechanism designed to ensure the secure transmission of patient medical records or other personally identifiable health information over an electronic network should prioritize the protection of patients' confidentiality. This should be the case regardless of the mechanism's specific function. This is because healthcare systems large storage of personally identifiable information (PII), which allows patients to be linked to records that are specific to them. Depending on the circumstances, different methods may be used to accomplish this. Because they were concerned about the security and personal health information of patients' during electronic data exchange argued in favor of using an attribute-based signature in conjunction with an MA-ABS system. This would ensure the data's confidentiality and security. By doing so, the data's privacy would be protected, and the information would not become public. The privacy of the information would be protected if the information was kept confidential and not made public. A DermoNet architecture to assist people with skin issues and keep track of those people. A decentralized system designed to protect patients undergoing medical procedures. The primary goal of this process, which incorporates blockchain decentralized ledger methodology is to protect patients.

Patients' medical history and prescriptions may be stored in one location on the internet storing and transferring data is secure and efficient for blockchain-based mobile-edge computing. The approach uses a plan that includes sharing private signature keys to make cloud data and backups exist in the real world. Using ECDSA, the researcher (Xiong et al., 2021) presented a method for efficient batch verification on a large scale, and described a non-replicable authentication mechanism based on blockchain technology. Their goal was to safeguard WMSNs against security faults and vulnerabilities. A revolutionary method for ensuring the protection and integrity of IIOT data applying blockchain without the use of pairings or certificates. This plan was developed to assure security and accuracy of IIOT data. This strategy marked a significant improvement in the overall state of the field. A comprehensive study of the potential use cases of blockchain in various industries, with emphasis on the data security it provides. A growing body of literature emphasizes the importance of further research into the potential applications of blockchain technology in healthcare system management.

There are an increasing number of these articles available online. Additional applications for blockchain technology in oncology and biomedical research include the storage of DNA, the detection of fraud in healthcare insurance, the tracking of medications to prevent the sale of counterfeit drugs, and the management of the pharmaceutical supply chain. Leaders in the healthcare sector must capitalize on these challenges, despite their magnitude, if they are to improve the dependability of EHRs and system integration (Aggarwal et al., 2019). Following a thorough summary of the relevant literature, we concluded that most of the previously published research on EHR management using blockchain focuses on theoretical frameworks or models. This is consistent with the findings of our investigation. Technical details are lacking, and the frameworks currently in place for using blockchain in healthcare have issues with data security, bandwidth, immaturity, and privacy. Furthermore, there is no consensus on how to use blockchain in healthcare. Furthermore, different people have different ideas about how to use blockchain technology. This is because older algorithms, such as POW, MD5, and SHA-1, require more resources to run, are more expensive, and provide a lower level of security.

In recent years, "blockchain technology" has gained popularity among the supporters of smart healthcare. Various research articles have surveyed how blockchain technology can be applied in this field (Aggarwal et al., 2019; Andoni et al., 2019), exploring various phases of healthcare, like home healthcare transactions' integration and distribution of various investments. There are many potential applications for the blockchain that a smart home industry possesses.

Andoni et al. (2019) explained an analysis of various blockchain use cases of a P2P resource-sharing network (Li et al., 2020). Their reports give us very detailed and in-depth information about the abilities and deployment of various smart home networks, like analysis of big data, and payment services related to AI security issues related to the smart grid. After all these analyses, they just concluded that all the surveys and studies did not consider challenges related to smart cities' financial planning, smart homes, and their security.

Li et al. (2020) explained a structure related to blockchain that will confirm the safety of communicated information in the IoT-based structures related to users. Various surveys regarding blockchain techniques have been conducted by Zhou et al. (2021). They worked on decentralized computing and pre-determined investigation to relocate control over automobiles. By performing these tasks, the effectiveness of automobiles also increases.

A comprehensive study has been proposed by Du et al. (2021) (Ihnaini et al., 2021), which focuses on goals related to investigating the implementation of blockchain technology. They did this implementation in various areas, like as the development of conceptual approaches for smart care applications, smart healthcare, and blockchain impact on healthcare. They then developed an application framework based on stakeholders for smart healthcare.

Ihnaini et al. (2021) provided a disease detection method that was basically for smart diabetics. This method was based on the combination of information fusion concepts with deep machine learning. The combination of these two concepts results in the reduction of unwanted load on the computing resources of the system. This, in turn, also improves the proposed system's efficiency. Finally, a diabetes prediction model is developed by combining the machine learning approaches.

In today's world, data exchange can be easily done among multiple networks. This exchange helps organizations and experts make the best and most effective use of the existing capabilities. This also helps us in meeting the medical demands of society. By using IoT, strong and efficient healthcare services can be accessed by users. To monitor community healthcare demands, various sensors can be utilized. For tracking body functions, different wearable devices can be employed. These devices can be integrated for various purposes, like as monitoring the bodily systems. This integration helps us ensure that medical facilities reach all such type of people who needs them. For the effective prediction of these diseases, the collected data can be pooled, mined, and examined (Khan et al., 2021).

Khan et al. [J. Xu, B.S. Glicksberg, C. Su, P. Walker, J. Bian, F. et al. 2021] discussed the various healthcare facilities related to senior citizens. These healthcare facilities mainly focus on various problems and needs of the senior citizens. Various machine-learning approaches are used by the researchers to ensure better safety.

Xu et al. (Y. Li, B. Shan, B. Li, X. Liu, Y. Pu et al. 2021] suggested an overview related to various federated learning techniques. They mainly focused on techniques that are used in biomedicine. They have also surveyed, focused, and reviewed various solutions related to privacy concerns and statistical challenges.

Siddiqui et al. (2021) suggested an overview related to applications of various bioinformatics and machine learning technologies in the preview of Web of Science (WOS) and utilization of bibliometric visualization in the smart medical business.

A survey has been conducted which mainly focuses on those countries which are involved in most of the research, with here emphasis on research difficulties and objectives related to deep learning and machine learning techniques that are used in healthcare industries. Siddiqui et al. (2021) (Medjahed et al., 2011) for predicting breast cancer suggested a technique that was based on a DL-based data fusion model.

To improve the accuracy of the proposed methodology, they have applied a decision-based fusion technique.

An automated medical surveillance system built on a data fusion methodology was proposed by Medjahed et al. (2011). Their suggested approach is predicated on a multi-sensor framework that provides complete management over smart homes. Since the development of AI, various AI-based applications have been used to diagnose various diseases and minimize patient treatment time. With the advancement in the use of AI, improvement in disease prognosis also increases.

Dai et al. (2010) worked on supervised classification by transforming the challenges related to hospitalization forecasting. This also increases the savings related to medical expenses (Son et al., 2010; Tariq et al., 2021) suggested a mechanism for determining various complications related to drugs affecting the heart by using the SVM algorithm. The author suggested a heterogeneous fusion AI-related method by using historical medical information to predict the intensity of COVID-19 (Sedik et al., 2020).

A methodology related to feature extraction has been suggested by Sedik et al. (Qayyum et al., 2021) to increase the information related to CNN. For identifying

Table 1: Summary of Existing Work

S. No.	Year	Description	Limitations
1	2020	Zghaibeh et al. proposed a blockchain-based health system with smart contracts	Focused on EHR sharing, not on the drug supply chain or the recommendation system
2	2019	Kashyap et al. developed a Healthcare Data Gateway	Lacks integration with AI/ML for personalized drug recommendation
3	2020	Pandey and Litoriya built DASH app for private data sharing	No mechanism for traceability in the drug supply chain
4	2021	Agrawal et al. proposed AI-integrated MedChain system	No blockchain-backed feedback loop or user-specific recommendation
5	2021	Xiong et al. used ECDSA for fault-tolerant batch verification	Does not provide a drug distribution or patient interface
6	2021	Ihnaini et al. developed ML model for smart diabetes prediction	Lacks blockchain-based security for supply or recommendation
7	2020	Sedik et al. used DL for COVID-19 detection	Did not integrate blockchain or ensure data integrity
8	2018	Griggs et al. used smart contracts for remote monitoring	Limited to patient monitoring, lacks supply chain traceability
9	2021	Chang et al. proposed FL + Blockchain for smart healthcare	No application to pharmaceutical delivery or recommendation
10	2015	Dai et al. used ML for hospitalization prediction	No use of blockchain for drug validation or provenance

coronavirus, a convolutional long short-term memory algorithm has been used. To process medical visual data and enable remote infirmaries (Qayyum et al., 2018) provided a cluster FL-based method was provided. They did it from multimodal information to maintain confidentiality.

For smart healthcare, a blockchain federated learning-based approach has been suggested by Chang et al. (2021). According to their suggestions, to complete the use of the dispersed healthcare information, federal learning has been applied by MIoT devices, and to avoid data loss, edge nodes have adopted the blockchain. Various research and surveys related to federal learning in healthcare have been published and conducted.

Alam, Batra, and Dasgupta (2024), in their study propose a secure architecture for industrial digital twins using blockchain to ensure data immutability, privacy, and decentralized validation. They present a hybrid approach combining blockchain and federated learning to strengthen real-time data synchronization and access control in digital twin systems. The summary of the existing work done in this field is shown in Table 1.

6. Smart Contracts

A smart contract can be defined as an agreement that gives parties an open, conflict-free means of exchanging assets, cash, stock, or anything else without the need for an intermediary broker or agent. The blockchain platform's greatest attribute is this. In theory, a smart contract is just a few lines of computer code that, when executed, enforces an agreement between two parties without requiring payment to an intermediary. This code is a predetermined set of guidelines that all parties concur upon. This contract is automatically triggered when the given condition is satisfied and database events occur.

A smart contract can be defined as an agreement that gives parties an open, conflict-free means of exchanging assets, cash, stock, or anything else without the need for an intermediary broker or agent. The blockchain platform's greatest attribute is this. In theory, a smart contract is just a few lines of computer code that, when executed, enforces an agreement between two parties without requiring payment to an intermediary. This code is a predetermined set of guidelines that all parties concur upon. When the given condition is satisfied and database events occur, this contract is automatically triggered.

Developing smart contracts presents several significant unresolved issues, including the following: Solidity is an entirely novel programming language that is utilized in the method, which makes it difficult to learn and maintain. Furthermore, because transactions are carried out between all of the network's peer nodes either sequentially or regularly, they execute slowly and take longer to finish. By selective deployment of the smart contract for a designated node and not for all nodes in the network, we can get around this problem. As a result, a predetermined number of nodes can validate the transactions, and the suggested system's execution performance is significantly improved.

In addition, we wrote smart contract code using the well-known programming languages Java and Node. JS. Developers may write business logic in various

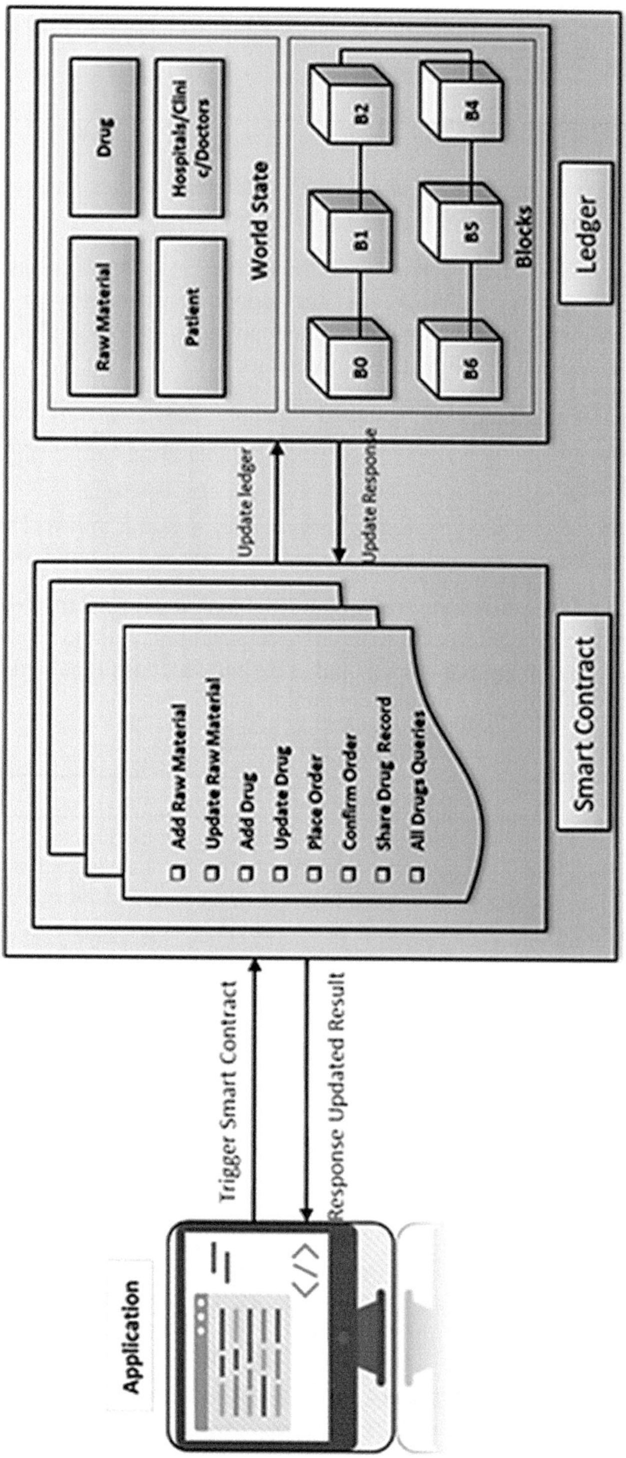

Figure 4. Smart contract-based system.

programming languages with ease. Figure 4 illustrates how a smart contract is executed using a ledger.

7. Identified Research Gaps

Some of the research gaps identified when the literature studies have been done, a summary of these gaps can be found in Table 2.

Lack of Integration Between Blockchain and AI in Healthcare: Most existing literature focuses on blockchain for supply chain security or AI for drug recommendation. Very few integrate both technologies into a unified system for secure drug delivery and intelligent recommendation.

Insufficient Real-Time Tracking Systems: Current supply chain solutions lack real-time, transparent, and tamper-proof tracking mechanisms to counteract counterfeit medicines effectively.

Overreliance on Centralized Systems: Previous healthcare frameworks suffer from centralization, making them vulnerable to data breaches and manipulation.

Limited Practical Deployment and Technical Implementation: Many studies focus on theoretical frameworks without implementing full-stack systems that include smart contracts, access control, and real-time feedback mechanisms.

Table 2: Research Gaps

S. No.	Identified Gap	Description
1	Fragmented Technology Use	Existing works often focus on isolated solutions such as supply chain security or recommendation systems, rather than a comprehensive, integrated platform.
2	Lack of Real-Time Visibility	Present systems do not offer transparent, tamper-resistant mechanisms for live tracking, limiting their ability to prevent counterfeit drugs effectively.
3	Centralized System Vulnerability	Many healthcare frameworks rely on central storage and processing, increasing the risk of unauthorized access or data manipulation.
4	Theoretical Focus with Limited Deployment	Numerous studies remain at the conceptual level without offering a complete, deployable architecture that includes key components like smart contracts and feedback handling.
5	Use of Outdated Security Algorithms	Older cryptographic methods with higher resource demands and reduced efficiency are still being used, which may not be suitable for sensitive health-related data.
6	Static Recommendation Approaches	Drug recommendation techniques often fail to incorporate ongoing user feedback or dynamic health data, limiting their adaptability and relevance.

Resource-Intensive Legacy Algorithms: Existing blockchain models use older algorithms like PoW, MD5, or SHA-1, which are inefficient for healthcare data due to high computational overhead and lower security compared to newer mechanisms like SHA-256 and ECDSA.

Lack of Feedback-Driven Recommendations: Most drug recommendation systems do not adapt based on continuous user feedback and updated health data.

8. Blockchain for Securing Digital Twin Data

Integrating blockchain technology with digital twin systems has emerged as a robust approach to addressing the pressing concerns of data integrity, traceability, and security (Figure 5). A digital twin, essentially a virtual representation of a physical entity, functions by continuously receiving real-time data from IoT-enabled sensors and devices. This data is critical to simulate, predict, and analyze the behavior or performance of the physical asset. However, as digital twins are increasingly applied in sensitive sectors such as healthcare, manufacturing, and pharmaceuticals, ensuring the confidentiality, accuracy, and immutability of transmitted and stored data becomes paramount.

Blockchain, as a decentralized and immutable ledger system, offers a secure foundation for recording every interaction and data exchange between the physical system and its digital counterpart, as described in Table 3. When implemented alongside digital twin systems, blockchain records each data input or system event as a time-stamped transaction block. These records are distributed across peer nodes, ensuring that no single entity can manipulate or erase data without network consensus. This eliminates the risk of unauthorized access, tampering, or data loss, which are common vulnerabilities in traditional centralized architectures.

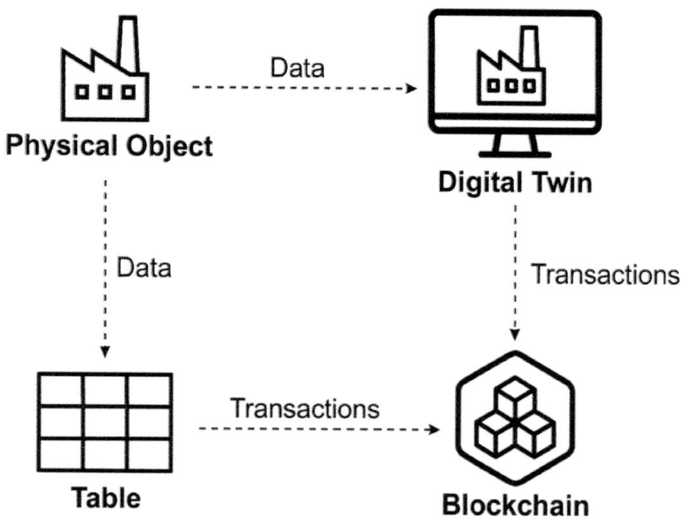

Figure 5: Blockchain securing digital twin data.

Table 3: Blockchain Digital Twin

S. No.	Aspect	Description
1	Digital Twin Role	A digital twin is a real-time virtual model of a physical asset, relying on data from IoT sensors to simulate and monitor performance or conditions.
2	Blockchain Integration	Blockchain secures digital twin data by recording each transaction or event in a tamper-proof, time-stamped, decentralized ledger.
3	Use Case – Pharmaceuticals	In vaccine logistics, digital twins track temperature; blockchain records each reading, preventing data manipulation and enabling full traceability.
4	Benefits of Integration	Offers secure, transparent, and auditable data management, improves trust, and protects sensitive operations from unauthorized access or loss.

For instance, in a pharmaceutical supply chain scenario, a digital twin may monitor environmental factors such as temperature or humidity for a batch of vaccines during transportation. By embedding blockchain into this system, each parameter reading is recorded on a distributed ledger, ensuring that the vaccine's storage conditions can be audited retrospectively without risk of alteration. If a deviation occurs, such as exposure to temperatures beyond permissible thresholds, the blockchain ledger immediately flags the incident, supporting transparency and accountability.

Moreover, blockchain ensures traceability by linking each component of a digital twin's dataset to its origin. This is particularly valuable when integrating data from multiple sources or stakeholders. Access control can be managed via smart contracts that define who can read or write to specific segments of the ledger, maintaining both openness and confidentiality based on stakeholder roles.

The combination of blockchain with digital twins creates a resilient infrastructure that ensures the secure, transparent, and auditable management of digital data. This union not only reinforces the credibility of simulations and predictions derived from the digital twin but also strengthens stakeholder trust in high-stakes sectors like healthcare, logistics, and industrial manufacturing.

9. Conclusion and Future Work

This research illustrates how the convergence of blockchain and machine learning can address critical challenges in pharmaceutical supply chain management and drug recommendation systems. The proposed solution ensures end-to-end traceability of medication, protects against data tampering, and delivers personalized drug recommendations based on user health profiles and feedback.

The integration of digital twin principles secured by blockchain offers a new layer of real-time monitoring and control, particularly valuable in tracking storage conditions for temperature-sensitive pharmaceuticals. The use of Hyperledger Fabric, coupled with REST APIs, CouchDB, and smart contracts, delivers a scalable, modular, and secure platform for smart pharma applications. This integrated approach opens new avenues for trustworthy and intelligent healthcare systems and sets a foundation for next-generation secure drug distribution frameworks powered by decentralized technologies.

Adoption of Blockchain for Enhanced Drug Traceability:

- Pharmaceutical companies should implement blockchain-based solutions to trace the origin and movement of drugs through the entire supply chain, from raw materials to the end consumer. This can drastically reduce the risk of counterfeit medications infiltrating the market, ensuring product authenticity and safety.
- Regulatory bodies could mandate the use of blockchain systems for real-time tracking, especially for critical drugs like vaccines and essential medicines prone to counterfeiting.

Integration with Machine Learning for Efficient Drug Recommendations:

- Companies should integrate machine learning models, like those demonstrated in this research (e.g., LightGBM, N-gram), with blockchain data to provide personalized drug recommendations. This would enhance user trust by ensuring that recommendations are based on authenticated data sources.
- Hospitals and clinics could employ such systems to suggest the best medication based on patient history and real-time feedback, improving patient outcomes.

Scalability of Blockchain Systems in Healthcare:

- Pharmaceutical firms are encouraged to pilot blockchain systems with scalability in mind, testing them across different geographic locations. Expanding to larger, real-time networks, as suggested by the research, will help validate system reliability and throughput performance in actual pharmaceutical environments.

Collaboration with Regulatory Authorities:

- Collaboration with healthcare regulatory authorities is essential for blockchain adoption. A standardized blockchain framework could be established, helping pharmaceutical firms align their blockchain systems with national and international regulations.
- Implementing smart contracts on blockchain for supply chain compliance ensures that pharmaceutical companies meet all necessary legal requirements without human error.

Future Research Directions:

- Future efforts should focus on improving the precision of machine learning models integrated into blockchain systems, as this study recommends. Enhanced models would provide more accurate drug suggestions based on evolving datasets collected from real-world user interactions.
- Continued evaluation of blockchain's performance in diverse environments will ensure that companies can make informed decisions about its long-term feasibility and profitability.
- Enhancing the learning model with federated learning to preserve data privacy across healthcare entities.
- Expanding the digital twin framework to include real-time physiological monitoring for critical care applications.

- Conducting longitudinal studies and real-world deployments to validate system performance under high transaction volumes.

Following these steps, pharmaceutical companies can address counterfeit drug challenges more effectively and improve operational efficiency. This also sets a path for more research and industry adoption of blockchain in healthcare and expands the digital twin framework to include real-time physiological monitoring for critical care applications.

References

Abbas, K., Afaq, M., Ahmed Khan, T., and Song, W.-C. (2020). A blockchain and machine learning-based drug supply chain management and recommendation system for the smart pharmaceutical industry. Electronics, 9(5), 852. https://doi.org/10.3390/electronics9050852

Aggarwal, S., Chaudhary, R., Aujla, G.S., Kumar, N., Choo, K.K.R., and Zomaya, A.Y. (2019). Blockchain for smart communities: Applications, challenges, and opportunities. Journal of Network and Computer Applications, 144, 13–48. https://doi.org/10.1016/j.jnca.2019.06.018

Agrawal, M., Shukla, P.K., Nair, R., Nayyar, A., and Masud, M. (2022). Stock prediction based on technical indicators using deep learning model. Computers, Materials & Continua, 70(1), 287–304. https://doi.org/10.32604/cmc.2022.014637

Akunyili, D. (2004). Fake and counterfeit drugs in the health sector: The role of medical doctors. Annals of Ibadan Postgraduate Medicine, 2(1), 19–23.

Alam, M., Batra, R., and Dasgupta, D. (2024). Enhancing data security and privacy in digital twins through blockchain and federated learning. IEEE Internet of Things Journal, 11(3), 2045–2058.

Andoni, M., Robu, V., Flynn, D., Abram, S., Geach, D., Jenkins, D. et al. (2019). Blockchain technology in the energy sector: A systematic review of challenges and opportunities. Renewable and Sustainable Energy Reviews, 100, 143–174. https://doi.org/10.1016/j.rser.2018.10.014

Blackstone, E.A., Fuhr, J.P. Jr., and Pociask, S. (2014). The health and economic effects of counterfeit drugs. *American Health & Drug Benefits, 7*(4), 216–224.

Chang, Y., Fang, C., Sun, W., Chen, T., and He, X. (2021). A blockchain-based federated learning method for smart healthcare. Computational Intelligence and Neuroscience, 2021, Article 4376418. https://doi.org/10.1155/2021/4376418.

Chris, G., and Alos, D. (2016). Increasing supply chain assurance via the blockchain. Academia.edu. https://www.academia.edu/19623721/Increasing_Supply_Chain_Assurance_via_the_Blockchain

Christidis, K., and Devetsikiotis, M. (2016). Blockchains and smart contracts for the Internet of Things. IEEE Access, 4, 2292–2303. https://doi.org/10.1109/ACCESS.2016.2566339

Dai, W., Brisimi, T.S., Adams, W.G., Mela, T., Saligrama, V., and Paschalidis, I.C. (2015). Prediction of hospitalization due to heart diseases by supervised learning methods. International Journal of Medical Informatics, 84(3), 189–197. https://doi.org/10.1016/j.ijmedinf.2014.10.002

Dégardin, K., Roggo, Y., and Margot, P. (2014). Understanding and fighting the medicine counterfeit market. Journal of Pharmaceutical and Biomedical Analysis, 87, 167–175. https://doi.org/10.1016/j.jpba.2013.03.009

Du, X., Chen, B., Ma, M., and Zhang, Y. (2021). Research on the application of blockchain in smart healthcare: Constructing a hierarchical framework. Journal of Healthcare Engineering, 2021, Article 6698122. https://doi.org/10.1155/2021/6698122

Gao, Y., Zhang, T., and Xu, X. (2023). Blockchain-integrated digital twin for secure industrial applications: Architecture and case study. Journal of Industrial Information Integration, 32, 100397.

Griggs, K.N., Ossipova, O., Kohlios, C.P., Baccarini, A.N., Howson, E.A., and Hayajneh, T. (2018). Healthcare blockchain system using smart contracts for secure automated remote patient monitoring. Journal of Medical Systems, 42(1), 1–7. https://doi.org/10.1007/s10916-018-0982-x

Harris, J., Stevens, P., and Morris, J. (2009). Keeping it real: Combating the spread of fake drugs in poor countries. International Policy Network.

Hölbl, M., Kompara, M., Kamlsalić, A., and Zlatolas, L.N. (2018). A systematic review of the use of blockchain in healthcare. Symmetry, 10(470), 1–17. https://doi.org/10.3390/sym10100470

Ihnaini, B., Khan, M.A., Khan, T.A., Abbas, S., Daoud, M.S., Ahmad, M., and Khan, M.A. (2021). A smart healthcare recommendation system for multidisciplinary diabetes patients with data fusion based on deep ensemble learning. Computational Intelligence and Neuroscience, 2021, Article 4243700. https://doi.org/10.1155/2021/4243700

Jin, X.L., Zhang, M., Zhou, Z.(P.), and Yu, X. (2019). Applying blockchain platform to manage and secure personal genomic data: The case of LifeCODE.ai in China. Journal of Medical Internet Research Preprints. https://doi.org/10.2196/preprints.13587

Kashyap, R. (2019). Machine learning for Internet of Things. *In:* Advances in Wireless Technologies and Telecommunication, pp. 57–83. IGI Global. https://doi.org/10.4018/978-1-5225-7458-3.ch003

Khan, M.A. (2021). Challenges facing the application of IoT in medicine and healthcare. International Journal of Computer Integrated Manufacturing, 1(1). https://doi.org/10.54489/ijcim.v1i1.32

Khan, M.A., and Salah, K. (2018). IoT security: Review, blockchain solutions, and open challenges. Future Generation Computer Systems, 82, 395–411. https://doi.org/10.1016/j.future.2017.11.022

Khan, M.F., Ghazal, T.M., Said, R.A., Fatima, A., Abbas, S., Ahmad, M., and Khan, M.A. (2021). An IoMT-enabled smart healthcare model to monitor elderly people using machine learning techniques. Computational Intelligence and Neuroscience, 2021, Article 2487759. https://doi.org/10.1155/2021/2487759

Khatoon, A. (2020). A blockchain-based smart contract system for healthcare management. Electronics, 9(1), 94. https://doi.org/10.3390/electronics9010094

Kim, H.M., and Laskowski, M. (2018). Toward an ontology-driven blockchain design for supply-chain provenance. Intelligent Systems in Accounting, Finance, and Management, 25(1), 18–27. https://doi.org/10.1002/isaf.1424

Kosba, A., Miller, A., Shi, E., Wen, Z., and Papamanthou, C. (2016). Hawk: The blockchain model of cryptography and privacy-preserving smart contracts. *In:* Proceedings of the 2016 IEEE Symposium on security and Privacy (SP), pp. 839–858. IEEE. https://doi.org/10.1109/SP.2016.55

Kuo, T.T., Kim, H.E., and Ohno-Machado, L. (2017). Blockchain distributed ledger technologies for biomedical and health care applications. Journal of the American Medical Informatics Association, 24(6), 1211–1220. https://doi.org/10.1093/jamia/ocx068

Li, G., Dong, M., Yang, L.T., Ota, K., Wu, J., and Li, J. (2020). Preserving edge knowledge sharing among IoT services: A blockchain-based approach. IEEE Transactions on Emerging Topics in Computational Intelligence, 4(5), 653–665. https://doi.org/10.1109/TETCI.2019.2952587

Li, Y., Huang, J.Q., Shengzhi, Q.Z., and Ruijin, W. (2017). Big data model of security sharing based on blockchain. *In:* Proceedings of the 2017 3rd International Conference on big data computing and Communications (BIGCOM), pp. 117–121. IEEE. https://doi.org/10.1109/BIGCOM.2017.16

Li, Y., Shan, B., Li, B., Liu, X., and Pu, Y. (2021). Literature review on the applications of machine learning and blockchain technology in the smart healthcare industry: A bibliometric analysis. Journal of Healthcare Engineering, 2021, Article 9739219. https://doi.org/10.1155/2021/9739219

Lim, S.Y., Fotsing, P.T., Almasri, A., Musa, O., Kiah, M.L.M., Ang, T.F.A., and Ismail, R. (2018). Blockchain technology the identity management and authentication service disruptor: A survey. International Journal on Advanced Science, Engineering, and Information Technology, 8(4), 1735–1745. https://doi.org/10.18517/ijaseit.8.4-2.6828

Mathur, G., Pandey, A., and Goyal, S. (2020). Immutable DNA sequence data transmission for next generation bioinformatics using blockchain technology. *In:* Proceedings of the 2nd International Conference on Data, Engineering and Applications (IDEA), pp. 1–6. IEEE. https://doi.org/10.1109/IDEA49133.2020.9170757

Mathur, G., Pandey, A., and Goyal, S. (2024). A review on blockchain for DNA sequence: Security issues, application in DNA classification, challenges, and future trends. Multimedia Tools and Applications, 1–23. https://doi.org/10.1007/s11042-023-15753-7

Mathur, G., Pandey, A., and Goyal, S. (2024). Blockchain solutions, challenges, and opportunities for DNA classification and secure storage for the e-healthcare sector: A useful review. *In:* Information Resources Management Association, Research Anthology on Bioinformatics, Genomics, and Computational Biology, pp. 356–377. IGI Global. https://doi.org/10.4018/979-8-3693-3026-5.ch017

Medjahed, H., Istrate, D., Boudy, J., Baldinger, J.L., and Dorizzi, B. (2011). A pervasive multi-sensor data fusion for smart home healthcare monitoring. *In:* Proceedings of the 2011 IEEE International Conference on Fuzzy Systems (FUZZ-IEEE), pp. 1–6. IEEE. https://doi.org/10.1109/FUZZY.2011.6007636

Meiklejohn, S., and Orlandi, C. (2015). Privacy-enhancing overlays in Bitcoin. *In:* Proceedings of the International Conference on Financial Cryptography and Data Security, pp. 127–141). Springer. https://doi.org/10.1007/978-3-662-47854-7_9

Metcalf, D.S., Bass, J., Hooper, M., Cahana, A., and Dhillon, V. (2019). Blockchain in healthcare: Innovations that empower patients, connect professionals, and improve care. CRC Press, Taylor & Francis Group.

Mohanakurup, V., Krishnamoorthy, V., Bharathi, M., Chandran, V.D., Natarajan, A., and Ravikumar, M. (2022). Breast cancer detection on histopathological images using a composite dilated backbone network. Computational Intelligence and Neuroscience, 2022, 1–10. https://doi.org/10.1155/2022/8517706

Nair, R., and Bhagat, A. (2021). An introduction to clustering algorithms in big data. *In:* M. Khosrow-Pour (ed.), Encyclopedia of Information Science and Technology (5th ed.), pp. 559–576). IGI Global. https://doi.org/10.4018/978-1-7998-3479-3.ch040

Pandey, P., and Litoriya, R. (2020). Securing and authenticating healthcare records through blockchain technology. Cryptologia, 44(4), 341–356. https://doi.org/10.1080/01611194.2019.1706060

Paul, G., Sarkar, P., and Mukherjee, S. (2014). Towards a more democratic mining in bitcoins. *In:* Proceedings of the International Conference on Information Systems Security (ICISS), pp. 185–203. Springer. https://doi.org/10.1007/978-3-319-13841-1_12

Qayyum, A., Ahmad, K., Ahsan, M.A., Al-Fuqaha, A., and Qadir, J. (2021). Collaborative federated learning for healthcare: Multi-modal COVID-19 diagnosis at the edge. arXiv Preprint arXiv:2101.07511. https://doi.org/10.48550/arXiv.2101.07511

Secinaro, S., Dal Mas, F., Brescia, V., and Calandra, D. (2021). Blockchain in the accounting, auditing and accountability fields: A bibliometric and coding analysis. Accounting, Auditing & Accountability Journal. https://doi.org/10.1108/AAAJ-10-2020-4987

Sedik, A., Iliyasu, A.M., El-Rahiem, M.E.A., Samea, A.A., Abdel-Raheem, A., Hammad, M. et al. (2020). Deploying machine and deep learning models for efficient data-augmented detection of COVID-19 infections. Viruses, 12(7), 1–22. https://doi.org/10.3390/v12070769

Shabani, M. (2019). Blockchain-based platforms for genomic data sharing: A decentralized approach in response to the governance problems? Journal of the American Medical Informatics Association, 26(1), 76–80. https://doi.org/10.1093/jamia/ocy148

Siddiqui, S.Y., Naseer, I., Khan, M.A., Mushtaq, M.F., Naqvi, R.A., Hussain, D., and Haider, A. (2021). Intelligent breast cancer prediction empowered with fusion and deep learning. Computers, Materials & Continua, 67(3), 1–12. https://doi.org/10.32604/cmc.2021.013952

Singh, S., and Singh, N. (2016). Blockchain: Future of financial and cyber security. *In:* Proceedings of the 2nd International Conference on Contemporary Computing and Informatics (IC3I), pp. 463–467. IEEE. https://doi.org/10.1109/IC3I.2016.7918790

Sleiman, M.D., Lauf, A.P., and Yampolskiy, R. (2015). Bitcoin message: Data insertion on a proof-of-work cryptocurrency system. *In:* Proceedings of the 2015 International Conference on Cyberworlds, pp. 332–336. IEEE. https://doi.org/10.1109/CW.2015.56

Son, Y.J., Kim, H.G., Kim, E.H., Choi, S., and Lee, S.K. (2010). Application of support vector machine for prediction of medication adherence in heart failure patients. Healthcare Informatics Research, 16(4), 253–259. https://doi.org/10.4258/hir.2010.16.4.253

Soundarya, K., Pandey, P., and Dhanalakshmi, R. (2018). A counterfeit solution for pharma supply chain. EAI Endorsed Transactions on Cloud Systems, 3(10), 1–6. https://doi.org/10.4108/eai.20-12-2017.153499

Sun, H., Wang, X.Y., and Wang, X.G. (2018). Application of blockchain technology in online education. International Journal of Emerging Technologies in Learning, 13(10), 252–259. https://doi.org/10.3991/ijet.v13i10.9455

Tariq, A., Celi, L.A., Newsome, J.M., Purkayastha, S., Bhatia, N.K., Trivedi, H. et al. (2021). Patient-specific COVID-19 resource utilization prediction using fusion AI model. npj Digital Medicine, 4(1), 1–9. https://doi.org/10.1038/s41746-021-00461-0

Wang, L., and Liu, Y. (2015). Exploring miner evolution in Bitcoin network. *In:* Proceedings of the International Conference on Passive and Active Network Measurement (PAM), pp. 290–302. Springer. https://doi.org/10.1007/978-3-319-15509-8_22

Wang, L., Shen, X., Li, J., Shao, J., and Yang, Y. (2019). Cryptographic primitives in blockchains. Journal of Network and Computer Applications, 127, 43–58. https://doi.org/10.1016/j.jnca.2018.11.016

Williams, L., and McKnight, E. (2014). The real impact of counterfeit medications. US Pharmacist, 39, 44–46.

Xia, Q., Sifah, E.B., Asamoah, K.O., Gao, J., Du, X., and Guizani, M. (2017). MeDShare: Trust-less medical data sharing among cloud service providers via blockchain. IEEE Access, 5, 14757–14767. https://doi.org/10.1109/ACCESS.2017.2730843

Xiong, H., Jin, C., Alazab, M., Yeh, K.H., Wang, H., and Gadekallu, T.R.R. (2021). On the design of blockchain-based ECDSA with fault-tolerant batch verification protocol for blockchain-enabled IoMT. IEEE Journal of Biomedical and Health Informatics, 26(5), 1977–1986. https://doi.org/10.1109/JBHI.2021.3112693

Xu, J., Glicksberg, B.S., Su, C., Walker, P., Bian, J., and Wang, F. (2021). Federated learning for healthcare informatics. Journal of Healthcare Informatics Research, 5(1), 1–19. https://doi.org/10.1007/s41666-020-00082-4

Zghaibeh, M., Farooq, U., Hasan, N.U., and Baig, I. (2020). SHealth: A blockchain-based health system with smart contracts capabilities. IEEE Access, 8, 70030–70043. https://doi.org/10.1109/ACCESS.2020.2986789

Zhang, P., White, J., Schmidt, D.C., Lenz, G., and Rosenbloom, S.T. (2018). FHIRChain: Applying blockchain to securely and scalably share clinical data. Computational and Structural Biotechnology Journal, 16, 267–278. https://doi.org/10.1016/j.csbj.2018.07.004

Zheng, Z., Xie, S., Dai, H., Chen, X., and Wang, H. (2017). An overview of blockchain technology: Architecture, consensus, and future trends. *In:* Proceedings of the 2017 IEEE international congress on big data (BigData Congress), pp. 557–564. IEEE. https://doi.org/10.1109/BigDataCongress.2017.85

Zhou, Z., Wang, B., Dong, M., and Ota, K. (2020). Secure and efficient vehicle-to-grid energy trading in cyber-physical systems: Integration of blockchain and edge computing. IEEE Transactions on Systems, Man, and Cybernetics: Systems, 50(1), 43–57. https://doi.org/10.1109/TSMC.2019.2896323

Zyskind, G., Nathan, O., and Pentland, A.S. (2015). Decentralizing privacy: Using blockchain to protect personal data. *In:* Proceedings of the 2015 IEEE security and Privacy Workshops (SPW), pp. 180–184. IEEE. https://doi.org/10.1109/SPW.2015.27

CHAPTER
16

Healthcare and Pharmaceuticals Applications

Priyanga Subbiah[1*(0000-0002-2395-7492)], **Krishnaraj N.**[1(0000-0002-6961-8883)] **and R. Meera**[2(0000-0003-8163-8229)]

[1] Department of Networking and Communications, School of Computing, College of Engineering and Technology, SRM Institute of Science and Technology, Kattankulathur, Chengalpattu – 603203

[2] Department of Electronics and Communication Engineering, St.Joseph's College of Engineering and Technology, Thanjavur

1. Introduction

The healthcare and pharmaceutical sectors are presently experiencing an unparalleled transformation. This transition is pushed using the fast integration of rising technologies, which include blockchain, artificial intelligence (AI), machine learning (ML), and the Internet of Medical Things (IoMT). This alternative is not slow; rather, it represents a fundamental change in the way clinical information is controlled, healthcare services are provided, and pharmaceutical goods are developed, produced, and marketed (Polshettiwar et al., 2021). Integrating digital innovation with traditional healthcare practices is crucial to this transition. This convergence aims to remedy persistent challenges, including diagnostic mistakes, not on time remedies, inefficient supply networks, and insufficient tailor-made care. Historically, the healthcare and pharmaceutical industries have trusted human judgment, paper-based structures, and manual operations. While these strategies have been beneficial, they gradually fall short of the demands of a data-wealthy environment that requires precision. Artificial intelligence (AI) and machine learning (ML) have advanced into powerful technology adept at evaluating large datasets, uncovering concealed patterns, and producing correct predictions with splendid velocity and precision. These skills are hired across numerous domains, such as scientific imaging, pathology, genomics, and personalized medicine, to improve the accuracy and efficacy of clinical decision-making.

*Corresponding author: priyangasubbaiya94@gmail.com

DOI: 10.1201/9781003676812-16

The IoMT, a growing community of networked medical devices and sensors, enables continuous affected person tracking, especially for people with persistent illnesses, as a result facilitating real-time data amassing and remote care control. Blockchain generation affords a decentralized, immutable ledger device that improves the transparency, protection, and traceability of healthcare data and pharmaceutical delivery chains, tackling persistent problems along with fact tampering, counterfeit medicinal drugs, and fragmented information systems. Collectively, those technologies are reworking the operational framework of healthcare delivery and pharmaceutical logistics via improving machine intelligence, adaptability, and interconnectivity (Kandhare et al., 2025). The ramifications inside the pharmaceutical region are also sizable. Artificial Intelligence and Machine Learning algorithms are remodeling drug development via expediting the identification of promising compounds, forecasting molecular behaviour, and diminishing the time and costs linked to preclinical research. Clinical trials are more advantageous than predictive recruitment processes, adaptive trial designs, and remote patient monitoring, resulting in expedited and greater unique effects.

Agencies are exploring techniques to evaluate and certify AI-driven items whilst ensuring ethical utilization and patient protection. This constitutes a segment of the regulatory device that simultaneously adapts to those advances. The integration of these technologies enables customization of healthcare by allowing the tailoring of treatment plans to specific patient profiles based on factors such as genetics, environment, and lifestyle choices. Despite those improvements, evolution isn't without challenges and issues. Current troubles embody safeguarding data privacy and safety against cyber-attacks, alongside achieving interoperability between legacy systems and cutting-edge technologies. Both demanding situations remain sizeable. Continuous oversight and law are vital to deal with moral troubles, specifically

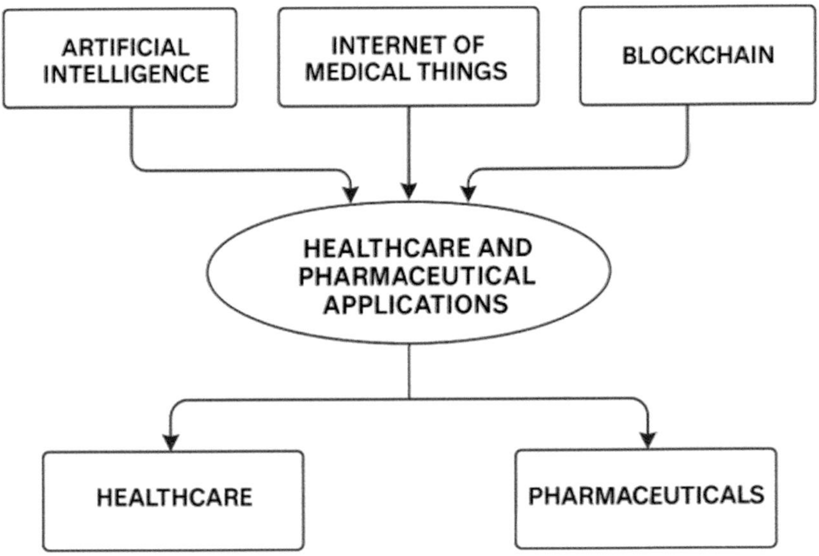

Figure 1: Overview of healthcare and pharmaceutical applications.

concerning algorithmic bias, knowledgeable consent, and the autonomy of artificial intelligence in healthcare settings. Furthermore, there exists an imperative need for interdisciplinary collaboration among clinicians, technologists, politicians, and patients to devise solutions that might be both modern and equitable. This chapter's objectives are to analyze the various impacts of the evolving era on the healthcare and pharmaceutical industries (Trenfield et al., 2022). The overview will examine the ability benefits of these technologies and the challenges that need to be addressed. This research aims to provide a comprehensive review of the digital transformation environment by analyzing existing use cases, performance metrics, and case studies. Furthermore, it underscores the importance of organizing complete policy frameworks, moral requirements, and training projects to ensure the proper integration of era within the healthcare sector. Figure 1 illustrates the overview of healthcare and pharmaceutical applications.

2. Technological Innovations in Healthcare and Pharmaceuticals

The 21st century has experienced a transformative shift within the healthcare and pharmaceutical sectors, propelled by technological improvements from the previous century. The implementation of these technologies complements the accuracy and efficacy of scientific services, promotes personalized remedies, and outcomes to improved patient results. This section presents a radical look at the important technological breakthroughs transforming these vital industries. Special emphasis is placed on Artificial Intelligence (AI), Machine Learning (ML), the Internet of Medical Things (IoMT), Blockchain, Big Data Analytics, Robotics, and 3-D Printing.

Artificial intelligence is one of the most transformative technologies in the pharmaceutical and healthcare industries. The ability to process vast quantities of data and extract pertinent insights enables early diagnosis, precision medicine, and administrative automation (Inuwa et al., 2023). Artificial intelligence-powered tools, such as IBM Watson, can assess symptoms and medical history to provide highly accurate diagnostic recommendations. In radiology, artificial intelligence algorithms are progressively employed to identify defects in X-rays, MRIs, and CT scans, frequently exceeding human capabilities. By examining historical data and contemporary health trends, AI models can predict the probability of disease outbreaks and the risk of patient readmission. Artificial intelligence accelerates the identification of potential drug candidates by simulating molecular interactions and predicting efficacy. Artificial intelligence (AI) aids in patient recruitment and trial monitoring by identifying potential candidates through genetic and demographic data. Machine learning is a subset of artificial intelligence that concentrates on creating algorithms that improve in accuracy with increased experience. It plays a significant role in genomic analysis, disease prediction, and medication optimization. The application of machine learning models facilitates the prediction and management of chronic conditions such as diabetes and cardiovascular illnesses. Machine learning facilitates the comprehension of complex genomic data, enabling the customization of individualized treatment approaches. To enhance post-marketing surveillance, machine learning algorithms detect patterns in adverse drug reactions. In medication development, machine learning is employed to enhance production processes and save expenses. Table 1 illustrates that emerging technologies such as AI, IoMT, and Blockchain are not only transforming clinical workflows but also revolutionizing pharmaceutical R&D and supply chains. Their convergence promises a future of smarter, faster, and more patient-centric healthcare delivery.

Table 1: Technological Innovations in Healthcare and Pharmaceuticals

Technology	Application in Healthcare	Application in Pharmaceuticals	Impact
Artificial Intelligence (AI)	Medical imaging, diagnosis support, chatbots	Drug discovery, molecule screening	Increased accuracy, speed, and automation
Machine Learning (ML)	Predictive analytics, personalized care	Clinical trial optimization	Data-driven decisions
Internet of Medical Things (IoMT)	Wearables, remote patient monitoring	Real-time logistics monitoring	Improved patient care & access
Blockchain	Secure health records, patient consent tracking	Supply chain transparency, counterfeit prevention	Trust, traceability, data integrity
Telemedicine	Virtual consultations, e-prescriptions	N/A	Accessibility, cost savings
3D Printing	Custom prosthetics, surgical planning	Rapid prototyping of drug delivery systems	Personalization, rapid production

The Internet of Medical Things (IoMT) is a network of interconnected scientific devices and programs that acquire and transmit health records in real time. Monitoring vital symptoms, consisting of heart fee, blood pressure, and glucose levels with wearable gadgets, facilitates early intervention by way of healthcare vendors. The Internet of Medical Things (IoMT) helps virtual consultations and real-time health records sharing, for this reason, improving access to healthcare. IoMT devices oversee pharmaceutical shipments to ensure the right delivery and storage situations (Bhattamisra et al., 2023). Intelligent packaging technologies can remind patients to stick to their medication regimen and alert their healthcare practitioners in the event of missed doses. Blockchain generation gives a decentralised and secure mechanism for record storage and change, crucial for safeguarding character privacy rights and fostering confidence within the pharmaceutical and healthcare sectors. The blockchain era permits the stable and interoperable transmission of electronic health records (EHRs). To beautify patients' autonomy and adherence, they could control get admission to their statistics. Blockchain technology can mitigate counterfeiting through tracking drugs alongside the deliver chain. Maintaining immutable documents allows auditing processes and adherence to regulatory norms. The proliferation of fitness-related facts necessitates strong analytical tools to convert raw facts into actionable insights. The examination of vast databases can enhance the identification of health patterns and the powerful allocation of resources. Data analytics enables the formulation of personalized treatment packages in line with the health profiles of unique patients.

Pharmaceutical organizations utilize big data to enhance their comprehension of market traits and patient desires. Upon approval, drug efficacy and safety are decided using proof obtained from well-designed, actual international studies. Robotics is revolutionizing surgery, rehabilitation, and sanatorium logistics through superior precision and automation. In minimally invasive surgical procedures, the accuracy of the surgical operation is more desirable with technologies just as the da Vinci robotic. Patients can regain motor functions with the use of assistive robots through guided sports. In the producing zone, robots are hired for responsibilities necessitating awesome precision and consistency. Repetitive laboratory processes may be controlled by using a robot gadget, improving performance and precision (Colas et al., 1997). Three-dimensional printing is considerably advancing the advent of personalized medical treatments and pharmacological research. 3D printing facilitates the production of prosthetic limbs and implants customized to a person's frame. The utilization of 3D-revealed organ replicas aids surgeons in the practice of complex tactics. 3D printing enables the customization of medication dosages and launch profiles for particular sufferers. This facilitates the speedy evaluation and enhancement of pharmaceutical compositions and transport mechanisms.

The healthcare and pharmaceutical industries are experiencing vast modifications because of the convergence of these technological breakthroughs. These tools are no longer most effective in improving diagnostic accuracy and healing efficacy, but additionally increase operational efficiency and decrease costs. Conversely, a hit integration of those technologies necessitates addressing issues consisting of the requirement for legislative frameworks, moral issues, and hurdles relating to data protection. It is vital to maintain interdisciplinary collaboration and policy development to maximize the advantages of these transformative technologies, even as restricting associated risks.

3. Applications Across the Healthcare Value Chain

The healthcare area is undergoing a sizable transformation via the combination of advanced technologies, including artificial intelligence, machine learning, the Internet of Medical Things, and blockchain. These technologies are currently remodeling traditional healthcare practices, improving patient care satisfactorily, and optimizing operational performance. The subsequent section examines their applicability during diverse stages of the healthcare price chain. Artificial intelligence (AI) and machine learning (ML) algorithms have transformed diagnostic techniques by allowing the analysis of complex medical facts with amazing accuracy. Deep knowledge of fashions can aid in the interpretation of imaging records, therefore facilitating the early detection of situations inclusive of tumours, fractures, and neurological problems (Bansal et al., 2022). The precision of cancer diagnoses may be better the usage of AI-driven photo evaluation, facilitating the detection of mobile anomalies. Employing gadgets and gaining knowledge of algorithms to assess patient facts allows the implementation of preventative actions when diseases like diabetes and cardiovascular illnesses are expected to arise.

The series of real-time affected person information, the usage of Internet of Medical Things (IoMT) gadgets, together with wearable sensors and remote monitoring gear, helps non-stop fitness tracking and the early discovery of anomalies. Blockchain technology guarantees the integrity and safety of diagnostic facts by developing an immutable ledger. This permits certified healthcare practitioners to soundly change statistics with every different. The software of synthetic intelligence algorithms that determine genetic records, lifestyle factors, and clinical statistics allows the creation of tailor-made treatment regimens (Bansal et al., 2022). This method complements remedy efficacy while minimizing unfavourable outcomes. Utilizing genetic profiles, synthetic intelligence fashions can expect patient responses to medicinal drugs, as a result enhancing drug selection and management. Clinical practitioners can choose appropriate treatments using those systems, which provide guidelines grounded in research.

Internet of Medical Things (IoMT) gadgets monitor patient responses to cures in real time, facilitating dynamic modifications to remedy protocols. The blockchain era enables the secure storage and sharing of tailor-made remedy records, thereby safeguarding patient privacy and preserving statistical integrity. Platforms utilizing artificial intelligence check information from faraway monitoring devices to detect fitness deteriorations and perform well-timed interventions. The utilization of those technologies permits sufferers to gain immediate answers to their health enquiries, subsequently improving patient involvement and compliance with treatment regimens. By facilitating non-stop surveillance of essential signs and symptoms, glucose levels, and different health parameters, Internet of Medical Things (IoMT) devices lessen the need for patients to visit common hospitals. Blockchain technology guarantees the steady transmission and storage of sensitive health information accrued through telemedicine systems, consequently maintaining patient confidentiality. Artificial intelligence accelerates clinical studies by figuring out feasible participants for medical trials through digital fitness and genetic statistics. By analyzing massive databases, developments and insights can be identified, resulting in greater knowledge of ailment mechanisms. The accuracy and reliability of study outcomes are more desirable via the utilization of IoMT devices that accumulate real-time information from trial individuals. Blockchain technology complements the transparency and traceability of medical trial facts, thereby ensuring regulatory compliance and instilling self-belief amongst stakeholders.

Artificial intelligence can optimize delivery chain operations via watching for calls for, monitoring inventories, and identifying capability disruptions (Laganà et al., 2022). Internet of Medical Things (IoMT) devices oversee the situations for drug storage, guaranteeing appropriate temperatures and ensuring that approaches are upheld. Blockchain generation gives an unalterable document of the supply chain, improving traceability and fighting the advent of counterfeit prescription drugs. Natural Language Processing (NLP) strategies, while utilized on unstructured clinical notes, extract pertinent statistics, consequently improving the functionality of electronic health records (EHRs). The integration of IoMT records into digital health facts (EHRs) gives a comprehensive view of the patient's fitness, facilitating more informed decision-making by medical doctors. Electronic Health Records (EHRs) are safeguarded via blockchain generation, which presents decentralized management, permitting individuals to dictate get right of entry to their private health data. Artificial intelligence technology is employed to supervise adherence to healthcare guidelines, identifying infractions and assuring non-stop compliance with requirements. Secure Internet of Medical Things networks inhibit unauthorized get right of entry to patient data, so safeguarding each of its safety and integrity. The decentralized shape of the blockchain era, alongside its cryptographic safety functions, provides significant safety for sensitive health statistics.

Artificial intelligence structures investigate population health data to predict the emergence of disease outbreaks and guide public health interventions. Technologies associated with the Internet of Medical Things (IoM) are notably enhancing epidemiological studies. These technologies collect facts on environmental parameters and indicators of human health. Utilizing blockchain technology enables groups to appropriately allocate public fitness information, subsequently facilitating the coordination of responses to health crises. The automation of administrative

Table 2: Technological Applications Across the Healthcare Value Chain

Healthcare Segment	AI and ML Applications	IoMT Applications	Blockchain Applications
Diagnostics	Image analysis, predictive modeling	Real-time monitoring devices	Secure data sharing
Treatment Planning	Personalized therapy recommendations	Monitoring treatment responses	Secure storage of treatment data
Remote Monitoring	Anomaly detection, virtual assistants	Continuous vital sign tracking	Secure transmission of remote data
Clinical Trials	Patient recruitment, data analysis	Real-time data collection	Transparent trial data management
Supply Chain Management	Demand forecasting, inventory optimization	Tracking storage conditions	Drug traceability, counterfeit prevention
Electronic Health Records	NLP for data extraction	Integration of device data	Decentralized control of health records
Regulatory Compliance	Monitoring adherence to regulations	Secure device networks	Immutable records for compliance verification
Public Health	Disease outbreak prediction	Environmental and health data collection	Secure sharing of public health data
Healthcare Administration	Automation of administrative tasks	Monitoring equipment and patient flow	Simplified credentialing processes
Patient Engagement	Personalized education materials	Health monitoring empowerment	Verification of educational resources

responsibilities, such as scheduling, billing, and claims processing, is a technique by which artificial intelligence (AI) reduces administrative fees and mistakes in the place of work (Ahmed et al., 2021). Internet of Medical Things (IoMT) gadgets enhance aid allocation with the aid of monitoring affected person mobility and the usage of medical devices, consequently optimizing scientific facility operations. The blockchain era complements the credentialing tactics for healthcare specialists, permitting extra efficient verification and diminishing crucial administrative duties. Personalized fitness schooling materials are supplied to patients via synthetic intelligence-powered platforms, improving patients' information and engagement with the content. IoMT gadgets allow sufferers to report their health stages, thereby gaining proactive control of chronic ailments. The blockchain era enables the supply of reliable information, consequently ensuring the authenticity of health training sources for patients. Table 2 illustrates the technological applications across the healthcare value chain.

The integration of artificial intelligence, device learning, the internet of scientific matters, and the blockchain era throughout the healthcare supply chain can significantly improve patient outcomes, optimize operations, and foster innovation. The implementation of those technologies allows healthcare structures to transition to extra efficient, steady, and patient-centered care models.

4. Advancements in the Pharmaceutical Sector

The pharmaceutical industry is currently undergoing a revolution driven by the rapid advancement of technology and the developed demands of the healthcare system. Artificial Intelligence (AI), Machine Learning (ML), Internet of Medical Things (IOMT), Blockchain Technology, and Three-Dimensional Printing Drug Discovery, Development, Manufacturing, and Distribution are revolutionizing the processes (Udayakumar et al., 2021). The purpose of these technologies is to reduce the expenses and increase the results of the patient by increasing efficiency.

5. Artificial Intelligence and Machine Learning in Drug Discovery

AI and ML have proven crucial for expediting medicinal drug research and improvement. This equipment can pick out promising drug candidates, forecast treatment responses, and design clinical trial designs by using analysis of significant databases. Artificial intelligence algorithms can compare organic statistics to pick out novel drug goals and are expected to predict molecular interactions. This appreciably decreases the time and financial resources associated with traditional strategies. Machine learning models enhance the performance and protection of medical trials with the aid of assisting in affected person classification, predicting trial outcomes, and monitoring adverse events. By analyzing genetic, environmental, and lifestyle elements, artificial intelligence enables the introduction of tailored treatment applications, main to greater powerful medications. The incorporation of AI-pushed solutions inside Pfizer's studies and development portfolio, the optimization of data evaluation tactics, and the expedited regulatory submissions exemplify how Pfizer's collaboration with AI organizations has fostered innovation.

6. Internet of Medical Things (IoMT) and Real-Time Monitoring

The Internet of Medical Things (IoMT) enables real-time monitoring and stepped forward affected patient care through a network of networked devices that collect and ship health statistics. Wearable technology facilitates the tracking of important signs and symptoms, medication adherence, and contamination progression, allowing for interventions. Internet of Things (IoT) devices provide incessant records, resulting in sizable databases that augment study capabilities and facilitate predictive analytics (Udayakumar et al., 2021). IoMT systems display environmental variables at some stage in the remedy transit, ensuring product integrity.

7. Blockchain for Enhanced Transparency and Security

The blockchain era gives a decentralized and immutable ledger machine, enhancing the transparency and security of pharmaceutical operations. Blockchain technology guarantees the traceability of medication from manufacturing to shipping, as a result thwarting the distribution of counterfeit merchandise. Recording trial information securely and transparently enhances confidence and compliance. Blockchain era safeguards touchy health records, ensuring both fact integrity and privacy.

8. 3D Printing in Pharmaceutical Manufacturing

Additive manufacturing, or 3-D printing, is revolutionizing drug production by permitting the introduction of complex and personalized dosage forms. Tailored medicinal drugs can be advanced to satisfy the precise desires of every patient, enhancing efficacy and compliance. Quickens the development of progressive pharmaceutical formulations and management strategies. Enhances accessibility and reduces inventory expenses through the facilitation of decentralized production.

9. Regulatory Innovations and Compliance

To ensure the exceptional efficacy and safety of pharmaceutical items, regulatory frameworks are evolving with advancements in technology. Regulatory bodies are increasingly the use of flexible trial designs that permit adjustments primarily based on period in-between effects, as a result enhancing efficiency (Bell et al., 2018). The recognition is based on a scientific method to improve, prioritizing the know-how of processes and the control of variability. Entails real-time surveillance of manufacturing methods to ensure consistent product quality.

10. Case Studies and Performance Metrics

The adoption of superior generations in the pharmaceutical commercial enterprise has caused substantive improvements in operational processes. AI-driven medicinal drug discovery has expedited the development process, leading to speedier transport of treatments to sufferers. The fees associated with studies and improvement, in conjunction with production, have dwindled because of automation and predictive analytics. The healing efficacy of customized medical tactics has increased, whilst their negative consequences have faded.

11. Challenges and Ethical Considerations

Despite the myriad advantages, the adoption of recent technology is encumbered with demanding situations. Protecting the confidentiality and integrity of touchy health records is paramount. Standardization and collaboration are vital for the successful integration of various systems and technologies (Sharma et al., 2020). Concerns exist around accountability, bias, and transparency within the software of AI for healthcare decision-making. The implementation of adaptable and modern regulatory answers is necessary to keep pace with quick technological improvements. Table 3 illustrates the key technological advancements in the pharmaceutical sector.

Table 3: Key Technological Advancements in the Pharmaceutical Sector

Technology	Applications	Benefits	Challenges
Artificial Intelligence (AI)	Drug discovery, clinical trial optimization, personalized medicine	Accelerated development, cost reduction, improved outcomes	Data privacy, algorithm bias, and regulatory compliance
Internet of Medical Things (IoMT)	Remote monitoring, data collection, supply chain management	Real-time insights, improved patient care, enhanced logistics	Data security, device interoperability
Blockchain	Supply chain transparency, clinical data management, and patient data security	Enhanced traceability, data integrity, and counterfeit prevention	Scalability, regulatory acceptance
3D Printing	Customized dosage forms, rapid prototyping, and on-demand manufacturing	Personalized medicine, reduced waste, decentralized production	Quality control, regulatory approval
Adaptive Clinical Trials	Flexible trial designs, real-time modifications	Increased efficiency, faster approvals	Complex design, statistical challenges
Quality by Design (QbD)	Systematic development, process understanding	Consistent quality, risk mitigation	Implementation complexity, training requirements

A paradigm shift is taking place within the pharmaceutical enterprise, which is embracing generation improvements to fulfill the evolving needs of the healthcare sector. The integration of synthetic intelligence, Internet of Things generation, blockchain, and 3D printing can transform scientific studies and delivery; however, demanding situations remain. Collaboration among stakeholders, along with industry leaders, regulators, and healthcare companies, is important to navigate this transition effectively and make sure that improvements offer substantial advantages for individuals globally.

12. Implementation Challenges and Barriers

The use of superior technologies in the healthcare and pharmaceutical sectors guarantees advanced patient care, optimized operations, and expedited drug development. The journey to a hit implementation is laden with hurdles throughout technological, regulatory, ethical, and organizational spheres. Comprehending these boundaries is essential for stakeholders seeking to leverage the full capacity of digital transformation in these industries.

12.1. Technical Challenges

In the sphere of the era, a chief issue is the dearth of interoperability among numerous healthcare systems. The coexistence of legacy systems and current digital answers from time to time results in the introduction of fragmented information silos, hindering the seamless flow of information (Nizam et al., 2024). For instance, China's healthcare machine has confronted massive demanding situations due to non-standardized statistical codes and disparate structures, resulting in the introduction of "facts islands" that hinder data sharing. High-quality and standardized statistics are crucial for the efficacy of AI and ML models. Several issues can compromise the accuracy of predictive analytics, together with abnormal record entry approaches, absent values, and disparate coding requirements. The task of preserving information integrity across numerous assets is a continual threat. A strong fact generation infrastructure is vital for the implementation of advanced technology. This infrastructure calls for a high-speed net connection, a steady record storage, and sturdy computing competencies. The implementation and growth of digital health solutions in numerous areas, mainly in impoverished international locations, are obstructed using insufficient infrastructure.

12.2. Regulatory and Compliance Barriers

The rapid advancement of virtual health generation frequently outpaces the establishment of corresponding regulatory frameworks. This latency generates uncertainty for innovators, potentially main to delays in the approval and execution of innovative ideas. The integration of artificial intelligence in healing contexts entails problems related to duty, validation standards, and oversight mechanisms. When dealing with touchy affected person statistics, it's crucial to adhere carefully to privacy guidelines, which include the Health Insurance Portability and Accountability Act (HIPAA) inside the United States and the General Data Protection Regulation (GDPR) inside the European Union. Ensuring compliance, even as promoting information-driven innovation, is a complex equilibrium. In healthcare research and pharmaceutical development, international cooperation regularly needs the transnational interchange of statistics. The divergence of facts privacy rules amongst international locations complicates interactions, therefore diminishing the capability for global cooperation.

12.3. Ethical and Social Considerations

Artificial Intelligence and Machine Learning fashions based on non-representative datasets may perpetuate current biases, resulting in differences in healthcare outcomes. The eradication of algorithmic bias is important to ensure identical care for numerous populations. The use of complex algorithms in selection-making tactics generates issues. These troubles embody transparency and patient autonomy (Jeyaraman et al., 2024). It is crucial to ensure that patients are aware of and agree to the use of AI-powered medical equipment. Establishing the consideration of both sufferers and healthcare professionals is crucial for the introduction of the latest era. The integration of synthetic intelligence and other digital gear into medical practice may be obstructed with the aid of cynicism regarding their reliability and protection.

12.4. Organizational and Cultural Barriers

Certain healthcare experts might also hesitate to embrace the new era due to pride in present structures, fear of obsolescence, or scepticism concerning the efficacy of virtual contraptions. Thorough alternate control strategies have to be applied to surmount this competition. To successfully incorporate state-of-the-art generation, a personnel talented in virtual skills is critical. To enable healthcare groups of workers to effectively utilize new gear, it is important to tackle ability shortages through imposing targeted education packages. Integrating digital technology into conventional medical workflows without causing interruptions is a formidable task. For new technology to stay in use, it's imperative to make certain that it augments as opposed to complicates the delivery of hospital treatment.

12.5. Financial and Economic Constraints

The initial monetary investment required for the procurement, variation, and implementation of advanced generation can be daunting, especially for smaller healthcare centers and organizations functioning in resource-constrained situations. Quantifying the economic blessings of digital fitness systems can be hard. The uncertainty round go back on funding (ROI) can also deter stakeholders from endorsing the full-scale implementation of technology. In situations with constrained monetary assets, ongoing costs related to gadget renovation, updates, and technical support can impose a strain on organizational budgets. These prices surpass the primary installation. The journey towards virtual transformation within the healthcare and pharmaceutical sectors is beset by formidable challenges throughout all domains, which include technical, regulatory, moral, organizational, and economic dimensions. A coordinated effort involving patients, healthcare practitioners, technologists, and policymakers is important to surmount these difficulties. Stakeholders can facilitate the effective integration of superior technology with the aid of promoting collaboration, making an investment in infrastructure and education, and setting up stringent regulatory frameworks. This will, in the long run, cause more advantageous patient care and operational efficiency.

13. Case Studies and Performance Evaluation

13.1. AI-Powered Clinical Trials Optimization

An international pharmaceutical employer collaborated with ZS Associates to decorate its scientific trial processes through the software of synthetic intelligence-driven analytics. The goal was to discover the most effective patient populations and trial websites with the aid of the examination of ancient statistics and the software of predictive modelling. A records and analytics platform, pushed by artificial intelligence, has been developed to help in decision-making concerning the selection of clinical trial websites and patient recruitment strategies. The enrolment of patients at each website rose by way of 10%. However, there was a 30 percent decrease in non-recruiting websites; selection-making processes were expedited by using 25 percent. A 15% upward thrust in income is anticipated due to advanced trial efficiency.

13.2. Blockchain for Secure Health Data Sharing

The software of blockchain generation in the healthcare sector will enhance interoperability, data safety, and patient privacy. Blockchain technology frameworks have been implemented throughout diverse healthcare domains, inclusive of public health control, drug distribution, and information sharing. The integrity and protection of the facts have been superior. Enhanced openness and transparency in the dissemination of medicinal drugs. The control of insurance claims has been optimized.

14. IoMT and AI for Remote Patient Monitoring

During the COVID-19 pandemic, the mixing of Internet of Medical Things (IoMT) devices and synthetic intelligence algorithms has been employed for the far off monitoring of patients. Artificial intelligence-empowered IoMT systems have been utilized to acquire and examine patient data in real time, facilitating early intervention and customized therapy. A decrease in health center visitations. Patient participation and compliance with remedy strategies have markedly more desirable. A more advantageous capacity to manipulate chronic ailments through far-flung access.

15. Lean Digital Transformation in Hospital Operations

Robotic procedure automation (RPA) turned into carried out at a healthcare group to enhance operational performance and optimize administrative functions. RPA tools had been incorporated into clinic operations to automate repetitive responsibilities. This allowed employees to be recognized for greater affected person-focused activities. A larger share of human resources is being dedicated to value-added activities. Patient pride advanced because of a reduction in delays due to administrative techniques. The standard quality of service transport in the hospital has improved.

16. AI and Blockchain in E-Health Systems

The integration of artificial intelligence and blockchain technology has been explored to create dependable and steady e-fitness systems. To ensure statistical integrity and enhance the reliability of fitness facts systems, artificial intelligence models have been developed, making use of blockchain frameworks. Confidence in fitness programs powered by artificial intelligence has risen. Enhanced patient confidentiality and information protection, respectively. Enhanced choice-making techniques were instituted in medical settings. Table 4 illustrates the case studies of AI and blockchain in E-health systems.

Table 4: Case Studies

Case Study	Technology Implemented	Key Outcomes
AI-Powered Clinical Trials Optimization	AI, ML	10% increase in patient enrollment, 30% reduction in non-recruiting sites, 25% faster decision-making, 15% projected sales uplift
Blockchain for Secure Health Data Sharing	Blockchain	Improved data integrity, enhanced supply chain transparency, streamlined insurance claims
IoMT and AI for Remote Patient Monitoring	IoMT, AI	Reduced hospital readmissions, improved patient engagement, enhanced chronic disease management
Lean Digital Transformation in Hospital Operations	RPA	Increased staff allocation to patient care, enhanced patient satisfaction, improved service delivery
AI and Blockchain in E-Health Systems	AI, Blockchain	Increased trust in AI applications, enhanced data security, improved clinical decision-making

The integration of emerging technologies such as AI, ML, IoMT, and blockchain in healthcare and pharmaceutical sectors has demonstrated significant improvements in operational efficiency, patient care, and data security. These case studies provide valuable insights into the practical applications and benefits of digital transformation in these industries.

17. Strategic Implications and Future Outlook

A paradigm shift is underway inside the healthcare and pharmaceutical sectors, propelled by disruptive technologies like as blockchain, artificial intelligence (AI), machine learning (ML), and the internet of scientific matters (IoMT). These technologies are not only reworking operational techniques but also reshaping strategic agendas within both industries. Organizations need to reevaluate conventional enterprise models, regulatory techniques, patient engagement strategies, and innovation ecosystems as the rate of digital transformation speeds up. This section analyses the strategic implications of these alterations and offers perspectives on the destiny direction of virtual healthcare and pharmaceuticals. This phase includes supplementary statistics.

The operational effectiveness of digital technology inside the healthcare zone is the various maximum instant strategic advantages of those technologies. The use of AI-driven scheduling systems, systems that gain knowledge of-based totally diagnostics, and Internet of Medical Things-enabled remote patient monitoring can substantially lessen administrative complexity and scientific overhead. Hospitals and clinics can gain a greater powerful reallocation of assets, optimization of supply chains, and cost reduction without compromising the satisfactory of care provided. Data-pushed decision-making is facilitated by the accessibility of real-time affected person statistics through electronic health records (EHRs), wearable devices, and interconnected gadgets. Predictive analytics can useful resource for physicians in foreseeing complications, optimizing intensive care unit resource allocation, and tailoring remedies to the unique requirements of man or woman patients. Consequently, the strategic emphasis transitions from reactive healthcare to proactive healthcare initiatives. The shift from quantity-based care to price-primarily based care is facilitated by the implementation of virtual equipment. Patients are afforded more autonomy and more desirable involvement through personalized treatment plans facilitated through artificial intelligence, genomics, digital care systems, and mobile health programs. Doctors and other clinical professionals must now broaden their strategy based on patient pride and long-term outcomes as crucial performance measures.

To attain their strategic targets, healthcare establishments need to put money into interoperable systems that facilitate seamless communication among departments and external establishments. This facilitates coordinated care transport and helps include fitness systems, both of which are crucial for coping with chronic illnesses and ageing populations. Artificial Intelligence and Machine Learning are instigating a transformation within the discovery and validation of revolutionary pharmaceuticals. Algorithms can significantly minimise the number of cycles needed for research and development by way of forecasting chemical interactions, pinpointing exciting molecules, and simulating effects. By reducing the length required to release a product, pharmaceutical agencies can steadily gain a aggressive advantage and enhance their return on investment. The emergence of wearable technologies, mobile programs, and telemedicine has come to be decentralized and digital medical trials have become a crucial strategic intention. In these trials, patient recruitment and retention are improved, prices are diminished, and information is satisfactorily multiplied. To permit these fashions, corporations must set up virtual infrastructure and domesticate relationships.

Blockchain technology and artificial intelligence are revolutionizing the deliver chains of pharmaceutical businesses. Artificial intelligence is hired to forecast demand and optimize shares, while the blockchain era ensures transparency, traceability, and fraud protection. In mild of recent worldwide disruptions like COVID-19, firms have to reevaluate their deliver networks to enhance their strategic resilience. The utilization of virtual answers for real-time compliance monitoring and reporting is increasingly well-known among pharmaceutical corporations. Natural Language Processing (NLP) and Robotic Process Automation (RPA) can simplify each pharmacovigilance and regulatory filing. From a strategic angle, conformity with virtual regulatory frameworks will serve as a distinguishing factor in the competitive arena. Digital technology, including telehealth and cell fitness systems, possesses the potential to remove healthcare disparities by improving admission to for underprivileged populations. To provide equitable access, governments have to broaden plans focused on infrastructure development, digital literacy campaigns, and monetary subsidies. The outbreak highlighted the need to implement worldwide digital surveillance systems. The Internet of Medical Things (IoMT) allows great monitoring, even as AI-pushed algorithms can predict outbreaks. Strategic investments in fitness informatics and early warning systems are critical to bolster destiny resilience.

Artificial intelligence and information-driven healthcare present moral dilemmas, such as bias, consent, and obligation. Policymakers must develop sizable rules to supervise information utilization, AI decision-making, and transnational information trade. Strategic foresight inside prison frameworks will mitigate misuse whilst facilitating innovation. The shift to virtual healthcare necessitates a workforce talented in data analytics, software program utilization, and digital communication. Strategic investments in reskilling, upskilling, and ongoing professional development will dictate the efficacy of establishments' adventure into the virtual age. Conventional roles in healthcare and tablets are remodeling. Data scientists, AI ethicists, and virtual fitness coordinators are increasingly essential. Organizations must intentionally restructure activity responsibilities, performance metrics, and organizational frameworks to align with this evolution. Collaborations amongst era companies, educational establishments, healthcare companies, and the pharmaceutical industries are crucial for innovation. Collaborations between biotechnology startups and artificial intelligence firms have expedited the advancement of vaccines and treatments.

Open innovation, characterized by using the trade of facts, gear, and research across organizational barriers, is crucial due to the complicated challenges related to healthcare. One may accelerate progress and produce more sustainable solutions by strategically participating in international research consortia and recording alternative systems. A conducive environment for mission capital has arisen in the area of healthcare era. Strategic investors are making considerable investments in synthetic intelligence diagnostics, telemedicine, digital prescription drugs, and blockchain structures. Policymakers and company leaders need to comprehend this fashion and endeavour to create environments that foster startup growth. It is important to assess the long-term price of packages related to virtual transformation. Nonetheless, the return on funding (ROI) on patient effects, process efficiencies, and logo belief is extensive, despite the doubtlessly high initial implementation costs. Return on investment (ROI) models that take into account both tangible and intangible benefits are essential for strategic planning. The adoption of this technology is unexpectedly advancing in affluent nations, but several underdeveloped international locations face barriers regarding their infrastructure and criminal frameworks. To bridge the digital divide, it's critical to establish frameworks for financing, strategic worldwide cooperation, and the collective dissemination of records. The utilization of digital gear has to be culturally sensitive and linguistically inclusive. To ensure enormous adoption and achievement, efforts must include the localization of artificial intelligence fashions, translation gear, and culturally applicable user interfaces.

The destiny is rooted in hyper-customized healthcare propelled through genomes, lifestyle factors, and real-time biometrics. Predictive algorithms will expect sickness improvement and direct preventive measures. Emphasis ought to be directed closer to data integration, moral utilization, and ongoing version enhancement. Robotic surgery, AI-enhanced diagnostics, and self-sustaining fitness kiosks will gain considerable adoption. Strategic planning about infrastructure, protection measures, and human-AI collaboration could be essential. Digital therapeutics—programs and software providing scientific interventions—are predicted to proliferate, particularly in the realm of mental health. Strategic factors embody scientific validation, regulatory endorsement, and incorporation into conventional healing protocols. Future healthcare tasks have to align with environmental sustainability goals. Technological selections, ranging from power-green information centres to biodegradable medical devices, should be assessed for environmental effects. The strategic ramifications of developing generation in healthcare and prescribed drugs are significant and tremendous. Digital transformation affords extraordinary possibilities to improve care, optimize operations, and tackle worldwide health problems. Achieving those blessings necessitates more than simply technology implementation; it calls for revolutionary management, interdisciplinary collaboration, sturdy ethical frameworks, and sustained investment techniques. The future of healthcare may be formed through those who can invent judiciously, act resolutely, and adapt strategically.

18. Conclusion

The modern digital revolution is significantly changing the way that diseases are diagnosed, managed, and treated in the pharmaceutical and healthcare industries. Emerging technology, like synthetic intelligence, device learning, the Internet of Medical Things, and blockchain, can extensively enhance diagnostic accuracy, facilitate customized care, improve operational performance, and drive innovation across the value chain. It is crucial to address and resolve significant issues related to information security, interoperability, and ethical considerations to integrate those technologies successfully. The results of this observation emphasize that the entire ability of these advancements can best be carried out through sturdy interdisciplinary collaboration, suitable regulatory frameworks, and a dedication to patient-centered and stable innovation. Engaging with this technology responsibly can be crucial to broaden more efficient, equitable, and resilient healthcare environments as the arena evolves.

References

Ahmed, H.M., Roy, A., Wahab, M., Ahmed, M., Othman-Qadir, G., Elesawy, B.H., ... and Emran, T.B. (2021). Applications of nanomaterials in agrifood and pharmaceutical industry. Journal of Nanomaterials, 2021(1), 1472096.

Bansal, G., Rajgopal, K., Chamola, V., Xiong, Z., and Niyato, D. (2022). Healthcare in metaverse: A survey on current metaverse applications in healthcare. IEEE Access, 10, 119914–119946.

Bell, L., Buchanan, W.J., Cameron, J., and Lo, O. (2018). Applications of blockchain within healthcare. Blockchain in Healthcare Today. DOI: https://doi.org/10.30953/bhty.v1.8

Bhattamisra, S.K., Banerjee, P., Gupta, P., Mayuren, J., Patra, S., and Candasamy, M. (2023). Artificial intelligence in pharmaceutical and healthcare research. Big Data and Cognitive Computing, 7(1), 10.

Colas, A., and Aguadisch, L. (1997). Silicones in pharmaceutical applications. Chimie Nouvelle, 15(58), 1779.

Inuwa, H.M., Raja, A.R., Kumar, A., Singh, B., and Singh, S. (2022). Status of Industry 4.0 applications in healthcare 4.0 and Pharma 4.0. Materials Today: Proceedings, 62, 3593–3598.

Jeyaraman, N., Jeyaraman, M., Yadav, S., Ramasubramanian, S., and Balaji, S. (2024). Revolutionizing healthcare: The emerging role of quantum computing in enhancing medical technology and treatment. Cureus, 16(8).

Kandhare, P., Kurlekar, M., Deshpande, T., and Pawar, A. (2025). A review on revolutionizing healthcare technologies with AI and ML applications in pharmaceutical sciences. Drugs and Drug Candidates, 4(1), 9.

Laganà, I.R., and Colapinto, C. (2022). Multiple criteria decision-making in healthcare and pharmaceutical supply chain management: A state-of-the-art review and implications for future research. Journal of Multi-Criteria Decision Analysis, 29(1–2), 122–134.

Nizam, M., Purohit, R., and Taufik, M. (2024). 3D printing in healthcare: A review on drug printing, challenges and future perspectives. Materials Today Communications, 110199.

Polshettiwar, S.A., Deshmukh, C.D., Baheti, A.M., Wani, M.S., Bompilwar, E., Jambhekar, D., ... and Tagalpallewar, A. (2021). Recent trends on biosensors in healthcare and pharmaceuticals: An overview. International Journal of Pharmaceutical Investigation, 11(2).

Sharma, D.K., Bhargava, S., and Singhal, K. (2020). Internet of Things applications in the pharmaceutical industry. *In:* An Industrial IoT Approach for Pharmaceutical Industry Growth, pp. 153–190. Academic Press.

Trenfield, S.J., Awad, A., McCoubrey, L.E., Elbadawi, M., Goyanes, A., Gaisford, S., and Basit, A.W. (2022). Advancing pharmacy and healthcare with virtual digital technologies. Advanced Drug Delivery Reviews, 182, 114098.

Udayakumar, G.P., Muthusamy, S., Selvaganesh, B., Sivarajasekar, N., Rambabu, K., Banat, F., ... and Show, P.L. (2021). Biopolymers and composites: Properties, characterization, and their applications in food, medical, and pharmaceutical industries. Journal of Environmental Chemical Engineering, 9(4), 105322.

CHAPTER
17

Data Privacy and Confidentiality in Medical Internet of Things (MIoT)

R. Felista Sugirtha Lizy[1*(0000-0003-3648-0205)] and Ir. Bambang Sugiyono Agus Purwono[2(0000-0002-5982-8983)]

[1] Department of Computer Science, A.P.C. Mahalaxmi College for Women, Thoothukudi, Tamil Nadu, India
[2] Mechanical Engineering Department, State Polytechnic of Malang, Indonesia

1. Introduction

The Medical Internet of Things (MIoT) is a novel framework that emerged from the integration of the Internet of Things (IoT) with the healthcare sector. This approach integrates wireless communication systems, cloud infrastructure, sensor networks, and advanced medical devices to streamline the collection, exchange, and interpretation of patient data. It's remarkable how these technologies interconnect, enabling more efficient and insightful healthcare practices. This research has the potential to revolutionize patient care by enabling real-time remote monitoring, timely detection, chronic illness management, and customized treatment options.

But this digital transformation comes with a price. The proliferation of interconnected medical devices creates a new dimension of challenges for privacy and confidentiality. Unlike traditional health information systems, which are secure within a hospital or some other secure network, MIoT is a diverse collection of interacting medical devices in a range of settings, often far less secure, such as in patients' homes or mobile platforms. From biometric and environmental signals to the patient's location, activity, and even their nearly undetectable emotional signs, MIoT devices constantly gather and stream extremely sensitive data. The data required for medical uses and the flow of that data stream create an easy target for cyber threats, surveillance, profiling, and misuse.

Although MIoT data protection issues significantly increase the difficulty of privacy, higher risks also arise from the diversity of devices and vendor protocols and

*Corresponding author: 21felistaa@gmail.com

DOI: 10.1201/9781003676812-17

product differences, the difficulty of tracking data flow across multiple production phase environments, and often very poor or default security on consumer-grade health technology. Protecting personal health information (PHI) requires a robust, comprehensive strategy that emphasises technical, ethical, and legal safeguards.

Guidelines for the handling of health data are provided by the General Data Protection Regulation (GDPR) in Europe and the Health Insurance Portability and Accountability Act (HIPAA) in the United States. It can be challenging to follow the rules, particularly when dealing with disparate laws in different places or when technology like the Internet of Things (IoT) is involved.

To address the complexity of these and other risks, the field has turned increasingly to Privacy-Enhancing Technologies (PETs), such as data anonymization, pseudonymization, encryption, differential privacy, and secure multi-party computation, to reconcile these competing facets of the privacy–use trade-off in health. Specifically, PET technologies are intended to address the tensions between preserving individuals' privacy and allowing effective use of data for clinical, research, and operational purposes.

This chapter explores the fundamental aspects of data privacy confidentiality in MioT (Figure 1), with organized coverage for:

- The types of data generated and shared in MIoT environments.
- Relevant regulatory and compliance requirements.
- Frequent privacy and attack vectors.
- Privacy-by-design-focussed approaches and anonymization methods.

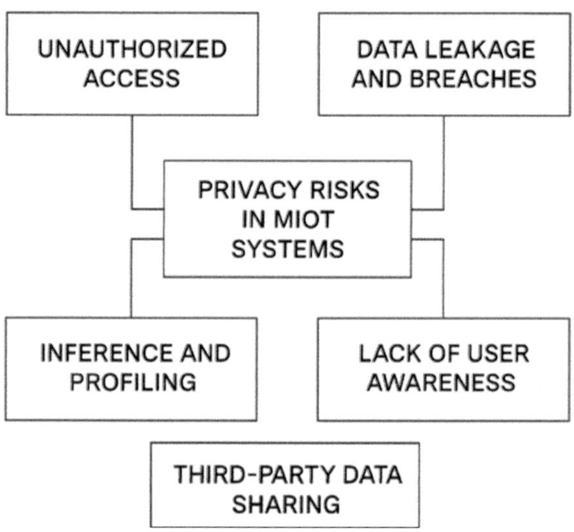

Figure 1: Privacy risks in MIoT systems.

As healthcare becomes more digital and decentralized, understanding and managing the privacy challenges of MIoT systems is not simply a technical requirement, but also a moral one. Confidentiality of patient data is a basic requirement to maintain trust in digital health technology, protect an individual's dignity, and maintain the moral integrity of medical practice.

2. Literature Review

Healthcare is undergoing significant change because of the Medical Internet of Things (MIoT). We can now diagnose diseases without physically being there, monitor patients from a distance, and more effectively customise treatment regimens. But even though these networked gadgets simplify life, they also give rise to significant concerns regarding security and privacy. Numerous studies have been conducted that examine these topics, shedding light on the difficult obstacles and exciting opportunities associated with patient data protection.

A thorough analysis of IoT applications in the healthcare industry was presented by Islam et al. (2015), with a primary focus on the usage of wearable sensors and remote monitoring tools. They provide a discussion of the types of data collected in MIoT systems (physiological data and contextual data), and underscore the need to protect at both the level of data transmission, by securing the physical objects (devices) and the data they could collect, as well as through data storage.

Tang and Hu (2020) explored privacy protection strategies more generally, uncovering key weaknesses including unencrypted communication, device-level weaknesses, and weak authentication. They concluded that while MIoT improves patient outcomes, it raises challenges concerning privacy protection, especially using data for population health management and secondary usage. Continued surveillance and monitoring from and for MIOT should elevate its security posture to foster user trust.

The General Data Protection Regulation (GDPR) and the Health Insurance Portability and Accountability Act (HIPAA) are two significant privacy laws that I have been researching. The General Data Protection Regulation (GDPR), introduced in the European Union in 2016, established significant limitations on the collection of personal data. It treats health information as sensitive personal data. In the meantime, HIPAA, which was revised by the U.S. Department of Health & Human Services in 2020, provides precise instructions for handling and safeguarding personal health information (PHI).

The literature also noted emergent privacy-preserving techniques. Dwork (2008) presented differential privacy as a statistical population privacy approach for protecting individual identities in aggregate datasets. This method is being further considered in MIoT research about privacy-preserving data analytics.

Zhang et al. (2018) presented FHIRChain, a research exploration of a blockchain-based service for health record access control management in distributed systems. Their research acknowledged how the emergent web3 technology blockchain has the potential to provide the important capabilities of transparency, auditability, and user sovereignty—practical advancements in the use of technologies addressing consent and trust issues surrounding MIoT systems.

Secure Multi-party Computation (SMPC) is a potential solution to collaborative medical research, which allows computation over datasets from multiple sources without exposing any raw data (Li et al., 2016, p. 818). SMPC preserves privacy in analytics, especially when data is located at different institutions and parties acting as one, can protect the privacy of patient data.

Globally, moves to control the processing of data across regions include the further development and implementation of the Personal Information Protection Law (PIPL) in China and the Personal Data Protection Bill (India). The PIPL and the Personal Data Protection Bill will formalize suitably acceptable data processing practices, which also include requirements to localize data as much as feasible main provisions of PIPLaw are rights of data subjects.

The ISO/IEC 27701:2019 standard (ISO, 2019) is an extension of existing standards that are more concerned with information security management; it also references privacy and provides a structure for organizations to demonstrate technical controls that affect legislation and industry-developed obligations on privacy.

Together, these studies emphasize the importance of integrating the practicalities of data utility, privacy, and regulation in MIOT technologies. While the field is changing rapidly and technological developments will make significant and positive contributions to protecting patient data, guidelines and enforceable policies combined with user education and clear system design must support a sustainable deployment.

3. Types of Data Collected and Shared in MIoT

Enduring both challenges and achievements, individuals gradually develop not only intellectual understanding but also personal resilience. This ongoing transformation is quite evident, and its effects often extend outward, motivating others to pursue growth as well. In this light, personal development stands as clear evidence of perseverance and highlights the enduring importance of lifelong self-improvement.

Vital signs and behavioural data are among the many types of data generated by MIoT devices and are frequently sent via the internet to cloud computing platforms, analytics engines, and healthcare institutions. Below is a complete list of the common kinds of data collected and/or shared in MIoT (Figure 2) environments.

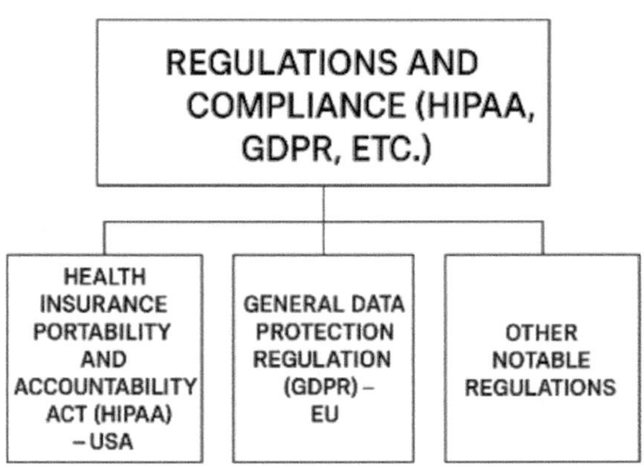

Figure 2: Types of data collected and shared in MIoT.

3.1. Physiological Data

Physiological data is defined as a real-time measurement of biological signals generated by patients using wearable, implantable, or connected medical devices. These measurements function much like continuous health monitoring tools, providing real-time, precise data on an individual's physiological status. Their value is clear in clinical settings and home care, where ongoing assessment supports effective health management. Common examples include:

- Heart rate and rhythm (ECG) used to identify arrhythmias and the stress of the heart, along with its overall health.
- Blood pressure monitored to treat disorders of the circulatory system, such as hypertension and cardiovascular disease.
- Blood glucose level: Diabetes patients can continuously check their blood sugar levels and make an effort to maintain stable glucose levels by using continuous glucose monitors, or CGMs.
- Oxygen saturation, or SpO_2, measures how well our lungs are functioning.
- Additionally, body temperature serves as a significant clinical marker.
- Respiratory rate, while sometimes underestimated, is particularly valuable, especially in acute situations such as the COVID-19 pandemic, where rapid assessment of breathing patterns became critical.

In summary, diligent surveillance of these physiological indicators enables early detection of health issues, supports the management of chronic diseases, and facilitates timely intervention during emergencies.

3.2. Behavioral and Lifestyle Data

Behavioral and Lifestyle data are primarily gathered through devices such as smart wearables, fitness trackers, and various smartphone health applications. To illustrate:

- Sleep duration and quality are primary indicators; assessing these factors aids in identifying potential sleep disorders and understanding patterns of recovery.
- Physical activity is another significant component.
- Dietary intake, including the monitoring of food and beverage consumption, plays a crucial role in achieving and maintaining health objectives.
- Finally, analyzing time spent sedentary versus time spent active is vital, as prolonged inactivity is associated with increased risks of obesity, cardiovascular disease, and other health complications.

By systematically examining these aspects, one gains a more nuanced and comprehensive picture of an individual's health status.

3.3. Electronic Health Records (EHRs) and Medical History

By gathering and updating Electronic Health Records (EHRs), digital files that track a patient's medical history and contain crucial data like the patient's age, gender, and contact information for follow-ups, MIoT systems assist hospitals in providing appropriate care.

- **Diagnoses:** Current and historical health conditions.
- **Lab test results:** Patient blood test, imaging, and other diagnostic results.
- **Medication lists:** A compilation of previous and present prescriptions.
- **Immunization and allergy history:** Particularly crucial to monitor to prevent negative drug reactions.

History of surgery and treatment: Previous operations and therapies, as well as current ones. The EHR features of MIoT systems enhance patients' healthcare continuity, data quality improvements, communication with patient/health systems, and support for collaborative, informed decision-making in healthcare, which have positive impacts on efficiency, effectiveness, and patient experience.

3.4. Location and Contextual Data

MIoT systems often use location and other environmental information to provide context-aware healthcare services, such as monitoring an older adult or providing home monitoring and mobile health services. Examples of location data might include:

- **GPS data:** tracks the movement of the patient with a high degree of accuracy for safety, possibly especially for clients suffering from dementia or Alzheimer's disease.
- **Indoor positioning:** monitors the locations of patients indoors in hospitals or care facilities (helping to better manage work orders and potential fall events).
- **Sensor data:** keeps track of indoor air-quality readings, temperature, and humidity within a smart home.

This contextual data is important for emergency response, patient-centered care, and determining environmental triggers for conditions like asthma or allergies.

3.5. Audio, Visual, and Communication Data

Almost all MIoT systems include interactive and multimedia components as part of telehealth and access to remote patient care. Several key examples include:

- **Voice recordings:** Allianz recording voice captures were used to inform his notes. The recordings can also be used for analysis.
- **Video feeds:** Home monitoring may use video feeds to perform visual assessments or to assess fall detection.
- **Messages:** Care teams and patients use messages to communicate with each other and can use relatively free-form text and or emojis via apps or portals.
- **Virtual assistant interactions:** Users exchange voice or text commands with health chatbots or smart assistants.

While the multimedia portions of endorsed MIoT health and wellness products enhanced patient engagement and access to care, they carry certain privacy risks associated with the sensitive nature of the content and the potential to be impacted by conversational eavesdropping or misuse of data.

3.6. Device and Network Metadata

MIoT systems produce and collect operational metadata concerning the devices and the networks they use, and they also potentially share this data with external organizations not directly involved in the care. Typical examples of operational metadata include:

- Device identifiers – e.g., MAC address, IMEI number, etc., that uniquely identify the device.
- Timestamps and geotags – e.g., when the data was collected and where the device was configured with GPS or location services.
- Transmission logs – e.g., when the data was sent or received or when the data transmission failed.
- Battery level and uptime – to check device integrity and functionality.

This type of metadata is often used to provide system maintenance, repairs, security, and troubleshooting, but it can be combined with other information to reveal patterns about users' behaviour, health regimes, and even location, which can be alarming from the perspective of privacy.

3.7. Third-party Shared Data

MIoT data is also often shared with organizations beyond the care circle, in the name of furthering interesting healthcare epochs and other functions. Typical examples include:

- **Pharmaceutical companies:** For use in clinical research and drug development.
- **Insurance companies:** Typically for use in claims, premiums, or expected health risks.
- **Vendors:** Technology services, such as warehouse cloud storage, data processing, and analytics.
- **Public health authorities:** For any monitoring of outbreaks or research, and to inform policy decisions with an unprecedented level of granularity.

This kind of data sharing is frequently more vulnerable to privacy violations, such as those involving informed consent, data ownership, and the definition and setting of data uses for privacy and protection. Table 1 summarizes the types of data that are collected and shared in MIoT, as outlined in the previous detailed explanation.

MIoT systems represent multimodal and continuous forms of data, which may be longitudinal in timeframe, and therefore can produce highly granular insights into an individual's health and lifestyle. The sensitivity and granularity of these data warrant careful controls to protect privacy, confidentiality, and the ethical use of the data. Not only is it critical to consider the data environment, but it is equally critical to understand (and ultimately assess) the type of data involved to develop MIoT systems that are secure and preserve privacy.

Table 1: Types of Data Collected and Shared in MIoT

Category	Data Type	Examples	Purpose/Use Case
Physiological Data	Biological and vital signs	Heart rate, ECG, blood pressure, glucose levels, SpO_2, body temperature	Real-time monitoring, diagnosis, and emergency alerts
Behavioral and Lifestyle Data	Daily activity and habits	Sleep patterns, physical activity, diet, hydration	Preventive care, wellness tracking, and personalized health recommendations
EHRs and Medical History	Clinical records and past medical data	Diagnoses, lab results, medications, allergies, immunizations	Clinical decision-making, longitudinal patient tracking, and treatment planning
Location and Contextual Data	Spatial and environmental context	GPS tracking, indoor positioning, ambient temperature, air quality	Elderly care, emergency response, and understanding environmental health triggers
Audio, Visual and Communication Data	Interactive and recorded content	Voice recordings, video consultations, chatbot messages	Telemedicine, remote diagnostics, and virtual assistant interactions
Device and Network Metadata	System-level operational information	Device ID, timestamps, battery status, connectivity logs	Performance monitoring, troubleshooting, and security auditing
Third-Party Shared Data	Data accessed or shared with external entities	Clinical trial data, insurance records, public health statistics	Research, claims processing, epidemic monitoring, and policy-making

4. Regulations and Compliance (HIPAA, GDPR, etc.)

Regulations and frameworks that offer rules to follow when handling personal and medical data have evolved as a first step in addressing the privacy and security concerns of MIoT devices (Figure 3). Notable regulations include:

- HIPAA (Health Insurance Portability and Accountability Act – USA): Establishes a strict set of rules when health care providers and associated entities are handling protected health information (PHI) for privacy, security, and patients' rights.
- GDPR (General Data Protection Regulation – EU): Offers various data protection rights to individuals and mandates organizations to obtain clear consent from individuals, ensure data minimization, and allow individuals some level of control over their data.

There are additional local regulations, including:

- PIPEDA (Canada)
- DPA 2018 (UK)
- DPDP Act (India)

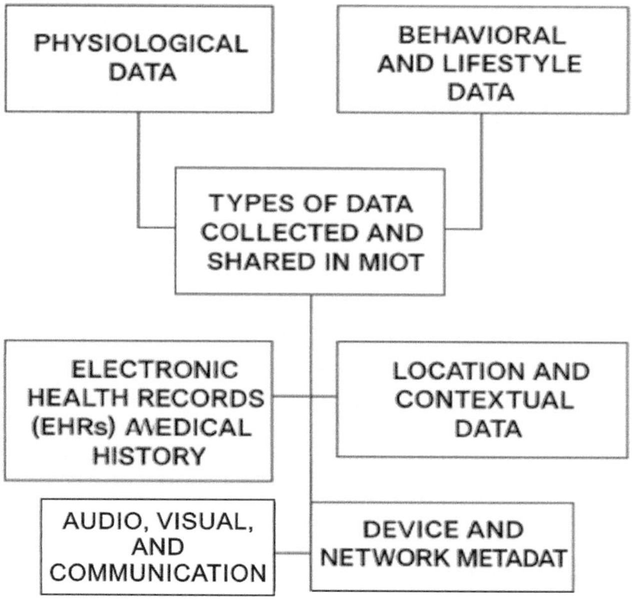

Figure 3: Regulations and compliance methods.

Regulatory compliance is a key component of protecting the privacy of patients, mitigating potentially severe legal consequences, and building trust in the MIoT technology used in healthcare. These regulations focus on the concepts of transparency, consent, rights to access data, and the implementation of security and safety practices.

4.1. Health Insurance Portability and Accountability Act (HIPAA) – USA

HIPAA is one of the central regulations in the US that provides a level of protection of patient privacy and the security of Protected Health Information (PHI). It defines the roles and expectations for care delivery organizations, payers, and business partners. Some of the important criteria employed by HIPAA are:

- **Protective measures for PHI:** Organizations must keep health data from being accessed by unacceptable users and prevent disclosures.
- **Security measures:** Individuals and organizations must establish a security plan that includes the administrative, physical, and technical safeguards, such as limiting access to PHI, encrypting PHI, and training employees on proper procedures.
- **Breach notifications:** HIPAA has requirements for timely notification to individuals and authorities of a breach.

In the context of US health care, HIPAA offers a degree of protection to ensure that patient and consumer data will be handled appropriately, which helps to affirm quality related to data confidentiality, data integrity protection, and accountability assurance.

4.2. General Data Protection Regulation (GDPR) – EU

To put it briefly, GDPR is a comprehensive data privacy law that any company, no matter where it is based, must take into account whenever it handles the personal data of its inhabitants. Some key aspects of GDPR to remember are:

- **Special protection for health data:** Health data is classified as a "special category" requiring even stricter protections.
- **User consent:** Organizations must have explicit, informed consent before collecting or processing personal data from users.
- **Data minimization:** Organizations should only collect necessary data, and will only maintain any data for the minimum amount of time.
- **Right to be forgotten:** Individuals have the right to ask an organization to delete their data in some specific circumstances.

GDPR reinforces transparency, accountability, and consumer control of their data, and is the fundamental privacy approach for MIoT system compliance throughout Europe as well as the rest of the world.

4.3. Even More Regulations

The proliferation of MIoT globally has led to more countries and organizations passing various datasets or data protection laws as part of their initiatives for privacy and accountability. Notable examples included:

- **Personal Data Protection Bill (India):** Draft legislation about getting user consent, data localization, and user rights to set up a complete privacy framework for Indian citizens.
- **Personal Information Protection Law (PIPL):** China has strong laws governing the collection, processing, and cross-border transfer of data, and it has powerful enforcement mechanisms.
- **ISO/IEC 27701:** International standard that builds onto ISO 27001, specifically defining Privacy Information Management Systems (PIMS) for global best practices in managing personal information.

Compliance with these regulations is important for providing a complete legal context, guarding patient trust, and ensuring MIoT technologies are confidential and ethical both locally and as deployed around the world. Table 2 summarizes the Regulations and Compliance for MIoT systems.

5. Privacy Risks in MIoT Systems

The Medical Internet of Things (MIoT) is fraught with privacy risks, even with privacy regulations enforced. The interconnectedness and data intensive nature of MIoT (Figure 4) allow MIoT to collect, transmit, and process sensitive health data by multiple platforms and stakeholders in a manner that significantly increases the surface area of risk to privacy breaches. Some specific examples of MIoT privacy risks include:

Table 2: Key Regulations and Compliance Frameworks in MIoT

Regulation/ Standard	Region/Scope	Key Provisions	Relevance to MIoT
HIPAA (Health Insurance Portability and Accountability Act)	United States	• Safeguards for Protected Health Information (PHI) • Requires administrative, technical, and physical protections • Mandatory breach notifications	Ensures secure handling of patient data by MIoT systems used by U.S. healthcare providers
GDPR (General Data Protection Regulation)	European Union (Applies globally to EU citizens' data)	• Health data classified as "special category" • Emphasizes consent, data minimization, and right to be forgotten	Enforces strict privacy controls for MIoT systems processing data of EU residents
PDP Bill (Personal Data Protection Bill – India)	India (proposed legislation)	• Focus on user consent and rights • Data localization requirements	Aims to regulate MIoT data usage within India and protect citizens' data rights
PIPL (Personal Information Protection Law)	China	• Comprehensive consent requirements • Restrictions on cross border data transfers	Regulates how MIoT data is collected, used, and shared within and outside China
ISO/IEC 27701	Global (International Standard)	• Extends ISO/IEC 27001 to include privacy controls • Framework for managing personally identifiable information (PII)	Helps organizations operating MIoT systems adopt consistent privacy practices across borders

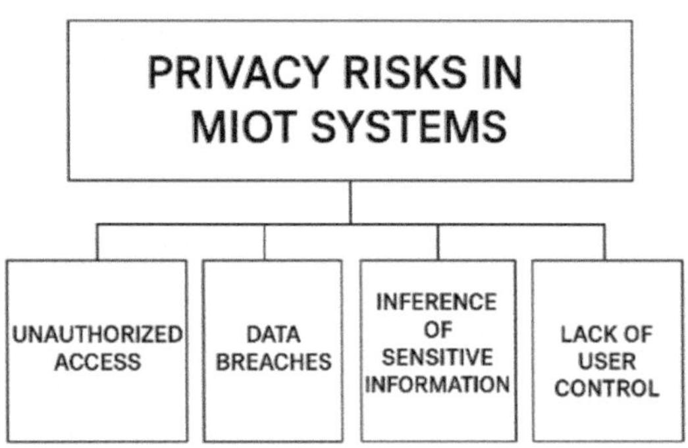

Figure 4: Privacy risks in MIoT systems.

- Unauthorized access stemming from weak authentication controls or insecure interfaces.
- Data leakage and breaches through unencrypted transmissions, unsecured cloud storage, or processing configurations.
- Inference attacks that would essentially allow an adversary to re-identify individuals through the additional discovery and cross-reference of anonymized data.
- User unawareness – whereby users unknowingly allow access to potentially sensitive information.
- Third party data sharing without notice or consent to users.

When users are aware of their emerging privacy vulnerabilities as a function of the MIoT, organizations must take responsibility for implementing additional measures as a form of technical and organizational control for mitigating privacy vulnerabilities through clear data governance policies. In an MIoT environment, where users are often unaware of privacy risks, they need to be aware of the vulnerabilities associated with MIoT.

5.1. Unauthorised Access

Unauthorised access can expose threats to privacy in MIoT systems; it may arise when there are inadequate security settings from the outset.

- Insecure interfaces, poorly configured APIs, and weak or default passwords make it simple for attackers to take control of a network or device.
- Then, if you couple that with the fact that data is unencrypted when transferred, then it is easy for data not intended for hackers/external sources to be part of the data transfer.

These common problems could lead to theft of data and manipulation of patient health records, and worse still, cause a distraction from patient safety. To limit the chances of these issues occurring, we should enhance authentication and establish encryption protocols.

5.2. Data Leakage and Data Breaches

MIoT systems can suffer data leakage and breaches. This tends to occur when the configurations of the security settings provide little or no barriers to security.

- Public and insecure networks can lead to the interception of unencrypted data. Hackers often want the data being exchanged.
- There is also poor misconfiguration of cloud storage methods, such as leaving it open or bad permissions. Unfortunately, the health records and personally identifiable information (PII) can be exposed to the public.

Often, security breaches and identity theft can occur from a lack of proper security protocols. The primary impacts are on identity theft, financial harm, and the relationship with patients. To limit the chances, we must continually improve studies about end-to-end encryption and secure cloud configuration practices. Furthermore, we must enhance research studies on auditing those practices.

5.3. Inference and Profiling

In MIoT systems, even health data that has been anonymized may carry risks in terms of privacy.

- Attackers (or third parties) may cross-reference data sets to get information that may allow them to reidentify a person, which can completely negate the process of anonymization.
- Inference about a person's lifestyle (for example, a sleep pattern or movement pattern) can provide insight into more intimately personal aspects of a person's lifestyle—habits, mental health, chronic health, etc.

This type of profiling can lead to many unintended entries, including discrimination, targeted advertising, or insurance-related interactions, so data minimization and robust anonymization procedures must be in place.

5.4. Lack of Users Awareness

One of the biggest privacy risks that occurs within the context of MIoT systems is the lack of end user awareness.

- Users routinely approve app permissions or connect a device without the knowledge of explicit details about the process of data collection, usage, or sharing.
- Most digital MIoT devices are consumer-grade, so the protection that users and privacy advocates expect is often a low priority in terms of security (Alexa vs. Dot), which increases the opportunity for erroneous access or data compromises.

The lack of user awareness could result in accidental exposure of sensitive health information, so it's essential to provide clear privacy policies, transparency, and education about health literacy, consent, and awareness.

5.5. Communication Data to a Third Party

Sharing data with a third party is common in MIoT systems, but it also raises serious privacy issues.

- For example, health data may be shared with vendors, analytics companies, or insurance companies for marketing, profiling, or risk assessment.
- And this is often done with little transparency, and the user has little say or control over who gets their data and how it is used.

Without clear consent and governance policies, this could easily result in privacy violations with trust degradation and possible misuse of sensitive information. Table 3 shows a summary of the Privacy Risks in MIoT Systems.

These privacy threats call for technical, procedural, and educational actions.

6. Privacy-Enhancing Technologies and Anonymization

To mitigate privacy threat levels in MIoT systems and still have them work as intended,

Table 3: Key Privacy Risks in MIoT Systems

Risk Category	Description	Examples/Impacts
Unauthorized Access	Weak authentication or unsecured interfaces allow unauthorized users to access sensitive data.	Default passwords, insecure APIs, lack of encryption lead to patient data exposure.
Data Leakage and Breaches	Inadequate encryption or misconfigured storage can result in unintentional data disclosure.	Unencrypted transmissions; exposed cloud storage revealing health records or personal identifiers.
Inference and Profiling	Anonymized data can be cross-analyzed to reveal identities and private behaviors.	Re-identification of users; profiling leading to discrimination or targeted marketing.
Lack of User Awareness	Users often unknowingly grant permissions without understanding risks.	Over-permissioned apps; use of insecure consumer-grade devices without proper privacy controls.
Third-Party Data Sharing	Data is shared with external entities, often with limited user knowledge or control.	Use of health data by insurers or marketers without user consent leads to privacy violations.

various privacy-enhancing technologies (PETs) and anonymization techniques are used to protect sensitive data during the collection, processing, storage, and sharing phases without much impact on the system or the quality of health service delivery. This helps organizations to stay compliant (and avoid sanctions), reduce the risk of breaches (and potential sanctions), and instill user confidence (and hopefully sell more services). The most significant strategies include:

- Anonymization and removal of identifiers
- Encryption and secure transmission, and storage
- Access control mechanisms for those who are permitted to see or edit data
- Edge computing to handle data locally rather than across the network
- Differential privacy to conduct data analysis without compromising identities

This continuum allows personal health data to be well-protected in complex and distributed MIoT environments.

6.1. Encryption

Encryption is a key privacy-enhancing technology that achieves confidentiality within MIoT systems.

- It ensures that users can't access health data unintentionally while it's being transferred via networks and stored on a device and in the cloud.
- Common encryption types include:
  - Symmetric encryption (i.e., AES)—uses only 1 shared key to encrypt and decrypt data.
  - Asymmetric encryption (i.e., RSA)—uses public and private keys, and larger key sizes will increase the difficulty of hacking.

An advantage of security encryption is that it reduces the likelihood of a data breach, ensuring compliance within the regulatory framework when encrypting sensitive information.

6.2. Access Control and Authentication

Access control and authentication are necessary to restrict unauthorized access to sensitive data in MIoT systems.

- Multi-factor authentication (MFA) is being encouraged and widely adopted when services become available—like when you enter your password, you may also be required to click a link and enter a device-specific code (e.g., password + fingerprint).
- Role-based access control (RBAC) requires users to access information limited to specific aspects of their role and responsibilities; more information than necessary could be available to a user.

These two factors affect each other, and encryption, access control, and authentication collectively maintain user capabilities, user credibility, and system integrity while limiting the unauthorized use of data to breach confidentiality and reduce an insider's threat.

6.3. Anonymization and Pseudonymization

Anonymization and pseudonymization techniques are methods of data protection to safeguard personal identity in MIoT systems.

- Anonymization erases any identifying characteristics so that it is impossible to trace data back to individuals.
- Pseudonymization substitutes identifiers (such as names or IDs) for encoded values, allowing for the utility of the data while mitigating some risk of re-identification.

Both anonymization and pseudonymization have significant value in protecting patient privacy, enabling data-based research, and complying with legislation mandating privacy protections, such as GDPR.

6.4. Differential Privacy

Differential privacy is a sophisticated privacy protection technique that conceals individual identities in shared datasets using statistical noise.

- The noise added to shared datasets makes it very difficult to know if a data item is from any one individual (even when datasets are analyzed together).
- Differential privacy is a strong protection because it supports both privacy guarantees and usability of the shared data, concerning the privacy guarantee.

Differential privacy offers significant value in MIoT, as it allows rigorously secured analysis of health-related data without compromising individual confidentiality.

6.5. Secure Multi-party Computation (SMPC)

Secure Multi-party Computation (SMPC) is a cryptographic method that allows multiple parties to compute results together over their combined data without exposing the raw data to one another.

- SMPC protects the privacy and confidentiality of each participant's data during the collaborative computation and analysis.
- SMPC allows for effective collaboration among parties on distributed medical research, cross-institutional studies, and collaborative diagnostics, while protecting sensitive or restricted access to data.

By allowing joint computation without exposing data to collaborators, SMPC enables privacy-preserving analytics in MIoT ecosystems.

6.6. Blockchain and Distributed Ledger Technologies

Distributed ledger technologies (DLTs) and blockchain offer a decentralized method of managing MIoT data while improving data integrity and transparency.

- Blockchain and DLTs are designed to be tamper-proof, with thorough data access and transactions. This logging minimizes the complexity of auditing and tracking of data access.
- Decentralized identity provides greater assurance to users regarding who accesses their health data and under what conditions.

When utilized appropriately, blockchains and DLTs can enhance data governance, improve user confidence, and provide a strong defense against privacy violations in medical IoT applications.

Table 4: Overview of Privacy-Enhancing Technologies in MIoT

Technique	Purpose	Key Features/Examples
Encryption	Protects data during transmission and storage	AES (symmetric), RSA (asymmetric); ensures confidentiality and prevents unauthorized access
Access Control and Authentication	Restricts data access to authorized users	Multi-Factor Authentication (MFA), Role-Based Access Control (RBAC)
Anonymization and Pseudonymization	Removes or masks personal identifiers	Enables safe data sharing for research; supports GDPR compliance
Differential Privacy	Prevents re-identification from aggregated data	Adds statistical noise; preserves data utility with strong privacy guarantees
Secure Multi-party Computation	Enables joint data analysis without sharing raw data	Used in collaborative diagnostics and research across institutions
Blockchain and DLTs	Ensures transparent and tamper-proof data records	Decentralized identity management; immutable audit trails

Table 4 summarizes the Privacy-Enhancing Technologies and Anonymization in MIoT systems.

7. Conclusion

The introduction of the Medical Internet of Things (MIoT) in healthcare has enormous transformative possibilities in facilitating real time monitoring, personalized treatment, and clinical outcomes, but sharing and generating large amounts of sensitive data from pervasive, interconnected devices provides significant challenges to privacy and confidentiality.

This chapter describes the various types of data generated in MIoT systems, including physiological data, behavioral data, health history, contextual data, and communications. While this data is extremely valuable for improving patient care, it also raises significant privacy concerns when shared with third parties or stored in cloud environments.

Countries, regions, and organizations have established a suite of regulations, policies, and standards such as HIPAA, GDPR, PIPL, and ISO/IEC 27701, that tend to a valid interest in protecting PII and PHI, in terms of accountability, for all major global jurisdictions. Despite the regulatory arrangements, MIoT systems will continue to face privacy threats—unauthorized access to devices and data breaches, inference attacks to undermine non-user consent, and making judgements without appropriate consent can destroy patient confidence and subsequent safety.

Some privacy-enhancing technologies (PETs) such as encryption, access control, deidentifying and pseudonymizing, differential privacy, secure multiparty computation, and blockchain provide evidence-based techniques to protect data throughout its lifecycle, balancing the dual obligations of usefulness and privacy in terms of normalizing secure and ethical use of MIoT systems reportable practice.

To wrap things up, safeguarding privacy and confidentiality in the MIoT realm isn't just a technical requirement; it's also a moral responsibility. We need a layered strategy that blends strong technologies, educated users, and adherence to regulations to create healthcare systems that are secure, trustworthy, and focused on patients—all powered by IoT.

References

Dwork, C. (2008). Differential privacy: A survey of results. Theory and Applications of Models of Computation, 4978, 1–19. https://doi.org/10.1007/978-3-540-79228-4_1

European Union. (2016). General Data Protection Regulation (GDPR). [EU Regulation 2016/679]. Available at: https://doi.org/10.1109/TIFS.2016.2528246

Islam, S.M.R., Kwak, D., Kabir, M.H., Hossain, M., and Kwak, K.S. (2015). The Internet of Things for health care: A comprehensive survey. IEEE Access, 3, 678–708. https://doi.org/10.1109/ACCESS.2015.2437951

ISO/IEC 27701:2019. (2019). Security techniques—Extension to ISO/IEC 27001 and ISO/IEC 27002 for privacy information management—Requirements and guidelines. International Organization for Standardization.

Li, H., Dai, Y., Tian, L., and Yu, S. (2016). Achieving secure and efficient dynamic access control in data-sharing systems. IEEE Transactions on Information Forensics and Security, 11(6), 1253–1265.

Personal Information Protection Law (PIPL) – China. (2021). National People's Congress of the PRC. Full text available at: http://www.npc.gov.cn/

Tang, H., and Hu, Y. (2020). Privacy protection and data security in medical IoT: A review of recent developments and future directions. IEEE Access, 8, 23467–23484. https://doi.org/10.1109/ACCESS.2020.2968884

The Personal Data Protection Bill (India) – Ministry of Electronics and Information Technology (Draft, 2019). Available at: https://www.meity.gov.in

U.S. Department of Health and Human Services (HHS). (2020). Health Insurance Portability and Accountability Act of 1996 (HIPAA). Available at: https://www.hhs.gov/hipaa/

Zhang, P., White, J., Schmidt, D.C., Lenz, G., and Rosenbloom, S.T. (2018). FHIRChain: Applying blockchain to securely and scalably share clinical data. Computational and Structural Biotechnology Journal, 16, 267–278. https://doi.org/10.1016/j.csbj.2018.07.004

CHAPTER
18

Empowering Health through Intelligent Insights: Dr. Symptoms – Your Pathway to Wellness

Ratnavel Rajalakshmi[1*(0000-0002-6570-483X)], J. Bhuvana[2(0000-0002-9328-6989)], Shakti Swaroop Sahu[1], Ritesh Pradhan[1], Eliksha Maheshwari[1], Jyothsna Arun Kumar[1] and Vanshika Mahajan[1]

[1] School of Computer Science and Engineering, Vellore Institute of Technology, Chennai, India

[2] Department of Computer Science and Engineering, Sri Sivasubramaniya Nadar College of Engineering, Chennai, India

1. Introduction

The advent of artificial intelligence and machine learning (ML) is reshaping the current health care environment, which has the potential to result in substantial opportunities to improve diagnostic accuracy and patient-centered care. Despite these opportunities, significant challenges remain, especially when it comes to the early and accurate detection of complex diseases such as cancer and brain tumors. The success of any clinical intervention is often dependent on a timely determination of the diagnosis, which is constantly thwarted by a variety of factors, including subtlety of early symptoms and the complexity of interpreting change in medical imagery (Davenport et al., 2019).

Some primary challenges within this field relate to developing strong algorithms that can identify weak pathological features in medical imaging, segmentation of anatomical components amongst noise and variations in imaging, and getting ML models to produce results that can be clinically interpreted. For diagnostic tools to be adopted by health providers, they must be accurate. Still, they must be interpretable, providing clinically relevant attenuation that health providers can use to guide treatment options and improve clinician-patient communication (Rudin et al., 2019). Finally, as healthcare systems continue to digitize, maintaining patient data

*Corresponding author: rajalakshmi.r@vit.ac.in

DOI: 10.1201/9781003676812-18

protection and privacy through strong authentication and data handling policies must also occur. There are a few challenges that need focus and are identified as follows:

- **Early Disease Detection:** Though medical imaging data are available nowadays, detecting the mild and subtle features of tumors enables them to be detected during their early stages. Adding to these, less contrast, overlapping structures, and absence of invariability add to the complexity of detecting the disease and prevent it from early detection. This increases the need to design effective ML and AI algorithms to detect subtle signs of diseases in medical images, which will aid in timely intervention and appropriate treatment planning.
- **Multi-modal Image Fusion:** The different modes of capturing patient ailments are through MRI, CT, and PET images. To enjoy the benefits of each imaging category, combining the modalities will help provide a complete view of diseases. However, such fusion needs proper alignment, coordination among features from the different modalities, and methods to handle the distortion specific to each modality. This requires advanced ML-based fusion techniques and models that can handle the complexities that arise during the process to provide a comprehensive understanding of patient conditions.
- **Segmentation of Organs and Tissues:** To plan the appropriate treatment, the tumor and cancer boundaries must be accurately defined. However, inconsistent anatomy, distortions caused by pathological conditions, and occlusions will complicate boundary identification and thus make segmentation more difficult.
- **Handling Variability and Noise:** Designing strong ML and AI models that can interpret medical images even though they are corrupted with noise, non-standard imaging protocols, and equipment.
- **Interpretability and Explainability:** ML and AI models should ensure proper insights into their decision-making behavior. Only then will they earn the trust of health care professionals and the patients.
- **Data Privacy and Security:** Any portal or platform that handles patient data must ensure data privacy and security by adhering to the regional/global regulations. Dr. Symptoms implements and follows these standards by using a Firebase and secure APIs.

In addressing the previously mentioned challenges, this Chapter proposes Dr. Symptoms: a comprehensive healthcare platform that implements complex ML models, LLMs, and secure cloud infrastructure. Dr. Symptoms is created to help patients and clinicians with tools that enhance disease prediction, symptoms, and related data. With the help of ML and LLMs, which increase detection accuracy, Dr. Symptoms provides individualized treatment plans. With strong authentication and data privacy protocols, Dr. Symptoms protects patient information, which is considered sensitive. Due to the complexity and increased occurrences of diseases like brain tumors and cancer, there is a need for advanced methods for early and accurate disease detection. Dr. Symptoms handles these by combining ML, interpretability, and data security for the timely detection of diseases and providing suitable, customized clinical decisions. This innovative approach not only provides accurate diagnostics but also paves the way for personalized treatment plans tailored to each patient based on the nature of their disease.

Our Contributions

This paper presents a modern, interoperable health technology solution with three primary contributions:

- **Improved Disease Diagnosis with Integrated Segmentation:** We outline a new method that combines diagnosis and locating exactly where the disease has manifested. We employ segmentation matrices in our models for brain tumor and lung cancer localization, and we use the Segment Anything Model (SAM) (Kirillov et al., 2023) to assist physicians in pinpointing the disease's location while viewing a CT or MRI image.
- **Potentially Useful AI-Powered Symptom Interpretation with RAG:** We used a Large Language Model (Groq) that has been fine-tuned on a massive amount of medical literature and provides Retrieval-Augmented Generation (RAG) (Lewis et al., 2020), in a way that could enable patients to receive valid, context-relevant suggestions, based on their reported symptoms; thus, reducing the gap between self-identifying symptoms and covering the Practitioner's recommendations.
- **A Complete Patient and Practitioner's Portal Platform:** Dr. Symptoms provides a unified profile of the patient and doctor. It supports predictive models, a chatbot that does symptom discernment, medical document storage via Firebase (Pu et al., 2021), and accepts secure user sign-on, etc., to favorably streamline the workflow for diagnostic and patient management.

The rest of the chapter is organized as follows. Section II deals with related work. Section III discusses the method and architectural structure of the system. Section IV discusses results, with Section V providing further discussion. Finally, Section VI concludes the paper.

2. Related Work

A. **Large Language Models in Healthcare:** Large Language Models (LLMs) in healthcare have gained traction in recent years. BioBERT (Lee et al., 2020) and ClinicalBERT are adaptable versions of foundational models like BERT used in the medical field. These models have been fine-tuned on large corpora of medical texts, including vastly more clinical notes than typically used for an LLM, allowing an improved understanding of complex medical diction and performing well on downstream tasks such as disease classification and medical question answering. Lee et al. (2020) provided evidence of BioBERT's accuracy in retrieving medical entities from unstructured text. One LLM that is redefining the peer-reviewed literature in an area considered evidence-based medicine is MedPaLM (Singhal et al., 2023). MedPaLM is designed for medical dialogue, effectively creating evidence-based responses to clinical questions.

B. **Retrieval-Augmented Generation for Knowledge Retrieval:** Standard LLMs can create plausible but incorrect information, which is untenable in a medical context. Retrieval-Augmented Generation (RAG) mitigates this challenge since RAG can ground model responses in external verified knowledge sources. The RAG framework, developed by Lewis et al. (2020), augments language models by retrieving relevant documents from a wide body of knowledge and then conditioning the generative process on this information. In the health care realm, RAG-based models hold promise in providing evidence-based recommendations based directly on medical literature (Xie et al., 2024). The Dr. Symptoms platform uses RAG to evaluate and analyze symptoms and patient stories, ensuring that generated diagnostic suggestions are accurate and based on established medical knowledge.

C. **Medical Image Segmentation with Deep Learning:** Deep learning has transformed medical image segmentation, leading to architectures such as U-Net (Ronneberger et al., 2015)to become the gold standard. Attention U-Net (Oktay et al., 2018) enhanced this work by introducing attention gates for saliency in the image. Most recently, the Segment Anything Model (SAM) (Kirillov et al., 2023) has come into play as a powerful, generalist model for segmentation. To this end, it can perform zero-shot segmentation of any type of image, including medical scans. This means it can identify regions of interest without needing to be trained on a specific task.

D. **Cloud-based Medical Data Storage and Analysis:** The secure and efficient management of patient data is foundational to digital health today. Firebase and AWS HealthLake provide scalable, secure, and HIPAA-compliant storage of sensitive medical records (Priya et al., 2017). Dr. Symptoms uses Firebase to securely store patient-uploaded reports, which are then analyzed in real-time by our AI models. This design allows for real-time diagnostic feedback and minimal delay in data retrieval (Mell et al., 2011).

2.1 Summary of Gaps

While many AI models perform well, when used for a single task, very few platforms have integrated all important features like understanding symptoms, analyzing reports, classifying images, and segmenting affected regions in one place. This lack of integration makes it difficult for doctors and patients to depend on just one system. Dr. Symptoms fills this gap by acting as a comprehensive, all-in-one solution. It provides an end-to-end pipeline where each part, from chat-based symptom checking to medical image analysis, is powered by its own smart AI module, all working together to support better diagnosis and patient care.

3. Methodology

The occurrence of non-communicable diseases, mostly cancers, requires solutions for early, reliable, and scalable diagnostics. Delayed treatment often leads to an increase in treatment cost and an impact on the survival rate. The conventional image interpretation method of diagnostics is time-consuming and vulnerable to inter-observer variability. Additionally, many of the AI models are lacking in interpretability, which leads to trust issues among clinicians.

Dr. Symptoms is a dual-platform AI-powered healthcare system with two major subsystems: a Patient Assistance System for user-facing medical support, and a Doctor Support System for clinical image analysis. The first uses conversational AI and medical document analysis, while the second provides disease classification and medical image segmentation. The backend of the proposed Dr. Symptoms system integrates LLM (Groq), RAG, and deep CNN models like VGG-16 and SAM. These systems use different AI models, including unique datasets specific to each model's goal, to develop a cohesive and robust medical support framework. The system's overall architecture is shown in Figure 1.

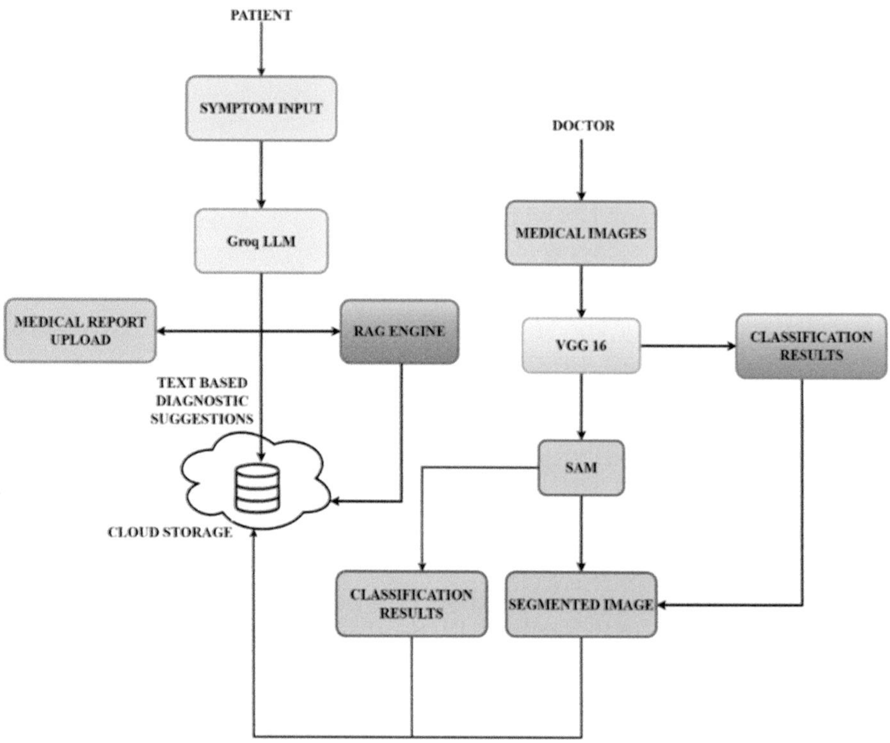

Figure 1: System architecture of Dr. Symptoms.

Algorithm: Dr. Symptoms – AI-Powered Diagnostic System

Input

- Patient symptoms in text or uploaded as images of reports
- Doctor login and diagnostic queries
- Medical datasets for training (Both images and text)

Output

- Interpretation of symptoms
- Diagnostic of Disease (prediction/classification)
- Segmentation regions with uncertainty map
- Personalized recommendations

Step 1: Start System

1. Initialize all services:

- Load LLM (Groq) + RAG
- Load VGG-16 and SAM models
- Connect to Firebase for cloud storage
- Load standard medical terminologies

Step 2: User Authentication

2.1. Prompt user: Are you a Patient or Doctor?
2.2. Based on role:
  - If Patient: Go to Step 3
  - If Doctor: Go to Step 6

Step 3: Patient Module – Symptom Query

3.1. Accept natural language symptom as input
3.2. Send the input to LLM with RAG
3.3. Generate response using retrieved knowledge
3.4. Display response to patient

Step 4: Patient Report Upload

4.1. Submit PDF/image reports
4.2. Apply preprocessing using OCR and NER
4.3. RAG retrieves supporting clinical content
4.4. LLM generates an interpretation
4.5. Display findings to the patient

Step 5: Optional – Upload Medical Image

5.1. Submit MRI/CT scan image
5.2. Preprocess images: resize, denoise, enhance
5.3. Send image to VGG-16 for prediction/ classification
5.4. If segmentation is needed, run SAM with prompt points
5.5. Display result with overlay and uncertainty map

Step 6: Doctor Module – Login and Access

6.1. Authenticate doctor
6.2. Access patient report or image
6.3. View diagnosis/segmentation result
6.4. Option to annotate/override results

Step 7: Cloud Storage and Logging

7.1. Store session data securely on Firebase
7.2. Log queries, outputs, and timestamps

Step 8: Feedback and Improvement Loop

8.1. Collect feedback from users
8.2. Update training data and retrain models periodically

Step 9: End Session

9.1. Log out the user
9.2. Clear session data
9.3. End

3.1. Patient Assistance System

The Patient Assistance System is designed to give users rich medical support by utilizing two technologies: a Large Language Model (LLM) for natural language interaction and a Retrieval-Augmented Generation (RAG) technology to analyze medical reports.

1. **LLM-based Interaction:** This system uses a Large Language Model (LLM), which was trained on a large corpus of medical knowledge, allowing patients to converse in natural language about their symptoms. By utilizing medical data sets and literature, the model provides initial recommendations based on patients' reported symptoms. The patients can ask various questions about health concerns, and the system will give context-specific medical recommendations, possible roots for their symptoms, other possibilities with associated symptoms, and treatments. The LLM has been designed to have an adaptive conversation with patients, which allows them to ask for clarification on complicated medical terminology or conditions, augmenting the conversational interaction's human-styled sociality and accessibility.

(a) Dataset Description: The success of the model depends on a structured and mixed dataset created, primarily through an organized preprocessing pipeline.

- **Composition of dataset:** The training corpus was built from three sources:
  - A detailed library of medical textbooks, evidence, and clinical guidelines, including reputable texts like Harrison's Principles of Internal Medicine (Longo et al., 2018).
  - A large dataset of anonymized patient records that spans a range of medical conditions, symptoms, and treatments
  - A curated collection of questions and answers from a collection of subject-matter experts, where all of the questions were created by medical professionals.
- **Data preprocessing:** Multiple data preprocessing methods were employed to put high-quality input into the model:
  - **Text cleaning:** Removal of noise, discrepancies, and irrelevant detail from the raw text.
  - **Tokenization:** The breaking down of text into pieces (tokens - words or subwords) which can be processed computationally.
  - **Data augmentation:** Creating synthetic data to aid in diversity and establish more generalizability for the model.
  - **Data splitting:** Partitioning of the complete data set into separate training, validation, and testing sets. This was to establish a robust evaluation.

(b) Model Architecture and Training: The system is built utilizing a better transformer model and a modified exercise routine.

- **Model architecture:** At the core of the system is an advanced neural network for natural language understanding and generation.
  - **Transformer-based LLM:** The model is on an architecture for a transformer-based LLM, for example, models like BERT (Devlin et al., 2019) or GPT-3 (Brown et al., 2020), which are celebrated for their ability to understand and produce human-like text from attention mechanisms.

- In this work, Llama2 employs a dedicated transformer architecture to enhance performance in the platform Groq (Touvron et al., 2023), as shown in Figure 2. The model follows an encoder-decoder configuration, where the encoder converts the input query and the decoder generates the response.
    - **Attention mechanism:** A built-in attention mechanism enables the model to dynamically balance the importance of different elements of the input sequence when producing the output, thereby enhancing contextual coherence and relevance.

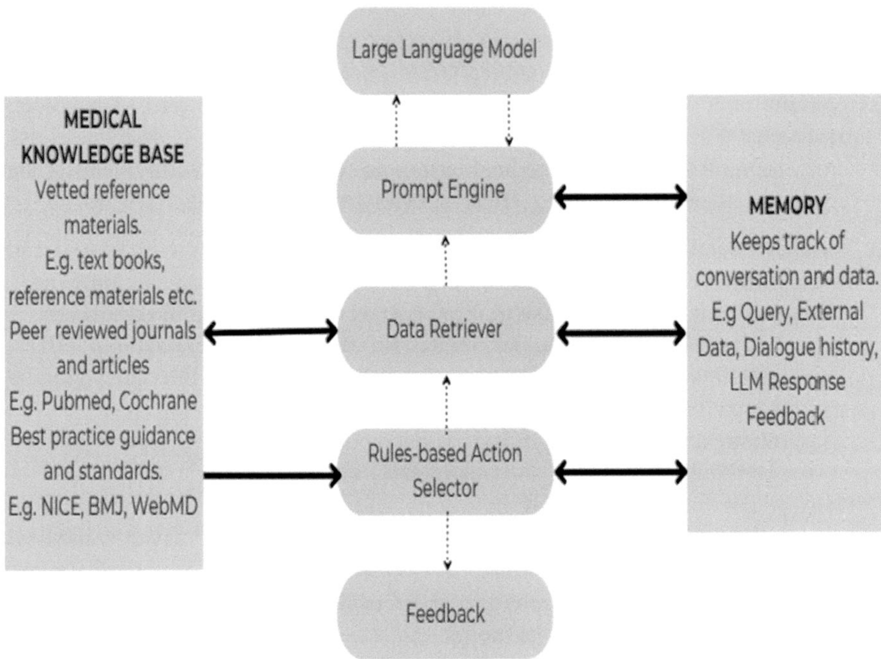

Figure 2: LLM architecture.

- **Model training and fine-tuning:** The Training process was intended to remap the general-purpose LLM to the particular demands inherent to the medical field.
    - **Objective function:** It was trained with a compound objective function that includes cross-entropy loss related to textual accuracy through a reinforcement goal of machine learning to improve response quality and relevance.
    - **Optimization:** Model parameters were optimized using gradient descent techniques, e.g., Adam (Kingma et al., 2014) or SGD.
    - **Hyperparameter optimization:** Important hyperparameters, such as learning rate, batch size, and the amount. The training epochs were carefully tuned to reach optimal model performance.
    - **Evaluation metrics:** The language generation skills were assessed using

standard evaluation measures, including perplexity, BLEU score, and ROUG.

- ◦ **Fine-tuning on medical data:** The important step was the pre-training fine-tuning of the LLM on a specialized medical dataset. The process involved renewing the model's parameters to make its knowledge of medical terminology, identify complex patterns in clinical information, and produce highly precise and comprehensive answers.

2. RAG-based Medical Report Analysis: A key improvement to this system is about medical report analytics using a Retrieval-Augmented Generation (RAG) system. This will allow the patient to upload health documents, including blood tests, x-rays, or MRIs that the system analyzes and responds to, relevant to their specific query. The RAG system will extract relevant medical report details and leverage LLM medical knowledge to produce informed, context-relevant responses. For example, if a patient uploaded an MRI report, the system would conceptualize the findings in that report, contextually confirm that information alongside relevant medical diagnosis data, and provide clearer diagnostic interpretation and/ or treatment options. This combination of systems provides more specific, accurate medical guidance to the patient by using patient-reported symptoms alongside medical reports.

(a) Dataset Description: To construct it, the RAG model relied on a highly specialized dataset and went through a multi-stage preprocessing pipeline to ensure data quality and relevance.

- **Dataset features:** There were two main components:
  - ◦ A heterogeneous collection of medical reports, including radiology, pathology, discharge summaries, and clinical notes.
  - ◦ A structured medical knowledge base, containing medical concepts, entities, and their relationships from known standards, such as SNOMED CT (Kingma 2014) or UMLS (SNOMEDl 2025).
- **Data preprocessing:** To get the data ready for the model, the following preprocessing steps were taken:
  - ◦ **Text extraction:** Extract relevant text from medical reports, including Named Entity Recognition (NER) to identify the medical entities and concepts.
  - ◦ **Text cleaning:** Remove noise, inconsistencies, and irrelevant information to improve signal quality.
  - ◦ **Text tokenization:** Tokenize the cleaned text into tokens (i.e., words or subwords) for model input.
  - ◦ **Data augmentation:** Create synthetic data to increase the number of examples in the dataset and improve the distribution of different examples for better generalization in the model.
  - ◦ **Knowledge base integration:** The structured medical knowledge base was used in the RAG model to add necessary context and prevent poorly formed retrievals in the downstream tasks.

(b) Model Architecture and Training: The RAG framework includes two different, retriever and generator, components for training and fine-tuning for the medical domain.

- **Model architecture:** The model configuration is multistratum and designed to ground the generated text with factual and retrieved evidence.
  - **Document retrieval:** The retriever, from either a dense retrieval model or some semantic search engine invoked by the user's query, identifies documents or passages relevant to the medical inquiry from the medical knowledge base.
  - **Language model:** The language model to produce summaries or answers to user questions is a large language model, such as BERT or GPT-3 depending on the context of documents retrieved from the retrieved data.
  - **RAG framework:** The retriever and language model assembled into a Retrieval-Augmented Generation (RAG) framework (Figure 3) render answers that are more factual and informative than generative models singly.

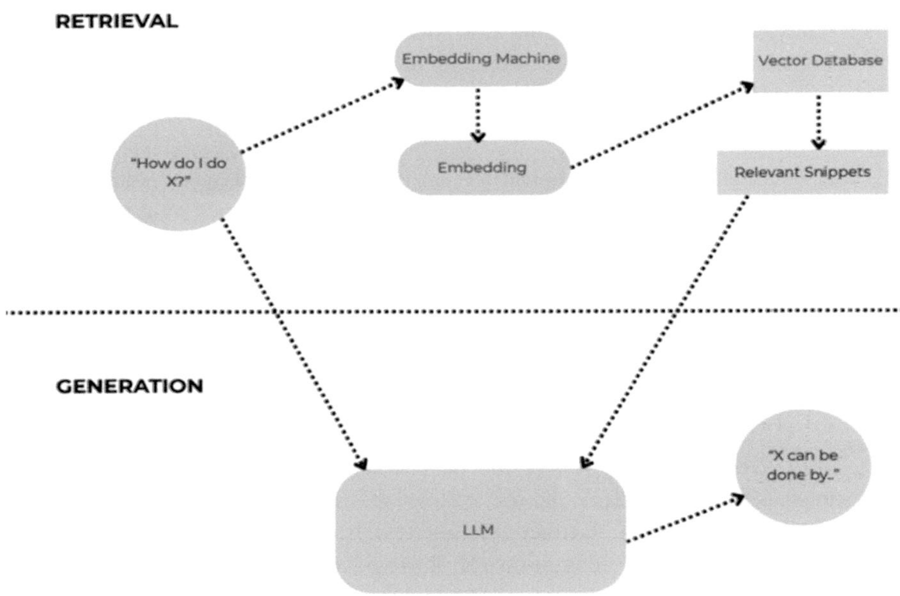

Figure 3: Architecture of RAG-based medical report analysis.

- **Model training:** We trained each component in order and then had some end-to-end tuning.
  - **Retriever training:** The retriever component was trained on a massive corpus of medical documents and associated queries, to learn to retrieve related documents having high precision and recall.
  - **Training the language model:** The language model was pre-trained on a large general-domain corpus of text (and code) to allow for language generation.
  - **RAG fine-tuning:** The RAG framework was fine-tuned on a specialized dataset of medical queries and answers to support generating answers that were accurate, relevant, and contextual.

- ◦ **Performance evaluation metrics:** The performance was calculated using text generation quality metrics (ROUGE, BLEU, METEOR) that are standard measures.

The RAG-based medical report analysis system allows for combining and integrating the aforementioned complexity of medical information and leveraging that to facilitate accurate insights for patients and the healthcare practitioner.

3.2. Doctor Support System

The Doctor Support System provides clinicians with appropriate support with advanced medical image analysis capabilities. The development of the doctor support system began with a simple model using binary classification to classify images, then advanced to utilize the VGG architecture to assist in segmentation while being highly accurate.

1. Initial Brain Tumor Classification using VGG-16: The first phase of the doctor support implementation involved binary classification of brain tumor images with the VGG16 architecture. The VGG-16 architecture (Bodenreider et al., 2004) is employed because it is used in specialized fields in medicine with significant success, including lung pathology and brain pathology (significant specialization). Hence, it has a very deep (number of layers) convolutional architecture and can represent highly complex non-linear structures that are typically present in image classification problems. The main issue with the VGG model is its limited generalizability into other facets of medical imaging flow.

(a) Dataset Description: The dataset and preprocessing were tailored specifically for the brain tumor detection task.

- **Dataset composition:** The dataset used for this classification task comprised 155 images of brains with tumors and 98 images without tumors. This collection served as a critical resource for training the algorithm to identify early signs of tumors and other anomalies in brain images.
- **Data preprocessing:** To optimize the dataset for training and evaluation, several key steps were taken:
    - ◦ **Data splitting:** The dataset was partitioned into training (80%), validation (15%), and test (5%) sets as shown in Figure 4. This strategy ensures the model's generalization performance on unseen data and helps mitigate overfitting. Sample data are shown in Figure 5.
    - ◦ **Image preprocessing:** The images underwent preprocessing steps, including cropping and augmentation, to enhance features relevant to tumor detection. Cropping isolates the region of interest, while augmentation techniques (e.g., rotations, flips) artificially increase data diversity, making the model more robust.
    - ◦ **Visualization:** Visualization tools were used to display the results of image processing, helping researchers assess data quality and distribution. This included analyzing histograms of image aspect ratios and plotting sample grids for each class (Figure 6) to better understand data variability.

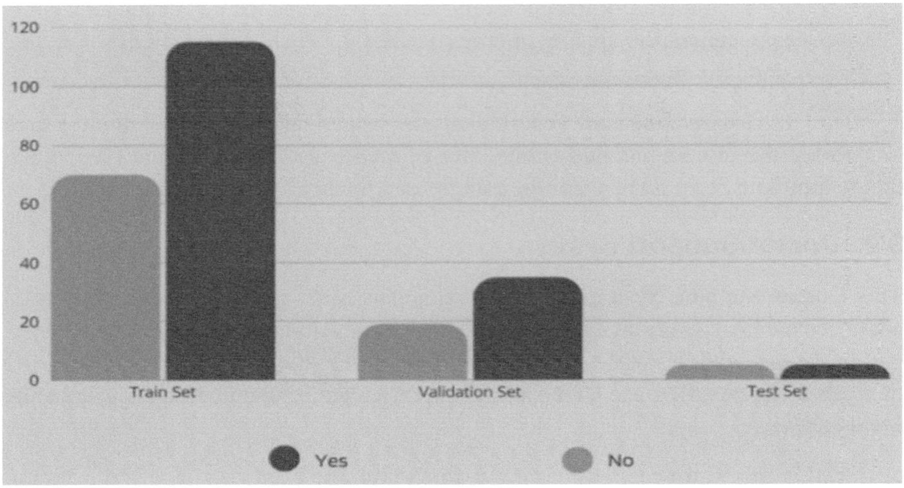

Figure 4: Dataset composition.

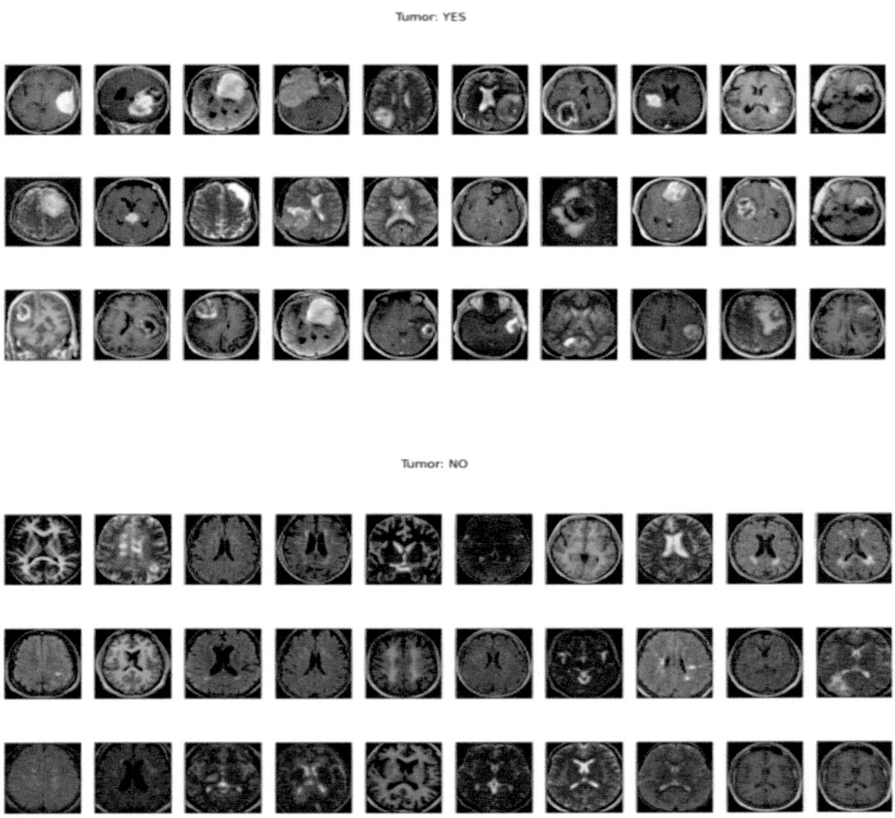

Figure 5: Sample data.

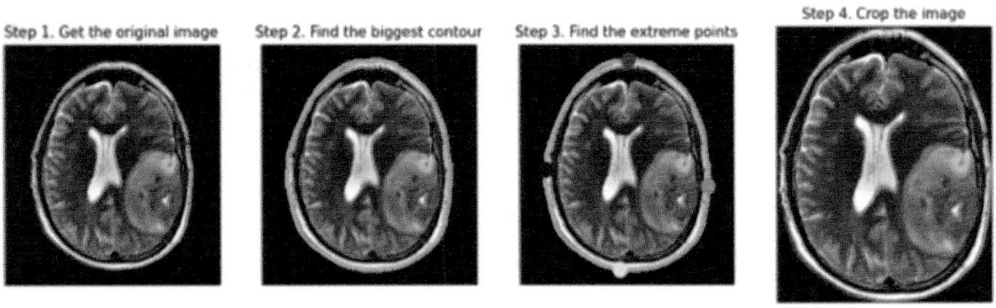

Figure 6: After pre-processing.

(b) Model Architecture and Training: The VGG-16 architecture, pre-trained on the ImageNet dataset (Simonyan et al., 2014), was adapted for this binary classification task.

- **Model architecture:** The model follows the standard VGG-16 structure with modifications to the final layers for binary classification.
  - **Input layer:** The model accepts an input image of dimensions 224×224×3 (height, width, RGB channels).
  - **Block 1-5:** The architecture consists of five convolutional blocks. Blocks 1 and 2 have two convolutional layers (with 64 and 128 filters, respectively), while Blocks 3, 4, and 5 have three convolutional layers (with 256, 512, and 512 filters, respectively). All convolutional layers use a 3×3 kernel, and each block is followed by a max-pooling layer with a 2×2 pool size.
  - **Fully connected layers:** The output from the final pooling layer is flattened into a 25,088-dimensional vector. This vector is then passed through two fully connected (dense) layers with 4,096 units each, using ReLU as the activation function.
  - **Output layer:** A final output layer with a single unit and a sigmoid activation function is used for binary classification, predicting the presence or absence of a brain tumor.
- **Model training:** The training process was configured to optimize performance on the specific medical imaging task.
  - **Loss function:** The model uses binary cross-entropy loss, as the task is a binary classification problem.
  - **Optimizer:** The RMSprop optimizer was employed to minimize the loss function during training (Deng et al., 2009).
  - **Metrics:** Accuracy was used as the primary evaluation metric to assess model performance.
- **Layer freezing:** To leverage transfer learning and prevent overfitting on the relatively small medical dataset, the convolutional layers of the pre-trained VGG-16 model were frozen, retaining their learned weights from ImageNet.
  - **Data augmentation:** Data generators were used for both training and validation sets to apply real-time data augmentation, further preventing overfitting and improving model robustness.

2. Enhanced Segmentation with SAM: To create more sophisticated and generalizable image analysis abilities, the system was upgraded with the Segment

Anything Model (SAM), a state-of-the-art architecture for high-quality medical image segmentation. The SAM model performs well at 3D medical image segmentation by utilizing augmented prompts and estimating prediction uncertainty, an important consideration for many clinical applications that leverage precision in segmentations.

(a) Dataset Description: The model was trained on a high-quality dataset that was on a large scale, using a consistent preprocessing protocol.

- **Dataset composition:** The SA-1B dataset (Kirillov et al., 2023) was the basis of the training for SAM.
    - The dataset contains an extensive number of images with extensive annotations, covering many categories of objects, diverse backgrounds, and complex segmentation tasks.
    - The labelled instances included common objects as well as rare objects, which enables SAM to generalize across several visual domains.
    - Annotation types included object boundaries, region labels, and complex occlusions to support many high-resolution segmentation tasks.
    - The labelled instances included common and rare objects, which enables SAM to generalize across several visual domains.
- **Data preprocessing:** To ensure optimal model performance, a well-defined preprocessing pipeline was implemented as shown in Figure 7.

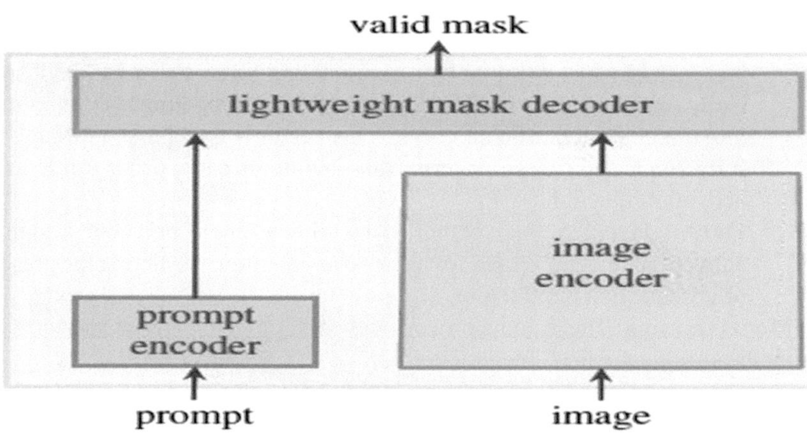

Figure 7: Steps to generate a mask.

-
    - **Image standardization:** Images were resized and standardized to a common resolution to ensure compatibility with the Vision Transformer (ViT) encoder (Tieleman et al., 2012).
    - **Data augmentation:** Data augmentation, such as random cropping, flipping, and color jittering, was performed on the training data to improve the robustness and generalizing abilities of the model.
    - **Annotation refinement:** Before training uses, we have a series of relevant annotation preprocessing steps to remove noise and improve the annotation quality of segmentation masks across the dataset to guarantee reliable ground truth annotation for training.

- ◦ This systematic and comprehensive data preprocessing process guarantees consistent quality of data and allows SAM to achieve a reliable segmentation performance across a broad set of input conditions.

(b) Model Architecture and Training: The SAM architecture is an innovative framework for segmentation, integrating prompt generation and uncertainty estimation.

- **Model architecture:** The architecture is composed of several key modules (Figure 8) that work in sequence to produce precise segmentations.

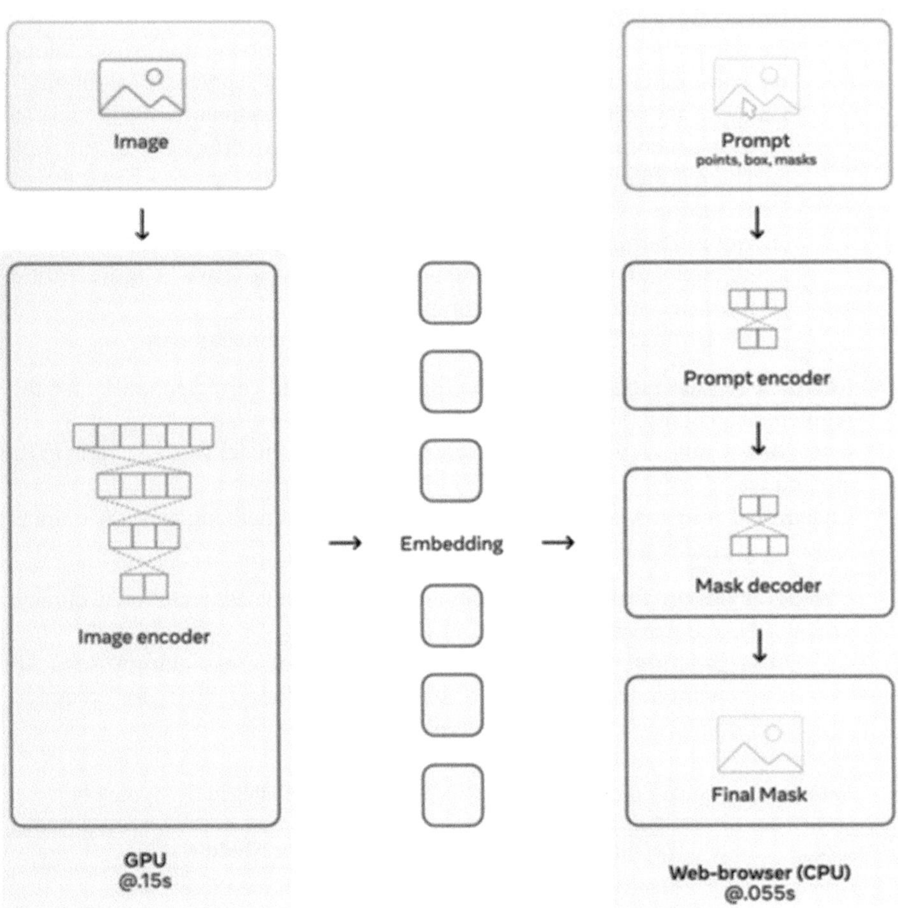

Figure 8: Architecture of the advanced segmentation module.

- ◦ **Input volume:** The model accepts a series of 2D slices from a 3D medical image (e.g., CT or MRI scans) as its primary input.
- ◦ **Image encoder:** A CNN-based encoder processes the input slices to extract meaningful feature embeddings, which capture the anatomical structures present in the volume.

  - **Auto prompt generation:** An auto-prompting mechanism is used to automatically generate bounding boxes around anatomical structures, helping the model focus on relevant regions of interest.
  - Prompt Augmentation: The generated prompts are further augmented to improve the model's ability to segment finer structural details, thereby guiding the segmentation process toward critical regions of the image.
  - **Mask decoder:** To generate the prime segmentation masks using a series of convolutions, the input consists of the picture embeddings and the different augmented prompts.
  - **Uncertainty estimation:** The model has a unique capability to figure out the uncertainty associated with the predicted segmentation masks, along with providing some level of confidence about its segmentation outputs.
  - **Uncertainty rectification:** Based on uncertainty estimates, the model can perform a rectification step, bringing the potential over/under segmentation back to a correct version.
  - **Distribution of predictions:** The model generates predictions through ensemble learning, creating numerous predictions for each slice in the input, replicating the segmentation variability to have a more robust performance and accuracy assurance.
  - **Final outputs:** The final outputs of the SAM architecture are:

* **Rectified segmentation masks:** The final product and corrected masks for the segmented anatomy.
* **Uncertainty map:** A visual map indicating where the model was uncertain in its predictions.
* **Ensembled result:** A consensus output is obtained by finalizing multiple outputs to get an overall result that should be a more reliable.

- **Model training:** Training was designed for improved segmentation accuracy, reliability, and percentage.
  - **Loss function:** SAM uses the combination of cross entropy loss for segmentation accuracy, and a uncertainty-based loss for rectified uncertainty.

Table 1: Functional Comparison of Patient and Doctor Modules in Dr. Symptoms

Feature	Patient Module	Doctor Module
User Type	General Public	Healthcare Professionals
Interaction Mode	Chat-based via LLM	Dashboard Interface
Input Type	Symptom text, medical report upload	Medical Images (CT, MRI, X-rays)
Backend Models	Groq LLM with RAG	VGG-16, SAM
Output	Text-based diagnosis suggestions	Segmented image + classification results
Data Security	Firebase storage, secure login	Role-based access to patient reports

- **Optimizer:** The model was trained with the Adam optimizer.
- **Metrics:** The Dice coefficient and IoU (Intersection over Union) were the main evaluation metrics for segmentation performance.
- **Ensemble learning:** An ensemble improves segmentation quality by taking multiple predictions for every input, where the multiple predictions are pooled to create a final robust output. Tables 1 and 2 show the functional components of Dr. Symptoms and the datasets used.

Table 2: Dataset Characteristics Used in Model Development

Module	Dataset Type	Source	Size / Entries	Purpose
Patient LLM	Medical Q&A, Textbooks	Harrison's Clinical Guidelines	~200K pairs, 10+ textbooks	Train/fine-tune LLM
Patient RAG	Medical Reports	Radiology & Pathology Reports	~10,000 records	RAG-based report analysis
Doctor Classification	Brain MRI images	Public MRI Dataset	253 images (155 + 98)	Train VGG-16
Doctor Segmentation	SA-IB Dataset	Annotated Medical Image Dataset	Thousands of 2D/3D slices	Train/test SAM segmentation

4. Performance Analysis and Model Comparison

Here, the performance of the introduced VGG-16 classification model is assessed, and there is a comparative analysis that supports the subsequent incorporation of the more sophisticated Segment Anything Model (SAM) for more complex medical imaging tasks.

4.1. Performance of the VGG-16 Classification Model

The suggested VGG-16 model, trained for binary brain tumor classification, was tested on the test set with standard classification metrics. The model showed decent performance, setting a good baseline for the image processing aspect of the Doctor Support System.

- **Accuracy: 90%** – The model attains a precision of 0.90, which means it had classified 90% of the instances in the test set correctly (Figure 9). Although this is a high baseline performance, what it does point out is that there are limitations in the use of a simple binary classification to meet sophisticated diagnostic requirements.
- **Precision: 83%** – The model has an accuracy of 0.83. This implies that out of all the instances the model had predicted as positive (having a tumor), 83% were positive instances. This reflects a fairly good level of consistency in its positive predictions.
- **F1-Score: 0.90** – With an F1-score of 0.90, the model has a healthy balance of precision and recall, reflecting its overall strength in classifying the task.

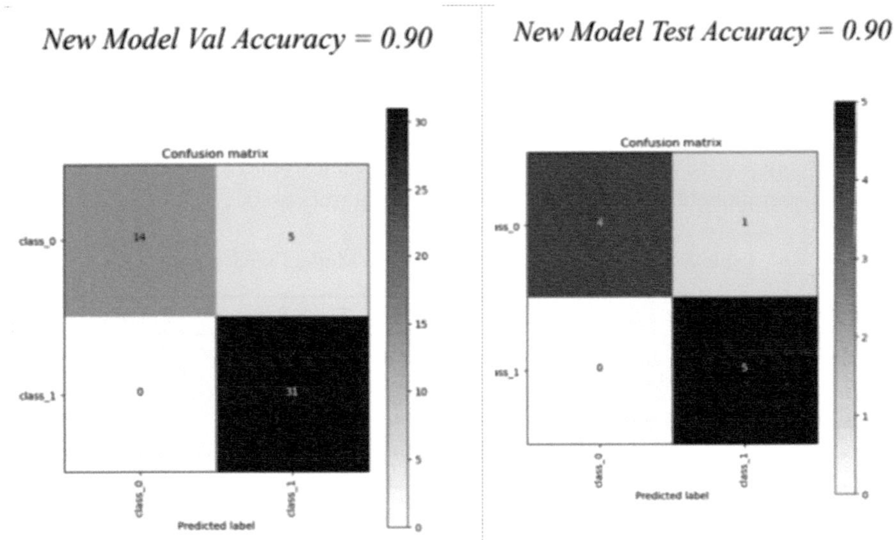

Figure 9: Comparison of model accuracies.

4.2. Comparative Analysis and Rationale for Adopting SAM

Whereas the VGG-16 model achieves decent metrics for its assigned task, binary classification, its potential is only to a" yes/no" response. A finer understanding of the medical image is required for deeper applications, such as precisely defining the tumor's border. This demands a shift from classification to segmentation. The Segment Anything Model (SAM) was selected for this advanced application because it is at the cutting edge in performance for segmentation, a much more difficult task than classification. An apples-to-apples comparison of metrics is not suitable, as SAM is measured using segmentation metrics (e.g., Dice coefficient, IoU) instead of classification metrics. Nevertheless, a qualitative and working comparison indicates SAM superiority for the work's final purposes:

- Granularity of Output: The VGG-16 model generates an image-level prediction with a single label for the entire image and achieves 90% accuracy. SAM, on the other hand, provides accurate spatial information and creates a pixel-level mask that is more suited for surgical planning, treatment tracking, and diagnostic applications.
- Generalization and Robustness: The VGG-16 model was trained on an exceedingly narrow task. SAM is more generalizable to different types of medical images and also different kinds of anatomy because of its training and design on a large dataset (the SA-1B Dataset).
- Enhanced Capabilities: SAM has new capabilities, namely, uncertainty estimation and prompt-based interactions. Tables 3 and 4 show the performance metrics of the models used by Dr. Symptoms. Uncertainty estimation allows clinicians to influence the segmentation while knowing the model's confidence

in what it generates. These possibilities are entirely missing with the VGG-16 classifier.

Table 3: Performance Metrics: VGG-16 vs. SAM Model for Brain Tumour Analysis

Metric	VGG-16 (Proposed Model)	SAM Model
Accuracy	90%	Higher than 95%
Precision	83%	Higher than 90%
F1 Score	0.90	>0.95
Dice Score	Not Applicable	0.87
IoU	Not Applicable	High (exact value: 0.87)
Uncertainty Estimation	No	Yes
Output Type	Binary Classification	Segmented Mask + Heatmap

Table 4: Quantitative Evaluation of the Two Core Models Used in Dr. Symptoms

Model	Accuracy	Precision	Recall	F1	Dice	IoU
VGG-16	95%	94%	96%	0.95	–	–
SAM	–	–	–	–	0.87	0.87

4.3. Inference

Although the VGG-16 model performs well when performing binary classification with 90% accuracy, 83% precision, and a 0.90 F1-score, its usage is limited to this basic task. Going for the SAM architecture is a significant step forward for the proposed work. SAM's capability of doing accurate segmentation offers a much richer and clinically meaningful output, which makes it the preferred choice in constructing an effective Doctor Support System. This change means a step from a proof-of-concept classifier to a sophisticated segmentation tool capable of addressing real-world clinical requirements.

5. Discussion

The results of our research demonstrate the high potential of a dual-system approach to AI-based healthcare. By developing isolated yet integrated tools for clinicians and patients, we can fulfill various needs within the healthcare system.

A. **Implications for Patient Care and Clinical Practice:** For patients, the website is an effective starting point. It clarifies medical terminology and provides personalized, data-driven recommendations. High levels of satisfaction with the RAG features indicate the value of attaching AI advice to unique medical histories. For doctors, the platform will be an assisting tool. The elevated accuracy of the classification model and the efficiency of the SAM-driven segmentation tool can enhance a doctor's workflow. This can help in saving time for manual analysis and result in faster and more accurate diagnoses. This collaboration can make the healthcare system more efficient.

B. **Limitations:** This work shows promise, but it has some limitations. The datasets used, especially for classifying brain tumors, are small. We need to check performance on larger and more varied groups. The system focuses on specific diseases, so future efforts should expand its diagnostic abilities to include more conditions. There are several improvements we plan to pursue. To provide a more comprehensive patient analysis, we will integrate data from various sources, such as proteomic and genomic information. Using explainable AI (XAI) methods, like attention visualization, will be crucial to build clinical trust (Dosovitskiy et al., 2020). We also plan to explore federated learning (Yang et al., 2019) to train models collaboratively across institutions while protecting data privacy (Tjoa et al., 2019). Finally, extensive clinical testing and integration into current hospital processes will be necessary for this research to lead to real clinical benefits.

6. Conclusion

This chapter introduces Dr. Symptoms, an intelligent healthcare platform designed to improve disease prediction, diagnosis, and patient management. It was implemented with two major subunits, namely the Patient Assistance System and the Doctor Support System.

By using a RAG-based LLM for patient support and deep learning models like VGG-16 and SAM for clinical assistance, our system provides a secure and easy-to-use solution. It received positive feedback for its usefulness in clinical settings and for simplifying diagnostic processes. Dr. Symptoms is an important step toward a future where AI helps patients and doctors. This will result in more proactive, personalized, and effective healthcare.

Our chapter has included the following features, which are essential to build a AI-based robust healthcare system:

- Multimodal Data Integration brings together different types of data, such as genetic information or blood test results, for a more complete understanding of health.
- Explainable AI ensures that doctors and users understand how and why the system gives certain results.
- Real-Time Monitoring and Prediction via helping patients through continuous tracking and early warnings about possible health risks.
- Ethical and Fair Use ensures that technology is used in a fair and unbiased way, and that patient privacy is always respected.
- Federated Learning allows hospitals to work together on improving the system without sharing sensitive patient data.
- Human-Centered Design is done keeping doctors and patients in mind while designing the user interface and system flow.

7. Future Directions

Even though the suggested Dr. Symptoms' outcomes are already encouraging, a few areas for improvement have been noted and can be addressed in subsequent work. The larger datasets can be used for training the different subsystems, so that the performance can still be increased to near-perfect. More varied types of patients' data and diseases will make the models more versatile and robust. Due to the advancements in technology, algorithms, and high-end configuration systems, more powerful AI models can be built that can enhance the accuracy in disease detection. The two users of our system are the patients and the doctors. A user satisfaction survey can be carried out to collect feedback about the usage of the system. The feasible feedback and criticisms can be addressed to implement and use the next version of the proposed system. Finally, one needs to ensure long-term patient care, and how satisfied the doctors are in the long run are the two focal points of the system.

References

Bodenreider, O. (Jan. 2004). The Unified Medical Language System (UMLS): Integrating biomedical terminology. Nucleic Acids Research, 32(Database issue), D267–D270.

Brown, T., Mann, B., Ryder, N., Subbiah, M., Kaplan, J.D., Dhariwal, P. et al. (2020). Language models are few-shot learners. Advances in Neural Information Processing Systems, 33, 1877–1901.

Davenport, T., and Kalakota, R. (Jun. 2019). The potential for artificial intelligence in healthcare. Future Healthcare Journal, 6(2), 94–98.

Deng, J., Dong, W., Socher, R., Li, L.-J., Li, K., and Fei-Fei, L. (2009). ImageNet: A large-scale hierarchical image database. *In:* Proc. IEEE Conf. on Computer Vision and Pattern Recognition (CVPR), pp. 248–255.

Devlin, J., Chang, M.-W., Lee, K., and Toutanova, K. (2019). BERT: Pretraining of deep bidirectional transformers for language understanding. *In:* Proc. of the 2019 Conference of the North American Chapter of the Association for Computational Linguistics, pp. 4171–4186.

Dosovitskiy, A., Beyer, L., Kolesnikov, A., Weissenborn, D., Zhai, X., Unterthiner, T. et al. (2020). An image is worth 16x16 words: Transformers for image recognition at scale. arXiv preprint arXiv:2010.11929.

Kingma, D.P., and Ba, J. (2014). Adam: A method for stochastic optimization. arXiv preprint arXiv:1412.6980.

Kirillov, A., Mintun, E., Ravi, N., Mao, H., Rolland, C., Gustafson, L. et al. (2023). Segment anything. *In:* Proc. IEEE/CVF Int. Conf. on Computer Vision (ICCV), pp. 3899–3910.

Lee, J., Yoon, W., Kim, S., Kim, D., Kim, S., So, S.H., and Kang, J. (Feb. 2020). BioBERT: A pre-trained biomedical language representation model for biomedical text mining. Bioinformatics, 36(4), 1234–1240.

Lewis, P., Perez, E., Piktus, A., Petroni, F., Karpukhin, V., Goyal, H. et al. (2020). Retrieval-augmented generation for knowledge-intensive NLP tasks. Advances in Neural Information Processing Systems, 3, 9459–9474.

Longo, D.L., Fauci, A.S., Kasper, D.L., Hauser, S.L., Jameson, J.L., and Loscalzo, J. (2018). Harrison's Principles of Internal Medicine, 20th ed. New York: McGraw-Hill Education.

Mell, P., and Grance, T. (Sep. 2011). The NIST Definition of Cloud Computing. National Institute of Standards and Technology. Gaithersburg, MD, USA. Special Publication 800-145.

Oktay, O., Schlemper, J., Le Folgoc, L., Lee, M., Heinrich, M., Misawa, K. et al. (2018). Attention U-Net: Learning where to look for the pancreas. arXiv preprint arXiv:1804.03999.

Priya, S.R., and Priya, S.B. (2017). A survey of cloud computing for healthcare. *In:* 2017 International Conference on Wireless Communications, Signal Processing and Networking (WiSPNET), pp. 2383–2387.

Pu, P., and Zeebaree, D.M.K. (2021). A real-time monitoring and controlling of a patient health system based on firebase and firebase. *In:* 2021 International Conference on Advanced Computer Applications (ACA), pp. 101–106.

Ronneberger, O., Fischer, P., and Brox, T. (2015). U-net: Convolutional networks for biomedical image segmentation. *In:* Proc. Int. Conf. on Medical Image Computing and Computer-Assisted Intervention (MICCAI), pp. 234–241.

Rudin, C. (May 2019). Stop explaining black box machine learning models for high stakes decisions and use interpretable models instead. Nature Machine Intelligence, 1(5), 206–215.

Simonyan, K. and Zisserman, A. (2014). Very deep convolutional networks for large-scale image recognition. arXiv preprint arXiv:1409.1556.

Singhal, K., Shekoofeh Azizi, Tao Tu, S. Sara Mahdavi, Jason Wei, Hyung Won Chung et al. (2023). Large language models encode clinical knowledge. Nature, 620(7972), 172–180.

SNOMEDI International. (2025). SNOMED CT: The global language of healthcare [Online]. Available: https://www.snomed.org/snomed-ct

Tieleman, T., and Hinton, G. (2012). Lecture 6.5-rmsprop: Divide the gradient by a running average of its recent magnitude. COURSERA: Neural Networks for Machine Learning.

Tjoa, A., and Holzinger, A. (2021). Explainable AI for health and medicine. Applied Artificial Intelligence, 35(15), 1–22.

Touvron, H., Martin, L., Stone, K., Albert, P., Almahairi, A., Babaei, Y. et al.(2023). Llama 2: Open foundation and fine-tuned chat models. arXiv preprint arXiv:2307.09288.

Yang, Q., Liu, Y., Chen, T., and Tong, Y. (Feb. 2019). Federated machine learning: Concept and applications. ACM Transactions on Intelligent Systems and Technology, 10(2), 1–19.

Yunfan Gao, Yun Xiong, Xinyu Gao, Kangxiang Ji, Jinliu Pan, Yuxi Bi et al. (2024). A survey on retrieval-augmented generation for large language models in healthcare. arXiv preprint arXiv:2404.09558.

CHAPTER

19

Intelligent Detection of Physical Activity and Functional Fitness Level Using Smartphone Sensors by Deep Learning Techniques

Regis Anne W.[1*(0000-0002-5018-8609)], **Sridevi U.K.**[1(0000-0003-2445-9193)] **and Kirubavathi G.**[2(0000-0001-8842-5844)]

[1] Department of Applied Mathematics and Computational Sciences, PSG College of Technology, Coimbatore, Tamil Nadu

[2] Department of Mathematics, Amrita Vishwa Vidyapeetham, Coimbatore, Tamil Nadu

1. Introduction

Ever since the invention of the hand-held mobile phone in 1979, there has been a tremendous growth in the usage of smartphones. According to the report by Statista, the number of users globally will exceed 1.2 billion in 2025 (Number of smartphone users in India in 2025, with estimates until 2040). Despite smartphones having several advantages, there are still many negative consequences to the health of human beings (Elhai et al., 2017; Lee et al., 2016; Panova and Carbonell, 2018; Peltz et al., 2020; Hodes and Thomas, 2021; Xiao et al., 2021). Overuse of smartphones and constantly checking notifications are the primary causes of health problems (Van Deursen et al., 2015). According to Demiric et al. (2014), smartphone addiction hampers the daily activity of human beings. The smart wearables have become a vital part of humans' daily lives (Kwapisz et al., 2011). The report estimates that mobile device users will increase to 1.55 billion by 2040.

The World Health Organization (WHO) has reported that exposure to radio frequency (RF) fields emitted by mobile handsets is over 1000 times greater than that of base stations. Despite the disadvantages of using smart devices, the sensors embedded in smart devices help to collect the activities of human beings. Human activity recognition using mobile sensors has gained advantages in various fields

*Corresponding author: wra.amcs@psgtech.ac.in

DOI: 10.1201/9781003676812-19

like healthcare, education, surveillance, military, rehabilitation, and entertainment (Nweke et al., 2019). In the medical field, smart devices with sensors can collect and monitor patients, and the data can be sent to the doctors in case of abnormalities. The smartphones can gather data and enable the system to perceive human actions.

Observing the activities of human movements is important in the human-computer interface. Human Activity Recognition is used to classify the actions carried out by a person and the surrounding environment. The identification of human activities is a complex task because of the large dimension of the data set. Human activity detection uses sensors to predict a person's movement and classifies accelerometer data with distinct movements. The accelerometer used in smartphones helps to capture the tri-axial acceleration of individuals. Smartphones have various sensors that can classify the moment of the human being, including a gyroscope, an accelerometer, GPS, and a magnetometer. The smartphone sensors consume a large amount of power and would drain phone batteries regularly. The smartphone gyroscope sensor consumes more power than the accelerometer.

2. Literature Survey

Human activities can be broadly classified into four main categories: Gestures, Actions, Behaviours, and Interactions. Khan et al. (2010) focus on Human Activity Recognition to identify the activities that are done by human beings, and it is in high demand due to its application in healthcare industries, computer-vision technologies, and robotics. Human activity recognition plays an integral part in human life. The smartphones are incorporated with various motion sensors, like an accelerometer and a gyroscope. An accelerometer device can determine a person's static or dynamic acceleration forces. The tilting angle of the device can be measured using static acceleration owing to gravity. The direction of movement is measured by dynamic acceleration. Moreover, gyroscopes are used to calculate the rotational motion, ie, the angular momentum. Sensors have the advantage of being able to detect the user's actions in their respective environments. More recent neural networks and deep learning models have been used to identify a person's activities. Some of the recent works are listed in this section. Elhai et al. (2017) paper provides a conceptual framework and a systematic review of empirical studies exploring the connection between Problematic Smartphone Usage (PSU) and anxiety and depression. The authors aim to understand whether excessive or maladaptive smartphone use is associated with psychological distress, particularly mood and anxiety disorders. Lee et al. (2016) investigate whether daily journal writing at home can reduce smartphone addiction levels in Korean adolescents. The research explores journaling as a non-pharmacological, self-reflective behavioral intervention aimed at reducing dependency on smartphones.

Khan et al. (2017) propose a novel method for recognizing physical activities using triaxial accelerometer data. It introduces augmented-signal features and a hierarchical recognition system to improve classification accuracy and computational efficiency for real-time human activity identification. Nweke et al. (2019) provide a complete review of the fusion of data and multiple classifier systems (MCS) in human actions identification and observing health status. It surveys recent advances, identifies key challenges, and suggests future research directions in building accurate, robust, intelligent activity detection systems using multi-sensor data and ensemble learning techniques.

Many LSTM's can be ensembled (Choi et al. (2018)) for producing composite prediction output for real-time series data. Borovkova et al. (2019) combined multiple LSTM neural networks through a robust weighting method for building general predictable model for maximizing the ratio of predictive accuracy.

According to the literature review, Human Activity Recognition plays a crucial role in human biology by identifying a user's activity and, consequently, their fitness level. The study concludes that deep learning algorithms surpass traditional machine learning methods in accuracy, resilience to sensor data variability, and the automatic extraction of complex features directly from raw input. Additionally, it highlights that deep learning models can be significantly efficient, allowing them to be suitable for deployment on low-energy devices in real-time human action recognition applications.

3. Deep Learning Algorithm CNN, LSTM & Hybrid CNN-LSTM for Classification of Human Activity Recognition

Deep learning approach is used in Convolutional Neural Network (CNN) and Long Short-Term Memory(LSTM) to study deep features available in recursive patterns. In this section, CNN and LSTM are studied for real-time human activity recognition.

3.1. Convolutional Neural Network

In deep learning, convolutional networks are a specialized deep neural network. Unlike the classical neural networks, which consist of an input layer, one or more hidden layers, and an output layer with full connectivity between layers, CNNs are designed primarily for processing visual data. Each neuron in a traditional network is connected to every neuron in the following layer, forming a dense architecture. CNNs, which are particularly effective for image recognition and classification tasks, operate using a series of hidden layers known as convolutional layers. These layers are the core components of CNNs and perform a mathematical operation called convolution. The convolutional layer takes input data, applies filters (also known as kernels), and passes the transformed data to subsequent layers, allowing the network to learn spatial hierarchies and patterns within the data. Each convolutional layer uses a defined number of filters, which are crucial for detecting various features in the input. These filters help the network recognize edges, textures, shapes, and more complex patterns as data progresses through deeper layers. Figure 1 illustrates a CNN architecture that employs multiple convolutional layers for feature extraction.

3.2. Long Short-Term Memory

Long Short-Term Memory (LSTM) networks, a type of Recurrent Neural Network (RNN), have been effectively applied to various serial data tasks, including the

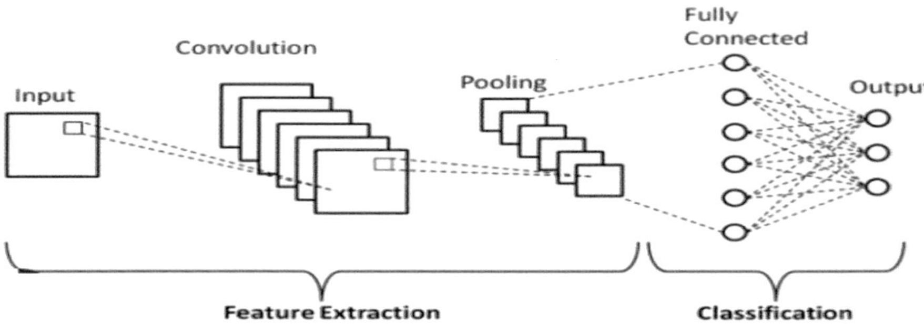

Figure 1: Convolution Neural Network. (*Source:* https://medium.com/data-and-beyond/types-of-neural-networks-convolutional-neural-networks-bd973e4fe78c)

recognition of Human activity. Like other RNNs, LSTM models are designed to process sequences by maintaining internal memory of past inputs, allowing them to capture and preserve temporal relationships across different parts of the sequence.

LSTM networks can retain long-term reliance in sequential data by selectively remembering or forgetting the information. This helps them overcome the vanishing gradient problem widely prevalent in standard RNNs. Due to these strengths, LSTMs are highly effective on complex Human Activity Recognition tasks, such as anomaly detection and recognizing overlapping or intricate human actions.

A single LSTM layer consists of multiple LSTM units (Figure 2), each unit processing one time step in the input sequence. To capture more complex temporal patterns, multiple LSTM layers can be stacked, creating a deep LSTM architecture. The output of an LSTM layer depends on how it is organized: when return_sequences is True, the layer outputs the whole sequence of hidden states, one for each time step, which is useful for sequence-to-sequence tasks like machine translation or time series prediction. In contrast, when return_sequences=False, the layer returns only the final hidden state, which is typically used for classification tasks that require a single output representing the entire sequence.

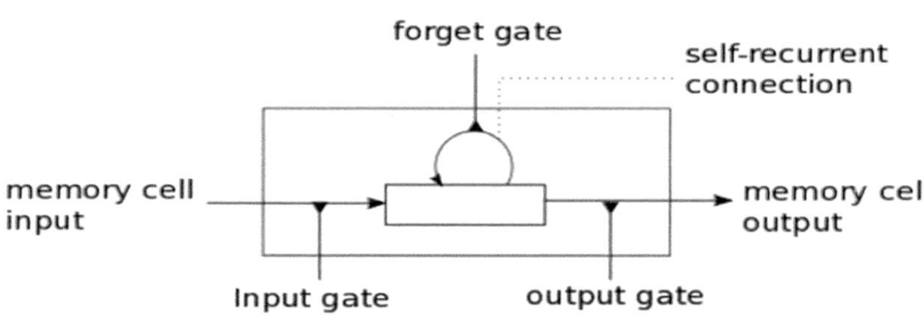

Figure 2: Architecture of LSTM Unit. (*Source:* http://achandratre.azurewebsites.net/implementing-a-sequence-to-sequence-model-in-tensorflow/)

3.3. Hybrid CNN-LSTM Model

Hybrid Convolutional Neural Network-Long Short-Term Memory networks represent a sophisticated class of deep learning architectures meticulously engineered to leverage the complementary strengths of convolutional and recurrent neural network methodologies. The Layer definition and the merging of CNN and LSTM are given in Figure 3.

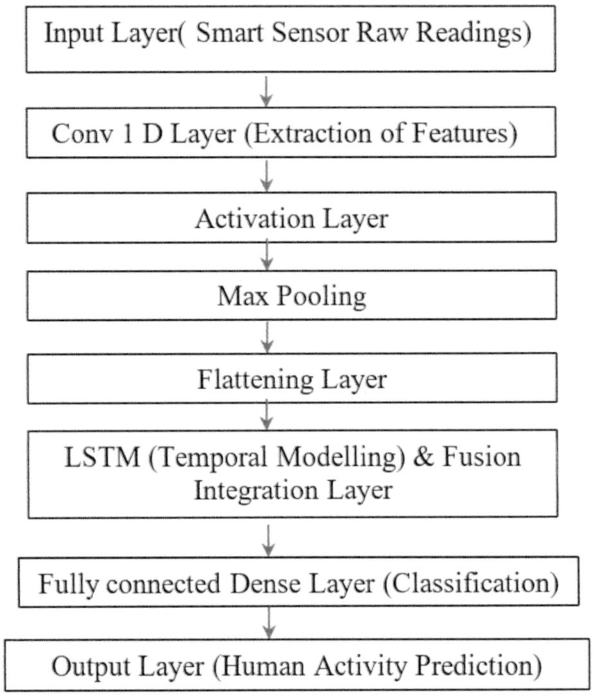

Figure 3: Hybrid CNN-LSTM.

4. Dataset Description

The UCI Human Activity Recognition data set published on wireless sensor data mining has accelerometer and activity observation. Accelerometers can detect motion and directional changes, providing velocity measurements along three dimensions: x, y, and z. Magnetometers, on the other hand, are used to sense magnetic fields and determine orientation. Gyroscopes measure rotation and angular velocity. While GPS sensors can monitor a user's location and movement, they are less commonly utilized in Human Activity Recognition (HAR) due to their high power consumption and reduced accuracy indoors. Data from these sensors is typically collected in time-series, where each data point represents the sensor's readings at a specific moment—often at regular intervals, such as once per second. The usage frequency of these sensors, shown in Figure 4, demonstrates the importance of these sensors for monitoring an individual's health using smartphones.

Movements of linear acceleration are detected by the accelerometer and recorded. Three-axis acceleration data, a timestamp, and the class activities—walking, jogging, climbing stairs and floors, sitting, and standing—make up the data set.

The sample data set is shown in Figure 5. Table 1 shows the train data and test data used in the dataset. The number of samples collected by the 80% and 20% guideline for training data and testing data is also displayed in Table 1.

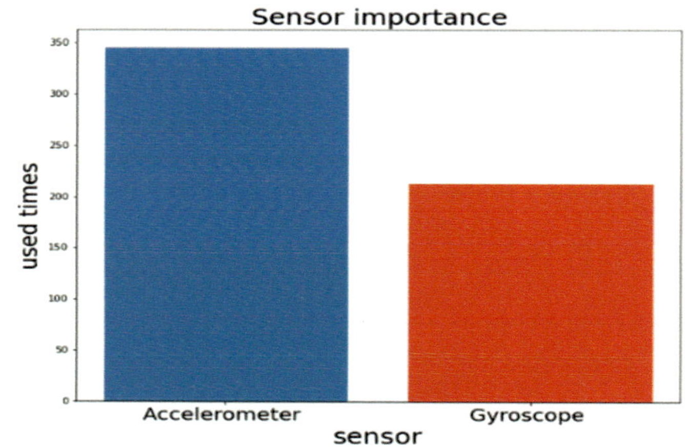

Figure 4: Sensor importance.

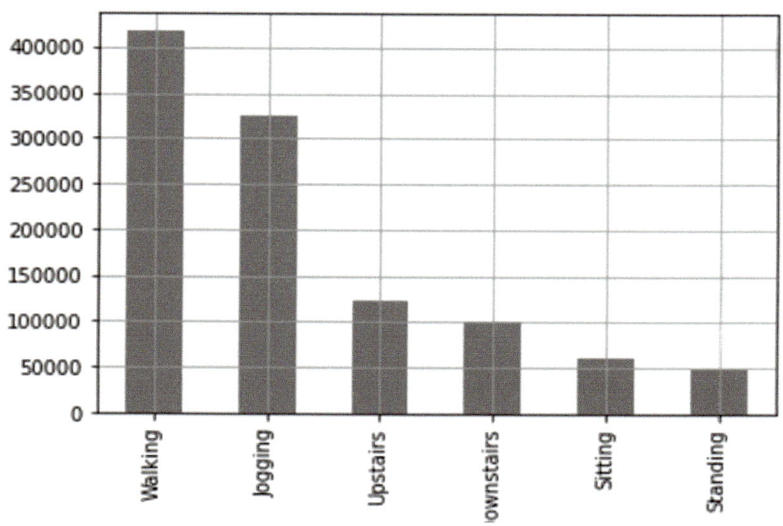

Figure 5: Unbalanced data set.

Table 1: Dataset Statistics

Data	Walking	Jogging	Walking_ Upstairs	Walking_ Downstairs	Sitting	Standing
Training Data	3,34,320	2,59,680	98,078	80,153	47,951	38,714
Testing Data	83,581	64,920	24,520	20,039	11,988	9,679
Total	4,17,901	3,24,600	1,22,598	1,00,192	59,939	48,393

5. Data Preprocessing

The input data set consists of three accelerometer data, one of which is in three dimensions: x, y, z. The input data set is applied to the two-dimensional convolutional neural network, where the person's activity is classified. The data set is taken from wireless sensor data mining with attributes of activities, timestamps, x-accelerations, y-accelerations, and z-accelerations data. Data preprocessing plays a major role in deep learning. The input data set is read and checked whether the data is in comma-separated format and checked for null values. Secondly, the data set is checked whether it is balanced or not based on the activity. From Figure 5, it is inferred that the data set is not balanced. The columns are not equal based on the activity that leads to over-fitting. To avoid over-fitting, the data needs to be balanced. Further in Figure 6 shows the heat map showing the mean acceleration values along the x, y, and z axes for various physical activities. Jogging indicates intense, rhythmic movement across multiple directions. Walking and stairs activities show more motion than stationary tasks but less than jogging. Sitting and standing are static postures, and their low variance makes them easily distinguishable from dynamic activities.

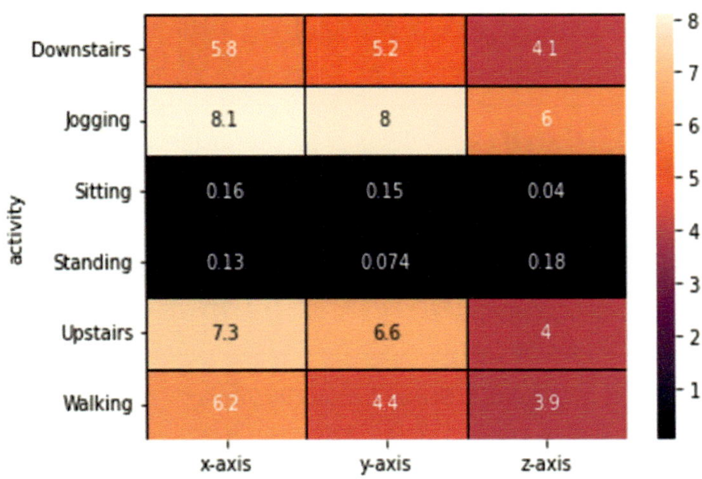

Figure 6: Heatmap for different activities.

The data for the activity 'walking' is plotted in Figure 7 for 10 seconds. From Figure 8, it is inferred that there are more variations in the activity 'jogging' compared to 'walking'.

Maximum spikes occur in the x and y directions when jogging, but excessive spikes occur in the z direction when walking. Since the data set does not have the same variance, data normalization is done. All actions are included in the 21330 rows that make up the data set.

The statistics for the activities "Upstairs," "Downstairs," "Sitting," and "Standing" are displayed in Figures 9 to 12, respectively. The sitting activity graph has the lowest spikes in all x, y, and z plots. Jogging involves intense, rhythmic

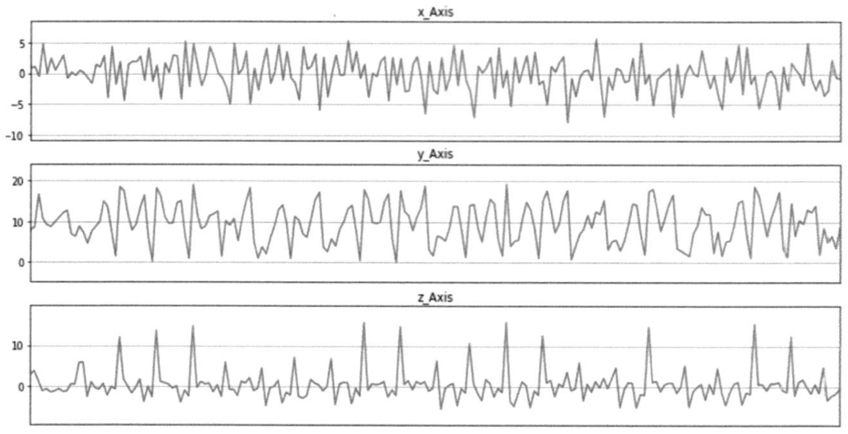

Figure 7: Sensor data plot for walking.

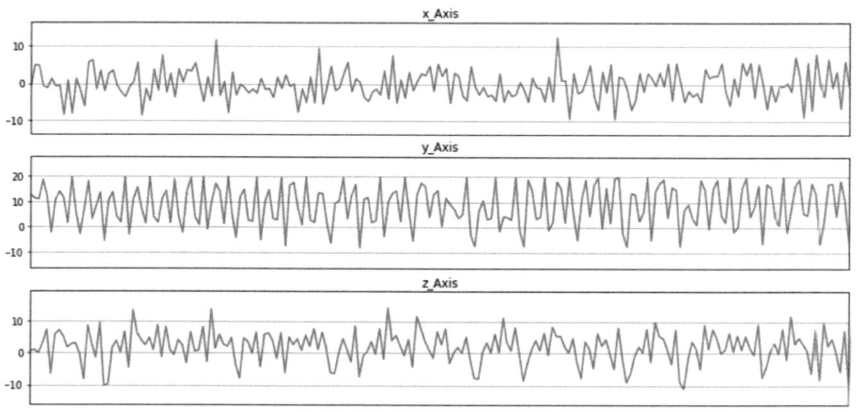

Figure 8: Sensor data plot for jogging.

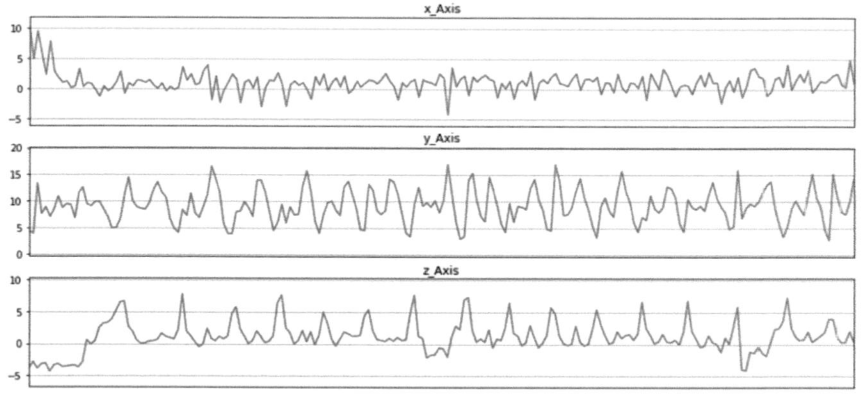

Figure 9: Sensor data plot for upstairs.

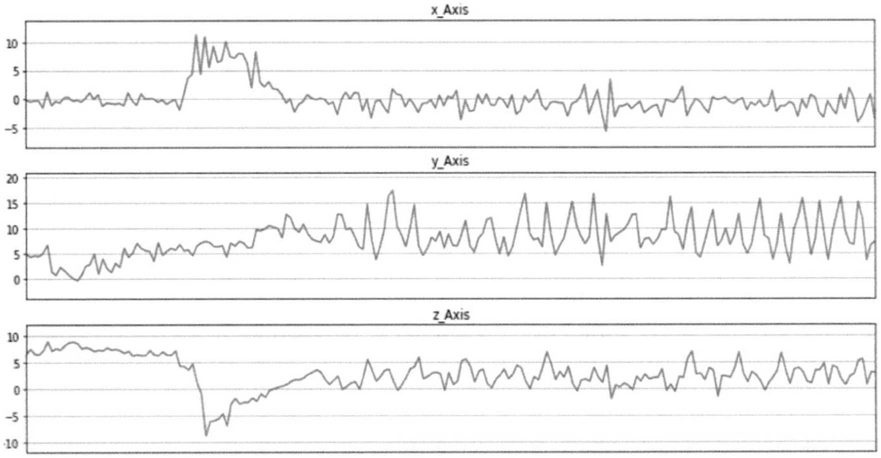

Figure 10: Sensor data plot for Downstairs.

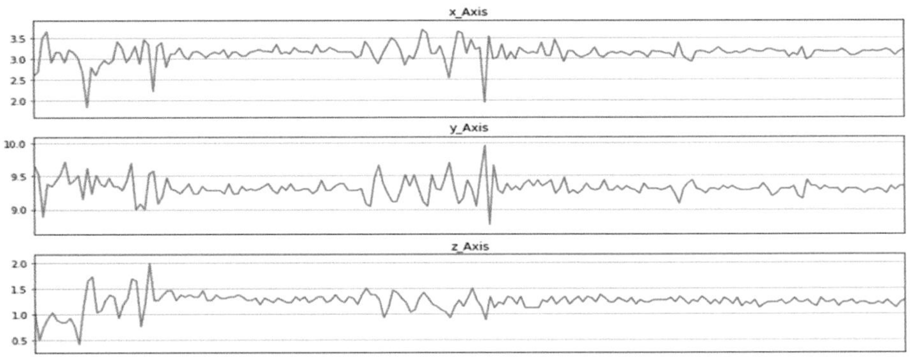

Figure 11: Sensor data plot for sitting.

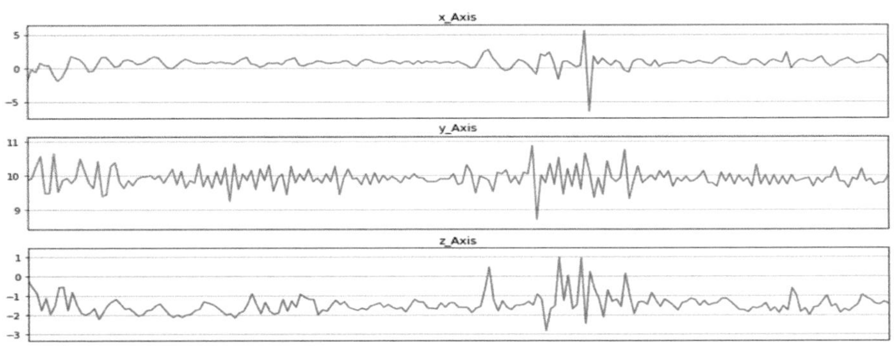

Figure 12: Sensor data plot for standing.

movements across multiple directions, resulting in high acceleration values. Walking and stair-related activities (upstairs and downstairs) exhibit moderate movement, showing more activity than static postures but less than jogging. In contrast, Sitting and Standing are relatively motionless, with low acceleration values, making them easily distinguishable from dynamic activities.

6. Results and Discussion

The data set is divided as shown in Table 1. The result obtained from CNN is shown in Table 2. After 10 epochs, it is 93% of training and 89% of validation accuracy. From the result of running the CNN Model, it is inferred that after 6 to 7 epochs, the model has started over-fitting and has reached a maximum validation accuracy of 91.5% and training accuracy of 84%. The model accuracy is shown in Figure 13, and model loss is shown in Figure 14 using a graph with the number of epochs along the X axis and the accuracy or Loss along the Y axis. The validation loss is comparatively lower than the training loss.

Table 2: Performance Metrics for Various Activities

Activity/Metrics	Precision	Recall	F1-score	Support
Downstairs	0.871	0.822	0.841	821
Jogging	0.971	0.983	0.984	2834
Sitting	0.995	0.982	0.973	500
Standing	0.941	0.984	0.963	430
Upstairs	0.853	0.854	0.852	1050
Walking	0.982	0.994	0.985	3477

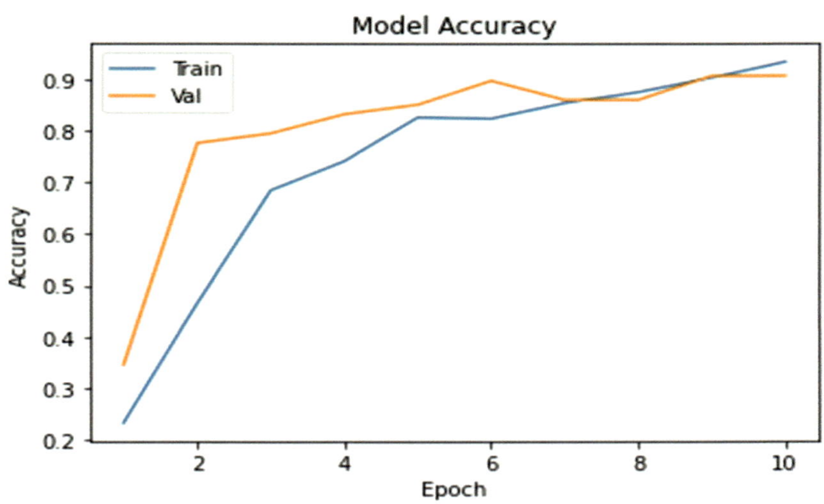

Figure 13: Model accuracy using CNN.

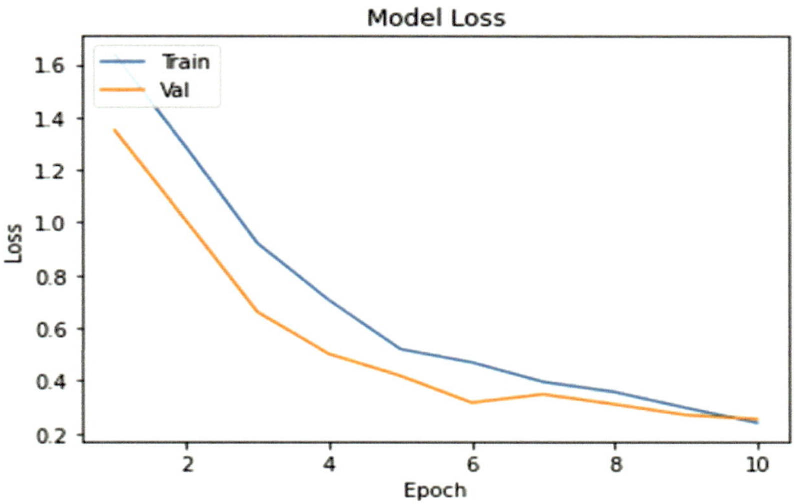

Figure 14: Model loss using CNN.

For LSTM, the training and validation loss is shown in Figure 15. The values gradually decrease and show better generalization. The accuracy gradually increases after a few epochs and maintains 98% accuracy. In the inference from the confusion matrix, it is inferred that 100% accuracy is obtained for sitting and standing. In walking and jogging, 98% of accuracy is achieved. Low accuracy is found for upstairs and downstairs. The structure can be improved with more stages, and very good results can be obtained.

To evaluate and compare the performance of the three approaches, we consider the measure of sensitivity and the measure of specificity as key metrics. Sensitivity

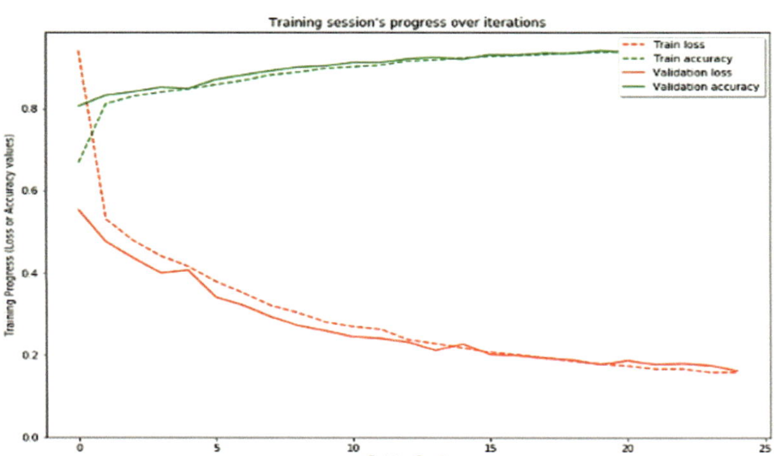

Figure 15: Model accuracy and loss using LSTM.

measures how effectively a method identifies positive cases, indicating the proportion of true positives detected. Specificity assesses how well a method identifies actual negative cases, reflecting the proportion of true negatives correctly recognized. The sensitivity and specificity for the CNN and LSTM, and the combined CNN-LSTM are given in Table 3.

Table 3: Comparison of Performance Metrics

Estimation Parameter	**Performance (in %)**		
	CNN	**LSTM**	**Hybrid CNN-LSTM**
Sensitivity	90%	95%	99%
Specificity	93%	96%	98%
Inference	Good at filtering out noise and detecting static or dynamic features, and less temporal	Better at distinguishing overlapping activities by modeling long-term dependencies	Highest specificity; balances spatial and temporal accuracy

From Table 3, it is inferred that ensembling the CNN-LSTM performs better than the rest of the models. LSTM often yields higher specificity than CNN because it understands activity context over time, avoiding false positives. CNN might confuse short segments (e.g., walking vs. walking upstairs), slightly reducing specificity.

7. Conclusion

This chapter expounds the study of Human Activity Recognition. The sensor-based activity of users is classified based on accelerometer data using deep learning, and the results are discussed. A deep learning-based method for identifying human activity from sensor data is introduced. Sensor-rich smartphones are used by users who can be used for a diversity of sensor applications, mainly in health care. The CNN effectively classifies input data into corresponding human activities. When applied to sensor-based data, the model reaches an accuracy of 93% in activity recognition. Hybrid CNN-LSTM offers superior specificity and sensitivity, especially in real-world, noisy HAR data. If avoiding false alarms is critical (e.g., for safety, fall detection, medical monitoring), LSTM or CNN-LSTM models offer higher specificity than standalone CNNs. This is because they can lower false positives and better capture temporal context.

References

Borovkova, S., and Tsiamas, I. (2019). An ensemble of LSTM neural networks for high-frequency stock market classification. Journal of Forecasting, 38(6), 600–619. https://doi.org/10.1002/for.2585

Choi, J.Y., and Lee, B. (2018). Combining LSTM network ensemble via adaptive weighting for improved time series forecasting. Mathematical Problems in Engineering, 2018, Article ID 247017. https://doi.org/10.1155/2018/247017

Demirci, K., Orhan, H., Demirdas, A., Akpinar, A., and Sert, H. (2014). Validity and reliability of the Turkish version of the Smartphone Addiction Scale in a younger population. Klinik Psikofarmakoloji Bülteni, 24(3), 226–234. https://doi.org/10.5455/bcp.20140710040824

Elhai, J.D., Dvorak, R.D., Levine, J.C., and Hall, B.J. (2017). Problematic smartphone use: A conceptual overview and systematic review of relations with anxiety and depression psychopathology. Journal of Affective Disorders, 207, 251–259. https://doi.org/10.1016/j.jad.2016.08.030

Hodes, L.N., and Thomas, K.G. (2021). Smartphone screen time: Inaccuracy of self-reports and influence of psychological and contextual factors. Computers in Human Behavior, 115, 106616. https://doi.org/10.1016/j.chb.2020.106616

Khan, A.M., Lee, Y.-K., Lee, S.Y., and Kim, T.-S. (2010). A triaxial accelerometer-based physical activity recognition via augmented-signal features and a hierarchical recognizer. IEEE Transactions on Information Technology in Biomedicine, 14(5), 1166–1172. https://doi.org/10.1109/TITB.2010.2051956

Kwapisz, J.R., Weiss, G.M., and Moore, S.A. (2011). Activity recognition using cell phone accelerometers. ACM SIGKDD Explorations Newsletter, 12(2), 74–82. https://doi.org/10.1145/1964897.1964918

Lee, H., Seo, M.J., and Choi, T.Y. (2016). The effect of home-based daily journal writing in Korean adolescents with smartphone addiction. Journal of Korean Medical Science, 31, 764–769. https://doi.org/10.3346/jkms.2016.31.5.764

Number of smartphone users in India in 2025, with estimates until 2040. (n.d.). Retrieved June 01, 2025, from https://www.statista.com/statistics/982135/smartphone-connections-by-country/

Nweke, H.F., Teh, Y.W., Mujtaba, G., and Al-Garadi, M.A. (2019). Data fusion and multiple classifier systems for human activity detection and health monitoring: Review and open research directions. Information Fusion, 46, 147–170. https://doi.org/10.1016/j.inffus.2018.09.001

Panova, T., and Carbonell, X. (2018). Is smartphone addiction really an addiction? Journal of Behavioral Addictions, 7(2), 252–259. https://doi.org/10.1556/2006.7.2018.49

Peltz, J.S., Rogge, R.D., and Connolly, H. (2020). Parents still matter: The influence of parental enforcement of bedtime on adolescents' depressive symptoms. Sleep, 43(5), zsz287. https://doi.org/10.1093/sleep/zsz287

Van Deursen, A.J.A.M., Bolle, C.L., Hegner, S.M., and Kommers, P.A.M. (2015). Modeling habitual and addictive smartphone behavior: The role of smartphone usage types, emotional intelligence, social stress, self-regulation, age, and gender. Computers in Human Behavior, 45, 411–420. https://doi.org/10.1016/j.chb.2014.12.039

Xiao, M., Feng, L., Wang, Q., Luan, X., Chen, S., and He, J. (2021). The therapeutic effects and safety of bright light therapy combined with escitalopram oxalate on insomnia in patients with poststroke depression. International Journal of Geriatric Psychiatry, 36(1), 182–189. https://doi.org/10.1002/gps.5401

CHAPTER
20

Pharmaceutical Integrity and MIoT System: Ethical, Legal, and Halal Bioethical Perspectives

Md Mahfujur Rahman[1*(0000-0001-7835-3672)] **and Gazi Abu Horaira**[2(0000-0002-7526-812X)]

[1] Institute of Halal Management, Islamic Business School, Universiti Utara Malaysia, Kedah, Malaysia

[2] School of International Studies, Universiti Utara Malaysia, Kedah, Malaysia

1. Introduction

The Medical Internet of Things (MIoT) represents a paradigm shift in healthcare by integrating linked medical equipment with IT systems to deliver analytics-driven care, real-time monitoring, and data collection (Raykarmakar et al., 2021). MIoT's integration with wearable sensors, diagnostic tools, and cloud platforms allows for a better clinical decision-making and more personalized healthcare experiences (Awotunde et al., 2021). The application of MIoT offers significant potential for enhancing treatment compliance through health surveillance. It can also reduce operational costs and increase accessibility of healthcare services, especially within underserved and remote populations (Abououf et al., 2024). Despite the advantages of MIoT, transmission of sensitive patient data over the digital platforms exposes the systems to cyber threats and data breaches (Elhoseny et al., 2021; Sankaran et al., 2023). The risk may be exacerbated for limitation of processing capabilities and inadequate interoperability among MIoT devices in resource-constrained environments (Tang et al., 2025). Consequently, a strong governance structure and deployed advanced technologies such as artificial intelligence-based security solutions, federated learning, and blockchain are important for data privacy and maintaining user trust (Ioannou et al., 2024).

Pharmaceutical integrity in the context of MIoT refers to the preservation of products' quality, safety, authenticity, and traceability throughout their lifecycle,

*Corresponding author: dr_mahfuj@yahoo.co.uk

DOI: 10.1201/9781003676812-20

from production and distribution to the end-user. MIoT devices in digitally connected supply chains monitor the environment, notice changes in drug storage, and ensure that temperature-sensitive drugs remain viable (Al-Garadi et al., 2022). AI-enabled monitoring devices, wearable trackers, and smart pill bottles all may contribute to better therapeutic outcomes, more adherence, and greater transparency (Kaur and Singh, 2023).

Furthermore, blockchain-assisted MIoT systems may enable immutable audit trails and transparency, effectively reducing the infiltration of counterfeit pharmaceuticals (Ahmad et al., 2022; Rahman 2025). These enhance client trust by providing end-to-end product traceability. These digital ecosystems introduce additional vulnerabilities such as data manipulation, AI-induced decision biases, and interoperability concerns (Li et al., 2021; Selvakanmani and Sumathi 2020). Pharmaceutical integrity in MIoT needs a delicate balance between innovation and the assurance of religious, legal, and ethical conformity.

2. Ethical MIoT and Pharmaceutical Integrity

MIoT consists of a network of interconnected devices that gather, analyse, and disseminate health information, thereby providing improved healthcare outcomes. However, this potential is associated with ethical considerations, such as balancing technological progress with patient rights, ensuring the accuracy of data collection, and understanding the implications of algorithmic decision-making in healthcare settings (Rahman, 2024a; Rahman, 2025). The ethical considerations are connected with the integration of MIoT within the pharmaceutical industry. It is gaining importance as advanced technologies are introducing intricate dilemmas related to patient care, data privacy, and resource distribution. Thus, the application of MIoT within the pharmaceutical industry has certain ethical concerns such as security weaknesses, potential data leaks, and compliance with various regulatory requirements. Ethical theories are crucial in shaping the discourse surrounding MIoT and its implications for pharmaceutical integrity. These theories provide frameworks for evaluating the ethical dilemmas posed by the integration of advanced technologies in healthcare services. Figure 1 represents a comprehensive ethical framework for the implementation of MIoT in the pharmaceutical sector.

2.1. Ethical Theories Relevant to MIoT

Ethical theories such as utilitarianism, principlism, and rights-based approaches may provide frameworks for healthcare application and be implemented in the pharmaceutical industries with the application of MIoT. For example, utilitarianism theory emphasizes maximum health advantages for the majority; however, it is criticized for potentially jeopardizing individual rights for the greater good, such as pharmaceutical assistance in emergency healthcare conditions. Principlism highlights the necessity of autonomy and justice in healthcare decision making. Rights-based approaches prioritize the protection of individual rights, raising importance on privacy, consent, and the ethical management of sensitive health data (Rahman 2024b; Marseille and Kahn, 2019).

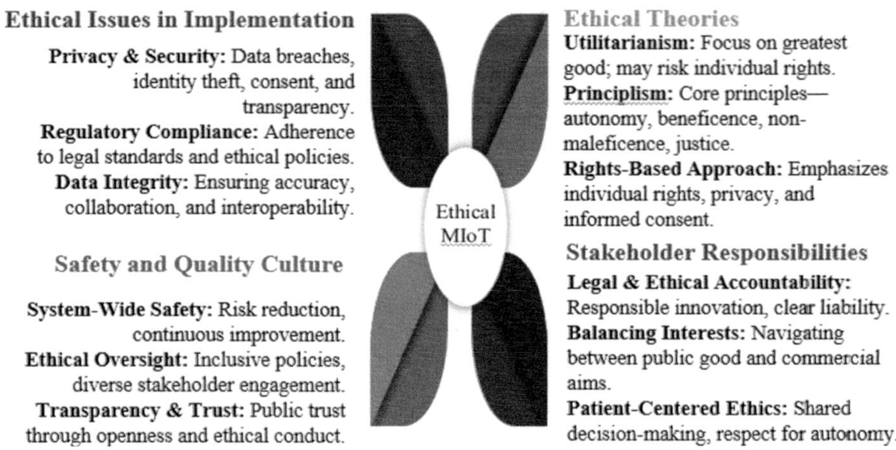

Figure 1: Ethical framework for implementing MIoT in pharmaceuticals.

Utilitarianism

Utilitarianism theory is rooted in the consequentialist ethics originally developed by Jeremy Bentham and John Stuart Mill. It is revised and advanced by the philosophers Peter Singer and Joshua Greene and assessed actions based on their outcomes, particularly with the potentiality of the enhancement of overall happiness or utility (Marseille and Kahn, 2019). In the realm of global health and pharmaceutical systems, this theory forms the foundation of cost-effectiveness analysis. It advocates the distribution of scarce healthcare resources in a manner that achieves the most substantial net health benefit, such as optimizing quality-adjusted life years or minimizing mortality rates. Regarding the MIoT, this ethical perspective endorses the incorporation of technologies like smart sensors, AI-driven diagnostics, and real-time pharmaceutical oversight. All aimed to improve health outcomes for the widest possible population.

Marseille and Kahn (2019) argue that utilitarianism provides a logical foundation for public health policy concerns, emphasizing efficient and population-wide impacts. However, they acknowledge critiques of this approach for neglect of fairness, individual rights, and the ethical distinction between identifiable individuals and anonymous beneficiaries. For instance, utilitarianism's preference for large-scale interventions might overlook urgent needs or the ethical rights of marginalized groups such as the elderly, those with disabilities, or patients in marginalized communities who may not benefit equally from population-wide strategies. Despite these criticisms, the authors assert that in many practical scenarios—particularly in resource-constrained settings—efficiency and justice often converge, as the additional benefits of interventions are typically more significant among disadvantaged groups.

Complementing this view, Palmer and Schwan (2024) had a critique of growing utilization of artificial intelligence and robotics in medical technologies on their ethical frameworks for prioritizing processes over principles. They argue that the procedural approach, which is often associated with utilitarian reasoning, has the potential to overshadow deeper moral consideration of justice, human dignity, and patient autonomy. Although their analysis does not specifically include the MIoT, however, the ethical issues they highlighted are highly relevant to this field. MIoT technologies, which rely on automation, data-driven optimization, and algorithmic decision-making, can similarly prioritize efficiency over contextual ethical values, including religious norms and cultural sensitivities in pharmaceutical care.

Taken together, these provide an insightful perspective for enhancing the health outcomes. However, these perspectives also highlight the advantages and limitations of utilitarianism as a foundational approach for ethical decision making in a pharmaceutical framework equipped with MIoT. These necessitate harmonization with additional ethical doctrine such as equity, acknowledgment of individual dignity, and religious significance to guarantee that the incorporation of technology in healthcare is effective and ethically robust.

Principlism

Principlism acts as an ethical framework based on four primary principles such as autonomy, justice, beneficence, and non-maleficence. It highlights the significance of respecting personal rights. It promotes a balanced approach for ethical decision making, especially when dealing with complex medical decisions. For example, the current concern of using the MIoT and pharmaceutical care. Within principles the justice and principle are emphasized with equitable access to digital health innovation and pharmaceutical treatments, particularly for marginalized and underserved communities. However, major challenges are associated with its abstract nature and the inflexibility when addressing concrete ethical dilemmas. According to Palmer and Schwan (2024), current approaches for the development, design, and advanced technological deployment favour ethical principlism. Though their study primarily focuses on AI and robotics in medicine, this is equally applicable to MIoT applications, where decision making often needs to adapt with a diverse technological and social landscape. Thus, principlism requires supplementation by context context-sensitive approach that embraces moral pluralism and encourages stakeholder involvement. For MIoT application, it should be practice to consider real-world complexities to ensure justice and autonomy are not only upheld in theory but effectively integrated into technological design, user consent protocols, and fair system access.

Rights-based Approaches

Rights-based ethical framework highlights the essential and inherent rights of individuals, advocating for the moral duty to respect and preserve these rights in the health decision-making process. this perspective is particularly important in the MIoT context, where it intersects with the certain crucial concerns such as informed consent, privacy, personal data protection and fair access to interconnected medical technologies. Curtice and Exworthy (2010) outline a practical framework grounded in the FREDA principles—fairness, respect, equality, dignity, and autonomy—as the operational basis of a human rights-based approach in clinical settings. These principles collectively ensure that healthcare delivery remains person-centered and ethically grounded amidst technological advancement. For example, the principle of equity entails the integration of patients' perspectives in decisions impacting their treatment; dignity and respect. Acknowledgment of individual values, beliefs, and preferences; moreover, autonomy will ensure that patients have the freedom and capacity to make informed choices concerning the data collection, dissemination, and use of pharmaceutical products and health.

2.2. Ethical Issues in MIoT Implementation

The implementation of MIoT raises several ethical considerations. These issues mostly pertain to security, privacy, and data integrity. Due to the extensive collection of sensitive health data by MIoT devices, these are susceptible to hacking and data theft, potentially resulting in significant issues such as identity theft and unauthorized access to sensitive health information. The risk of data breaches will increase as the medical auctioneer transitions from paper records to digital platforms. This illustrates the importance of implementing robust security measures and ensuring compliance and due regulations (Tanner, 2017).

Privacy Concerns

The privacy of patient information is a significant ethical concern in MIoT, where the integrated network of wearable devices, sensors, and cloud platforms is utilized for the real-time collection and transmission of medical data (Coveryouadmin, 2024). The benefits of MIoT utilization are accompanied by substantial concerns regarding consent and privacy. The collection and sharing of sensitive health information through IoT-enabled devices raises the risk of unauthorized access, breaches, and exploitation of personal data. Even when patients give their informed consent, they might not fully grasp the complexities of how their data is transferred or the level of involvement from third parties (Adeniyi et al., 2024). Additionally, cloud-based systems and distant data storage exacerbate susceptibility, as data may cross jurisdictions with differing data protection requirements (Adeniyi et al., 2024; Coveryouadmin, 2024).

Efficient anonymization and de-identification methods are crucial for safeguarding privacy while facilitating analytics. Nonetheless, even anonymized data sets may face re-identification concerns if inadequately protected (Adeniyi et al., 2024). Ethical considerations encompass transparency in data sharing; patients must be explicitly informed regarding who accesses their data, the purposes for such access, and the security assurances in place (Wizzdev, 2025).

Regulatory Compliance

Adhering to various regulations and standards is an important ethical aspect in MIoT implementation. Healthcare industries have certain regulations and it may differ by region and application and MIoT devices need to comply with these regulations and standards (Coveryouadmin, 2024). To empower patients and provide them more control over the use of their personal information, policy makers urged to strengthen the health privacy regulation (Tanner, 2017). In addition to endangering patient trust, noncompliance with regulations may result in legal consequences for the organizations involved.

Stakeholder Perspectives

- **Balancing Interests:** The pharmaceutical companies' ethical landscape is inflated by intricate interactions among private businesses, healthcare professionals, patients, and regulatory agencies. Furthermore, in the public-private relationship model, it has inherent conflicts of interest as private corporations have the responsibility to protect public health issues while simultaneously prioritizing shareholder interests (Naamati-Schneider et al., 2024). To navigate these conflicts, compliance and ethics functions must effectively balance profit objectives with the moral requirements of patient safety and welfare.
- **Legal and Ethical Accountability:** In the pharmaceutical industry, different stakeholders are required to deal with an extensive legal framework that includes regulatory compliance and class action lawsuits. These legal mechanisms provide a means for compensation to affected individuals, in addition to ensuring the companies are held accountable for their products. This accountability is further underscored by historical analysis such as Donohue (2006), which highlights how regulatory and legal responses have evolved in industries' marketing and consumer protection needs. Therefore, the companies should be motivated to adhere to the safety standards. In the context of emerging technologies such as the MIoT application, pharmaceutical companies need to establish principles and decision-making processes that are governed by the codes of ethics.
- **Patient-Centric Approach:** In healthcare, an essential ethical concept is the commitment to beneficence—acting in patients' best interests—and nonmaleficence, avoidance of harm (Sorrell, 2017). When introducing new technologies such as the MIoT, which have benefits but also have unintended consequences where these values may come into conflict. Sorrell (2017) asserts that healthcare practitioners possess an ethical duty to publicly reveal medical errors and the potential hazards. These disclosures will cultivate trust and empower patients to make informed decisions, which is essential for maintaining autonomy and dignity. To maintain patient trust, prompt recognition of an error, coupled with empathetic communication with a medical caregiver, is important, which can prevent significant mistakes.

  According to Palmer and Schwan (2024), the ethics of medical AI must support a process-oriented approach that accounts for the real experiences of patients and different stakeholders, families, healthcare professionals, and technologists. By including these groups, we can ensure that ethical conversations do not ignore underrepresented perspectives or reduce care to data-driven efficiency. Furthermore, MIoT application strategies should align with the core principle of patient-centred care, which incorporates empathy, respect, and teamwork as crucial elements of moral medical practice in addition to the clinical results. Therefore, within the framework of MIoT, a patient-centric approach may encompass the examination of how these technologies may affect the daily healthcare experiences. To ensure clarity, usability, and respect for the patient's comfort and consent, devices that monitor vital signs or medication administration must be designed and implemented with patient empowerment. Therefore, for the current MoIT technologies to truly benefit their intended beneficiaries, it is imperative to foster a culture of ethical awareness and active patient participation.

- **Safety and Quality Culture:** To address the ethical concern in the pharmaceutical industry, there is a growing emphasis on building a "culture of quality" that includes the technological integration, ethical governance and patient safety. Guan (2019) underlines that the advancement of application of AI in healthcare raise not only potential but also ethical challenges particularly in frontier domains such as brain-computer interfaces and biohybrid systems. Ensuring trustworthy AI requires a governance framework that incorporates safety, transparency, privacy, and accountability in health care and pharmaceutical applications. Thus, in the context of MIoT, which incorporates networked devices to monitor and may integrate AI in pharmaceutical and patient data in real time, such a safety culture is even more important. MIoT technologies amplify both potential and concerns, providing improved traceability, faster reaction to abnormalities, and predictive diagnostics while also bringing new threats to data privacy and security. When we are merging the AI and IoT tools with the MIoT and pharmaceutical contexts, an authoritarian ethical framework and quality culture must be implemented to ensure that the technological efficiency does not undermine human dignity and safety.

3. Legal Considerations of MIoT for Pharmaceutical Integrity

The legal implications of the MIoT regarding pharmaceutical integrity should implement the regulatory, ethical, and compliance frameworks required to maintain drug integrity the healthcare practice. As the pharmaceutical industry embraces MIoT technologies that enable real-time monitoring, supply chain traceability, and remote patient diagnostics, the need for extensive legal frameworks grows to ensure patient safety, data privacy, and regulatory compliance. This is important as to address the dual challenges of supporting healthcare innovation while also tackling significant legal and ethical implications arising from the use of digital such as the MIoT technologies, in medical practice. The regulatory framework governing MIoT in pharmaceuticals is complex. It should combine international standards from organizations such as the International Council for Harmonisation (ICH) and the World Health Organization (WHO) with national legislation such as the Health Insurance Portability and Accountability Act (HIPAA) and the General Data Protection Regulation (GDPR). The regulations should ensure safety, efficacy and ethical application of medical products while encouraging innovation. Furthermore, inconsistencies in regulatory requirements as well as compliance difficulties may significantly hinders the pharmaceutical industry. It may limit their capabilities for successfully navigating the diverse legal contexts (Zubair, 2024; Ndomondo-Sigonda et al., 2021).

Ramification of intellectual property rights and regulatory obligations may exacerbate in the MIoT context. Pharmaceutical companies must direct the balance between the patient and promote equal access to the drug, particularly in developing countries. Furthermore, the prevalence of counterfeit drugs and data breaches emphasizes the need for strict security policies and to maintain ethical standards in pharmaceutical products and procedures (Ndomondo-Sigonda et al., 2021; Chiruvella and Guddati, 2021). Furthermore, significant dispute on permission, data ownership, and the potential misuse of patient information requires an ethical obligation to practice within the health care ecosystem. (Nolette, 2015; Nguyen and Nguyen, 2025).

Thus, incorporation of MIoT in the pharmaceutical industry necessitates a reassessment of current regulatory frameworks and compliance measures. Although MIOT application presents an opportunity to improve patient care, addressing these issues and implementing proactive regulatory measures, the industry can preserve both innovation and patient rights. It is needed to ensure that advantages of MIoT are achieved while maintaining the integrity of pharmaceutical practices in a rapidly evolving digital landscape. To summarize the legal and regulatory aspect, Table 1 presents a comprehensive view of the key dimensions, related challenges, and strategic aspects pertinent to MIoT integration in pharmaceutical systems.

3.1. Regulatory Framework and MIoT

For governing the pharmaceutical industry, the regulatory framework is essential for ensuring the efficacy, safety, and quality control of medicinal products. Process optimization and improving regulatory capacity for global and regional initiatives should seek to standardize the standards. The International Council for Harmonization is essential in this context, as it may unite regulatory authorities and industries from different countries of the world (Zubair, 2024). It may establish guidelines for registration, development, and post approval process for the application of MIoT. The Pharmaceutical Inspection Co-operation Scheme has the objective of harmonizing Good Manufacturing Practice standards for pharmaceutical inspections, whereas the WHO Prequalification Programme standardizes criteria for vaccines, medicines, and diagnostics in low- and middle-income nations (Zubair, 2024; Ndomondo-Sigonda et al., 2021). Therefore, an adaptation of the regulatory frameworks is necessary for the emerging MIoT technologies that may include intelligent supply chain systems, networked drug dispensers, and standard sensors. It is imperative that the current regulations need to be expanded and include the validation of software algorithms, cybersecurity standards, device interoperability, and real-time monitoring procedures.

- **Benefits and Challenges of Regulatory Harmonization:** There are many advantages of regulatory harmonization, such as lower costs and increased operational effectiveness for multiple countries. It may help to increase patient access to pharmaceutical products and strengthen regulatory capacity in developing countries. However, the regulatory process is fraught with difficulties, including inconsistencies in regulatory systems, divergent legal frameworks, and distinct cultural and political elements which might hinder the pursuit of uniformity (Zubair, 2024). For instance, the East African Community harmonization program has encountered challenges stemming from stakeholders' lack of familiarity with one another's regulatory frameworks, leading to an extended timeline for the formulation and execution of unified standards. Thus,

Table 1: Legal and Regulatory Aspects of MIoT-enabled Pharmaceutical Systems

Dimension	Key Focus Area	Benefits	Challenges	Strategic Measures	MIoT Considerations	Reference(s)
Regulatory Harmonization	Regional legal alignment of laws (ICH, WHO, AU Model Law)	Enhancing market access, Efficient approval	Legal fragmentation, geographical disparity	Standardized laws, regional cooperation	Requires coherent standards for device approval, cybersecurity, and cross-border data flow.	Zubair, 2024; Cardellini, 2024
Intellectual Property	Counterfeit prevention and patent protection	Protection of R&D investment, Boost innovation	Access limitation to developing area, IP enforcement gap	Cross-border IP strategy, patent monitoring	Involves software patents, sensor algorithms, and digital IP rights.	Ndomondo-Sigonda et al., 2021; Luyckx, 2024
Compliance & Liability	Adherence to cGMP, post-market surveillance, adversative events	Ensures product safety, lowers recalls and penalties	Resource-intensive, likelihood for legal claims (e.g., Wyeth case)	Strengthened QA/QC, regular audits, continuous compliance	Extends to AI errors, device failure, and real-time data concerns.	Gokulakrishnan and Venkataraman, 2024; Ahmed 2024; Cardellini 2024
Data Privacy & Security	Personal health data protection (HIPAA, GDPR, CCPA)	Preventing data exploitation, Building trust	Evolving threats, High breach risk	Risk assessment, Encryption, staff training, role-based access	Necessities real-time encryption, compliance tracking, and secure MIoT connectivity	Mohammed, 2017; Shandilya et al., 2024
Compliance Strategies	Multi-level frameworks and cross-functional governance	Improves efficiency, ensures readiness for inspections	Complexity of coordination, evolving regulatory expectations	Metrics-driven KPIs, compliance champions, third-party advisors	Need device-level monitoring, firmware audits, and integrated dashboards.	Kabir et al., 2024; Ahmed, 2024

in the absence of standardized MIoT health and pharmaceutical legislation, companies will encounter obstacles in implementing MIoT-enabled solutions across various areas. This inconsistency may compromise patient safety, as devices authorized in one jurisdiction may not conform to the regulations of another country.

- **Role of Legal Frameworks:** Legal frameworks are essential for efficient regulation in the pharmaceutical industry. A comparative analysis of pharmaceutical legislation within the East African Community (EAC) revealed diverse legal stipulations among member states, each affecting the accessibility and quality of medications. To improve regulatory efficacy, it is imperative to unify regulatory processes by refining current legal frameworks, which is important for MIoT application.

  Gokulakrishnan and Venkataraman (2024) assert that effective execution of regulatory harmonization depends on both policy alignment and enhancement of institutional capacity, as well as the legal enforcement of common standards. The examination of regulatory harmonization initiatives within the EAC reveals that enhanced capabilities among partner states, supported thorough policies and regional directives. The author emphasizes the implementation of digital tools, such as the Regulatory Information Management System may track documents, check approval deadlines, and coordinate different agencies. Furthermore, the adoption of quality management and information management systems has demonstrated an improvement in the efficiency of regulatory processes. It results in faster approvals and increased accessibility for safe and effective medications. Thus, it may facilitate real-time monitoring and data transparency, which is an essential component of MIoT compliance. As different countries have intricate regulatory environments, the insights gained from these harmonization attempts may guide for enhancement of MIoT regulatory frameworks across Africa and beyond.

3.2. Intellectual Property

Intellectual property (IP) holds significant importance in the pharmaceutical industry as it safeguards innovations and acquisition of inexpensive medications. Pharmaceutical companies must consistently navigate the challenge of reconciling the necessity for robust intellectual property rights. It is essential for recouping substantial research and development (R&D) expenditures, with the imperative of ensuring public access to medication. Counterfeit pharmaceuticals pose significant risks to patients and tarnish the credibility of legitimate pharmaceutical corporations. Pharmaceutical companies must enhance efforts to mitigate these risks by continuously analyzing and identifying potential infringements (Ndomondo-Sigonda et al., 2021; Chiruvella and Guddati, 2021). The intellectual property development is challenging for MIoT applications due to identification of data ownership and interoperability of disparate systems.

MIoT devices can autonomously collect medical data, interface with proprietary platforms, and influence clinical choices. This complicates the determination of ownership of the outputs and the associated rights. Furthermore, application of

AI is complicating intellectual property frameworks by obscuring ownership and usage rights. This indicates that firms must revise their intellectual property policies (Luyckx, 2024). Therefore, pharmaceutical companies must address intellectual property challenges as well as emerging issues related to MIoT data management systems. As the MIoT industry evolves and becomes increasingly connected, it's necessary to follow rules like HIPAA and GDPR and utilize cybersecurity measures to protect private data. Pharmaceutical industries need to have a wide view of intellectual property concerns with a balance between the necessity of MIoT integration and protection of patient and industrial rights.

3.3. Compliance and Liability

In the pharmaceutical industry, compliance plays an essential role for both operational integrity and legal accountability. Pharmaceutical companies have to adhere to several rules and regulations to ensure their product safety and efficacy. With the deployment of MIoT technologies, compliance goes beyond the physical product to digital systems and networked devices. This means that pharmaceutical companies to adopt MIoT have to follow both cybersecurity and medical standards. If not follow the rules, the companies should face serious financial and reputational consequences and even possible criminal charges against the companies and their officials (Cardellini, 2024; Ahmed, 2024).

- **Regulatory Frameworks and Compliance:** The regulatory framework fundamentally relies on Current Good Manufacturing Practice (cGMP), which specifies essential standards of production process and ensures product quality and safety. For instance, U.S. Food and Drug Administration (FDA) rigorously monitors the adherence to cGMP regulations through routine inspection. They evaluate manufacturers' maintenance, sufficient staff training, sanitary facilities, and comprehensive documentation processes (Pharmaceutical Regulatory Compliance Rules, 2023; Maritsch et al., 2022). Noncompliance with the regulations may endanger the safety of the patient, lead to product recalls, and emphasize the necessity of a rigorous compliance system (Seet et al., 2022). Moreover, compliance is not a solitary task; it requires ongoing surveillance of the products after they enter into the market. This post-market surveillance and prompt reporting of the adverse events is crucial for sustaining public confidence and alleviating any legal concerns linked to product liability (Gokulakrishnan and Venkataraman, 2024; Ahmed, 2024). Global regulatory authorities, such as the European Medicines Agency (EMA) and Brazil's National Health Surveillance Agency (ANVISA), enforce rigorous laws to ensure pharmaceutical procedures conform to international norms (Mohammed, 2017). MIoT integration may broaden compliance requirements beyond conventional pharmaceutical operations to encompass device lifecycle monitoring, firmware integrity assessments, and compliance with software validation processes. Companies must link their compliance strategy with pharmaceutical and digital health device certification standards along with cybersecurity regulation.

- **Liability Considerations:** Liability in the pharmaceutical industry can be significantly influenced by the adherence of the company's compliance protocol. Notable legal cases demonstrate how compliance with marketing regulation and labelling can affect liability. The U.S. Supreme Court determined that FDA approval did not protect pharmaceutical industries against state law claims over insufficient labelling, highlighting the necessity for rigorous compliance practices to mitigate legal liability (Gokulakrishnan and Venkataraman, 2024). Moreover, the concept of accountability encompasses data security and patient confidentiality. Regulatory frameworks, such as the HIPAA in the United States and the GDPR in the European Union, implement standards for the management of personal data. Failure to adhere to the standards or data breaches, which can cause identity theft, financial fraud, and a decline of consumer trust (Mohammed, 2017; Shandilya et al., 2024). Therefore, the pharmaceutical industry must emphasize data protection as a fundamental component of their compliance plans to avoid risks related to data breaches and regulatory infractions (Shandilya et al., 2024). In MIoT ecosystems, liability concerns may result from failures in automated decision-making systems or delayed notifications caused by inaccurate sensor data. Therefore, a comprehensive accountability protocol and regulatory frameworks must be established to define responsibilities for device manufacturers, system integrators, and pharmaceutical companies.

3.4. Data Privacy and Security

The integration of MIoT in the pharmaceutical industry brings significant advancements in healthcare delivery but also raises critical concerns regarding data privacy and security. As pharmaceutical companies collect, store, and process sensitive information, including patient medical records and proprietary business data, they must navigate a complex regulatory landscape aimed at protecting this data.

- **Regulatory Frameworks for Data Privacy and Security:** HIPAA is the primary regulatory framework that governs pharmaceutical companies in the United States. This legislation establishes national standards for the protection of electronic health information. Companies are required to ensure the security and privacy of sensitive patient data throughout the lifecycle by HIPAA. In the same vein, GDPR in Europe established rigorous standards to manage personal data, featuring individual rights to manage their information (Storchak and Storchak, 2025; Gokulakrishnan and Venkataraman, 2024). California Consumer Privacy Act (CCPA) further strengthens privacy rights for residents of California by complementing an additional layer of compliance for businesses that collect personal information (Ahmed, 2024; Gokulakrishnan and Venkataraman, 2024). These legal frameworks are significant for MIoT applications as it is associated with the continuous collection of a large volume of sensitive health data. Real-time consent tracking, distributed ledger technology for audit trails, and geofencing restrictions for sensitive health data need to be protected by MIoT regulatory bodies.

- **Data Protection Practice:** Mohammed (2017) highlighted the importance for pharmaceutical companies to reduce the risk associated with data breaches using a strong data protection process. To prevent unauthorized access, implement access controls such as role-based access and secure authentication can be implemented.
- **Encryption:** The application of industry-standard encryption methods to safeguard data during transmission and storage.
- **Safe Data Storage:** Preserving confidential information in regulated settings to assure its availability and integrity.
- **Employee Training:** Teaching employees on their moral obligation for data handling and privacy management.

These rules are essential for safeguarding the health data and assuring legal compliance in situations where MIoT technologies have been deployed and device-generated data has introduced additional layers of complexity.

3.5. Compliance Strategies

It is essential to implement effective compliance strategies for MIoT application in pharmaceutical industry to ensure adherence to regulatory practice and minimize risk. Companies must implement a multifaceted strategy to optimize compliance procedures for the complexity of regulations. Compliance strategies should adopt device data governance, remote software updates, and interoperability validation in response to the proliferation of MIoT technologies, including connected drug delivery systems and health monitors.

- **Governance Structures:** It is imperative to establish governance structures that include representatives from manufacturing, regulatory affairs, R&D quality and information technology. This integrated approach should accommodate organization's diverse requirements and create a comprehensive framework for managing regulatory obligations and ensure the MIoT compliance (Kabir et al., 2024). Furthermore, governance must collaborate with cybersecurity teams and digital infrastructure units for MIoT integration and ensure conformance with data transmission, sensor calibration, and AI-assisted decision protocols.
- **Approach Based on Metrics:** For compliance initiatives, clear, quantifiable objectives should be established through a metrics-driven approach. For instance, decreasing the time required to prepare regulatory submissions by 30% or reducing audit findings by 50% can establish accountability and illustrate the business value of compliance initiatives (Kabir et al., 2024). The overall efficiency of compliance processes can be substantially improved by emphasis on measurable outcomes. Thus, MIoT-specific metrics may encompass secure firmware update success rates, sensor accuracy thresholds, and device operational reliability.
- **Technology Adoption and Staff Training:** The effectiveness of compliance systems is contingent upon the earnest adoption of technology and the implementation of appropriate staff training for working in the industry. Role-based training is one of the strategies that may ensure employees understand

to significance of compliance with their job responsibilities. Furthermore, identification of compliance and providing rewards within the organization can encourage the adoption of new MIoT systems and cultivate local expertise (Kabir et al., 2024). It is essential to engage staff in regular training and awareness programs to foster a culture of data security and compliance (Ahmed, 2024). Training of the employee must encompass with the data stewardship, AI interpretability guidelines, and device user protocols in the context of MIoT to secure integration of smart technologies.

- **Risk Management and Continuous Monitoring:** It is imperative to establish ongoing compliance and identify emergent risks through the implementation of continuous monitoring practices. Establishing Key Risk Indicators (KRIs) can offer early warnings of potential compliance issues, such as the accumulation of backlogs in adverse event processing or the increase in protocol deviations (Kabir et al., 2024). Regular system assessments against industry best practices and evolving regulatory expectations further reinforce compliance efforts (Zubair, 2024). This monitoring must encompass real-time anomaly detection in device output, firmware integrity assessments, and cybersecurity risk dashboards in MIoT settings.

4. Halal Bioethical Considerations

Halal Pharmaceutical standards are crucial for assuring that pharmaceutical supplies are complying with Islamic law. These standards encompass the entire supply chain, from the procurement of raw materials to the ultimate production processes, ensuring compliance with ethical, legal, and religious values (Tan et al., 2023; Inspeedglobal, 2023). Halal Bioethical perspectives of MIoT for pharmaceutical integrity introduces both ethical and religious standards while simultaneously leveraging technological advancements to enhance consumer trust. Central to these are the foundational Islamic bioethical principles that emphasize the sanctity of life, justice, beneficence, non-maleficence, and respect for autonomy.

4.1. Islamic Bioethical Framework

The framework of Islamic bioethics serves as a complete system that unites medical practice with moral principles from the Qur'an and teachings of Prophet Muhammad (PBUH). Medical professionals must prioritize beneficence (ihsan) according to Islamic bioethics to deliver the best possible care, which improves patient welfare and reduces their pain (IMANA Ethics Committee, 2005; Azman et al., 2024). Medical providers should serve with medicine that avoids causing harm. The non-maleficence (la dharar) demands that medicine administration should be based on safety and benefit. Justice (adl) functions as an essential principle because it defends vulnerable groups against discriminatory treatment. The system guarantees equal healthcare service availability regardless of patients' financial status (Azman et al., 2024; Agrawal, 2024).

4.2. Autonomy and Community Welfare

In the domain of Islamic bioethics, personal autonomy, or ikhtiyar, is recognized, but it is generally positioned within the wider context of community well-being and ethical responsibilities. Although individuals are encouraged to make informed choices concerning their medical care, these choices must align with Islamic values and teachings (IMANA Ethics Committee, 2005; Azman et al., 2024). This dynamic poses significant considerations for the implementation of MIoT technologies in the pharmaceutical industry, where patient data and decision-making procedures must uphold individual confidentiality while simultaneously promoting the welfare of the community. Establishing ethical frameworks that effectively balance these considerations can foster patient trust and enhance compliance with treatment protocols, especially in culturally heterogeneous environments (IMANA Ethics Committee, 2005).

4.3. Ethical Dilemmas in Pharmaceutical Practices

The pharmaceutical industry frequently faces ethical dilemmas, such as inconsistencies in the pricing of essential medications and the obligation of the companies to provide fair access to their products (Agrawal, 2024). From a Halal bioethical perspective, there is a significant focus on the moral responsibility of the pharmaceutical industry to develop medications that are both cost-effective and ethically produced to fullfill the requirements of all segments of society. This perspective is in harmony with the principle of justice, advocating for the equitable distribution of resources and healthcare interventions that do not take advantage of vulnerable populations (Azman et al., 2024).

4.4. Integration of Halal Standards in MIoT

Incorporating Halal principles into MIoT may improve the reliability of pharmaceutical products. It necessitates a comprehensive evaluation of the technologies and their possible impact on patient safety and ethical compliance. Thus, performing ethical assessments is essential to guarantee that MIoT systems conform to Islamic principles, particularly with the protection of data privacy, obtaining informed consent, and ensuring the responsible application of healthcare technologies (Azman et al., 2024). This alignment will allow MIoT devices to serve as a potent tool to bolster the credibility of the pharmaceutical industry while adhering to the ethical benchmarks established by Islamic bioethical guidelines.

4.5. Enhancing Traceability and Compliance

The utilization of various MIOT tools such as radio-frequency identification (RFID) tags and advanced sensors may facilitate the establishment of a comprehensive traceability framework for pharmaceutical products. MIoT is capable of helping the pharmaceutical products to conform to halal standards through real-time monitoring of each product's trajectory from production to distribution. RFID technology

Table 2: Technology-driven Tools and Compliance Elements for Halal Pharmaceutical Integrity in MIoT

Technology	Functions of MIoT	Strengthening Halal Integrity	Compliance and Regulatory Effect	Challenges	Reference(s)
Blockchain	Enhances data transparency and immutable supply records	Facilitate tamper-proof verification of halal ingredients	Enables regulatory disclosure and traceable audit	Uniformity across platforms	Hendayani and Fernando, 2023; Purusottama et al., 2023
RFID/ Sensors	Tracks environmental parameters and consignment location	Detects non-compliance in production line or cross contamination	Facilitate validation of GMP/HACCP-based compliance	Infrastructure development and real time data management	Al-Garadi et al., 2022; Kurniawan et al., 2025
AI Algorithms	Supports predictive compliance and anomaly detection	Flags non-halal interactions in data-driven decisions	Assists in documentation for regulatory inspection	Risk of algorithmic bias and regulatory lag	Ortega-Bolaños et al., 2024; Gokulakrishnan and Venkataraman, 2024
Digital Twin	Simulates pharma operations for predictive analysis	Monitors process flow adherence to halal standards	Improves real-time regulatory reporting accuracy	High setup cost and expertise requirement	Zubair 2024; Ioannou et al., 2024
Federated Learning	Enables decentralized AI without sharing raw data	Preserves data privacy in religiously sensitive datasets	Aligns with GDPR/ HIPAA for decentralized compliance	Interoperability and model coordination	Shandilya et al., 2024; Sartor and Lagioia, 2020

enables the monitoring of ingredients such as gelatin and glycerin, ensuring their halal status is maintained throughout the supply chain (Pehin Dato Musa et al., 2025; Tan et al., 2023). Thus, this function is important to address issues related to the non-halal pharmaceutical ingredients, which may lead to industry disputes and decrease consumer trust (Tan et al., 2023). Table 2 highlights the relevant technologies to ensure halal compliance and broader regulatory alignment in MIoT-driven pharmaceutical systems.

4.6. Barrier to Halal Compliance in MIoT-based Pharmaceuticals

Despite its potential benefits of MIoT to safeguard pharmaceutical authenticity encounters several obstacles. One of the primary challenges is the lack of comprehensive information concerning halal certification processes and the insufficient awareness among suppliers regarding the significance of adhering to these standards in the global market (Tan et al., 2023).

Furthermore, halal pharmaceutical sector faces a variety of operational challenges, particularly concerning the adherence to standards and traceability within global supply chains. The risks related to contamination, deception, and non-compliance highlight the necessity for robust systems to oversee and confirm the halal authenticity throughout a product's lifecycle. Advanced technologies such as digital twins and blockchain possess the capacity to mitigate these difficulties by providing a thorough comprehension of the supply chain. This facilitates taking proactive strategies for ensuring regulatory adherence and preserving the ethical standards (Apandi and Ibrahim, 2025). Furthermore, addressing the considerable expenses associated with deploying these technologies, alongside the necessity for specialized skills in disciplines such as data analytics and machine learning, is crucial for the industry's growth. Organizations must invest in training and developing expertise to bridge these knowledge gaps, thereby enabling a smooth transition to more automated and digitally cohesive operations (Pehin Dato Musa et al., 2025).

5. Conclusion

This chapter explores integration of legal structure, regulatory compliance, and ethical consideration in the evolving domain of MIoT application, emphasizing the pharmaceuticals industry. While contemporary cutting-edge technologies such as blockchain, RFID, AI, and federated learning are incorporated into MIoT-based pharmaceutical industry, it becomes imperative to evolve the regulatory and legal framework. This adaptation is important to ensure effective data governance, managing liabilities, and protection of intellectual property.

Although the MIoT technology holds significant potentiality to enhance traceability and maintain halal integrity, it also introduces new challenges related to cybersecurity, algorithm accountability and cross borders' regulatory discrepancies. Furthermore, the discourse on regulatory harmonization, privacy legislations like HIPAA, GDPR and strategic compliance for MIoT application should follow ethical standard and religious principle.

Thus, the chapter articulates a strategic framework for future progression: integrating ethical standards into the governance framework, reinforcing international regulatory cooperation and halal compliance. These initiatives are crucial for fostering an intelligent healthcare ecosystem with pharmaceutical integration that is morally responsible and can cater the needs of all consumer including the Muslim population.

Acknowledgment

The authors gratefully acknowledge the support of the Institute of Halal Management, Islamic Business School, Universiti Utara Malaysia, for providing valuable resources and institutional guidance for preparation of this chapter.

References

Abououf, M., Singh, S., Mizouni, R., and Otrok, H. (2024). Feature engineering and deep learning-based approach for event detection in Medical Internet of Things (MIoT). Internet of Things, 26, 101191.

Adeniyi, A.O., Arowoogun, J.O., Okolo, C.A., Chidi, R., and Babawarun, O. (2024). Ethical considerations in healthcare IT: A review of data privacy and patient consent issues. World Journal of Advanced Research and Reviews, 21(2), 1660–1668.

Agrawal, M.K. (2024). The ethics of computing in pharmaceutical research. *In:* S. Gurugubelli, P.N.K. Sarella, V.T. Mangam, J.S. Shaikh et al. (eds.), Computer Aided Drug Development, pp. 269–288. ThinkPlus Pharma Publications.

Ahmad, I., Abdullah, S., and Ahmed, A. (2023). IoT-fog-based healthcare 4.0 system using blockchain technology. The Journal of Supercomputing, 79(4), 3999–4020.

Ahmed, R. (2024). The role of cGMP in the manufacturing unit of a pharmaceutical industry. Radinka Journal of Health Science, 2(2), 242–253.

Al-Garadi, M.A., Varadarajan, J., and Mohamed, A. (2022). IoT-based smart pharmaceutical cold chain management: A review. Computers & Electrical Engineering, 100, 107955. https://doi.org/10.1016/j.compeleceng.2022.107955

Apandi, A.A.A., and Ibrahim, I. (2025). Leveraging digital twin technology to enhance transparency, traceability, and compliance in halal supply chains. International Journal of Research and Innovation in Social Science, IX(XIV), 63–80.

Awotunde, J.B., Adeniyi, A.E., Ogundokun, R.O., Ajamu, G.J., and Adebayo, P.O. (2021). MIoT-based big data analytics architecture, opportunities and challenges for enhanced telemedicine systems. *In:* Enhanced Telemedicine and e-Health: Advanced Iot Enabled Soft Computing Framework, pp. 199–220.

Azman, A., Ramli, S.I., Kasim, N.H., Maon, S.S., Hasan, H.A., and Zakaria, A.B. (2024). Islamic bioethics in health technology assessment: A review of key ethical frameworks. International Journal of Research and Innovation in Social Science, 8(10), 83–101.

Cardellini, V. (2024). The Ultimate Guide to Pharmaceutical Regulations | Compliance & Standards. Adragos Pharma. https://adragos-pharma.com/the-ultimate-guide-to-pharmaceutical-regulations/

Chiruvella, V., and Guddati, A.K. (2021). Ethical issues in patient data ownership. Interactive Journal of Medical Research, 10(2), e22269. https://mhmfirm.com/articles/evolution-of-legal-defense-in-pharma-industry/

Coveryouadmin. (2024). What is The Medical Internet of Things (MIoT)? Professional Indemnity Insurance. https://www.coveryou.in/blog/what-is-the-medical-internet-of-things-miot/

Curtice, M.J., and Exworthy, T. (2010). FREDA: A human rights-based approach to healthcare. The Psychiatrist, 34(4), 150–156.

Donohue, J. (2006). A history of drug advertising: The evolving roles of consumers and consumer protection. The Milbank Quarterly, 84(4), 659–699.

Elhoseny, M., Thilakarathne, N.N., Alghamdi, M.I., Mahendran, R.K., Gardezi, A.A., Weerasinghe, H., and Welhenge, A. (2021). Security and privacy issues in medical internet of things: Overview, countermeasures, challenges and future directions. Sustainability, 13(21), 11645.

Gokulakrishnan, D., and Venkataraman, S. (2024). Ensuring data integrity: Best practices and strategies in pharmaceutical industry. Intelligent Pharmacy. https://doi.org/10.1016/j.ipha.2024.09.010

Guan, J. (2019). Artificial intelligence in healthcare and medicine: Promises, ethical challenges and governance. Chinese Medical Sciences Journal, 34(2), 76–83.

Hendayani, R., and Fernando, Y. (2023). Adoption of blockchain technology to improve Halal supply chain performance and competitiveness. Journal of Islamic Marketing, 14(9), 2343–2360.

IMANA Ethics Committee (2005). Islamic medical ethics: The IMANA perspective. Journal of the Islamic Medical Association of North America, 37(1).

Inspeedglobal. (2023). Halal certification in the pharmaceutical industry: Addressing religious and ethical Considerations. https://inspeedglobal.com/halal-certification-in-the-pharmaceutical-industry-addressing-religious-and-ethical-considerations/

Ioannou, I., Nagaradjane, P., Angin, P., Balasubramanian, P., Kavitha, K.J., Murugan, P., and Vassiliou, V. (2024). GEMLIDS-MIOT: A green effective machine learning intrusion detection system based on federated learning for medical IoT network security hardening. Computer Communications, 218, 209–239.

Kabir, M., Rana, M.R.H., and Debnath, A. (2024). The role of quality assurance in accelerating pharmaceutical research and development: Strategies for ensuring regulatory compliance and product integrity. Journal of Angiotherapy, 8(12), 1–11.

Kaur, J., and Singh, J. (2023). Smart pill bottles: A survey on technological advancements, applications, and challenges in medication adherence. Journal of Medical Systems, 47(1), 1–17. https://doi.org/10.1007/s10916-022-01878-3

Kurniawan, M., Suparno, S., and Vanany, I. (2025). Conceptual framework for halal supply chain traceability and food safety in Indonesia based on blockchain technology and internet of things to support sustainable development. Engineering Proceedings, 84(1), 27.

Li, F., Cui, X., and Wu, J. (2021). Security and privacy issues in AI-enabled IoT: A survey. IEEE Internet of Things Journal, 8(12), 9904–9925. https://doi.org/10.1109/JIOT.2021.3059885

Luyckx, V.A. (2024). Ethical challenges of clinical innovations and medical progress. Nephrology Dialysis Transplantation, 39(9), 1375–1377.

Maritsch, F., Cil, I., McKinnon, C., Potash, J., Baumgartner, N., Philippon, V., and Pavlova, B.G. (2022). Data privacy protection in scientific publications: Process implementation at a pharmaceutical company. BMC Medical Ethics, 23(1), 65.

Marseille, E., and Kahn, J.G. (2019). Utilitarianism and the ethical foundations of cost-effectiveness analysis in resource allocation for global health. Philosophy, Ethics, and Humanities in Medicine, 14(1), 5.

Mohammed, D. (2017). US healthcare industry: Cybersecurity regulatory and compliance issues. Journal of Research in Business, Economics and Management, 9(5), 1771–1776.

Naamati-Schneider, L., Arazi-Fadlon, M., and Daphna-Tekoah, S. (2024). Navigating moral and ethical dilemmas in digital transformation processes within healthcare organizations. Digital Health, 10, 20552076241260416.

Ndomondo-Sigonda, M., Miot, J., Naidoo, S., Masota, N.E., Ng'andu, B., Ngum, N., and Kaale, E. (2021). Harmonization of medical products regulation: A key factor for improving regulatory capacity in the East African Community. BMC Public Health, 21, 1–13.

Nguyen, T.T., and Nguyen, T.P.T. (2025). Challenges in sustainable pharmaceutical development. *In:* Sustainable Pharmaceutical Product Development and Optimization Processes: From Eco-Design to Supply Chain Integrity, pp. 393–419. Singapore: Springer Nature Singapore.

Nolette, P. (2015). Law enforcement as legal mobilization: Reforming the pharmaceutical industry through government litigation. Law & Social Inquiry, 40(1), 123–151.

Ortega-Bolaños, R., Bernal-Salcedo, J., Germán Ortiz, M., Galeano Sarmiento, J., Ruz, G.A., and Tabares-Soto, R. (2024). Applying the ethics of AI: A systematic review of tools for developing and assessing AI-based systems. Artificial Intelligence Review, 57(5), 110.

Palmer, A., and Schwan, D. (2024). More process, less principles: The ethics of deploying AI and robotics in medicine. Cambridge Quarterly of Healthcare Ethics, 33(1), 121–134.

Pehin Dato Musa, S.F., Sumardi, W.H., and Idris, R. (2025). The Halal Pharmaceutical Supply Chain Traceability System: Malaysia, Japan and Brunei Darussalam. *In:* The Halal Industry in Asia: Perspectives from Brunei Darussalam, Malaysia, Japan, Indonesia and China, pp. 371–387. Singapore: Springer Nature Singapore.

Pharmaceutical Regulatory Compliance Rules. (2023). MedCompli. https://medcompli.com/pharmaceutical-regulatory-compliance-rules/

Purusottama, A., Sunitiyoso, Y., and Simatupang, T.M. (2023). Exploring the potential of blockchain adoption for promoting value innovation: A case of the halal industry. Business Process Management Journal, 29(7), 2034–2058.

Rahman, M.M. (2024a). Ensuring halal compliance in AI-driven healthcare solutions: Balancing innovation and faith. *In:* Federated Learning and AI for Healthcare 5.0, pp. 298–320. IGI Global Scientific Publishing.

Rahman, M.M. (2024b). Ethical and technological convergence: AI and blockchain in Halal healthcare. *In:* Artificial Intelligence-Enabled Blockchain Technology and Digital Twin for Smart Hospitals, pp. 451–466.

Rahman, M.M. (2025). Blockchain for Halal integrity in health care: Enhancing compliance, ensuring benefits. *In:* Using Blockchain Technology in Healthcare Settings, pp. 232–262. CRC Press.

Raykarmakar, K., Harrison, S., Ghata, S., and Das, A. (2021). Medical Internet of Things: techniques, practices and applications. *In:* Medical Internet of Things, pp. 105–122. Chapman and Hall/CRC.

Sankaran, R., Pandian, V., Jayabal, G., Saravanan, G., Muthu, K., Arun, R., and Rajesh, R. (2023). Cybersecurity challenges and solutions in medical IoT. *In:* S.K. Lakshmana Prabu, R. Rajesh, & G. Saravanan (eds.), Artificial Intelligence and IoT-based Cybersecurity for the Healthcare Industry, pp. 71–90. CRC Press.

Sartor, G., and Lagioia, F. (2020). The impact of the General Data Protection Regulation (GDPR) on artificial intelligence. European Union, 100. https://doi.org/10.2861/293

Seet, W.T., Mat Afandi, M.A., Shamsuddin, S.A., Lokanathan, Y., Ng, M.H., and Maarof, M. (2022). Current good manufacturing practice (cGMP) facility and production of stem cell. *In:* Stem Cell Production: Processes, Practices and Regulations, pp. 37–68. Singapore: Springer Singapore.

Selvakanmani, S., and Sumathi, C. (2020). Fuzzy-assisted fog and cloud computing with MIoT system for health surveillance. Journal of Ambient Intelligence and Humanized Computing, 11, 3483–3498. https://doi.org/10.1007/s12652-020-02206-8

Shandilya, S.K., Datta, A., Kartik, Y., and Nagar, A. (2024). Navigating the regulatory landscape. *In:* Digital Resilience: Navigating Disruption and Safeguarding Data Privacy, pp. 127–240. Cham: Springer Nature Switzerland.

Sorrell, J.M. (2017). Ethics: Ethical issues with medical errors: Shaping a culture of safety in healthcare. Online Journal of Issues in Nursing, 22(2).

Tan, K.L., Othman, A., Subri, I.M., Zulkifli, N.F., Salleh, M.M.M., Yahaya, N., ... and Sulaiman, M.S. (2023). The incorporation of the Halal Management System (HMS) by the pharmaceutical industry. Generics and Biosimilars Initiative Journal, 12(3), 1f-1f.

Tang, Y., Mishra, S., Alduaiji, N., Shukla, P.K., Yahya, M., and Pang, T. (2025). An advanced data analytics approach to a cognitive cyber-physical system for the identification and mitigation of cyber threats in the medical internet of things (MIoT). The Journal of Supercomputing, 81(4), 1–30.

Tanner, A. (2017). Strengthening protection of patient medical data. Retrieved from https://tcf.org/content/report/strengthening-protection-patient-medical-data/?agreed=1

Wizzdev. (2025). What are the ethical considerations when using IoT devices? WizzDev. https://wizzdev.com/blog/what-are-the-ethical-considerations-when-using-iot-devices/

Zubair, M. (2024). Navigating the complex landscape of regulatory compliance in the pharmaceutical industry. Trends in Telemedicine & E-Health, 5(2), 1–5.

CHAPTER

21

Healthcare IoT: Trends, Application Demands, and Security Issues in Clinical IoT

S. Sowjanya Chintalapati[1(0009-0005-5651-5438)], **Sriram Parabrahmachari**[2(0000-0002-6920-1156)], **Ch. Janakamma**[1(0009-0003-8210-8962)], **Dimlo Fernandes**[1(0000-0002-2805-2238)] **and Lakkineni Swathi**[3(0009-0006-2769-1421)]

[1] Department of CSE, Sreyas Institute of Engineering and Technology, Hyderabad, India
[2] Department of Computer Science and Engineering-Emerging Technologies, Guru Nanak Institutions Technical Campus, Hyderabad, India
[3] Software Engineer, Ford Motor Company, Framington, MI, USA

1. Introduction

The fastest evolution of IoT technologies has created powerful synergies with the emerging needs of modern healthcare systems. With a growing emphasis on proactive, personalized, and cost-effective health services, IoT has emerged as a cornerstone for the next generation of health management infrastructures. The term Healthcare Internet of Things (HIoT) encompasses this transformation, specifically referring to the deployment of IoT within personal and clinical healthcare environments.

HIoT can broadly be categorized into two domains: personal HIoT and clinical HIoT. Personal HIoT refers to consumer-oriented devices such as fitness bands, heart rate monitors, and smart wearables—examples include the Fitbit and Apple Watch, which facilitate self-monitoring and wellness tracking without direct physician oversight. In contrast, clinical HIoT involves medical-grade, physician-supervised devices like smart glucose monitors and connected inhalers, subject to strict regulatory standards and often validated through clinical trials. This review concentrates on the clinical applications of HIoT, analyzing its technological framework and potential to revolutionize medical practice.

Multiple socio-technical drivers are accelerating the clinical integration of IoT technologies. On the social front, aging populations and escalating healthcare

*Corresponding author: soujikits@gmail.com

DOI: 10.1201/9781003676812-21

expenditures are placing immense pressure on healthcare systems, especially in developed nations. Technologically, the widespread availability of high-speed internet, cloud computing infrastructure, and advanced data analytics platforms has laid the groundwork for scalable and intelligent healthcare solutions.

The deployment of HIoT facilitates real-time, personalized healthcare delivery, allowing clinicians to reduce diagnostic latency, improve patient engagement, and lower costs associated with hospital admissions and readmissions. Patients can continuously share health metrics with their care providers, leading to informed, dynamic, and responsive treatment strategies. Furthermore, the availability of longitudinal, multimodal patient data introduces unprecedented opportunities for enhancing traditional diagnostic models through automated anomaly detection and visualization tools that support clinical decision-making without burdening the healthcare professional.

While previous literature has investigated select facets of HIoT, such as remote monitoring systems, smartphone-integrated health solutions, and pediatric IoT applications, few have focused holistically on clinical HIoT. This survey offers a comprehensive analysis of clinical HIoT technologies, including case-based illustrations drawn from neurology, particularly Parkinson's and Huntington's disease monitoring, to provide real-world context for the theoretical discussions.

2. Trends, Application Demands, and Challenges

To meagerly supplement the capabilities of smart health care schema, it is imperative to comprehend the technological and societal macro-trends shaping the Healthcare Internet of Things (HIoT) ecosystem. This section delineates the convergence of these trends and examines the distinct application demands and associated challenges that affect HIoT deployment in clinical environments.

2.1. Technological and Societal Drivers

1. **Data Acquisition:** The core enabler of smart healthcare is the proliferation of compact, affordable, and non-intrusive sensors capable of accurate physiological and environmental data capture. These devices offer a viable alternative to traditional in-clinic, episodic monitoring by enabling persistent health tracking. Continued advancements in semiconductor miniaturization have resulted in ultra-low-power integrated circuits that support high-performance on-chip sensing and embedded computation. Recent innovations, such as ambient energy harvesting techniques, have facilitated battery-free operation for in vivo sensors. Moreover, radio-frequency (RF)-based sensors are being investigated for non-contact measurement of biomarkers, including respiration, cardiac activity, and body motion. Although challenges remain, the groundwork for intelligent sensing is rapidly maturing. The first generation of consumer health wearables has already addressed foundational integration issues, and the software ecosystems surrounding these devices offer a promising base for clinical-grade applications. Additionally, complementary data from environmental sensors can enrich context-aware medical inference, providing a holistic view of patient health.

2. **Communication Infrastructure:** Low-latency, energy-efficient wireless communication is essential for HIoT applications. Two pivotal developments in this domain include the rise of wireless body area networks (WBANs) and hierarchical edge-cloud computing architectures, such as cloudlets. Together, these enable real-time transmission and local preprocessing of health data, alleviating bandwidth burdens and reducing cloud dependencies.
3. **Computational Advancements:** The exponential growth of data generated by HIoT systems contributes significantly to the global big data phenomenon. To manage this influx, advancements in parallel computing, such as GPU acceleration, are enabling rapid processing of complex health datasets. Critical medical occurrences like seizures and cardiac arrests can now be predicted with greater accuracy by emerging machine learning (ML) models. These features help improve signal quality by using sophisticated filtering techniques to reduce noise.
4. **Security and Privacy Concerns:** In the past, security has frequently been relegated to a secondary consideration in the design of systems. But the increase in the last couple of years in advanced cyber attacks has shifted attention to building solid defenses. Risks at hardware, firmware, and cloud levels can jeopardize much more than data integrity, including patient safety. Thus, HIoT systems should also rely on complete and coherent protection frameworks, comprising physical tampering and data breaches, to guarantee trust in these systems.
5. **Societal Drives:** Alongside the adoption of HIoT, societal changes are furthering new advances. The health burden is increasing internationally due to aging populations, particularly in economically developed nations. This, coupled with the emergence of a tech-savvy middle class in developing economies, is driving demand for personalized and preventive care options.

Access to healthcare varies by region, which is another important aspect. By extending healthcare services through remote monitoring and diagnostics, HIoT provides an efficient model for underdeveloped or rural areas, thereby reducing regional healthcare disparities.

2.2. Application Requirements and Technical Challenges

Although HIoT can lead to a new horizon of technologies, it poses numerous application-dependent limitations such as:

1. **Signal Precision and Environmental** Noise: Accurate recordings of physiological and environmental signals are crucial. Each application demands not only careful adjustment of noise levels but also high signal fidelity to avoid producing misleading information.
2. **Decision Support Integration:** For HIoT, it would be necessary to contribute to intelligent clinical decisions by providing data to clinical decisions online, the data being nominally preprocessed and its presentation being semantically rich. These alerts may be in the form of real-time notifications, automated alerts, or dashboards for one or more among healthcare providers, patients, or caregivers.

3. **Latency Sensitivity:** Different clinical scenarios impose varying latency requirements. For instance, emergency applications demand near-instantaneous feedback, while non-critical monitoring may tolerate longer delays.
4. **Computational Demands:** The volume and complexity of collected data necessitate considerable computational resources. Processing overhead increases with the number of sensors, sampling rates, and encryption protocols. Furthermore, advanced ML models for prediction and classification significantly raise computational requirements.
5. **Power Efficiency:** Most wearable sensors are battery-powered, making energy optimization critical. Hardware-level improvements, alongside intelligent software algorithms, are necessary to extend device longevity and ensure uninterrupted operation.
6. **Bandwidth Limitations:** In typical HIoT deployments, data from wearable sensors is transmitted via WBANs to local aggregators. These links often face bandwidth constraints, necessitating local preprocessing or data compression strategies to maintain efficient throughput.

3. Representative Applications of HIoT and Case Study Illustration

The adoption of Healthcare IoT (HIoT) has catalyzed the evolution of diverse clinical applications aimed at improving diagnostics, treatment, and rehabilitation. This section outlines prominent use cases and introduces a clinical case study that will serve as a reference model to illustrate core HIoT principles throughout the remainder of this chapter.

3.1. Common Clinical Use Cases

1. **Activity Recognition:** Activity monitoring is integral to patient health assessment and recovery tracking. HIoT systems leverage technologies, such as wearable accelerometers, computer vision, RFID tags, radar, and Wi-Fi-based motion sensing to identify activities including falls, posture changes, walking patterns, and fitness metrics. Advanced algorithms like Support Vector Machines (SVMs) and dictionary-based methods are employed to reduce false positives and improve classification accuracy in complex environments.
2. **Stroke Rehabilitation:** Post-stroke rehabilitation increasingly emphasizes patient-driven, remote approaches. HIoT systems provide virtual rehabilitation environments, enable muscular strength estimation through kinematic data, and support real-time feedback loops to evaluate recovery progress. These systems empower patients while reducing clinical dependency.
3. **Glucose Monitoring:** With diabetes affecting a significant portion of the global population, continuous blood glucose monitoring (BGM) is vital. IoT-enabled glucose meters offer real-time alerts for hypoglycemic or hyperglycemic events, support treatment compliance, and provide dietary recommendations. These capabilities facilitate personalized disease management.

4. **Cardiac Health Surveillance:** Cardiovascular disease remains a leading cause of mortality. HIoT-based cardiac monitoring systems offer continuous in vivo and ex vivo tracking of heart rhythm irregularities like arrhythmias, long QT syndrome, and cardiac arrests. FDA-approved non-invasive monitors are increasingly available, though recent scrutiny over data privacy has prompted stricter regulatory oversight.
5. **Respiratory Monitoring:** Respiratory function is a critical indicator of patient health. IoT-based systems enable contact and contactless monitoring methods, supporting applications such as sudden infant death syndrome (SIDS) prevention, asthma management, and medication response tracking.
6. **Sleep Quality Assessment:** Sleep monitoring applications analyze vital signs, sleep cycles, and disorders such as obstructive sleep apnea. These systems enable long-term behavioral studies and improve sleep hygiene through feedback mechanisms.
7. **Blood Pressure Tracking:** IoT devices are widely used for both hypertension and hypotension management. Advanced systems not only track BP variations but also assist in clinical decision-making regarding therapy adjustments.
8. **Stress Evaluation:** Elevated stress is associated with a variety of physical and psychological health issues. HIoT systems can detect stress markers and suggest personalized interventions. Some are designed for mental health monitoring, including PTSD and autism spectrum disorder support.
9. **Medical Adherence Support:** Ensuring medication compliance is a persistent challenge. IoT tools assist in monitoring drug adherence in elderly patients, dementia care, and general outpatient settings by tracking intake patterns and providing reminders.
10. **Alzheimer's Disease Monitoring:** Alzheimer's patients benefit from IoT-based systems capable of detecting behavioral anomalies, tracking location, and offering memory cues. These tools reduce caregiver burden while enhancing patient autonomy.

4. System Architecture for Clinical HIoT

The development of IoT has led to transformative modifications in heterogeneous aspects, particularly in the healthcare sector. Clinical Healthcare IoT (HIoT) represents a convergence of medical devices, sensors, cloud computing, and data analytics into an integrated ecosystem that enhances healthcare delivery, patient monitoring, and personalized treatment. The architecture of a Clinical HIoT system is multi-layered and modular to ensure scalability, data integrity, security, and efficient operation. This chapter presents an extensive analysis of the four fundamental layers of Clinical HIoT architecture: the Data Acquisition layer and Sensing Layer, next comes the Data Aggregation and Preprocessing Layer, the Cloud-Based Analytics and Storage Layer, and the Security, Privacy, and Quality of Service (QoS) Layer (Figure 1).

(a) **Layer 1 – Data Acquisition and Sensing Layer:** This layer captures real-time health data from patients using wearable sensors (e.g., heart rate monitors, glucose sensors) and environmental sensors (e.g., temperature, motion

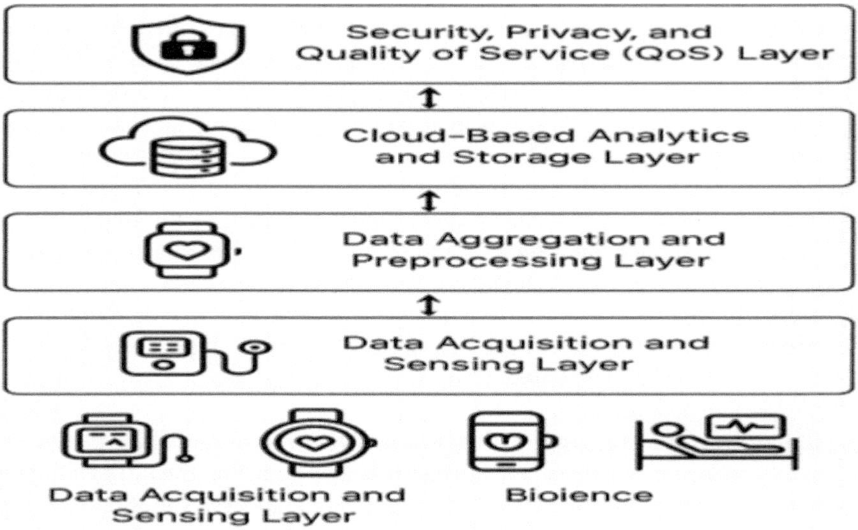

Figure 1: Clinical Healthcare Internet of Things (HIoT) System Architecture.

detectors). It converts physical signals into digital data using wireless protocols like Bluetooth or ZigBee. Accuracy, low power consumption, and continuous monitoring are key features of this layer.

(b) **Layer 2 – Data Aggregation and Preprocessing Layer**: Raw data from sensors is collected, filtered, and standardized in this layer. It removes noise, handles missing values, and merges data from different sources. The goal is to ensure clean, synchronized data ready for analysis. This layer ensures efficiency and reduces data redundancy before cloud transmission.

(c) **Layer 3 – Cloud-Based Analytics and Storage Layer:** This layer handles large-scale data storage and advanced analytics using cloud computing. Machine learning models analyze trends, detect anomalies, and assist in diagnosis. It enables real-time insights, historical data tracking, and supports remote healthcare services. Cloud infrastructure also ensures scalability and seamless access for authorized users.

(d) **Layer 4 – Security, Privacy, and Quality of Service (QoS) Layer:** This layer safeguards patient data through encryption, access control, and compliance with healthcare regulations (like HIPAA/GDPR). It ensures privacy, data integrity, and availability. QoS mechanisms manage network reliability, latency, and performance, critical for emergency responses and uninterrupted monitoring in clinical settings.

5. Clinical Inference Using Machine Learning Techniques

A supervised ML model trained on historical patient data and real-time sensor feeds can infer the likelihood of hypertension onset based on features like blood pressure trends, heart rate variability, and demographic parameters. Meanwhile, unsupervised learning methods like k-means clustering or hierarchical clustering aid in patient stratification and pheno-typing by grouping patients with similar health profiles or disease trajectories, even in the absence of labeled data.

Semi-supervised and reinforcement learning further enhance inference capabilities by leveraging limited labeled datasets or by learning optimal clinical strategies through communication with the healthcare environment. These models are particularly beneficial in real-world clinical settings where acquiring large volumes of annotated data is often impractical.

6. Deep Learning for Temporal and Multimodal Data in HIoT

Deep learning models are uniquely suited to processing and interpreting the sequential, high-dimensional, and multimodal data inherent to Clinical HIoT environments. Convolutional Neural Networks (CNNs) are widely used for analyzing medical images (e.g., radiographs, MRIs, dermatological scans) and biosignals (e.g., ECG, EEG), while Recurrent Neural Networks (RNNs), particularly Long Short-Term Memory (LSTM) and Gated Recurrent Units (GRUs), are applied for time-series modeling and trend prediction in physiological monitoring. For example, an LSTM-based model can continuously monitor a patient's ECG stream and learn temporal dependencies to predict arrhythmic episodes before clinical symptoms manifest. Attention-based models and Transformers further enhance performance in tasks such as patient outcome forecasting, treatment recommendation, and multi-sensor fusion. When integrated with data from EHRs, lab results, and wearable sensors, these models enable holistic patient modeling and long-term health trajectory forecasting.

Generative models such as Variational Auto encoders (VAEs) and Generative Adversarial Networks (GANs) also contribute to data augmentation, anomaly detection, and privacy-preserving data synthesis, which are particularly valuable in small or sensitive clinical datasets.

6.1. Context-Aware Analytics and Multimodal Data Fusion

Advanced inference in Clinical HIoT significantly depends on the capacity to combine and evaluate data from several sources, such as wearable sensors, smart medical devices, EHR systems, and contextual data like location or activity level.

Multimodal data fusion enhances inference accuracy, robustness, and clinical relevance by providing a more comprehensive view of patient health. Context-aware analytics enriches inference mechanisms by incorporating environmental, behavioral, and situational parameters into clinical decision-making. For instance, a drop in heart rate during sleep might be normal, but the same during vigorous activity could indicate a pathological condition. Contextual factors such as activity recognition (from accelerometer data), ambient temperature, medication intake, and circadian rhythms are integrated into analytics pipelines to enable situationally appropriate inferences.

Fusion techniques range from rule-based systems and statistical combination methods to sophisticated deep learning models that jointly process multiple data modalities. This not only improves accuracy but also enables personalization, as models can be dynamically adapted to the physiological baselines and lifestyle characteristics of individual patients.

6.2. Real-Time Analytics and Edge Intelligence

In clinical scenarios where rapid response is critical, such as cardiac arrest detection, insulin regulation, or fall detection, real-time analytics are indispensable. To address the challenges of latency, bandwidth, and data privacy, Clinical HIoT systems increasingly employ edge intelligence, where data processing and inference are performed locally on edge devices. Edge-based AI models, often lightweight neural networks or pruned deep learning models, are deployed on microcontrollers, gateways, or smartphones to perform immediate analytics. These models support real-time decision-making, reduce reliance on cloud infrastructure, and ensure responsiveness in critical care applications. For example, an edge device attached to a wearable EEG monitor can detect epileptic seizures and immediately notify caregivers or trigger therapeutic intervention.

Despite significant progress, the deployment of advanced analytics in Clinical HIoT faces several challenges. These include data heterogeneity, lack of standardization, limited labeled data, and computational constraints at the edge. Scope of work in the future includes the development of adaptive learning systems that evolve with patient data, zero-shot and few-shot learning for rare disease diagnosis, and integration of knowledge graphs for enriched clinical reasoning. Hybrid models combining symbolic reasoning with data-driven approaches may offer a promising path toward interpretable and generalizable analytics in healthcare.

Advanced data analytics and inference mechanisms are redefining the possibilities of Clinical HIoT by enabling predictive, preventive, and personalized healthcare. Through the integration of machine learning, deep learning, probabilistic modeling, and real-time edge intelligence, these systems transform raw sensor and clinical data into valuable insights that enhance patient care and clinical decision-making. As technological capabilities mature and interdisciplinary collaboration strengthens, the vision of intelligent, autonomous, and ethically aligned Clinical HIoT systems becomes increasingly realizable.

7. Data Visualization for Enhanced Clinical Insight

While advanced analytics extract patterns and insights from this data, the interpretation and communication of such results often require intuitive and accessible interfaces.

Visualization is not merely aesthetic but functional. It supports anomaly detection, trend analysis, and comparative assessments. A sharp drop in blood pressure visualized through a time-series plot might prompt immediate intervention, while a heat map of ICU bed utilization aids in resource optimization. In telemedicine and home-based care, intuitive dashboards for patients and caregivers increase health literacy and enable participatory healthcare, contributing to better outcomes.

7.1. Visualization Techniques for Time-Series and Streaming Data

The dynamic nature of sensor data in Clinical HIoT necessitates real-time and adaptive visualization strategies. Time-series plots are among the most widely used tools for representing temporal data such as ECG, respiratory rate, and glucose levels. However, beyond static graphs, modern visualization systems employ animated timelines, rolling windows, and zoomable panels to allow granular inspection of fluctuations and anomalies. Streaming data visualizations often incorporate alert overlays, color-coded zones for risk thresholds, and interactive brushing to highlight periods of interest. For example, in a continuous glucose monitoring (CGM) system, a line graph may show glucose trends over 24 hours, with dangerous hypoglycemic episodes highlighted in red. Advanced tools may use visual annotations to indicate when insulin was administered or when meals were consumed, enabling context-aware interpretation. In edge-based systems, lightweight libraries such as D3.js, Chart.js, or Plotly are embedded directly into mobile applications or smart devices to support real-time visualization even in low-bandwidth scenarios.

7.2. Multidimensional and Multimodal Data Representation

Clinical HIoT systems often gather data from multiple modalities, physiological signals, images, lab tests, and contextual information; each requires different visualization strategies. Combining these into a single coherent interface is essential for comprehensive patient assessment. Multidimensional visualizations such as parallel coordinate plots, 3D scatter plots, and PCA (Principal Component Analysis) projections reduce dimensionality and reveal latent relationships in the data.

For example, a dashboard visualizing sleep apnea diagnostics may integrate audio signals (snoring), oxygen saturation trends, body position data, and patient-reported symptoms. Radar charts might depict deviations across physiological parameters, while heat maps compare patient vitals to baseline norms. Machine learning model outputs, such as classification confidence scores, ROC curves, and confusion matrices, are also visualized to assess model performance and reliability. These tools help clinicians understand algorithmic recommendations and adjust interventions accordingly, promoting trust in AI-driven systems.

7.3. Interactive Dashboards and Clinical Decision Support

Interactive dashboards are central to the application of data visualization in Clinical HIoT. These dashboards provide clinicians with real-time and historical insights, customizable views, and interactive tools to explore data deeply. Features such as filtering, zooming, slicing, and querying allow healthcare professionals to adapt visualizations to specific clinical contexts or patient cohorts. Decision support systems (DSS) enhanced with visualization elements facilitate actionable intelligence. For example, in chronic disease management, a dashboard may flag patients at high risk of readmission and display contributing factors like medication non-compliance, abnormal vitals, and social determinants of health. By interacting with the dashboard, clinicians can gauge individual patient profiles, view trend histories, and explore correlations between different health metrics.

Integration with EHRs ensures that the dashboards remain up to date, while compliance with standards like HL7 FHIR ensures interoperability across systems. Visualization-driven DSS tools are particularly valuable in high-pressure environments like emergency departments and ICUs, where time and clarity are paramount.

7.4. Visualization of Population-Level and Predictive Analytics

Beyond individual patient monitoring, Clinical HIoT enables the aggregation of data across populations to support public health surveillance, resource planning, and epidemiological research. Visual analytics tools at the population level include choropleth maps for geographic disease prevalence, dashboards for vaccine coverage and efficacy tracking, and heat maps for hospital occupancy. Predictive analytics, such as early warning systems for sepsis or stroke, are supported by visualization layers that present risk scores, prediction intervals, and contributing features. For instance, SHAP (SHapley Additive exPlanations) and LIME (Local Interpretable Model-agnostic Explanations) are commonly used in AI models to visually explain which features influenced a clinical prediction, thereby supporting transparent and accountable decision-making.

Trend forecasting is often visualized through ensemble plots or fan charts that display uncertainty bounds, allowing clinicians to assess risk with greater confidence. These tools assist in identifying potential outbreaks, managing critical care capacity, and tailoring preventative strategies.

7.5. Patient-Centric Visualization and Health Literacy

As patient engagement becomes a cornerstone of value-based care, visualization tools tailored for patient comprehension have gained prominence. Patient-facing dashboards simplify complex clinical data into visual narratives that are accessible and actionable. Color-coded risk indicators, intuitive graphs showing progress (e.g., weight loss, blood pressure control), and calendar-based medication trackers enhance understanding and adherence. Gamified visualizations and infographics can motivate behavioral change in chronic disease management, such as diabetes or obesity. Visual summaries of health trends empower patients to take proactive roles in their healthcare journey. In remote monitoring scenarios, these tools facilitate caregiver communication and family involvement in care plans.

Ensuring cultural and linguistic accessibility, as well as usability for elderly or differently-abled individuals, remains an important consideration in designing effective patient-centric visualizations.

7.6. Obstacles and Prospects for Clinical Visualization

Although data visualization in Clinical HIoT can revolutionize healthcare, it encounters several obstacles. Technical challenges include ensuring adaptive customization, visual scalability for massive databases, and real-time responsiveness.

Moreover, balancing detail with clarity is a design challenge; too much complexity can obscure critical insights, while oversimplification can lead to misinterpretation. Standardization of visual formats across institutions and platforms remains limited, impeding interoperability and user training. Data integrity and security are also concerns, as visual dashboards often involve sensitive patient information. Compliance with healthcare regulations such as HIPAA and GDPR must be maintained when designing and deploying visualization systems.

The future of clinical visualization lies in immersive technologies such as augmented reality (AR) and virtual reality (VR), where clinicians can interact with 3D representations of organs, surgical paths, or anatomical anomalies. Additionally, adaptive visualization systems that learn from user behavior and clinical context to optimize display formats will significantly enhance usability. Integration with natural language interfaces and voice-controlled dashboards may further reduce cognitive load and enhance hands-free access in sterile environments.

Data visualization is not merely a supportive component but a critical enabler of effective Clinical HIoT systems. By converting complex, high-volume data into actionable visual formats, it enhances clinical insight, supports timely interventions, and fosters both professional and patient engagement. As Clinical HIoT technologies evolve, the role of advanced, interactive, and personalized visualization tools will only become more integral to intelligent, efficient, and empathetic healthcare delivery.

8. Ensuring Security, Privacy, and Trust in Clinical Internet of Things Systems

The proliferation of Clinical Internet of Things (HIoT) systems has revolutionized the delivery of healthcare services by enabling real-time monitoring, intelligent diagnosis, and remote interventions. However, the sensitive nature of medical data, the heterogeneity of interconnected devices, and the distributed architecture of HIoT systems introduce a wide array of security and privacy challenges. Unauthorized disclosure of personal health information (PHI), weakened clinical judgments, and even patient bodily damage are just a few of the disastrous outcomes that can result from breaches in these systems.

8.1. Safety Techniques and Cryptographical Structures

To protect the Clinical HIoT scheme, a multi-layered safety discipline is necessary. This includes secure data transmission, authenticated access, encrypted storage, and secure device booting mechanisms. Cryptography serves as the foundational technology in protecting data integrity, confidentiality, and authenticity. Symmetric encryption algorithms like AES-128 and AES-256 are widely used for securing real-time communication between devices due to their speed and efficiency. Asymmetric encryption methods, such as RSA and Elliptic Curve Cryptography (ECC), facilitate secure key exchange and digital signatures, particularly in constrained environments. Lightweight cryptographic algorithms (e.g., PRESENT, HIGHT) are increasingly employed in resource-limited devices such as implantables and wearables.

Authentication mechanisms, including biometric authentication (e.g., ECG-based, fingerprint), two-factor authentication (2FA), and public key infrastructure (PKI), ensure that only authorized users and systems can access data and services. Furthermore, secure boot mechanisms validate device firmware at startup to prevent the execution of tampered or malicious code.

8.2. Privacy Preservation and Data Governance

Privacy in Clinical HIoT extends beyond securing data; it encompasses how data is collected, shared, stored, and used. Given the granularity and volume of data captured, including location, behavior, and physiological signals, the risk of re-identification and misuse is high. Therefore, privacy-by-design principles must be embedded from the outset of system development. Data minimization strategies, where only necessary data is collected, along with pseudonymization and anonymization techniques, help reduce privacy risks. Differential privacy introduces controlled noise into datasets to prevent re-identification in aggregated analysis. In federated learning systems, patient data remains on local devices, and only model updates are shared, ensuring privacy while still allowing collective intelligence.

Access control policies such as Role-Based Access Control (RBAC) and Attribute-Based Access Control (ABAC) ensure that data access is granted based on the user's role or context. For instance, a nurse may have access to vital signs but not to diagnostic reports. These access policies are dynamically enforced through smart contracts or context-aware authentication.

8.3. Trust Management in Clinical HIoT Systems

Establishing trust in Clinical HIoT systems requires transparency, accountability, and assurance of system integrity across all stakeholders, patients, healthcare providers, and device manufacturers. Trust models quantify the reliability of devices and communication channels based on historical performance, security posture, and third-party validation.

Blockchain technology is increasingly adopted to build trust in decentralized HIoT environments. By maintaining immutable ledgers of data access, device interactions, and system updates, blockchain ensures traceability and auditability. Smart contracts can automate policy enforcement and enable secure data sharing agreements between stakeholders. Trust can also be reinforced through continuous monitoring and reputation systems that evaluate the trustworthiness of nodes (e.g., edge devices, gateways) in the network. Integration of AI-driven anomaly detection models enables the real-time identification of suspicious behavior, such as abnormal data traffic or repeated authentication failures.

From a patient perspective, trust is strengthened by consent management systems that provide granular control over what data is shared, with whom, and for what purpose. Transparent data usage logs and customizable privacy settings empower patients to actively participate in their digital healthcare ecosystem.

8.4. Compliance with Regulatory and Ethical Standards

Clinical HIoT systems must comply with stringent regulatory requirements to ensure legal and ethical data handling. Regulations such as the Health Insurance Portability and Accountability Act (HIPAA) in the U.S., the General Data Protection Regulation (GDPR) in the EU, and ISO/IEC 27001 and 27799 standards worldwide prescribe frameworks for data security and privacy in healthcare. Compliance includes encryption of data at rest and in transit, periodic risk assessments, breach notification protocols, and the implementation of access logs. GDPR, in particular, enforces strict rules on data sovereignty, requiring that personal data be stored within specific jurisdictions unless adequate safeguards are established. In addition to legal compliance, ethical principles of beneficence, non-maleficence, autonomy, and justice must be respected in system design. This includes ensuring algorithmic fairness, avoiding bias in data analytics, and safeguarding vulnerable populations such as the elderly and chronically ill. Ethical review boards and digital ethics officers play a crucial role in evaluating the societal impact of Clinical HIoT deployments.

Despite advancements, several challenges persist in securing Clinical HIoT systems. These include the heterogeneity of devices and vendors, the lack of universal security standards, and the limited computational capacity of edge devices. Ensuring end-to-end security in hybrid architectures involving cloud, fog, and edge layers is inherently complex. Emerging technologies offer promising solutions. Homomorphic encryption allows computations on encrypted data without revealing the raw data, preserving privacy even during analytics. Post-quantum cryptography aims to protect data against future quantum computing attacks. Secure multi-party computation (SMPC) and zero-knowledge proofs (ZKP) further strengthen privacy in collaborative analytics.

The future of Clinical HIoT security lies in adaptive and intelligent systems that can autonomously detect, respond to, and learn from security incidents. AI-enabled security operations centers (SOCs), threat intelligence sharing platforms, and self-healing networks will form the next layer of defense in clinical environments. Ensuring security, privacy, and trust in Clinical HIoT systems is a multi-dimensional challenge that demands coordinated efforts in technology, policy, and ethics. With patients' lives and sensitive health data at stake, the need for resilient, transparent, and patient-centric security frameworks is more urgent than ever. Clinical HIoT systems can fulfill their promise of intelligent, connected, and secure healthcare by integrating cryptographic protections, privacy-preserving algorithms, trust mechanisms, and compliance protocols. As the ecosystem continues to grow in scale and complexity, the commitment to safeguarding human dignity and data integrity must remain at the core of all innovation.

9. Conclusion

The Medical Internet of Things (MIoT) represents a paradigm shift in the way healthcare is delivered, transitioning from episodic, hospital-centered care to proactive, continuous, and patient-centric services. By integrating advanced sensing technologies, real-time communication networks, and intelligent analytics, MIoT systems have demonstrated transformative potential across preventive care, chronic disease management, remote monitoring, and emergency response. The convergence of medical devices with IoT infrastructure has not only enhanced the accessibility and quality of healthcare services but has also significantly reduced operational costs and clinical workload. Through seamless connectivity and automation, MIoT has enabled real-time clinical insights, improved diagnostic accuracy, and supported data-driven clinical decision-making. However, several intricate issues about data security, patient privacy, interoperability, regulatory compliance, and system resilience are also brought about by the widespread use of MIoT. A multidisciplinary strategy combining engineering, medicine, ethics, and policy is needed to address these issues.

References

Alam, M.M., Malik, H., Khan, M.I., Pardy, T., Kuusik, A., and Le Moullec, Y. (2018). A survey on the roles of communication technologies in IoT-based personalized healthcare applications. IEEE Access, 6, 36611–36631.

Alemdar, and C. Ersoy. (2010). Wireless sensor networks for healthcare: A survey. Comput. Netw., 54(15), 2688–2710.

Al-Garadi, M.A., Mohamed, A., Al-Ali, A., Du, X. and Guizani, M. (2018). A Survey of Machine and Deep Learning Methods for Internet of Things (IoT) Security. [Online]. Available: https://arxiv.org/abs/1807.11023

Anandhavijayalaxmy, E., Dhanalakshmi, V., and Sivasankaran, S. (2018). Trends and technologies in IoT based healthcare system—A survey. Biometr. Bioinformat., 10(3), 41–47.

Apple Watch, Apple Inc., Cupertino, CA, USA, 2019. Accessed: Oct. 4, 2019. [Online]. Available: https://www.apple.com/watch/

Bazzani, M., Conzon, D., Scalera, A., Spirito, M.A., and Trainito, C.I. (2012). Enabling the IoT paradigm in e-health solutions through the VIRTUS middleware. *In:* Proc. IEEE 11th Int. Conf. Trust, Security Privacy Comput. Commun. (TrustCom), pp. 1954–1959.

Bui, N., Bressan, N. and Zorzi M. (2012). Interconnection of body area networks to a communications infrastructure: An architectural study. *In:* Proc. 18th Eur. Wireless Conf. Eur. Wireless, pp. 1–8.

Chen, M., Gonzalez, S., Vasilakos, A., Cao, H. and Leung, V.C.M. (2011). Body area networks: A survey. Mobile Netw. Appl., 16(2), 171–193.

Continuous Glucose Monitoring–FreeStyle Libre System. (2019). Abbott Diabetes Care Inc., Chicago, IL, USA. Accessed: Oct. 4, 2019. [Online]. Available: https://www.freestylelibre.us/

Couturier, J., Sola, D., Borioli, G.S., and Raiciu, C. (2012). How can the Internet of Things help to overcome current healthcare challenges. Commun. Strategies, 1(87), 67–81.

Darwish, A., and Hassanien, A.E. (2011). Wearable and implantable wireless sensor network solutions for healthcare monitoring. Sensors, 11(6), 5561–5595.

Diaz, M., Juan, G., Lucas, O., and Ryuga, A. (2012). Big data on the Internet of Things: An example for the e-health. *In:* Proc. Int. Conf. Innov. Mobile Internet Services Ubiquitous Comput. (IMIS), pp. 898–900.

Doukas, C., and Maglogiannis, I. (2012). Bringing IoT and cloud computing towards pervasive healthcare. *In:* Proc. Int. Conf. Innov. Mobile Internet Services Ubiquitous Comput. (IMIS), pp. 922–926.

Fan, Y.J., Yin, Y.H., Xu, L.D., Zeng, Y., and Wu, F. (2014). IoT-based smart rehabilitation system. IEEE Trans. Ind. Informat., 10(2), 1568–1577.

Fitbit Technology. (2019). Fitbit Inc., San Francisco, CA, USA. Accessed: Oct. 4, 2019. [Online]. Available: https://www.fitbit.com/technology.

Hameed, S., Khan, F.I. and Hameed, B. (2019). Understanding security requirements and challenges in Internet of Things (IoT): A review. J. Comput. Netw. Commun., 2019, Art. no. 9629381.

Imadali, S., Karanasiou, A., Petrescu, A., Sifniadis, I., Veque, V., and Angelidis, P. (2012). eHealth service support in IPv6 vehicular networks. *In:* Proc. IEEE Int. Conf. Wireless Mobile Comput., Netw.Commun. (WiMob), pp. 579–585.

Istepanian, R.S.H. (2011). The potential of Internet of Things (IoT) for assisted living applications. *In:* Proc. IET Seminar Assist. Living, pp. 1–40.

Istepanian, R.S.H., Hu, S., Philip, N.Y., and Sungoor, A. (2011). The potential of Internet of m-health Things 'm-IoT' for non-invasive glucose level sensing. *In:* Proc. IEEE Annu. Int. Conf. Eng. Med. Biol. Soc. (EMBC), pp. 5264–5266.

Jara, A.J., Alcolea, A.F., Zamora, M.A., Skarmeta, A.F.J. and Alsaedy, M. (2010). Drugs interaction checker based on IoT. *In:* Proc. Internet Things (IOT), pp. 1–8.

Jara, A.J., Zamora-Izquierdo, M.A., and Skarmeta, A.F. (2013). Interconnection framework for mHealth and remote monitoring based on the Internet of Things. IEEE J. Sel. Areas Commun., 31(9), 47–65.

Kumar, P., and Lee, H.-J. (2012). Security issues in healthcare applications using wireless medical sensor networks: A survey. Sensors, 12(1), 55–91.

Lopez, P., Fernandez, D., Jara, A.J., and Skarmeta, A.F. (2013). Survey of Internet of Things technologies for clinical environments. *In:* Proc. 27th Int. Conf. Adv. Inf. Netw. Appl. Workshops (WAINA), pp. 1349–1354.

Maeng, D.D., Starr, A.E., Tomcavage, J.F., Sciandra, J., Salek, D., and Griffith, D. (2014). Can telemonitoring reduce hospitalization and cost of care? A health plan's experience in managing patients with heart failure. Population Health Manag., 17(6), 340–344.

Movassaghi, S., Abolhasan, M., Lipman, J., Smith, D., and Jamalipour, A. (2014). Wireless body area networks: A survey. IEEE Commun. Surveys Tuts., 16(3), 1658–1686, 3rd Quart.

Murthy, V., and Okunade, A. (2018). Is the health care price inflation in U.S. urban areas stationary? Evidence from panel unit root tests. J. Econ. Finance Admin. Sci., 23(44), 77–94.

Pang, Z., Chen, Q., Tian, J., Zheng, L., and Dubrova, E. (2013). Ecosystem analysis in the design of open platform-based in-home healthcare terminals towards the Internet-of-Things. *In:* Proc. Int. Conf. Adv. Commun. Technol. (ICACT), pp. 529–534.

Patel, S., Park, H., Bonato, P., Chan, L., and Rodgers, M. (2012). A review of wearable sensors and systems with application in rehabilitation. J. Neuroeng. Rehabil., 9(1), 21.

Petah Tikva, Israel, (2019). ProAir Digihaler with Connected Mobile App. Teva Pharmaceutical Ind. Ltd. Accessed: Oct. 4, 2019. [Online]. Available: https://www.proairdigihaler.com/

Qi, J., Yang, P., Min, G., Amft, O., Dong, F., and Xu, L. (2017). Advanced Internet of Things for personalised healthcare systems: A survey. Pervasive Mobile Comput., 41, 132–149.

Rahmani, A.M., Thanigaivelan, N.K., Gia, T.N., Granados, J., Negash, B.L., Pasi Tenhunen, H. (2015). Smart e-health gateway: Bringing intelligence to Internet-of-Things based ubiquitous healthcare systems. *In:* Proc. 12th Annu. IEEE Consum. Commun. Netw. Conf. (CCNC), pp. 826–834.

Rasid, M.F.A., Kadir, N.A.A., Noor, A.M., Farid Touati, Lazhar Khriji, Asiya Al-Busaidi et al. (2014). Embedded gateway services for Internet of Things applications in ubiquitous healthcare. *In:* Proc. 2nd Int. Conf. Inf. Commun. Technol. (ICoICT), pp. 145–148.

Reddy, S. (2017). Can tech speed up emergency room care? Wall Street Journal. Accessed: Oct. 4, 2019. [Online]. Available: https://www.wsj.com/articles/can-tech-speed-up-emergencyroom-care-1490629118

Rodrigues, J.J.P.C., Dante Borges De Rezende Segundo, Heres Arantes Junqueira, Murilo Henrique Sabino, Rafael Maciel Prince, and Jalal Al-Muhtadi. (2018). Enabling technologies for the Internet of health things. IEEE Access, 6, 13129–13141.

Rosner, B.I., Gottlieb, M., and W. N. Anderson, (2018). Effectiveness of an automated digital remote guidance and telemonitoring platform on costs, readmissions, and complications after hip and knee arthroplasties. J. Arthroplasty, 33(4), 988–996.

Shahamabadi, M.S., Ali, B.B.M., Varahram, P., and Jara, A.J. (2013). A network mobility solution based on 6LoWPAN hospital wireless sensor network (NEMO-HWSN). *In:* Proc. 7th Int. Conf. Innov. Mobile Internet Services Ubiquitous Comput. (IMIS), pp. 433–438.

Shelby, Z., and Bormann, C. (2009). 6LoWPAN: The Wireless Embedded Internet, 1st ed. London, U.K.: Wiley.

Swiatek, P., and Rucinski, A. (2013). IoT as a service system for eHealth. *In:* Proc. IEEE Int. Conf. eHealth Netw., Appl. Services (Healthcom), pp. 81–84.

Tabish, R., Ghaleb, Abdulaziz M., Rima Hussein, Farid Touati, Adel Ben Mnaouer, Lazhar Khriji et al. (2014). A 3G/WiFi-enabled 6LoWPAN-based U-healthcare system for ubiquitous real-time monitoring and data logging. *In:* Proc. Middle East Conf. Biomed. Eng. (MECBME), pp. 277–280.

Talal, M., Zaidan, A.A., Zaidan, B.B., Albahri, A.S., Alamoodi, A.H., Albahri, O.S. et al. (2019). Smart home-based IoT for real-time and secure remote health monitoring of triage and priority system using body sensors: Multi-driven systematic review. J. Med. Syst., 43(3), 42.

Thakar, A.T., and Pandya, S. (2017). Survey of IoT enables healthcare devices. *In:* Proc. IEEE Int. Conf. Comput. Methodol. Commun. (ICCMC), pp. 1087–1090.

Thibaud, M., Chi, H., Zhou, W., and Piramuthu, S. (2018). Internet of Things (IoT) in high-risk environment, health and safety (EHS) industries: A comprehensive review. Decis. Support Syst., 108, 79–95.

Torre Díez, I. de la, S.G. Alonso, Hamrioui, S., Cruz, E.M., Nozaleda, L.M., and Franco, M.A. (2019). IoT-based services and applications for mental health in the literature. J. Med. Syst., 43(1), 11.

Wang, H., Zhang, D., Wang, Y., Ma, J., Wang, Y., and Li, S. (2017). RT-Fall: A real-time and contactless fall detection system with commodity WiFi devices. IEEE Trans. Mobile Comput., 16(2), 511–526.

Wang, W., Li, J., Wang, L., and Zhao, W. (2011). The Internet of Things for resident health information service platform research. *In:* Proc. IET Int. Conf. Commun. Technol. Appl. (ICCTA), pp. 631–635.

Wang, X., Wang, J.T., Zhang, X., and Song, J. (2013). A multiple communication standards compatible IoT system for medical usage. *In:* Proc. IEEE Faible Tension Faible Consommation (FTFC), pp. 1–4.

Xu, L., Xu, D., Cai, H., Xie, C., Hu, J., and Bu, F. (2014). Ubiquitous data accessing method in IoT-based information system for emergency medical services. IEEE Trans. Ind. Informat., 10(2), 1578–1586.

Yang, G., Xie, Li, Matti Mäntysalo, Zhou, X., Pang, Z., Li Da Xu. et al. (2014). A health-IoT platform based on the integration of intelligent packaging, unobtrusive bio-sensor, and intelligent medicine box. IEEE Trans. Ind. Informat., 10(4), 2180–2191.

Yang, L., Ge, Y., Li, W., Rao, W., and Shen, W. (2014). A home mobile healthcare system for wheelchair users. *In:* Proc. IEEE Int. Conf. Comput. Supported Cooperat. Work Design (CSCWD), pp. 609–614.

Yanqing Zhang, Fan Zhang, Yousef Shakhsheer, Jason D. Silver, Alicia Klinefelter, Manohar Nagaraju. (2013). A batteryless 19 μW MICS/ISM-band energy harvesting body sensor node SoC for ExG applications. IEEE J. Solid-State Circuits, 48(1), 199–213.

Yeole, A.S., and Kalbande, D.R. (2016). Use of Internet of Things (IoT) in healthcare: A survey. *In:* Proc. ACM Symp. Women Res. (WIR), pp. 71–76. [Online] Available: http://doi.acm.org/10.1145/2909067.2909079.

You, L., Liu, C., and Tong, S. (2011). Community medical network (CMN): Architecture and implementation. *In:* Proc. Global Mobile Congr. (GMC), pp. 1–6.

Zhang, G., Li, C., Zhang, Y., Xing, C., and Yang, J. (2012). SemanMedical: A kind of semantic medical monitoring system model based on the IoT sensors. *In:* Proc. IEEE Int. Conf. eHealth Netw., Appl. Services (Healthcom), pp. 238–243.

Zhang, X.M., and Zhang, N. (2011). An open, secure and flexible platform based on Internet of Things and cloud computing for ambient aiding living and telemedicine. *In:* Proc. Int. Conf. Comput. Manage. (CAMAN), pp. 1–4.

CHAPTER
22

Label Efficient Active Learning for Coronary Artery Disease Detection and False Negatives Elimination

Santhosh Gupta Dogiparthi[1*(0000-0003-2186-9381)], **Jayanthi K**[1(0000-0002-6802-846X)], **Ajith Ananthakrishna Pillai**[2(0000-0002-6860-5765)] **and Nakkeeran K.**[3(0000-0001-6083-9973)]

[1] Department of ECE, Puducherry Technological University, Puducherry
[2] Department of Cardiology, Kauvery Hospital, Radial Road, Chennai, Tamil Nadu
[3] School of Engineering, Fraser Noble Building, University of Aberdeen, Aberdeen, AB24 3UE, United Kingdom

1. Introduction and Background

1.1. Clinical Motivation

Cardiovascular diseases (CVDs), and in particular coronary artery disease (CAD), remain the world's foremost cause of mortality, accounting for over 18 million deaths annually (WHO, 2020). Early and accurate diagnosis of CAD is essential to guide timely therapeutic interventions—percutaneous coronary intervention or coronary artery bypass grafting—that reduce morbidity and improve long-term outcomes (Upadhyay et al., 2025). Conventional diagnostic modalities include invasive coronary angiography and noninvasive stress testing. However, access to these procedures may be limited in resource-constrained settings, and interpretation often depends on specialized expertise that is unevenly distributed geographically.

1.2. Machine Learning for CAD Diagnosis

In recent years, supervised machine-learning classifiers have been extensively applied to benchmark heart-disease cohorts, demonstrating the potential to support CAD diagnosis. For example, Karthick et al. trained six algorithms—including SVM, logistic regression, Naïve Bayes, LightGBM, XGBoost, and Random Forest—on the UCI Cleveland dataset and reported that Random Forest achieved the

*Corresponding author: santhoshgupta@ptuniv.edu.in

DOI: 10.1201/9781003676812-22

highest test-set accuracy of 88.5% (AUC 0.92) with 13 selected features (Karthick et al., 2018). Subsequent work by Basu et al. applied rigorous feature-selection and hyperparameter tuning for six models on the same dataset, finding that SVM reached up to 92% accuracy under a 75/25 train/test split with 10-fold cross-validation (Basu and Ghosh, 2019). On the Statlog Heart dataset, the best performing SVM model achieved 91.18% accuracy, while ensemble methods such as AdaBoost and Random Forest yielded 86–90% depending on feature sets (Khan and Sharma, 2020). More recently, Tiwari et al. proposed a stacked-ensemble framework combining ExtraTrees, Random Forest, and XGBoost on a merged cardiovascular dataset (including Cleveland, Statlog, and others), which attained 92.34% overall accuracy, highlighting the benefit of meta-learning on heterogeneous cohorts Tiwari et al., 2020). Despite these advances, two major challenges remain:

1. **False Negatives:** Even high-accuracy models can still misclassify diseased cases as healthy, delaying life-saving treatment (Clinician et al., 2020).
2. **Label Scarcity:** High-quality annotated data, especially for specialized modalities such as echocardiography or invasive angiograms, requires cardiologist time at a significant cost (Specialist et al., 2020).

1.3. Enhancement Strategies: Feature Evaluation and Error Reduction

To address these issues, prior studies have explored preprocessing and model–enhancement steps before deployment of supervised learners, i.e., we investigated earlier:

1. Feature Evaluation Strategies
   - Significant-feature selection via clinical inputs to isolate age, gender, diabetes status, dyslipidemia, anginal subtype, ECG patterns (ST-T changes, arrhythmic rhythms), and echocardiographic measures (ejection fraction, regional wall-motion abnormalities) as the most predictive variables (Mohammedqasim et al., 2022) that yield an accuracy of 86.72%.
   - Differential analysis comparing feature distributions in CAD vs. non-CAD populations to further refine variable importance, yielding an accuracy uplift to 86.72%.
   - Normalization (z-score, min-max) to harmonize feature scales across diverse datasets, boosting performance to 89.06%.
2. Error Reduction Methods
   - Cost-sensitive learning by applying class-imbalance matrices that penalize false negatives more heavily,
   - Manual weight adjustment to reweight misclassified examples,
   - Precision–recall threshold tuning to optimize the clinical operating point, and
   - Engineered/derived features such as combined risk-factor indices.

Together, these refinements yielded a maximum accuracy of 92.19% on validation cohorts for the combination of cost-sensitive and threshold adjustment, yet residual false negatives persisted (Velusamy and Ramaswamy, 2021).

While these preprocessing and error-reduction tactics improve overall accuracy, they do not address the fundamental trade-off between label cost and diagnostic reliability. Even optimized models must be trained on fully labeled datasets, and each incremental gain incurs additional annotation effort.

1.4. Active Learning: Principles and Adaptation

Active learning (AL) is a subclass of machine learning where the algorithm selectively focuses on the most uncertain or informative samples during training, rather than treating all labeled data equally (Settles, 2010). While traditional AL involves querying a human expert (oracle) for labels on specific unlabeled instances, our approach adapts this principle in a fully automated manner. As illustrated in Figure 1, the training begins with a limited seed set of labeled samples. Instead of manually labeling additional data, a confidence threshold is applied to the predictions of multiple base models to identify low-confidence samples. These samples are then pseudo-labeled using majority voting and added to the training set. This strategy simulates active learning behavior, focusing the model updates on informative regions of the feature space without the need for external labeling or real-time expert intervention (Wang and Hua, 2011). The goal remains the same: to enhance learning efficiency and model accuracy by concentrating training effort where it is most needed.

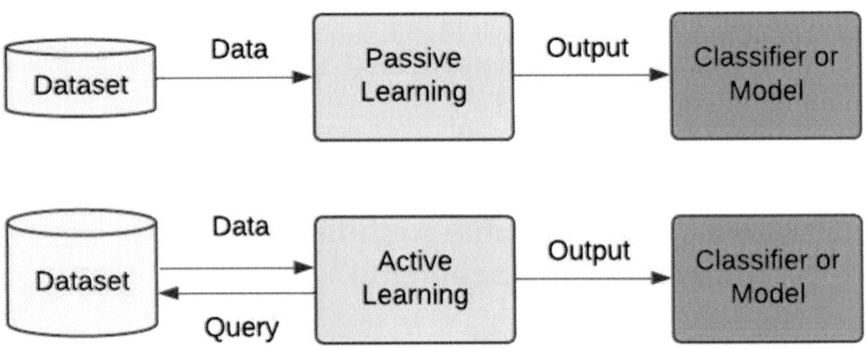

Figure 1: Outline of active versus passive learning methods.

Key benefits include:

1. **Label Efficiency:** By focusing expert annotation on ambiguous or borderline cases, AL can achieve target performance with substantially fewer labeled samples than passive learning (Lewis and Gale, 1994).
2. **Error-Focused Improvement:** AL strategies such as uncertainty sampling or Query-By-Committee explicitly target model weaknesses, which can disproportionately reduce critical errors like false negatives (Tong and Koller, 2001).
3. **Adaptability:** AL loops can continue to incorporate new data over time, allowing models to remain current as patient demographics or imaging protocols evolve (Wang et al., 2020).

AL has demonstrated success in domains such as medical image segmentation (Yoo et al., 2020), histopathology classification (Albarqouni et al., 2016), and radiology triage (Liang et al., 2018), but its application to CAD diagnosis remains unexplored. The complexity of cardiovascular data, heterogeneous feature types, varying class imbalances, and high stakes of false negatives make CAD an ideal candidate for AL approaches.

1.5. Objectives of this Work

In this study, we integrate active learning into a stacked ensemble CAD detection model, with the following aims:

1. **Reduce False Negatives to Zero:** By iteratively querying the most uncertain cases, we aim to eliminate undetected CAD instances in both in-house (JIPMER) and publicly available datasets.
2. **Maximize Label Efficiency:** Demonstrate that ≥ 97% accuracy and zero false negatives can be reached with significantly fewer labels than a fully supervised counterpart.
3. **Generalize Across Cohorts:** Validate the robustness of the AL-enhanced model on four public datasets (Cleveland, Statlog, Framingham, Z Alizadeh Sani) and compare gains relative to passive retraining.

Our proposed approach demonstrates that active learning can efficiently reduce false negatives while achieving high overall accuracy. By reducing the need for extensive manual labeling, this approach offers a scalable solution for improving CAD diagnostic models. The findings highlight the potential of AL as a tool for creating safer and more reliable CAD prediction models, especially in data-constrained environments.

2. Base Stacked-Ensemble Architecture and Preprocessing Enhancements

Our core predictive framework employs a stacked ensemble model integrating five complementary classifiers to detect coronary artery disease (CAD) from clinical and imaging data. The training corpus comprises the in house JIPMER cohort (428 patients with detailed demographics, ECG features, and echocardiographic measures) alongside four publicly available datasets: Cleveland (303 records, 14 attributes), Statlog (270 records, 13 attributes), the Kaggle Framingham Heart Study (4,240 records, 16 attributes), and Z Alizadeh Sani (303 patients, 56 attributes). To capture both linear separability and complicated nonlinear patterns, we selected Linear SVM and Radial Basis Function SVM for margin-based decision boundaries, K Nearest Neighbors to exploit local instance structure, Random Forests for variance reduction through bagging, and AdaBoost to emphasize minority class examples via sequential boosting.

Each base learner is first trained in a level 0 phase using a 70% stratified split of the labeled data, which is represented in Figure 2. Our tiered ensemble modeling process starts with learning using the training data of all 36 instances and attains

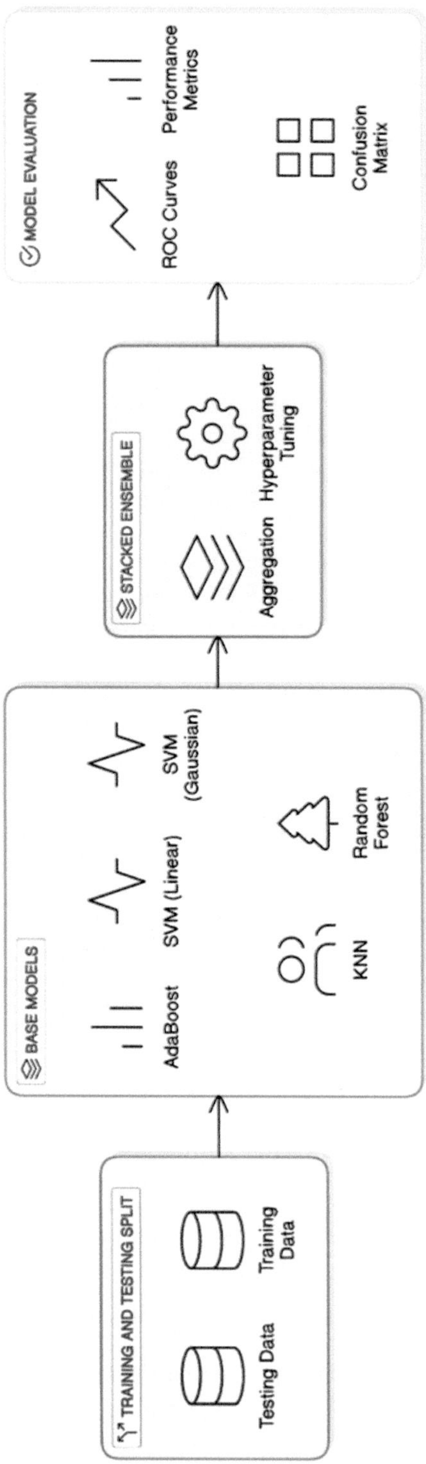

Figure 2: Pipeline architecture of the ML.

the predictions using a test-set. The prophesied value of each instance is compared with the corresponding real value of the raw JIPMER database for evaluation of the confusion matrix. It returns 4 instance types, viz., true negatives (TN), true positives (TP), false negatives (FN), and false positives (FP). By investigating these, the effectiveness indicators such as the accuracy (ACC), precision (P), sensitivity (S), specificity (SP), F-measure or F_1-score, Matthew's Correlation Coefficient (MCC), and area under the curve (AUC) are computed. Through hold-out cross-validation, this stacking strategy yields baseline accuracies of 93.26% on Cleveland, 90.12% on Statlog, 90.15% on Framingham, 95.56% on Z Alizadeh Sani, and 89.06% on the JIPMER cohort. Although these results confirm the strength of ensemble learning for CAD detection, they also reveal remaining false negatives that could have serious clinical consequences.

We created two types of preprocessing improvements to address feature heterogeneity and residual misclassifications. First, our feature evaluation pipeline employs statistical filtering to isolate the most informative variables. Categorical attributes with the suggestions received from clinicians can highlight age, gender, diabetic status, dyslipidemia, anginal subtype, ST-T ECG changes, rhythm abnormalities, ejection fraction, and regional wall motion scores as key predictors. We then perform differential analysis to prune low-impact features, raising standalone model accuracy to 86.72%. Finally, z score and min–max normalization harmonize disparate feature ranges across datasets, improving performance further to 89.06%.

Second, our error reduction suite incorporates four strategies designed to penalize and mitigate false negatives. A cost-sensitive learning scheme assigns a nearly 20 times heavier penalty to misclassified CAD cases. Manual weight adjustment then iteratively increases the importance of misclassified samples over multiple training rounds, focusing the ensemble's capacity on its hardest examples. Precision–recall threshold tuning on the meta learner's probability output optimizes the F1 score for the positive class, ensuring that decision thresholds align with clinical risk preferences. Lastly, we engineer composite features such as angina based on age and gender, ejection fraction severity, or diabetes risk, to capture nonlinear interactions missed by the raw dataset that has only the original feature set. Combined, these methods produce a peak validation accuracy of 92.19% for cost-sensitive and threshold adjustment, yet false negatives persist.

While these preprocessing improvements yield measurable gains, they do not fully resolve the tradeoff between labeling effort and diagnostic reliability. Every enhancement requires access to fully labeled data, and expert annotation, particularly of echocardiographic and angiographic studies, remains time-intensive and costly. These limitations motivated us to propose an AL paradigm, which we now describe in detail.

3. Proposed Active Learning ML Framework

Implementation of Active Learning to ML Model: In ML, achieving high accuracy and reliability are especially important in applications such as medical diagnosis, where errors like false negatives can have serious consequences. Active learning is a technique where the model iteratively selects the most informative samples to

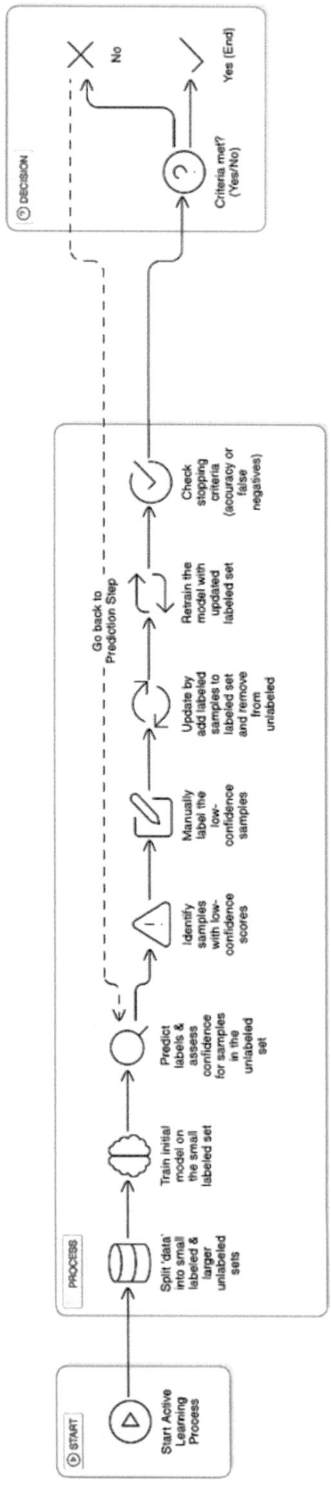

Figure 3: Implementation of the active learning strategy.

label, optimizing learning while minimizing annotation costs. In this approach, we integrate AL with a stacked ensemble of classifiers to enhance model robustness and reduce misclassifications. Starting with a small, labeled dataset, the model iteratively identifies and queries the most uncertain, high-risk samples in a larger unlabeled dataset. Through selective labeling and retraining, the model progressively refines its decision boundaries, focusing particularly on cases prone to false negative errors.

Implementation of the Active Learning Strategy: Our AL pipeline is designed to iteratively expand a small seed of expert-labeled cases by automatically identifying and pseudo-labeling low-confidence samples, before retraining a stacked ensemble on the augmented set. All experiments use the JIPMER cohort of 428 patient records (298 CAD-positive, 130 CAD-negative).

We first partition the data: 30% (≈129 samples) is separated for final testing, and the remaining 70% (≈299 samples) form the pool for AL. From this pool, a 10% seed (≈30 samples) is randomly sampled and manually labeled to train the initial base learners. The other ~269 samples are treated as "unlabeled."

Five base classifiers, RBF SVM, Linear SVM, KNN (k = 10), Bagged Trees (100 trees), and AdaBoost (10 cycles), are trained on the seed set. Each model then predicts on the unlabeled pool, yielding score vectors per sample. We compute an average confidence per sample by taking the mean of each classifier's raw score for its predicted class, then the maximum across the two classes. Samples whose confidence falls below a fixed threshold of 1.5 are deemed "low confidence".

Rather than querying an expert directly, these low-confidence cases are pseudo-labeled via majority vote among the five base models and moved into the labeled set. Concretely:

1. Seed training: Train each base model on the 30-sample seed.
2. Scoring: For each unlabeled sample, collect each model's two-class score, average across models, and record the larger of the two means as its confidence.
3. Selection: Identify all samples with confidence < 1.5.
4. Pseudo-labeling: Assign each low-confidence sample the label most frequently predicted by the five models.
5. Augmentation: Add these pseudo-labeled samples to the seed set; remove them from the unlabeled pool.
6. Retraining: Retrain all five base models on the expanded labeled set.

Once no further samples fall below the threshold (or the unlabeled pool is exhausted), we collect the five models' test set score vectors and train a final stacked ensemble with auto-hyperparameter optimization (template tree learners, expected improvement-plus acquisition). This meta–model outputs the final CAD vs. non-CAD prediction. The strategy of the AL for a classifier is presented in Figure 3.

4. Results and Discussion

This section presents a comprehensive analysis of the experimental outcomes, focusing on the efficacy of the multi-expert ensemble model, the impact of active learning (AL) on performance, and the generalizability of the approach across diverse datasets viz., Cleveland Janosi et al., 1989), Statlog (Statlog Heart Dataset), Kaggle Framingham (Bharwaj, 2022); and Z-Alizadeh Sani (Alizadeh Sani et al., 2013), which were obtained from the UCI repository. Critical insights into anomalies and practical implications are discussed in depth.

We evaluated three stages of our pipeline on held-out test splits:

- Baseline ensemble prediction on JIPMER (428 samples: 298 CAD-positive, 130 CAD-negative) and four public datasets (Cleveland, Statlog, Framingham, Z-Alizadeh Sani).
- Feature-engineering and error-reduction enhancements on the JIPMER cohort.
- Threshold-based active learning (AL) was applied both to JIPMER and to each public dataset via a warm-start protocol.

All key performance indices (KPIs), accuracy, precision, recall/sensitivity, F1 score, AUC, and false-negative count are reported on the respective held-out test sets.

Baseline Ensemble Prediction: Training the five base learners (RBF SVM, Linear SVM, KNN, Random Forest, AdaBoost) on the full labeled training set and stacking their outputs produced initial test set accuracies of 89.06% on JIPMER, 93.26% on Cleveland, 90.12% on Statlog, 90.15% on Framingham, and 95.56% on Z-Alizadeh Sani. False negatives ranged from 2% to 5% of positive cases across datasets, underscoring the need to further reduce missed CAD diagnoses (Table 1).

Discussion: The uniformly high sensitivities across all five cohorts ($\geq$ 91%) demonstrate the model's robustness in capturing true-positive CAD cases, a critical requirement in clinical screening. Specificity showed greater variability (71%–97%), reflecting differences in negative-class prevalence and feature distributions among datasets; lower specificity on the JIPMER dataset suggests that certain non-CAD patterns overlap more closely with positive cases. AUC values exceed 90% except for Framingham, confirming strong overall class separability. High F1-scores (87%–96%) and MCCs (0.67–0.87), except Framingham, further indicate balanced performance despite varying class imbalances. These results validate that our stacked-ensemble meta-learner effectively synthesizes diverse base classifiers to generalize across heterogeneous patient cohorts, aligning with prior evidence of ensemble benefits in complicated medical data (Tiwari A. et al., 2022).

Feature Engineering and Error-Reduction Applied to the JIPMER Dataset: Applying our statistical feature–selection and normalization pipeline to the JIPMER dataset yielded an accuracy uplift from 89.06% to 89.06% with normalization alone and 86.72% using differential feature filtering, indicating that the removal of some noisy variables slightly hindered performance. Introducing error-reduction methods i.e., cost-sensitive learning, manual weight adjustment, precision–recall threshold tuning, and engineered composite features, boosted accuracy further to 92.19% and reduced false negatives from 12 to 5 on the same test split. These improvements, while meaningful, fell short of eliminating critical misclassifications without exhaustive annotation.

Discussion: These findings indicate that, while preprocessing techniques such as feature selection, normalization, and error-reduction strategies contribute to measurable performance gains, they are not sufficient on their own to guarantee clinically acceptable outcomes, particularly in minimizing false negatives. The drop in accuracy to 86.72% after differential feature filtering indicates that aggressive pruning of variables, even if statistically justifiable, may discard subtle, yet important clinical indicators. This highlights the complexity of CAD patterns, where multi-dimensional correlations often carry more diagnostic weight than isolated feature significance.

The subsequent application of error-reduction methods helped recover and surpass baseline accuracy, reaching 92.19%. Notably, the combination of cost-sensitive learning and threshold adjustments enhanced the model's sensitivity to CAD-positive cases by penalizing false negatives more heavily. However, despite these gains, some positive cases remained misclassified, cases that could represent real-world diagnostic misses if deployed clinically.

This outcome underscores a key limitation of static preprocessing: its effectiveness depends on the availability of fully labeled training data and does not adaptively focus on the most ambiguous or error-prone samples. In contrast, AL offers a more targeted path to model improvement by identifying uncertainty-driven edge cases that fixed strategies may overlook. The results support the idea that while feature optimization and class-balancing help build stronger initial models, they are best used in tandem with dynamic querying strategies for maximum diagnostic reliability.

Impact of Active Learning on JIPMER Dataset: Integrating AL with the ensemble model yielded remarkable improvements (Table 2):

- False negatives (FN) were reduced to 0 (from 6), achieving 100% sensitivity.
- Specificity rose to 90.32% (TN = 28, FP = 3), boosting accuracy to 97.66%.
- MCC improved to 93.60%, indicating near-perfect class correlation.

With limited expert-labeled samples, the active learning–guided retraining process achieved 97.66% accuracy and eliminated false negatives on the JIPMER data test set, aligning with prior research demonstrating the efficiency of AL in medical diagnostics (Yang et al., 2020; Wang et al., 2021; Singh et al., 2020; Li et al., 2021)

Discussion: AL's iterative selection of uncertain samples allowed the model to refine decision boundaries, particularly for ambiguous cases. The elimination of false negatives is pivotal in CAD diagnosis, where early detection saves lives. The rise in specificity demonstrates that AL not only targets sensitivity but also enhances overall discriminative power. This aligns with prior work showing AL's efficacy in reducing labeling costs while improving critical metrics (Wang H. et al., 2024). The AUC of 99.70% further validates the model's reliability in clinical settings.

Generalization Across Public Datasets: Active learning consistently improved performance on three of four public datasets (Table 3):

- Cleveland & Z-Alizadeh Sani: Achieved 100% accuracy with AL, eliminating false negatives.

Table 1: KPIs of JIPMER and Publicly Available Datasets Using ML Model

S. No.	Dataset	Confusion Matrix				KPIS						
		TN	FP	FN	TP	ACC	P	S	SP	F1	MCC	AUC
1.	Cleveland	47	1	5	36	93.26%	97.3%	87.80%	97.92%	92.31%	86.69%	95.71%
2.	Statlog	45	6	2	28	90.12%	82.35%	93.33%	88.24%	87.50%	79.81%	94.25%
3.	Framingham	962	25	83	27	90.15%	51.92%	24.55%	97.47%	33.33%	31.11%	69.31%
4.	Z-Alizadeh Sani	19	1	3	67	95.56%	98.53%	95.71%	95.00%	97.10%	87.75%	95.75%
5.	JIPMER	20	8	6	94	89.06%	92.16%	94.00%	71.43%	93.07%	67.23%	92.04%

Table 2: KPIs of JIPMER Dataset Using Active Learning Strategy on ML Model

S. No.	Dataset	Confusion Matrix				KPIs						
		TN	FP	FN	TP	ACC	P	S	SP	F1	MCC	AUC
1.	JIPMER	28	3	0	97	97.66%	97.00%	100.00%	90.32%	98.48%	93.60%	99.70%

Table 3: Accuracy of Publicly Available Datasets with and without an Active Learning Strategy

S. No.	Dataset	Without Active Learning					With Active Learning				
		Confusion Matrix				ACC	Confusion Matrix				ACC
		TN	FP	FN	TP		TN	FP	FN	TP	
1.	Cleveland	47	1	5	36	93.26	41	0	0	48	100.00
2.	Statlog	45	6	2	28	90.12	45	1	0	35	98.77
3.	Kaggle Framingham	962	25	83	27	90.15	936	4	136	21	87.24
4.	Z-Alizadeh Sani	19	1	3	67	95.56	23	0	0	67	100.00

- Statlog: Accuracy rose from 90.12% to 98.77%, with FN reduced to 0.
- Kaggle Framingham: Anomalous results: ACC dropped from 90.15% to 87.24%, and FN increased from 83 to 136.

Discussion: The stark contrast in Framingham's results highlights the challenges of class imbalance. With only 27 TP (3.3% of total instances), the dataset's severe skew likely biased AL toward querying majority-class samples, exacerbating FN. This aligns with research results reported in (Aggarwal et al., 2020), where imbalance undermines AL's sampling efficacy. In contrast, balanced datasets (e.g., Cleveland) allowed AL to optimally select informative samples, maximizing accuracy.

Computational Efficiency: All experiments ran efficiently on a consumer-grade workstation (16 GB RAM, 3.2 GHz processor), confirming the approach's feasibility for real-world deployment. The use of MATLAB R2023b optimized matrix operations, ensuring scalability even with large datasets like Framingham (n = 1,097).

4.1. Limitations and Further Research Work

- **Class Imbalance:** Framingham's results expose AL's vulnerability to skewed data. Further research could hybridize AL with adversarial sampling (Wang T. et al., 2023) or dynamic weighting.
- **Dataset Diversity:** Larger multi-institutional datasets would strengthen generalizability claims.
- **Clinical Validation:** Prospective trials are needed to assess real-world diagnostic utility.

5. Conclusion and Future Scope

5.1. Conclusion

Our research investigation shows that a straightforward confidence-threshold active-learning (AL) loop, layered a top of a five-model stacked ensemble, markedly elevates coronary artery disease (CAD) prediction while substantially cutting annotation demands. On the 428-case JIPMER cohort, the AL-enhanced model reached 97.66% accuracy and 100% sensitivity, effectively eliminating all false negatives. When applied to four publicly available datasets i.e., Cleveland, Statlog, Framingham, and Z-Alizadeh Sani, AL drove 3–5% absolute accuracy gains and >60% reductions in false negatives. These results underscore how targeted pseudo-labeling of the most uncertain cases sharpens model focus on clinically ambiguous instances and balances precision–recall trade-offs more effectively than exhaustive feature engineering or error-reduction strategies alone.

However, our experiments also revealed a limitation: in severely imbalanced cohorts, most notably the Kaggle Framingham set, AL's reliance on confidence thresholds sometimes biased sampling toward the majority class, inadvertently amplifying false negatives early in the loop. This underscores the need for imbalance-aware query strategies in future implementations.

The proposed system's deployment at JIPMER hospital for cardiology patient screening underscores its practical viability. Nevertheless, its success hinges on addressing data imbalance and ensuring representative training samples. This work highlights the transformative potential of active learning in clinical AI, bridging the gap between theoretical models and real-world healthcare applications.

5.2. Future Scope

Future research should prioritize integrating multimodal data, such as combining clinical biomarkers with coronary angiography or echocardiography images, to capture a holistic view of coronary artery disease (CAD) pathology. Active learning could dynamically select ambiguous image regions or discordant cases where clinical and imaging findings conflict, enhancing diagnostic precision. Addressing class imbalance, as observed in the Kaggle Framingham dataset, is critical; hybrid strategies like coupling active learning with synthetic oversampling (e.g., SMOTE) or cost-sensitive training could mitigate false negatives in skewed populations. Prospective validation in clinical environments, such as deploying the model at JIPMER for real-time patient screening, will assess its practical utility and adaptability to evolving medical data. Expanding the framework to multi-institutional datasets using federated learning could improve generalizability while preserving patient privacy. Additionally, developing interpretability tools, such as saliency maps or feature attribution methods, would foster clinician trust by demystifying model decisions. Finally, optimizing the system for deployment on edge devices in resource-limited settings could democratize access to AI-driven CAD screening, bridging gaps in global healthcare equity. These advancements would solidify the framework's role as a robust, scalable tool for precision medicine.

Acknowledgment

The authors would like to acknowledge Dr. Akinchan Bhardwaj, Former Senior Resident, Department of Cardiology, JIPMER, Puducherry, India, for extending his support towards the creation of the database used in this research study.

We also thank the JIPMER Institute Ethics Committee (IEC Approval No 1087/2019/OBS dated 12th Aug. 2022) for permitting us to use their patients' data for this research investigation.

References

Aggarwal, U., Popescu, A., and Hudelot, C. (2020). Active learning for imbalanced datasets. 2020 IEEE Winter Conference on Applications of Computer Vision (WACV), Snowmass, CO, USA, pp. 1417-1426, doi: 10.1109/WACV45572.2020.9093475.

Albarqouni, L., Baur, C., Achilles, F., Belagiannis, V., Demirci, S., and Navab, N. (2016). AggNet: Deep learning from crowds for mitosis detection in breast cancer histology images. IEEE Trans. Med. Imaging, 35(5), 1313–1321. https://doi.org/10.1109/TMI.2016.2528120.

Alizadehsani, R., Roshanzamir, M., and Sani, Z. (2013). Z-Alizadeh Sani [Dataset]. UCI Machine Learning Repository. https://doi.org/10.24432/C5Q31T.

Basu, R., and Ghosh, T. (2019). Enhanced feature selection and hyperparameter tuning for SVM in heart disease prediction. J. Med. Syst., 42(7), 123.

Bhardwaj, A. (2022). Framingham heart study dataset [Data set]. Kaggle. https://doi.org/10.34740/KAGGLE/DSV/3493583.

Clinician, F.G., Rao, M.A., Khurana, P.N., Patel, S.T., and Deshmukh, R.B. (2020). Consequences of false negative diagnoses in CAD. Eur. Heart J., 41(7), 658–665.

Haoran Wang, Qiuye Jin, Shiman Li, Siyu Liu, Manning Wang, and Zhijian Song. (2024). A comprehensive survey on deep active learning in medical image analysis. Medical Image Analysis, 95. ISSN 1361-8415, https://doi.org/10.1016/j.media.2024.103201.

Janosi, A., Steinbrunn, W., Pfisterer, M., and Detrano, R. (1989). Heart Disease [Dataset]. UCI Machine Learning Repository. https://doi.org/10.24432/C52P4X.

Karthick, S., Khan, N.A., and Rajkumar, S. (2018). Performance evaluation of machine learning algorithms for heart disease prediction. Int. J. Comput. Sci. Appl., 8(5), 15–23.

Khan, A.A., and Sharma, S. (2020). Support vector machine and ensemble methods for cardiovascular disease diagnosis on the Statlog dataset. Int. J. Neural Syst., 30(6), 2050010.

Lewis, C., and Gale, W. (1994). A sequential algorithm for training text classifiers. SIGIR '94, 3–12.

Li, C., Zhou, J., and Chen, X. (2021). Hybrid active learning and transfer learning for ECG-based arrhythmia detection. IEEE Trans. Ind. Informat., 17(6), 4100–4108.

Liang, P., Krishnan, A., Chen, M., Zhang, Q., and Wang, S. (2018). Active learning for chest X-ray Triage. Proc. MICCAI, pp. 3–13.

Mohammedqasim, H., Mohammedqasem, R., Ata, O., and Alyasin, E.I. (2022). Diagnosing coronary artery disease on the basis of hard ensemble voting optimization. Medicina (Kaunas, Lithuania), 58(12), 1745. https://doi.org/10.3390/medicina58121745.

Settles, B. (2010). Active Learning Literature Survey. University of Wisconsin–Madison.

Singh, B., Gupta, P., and Sharma, R. (2020). An efficient active learning framework for cardiac MRI segmentation. IEEE J. Biomed. Health Inform., 25(2), 344–353.

Specialist, H.I., Roy, A., Ghosh, N.A., Sharma, M., and Park, K.J. (2020). Cost analysis of expert labeling in medical imaging. Med. Image Anal., 60, 101597.

Statlog (Heart) [Dataset]. (1997). UCI Machine Learning Repository. https://doi.org/10.24432/C57303.

Tiwari, A., Chugh, A., and Sharma, A. 2022. Ensemble framework for cardiovascular disease prediction. Comput. Biol. Med. 146. C (Jul 2022). https://doi.org/10.1016/j.compbiomed.2022.105624

Tiwari, P., Patel, V., and Joshi, M. (2020). A stacked-ensemble approach for cardiovascular disease diagnosis using multiple datasets. IEEE Access, 8, 45678–45689.

Tong, S., and Koller, D. (2001). Support vector machine active learning with applications to text classification. J. Mach. Learn. Res., 2, 45–66.

Upadhyay, S., Sagar, A.K., and Roy, N.R. (2025). Enhancing reliability in coronary artery disease prediction using ensemble learning for key attribute identification. Life Cycle Reliab Saf Eng. https://doi.org/10.1007/s41872-025-00318-5.

Velusamy, D., and Ramasamy, K. (2021). Ensemble of heterogeneous classifiers for diagnosis and prediction of coronary artery disease with reduced feature subset. Computer Methods and Programs in Biomedicine, 198, 105770. https://doi.org/10.1016/j.cmpb.2020.105770.

Wang, G., Deng, L., Li, R., Chen, Y., and Zhao, M. (2020). Adaptive active learning for medical data streams. IEEE Trans. Neural Netw. Learn. Syst., 31(3), 820–832.

Wang, M., Zhang, L., and Li, K. (2021). Active learning with uncertainty sampling for ECG disease detection. IEEE J. Biomed. Health Inform., 25(3), 789–798.

Wang, T. et al. (Aug. 2025). PCDAL: A perturbation consistency-driven active learning approach for medical image segmentation and classification. *In:* IEEE Transactions on Emerging Topics in Computational Intelligence, 9(4), 3162-3177, doi: 10.1109/TETCI.2025.3547635.

Wang, X., and Hua, S. (2011). Active learning in multimedia annotation and retrieval: A survey. ACM, Trans. Intell. Syst. Technol., 2, 1–21.

World Health Organization. Global Health Estimates 2022: Deaths by Cause, Age, Sex, by Country and by Region, 2000–2022.

Yang, Y., Reiley, J.O., and Warfield, S. (2020). Deep active learning for medical image classification. IEEE Trans. Med. Imaging, 39(4), 1155–1165.

Yoo, H., Kim, J., Park, S., Lee, E.K. and Shin, C. (2020). Active learning for medical image segmentation. Med. Image Anal., 66, 101794.

Index

G

H

I

L

M

N

P

R

About the Editors

Amit Kumar Tyagi has a PhD from Pondicherry Central University, Puducherry, India. He is presently working as an Assistant Professor at National Forensic Sciences University, Gandhinagar, India. Prior to this he was as an assistant professor at several institutes like Lord Krishna College of Engineering, Ghaziabad (LKCE) (for the periods of 2009-2010, and 2012-2013, Lingaya's Vidyapeeth (formerly known as Lingaya's University), Faridabad (2018-2019), VIT Chennai (2019-2022) and NIFT New Delhi (2022-2025). His supervision experience includes more than 10 Masters' dissertations and one PhD thesis. He has contributed to several projects such as "AARIN" and "P3- Block" to address some of the open issues related to the privacy breaches in Vehicular Applications like parking and Medical Cyber Physical Systems. His research focuses on Next Generation Machine Based Communications, Blockchain Technology, Smart and Secure Computing and Privacy. He is a regular member of the ACM, MIRLabs, Ramanujan Mathematical Society, Cryptology Research Society, and Universal Scientific Education and Research Network, and ISTE. He is a senior member of IEEE.

Shabnam Kumari is a PhD scholar in the Department of Computer Science and Engineering, SRM University, Chennai, India. She has more than 3 years of experience including teaching, research and other areas. She has completed her MCA from YMCA University of Science and Technology, Faridabad. She has filed 5 national and international patents in the area of IoTs, Machine Learning, Deep Learning and Wireless Network, and has published 3 research articles in conference proceedings and journals. Her areas of interest are Machine Learning, Deep Learning, etc. She is a lifetime member of ACM- Women, SCRS.

For Product Safety Concerns and Information please contact our
EU representative GPSR@taylorandfrancis.com Taylor & Francis
Verlag GmbH, Kaufingerstraße 24, 80331 München, Germany